AA

KEYGUIDE

VENICE

216

CONTENTS

115

76
166

UNDERSTANDING VENICE

Understanding Venice is an introduction to the city, its geography, economy,
history and its people. Living Venice gets under the skin of Venice today,
while The Story of Venice takes you through the city's past.

Venice is truly unique, a city built on water, threaded by canals, where water, stone and art combine to form a dazzling backdrop to an unparalleled way of life. Once mistress of the seas and controller of the Eastern trade routes, Venice used her riches to embellish her canals, streets and squares with churches and palaces, whose interiors house some of the greatest mosaics, paintings and sculpture to be found anywhere on earth. The march of history left this beautiful city stranded far from its former pre-eminence; Italian unification relegated Venice's political role to that of a small—and shrinking—regional city; the ever-increasing problems of pollution, decay and winter flooding place huge strains on the authorities responsible for keeping Venice functioning; and the summer visitors almost swamp the city. Despite everything, Venice continues to survive as a living, and still incomparably beautiful entity, with new conservation plans in the pipeline and a burgeoning international cultural role.

LAYOUT OF THE CITY

Venice is divided into six *sestieri* (wards/sixths), three of which lie on each side of the Grand Canal. Within each of these are several parishes, whose main church generally overlooks the area's central square, known in Venice as a *campo*. From each *campo* streets fan out, crossing, by means of bridges, the myriad canals that are Venice's alternative highways. Streets and canals are lined with wonderful *palazzi*, the mansions of the rich, whose architecture spans the full range of Venetian styles—Veneto-Byzantine, Venetian Gothic, Renaissance and baroque. Finding your way through this labyrinth of passages and alleys may be a challenge for the visitor, but it's also one of the great Venetian pleasures, with countless glimpses of everyday life and serendipitous discoveries along the way. The *sestieri* of San Marco, Cannaregio and Castello lie north of the Grand Canal; to the south are San Polo, Santa Croce and Dorsoduro. South of the city the lagoon opens out towards the islands of the Lido and Pellestrina, long thin land strips that provide the bulwark against the open seas of the Adriatic. North from the city, the lagoon, scattered with islands, stretches peacefully towards the mainland, the *terra firma*.

CLIMATE

Lying at the head of the Adriatic and backed by the foothills of the Alps, Venice has a climate as much influenced by central European weather systems as by those of the Mediterranean. Winters range from wet and foggy to bitingly cold, while summer is marked by periods of great heat punctuated by violent and dramatic storms. The city's maritime position contributes frequent high humidity, mist and damp, though there are days of clear brilliance, when the snow-capped Alps are clearly visible to the north and the air is fresh. October and November are the wettest months (around 80mm/ 3 inches of rain), July and August the hottest (26–28°C/ 79–82°F), making spring and early autumn the best time to visit the city.

POLITICS AND ECONOMY

Politics and economics are inextricably linked, with the city authorities attempting a delicate juggling act between the demands made on the city's infrastructure by visitors and the need for some sort of economic diversification away from tourism. There is also the pressing requirement to provide modern services for the Venetians themselves, without whom the city would be little more than an historic theme park. Under Mayor Paolo Costa, who stood down in 2005, great strides were made on all fronts; with his encouragement the city council, businesses and cultural associations started massive investment designed to give Venice 21st-century airport and port facilities, better communications within the city and a far larger range of cultural events. Steps were taken to solve the problems brought by the vast numbers of day-trippers—as many as 150,000 visit daily during the peak months, overwhelming the city while contributing little to the economy. The city council must also take into account the demands and needs of the other areas of the municipality, Mestre and the estuarine settlements, whose inhabitants far outnumber those of the historic centre. Venice has constantly reinvented itself through the years, and the growing numbers of 'serious' visitors, businesspeople and cultural enthusiasts may mark another role in the story of this city.

SOCIETY—PEOPLE AND LANGUAGE

Away from the major sights, everyday life goes on. Visitors have flocked to Venice for well over a thousand years, so Venetians are quite accustomed to seeing spellbound foreigners on every corner. Stunned by the physical actuality of the city, many tourists fail to grasp that, despite a population drop of more than 100,000 since 1950, Venice is still a functioning, prosperous provincial city, with a population of around 60,000 and all the facilities needed for their 21st-century lives. These numbers are swelled by a sizeable student presence, a growing band of devoted part-time foreign residents, and a daily influx of thousands of commuters from the mainland. The nature of the city makes it not only one of the safest urban areas in Europe, but also one of the most intimate, where neighbourhoods have a distinct village atmosphere and everyone seems to know everyone else. Venetians are generally civic-minded, tolerant and hard-working, attributes that have served them well throughout the centuries; though they have catered for outsiders they've never surrendered their own identity. They are helped in this respect by the existence of the Venetian dialect, a wonderfully vibrant tongue with which few foreigners come to terms. Characterized by sing-song rhythms, elisions, slurred vowels and softened consonants, it's rich in specialized vocabulary, stingingly pithy proverbs and down-to-earth wit, a language that cuts across all social boundaries and binds Venetian society together.

THE SESTIERI AND SHAPE OF THE CITY— THE ISLANDS AND THE GRAND CANAL

Venice is a mosaic of over 120 islands, linked by more than 400 bridges that span the canals between them. Since the 12th century, the city has been divided into six *sestieri*, each with its own distinct character. San Marco, Castello and Cannaregio lie to the north of the Grand Canal and are called the *sestieri de citra*, literally meaning 'on this side', referring to the Grand Canal. San Polo, Santa Croce and Dorsoduro lie to the south, and are known as the *sestieri de ultra*, 'on that side'. They are the most important political, economic and religious districts. **San Marco**, which includes the island of **San Giorgio Maggiore**, was the seat of Venice's secular power, home to the administration, the mint and the law courts, all grouped around the Piazza di San Marco, the only open space in Venice to qualify for the name Piazza. East of here, **Castello** was the original religious hub, where the city's cathedral, San Pietro in Castello, was sited, away from the central powerhouse of the Piazza. West of San Marco lies **Cannaregio**, developed through reclamation of sandbanks and lagoon shoals and historically one of the early city's most important areas, which borders with San Marco at the Rialto, medieval Europe's greatest financial and commercial centre. Across the Grand Canal lie San Polo and Santa Croce, and Dorsoduro to the south of the Canale della Giudecca. **San Polo** and **Santa Croce**'s boundaries are blurred, rather than being separated by canals; both were settled and were of major economic importance in early Venice. **Dorsoduro**, which includes, administratively, the island of the **Giudecca**, is home to some superb churches and museums, and has always been an immensely varied *sestiere*, firmly working-class to the north and west, elegant and well-heeled to the east and along the Grand Canal.

Opposite *The Rialto Bridge spans the Grand Canal*
Below *The Piazza di San Marco, a popular meeting place*

Since earliest times, the history of Venice has also been the history of the lagoon. The two are interdependent; the city has been much influenced by the ebb and flow of the tides in and out of the lagoon, and the lagoon inhabitants, who look on Venice as the metropolis, depend on the city for their livelihood.

THE LAGOON

The Venetian lagoon is a small inland sea whose waters are both brackish and salty. It covers an area of 550sq km (212sq miles), is 50km (31 miles) in length and ranges in width from 8km to 14km (5–9 miles). The lagoon is protected from the open sea by a chain of narrow strips of land; the curving peninsula of Punta Sabbioni to the north, and the islands of the Lido and Pellestrina to the south. Twice daily, tides surge through the gaps between these outer barriers, cleansing the lagoon waters and the canals that thread the lagoon itself. The largest of these channels follow the original paths of rivers that once flowed through the lagoon, which were diverted during the huge engineering works undertaken from the 15th to 17th centuries. These works maintained a vital balance between allowing the tides to cleanse the lagoon, and keeping out the full force of the sea. Maintaining this equilibrium has always been the primary preoccupation of the city. During the last 60 years of industrial development on the land around the lagoon, huge damage was done to this delicate balance, which is only now beginning to be addressed.

THE LAGOON LANDS

More than half of the area of the lagoon is permanently covered with water. The rest is a shifting landscape of islands, marshlands, shoals and mudflats, some firm enough to be used for cultivation and settlement, other areas only emerging from the sea at the lowest of tides. The firmest areas are the islands proper, a group of which contains Venice itself. The rest divides into *barene*, shoals or strips of land, covered with vegetation, which are only water covered at exceptionally high tides; *velme*, muddy, algae-cloaked stretches that emerge at low tide; and *valli di pesca chiuse*, areas mainly in the north and southwest of the lagoon where most of the fish farms are located. The *valli* have both permanent bodies of water and shoals, ideal for farming, and are surrounded by embankments to protect them from the ebb and flow of the tide. The best way to grasp the diversity of the lagoon is from the air on the approach to the airport, from where the marshes, shoals and water spread like a patchwork below.

THE LAGOON ISLANDS

The lagoon is scattered with islands, many of which were once inhabited, served as hospitals or military installations or housed religious communities. San Giorgio Maggiore and the Giudecca lie close to the south of the city; San Michele, the cemetery island, and Murano, the heart of Venice's glass-blowing industry, are a short hop to the north. Farther north are the islands of Burano, Mazzorbo and Torcello, a once important trio of settlements. The 'barrier' islands of the Lido and Pellestrina guard the lagoon entrances; of the two, the Lido is far more developed, due mainly to its 19th-century role as one of Europe's most fashionable resorts. Pellestrina, to the south, is still a lonely fishing community, a narrow strip of sandy land that feels a thousand miles from central Venice. Other important islands include bucolic Sant'Erasmo, a large agricultural island that still supplies many of the city's vegetables, and San Francesco del Deserto and San Lazzaro degli Armeni, both still retaining a monastic role. Smaller islands still in use are San Servolo, once a psychiatric hospital and now part of Venice International University; San Clemente, one of Venice's classiest hotels; and Sant'Andrea, a fortress island undergoing a lengthy schedule of restoration.

BOATS

Transport throughout the lagoon relies on boats, many of which are unique to Venice. As well as the ubiquitous *vaporetti*, taxis and goods barges, motorized boats include specifically modified vessels which act as refuse barges, fire engines, refrigerated transport, police boats and ambulances. In addition there is a variety of uniquely Venetian boats, whose design has evolved over the centuries for differing and specific uses in the shallow lagoon waters. Prime among these is the gondola (▷ 51); others include:

Topo—a sailing boat originating in Chioggia. They differ in size and were used for fishing. The middle part of the deck is left open to the hold so that the catch can be thrown in.
Puparin—an asymmetrical 10m-long (33ft) general-purpose boat, rowed from a small platform at the stern.
Sanpierota—a small, exceptionally stable craft, much used by families for excursions.
Caorlina—a streamlined rowing boat for six oarsmen, now mainly used for racing.

Clockwise from below *Navigation aids in the lagoon; the island of Torcello with Burano in the distance; green fields and canals characterize the rural island of Torcello*

S'ciopin—a water-hugging small boat, once used for duck shooting; the shallow draft makes it ideal for lagoon use.
Sandalo—a single-handed rowing boat propelled by a standing oarsman using crossed oars.
Mascareta—a light rowing skiff, usually used by women.
Gondolino—a very fast racing gondola, propelled by two oarsmen.

NAVIGATING THE LAGOON

Beneath the surface the water depth varies tremendously, and the lagoon is navigable only along channels, many of which have to be dredged constantly to prevent them from silting up. These are marked by various types of beacons and bollards, each of which follows a precise code of reference. Without them, the lagoon would be totally impassable. The pilings are driven deep into the bed of the lagoon and need replacing every 20 years. They provide attractive perches for the lagoon's birdlife, and the submerged parts support thriving colonies of anemones, barnacles, mussels, limpets, crabs, tiny fish and various seaweeds. The main types are:

Bricola—the massive groups of timber bound with iron hoops. These mark the limits of navigable channels and those along the main routes are illuminated at night.
Dama—generally a group of three large timbers. They mark the entrance to a channel or a junction between two navigable waterways.
Palina—the single poles, seen mainly along the city's canals, which are used as mooring posts. They are often painted with coloured stripes, which signify that the pole belongs to a specific family.

SAN MARCO AND SAN GIORGIO MAGGIORE

Acquapazza (▷ 94) Enjoy super-fresh fish in this modern restaurant where the tables spill out onto the area's prettiest square.

Basilica di San Marco (▷ 76–79) Experience the spiritual heart of Venice and one of Europe's most sublime medieval buildings.

Campo Santo Stefano (▷ 62) Relax with a drink in one of the *sestiere's* loveliest *campi.*

Ebrû (▷ 89) Shop here for Venice's finest marbled paper products in a rainbow of colours.

A gondola trip is a wonderful way to rekindle romance—embark at the Piazza San Marco.

Gritti Palace (▷ 96–97) Stay in a room overlooking the Grand Canal in this luxury hotel rated among the finest in Europe.

Palazzo Ducale (▷ 66–71) Visit the ultimate expression of the might and power of independent Venice, an incredible palace packed with artistic treasures.

San Giorgio Maggiore (▷ 74–75) Admire rational, intellectual and beautiful Palladian architecture at it finest.

Two panoramas: the Bacino di San Marco from the Molo and the view towards San Marco and the mouth of the Grand Canal from San Giorgio Maggiore.

CASTELLO

Anticlea Antiquariato (▷ 118) This tiny shop is a treasure house of antique beads for earrings and necklaces to be made up on the spot.

Bucintoro (▷ 122) Gaze across the Bacino from the windows of your well-appointed room in this nautically themed elegant hotel.

Campo Santa Maria Formosa (▷ 106) Stroll through this lovely square, the focal point of western Castello.

Corte Sconta (▷ 120) Sample a dazzling procession of imaginative dishes at Venice's original new-style restaurant, still rightly acclaimed for its food and ambiance 20-plus years down the line.

Palazzo Grimani (▷ 107) Wander through the frescoed and stuccoed rooms of this fascinating 16th-century Renaissance palace.

Santi Giovanni e Paolo (▷ 112) See the vast tombs and sarcophagi of many doges in this Gothic masterpiece that holds the best examples of Venetian church monuments.

Scuola di San Giorgio degli Schiavoni (▷ 115) Take in the charm and incident that's packed into this picture cycle by Vittore Carpaccio.

Above The glorious Basilica di San Marco

CANNAREGIO

Ca' Dogaressa (▷ 151) Stay in the heart of Cannaregio at this welcoming family-run hotel overlooking the lively Canale di Cannaregio.

Ca' d'Oro (▷ 132–133) Admire the city's most beautiful medieval Venetian merchant's house, superbly set on the Grand Canal, and its treasures.

Fondamenta della Sensa (▷ 144) Stroll hand-in-hand along this quiet quayside for a memorable romantic interlude.

Madonna dell'Orto (▷ 138–139) Soak in the peace of this Venetian Gothic church, packed with paintings by Tintoretto.

Santa Maria dei Miracoli (▷ 142–143) Gaze at the intricate detail of the polychrome marble in this serene Renaissance jewel of a church.

Vini da Gigio (▷ 150) Sample the finest Venetian cooking and superb wines at excellent prices at this temple of Venetian culinary expertise.

SAN POLO AND SANTA CROCE

Antiche Carampane (▷ 192) This tiny and welcoming restaurant is well tucked away, but up with the big players in terms of culinary expertise and imagination.

Campo San Giacomo dell'Orio (▷ 159) Relax with a drink and watch the local life in this focal square.

Campo San Polo (▷ 159) Spend time relaxing in this huge *campo*, Venice's second-largest open space.

Gilberto Penzo (▷ 189) Invest in an intricate model boat or snap up a build-it-yourself miniature gondola kit.

Iris (▷ 193) Enjoy the charms of this excellent-value, peaceful hotel set alongside a picturesque canal.

Rialto (▷ 172–173) Give your senses a feast while you browse the stalls of the city's oldest, biggest and best market, still sited where it's stood for a thousand years.

Santa Maria Gloriosa dei Frari (▷ 177–179) A lofty church that's home to two superb works by Titian and one of Giovanni Bellini's greatest paintings.

Scuola Grande di San Rocco (▷ 182–184) A staggering picture cycle by Tintoretto occupies a purpose-built *scuola grande*.

Above *Statue of the Madonna in Santa Maria dei Miracoli*
Below left *Venice is a popular venue for weddings—with a gondola ride on the Grand Canal for a truly romantic experience*

DORSODURO AND THE GIUDECCA

Accademia bridge (▷ 212) Stand on the Accademia bridge and drink in one of Venice's most iconic views— down the Grand Canal to the great church of the Salute.

La Calcina (▷ 230) Check in to this excellent mid-range hotel, overlooking the Giudecca canal, in a quiet and sought-after part of Dorsoduro.

Campo Santa Margherita (▷ 201) Spend time in Dorsoduro's most picturesque square, the focal point of the *sestiere* at every time of day.

Ca' Rezzonico (▷ 202–203) Get a taste of aristocratic style at this opulent *palazzo*, now a museum of 18th-century life, overlooking the Grand Canal.

Gallerie dell'Accademia (▷ 207–211) Trace the development of Venetian painting in this comprehensive gallery, home to some of Venice's greatest art.

Locanda Montin (▷ 228) Enjoy traditional Venetian cooking and service at one of the city's longest-established restaurants.

Mondonovo (▷ 224) You'll find the very best in handmade traditional and modern Carnival masks at this renowned store.

Punta della Dogana (▷ 214–215) Experience cutting-edge contemporary art in the wonderful surroundings of Venice's old customs house, now the city's newest and most exciting exhibition space.

TOP EXPERIENCES

Take vaporetto No. 1 down the Grand Canal
(▷ 163–169) to drink in the procession of *palazzi* on the world's most beautiful man-made waterway.

Don't miss the bronze horses when you visit the Basilica di San Marco (▷ 77–79). Dating from classical times, they're the oldest equestrian bronze group in the world.

Splash out on a drink at Florian's or Quadri's in the Piazza San Marco (▷ 61), listen to the band and relax in the surroundings of what Napoleon called the 'greatest drawing room in Europe'.

Buy an ice cream at Nico's (▷ 226) and stroll along the Zattere in the late afternoon; soft evening light and views over the water to the Giudecca add to the charms of the city's most sheltered promenade.

Cross the Grand Canal on a *traghetto* (▷ 45), one of the gondola ferries that have transported Venetians for more than a thousand years—and do it standing up.

Spend a day exploring the lagoon islands of Burano, Murano and Torcello (▷ 238, 240–243, 247): leave early and take a picnic to eat in the tranquil little park on Mazzorbo.

Join the well-heeled Venetians in and around Calle Vallaresso (▷ 268–269), home to the big Italian retail names—Fendi, Armani, Bottega Veneta and Gucci.

Watch the glass blowers at work in one of Murano's factories (▷ 240–241).

Take the lift up the Campanile di San Marco (▷ 79). The views over the city and lagoon are wonderful and it's a great way to get your bearings.

Head for the Giardini Pubblici (▷ 106) for green space and room to stretch your legs and, in season, the chance to experience the vibrancy of the international art scene of the Biennale (▷ 105).

Below *A bird's-eye view of Caffè Quadri in the Piazza San Marco from the top of the Campanile*

LIVING VENICE

Arriving in Venice in 1947, Robert Benchley cabled home to the *New Yorker*: 'Streets full of water; please advise'. He had a point, for the most essential fact about Venice is that there are no roads, and the city's main arteries are waterways. Alleys, wharves and squares exist, but the main street is the Grand Canal, from which radiates a 17km (10.5-mile) long spider's web of 177 lesser canals. They follow the old natural watercourses, which meandered through the islets of the lagoon before Venice was founded, and from their earliest days were integral to the everyday life of the city. Everything in the city, old or new, transient or permanent, at some stage has to travel by water. Until the 19th century boats plied incessantly through the Canale di Cannaregio from the mainland or docked in the Bacino; today most of the city's essentials are offloaded from trucks, trains and container ships in the dispiriting and frenzied surroundings of Piazzale Roma and transferred to the ubiquitous barges for onward transport on the canal network. Nowhere in Venice is more than a few metres from a canal, and the city itself is in reality a collection of 118 separate islands, linked by bridges. Beneath these glide gondolas—the city's symbol—grimy barges and refuse collectors, police boats and sleek white taxis, ambulances and fireboats, and myriad small craft. Water dictates the pace of life, and the Venetian existence is unlike that of any other city in the world.

STREET TRAFFIC

Venice's canals are used for delivering everything. Barges and smaller boats penetrate the side canals, offloading food, stores and equipment. From here, everything is transported on trolleys. Workers arrive by water, barges make daily refuse collections and the emergency services use the canal network for all their calls; around 300 fires are extinguished annually from the fire boats, and the white ambulance boats have their own water entrance to the main hospital on the Fondamente Nuove. Beneath the surface, pipes convey fresh water, gas is delivered and waste water empties into the canals. Most sewage nowadays is collected in *pozzi neri* (black wells), the septic tanks that are periodically emptied by specially designed barges.

Clockwise from above *Sightseeing on the Cannaregio Canal; decorated gondolas at their moorings; crossing the Rio di Sant'Anna*

BRIDGES

The canals are crossed by around 400 bridges, many of them dating from the Middle Ages. With a few exceptions, they have single semi-circular arches, and are high enough to provide a passage for gondolas and barges, while four of those on the Grand Canal, the Scalzi, the Accademia and the new Costituzione bridges, were specifically designed to allow enough height for *vaporetti*. Early bridges were wood, later replaced by stone and brick constructions whose foundations rest on wooden piles. Temporary bridges are built for two of Venice's main festivals; one across the Giudecca Canal for the feast of the Redentore in July, and the other across the Grand Canal to the church of the Salute in November. The average Venetian crosses 40 to 50 bridges daily, climbing and descending the equivalent of 120m (400ft) each way.

BOATS

The thoroughbred, streamlined gondola, Venice's 1,000-year-old city boat, is queen of the canals, but over the centuries Venice's boats have evolved to the point where there's a specialized craft for every conceivable function. Traditional boats, redolent with history and all rowed in the traditional Venetian manner, standing up, include the little *sandolo*, designed in the 13th century; the *mascareta*, rowed mainly by women; and the fast-moving *gondolino*, a greyhound of a craft. Modern boats are legion, the *vaporetti*, the public transport vessels and the barges being the real workhorses. Specialized motor boats serve as taxis, police boats, ambulances, fireboats and hearses, while out in the lagoon there are pleasure craft, fishing boats and beautiful, flat-bottomed, wooden sailing boats with square sails and a 10cm (4-inch) draught called *topi*.

KEEPING IT CLEAN

The tide is the first line of defence in keeping the canal system fresh, with the incessant twice-daily tides sweeping constantly in to fill and empty even the narrowest waterways. This is augmented by the regular dredging of the side canals, usually every two to three years, a noxious process whereby each end of the canal is sealed off with boarding and the canal pumped dry. Repairs are then made to the side walls, the bottom scraped of mud and deposits, and any pipe system below water level inspected and repaired if necessary. Despite this cleaning, high summer temperatures inevitably bring an unforgettable, and quintessentially Venetian, smell to many of the smaller side canals. Out in the lagoon, threaded by deepwater channels, dredgers are constantly at work removing the build-ups of silt and sand that the tides bring in.

STORMING THE DECKS

There was a lagoon-wide alert in winter 2004 when ACTV, the transport authority, realized a No. 51 *vaporetto* was missing from its berth near St. Mark's Basin. The vessel was tracked by global positioning technology moving at full throttle across the lagoon. Fearing a terrorist attack on the petrochemical works at Marghera, the police gave chase, upon which the *vaporetto's* mystery thief attempted to ram the much smaller police vessel. Officers eventually forced it into a U-turn, then stormed the ship and overwhelmed a man. He proved to be an extremely drunk, 36-year-old illegal Russian immigrant named Viktor Sobolev, who had taken the *vaporetto* because, in his own words, he 'missed being at sea'. He was charged with aggravated theft, resisting police officers, failing to provide immigration papers, and breaking various navigation laws.

Venice is 123cm (48 inches) lower in the water than in 1900, *acqua alta* ('high water', or flood) hits the city an average of 130 days a year, water levels in the Adriatic will rise 25–60cm (10–23 inches) by 2100, and experts believe the city will be uninhabitable within a hundred years unless new methods of protection from the water are installed. The causes are legion, but most vital of all for the city's survival is the equilibrium of the lagoon, a fragile environment that was actively destroyed during the boom years following World War II. The juggling act of balancing erosion and sedimentation was seriously threatened by indiscriminate tapping of the aquifers beneath the lagoon, undermining the foundations of the city. Pollution levels rocketed, with more than 3.5 million tonnes of waste being dumped daily into the lagoon. Channels 18m (59ft) were gouged into the lagoon bed for petrol tankers and cruise ships, landfill sites proliferated, and the lagoon became deeper, saltier and dirtier. Meanwhile, global warming drove the sea levels higher. Every year the situation worsened, causing huge damage to the city's fabric, exacerbated by the destruction of precious stonework by the chemicals from mainland refineries and industry. The worst of these practices has now been halted, and construction has started on the MoSE (Modulo Sperimentale Elettromeccanico) project; it remains to be seen whether help is coming too late.

HOLDING BACK THE WATERS

After many years of investigation, wrangling and procrastination, work started on the controversial, but vital, MoSE project in 2003. This will consist of 79 hinged floodgates lying flat on the seabed across the three main lagoon entry channels. When damagingly high tides are forecast they will be pumped full of air and will rise to an angle of 30 degrees to prevent flooding in the city, returning to the bottom once the danger is past. Opinion polls show Venetians broadly in favour, but environmentalists are concerned about the delicate ecological balance of the lagoon. In addition, the huge cost of MoSE is channelling public money away from the maintenance of the city's infrastructure. The barrier is scheduled for completion in 2011 at a cost of approximately €4 billion, and will cost €8 million a year to maintain.

Clockwise from above *Oil refineries and chemical plants on the lagoon shore at Mestre; dredging a canal in Cannaregio; the increasing number of tourists is one of the factors contributing to depopulation*

RAISING THE CASH

Restoration projects are costly and lengthy, leaving many of Venice's most iconic facades shrouded in scaffolding for years on end. Often, the scaffolding is covered with a hoarding picturing the hidden building, leaving tourists with an impression of what they're missing. But, in cash-strapped Venice, there's an increasing tendency for the *comune* (city council) to lease out these huge and prominent spaces for advertising, leaving unfortunate visitors, hoping for a photo opportunity of an historic *palazzo*, to find that their images are dominated by an advertisement for luxury leather goods or provocative underwear. Conservationists, art-lovers and academics are enraged, but advertising pays, and the city fathers point out that the money helps to keep the city, and its treasures afloat.

A CASE HISTORY

The church of Santa Maria dei Miracoli was first restored in the 1860s, when the marble facing was removed, cleaned and reattached with cement. By 1970 the underlying brickwork was waterlogged as the cement crumbled, and more work was needed. This restoration was only a temporary measure, as the marble itself was subsequently attacked by mineral salts, and in 1987 yet more work was needed. All walls were desalinated, cleaned and consolidated, crumbling stucco and masonry repaired using traditional techniques and materials, and iron supports replaced with steel ones. The work took more than 10 years to complete and cost $3 million, and, on the scale of Venetian restoration projects, was not considered a hugely difficult or expensive job.

MESTRE AND MARGHERA

Mestre-Marghera is one of the largest industrial complexes in Italy, with oil refineries and chemical plants—and it's just across the lagoon from Venice. Chemical pollution has fallen by 80 per cent since legislation in the 1970s, but the industrial zone is still a major source of pollution. Westerly winds blow the waste onto the historic quarter where the combination of gaseous acid with humidity and salt wreaks havoc. The surface amount eaten away annually is 6 per cent of marble and stone, 5 per cent of frescoes and 3 per cent of paintings on canvas and wood. In addition, giant tankers daily use the channels through the lagoon to ferry more than 12 million tonnes of chemicals and crude oil annually, and conservationists believe it's only a matter of time before a major shipping disaster totally destroys the ecological balance of the lagoon itself.

DEPOPULATION

Since 1946 about 110,000 people have left Venice to live on the mainland, leaving a population of around 60,000. This beautiful city is inconvenient and slow, housing is expensive both to buy and to maintain, and, with the closure of major city businesses—2,000 jobs alone went when Assicurazione Generali moved its headquarters—there is little work outside the tourist and service industries. The population drop has deprived those who have chosen to stay of local shops, tradesmen, workmen and entertainment facilities. The housing issue is being addressed by new construction projects, particularly on the Giudecca, but prices are high, and many new flats are snapped up by well-heeled out-of-towners, who spend little time or money in the city. A 2005 UNESCO report stated gloomily 'Venice is becoming a museum-city, and is no longer a residential one'.

In no other city are art and architecture as central to the essence of a place as they are in Venice. Every corner of this unique city contains buildings, paintings and sculpture that combine to form one of the world's most astonishing urban landscapes. Eastern influences shaped the unique Veneto-Gothic design of the early churches and palaces, the most individual architectural style the city ever produced, which segued in the 15th century into Venice's own take on the Renaissance. Two centuries later the classical forms of the High Renaissance evolved into the triumphantly opulent baroque. Down the line, artists were at work decorating the interior of these buildings; first, in the 11th and 12th centuries with glittering mosaics, and later with paintings on wood and then canvas. Technical expertise, rich hues, daring perspective and luminous light are the hallmarks of Venetian painting, found in the pictures in civic buildings, museums and churches throughout the city. Artists also celebrated the physical reality of their city and its inhabitants with a glorious procession of paintings of the city and its waters, piercing portraits of its citizens through the ages, and wonderfully quirky scenes of everyday life in the style known as *genre* painting. Trade and commerce may have given Venice its power and wealth, but it's the art, whether of paint, stone or gilded wood, that has created the physical reality of the city and still inspires people today.

TODAY'S GRAND TOURISTS

Visitors have been gazing open-mouthed at Venice treasures for centuries, and those on the Grand Tour have been replaced earnest academics and flocks. Well-to-do parent still send their offspring Venice for crash course in art history; some, like UK's John Halls', are firm aimed at students taking a year off, others, like the Venice International University offerings, tar undergraduates from all over the world. Budding academics have a great choice of libraries for research into the city's the Archivio di Stato, w more than 300 rooms of documents, the Fondazi Giorgio Cini, and the lib of the Architectural Fac of the University, one of best in Italy.

Clockwise from above *A scene from* The Wings of the Dove; *there are many delightful views for artists to capture; Caltrava's Ponte della Costituzione is a 21st-century contribution to the wealth of architecture*

A TOUCH OF THE NEW

There's a dearth of modern buildings in Venice. The reasons are myriad; the physical reality of the city, the difficulties of construction, the lack of space. But things are changing in the 21st century, with international architects making their mark. First on the scene was the 2002 high-tech airport terminal, designed by local architect Giampolo Mar, followed in 2008 by the opening of the fourth bridge over the Grand Canal, the work of Spanish super-star Santiago Calatrava. San Michele cemetery is expanding under the direction of UK-based David Chipperfield, while 2009 saw the opening of an exciting contemporary art space at the Punta della Dogana, a cutting-edge, supremely beautiful conversion of the interior of the old customs' building by the Japanese architect Tadao Ando, designed to display art works from the François Pinhault collection.

ON SET

Venice is one of the world's great movie locations, and the city has played starring and cameo roles in a string of films of varying artistic merit. It's the atmosphere, both voluptuous and sinister, that shines in Nicolas Roeg's 1973 adaptation of Daphne du Maurier's *Don't Look Now*, while David Lean's 1955 *Summertime*, starring Katharine Hepburn, captures the romance of Venice, and Visconti's *Death in Venice* its air of mist-laden nostalgia. But, above all, Venice sparkles in a costume drama, whether it's *The Wings of the Dove*, with Helena Bonham Carter making yet another corseted appearance, the decadent *Comfort of Strangers*, directed by Paul Schrader, or 2008's re-minted *Brideshead Revisited*, with Matthew Goode and Ben Wishaw as Charles Ryder and Sebastian Flyte, whiling away a self-indulgent golden summer in the Palazzo Contarini Polignac on the Grand Canal.

ART ON EVERY CORNER

Venice's museums are packed with great paintings, but the attraction for many visitors may well be a little something to take home—and there's plenty on offer. Pavement artists of varying talent are everywhere, knocking out canal scenes, lurid sunsets, gondolas and gondoliers and a hundred versions of the Bridge of Sighs. These artists congregate en masse at the Giardini ex Reali and along the Riva degli Schiavoni, where they exhibit their finished work and sketch out the work in progress. Most use vividly bright oils as a medium, though a few go for charcoal or watercolour, and will happily run up a special commission. Many of the subjects are pure pastiche, including canals that don't exist and buildings in the wrong place, but they're only following in a great Venetian tradition—Canaletto was guilty of the very same offence.

SAVING VENICE

The catastrophic floods of 1966 drew the world's spotlight on the perilous state of Venice and her treasures and was the impetus for one of the most audacious international conservation projects ever launched—a scheme to save not just a single building, but an entire city. Today, more than two dozen international organizations, under the umbrella guidance of UNESCO, work to raise funds for restoration and conservation. Topping the list are the British-based Venice in Peril fund, founded in the immediate aftermath of the 1966 floods as the result of an urgent phone call from the Italian director Franco Zeffirelli, and Save Venice Inc, operating with US money. All these private committees work closely with the Italian government and city authorities; Italy itself has provided more than 90 per cent of the money so far expended.

Once the 18th-century party capital of Europe, Venice still knows how to celebrate in style. There's a year-round procession of large-scale pageantry and fun, much of it aimed firmly at the Venetians themselves—though free-spending foreigners are always welcome. Historically festivals have always been part of city life, used by the powers-that-be in the great days of the Republic to bolster the power and prestige of the State, celebrate the feast days of local saints, give thanks for plague deliverances, and allow the citizenry to let off steam. Unsurprisingly, the feasts still dearest to the natives' hearts are those associated with water, which range from the superb Grand Canal pageantry of the Regata Storica and its accompanying races, to the chaotic fun of the Vogalonga (Long Row). Culture gets a good showing during the summer and autumn, when the internationally high-profile Biennale and the Film Festival bring in the artistic world's movers, shakers and beautiful people, while winter brings the start of the opera season and music in churches across the city. Things really get going in late winter, when Carnevale draws costumed and masked revellers from all over the world to pose against the magnificent backdrop of Venice itself. On a lower key, the year's rhythm is punctuated by more Venetian events—local saint's days, the city marathon, which crosses the lagoon and ends at the Riva degli Schiavoni, and open-air film events and children's traditional festivities.

THE MARITIME CELEBRATIONS

The first Sunday after Ascension sees the Vogalonga, the Long Row, a 33km (20.5-mile) row from St. Mark's Basin through the lagoon and back via the Canale di Cannaregio and the Grand Canal. Founded to encourage Venetian-style rowing—standing—the event now attracts entries from all over Europe and great effort goes into decorating some of the boats. The best place to watch is in Cannaregio, where the boats re-enter the bottleneck canal accompanied by cheering crowds. The Regata Storica in September is a far grander event, with a spectacular procession down the Grand Canal. Venetians love the races that follow, a series of four events for different boats that finishes at the Volta, the big curve on the Grand Canal at Ca' Foscari, where the prize-giving takes place on the Machina, a temporary floating grandstand.

Clockwise from above *Celebrating the Marriage of Venice to the Sea; Venetians processing across the pontoon bridge during the Festa del Redentore; a masked figure in an extravagant costume takes part in the Carnevale gondola procession along the Grand Canal*

CARNEVALE

Carnevale officially starts 10 days before *martedi grasso* (Shrove Tuesday, or Mardi Gras), so exact dates depend on when Easter falls. Well before the opening, traditional carnival goods appear in *pasticcerie*, such as *fritelle*, a fried spiced or cream-filled doughnut. The first Saturday sees a masked procession and party in the Piazza San Marco, followed the next day by the highlight of the first week, the *volo dell'angelo* (flight of the Angel), when a female acrobat swoops down a wire from the top of the Campanile to the Piazza below. *Giovedi grasso* (Thursday) sees the competition for the best costume, Friday a masked open-air ball in the Piazza, and Saturday a masked gondola procession along the Grand Canal. Carnevale culminates on Shrove Tuesday with clowns, acrobats and fireworks in the Piazza, and celebrations, parties and entertainment all over the city.

OUT AND ABOUT

Two events provide the counterbalance to a series of festivals that are heavy on tradition and culture; Su e Zo per I Ponti (Up and Down the Bridges) and the Venice Marathon. Su e Zo originated more than 20 years ago as an attempt to raise awareness of Venice, and consists of navigating your way through the city by means of a map and a list of checkpoints to tick off. There's a slew of opportunities for eating and drinking, both in the city's *bacari*, and at temporary official watering holes along the way—after the sixth refreshment stop, finishing the course tends to lose its importance. The October Marathon is a different story. This 42km 195m (26.2-mile) run starts on *terra firma* on the Riviera del Brenta, with runners crossing the lagoon via the Ponte della Libertà, running through the city to cross the Grand Canal on a pontoon bridge and finishing on the Riva dei Sette Martiri.

THE PLAGUE FESTIVALS

In 1576, Venice celebrated deliverance from a major plague outbreak with the construction of the church of Il Redentore (The Redeemer). Ever since, the third week of July sees the construction of a pontoon bridge across the Giudecca Canal to link the church with the main city, across which people process in the run-up to the Saturday celebrations. During the Saturday afternoon hundreds of little boats, laden with people, mass on the water to picnic and party while awaiting the spectacular firework finale. Another pontoon bridge goes up in November, this time across the Grand Canal to the church of the Salute, built after the 1631 plague. On 21 November each year, the Patriarch, the Cardinal of Venice, crosses the bridge from the Salute and processes to San Marco. People flock to the church to buy candles and enjoy the goodies sold at the stalls en route.

BIENNALE AND FILM FESTIVAL

The Biennale d'Arte Contemporanea was established in 1895 to showcase contemporary art, and now alternates with the Biennale d'Architettura Contemporanea, highlighting modern architecture, held in even-numbered years. Both attract visitors and exhibitors from all over the world, who showcase their work in the Giardini Pubblici, and in the Arsenale buildings. The Biennale runs concurrently with the Mostra Internazionale d'Arte Cinematografica, better known as the Venice Film Festival, held on the Lido. This major event runs for two weeks, showing films in three venues, the main one being the Palazzo del Cinema, and awarding a prestigious prize. In recent years, it has worked hard to attract the big-name stars, moving away from its art-house image, though the prizes still go to the non-commercial, indie offerings.

UNDERSTANDING LIVING VENICE

For all its charm, Venice is a city in the modern world, and there's a determination to hold its own against the vibrant economies of the prosperous towns of the Veneto. This is a decidedly left-leaning city in a region that's increasingly conservative, and its dynamic former mayor, Paolo Costa, used this attitude to full advantage when he was the moving force behind a letter, signed by mayors from all over the world, that urged President George Bush to change his stance on the Kyoto Treaty. In the run-up to the 2004 Iraq War, Venetians were outspoken in their criticism of British and American policy, an attitude that was perhaps a legacy of the city's Centro Pace (Peace Centre), founded by the city council in 1983 and now including more than 35 member organizations. Living in a treasure house that attracts more than 12 million visitors annually has brought a tolerance at grass-roots level to the Venetian character. This is helped by the recognition of the part played by the numerous international organizations working to preserve the city, who pump money into restoration projects. Venice has been welcoming foreigners for centuries, and lessons continue to be learned, with an increasing effort by the council, businesses and cultural associations to deal with the impact of the vast numbers of day-trippers by promoting the city as a vibrant cultural centre, rather than a historic theme park.

THE FOREIGN CONTINGENT

Venice has a large, and diverse, foreign population. Numerically high on the list are the academics, writers, researchers and students immersed in studying the city's past and preserving Venice for the future, but there's an increasing number of foreigners who simply want a holiday home. Demand for property is high, but it's a double-edged sword: foreigners have the desire, and money, to live in, and thus preserve, old buildings, but their homes are often empty for months on end and rising prices prevent Venetians from buying. Old-hand foreign residents wonder too, if the newcomers have missed the boat in terms of the Venetian dream; the city has changed hugely in the last ten years and living in Venice is an increasing story of struggling to maintain normal life in the face of massive tourism.

Clockwise from above *Putting the world to rights in Cannaregio; friends stop for a chat; boat building in Squero di San Trovaso*

A SMALL-TOWN CITY

Tourists may travel thousands of miles to marvel at Venice, but its inhabitants are firmly wedded to their own home patch, their *sestiere*. There are still plenty of Venetians who rarely get as far as St. Mark's Square and whose lives are focused on their own *campo* and *calle*. Living in a carless society, where everyone walks or takes a boat, brings a unique sense of community. Locals shop locally, bump into friends regularly and nurture a network of local concerns, bringing a marvellously village-like feeling to the city. Venice is remarkably safe and, give or take a pickpocket or two, crime rates are low; children can play and walk to school unattended and the streets are safe at night. Provincial it may be, but provincialism has its charms.

IT'S A MAN'S WORLD

They say gondoliers are born and not made, and it certainly helps to be both Venetian and male if that is your chosen career path. Of the 425 members of the Ente Gondola, the official gondoliers' co-operative, there is one sole woman, 23-year-old Georgia Boscolo, the daughter of a gondolier, who was formally accepted into the Ente in June 2009. With her family connections and expertise, she can now expect to earn anything up to €40,000 a year. In sad contrast, however, is the case of Alexandra Hai, a German-born would-be gondolier, who struggled for years to pass the exams, finally succeeding in 2007. Far from being accepted into the trade, the only suitable work she could find was private employment ferrying around guests from three Venetian hotels.

MASSIMO CACCIARI

Born in Venice, Massimo Cacciari, Mayor of Venice, is a Centre-Leftist philosopher and politician. Mayor between 1993 and 2000, he was re-elected in 2005 on an anti-MoSE ticket (▷ 16). He campaigned for a tourist tax on visitors to Venice—he's been known to suggest that all potential visitors should sit an exam in order to qualify for a visit—on the one hand, yet encouraged the development of still more accommodation on the other. He continues to hold strong views on the viability of the MoSE project, though, with the scheme nearing completion, this may prove irrelevant come election time. Venetians value him as a fellow Venetian, with a true understanding of the city and its problems, but, like many politicians, he has to balance his beliefs against the entrenched views of the officials and colleagues surrounding him.

THE CVN

Venice's biggest political hot potato is solving the ongoing problem of simply staying afloat. This means not only preventing further water damage within the city, but also safeguarding the lagoon environment, and the job is the responsibility of the Consorzio Venezia Nuovo. This body is funded by the Ministry of Public Works and the Venetian Water Authority and it's constituted so it can plan, organize and manage operations from start to finish. Its biggest initiative is the MoSE project, but it's also behind the funding and construction of higher-level canalside *fondamente*, silt dredging, reinforcing 46km (28.5 miles) of sea walls and ruling on the transit of big oil tankers through the lagoon. Some of its decisions have been contentious, but, as work on sea defences progresses, the benefits are starting to be seen.

THE CITY TODAY

Above *Performers at the Biennale festival*

Venetians are nothing if not determined—the mere existence of the lagoon city is proof of that. The problems are immense, but Venice has succeeded in selling itself as the property of the whole world, and its millions of admirers feel they have a stake in its future. Far-sighted planning and the desire for change into a cultural centre on a 21st-century scale may provide yet another makeover in the city's long history. Venetians are well aware they have to help themselves but know, too, they can count on the world's support to look to the future on a foundation of a glorious past. The authorities are finally addressing the problem of depopulation and excess visitors, though global warming remains the major threat. Even here, a strong recognition that action is needed may have emerged in the nick of time.

THE COMMUTING BUSINESS

Around 60,000 people live in Venice but the city is serviced by a massive daily influx of workers arriving from the mainland, who pour into the city by rail, bus or car across the causeway. The rush hour sees jam-packed *vaporetti* as workers fan out across the city, and two new projects are addressing this logjam. In 2008 a new bridge opened across the Grand Canal between the bus terminal at Piazzale Roma and the area immediately west of the railway station, a link which is encouraging commuters working in the western areas to walk the whole way to work. More *vaporetto* space was freed up too, by the sleek new monorail link running from the huge car parks at Tronchetto to Piazzale Roma which opened in April 2010.

CITY OF THE ARTS

Venice's future may well lie as a big-time player in the world cultural league. First steps to realizing this came in 1999 when the Biennale enlarged its scope to include not only the visual arts, architecture and film, but the performing arts as well, with international big names in theatre, music and dance visiting the city. If plans for the further revamp of the Arsenale, Venice's historic shipyards, go ahead, the area will become a huge cultural and exhibition space; parts are already used during the Biennale. Across St. Mark's Basin, the Fondazione Giorgio Cini, on the island of San Giorgio Maggiore, is continuing to enlarge its schedule of cultural conferences, and has restored and reopened the beautiful open-air Teatro Verde as a summer performance venue.

THE STORY OF VENICE

Venice, according to legend, was founded at midday on Friday 25 March 421; historical reality is less exact. As early as the eighth century BC there was some settlement of the lagoon by the Venetii and Euganei tribes from the adjoining mainland, and by 250BC Rome had conquered northeast Italy and founded important colonies at Padua, Verona and Aquileia. These thriving cities viewed the muddy islets of the lagoon as a place apart, attractive only for fishing and hunting forays. Attitudes changed around 375, when the barbarian Huns and Visigoths swept south to threaten the rich cities of the Veneto. The inhabitants fled to the lagoon, establishing settlements on the marshy islands, which became a duchy called Venetia. Vital to this was the stabilization of the existing land, the control of the rivers, which threatened to silt up the navigable channels, and the regulation of the tides to safeguard the settlements. Once this equilibrium of the lagoon waters was achieved, the embryonic state could thrive while the rest of Europe entered its darkest age. Politically and commercially, the early Venetians looked east to the more stable Byzantine Empire, gradually attaining sufficient autonomy to elect their first duke, or doge, in 697. The ninth century saw the construction of St. Mark's Basilica and the Doge's Palace, funded by a booming economy based on trade and shipping. By the start of the 11th century, Venice was a major mercantile power with a growing empire.

ANGELO PARTICIPAZIO

In 810 Pepin the Frank, son of Charlemagne, invaded Lombardy and swept through the mainland towns to besiege the lagoon communities, including Malamocco, the Venetians' main settlement. Things looked bad until a great leader, Angelo Participazio, emerged. He abandoned Malamocco, moving the capital to the Riva Alta, a settlement in the heart of the lagoon. From here, he sent his fleet first to head towards the Frankish ships massed outside the lagoon, then to feign terror and retreat into the shallow waters around the Rialto. The Franks, scenting cowardice, followed, only to run aground on the myriad sandbanks, allowing the Venetians to pick them off at their leisure and secure the lagoon. Angelo was elected doge, and it was during his reign that work started on the Doge's Palace and the lagoon communities were first formally called Venetia.

Clockwise from above *An intricate mosaic in Basilica di San Marco; St. Theodore and his crocodile still survey Venice from a column in the Piazzetta; two of the Palazzo Ducale's Four Moors, or tetrarchs, from the fourth century*

THE LIONS OF VENICE

The lion is the symbol of St. Mark and, like the saint, has become inextricably associated with Venice itself. St. Mark's lion still appears on the city's flag, on all official documents, on billboards and souvenir shops, and, in early times, was carved on the prows of warships; lions still guard the gates of the Arsenale. The Venetian lion, often winged, frequently appears with his paw on an open book—St. Mark's Gospel— engraved with the words '*Pax tibi, Marce*' (Peace be with you, Mark). There are hundreds of stone lions throughout the city, including 75 alone on the Porta della Carta, the main entrance to the Palazzo Ducale. Live lions were sometimes kept in the city gardens and their cubs fed at the expense of the state.

A PREMIER LEAGUE SAINT

The rising star of ninth-century Venice needed a saint to rival Rome's great patron, St. Peter. The Venetians chose St. Mark the Evangelist, whose remains lay in Alexandria in Egypt. To bolster the claim, stories were told of a visit to the lagoon by St. Mark and St. Paul, where they beheld a vision of Jesus appearing to Mark and saying '*Pax tibi Marcus Evangelista meus*' (peace be to you Mark, my evangelist). Despite this, the Christians of Alexandria were unwilling to give up St. Mark, so smuggling was the only answer. In 828, two merchants sailed to Egypt, seized St. Mark's body and, burying it under a cargo of pork to stop the Muslims and Jews searching too closely, brought the saint to his new home.

ST. THEODORE AND THE CROCODILE

Venice's first patron, St. Theodore, still occupies his perch on a column in the Piazzetta. He was born in Asia Minor, converted to Christianity, and became a brave soldier in the Roman army. Stationed in a remote mountain town in Persia, he slew a demon-possessed dragon with a bad habit of devouring local children, and generally annoyed his pagan superiors with his piety and good works. In 313 he was beheaded, canonized as a martyr and buried in Egypt. From here, his remains were shipped to southern Italy, where he came to the attention of the Venetians, who adopted him as their patron, using the dragon, now in the guise of a crocodile, as his symbol. St. Theodore's position was short-lived; with the rise of Venetian power the city dumped him in lieu of a higher-profile saint.

MARRIAGE TO THE SEA

The lagoon and Adriatic were vital to the city's wealth and safety, and Venice's reliance on the sea was first celebrated in 997 in a symbolic ceremony of marriage, which was enacted annually on Ascension Day until the fall of the Republic. The doge proceeded in the magnificent state barge called the *Bucintoro*, after Alexander the Great's horse, Bucephalus, to the Porto di Lido, the channel onto the open sea, where he threw a gold ring into the waters with the words 'I wed thee, oh Sea, in sign of perpetual dominion', a clear reminder to other nations of Venice's domination of the Adriatic. Hymns were sung before the procession returned to the Rialto for celebrations to mark the occasion, leaving the spectators free to dive into the sea and recover the ring for themselves, a case of finders, keepers.

With its growing merchant power, Venice was ready for expansion. The 11th century started well with the defeat of the Adriatic pirates by Doge Pietro Orseolo in 1000, a victory that brought much of Dalmatia, the northeastern coast of the Adriatic, under Venetian control. Farther south, the Normans still held sway, and looked increasingly aggressively towards the failing Byzantine Empire. In 1081, the Byzantine emperor appealed to Venice for help, and Venetian ships played a key role in the ensuing naval battles. Venice triumphed, establishing itself as the protector of the Empire, and securing the Adriatic shipping lines and advantageous trading rights with Byzantium, enshrined in the Golden Bull of 1082, a charter of alliance between Venice and the Byzantine emperor. Further opportunities for trade and territorial expansion came with the First Crusade, a pan-Christian expedition to free the Holy Land from Muslim occupation. The Venetians provided ships and finance, neatly reaping a profit while appearing piously to support this Christian enterprise, and extending the city's influence in the Aegean and Black Sea. In 1171, the six *sestieri*, the wards into which Venice is divided, were established. Fire destroyed the ninth-century Basilica di San Marco, but work started on a new structure, which was inaugurated in 1094. Churches such as San Giacomo al Rialto and San Nicolò dei Mendicoli were built, and the first grand *palazzi* went up around the growing commercial centre of the Rialto.

THE PEACE OF VENICE
In 1177, Venice achieved a major diplomatic coup when it persuaded the warring Pope Alexander III and the Holy Roman Emperor Frederick Barbarossa to meet in Venice. Worn out and almost bankrupt by years of struggle, the two made peace in Venice. It was the end of Frederick's attempt to establish his supremacy over the Pope, and he asked for forgiveness and received absolution at San Marco. Alexander was so delighted with his reception he gave Doge Zani a golden rose and a golden ring, which was used in the ceremony of the Marriage to the Sea.

Clockwise from above *Pope Alexander III presents the sword of office to Doge Ziani; a medieval Arabian perfumier at work; stunnning mosaics decorate the cupolas of San Marco*

SHIPS AND SHIPBUILDING

Venice's mastery of shipbuilding began early, with craftsmen being sent abroad to Dalmatia and Istria to learn construction techniques in the seventh century. By 1104 the Arsenale, the city's shipyards, were functioning initially as an arms and repair depot, with private yards responsible for the actual building. In emergencies workers were requisitioned by the doge, and shipbuilding became increasingly focused in one place. Teams of men, the *arsenalotti*, composed of carpenters, sawyers, caulkers and apprentices, worked together under a foreman, and could build up to six large galleys every two years. The merchant galleys were fast and light. They sailed in convoy for protection and specialized in transporting valuable cargoes of spices, silks, furs, gold, ivory and amber.

FIRST AMONG EQUALS

The first doges were presented to the people, in theory their electors, as *primus inter pares*, first among equals. In practice, early doges were despotic and thus prone to meet calamitous ends—of the 50 doges holding office up to 1172, 20 were exiled, murdered or deposed. In 1044 laws were drawn up to limit their power and they were barred from naming their successors. The Senate, a distinct council, evolved to supervise the doge's activities, and a complex electoral system was established. The doges ruled for life, leading to repeated elections of elderly men who, it was felt, would have less time to build up their own, potentially dangerous, power base. The average election age was 72, and by about the year 1200 the role of the doge had become similar to that of a modern European president.

OFFICINE ET LABORATOIRE D'UN PARFUMEUR CHIMISTE ARABE

THE *MAGGIOR CONSIGLIO*

In 1172 power passed from the doge to the *Maggior Consiglio*, the Great Council, founded by 35 members of Venice's leading patrician families. The council was responsible for legislation, and by 1297 had grown to more than 500, prompting the *Serrata del Maggior Consiglio* (the Closing of the Great Council), which limited membership to those on the original list of 500. This evolved in 1315 into the *Libro d'Oro*, the Golden Book, a closed register of noble families, from whose ranks were drawn council members and officers of state. From these names, too, the *Senato* and *Collegio* members were drawn, augmented by provincial and religious representatives. These two bodies remained virtually unaltered for more than 500 years.

THE ART OF MOSAIC

The glowing mosaic decoration of San Marco is a legacy of Byzantium, where this Greco-Roman skill continued throughout the Dark Ages. Mosaics are designed to cover large surfaces like a skin, and are composed of thousands of tiny pieces of tinted glass, fitted together to form a picture. They are created by first plastering the area to be covered, then tracing the design in fine detail on this surface. Each day, a layer of cement is applied and the *tesserae*, glass pieces, embedded in it. Glass of all hues is used, including gold and silver, made by applying the metals in leaf form to transparent glass, then fusing them with an over layer. The glass shards are deliberately set at different angles so the light will be refracted in varying ways to stunning visual effect.

POWER, TRADE AND WEALTH 1199–1453

In 1199 the Fourth Crusade was called, and by 1202 Crusaders from all over Europe were mustering in Venice to requisition ships and supplies, for which they were unable to pay in full. This provided Venice with the opportunity to persuade the Crusaders to let Venice both lead the expedition and make a detour to Constantinople, Christian capital of the Eastern Empire. Led by Doge Enrico Dandolo, the Crusaders attacked Constantinople in 1204, looted and sacked the city and carved up the Empire, Venice keeping every strategic port and island and gaining complete domination of the eastern Mediterranean trade routes. Sixty years later, aided by Genoa, the Byzantine emperor evicted the Venetians from Constantinople, leading to a Venetian-Genoese conflict that was finally resolved in 1381 with a decisive Venetian victory at the Battle of Chioggia. This heralded an era of unrivalled wealth and expansion, hardly dented by the 1348 Black Death, which left two-thirds of the city's population dead. It was during the 14th and 15th centuries that Venice assumed the architectural appearance it has today, with a reputation as the richest city in Christendom. At this time, too, the state increased its hold over the citizens, with measures to ensure that power remained in the hands of the elite and the Council of Ten, an all-powerful, secret commission whose spies were everywhere. It was a golden age, but for the blow inflicted in 1453, when Constantinople, the great trade centre, fell to the Turks.

DOGE ENRICO DANDOLO
Enrico Dandolo was nearing 90 and practically blind when the Crusaders approached him for help with the Fourth Crusade. He drove a hard bargain; for 85,000 silver marks he agreed to ship 33,500 men and their equipment to the Holy Land and to supply Venetian soldiers and warships for the expedition, with the proviso that he would lead the force. The Crusaders did not have the money, and found themselves blocked in the lagoon until they agreed to attack some ports on the Dalmatian coast and then detour to the Christian city of Constantinople. Dandolo himself led the attack, and encouraged the troops to plunder and destroy, thus making Venice 'Lords and Masters of a Quarter and a Half-quarter of the Roman Empire'.

Clockwise from above *The four bronze horses of San Marco; merchant adventurer Marco Polo (1254–1324); Doge Marin Falier (1274–1355), executed for aggrandizement*

MARCO POLO

In 1269 Marco Polo, a member of a family of merchant adventurers, left Venice to travel overland to Asia in pursuit of trade— sugar, spice, silk and cotton. Travelling along the Silk Road, he reached the court of the great Kublai Khan, ruler of the Mongol Empire, in 1274, and remained in China for 17 years, serving the Khan as governor and emissary. He was a great favourite, amply rewarded with money and precious jewels. These accompanied him home in 1292, via a route that took him south to Sumatra and Sri Lanka. He arrived, unrecognized, back in Venice in 1295, dictating his memoirs of 'a million wonders' while languishing in jail as a prisoner of war of the Genoese, and dying in 1324. His house, in the aptly named Corta Seconda del Milion, is still marked by a plaque.

BLACK DEATH

The first major outbreak of plague, in the shape of the Black Death, hit Venice in 1348. The disease originated in Mongolia and may have spread to Europe along the trade routes, or, as is more likely, was carried back by Genoese sailors. Called the Black Death because of the skin discolouration and black buboes that appeared in the groin, the plague, fatal in 99 per cent of all cases, took 37 days to incubate and kill. In Venice, 60 per cent of the population died over the course of 18 months, with deaths running at 500 to 600 a day at the height of the epidemic. Victims were buried on the now vanished island of San Marco in Boccalama. The Venetians learned a lot from this first epidemic and later introduced measures to isolate incoming ships and establish quarantine islands in the lagoon.

THE TIEPOLO CONSPIRACY

Following the closure of the Maggior Consiglio in 1297, many of the mercantile class were indignant to have missed their chance to participate in government. None more so than Baiamonte Tiepolo, who, in 1310, banded together with two conspirators to lead a revolt. The timing went wrong, his associates were captured, and Tiepolo was left marching through the main shopping street with a train of rebels. As they progressed, legend tells that an old woman, leaning from her window, dislodged a stone, which hit Tiepolo's standard-bearer on the head. Panic ensued, Tiepolo's troops fled and the rebellion failed. Tiepolo was sent into exile and his *palazzo* razed, and fear of a future conspiracy led to the establishment of the notorious Council of Ten.

THE COUNCIL OF TEN

Venice's most feared and powerful institution, the Council of Ten, was founded in 1310 to deal with insurrection and conspiracy. It had virtually unlimited powers, running the Inquisition, controlling the police and maintaining a network of spies. These were helped by ordinary citizens who were encouraged to denounce each other through anonymous letters, posted in the lion's head boxes that are still scattered about the city. No one was beyond the Council's reach, not even the Doge. In 1355 Doge Marin Falier was executed following an attempt to increase his powers and establish his family as hereditary leaders, the last attempt to attack the principle of rule by the Senate and Councils. In the series of dogal portraits in the Hall of the Maggior Consiglio, Falier is conspicuously absent, his place forever shrouded under a black cloth, with no likeness beneath.

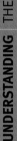

In 1544 Venice signed a peace treaty with Francesco Sforza of Milan, a move that marked the end of the Republic's annexation of territory in mainland Italy, begun in the 15th century. Venice now held much of the modern Veneto region, Udine and Friuli, Verona and its hinterland. This inland empire was to remain intact for nearly 300 years and did something to alleviate the gradual loss of overseas political and trading power. The first blow abroad had come in 1453 with the fall of Constantinople, causing the loss of Venice's crucial trading privileges, and in 1489 Vasco da Gama reached Calcutta by sea, putting an end to the Republic's monopoly of Far Eastern trade. Such was the city's accumulated wealth that the economic effects of these events were at first barely felt, and the 16th century saw an explosion of the decorative and performing arts within the city. But these riches fuelled dislike among the other European powers and the early 16th century was a story of warfare. By mid-century, mutual fear of the Ottomans united the European powers, led by Venice, and the Turks' advance was temporarily halted by their naval defeat at the Battle of Lepanto in 1571. This proved to be a hollow victory, swiftly followed by the secession of all the Venetian Mediterranean possessions to the Turks. The 17th century saw attempts to regain territory, but the trend was towards steady decline, and by 1718 Venice was virtually bankrupt and its government inert.

CATERINA CORNARO, QUEEN OF CYPRUS

Caterina Cornaro, a pawn in the hands of the Senate, was a member of the Corner family, a powerful clan with strong interests in Cyprus. With the Turks pressing hard in the eastern Mediterranean, the island was seen as a strategically vital Venetian possession and its loyalty was bolstered by the marriage of Caterina to the King of Cyprus in 1472. Only a year later he died and she was forced to surrender the island first to Venetian control, and then to the doge, abdicating in 1489. Caterina was given a hypocritically triumphant welcome back in Venice and then presented with the lordship of the town of Ásolo, where she held a cultured and sophisticated court until her death in 1510.

Clockwise from above The Miraculous Intervention of SS. Peter and Paul in the Battle of Lepanto *by Ottaviano Dandidi*; San Giorgio Maggiore *was designed by Palladio*; *detail from Tintoretto's* Last Supper *(1560) in San Trovaso*

MARCANTONIO BRAGADINO

Bragadino was a Venetian general captured by the Turks in Cyprus in 1571. Besieged for 11 months, he surrendered under the promise of safe passage for him and his men. Instead, the Turks slaughtered his men and then cut off Bragadino's nose and ears, before thrice withholding execution at the last moment. He was then paraded, laden with earth, around the Turkish camp, being forced to kiss the ground each time he passed the Pasha's tent, a regime only interrupted by hours spent suspended from the yardarms of a ship. He was finally chained to a stake and slowly skinned alive, the Turks stuffing his skin with straw and sending it back to Venice. Bragadino's skin is still preserved in an urn on his monument in the church of Santi Giovanni e Paolo.

THE BATTLE OF LEPANTO

Virtually unknown until 1300, by the 16th century the Ottoman Turks were a constant threat, and in 1570 an alliance of Venice, Spain and the Papal States mustered a huge fleet of 208 war galleys to sail against them to avenge previous defeats. Under the command of John of Austria, half-brother to Philip II of Spain, the fleet sailed to the Gulf of Corinth and encountered the Turkish force off Lepanto on 7 October 1571. It was the largest naval battle ever fought in the Mediterranean and a resounding victory for Venice and her allies, with 117 galleys captured. Back home, the news was greeted with an orgy of self-congratulation, but it was a shallow victory and the Turks remained as strong as ever. In 1573 Cyprus was handed to the Turks, and Crete, the final Venetian possession, fell in 1669.

LIFE ON THE MAINLAND

Land on the newly acquired Venetian *terra firma* rapidly became a must-have for the aristocracy during the 16th century. Rents and farming filled the coffers and the countryside was a welcome escape from the city. Access from Venice to the cool hills was easy along the Brenta, and it was in the hinterland of this river that many families built their summer villas. The architect of choice was Andrea Palladio (1508–80), who designed a staggering variety of classically influenced summer palaces throughout the provinces of Vicenza, Padua and Treviso. Best-known are the Villa Malcontenta, modelled on the lines of a Greek temple and the inspiration for thousands of other distinctive buildings; the beautifully set Villa Barbaro, inspired by traditional Veneto farm buildings; and the Villa Rotonda, a pleasure palace with a fine dome, built for a retired cleric.

THE VENETIAN RENAISSANCE

Despite a waning economy, the 16th and 17th centuries saw an explosion of art, architecture and music in Venice. The Renaissance started later here than in Tuscany, with the first clutch of big-name painters—the Bellinis, Cima da Conegliano and Carpaccio—active from the mid-15th century. They laid the foundations for the superstars of the 16th century: Giorgione, Titian, Tintoretto and Veronese, who worked all over the city, their paintings remaining in their original homes to this day. On the architectural front, Venice turned its back on its own unique Veneto-Gothic style and embraced classical ideals. The buildings designed by Palladio, Sanmicheli, Sansovino and Scamozzi illustrate this new style, and were, and still are, the perfect backdrop for the music of the Gabriellis and Venice's lauded composer, Antonio Vivaldi.

By 1718 the writing was on the wall for Venice as a political power. The city was still rich, but the funds were in the hands of patrician families rather than the state, and it was the aristocracy who fuelled Venice's reputation as the party capital of Europe. Carnevale ran for months at a time, playboys, embodied by that great lover, Casanova, roamed the streets, and fortunes were squandered in the city's gambling houses. The state, meanwhile, turned its last efforts against the perpetual threat of seas and tides, building the vast *murazzi* to protect the lagoon against the Adriatic. By the 1790s Venice was bankrupt and politically stagnant. When Napoleon invaded in 1797, there was no money left; the last doge, Lodovico Manin, was deposed and the once mighty Senate voted itself out of existence. Between 1797 and 1815, Venice was first Austrian, then French, then, with the fall of Napoleon, Austrian again. In 1848, two years after the construction of the railway bridge linking Venice to the mainland, there was a brief resurgence of the old independent spirit, when Venetians revolted against the occupying Austrians. An independent republican government was set up which held the city in a state of siege for five months. The uprising failed, and the Austrians renewed their grip. In 1866, the Austrians, badly weakened by defeats by the Prussians, handed over the city to the newly formed united Italian State.

MURAZZI (THE SEA WALLS)

The construction of the great *murazzi*, sea walls on the barrier island of Pellestrina, was the last great engineering work undertaken by the Republic. The maintenance of the water level in the lagoon had been a Venetian preoccupation since the city's foundation, and a special government department, the Magistrati alle Acque, was responsible for lagoon management. Sandy, low-lying Pellestrina had long been a weak link in the lagoon's defences and these great ramparts, 14m (46ft) wide and rising to 4.5m (14.75ft) above the mean tide level, were the final solution. Beautifully built of Istrian stone, they were erected between 1744 and 1782. They still stand, a monument to the everlasting struggle to keep the sea out and the city protected.

Clockwise from above *Paintings by Tiepolo in the church of Sant'Alvise; the opening of the Ponte dell'Accademia in 1854; Giacomo Casanova*

GIACOMO CASANOVA

Casanova, history's most noted libertine, was born in Venice in 1725, a man whose aim, as he wrote in his memoirs, was 'always to indulge my senses; I never knew anything of greater importance'. His life story is a monument to this philosophy, encompassing constant sexual adventures, gambling, drunkenness and other notoriously bad behaviour, which eventually led, in 1755, to accusations of witchcraft and imprisonment in the Palazzo Ducale. From here Casanova escaped by climbing through a hole in the ceiling and over the surrounding rooftops to emerge in the Piazza looking, in his own words, 'like a man of quality who had been beaten up in a brothel'. The next years were spent in exile, constantly on the move, one step ahead of creditors and enraged husbands. In 1774 he moved back to Venice, working as a government spy, but 10 years later, under threat of a libel suit, he fled to Bohemia, where he died in 1798.

THE DOWNSIDE OF PLEASURE

The great pox, syphilis, had first arrived in the city in 1450, and 18th-century Venice was one of the first states to try and control the disease by mandatory registration of brothels and prostitutes. Young visiting foreigners, as keen on nightlife and bedroom games as art and architecture, could buy a guidebook to the city brothels, and the Rio della Sensa, in Cannaregio, was famed for its daily afternoon procession of gondolas carrying the city's loveliest prostitutes. Prostitutes and courtesans with the disease were quarantined and given the dreaded mercury treatment—which often killed them—but ordinary citizens' behaviour was unchecked and by the 18th century it's estimated that around 20 per cent of Venice's population suffered from syphilis, including Casanova. A special hospital, the Incurabile, was built on the Zattere for those suffering from the horrific late stage of the disease.

NON-STOP PARTY TIME

Traditionally a festival held in the run-up to the penance-filled days of Lent, by the 17th and 18th centuries the Venetian Carnevale (Carnival) was occupying six months of the year, a non-stop round of parties and gambling, where, safe behind the universally worn masks, aristocrats and common people could mix and indulge in behaviour whose licentiousness was a byword throughout Europe. Elaborate stages were set up in the Piazza for acrobats, tumblers and wrestlers to perform, there was bear baiting in San Polo and bull fighting in Santo Stefano, while dancing and drinking went on around the clock. Small wonder, then, that John Evelyn, the diarist, recorded this entry in 1646: '…'tis impossible to recount the universal madnesses of this place during this time of license'.

THE LAST DOGE

In January 1789 Lodovico Manin, a member of a recently ennobled mainland family, was elected as the 120th doge. Rather than interrupt Carnevale, his accession was barely announced by the Senate, though one of the patrician Grand Council, Gradenigo, remarked, 'I have made a Friulian doge; the Republic is dead'. His words were prophetic; in 1797, Napoleon, conqueror of most of Italy and anxious to plunder Venice's wealth, attacked the city and Manin was deposed. He went quietly, removing his doge's cap, the symbol of the thousand-year-old Republic, and handing it to his valet with the words, 'Take this, I shall not be needing it again'. He is buried in the church of the Scalzi beneath a slab marked simply 'Cineres Manini' ('The Ashes of Manin').

Venice saw its fortunes improve with a revival of shipbuilding in the Arsenale and an upswing in glass production on Murano. The opening of the Suez Canal in 1869 brought renewed trade, and tourist numbers increased steadily, with luxury hotels opening in the city and on the newly fashionable Lido. This modest boom was halted by the outbreak of World War I, during which the Austrians pushed south through the Veneto almost to the borders of the lagoon. Shipbuilding was hard hit due to the proximity to the enemy front, a blow from which it never recovered. Against this background, the climate was ripe for the success of Fascism in the 1930s, and government funds financed the development of new industrial initiatives at Porto Marghera on the adjoining mainland. World War II left Venice virtually untouched, but the post-war years saw the mainland industries boom, bringing problems from pollution, and causing an exodus from the city as workers moved to the mainland; between 1946 and 2000 the population fell from 170,000 to around 58,000. Meanwhile tourism mushroomed, putting a huge strain on the city's infrastructure, as did increasing problems brought by the 1966 floods and high tides flooding the city. By the 1990s questions about Venice's future were high on the agenda, as international bodies became aware of the need to safeguard this unique city.

THE LAGOON BRIDGES
Venice was first directly linked to the mainland in 1846 when the rail bridge was built across the lagoon and Santa Lucia station was built. Physically, as well as psychologically, the bridge ended Venice's isolation, with easy, fast access to the mainland, and the transportation of goods now simpler. As road transport became increasingly common, it was inevitable that a road link be built, and a 3,657m-long (11,998ft), 222-arched viaduct bridge, the Ponte della Libertà, was constructed and opened in 1932. It was over this bridge that the Allies raced in 1945 to liberate the city; a story has the Allied tanks crossing the overpass to reach the bridge and seeing the Germans retreating on the road beneath.

Clockwise from above *A 19th-century image of the lagoon; the phoenix symbolizes La Fenice opera house's rise from the ashes; Venice in flood*

THE REGINA MARGHERITA

In 1881, the first mechanically propelled public transport vessel, a steamship named the *Regina Margherita (Queen Margaret)*, arrived in Venice. Gondoliers were up in arms, horrified at the competition, but the Venetians soon took the newcomer—reliable and cheap—to their hearts, and the following year a licence was granted to a French company to carry passengers on the Grand Canal. Its eight boats were built in France, sailing right around Italy to Venice, where they soon won the affectionate diminutive of *vaporetti* (little steamers), the name still given to the modern diesel-powered craft. Today, the *vaporetti* are run by ACTV, a company that carries approximately 180 million passengers annually and employs more than 3,000 personnel.

THE 1966 FLOODS

For centuries, Venice was prone to flooding when a combination of seasonal variation in the sea level, low atmospheric pressure and the southerly sirocco wind combined to trap water in the lagoon. Due to changes in the environment of the lagoon, these high waters increased in frequency, but remained largely ignored, throughout the 20th century. On 4 November 1966, at the same time as the disastrous floods in Florence, the city suffered the worst floods it has ever seen. Water flooded the Piazza to a height of 1.2m (4ft) and 100 per cent of the city streets were flooded, with more than 5,000 Venetians losing their homes and countless works of art damaged and destroyed. The flood finally forced international and national recognition of the peril facing the city.

PINK FLOYD IN VENICE

In 1989 the Venetian authorities gave permission for rock group Pink Floyd to give a free concert as part of the celebrations for the 15 July Festa del Redentore. It was a terrible mistake. More than 200,000 fans flooded into the city, many of them camping out for two days before the concert in a city that was totally unprepared, lacking even public lavatories and litter disposal for such an influx. During the concert, performed on a pontoon off the Piazzetta, fans climbed on lampposts and the Palazzo Ducale itself, damaging precious 10th-century stonework. When they left, the army had to be called in for a three-day clean-up, and a three-year repair to the Palazzo damage totalled nearly $46,000. The city council, faced with the wrath of citizens, art historians and conservationists, resigned en masse.

THE FENICE FIRE

During the night of 29 January 1996, fire broke out in Venice's beautiful opera house, La Fenice. With the nearest canal, which would have provided water for the fire fighters, closed for dredging, the blaze rapidly took hold, with flames clearly visible from the mainland, 10km (6 miles) away. All that remained of the theatre by the following morning was a blackened shell. More than a year later, two electricians were arrested and accused of starting the fire in an attempt to avoid incurring a 50 million lire fine for failing to complete a rewiring job on time. Rumour labelled the pair as fall guys for a far more sinister explanation, compounded by a series of court cases over insurance and the proposed rebuilding plan. La Fenice, triumphantly rebuilt, finally reopened to the public in time for the 2004–05 season.

Venice entered the 21st century with a renewed determination to tackle environmental problems that had spiralled during the second half of the 20th century, with initiatives launched for safeguarding the lagoon and tackling the ever-growing problem of *acqua alta*. Set against this is an awareness of the toll taken by the 12 million annual visitors, 80 per cent of whom are day-trippers, who contribute little economically but impose a heavy load on the city's fragile infrastructure; tour buses and boats are now charged an admission fee. The authorities, too, are committed to strengthening the port facilities, one of the world's largest cruise-ship docks, while expanding the airport complex and providing more parking. This means yet more visitors will descend on Venice, so measures have been introduced to control at least the visual impact of the hordes. Special tourist police now patrol the Piazza San Marco to discourage tourists from sitting on the paving, picnicking and parading around the city half-dressed.

THE LAST RITES

On 14 November 2009, under leaden skies, a funeral procession of gondolas set off down the Grand Canal. This was no ordinary interment, but a symbolic act to highlight what many saw as the beginning of the death of the city. The population of the *centro storico,* the historic centre, had dropped below the critical 60,000, and Matteo Secchi, the organizer, and his supporters wanted to draw attention to the relentless decline of everything that makes Venice a living city, rather than a mere tourist destination. The lack of affordable housing and rising cost of living are seen as the main culprits, and even city officials, who strongly refute the demographics, are forced to admit more needs to be done to encourage people to continue to live in central Venice.

WORLD RECESSION

When banks failed and stock markets crashed in 2008, the Venetian economy, like that of so many places reliant on tourism, was hard hit. The preceding years had seen an enormous increase in the amount of visitor accommodation, restaurants, and shops and services serving tourists; all were badly affected. Visitor numbers remained steady, but people stayed for shorter periods, and spent less. Luxury hotels and expensive shops suffered a huge drop in income, and many enterprises, opened in the heady years of credit-driven consumerism, went under as business rates and rents continued to rise and income dropped. For the rich visitor, this made Venice a buyer's market; for the modest traveller, and the Venetians themselves, it's still a case of weathering the storm.

Above *A cruise ship sails through the lagoon at sunrise*

ON THE MOVE

On the Move gives you detailed advice and information about the various options for travelling to Venice before explaining the best ways to get around the city once you are there. Handy tips help you with everything from buying tickets to finding an address.

BY AIR

Venice is served by two airports: Marco Polo and Treviso. Marco Polo is at Tessera, on the northern edge of the lagoon. By water, Marco Polo is 7km (4 miles) from central Venice; by road it is 12km (8 miles) from the city. Treviso airport is 26km (16 miles) north of Venice and is served from the UK by Ryanair.

AEROPORTO DI VENEZIA MARCO POLO (VCE)

The airport underwent a major expansion and modernization in 2002 and is now Italy's third-busiest airport, handling internal Italian traffic, international flights from all over Europe and daily flights to New York and Philadelphia.

The ground floor of the single terminal handles arrivals *(arrivi)*, and has cash dispensers *(bancomat)*, a currency exchange desk *(cambio)*, toilets and public telephones. There are car rental facilities, a hotel information and reservation desk, and transport, taxi and tourist information desks. A bar serves coffee, drinks and light refreshments, and a news kiosk, Hub, sells newspapers, books, snacks, drinks and souvenirs.

AEROPORTO DI TREVISO SANT'ANGELO (TSF)

Treviso airport has one terminal with a currency exchange desk *(cambio)*, transport information desk, toilets and car rental facilities. The snack bar is in the departure area. ATVO runs a bus service that connects with flight arrivals to Piazzale Roma via Mestre railway station. The journey time is around 45 minutes and a single ticket costs €6.40. Buy your ticket from the *cambio* in the arrivals hall and board the bus in the parking area outside the departures hall. Once at Piazzale Roma, walk to your hotel or transfer to the ACTV *vaporetto* service (▷ below and 41).

TRANSFERS FROM MARCO POLO AIRPORT INTO THE CITY

There are two options for getting into Venice from Marco Polo: by land,

using the route across the causeway to Piazzale Roma, and by water, across the lagoon.

By Land

The land route to Venice is inexpensive and takes between 20 and 40 minutes, depending on traffic. The quickest way is to take a taxi at the rank outside the arrivals area; the journey time is approximately 20 minutes and costs around €35.

Two bus services connect the airport with Piazzale Roma. ATVO runs a fast coach service (blue buses) to and from Piazzale Roma that coincides with most incoming flights. The service starts at 8.20am and, from 10.20am, runs half-hourly until 12.10am. The journey takes 20 to 35 minutes, depending on traffic. Tickets (€3.20) are available from the ATVO desk in the concourse to the left of the exit from the baggage reclaim area, and can be bought before boarding. Buses leave from the stop to the right of the exit from the arrivals area.

ACTV (Azienda Comunale per il Trasporto di Venezia, pronounced AhCheeTayVoo), Venice's public transport company, has a regular public service (orange buses) between Marco Polo and Piazzale Roma. Bus No. 5 runs from 4.08am until midnight, with departures half-hourly from 6.10am and a journey time of 25 to 40 minutes. Tickets (€2.20) are available from the ATVO kiosk in the concourse to the left of the exit from the baggage reclaim area, and buses leave from the stop to the left of the exit from the arrivals hall. You must validate your ticket on boarding the bus by

punching the ticket in one of the yellow boxes on the bus.

On arrival at Piazzale Roma, unless your hotel is within walking distance, you must transfer to the ACTV *vaporetto* service for onward travel by boat. The ACTV ticket offices are near the Grand Canal and are clearly marked. Once you have bought your ticket, go down the steps to the *imbarcarderi* (landings) along the pier *(fondamenta)* to your left to board the boats.

By Water

There are two options: a regular boat service, run by Alilaguna, or a water taxi. To get to the boats, exit the arrivals hall and take the shuttle bus *(navetta)* which runs regularly every 5 minutes to the lagoon edge. If you want to walk down, it's a 7- to

USEFUL TELEPHONE NUMBERS AND WEBSITES

MARCO POLO AIRPORT
- » Central operator, tel 041 260 6111
- » Flight information, tel 041 260 9260
- » Lost and Found, tel 041 260 9222
- » Customs, tel 041 269 9311
- » Car parking, tel 041 260 3060
- » Tourist information, tel 041 541 5887
- » Hotel Association, tel 041 541 5017
- » Alilaguna, tel 041 240 1701
- » ACTV, www.actv.it
- » ATVO, www.atvo.it
- » Taxi, tel 041 541 6363
- » Water taxi, tel 041 541 5084
- » www.veniceairport.it

TREVISO SANT'ANGELO
- » Central operator, tel 0422 315111
- » Ticket counter, tel 0422 315331
- » Customs, tel 0422 315260
- » www.trevisoairport.it

12-minute walk, turning left outside the terminal building.

The Società Alilaguna (tel 041 240 1701, www.alilaguna.com) runs an hourly boat service from Marco Polo to the city. There are five lines: Blu (blue), Arancio (orange), M, Oro (gold) and Rossa (red), serving different areas of the city and the lagoon islands, of which the Blu, Oro and Red are the most useful for the majority of visitors. Check their website before your arrival and choose the service that will take you as near as possible to your hotel; you may find that you will have to connect with an ACTV *vaporetto* for the last stages. Blu line services start at 6.10am and run hourly until 12.10pm; Oro at 9.30am hourly until 5.30pm; and Rossa from 9.15am hourly until 7.15pm. The Arancio and M lines serve Murano and the north of the city. Tickets cost €13 and can be bought on board; the journey time is around 75 to 90 minutes.

Water taxis are run by the Consorzio Motoscafi Venezia (tel 041 522 2303), whose desk is to the left of the exit from the baggage reclaim area in the arrivals hall. The main advantage of a water taxi is the sheer pleasure of the lagoon trip and the fact that taxis are able to deliver you, and your luggage, to the nearest water access point to your hotel, cutting out a walk over bridges with all your bags from the nearest *vaporetto* stop. The disadvantage is the price; they cost upwards of €100, depending on the number of people in your party and your destination. If there are four or more of you, it's worth considering. The journey across the lagoon takes about 15 to 20 minutes.

GETTING TO YOUR HOTEL

Before you leave home, ask your hotel to send you details of how to reach it. You need to know the nearest *vaporetto* stop, the name of the street as well as the *numero civico* (▷ 46), and the nearest landmark, such as a *campo*, church or museum. If you have a lot of heavy luggage, you can have it

delivered to your hotel by porter. This is charged per piece and must be booked in advance at Cooperativa Trasbagagli; tel 041 713 719 (8am–6pm), email info@trasbagagli.it.

RETURNING HOME

ATVO, ACTV and Alilaguna all run between the city and Marco Polo airport. ATVO buses run from 5am to 8.40pm and ACTV services from

4.40am to midnight. The Alilaguna Rossa service starts at 7.45am from the Zattere and runs until 8.45pm, and the Blu service from 4am to 10.25pm from San Marco. Both land and water taxis operate a 24-hour service. Note that buses to Treviso leave well in advance of flights to allow for delays, so check the timetable carefully on your arrival at Treviso.

GETTING TO CENTRAL VENICE FROM THE AIRPORT		
	MARCO POLO	**TREVISO SANT'ANGELO**
	Via Luigi Broglio, Tessera	Via Noalese, Treviso
	Tel 041 260 6111	Tel 0422 315111
	(central operator);	
	041 260 9260 (flight info)	
Taxi	€27, 30 minutes	
Bus		
ATVO	€3.20, 20–35 minutes	€6.40, 45 minutes
ACTV	€2.20, 25–40 minutes	
Water taxi	€100+	15–20 minutes
Boat		
Alilaguna	€12	75–90 minutes

AIRLINES			
Alitalia	tel 0870 544 8259 (UK)	tel 06 2222 (Italy)	www.alitalia.co.uk
British Airways	tel 0870 850 8850 (UK),	tel 199 712266 (Italy)	www.ba.com
Delta	tel 800/241-4141 (US)	tel 848 780376 (Italy)	www.delta-air-com
easyJet	tel 0905 821 0905 (UK)	tel 848 887766 (Italy)	www.easyjet.com
Ryanair	tel 0871 246 0000 (UK)	tel 899 678910 (Italy)	www.ryanair.com

from March to November, and runs from Victoria station (London) to Venezia Santa Lucia. The journey time is 31 hours and tickets cost between £1,595 (single) and £2,395 (return/round trip).

RAIL PASSES

If you are coming to Venice by train, or combining your visit with other European or Italian destinations, you may want to consider investing in some type of rail pass.

Inter-Rail Passes are valid for one month's unlimited rail travel within a specific zone; Italy is in Zone G, together with Turkey, Greece and Slovenia. You must be an EU citizen or have lived in Europe for six months to be eligible. The full fare is around €550 for adults and €367 for those under 26 for one month's unlimited travel. The ticket gives you discounts on cross-Channel services, including Eurostar.

Eurail Passes are available for North American visitors. They allow several days consecutive travel, or a certain number of days within a fixed time period in up to 17 countries. There are many combinations to choose from; check out www.raileurope.com for further information.

Trenitalia, the Italian state railway network, is heavily subsidized and journey prices are low—the cost of a return (round-trip) ticket from Venice to Florence is around €45. The company operates the Cartaviaggio system, offering a choice of different types of travel card, which enable the holder to obtain some reductions on travel and various other benefits in the form of shopping and hotel discounts. The cards are free, but unless you're doing a lot of travelling in Italy, not of great use to foreigners.

BY TRAIN

From the UK you can travel by train to Venice, routing, via the Channel Tunnel, through Paris. The choice of routes and fares is highly complex, but it's best to use the Eurostar service as far as Paris Gare du Nord, then transfer to Paris Bercy for the journey south. The old train and ferry route from London to Paris is now little used, and consequently badly timetabled.

Eurostar trains depart from London St. Pancras station and are scheduled to arrive in Paris in 2 hours 15 minutes. Check in 30 minutes before departure; you are allowed two suitcases and one item of hand luggage. Label all bags clearly with your name, address and seat number. You need your passport to clear immigration and customs.
» The total journey time from St. Pancras to Venezia Santa Lucia is 18 hours.
» Return (round-trip) prices range from £200 to £300 and include the cost of a couchette.

Eurostar and other fast European trains have facilities which include:
» 1st- and 2nd-class seating
» Sleeping cars
» Bar/restaurant cars
» Trolley service on daytime trains
» Baby-changing facilities on daytime trains
» Air-conditioning
» Telephones

» Toilets in each carriage (car); some are wheelchair accessible.

Note that if you are arriving in Venice by train from elsewhere in Italy some trains terminate in Venezia Mestre. If this is so, you need to change to a local train for the 10-minute hop across the lagoon. Trains from Mestre to Venice leave approximately every 10 minutes.

Sleeper accommodation varies from 3-, 4- and 6-berth couchettes to single and double sleepers with integral shower and lavatory. Your choice of accommodation will be reflected in the ticket price.

The Orient Express, the ultimate luxury train ride to Venice, operates

TRAIN INFORMATION AND TICKETS		
Eurostar	tel 0870 518 6186	www.eurostar.com
Rail Europe	tel 0870 584 8848	www.raileurope.co.uk
Trenitalia	tel 892021	www.trenitalia.com
The Man in Seat 61		www.seat61.com
Venice-Simplon-Orient-Express	tel 020 7805 5100	www.orient-express.com

BY CAR

If you're considering driving to Venice, bear in mind that you will have to organize and pay for parking while you are in the city. For information on how the parking areas work, ▷ 53.

You will need the following:
» Valid driver's licence
» Original vehicle registration document
» Motor insurance document (at least third-party insurance is compulsory)
» Passport
» A warning triangle
» A distinguishing nationality sticker if you do not have euro-plates
» A reflective vest in case of emergencies (this is compulsory)
» A set of replacement bulbs
» If you're driving in winter you may need winter tyres or snow chains for the Alpine passes.

BEFORE YOU GO
» Check what you must do to adjust your headlights for driving on the right. For newer cars, this adjustment may have to be made by a mechanic, so allow time for this.

» Remove any device to detect radar speed traps as they are banned in most European countries. Even if not in use, possession of such a device will incur a fine and may result in the confiscation of the car.
» Contact your car insurer or broker at least one month before departure.
» Have the car serviced and the tyres checked.
» Ensure you have adequate breakdown assistance cover. Contact driving organizations such as the AA in the UK (tel 0800 085 2721, www.theAA.com). In case of breakdown on non-motorway roads in Italy, you can get assistance from the Automobile Club d'Italia (ACI) by calling 803 116, or if you are using a foreign network mobile on 800 116 800. This is not a free service.

From the UK, you can cross the Channel either by ferry or through the Channel Tunnel. Heading for Venice, the main routes south to Italy run through France, Switzerland and Germany. All cross the Alps; the main passes are the St. Gotthard, the Great St. Bernard, Fréjus and Mont Blanc. The St. Gotthard tunnel is free; the cost for the others ranges from €20 to €35.

To reach the tunnels from Calais, take the E15 and E17 to Reims, then pick up the motorways towards the different passes. As an alternative route, you could drive east through Switzerland into Austria and cross the Alps from Innsbruck via the E45 motorway; which runs through the Brenner Pass. The E45 runs south to Verona, where you join the E70 to Venice.

There are toll-roads all along the routes south. You should allow between 11 to 15 hours driving time to reach the north Italian border.

BY FERRY

If you are travelling to or from Greece, there are two Greek ferry lines serving Venice. ANEK Lines has four weekly sailings (Monday, Thursday, Friday, Sunday) from Corfu and Patras, with a journey time of 27 and 36 hours respectively; Minoan Lines covers the same destinations on a daily basis, with Corfu trips taking 19 hours and Patras 29 hours.

The agent for ANEK Lines is ANEK Lines Italia srl, Stazione Marittima di Venezia, Magazzino 123, 30123 Venezia; tel 041 528 6522; you can book online for both companies at www.anek.gr/italian and www.minoan.gr.

Ferries and cruise ships dock at the Stazione Marittima in the heart of Venice.

Right *A huge cruise liner negotiates the Giudecca Canal*
Opposite *A fast inter-city train to Milan stops in Venice*

The best way to move around Venice is on foot; this is how the Venetians themselves get from place to place, combining walking with the judicious use of public transport in the shape of *vaporetti* (water buses) and *traghetti* (cross-Grand Canal ferries). Every Venetian carries in his head a mental map of the city, which he'll consult for main routes, short cuts and transport before he begins his journey. Visitors won't reach this state of expertise, but the satisfaction of rounding a corner, crossing a bridge and finding you're exactly where you want to be is huge, and the discoveries that walking brings are one of the intrinsic pleasures of the city.

Venice is divided into six *sestieri*, which roughly translates as 'quarters' or 'city wards'. Three—San Marco, Cannaregio and Castello—lie to the north of the Grand Canal, and three—San Polo, Santa Croce and Dorsoduro—to the south. The Grand Canal sweeps in a sinuous curve between the two halves of the city, crossed by four bridges, the Costituzione, the Scalzi, the Rialto and the Accademia, whose spans divide the Canal into four roughly equal sections. Myriad smaller canals *(rii)* branch off the Grand Canal, snaking their way through the city to form a spider's web of waterways. These are crossed by 400 or so bridges, linking neighbourhoods, streets and *campi* (squares). Making sense of this labyrinth and finding your way around is a challenge, and this section will help you to understand it better.

VAPORETTI

The *vaporetti* (▷ 48–49, 50, 51) can be a real help in getting around the city, and are a huge attraction to most visitors, but a glance at a map will show that, time-wise, they are often the slowest way to move about Venice. If you want to go from the Piazza San Marco to the Rialto, it's tempting to wait for a *vaporetto* and take the 8-stop, 20-minute boat trip. But if you cut through the streets running north out of the Piazza you can be at the Rialto in around 10 minutes. Along the Grand Canal, it's more than 20 minutes and 8 stops from the station to the *vaporetto* stop nearest the Frari church; the journey on foot takes around 10 minutes. The outer edges of Venice, up by the Fondamente Nuove in Cannaregio and down by the Zattere in Dorsoduro, take even longer to reach by *vaporetto*, and may involve complicated routes and changes of boats. So it makes sense, once you've begun to get your city bearings, to think twice before you automatically head for the *vaporetto*, and perhaps only use them for longer journeys; it is often quicker on foot, and you'll certainly see more of the city.

WALKING

Venice is a small city; roughly 3km (2 miles) long and a little less across at its widest point. Brisk walking—once you know the way—will take you from end to end in around an hour. Like all cities, it has its main through routes, important thoroughfares that link the city's major focus points. For many years, these routes have been helpfully signposted by the city council, and you'll see yellow signs, above head height, indicating the route to five central hubs: San Marco, the Rialto, the Accademia, Ferrovia (the station), and Piazzale Roma, where the causeway to the mainland starts. Follow these yellow signs, no matter how narrow and unlikely the street looks as a route, and they will take you to these end points. For the first couple of days, this will probably be all the help you need, but once you decide to explore further you will need to use your map. Spend a few minutes before you set out studying it and working out your route, and accept, too, that you will inevitably get lost, go around in circles or end up somewhere completely different from where you intended. If this

happens, console yourself with the thought that this is how you start to get to know one of the world's most topographically challenging cities.

» Follow the yellow signs for main cross-city routes.

» Remember that just because a street is very narrow it doesn't mean it's not an important route.

» Make a point of noticing key landmarks—churches, distinctive shop fronts, *campi*—so you can retrace your steps if necessary.

» Follow the crowds; even if you're lost in an out of the way corner, you'll be surprised how soon one person becomes two, then three, then six, until you're suddenly back on a main thoroughfare.

» Follow the disembarking crowds at *vaporetti* stops, some of which appear to be in the middle of

nowhere; the other passengers will lead you to sights and through routes.

» Wear comfortable shoes; street surfaces are hard and the bridges provide a lot of climbing.

TRAGHETTI

Traghetti (gondola ferries) ply back and forth from one side of the Grand Canal to the other at seven fixed points (for how they work, ▷ 51). Think of them as bridges, and it becomes clear they will save both time and unnecessary mileage. All *traghetti* have been operating for hundreds of years, and they exist primarily for the convenience of locals, but, once you're familiar with the system, judicious use of the *traghetti* will help get you quickly from point to point.

MOST USEFUL *TRAGHETTI*

Pescheria to Santa Sofia: connects the Rialto area with the Strada Nova. If you're staying near the Rialto, use it to access the Strada Nova, to join the walking route north via Santi Apostoli to the Fondamente Nuove (for boats to San Michele, Murano and Burano), to walk to Santi Giovanni e Paolo, Santa Maria dei Miracoli, the Ca' d'Oro and northern Cannaregio. From the Strada Nova side, it connects with the Rialto and the markets and the Campo San Polo area.

San Tomà to Ca' Garzoni: if you're staying in San Polo use it as the quickest way to San Marco by cutting through to Campo Santo Stefano and picking up the yellow signs from there. From the San Marco side, this *traghetto* gives easy access to the Frari and the Scuola Grande di San Rocco, and is a 5- to 10-minute walk from Campo Santa Margherita and Campo San Polo.

Ca' Rezzonico to San Samuele: useful link from Dorsoduro to San Marco and vice versa, but operates only in the mornings.

Santa Maria della Salute to Santa Maria del Giglio: from San Marco, this is the quickest way to reach the church of the Salute and the Collezione Peggy Guggenheim. If you're staying in eastern Dorsoduro it provides a quick link to the Piazza San Marco, by way of Calle XXII Marzo, and to the Rialto via Campo Sant'Angelo and Campo Manin; alternatively use the Dogana *traghetto* for the Piazza.

FINDING AN ADDRESS

Every *calle* and *campo* in Venice is clearly marked above eye-level with its name, written in black on a white background. These signs are called *nissioeti* and are written in Venetian dialect. The spelling therefore differs, sometimes considerably, from that marked on all maps of Venice, which always use normal Italian. However, written postal addresses for the city do not always give street names. The Venetian practice is to give the *sestiere* name, followed by its number, the *numero civico*. Venice is divided into six *sestieri*: San Marco, Cannaregio and Castello, to the north of the Grand Canal, and San Polo, Santa Croce and Dorsoduro to the south. In each of the six *sestieri, numeri civici* start at No. 1 and progress, seemingly at random and without logic, throughout the *sestiere* until every building has been covered; in the case of San Marco, this is more than 5,000. Your hotel's address therefore may officially read as San Marco 4563 or Dorsoduro 3118, with no indication of where in the *sestiere* it is. For this reason, it is essential to make certain you are given either the name of the street, or a local landmark, such as a church, important *campo*, or even a shop, to help you locate the address.

In this book, we have indicated street names in the Sights and Listings sections to make things easier. If you need to find somewhere and don't have the street name, invest in the comprehensive *Calli, Campielli e Canali* street guide. This gives the street name for every *sestiere* number, and marks them on clear maps, along with historical information about every building in Italian and English. It is available at good bookshops throughout the city (Edizioni Helvetia €19).

RULES OF THE ROAD

Venetians have considerable patience with visitors, but remember that locals live and work in the city and you should observe a few rules:
» Street traffic has to flow in both directions, so keep to the right and allow room for overtaking.
» Don't obstruct the middle of busy streets while you take photos or drink in the view.
» Venetians walk briskly so be aware of people behind you trying to pass in narrow streets.
» Pull in while you consult your map.
» Don't clutter bridges or junctions.
» Keep away from the main arteries at rush hour, and the main streets near San Marco and the Rialto at all times to avoid pedestrian traffic jams in high season.

VENETIAN STREET NAMES

Venice's idiosyncratic street names are one of the delights of the city, with the bonus of—just occasionally—providing clues to an address's location and history. Confusingly, you may find the same street name popping up more than once in different areas around the city, so, when checking street names of addresses, make sure you know which particular street of that name it is and in which *sestiere*. Unlike most Italian cities, the key nomenclatures of *Via* and *Piazza* are rare, so it makes sense to get a handle on Venice by coming to grips with its name-system (plurals in brackets).

TYPES OF STREET

Calle (calli): the commonest name for street, the equivalent of *Via* in other Italian towns
Campiello (campielli): a small *campo*
Campo (campi): the Venetian name for square, meaning field, comes from its origins as the central cultivated area on one of the islands that made up early Venice
Canale (canali): there are two main canals; the Canal Grande and the Canale di Cannaregio
Corte (corti): an even smaller *campo*
Crosera (crosere): crossroads, usually where important cross-city routes meet
Fondamenta (fondamente): a pier or street running beside a canal
Lista (liste): a street once occupied by an ambassador's residence

PIAZZALE ROMA

ALLA FERROVIA

Piazza (piazze): Venice has just one, the Piazza San Marco

Piazzale (piazzali): just one, the Piazzale Roma, where the causeway ends

Piazzetta (piazzette): there are only two; they flank the Basilica di San Marco, the Piazzetta on the water side, and the Piazzetta dei Leoni on the other side

Piscina (piscine): a paved area that was once the site of a pool

Ramo (rami): means branch; hence the name given to narrow side streets which may link two streets or a dead end

Rio (rii): the Venetian word for canal

Rio terà (rii terà): a street on the site of a filled-in canal

Riva (rive): a wide *fondamenta*, usually along the Grand Canal, a major *rio* or open water

Ruga (rughe): a street with shops

Sacca (sacche): originally a lagoon inlet

Salizzada (salizzade): the most important street in a neighbourhood; the word means 'paved'

Sotoportego (sotoporteghi): a covered street or archway

Via (vie): Venice has two, both laid out in the 19th century: Via Garibaldi in Castello, and Via (Calle) XXII Marzo in San Marco

MAPS

There is a street map of Venice at the back of this guide (▷ 289–301) and a *vaporetto* map in the inside back cover. Venice's APT has a free street map at all its offices and also sells, as do many newsstands and bookshops, other street maps of the

city. These vary greatly in accuracy, and it's generally accepted by the Venetians themselves that there's no such thing as a faultlessly accurate map of the city.

ACQUA ALTA

Acqua alta, high water, is becoming increasingly common between September and April. This occurs when higher than average tides coincide with low atmospheric pressure and a wind driving against the tidal outflow from the lagoon. Tides 100cm (3.2ft) above average will flood 3.5 per cent of central Venice; 110cm (3.6ft) puts 11.7 per cent of the city under water, 120cm (3.9ft) 35 per cent, 130cm (4.2ft) 68.7, and 140cm (4.5ft) will make more than 90 per cent of the city impassable for 2 to 3 hours each side of high tide. The worst months are October and November, but it can occur at any time during the late autumn and winter months.

» Two to three hours before an exceptionally high tide sirens around the city sound five 10-second wailing blasts. These may go off in the middle of the night.

» The water will gradually make its way through the city streets and into buildings, oozing up through the pavements and overflowing the *fondamente*.

» The city council will erect the *passarelle*, the raised walkways kept permanently on hand throughout the winter months, on major flood-prone routes. If the water rises above 130cm (4.2ft), these too will float, so in such circumstances it's better

to head for somewhere dry and sit it out.

» *Acqua alta* normally lasts for three days.

HOW TO COPE WITH *ACQUA ALTA*

» You can get advance information on tides by logging onto www. comune.venezia.it/maree; by calling 041 241 1996 to hear a taped 36-hour tide forecast, or by picking up a text message from your mobile by sending the word MAREA to 339 99 41041.

» If tide levels are high, it's worth either bringing Wellington boots *(stivali)* with you, or investing in a pair while you're in Venice. The disposable plastic leggings sold by street traders are not recommended, as they let in water and fall to pieces.

» Use the *passarelle* (raised walkways) to move around the city; wait your turn to get on them and walk carefully along the planks, keeping to the right. Venetians are polite and helpful to each other during *acqua alta* and expect visitors to be the same.

» Never splash; the *calli* may be under water, but they're still public streets and Venetians will not appreciate getting any wetter than is absolutely unavoidable.

» Remember that during *acqua alta* you cannot see where the pavement stops and the canal begins.

» *Vaporetti* continue to function up to a tide level of around 125cm (4.1ft); all stops have maps showing flood-prone areas, and the routes covered by the *passarelle*.

» You can get a copy of the *acqua alta* map from the tourist offices.

» Shops, bars and restaurants may temporarily close during *acqua alta* in order to try to keep water out, or pump it out; be patient—things will quickly get back to normal.

MAIN THROUGH ROUTES		
SESTIERE	**FROM WHERE TO WHERE**	**HOW TO WALK IT**
San Marco	Piazza San Marco to the Rialto	Follow yellow Rialto signs
San Marco	Piazza San Marco to Accademia	Follow yellow Accademia signs
San Marco	Rialto to the station	Follow yellow Ferrovia signs
San Marco	Piazza San Marco to Santi Giovanni e Paolo	Santa Maria Formosa, Calle Trevisana (blue sign)
Cannaregio	Rialto to station	Follow yellow Ferrovia signs
Cannaregio	Rialto to Fondamente Nuove	Santi Apostoli, Gesuiti, Fondamente Nuove
Dorsoduro	Accademia to the Rialto	Follow yellow Rialto signs
San Polo	Rialto to the station	Follow yellow Ferrovia signs
San Polo	Rialto to Piazzale Roma	Follow yellow Piazzale Roma signs

SIGNS

Note that yellow directional signs are very sparse in northern Cannaregio and eastern Castello.

BY BOAT

Although many journeys around Venice are quicker on foot, there's no doubt that for most visitors the *vaporetti* or waterbuses are a big draw. Until you start to get your city bearings, they can prove a lifeline, depositing you, from all over the city and lagoon, back on the familiar territory of the streets surrounding your hotel. They also provide a moving grandstand from which to drink in the beauty of the city—the palaces, the churches, the lagoon views—while the steady stream of local passengers will give you a real insight into the actuality of living in Venice.

Strictly speaking, the public service boats used by ACTV are not all *vaporetti*, the diminutive name used by all Venetians and coined more than a century ago when the first of these 'little steamers' appeared in Venice. ACTV operates three types of boat:

» *Vaporetti:* large, relatively slow vessels with rounded sterns, one large cabin and ample standing and luggage space on the foredeck. They cover the Grand Canal and Lido routes.

» *Motoscafi:* smaller, lower and faster boats with cabins fore and aft of the bridge and some outside seating at the back. They serve the stops on the periphery of the city and run to the Giudecca, San Giorgio and Murano.

» *Motonavi:* double-decker steamers that cross the lagoon to Burano, Torcello, Punta Sabbione and the Lido. The upper deck has plenty of outside seating.

There are three other types of public service vessel you will come across:

» *Taxi acquei:* water taxis are sleek, brown-and-white motorboats with comfortable cabins. Authorized taxis show a black registration number on a yellow background. They can take you all over the city via both the Grand Canal and many of the smaller *rii*.

» *Gondole:* Venice's own boats are by now almost solely devoted to tourism and few people use them to get around the city. In fact, they are the only boats that can penetrate even the narrowest and shallowest canals.

» *Traghetti:* these are inexpensive gondolas which cross the Grand Canal backwards and forwards at fixed points. They are extremely useful when moving about Venice on foot as they dispense with the need to take *vaporetti* or go out of your way to cross one of the Grand Canal bridges.

VAPORETTI ROUTES

If you are going to use the *vaporetti* a lot, it's worth investing in the ACTV *Orario* (Timetable), from the tourist information offices, the main ACTV/VeLa office at Piazzale Roma or any large ACTV booth (€0.60).

The Main Routes

» *No. 1:* slow route from Piazzale Roma down the Grand Canal and east along the Riva degli Schiavoni to the Giardini, Sant'Elena and the Lido; boats stop at every landing stage. Also operates in reverse.

» *No. 2:* a faster service with fewer stops from Vallaresso (San Marco) up the Grand Canal to Piazzale Roma, then around the southwestern edge of the city with stops at the Tronchetto parking areas, the islands of Sacca Fisola, Giudecca and San Giorgio Maggiore and back to San Marco. From June to September the service extends to the Lido. Also operates in reverse.

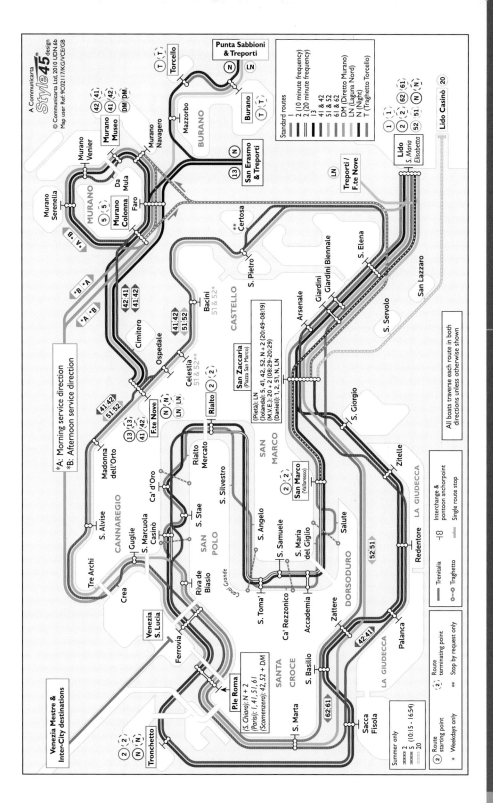

» *Nos. 41 and 42:* service running anticlockwise and clockwise around the outer edge of the main city from Murano, with stops on the northern side of the city, Piazzale Roma, the Giudecca, San Marco and Sant'Elena.

» *Nos. 51 and 52:* service running anticlockwise and clockwise from the Lido along the northern city edge and down the Canale di Cannaregio to Ferrovia and Piazzale Roma. It then returns to the Lido via the Canale della Giudecca, stopping at the Zattere and Sant'Elena.

» *Nos. 61 and 62:* fast service from Piazzale Roma to the Lido via the Zattere and Giardini.

» *DM:* the Diretto Murano is a non-stop service linking Piazzale Roma and Ferrovia with the island of Murano.

» *LN:* lagoon service (Laguna Nord) from the Fondamente Nuove to Murano, Mazzorbo and Burano, which returns via Treporti, Punta Sabbione and the Lido to San Zaccaria.

» *T:* Burano–Torcello service. Other routes serve the islands of Pellestrina, Vignole, Sant'Erasmo, San Servolo and San Lazzaro.

TIMETABLES

Vaporetti run to strict timetables, which are clearly displayed at all stops. On the main routes, services start around 5am and run to midnight or just after, when a regular night service (N), following the route of the No. 2, takes over. During the day, the No. 1 and No. 2 run every 10 minutes; the 41, 42, 51, 52, and 62 every 20 minutes; and the DM, LN and T half-hourly.

HOW TO USE THE *VAPORETTI*

If you're a stranger to Venice, the main pitfall of first using the *vaporetto* system is taking the wrong boat going in the wrong direction. As a general rule, if you're on the north side of the Grand Canal boats heading left are travelling towards San Marco, those heading right will take you towards the station or Piazzale Roma. Main stops have

two *imbarcaderi* (landings), one for each direction; both will be clearly marked with a route board showing the number of the *vaporetto* and the direction in which it will be heading. Smaller *imbarcaderi* serve boats going in both directions. If this is the case, check the destination board on the side of the boat which will indicate the number, final destination and stops en route. If you're still unsure, listen to the crewperson in charge of embarking who will shout out the final destination.

» Buy your ticket before boarding and pass it in front of the imob.venezia sensor (▷ 51, *Abbonamenti*) to validate it.

» As the boat arrives, stand back and allow passengers to disembark first.

» Board the boat, moving aft into the cabin if directed by the crew.

» Keep an eye open for the stop before yours and, once this is passed, start to work your way forwards for your own disembarkation, moving past other passengers by saying *permesso*. *Vaporetti* can be jam-packed and you don't want to be carried past your stop.

» Luggage should be stored where directed by the crew.

» Bear in mind *vaporetti* are extremely crowded during Venetian commuting hours, and at all times during the height of the tourist season.

TICKETS

Biglietti a tempo

For visitors, by far the best ticketing option is to invest in one of ACTV's *biglietti a tempo* (Travel Cards). These

MAIN *VAPORETTI* STOPS

Piazzale Roma is the stop for the causeway to the mainland

Ferrovia is the stop for the railway station

Rialto is the stop for the Rialto

Vallaresso, San Marco and San Zaccaria are the stops nearest to the Piazza San Marco

Piazzale Roma, Ferrovia and Fondamente Nuove can be used to reach Murano

Fondamente Nuove is the departure stop for Burano and Torcello

Rialto Mercato serves the market side of the Rialto (San Polo)

are valid for 12, 24, 36, 48 and 72 hours or 7 days and cost respectively €16, €18, € 23, €28, €33 and €50. They can be purchased at ACTV/ VeLa's main office at Piazzale Roma, the ticket booths at main stops and *tabacchi* (tobacconist shops) showing the ACTV logo. If the ticket is not already validated, you must do so by inserting it into the orange punch box at the *imbarcadero*. Validity starts from the moment it is punched.

Other Tickets

» A single ticket costs €6.50 and includes travel on the Grand Canal.

» A *traghetto* ticket, which gives a one-stop ferry service across open water, costs €2. Useful routes are: San Zaccaria–San Giorgio, Sant'Elena–Lido, Fondamente Nuove–Murano and Zattere–Palanca.

» Tickets for a return journey on No. 3 and 4 *vaporetti* (from Tronchetto parking to San Marco via the Grand Canal) cost €7.

» If you board without a ticket, ask a member of the crew for one immediately. Ticket inspections are frequent and the on-the-spot fine is €44.

Abbonamenti

If you are staying for several weeks or months in Venice, or planning to return frequently, consider applying for a *tessera di abbonamento*, which offers considerable savings on all ACTV routes. Primarily aimed at Venetian residents, it costs €40, and application forms, for which you will need a passport-sized photo, are available at main ACTV and VeLa offices. Take the photo, the form, your passport and the money in cash to one of the main offices (Piazzale Roma or Tronchetto) and the card will be issued on the spot. You can use it to buy either a monthly ticket (€33) or a book of ten tickets *(carnet)* for €10. ACTV has recently introduced the imob.venezia scheme which uses electronic, rechargeable, prepaid cards. Even if you have an *abbonamento*, you must have it read by swiping it in the sensor before you board the boat.

HOW TO USE THE *TRAGHETTI*

The *traghetti* are the best way of crossing from one side of the Grand Canal to the other; they're also a quintessential Venetian experience and a bargain way to have a gondola ride. The service is run by the gondoliers' cooperative in conjunction with the city council; fares are a standard €0.50 per crossing.

» *Traghetti* are marked by green *traghetto* boards with the name of the service.

» If there is a gondola waiting you can board at once; the service

will leave when the gondolier has enough passengers or feels those on board have been waiting long enough.

» Hand your money to the gondolier as you board—the right change is always appreciated.

» Move towards the back of the boat and remain standing. It's customary to stand so as many passengers can ride as possible, though you can sit down if the gondola isn't crowded.

» As you disembark, the gondolier will give you a helping hand if required.

WATER TAXIS

For moving to and from the airport and around the city, fast water taxis, seating up to eight people, are a solution. They are organized by the Consorzio Motoscafi Venezia, which operates the services both from ranks and via a telephone switchboard. Your hotel will order a taxi in advance to take you to the airport or around the city; it will arrive at the nearest *fondamenta* to your hotel. The main drawback is the cost; taxis are inordinately expensive. You can expect to pay between €90 and €100 for the trip into Venice from the airport; shorter, city rides will cost almost the same. Taxis charge a night supplement between 10pm and 7am of €5.50.

Bookings: tel 041 522 2303
www.motoscafivenezia.it

GONDOLAS

Gondolas today are almost solely used for tourist trips, the ultimate Venetian romantic experience. If you're planning a trip, you can discuss the itinerary beforehand with the gondolier; the route will

depend on where you're boarding, but most gondola trips will cover either the Bacino di San Marco and some side canals, or a section of the Grand Canal and some smaller *rii*. Fares are set by the *Istituzione per la Conservazione della gondola e tutela del gondoliere* (Gondola Board), tel 041 528 5075, www.gondolavenezia. it. Gondolas can carry up to six passengers; there are no discounts for smaller numbers. Expect to pay: between 8am and 8pm €80 for 50 minutes + €40 for each additional 25 minutes; between 7pm and 8am €100 for 40 minutes + €50 for each additional 20 minutes.

If you're in Venice on a package holiday, a gondola ride may be included in the deal.

TIPS

» If you're in Venice for 3 to 4 days and want to buy a 72-hour pass, it's worth working out when to buy it. You may find that you won't be using the *vaporetti* for your first or last day, so fit your boat travel into the middle three days to save money.

» New No. 1 *vaporetti* are gradually being introduced. The new boats no longer have the much-sought after front seats which give such superb views of the Grand Canal. If you're planning on using the No. 1 to sightsee, wait until one of the older type *vaporetti* comes along and try for a front seat.

» If you're planning a day to the lagoon islands use the timetable to plan your trip so you won't waste time waiting for infrequent boats.

TRAGHETTI STATIONS	
STATION	**TIMES**
San Marco to Punta di Dogana	Daily 9–12, 2–6
Giglio to Salute	Daily 8–6
San Samuele to Ca' Rezzonico	Mon–Sat 7.30am–1.30pm
Ca' Garzoni to San Tomà	Mon–Sat 7.30am–8.30pm; Sun 8–7.30
Riva del Carbon to Riva del Vin	Mon–Sat 8am–2pm
Santa Sofia to Pescheria	Mon–Sat 7.30am–8.30pm; Sun 8–7
San Marcuola to Fondaco dei Turchi	Mon–Sat 9–12.30

GONDOLA STATIONS
Bacino Orseolo (behind the Piazza San Marco)
Campo San Moisè (in front of the Grunwald hotel)
Ferrovia (railway station)
Piazzetta San Marco
Piazzale Roma
Riva degli Schiavoni (in front of Hotel Danieli)
Riva del Carbon (south end of Rialto bridge)
San Tomà (near *vaporetto* stop)
Santa Maria del Giglio (next to *vaporetto* stop)
Vallaresso (next to *vaporetto* stop)

BY BUS

If you're planning to visit other towns in the Veneto, you'll find many are easily accessible in a day by bus or train from central Venice. Both forms of transport are cheap, frequent and reliable, and you can find full travel information at either the ACTV and VeLa offices in Piazzale Roma or Santa Lucia station on the Grand Canal.

BUSES

The bright orange land buses serving the Venice area are run by ACTV to Mestre and Marghera on the mainland; ACTV also operates the island bus services on the Lido and Pellestrina and in the town of Chioggia.

» Buses for the mainland depart from Piazzale Roma.

» Lido and Pellestrina buses leave from outside the *vaporetto* stop on the Lido.

» Tickets cost €1.10 and are valid for 75 minutes, during which time you may use several buses, though not for a return journey.

» Buy the ticket before boarding and validate it on the bus by punching it in one of the yellow boxes.

» 24- and 72-hour travel passes are valid for Lido and Pellestrina buses.

» Tickets are available at the ACTV office at Piazzale Roma, ACTV ticket booths and *tabacchi* showing the ACTV logo.

» Buses leave from designated stands at Piazzale Roma; these are clearly marked with service numbers, final destinations, departure times and stops en route.

» Avoid bus travel at peak times in the morning (7.30–9) and evening (6–8).

» Board the bus through the front or rear doors (marked *entrata*) and leave from the middle (*uscita*).

» Night buses from Mestre, Marghera, the Lido and Pellestrina connect with the N nighttime *vaporetto* service.

FARTHER AFIELD

» ACTV buses connect Venice and Padova (Padua), stopping at several Palladian villas along the route; details from ACTV office, Piazzale Roma.

» SITA blue buses leave from Piazzale Roma and go directly to Padova along the motorway; details from the VeLa office at Piazzale Roma or tel 0421 383 671.

» FTV buses connect Padova and Vicenza, leaving from outside the railway station; for details tel 0444 223 115.

BY TRAIN

Few stations are as beautifully sited as Venezia Santa Lucia, where you exit the station to find yourself on the edge of the Grand Canal, an unforgettable arrival that outclasses Piazzale Roma in every way. Italian trains are excellent and, if you're sightseeing outside Venice, the most convenient form of transport. Verona is 90 minutes by train from the city, while Padova and Vicenza are close enough to make a day-trip to them both feasible.

TYPES OF TRAIN

Eurostar Italia (ES): a superfast service (250kph/155mph) connecting main Italian cities (e.g. Venice to Verona, Venice to Florence). First-class tickets are available and include newspapers and refreshments. All trains have a restaurant car and trolley service. Book ahead, either at the station; via Trenitalia agents; by telephone on 892021; or online at www.trenitalia.com.

Intercity (IC): high-speed trains connecting the main cities and important regional towns. Advance reservations are recommended (see above).

Treni Espressi (E): long-distance express trains; use them if you are

moving on from Venice to another part of Italy.

Diretti (D): trains stopping at larger stations only; useful from Venice for Padova and Verona.

Regionali (R): local trains that stop at every station within a 100km (62-mile) radius of their departure station. They are very slow, and it's often worth waiting a few minutes for a faster train. Seats cannot be reserved and smoking is not permitted.

TICKETS

» Italian trains offer the choice of first- or second-class tickets, which are calculated by the kilometre. A single (one-way) second-class ticket

between Venice and Padova costs around €6.

» Supplements are charged for the faster services, such as Intercity and Eurocity. These come in the form of a separate ticket and must be shown to the ticket inspector.

» There are no discounts for return (round-trip) tickets.

» Children aged 4–12 travel at a 50 per cent discount of the normal fare; children under 4 travel free.

» Tickets are valid for six months, but must be used within six hours of being validated.

AT THE STATION

» The ticket office is on the left of the front concourse of Santa Lucia station. There are separate windows for advance booking, and a useful travel information office, where English is spoken, to the right just before the entrance to the platforms.

» Ask for either *andata* (one-way) or *andata e ritorno* (return/round-trip). The distance and price are displayed on an electronic board. If you plan to travel by a fast train remember to ask for the supplement.

» Payment is normally by cash, though you can use a credit card for longer, more expensive journeys.

» Check your train's departure time and platform on the board; all platforms also have clear timetables for both arriving and departing trains (*arrivi* and *partenze*), and there is an information board, showing the next train's destination and departure time, at the head of each platform.

» Trains are numbered and almost always leave from the same platform.

» Validate your ticket by inserting it in one of the yellow boxes found at various points around the station and on the platforms. Failure to do this incurs an on-the-spot fine of around €17.

PARKING IN VENICE

If you arrive by car, you must leave your vehicle in one of the parking areas around the city, which are connected to Venice proper by public transport.

Parking costs are high, and mount up if you're staying for more than two to three days in the city. However, many Venetian hotels offer their guests discounts at parking areas, so it's worth checking when you make your hotel reservation.

Before you decide where to park, it's worth thinking about ease of access to the city as well as the cost. The multilevel parking areas at Piazzale Roma, at the end of the causeway, are virtually in the city itself, less than a 5-minute walk from the *vaporetto* stop. The artificial island of Tronchetto, northwest of

Piazzale Roma, is equally convenient and is served by its own *vaporetto* service, which connects with central Venice via the Grand Canal, though the walk to the *imbarcadero* is longer than at Piazzale Roma. Both these options are expensive. Across the lagoon on the mainland, the Fusina parking areas are cheaper, and have the convenience of an hourly boat service across the lagoon to the Zattere. Marco Polo airport has plenty of parking at competitive rates; if you park here, use the city transfer routes outlined on pages 40–41. There is additional, and very

cheap parking, around the station in Mestre, but finding a space can be difficult and parking cannot be pre-booked.

The best way to pre-book parking is online; follow the instructions on screen to send an email. The parking area will then confirm your reservation. You can pay by credit card or cash, and will be charged for each whole day or fraction of to the nearest hour. If your hotel negotiates reduced parking costs for you they will send you the necessary vouchers and paperwork.

CAR PARKS						
NAME	**ADDRESS**	**TEL/WEBSITE**	**PRICE**	**HOW TO GET THERE**	**ONWARD TRAVEL**	**OPEN**
Autorimessa Comunale	Piazzale Roma, Santa Croce 365B	041 272 7211; www.asmvenezia.it	€24 per day, €22.80 pre-booked online	Cross causeway and follow signs to Piazzale Roma	*Vaporetto* 1, 2, 41, 42, 51, 52 at Piazzale Roma	24 hours daily
Marco Polo Park	Marco Polo Airport, Via Luigi Broglio, Tessera	041 260 3060; www.veniceairport.it/	€16 per day, reduced rates for longer periods	Follow airport signs from A4, bus 5 to Piazzale Roma	*Vaporetto* 1, 2, 41, 42, 51, 52 at Piazzale Roma	24 hours daily
Park Terminal Fusina	Via Moranzani 79, Fusina	parcheggi 041 523 1337, 041 547 0160; www.terminalfusina.it	€12 up to 12 hours, €18 up to 24 hours	Exit A4 onto SS309 towards Ravenna and follow signs	Boat from Fusina to Zattere (8am–10pm)	Jun–end Sep 8am–11.30pm; Oct–end May 8am–9.30pm
Tronchetto	Ísola Nuova del Tronchetto	041 520 7555; www.veniceparking.it	€21 a day	Cross causeway and follow signs to Tronchetto	*Vaporetto* 2, 3, 4 at Tronchetto	24 hours daily

Unfortunately Venice presents particular problems for people with mobility disabilities, who will need the help of able-bodied companions to get around. Even with assistance, some areas of the city will be inaccessible, due particularly to the bridges. However, with some judicious planning, there's no reason why people with physical disabilities cannot experience at least some of Venice's special delights.

TRANSPORT INFORMATION FOR VISITORS WITH DISABILITIES

Marco Polo Airport
tel 041 260 9260
ACTV tel 0421 383672
Trenitalia tel 041 785 570

ARRIVING

Contact your airline to let them know what assistance you will need. Marco Polo airport has wheelchair access to all facilities, and airport buses, in theory, take wheelchairs. At Piazzale Roma, access to the *imbarcadero* for the No. 1 *vaporetto* service is straightforward.

CHOOSING A HOTEL

Elevators are rare in Venetian buildings, but the more expensive hotels have them, and some have wheelchair accessible rooms on the ground floor. Make sure there are no bridges between your hotel and the nearest *vaporetto* stop, preferably on the route of the No. 1 *vaporetto*, as these are easily accessible.

GETTING AROUND

You will find *vaporetto* crews helpful. Standard *vaporetti* and *motonavi* (▷ 48–49) have a large flat deck area and easy boarding; they operate on lines 1, 2, 3, 4, 5, LN, T and N. Venice has several bridges with wheelchair ramps. These are automated and need a key, available from tourist offices. Visitors with visual disabilities should note that not all canals have railings or walls.

SIGHTSEEING

Many Venetian museums have good access within the building. However, access to the building is a different matter, and you will not be able to visit all the main sights. Many churches are some distance from *vaporetti* stops and only accessible over several bridges.

EASILY ACCESSIBLE AREAS AND MAIN SIGHTS
(no bridges from *vaporetto*)

	Vaporetto No. and Stop
Basilica dei Frari	1, San Tomà
Basilica di San Marco	1, Vallaresso
Burano	LN, Burano
Ca' d'Oro (ask at the entrance to use the elevator)	1, Ca d'Oro
Campo Santo Stefano	1, San Samuele
Gallerie dell'Accademia (ask at the entrance to use the elevator)	1, 2 Accademia
Murano	LN, Murano Faro
Museo Civico Correr (ask at the entrance to use the elevator)	1, Vallaresso
Museo del Costume	1, San Stae
Palazzo Ducale (ask at the entrance to use the elevator)	1, Vallaresso
Piazza San Marco	1, Vallaresso
Rialto markets	1, San Silvestro
Scuola Grande di San Rocco	1, San Tomà
Zattere	1, Accademia

Other major sights may only involve negotiating as few as one or two bridges; careful study of the map will help you decide which to tackle.

INFORMATION

Informahandicap provides information on disabled travel in Venice and the Veneto. In conjunction with the tourist board, it produces a booklet listing hotels, restaurants and museums with disabled facilities, and the tourist offices have a map with wheelchair-accessible routes. Both maps and booklets are obtainable from:

INFORMAHANDICAP
Ca' Farsetti, San Marco 4136
Tel 041 274 8144 (Venezia);
41 274 6144 (Mestre)
www.comune.venezia.it/handicap

RADAR
12 City Forum, 250 City Road,
London EC1V 8AF
Tel 020 7250 3222
www.radar.org.uk

Before you go, you could also contact:
TOURISM FOR ALL
c/o Vitalise, Shap Road Industrial Estate,
Shap Road, Kendal, Cumbria LA9 6NZ
Tel 0845 124 9971
www.tourismforall.org.uk
A UK-based company that produces publications and information on accessibility.

SATH
347 5th Avenue, Suite 605,
New York City, NY 10016
Tel 212/447-7284
www.sath.org

REGIONS

This chapter is divided into five regions of Venice (▷ 7). Region names are for the purposes of this book only and places of interest are listed alphabetically in each region.

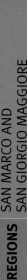

SAN MARCO AND
SAN GIORGIO MAGGIORE

Embraced by the sinuous southeast curve of the Grand Canal, and flanked to the east by Castello and to the west by Cannaregio, San Marco is Venice's busiest and most important *sestiere* (ward). It is a long-standing role, for San Marco was the hub of the machinery of state during the centuries of Venice's existence as an independent power, and the area still contains the principal buildings of that power. Clustering around Piazza San Marco, the city's largest open space, the Basilica, the Campanile and the sublime Palazzo Ducale are the architectural keynotes, drawing thousands of visitors. From here, the wide promenade of the Riva degli Schiavoni stretches east, while to the south, across the bustling waters of the Bacino di San Marco, rises the serene silhouette of Palladio's great church of San Giorgio Maggiore, superbly set on its own island.

Away from this honeypot cluster, two main routes fan out across the area, one leading roughly north to the Rialto, the other heading west to the Accademia bridge. The northern route is known as the Mercerie, a string of narrow alleys that connects the Piazza with the Rialto, and since the Middle Ages it has been the shopping heartland of the city, constantly thronged with crowds of both Venetians and visitors. The streets running west are broader, today lined with the emporia of some of Italy's most iconic names, offering retail therapy par excellence. Churches and *palazzi* are scattered everywhere, and there's culture too, in the shape of art spaces such as the Palazzo Grassi, home to a contemporary collection, and the rebuilt Teatro la Fenice, Venice's famous, and stunningly beautiful, opera house. Other *campi* (squares), such as Campo Santo Stefano, with its lovely Gothic church, punctuate the area and everywhere there are bars, restaurants and hotels, making San Marco the city's true tourist heartland.

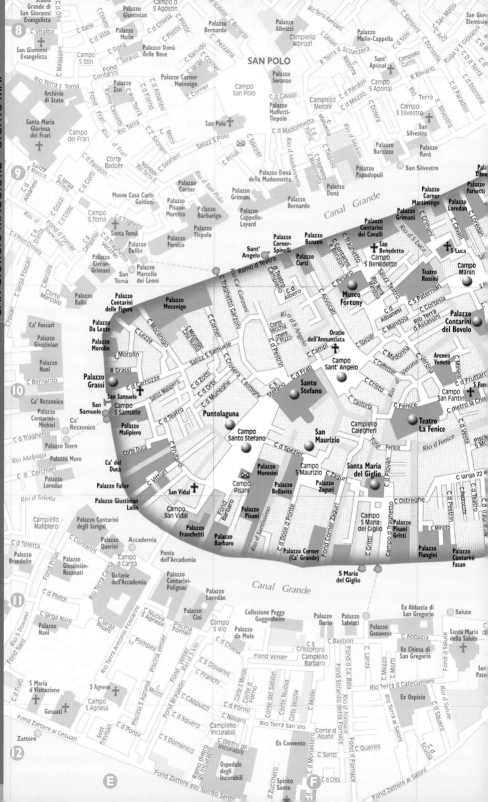

Scuola
Grande di
San Giovanni
Evangelista

C d Olio

Campo d
S Agostin

Rio Terra Rampani

Palazzo
Giustinian

C Zane

C Colalto

C d Pistor

C d Chiesa

Palazzo
Molin

Palazzo
Bernardo

C d Pezzana

Palazzo
Albrizzi

Campiello
Albrizzi

R Terra d. Scoazzera

Sant'
Aponal

Campiello
Curnis

Palazzo
Molin-Cappella

Ruga V S Giovanni

C d Sole

C Donnella

C d Terra

C d Storione

8

C Vitalba

C d Vida

C Dona

C Soranzo

Palazzo
Donà
delle Rose

C Sanudo

C larga Corner

C Corner

SAN POLO

Palazzo
Soranzo

Campo d
Aponal

R Ravano

C d Paradiso

San Giovanni
Evangelista

Campo
S Stin

Fond
Contarini

Campo
San Polo

C d Cavalli

Campiello
Meloni

C d Perdon

C d Mezzo

Campo
S Silvestro

S Silvestro

Archivio
di Stato

Rio Terra s Tomà

Palazzo
Zen

C d Albanesi

C Corner

Palazzo
Maffetti-
Tiepolo

Matassa

Rio Terra
d Dolera

Palazzo
Corner
Mocenigo

Santa Maria
Gloriosa
dei Frari

Campo
dei Frari

Rio d S Polo

San Polo

Salizz S Polo

C d Priuli

C Spezier

Palazzo
Donà
della Madonnetta

C d Madonetta

C Tiepolo

Palazzo
Grimani

Rio d Meloni

Palazzo
Barzizza

Palazzo
Rava

San Silvestro

9

Salizz
S Rocco

C larga
Prima

C larga
C Albanesi

C Gozzi

C d Cristo

Campo
S Tomà

C d Traghetto

Santa Tomà

Rio d San Polo

Corte
Badoèr

Rio d San Polo

Palazzo
Corner

Palazzo
Pisani-
Moretta

Palazzo
Barbarigo

Palazzo
Grimani

Palazzo
Cappello-
Layard

Canal Grande

Palazzo
Corner
Martinengo

Palazzo
Grimani

Palazzo
Loredan

Palazzo
Farsetti

C Crivran

C Cavalli

C Loredan

Fond d Forner
Frescada

C d Preti Crosera

Fond
Frari

Rio d
Frari

Museo Casa Carlo
Goldoni

Palazzo
Tiepolo

Palazzo
Persico

Palazzo
Benzon

Palazzo
Contarini
dei Cavalli

C Contarini
e Benzon

Rio d S Luca

San
Benedetto

Campo
S Benedetto

Teatro
Rossini

S Luca

Campo
Manin

S Paternian

Santa Tomà

Palazzo
Dolfin

Civran-
Grimani

San
Tomà

Palazzo
Marcello
dei Leoni

Sant'
Angelo

Palazzo
Corner-
Spinelli

Palazzo
Curti

d teatro
Campiello

d teatro

C Pestrin

Avvocati

Museo
Fortuny

C Albanesi

C Mandola

C Cortesia

Palazzo
Contarini
del Bovolo

C Teatro

C d Albero

Oratio
dell'Annunziata

C Campi

Campo
Sant'Angelo

C Frati

C Cristo

C d Verona

Areneo
Veneto

Minelli

10

Palazzo
Balbi

Palazzo
Contarini
delle Figure

Palazzo
Mocenigo

C Mocenigo

Ca Mocenigo
Casa Nuova

Rio d S Angelo

C Caffetier

C Verona

Fruttarol

S Fan

Ca' Foscari

Palazzo
Da Lezze

C Lezze

Corte
Vecchia
chiere

C d Pizzo

Oratio
dell'Annunziata

Santo
Stefano

Campo
San Fantin

C d dietro la Chie

Palazzo
Giustinian

Palazzo
Nani

C Bernardo

R Grassi

Palazzo
Morolin

Morolin

Salizz S Samuele

Salizz Malipiero

C Corner

C Crosera S Samuele

C d Botteghe

C S Stefano

Santo
Stefano

C Fenice

Teatro
La Fenice

**Palazzo
Grassi**

C d Carrozze

C d Zotti

C d Orbi

C d Muneghe

C Caotorta

Fond
Fenice

Ca' Rezzonico

Palazzo
Contarini-
Michiel

C d Traghetto

San
Samuele

Campo
S Samuele

Ca'
Rezzonico

Palazzo
Malipiero

C d Teatro

C Frutarol

C Frutarol

Puntolaguna

Campo
Santo Stefano

San
Maurizio

Campiello
Caleghieri

C d Spezier

Santa Maria
del Giglio

Rio d Fenice

C dietro la Chie

Piscia
S M

Rio Malpaga

Palazzo
Moro

C d Cerchieri

Palazzo
Loredan

Rio d Toletta

Palazzo
Stern

Ca' del
Duca

Corte Duca

C Vitturi

San Vidal

Palazzo
Falier

Palazzo
Giustinian
Lolin

Campo
San Vidal

Campo
Pisani

Palazzo
Morosini

San
Maurizio

Campo
S Maurizio

C S Zaguri

Palazzo
Bellavite

Palazzo
Zaguri

C d Piovan

Campo
S Maria
del Giglio

C d Traghetto

Palazzo
Pisani
Gritti

C Larga 22

C Piscina

C Pedrocchi

C d Teatro

C Minoto

Campiello
Malipiero

Palazzo
Contarini
degli Scrigni

C d Toletta

C Contarini

Palazzo
Querini

Accademia

Campo
di Carità

Ponte
dell'Accademia

Palazzo
Franchetti

Fond
Barbaro

Palazzo
Pisani

Palazzo
Barbaro

Fond d Ponte

Rio d Santissimo

Fond Corner Zaguri

Palazzo
Corner
(Ca' Grande)

C Gritti

Palazzo
Flangini

Palazzo
Contarini
Fasan

Palazzo
Brandolin

Fond Priuli

Palazzo
Giustinian-
Recanati

Gallerie
dell'Accademia

Rio Terra Antonio Foscarini

C d Pistor

C larga Nani

C larga Pisani

Nuova
S Agnese

Piscina
Forner

Palazzo
Contarini-
Polignac

Palazzo
Loredàn

Collezione Peggy
Guggenheim

Palazzo
Dario

Palazzo
Salviati

Ex Abbazia di
San Gregorio

Salute

11

S Trovaso

C larga Nani

Palazzo
Nani

C Pistor

Palazzo
Cini

Campo
S Vio

Palazzo
da Mula

Palazzo
Genovese

C Abbazia

Santa Maria
della Salute

Ser
Pate

S Maria
d Visitazione

S Agnese

Campo
S Agnese

Piscina S Agnese

C d Mezzo

C Pompea Venier

C d Venier

C S Giovanni

C Franchi

C S Vio
C d Chiesa

Collezione Peggy
Guggenheim

Palazzo
da Mula

S
Cristoforo

Fond Venier

Campiello
Barbaro

C Bastion

C d Mezzo

C Morti

Ex Chiesa di
San Gregorio

Ex Ospizio

Rio d Salute

C d
Squero

Gesuati

Fond Zattere ai Gesuati

Campo
S Agnese

C d Mende

Corte
d Forno

Corte
Vecchia

C Navaro

Rio Terra San Vio

Corte d Abate

Fond Soranzo detto Fornace

Fond d'Fornace

Rio Terra a Catecumeni

Ex Ospizio

Rio d Salute

Zattere

Sott
Trevisan

C d Ponte

S Domenico

Campiello
Incurabili

C dietro gli
Incurabili

Rio Terra San Vio

C Molin

Ex Convento

C Santi

Rio d Fornace

Fond d Fornace

12

Fond Zattere ai Gesuati

Rio dietro gli
Incurabili

Ospedale
degli
Incurabili

Fond Zattere allo spirito Santo

Spirito
Santo

Rio d Zucchero

Rio d Monastero

C d Crea

E

F

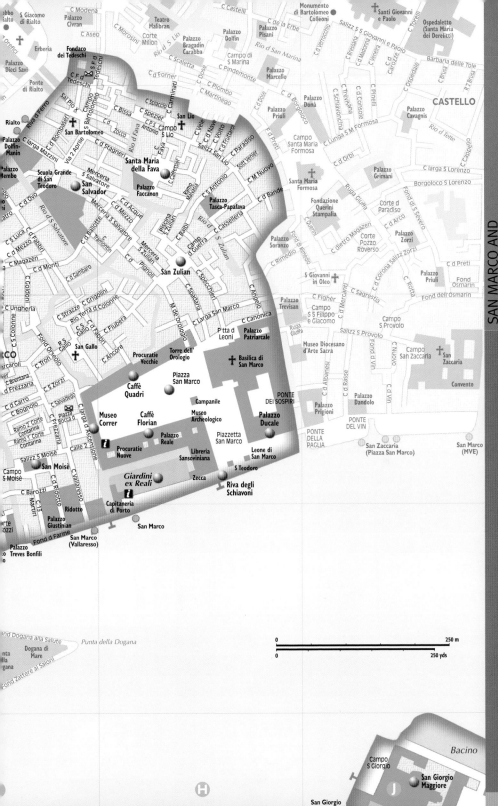

CASTELLO

Bacino

San Giorgio Maggiore

San Giorgio

MANIN

CAFFÈ FLORIAN

www.caffeflorian.com

Sitting with a drink in the Piazza San Marco is as much a part of the Venetian experience as visiting the Basilica or going down the Grand Canal. Café life has been an essential part of the city since the 18th century and still is today, whether you're sitting at a table in the sunshine, or relaxing in the warmth of one of the charming rooms in winter.

The Caffè Florian (▷ 94) has been in business since 1720, when Floriano Francesoni established a coffee-house known as Venezia Trionfante. By the early 1800s it was very popular with Venetians, and it gained the upper hand among the Piazza cafés during the Austrian occupation (1815–66), when loyal citizens drank here to escape the army officers in Caffè Quadri (▷ below) across the Piazza.

The present warren of intimate and elegant rooms dates from 1859, while marble tables and upholstered benches spill out onto the arcade and into the Piazza. As you listen to the orchestra and sip your inordinately expensive *cioccolata calda con panna* (hot chocolate with whipped cream on top) or Bellini *(prosecco* with white peach juice) you'll be in good company—Lord Byron and the German writer Goethe were enthusiastic patrons.

➕ 59 H10 ✉ Piazza San Marco 56, San Marco ☎ 041 520 5641 🕐 May–end Oct daily 9.30am–12am; Nov–end Apr Thu–Tue 9.30am–12am 🚤 San Marco

CAFFÈ QUADRI

www.quadrivenice.com

Founded as early as 1638, not long after the introduction into Venice—and thus Europe—of coffee, the coffee-house known as Il Remedio was purchased in 1775 by Giorgio Quadri, who quickly established it as a popular meeting place that attracted society figures and politicians alike. It was the first Venetian café to serve the super-concentrated *caffé alla turca,* the precursor to today's *espresso.*

Above *Caffè Quadri on Piazza San Marco is popular with Venetian society and tourists alike*
Opposite *A bronze statue of Daniele Manin stands in the centre of Campo Manin*

During the Austrian occupation it was a firm favourite with officers from the occupying army, and the then owners, the Vivarini brothers, sought to win back a Venetian clientele with the opening of the upstairs restaurant rooms and the fashionable redecoration of the café itself. The interior remains today: light, bright and elegant, with clear colours and charming stucco and fresco decoration. Outside tables give superb views over the Piazza, the perfect place to view the square while listening to the orchestra and enjoying a drink (▷ 94–95).

Celebrities have frequented Quadri down the years, and today's habitués range from Pierce Brosnan, Claudia Schiffer and Brad Pitt to Italian heavyweight political players such as Silvio Berlusconi.

➕ 59 H10 ✉ Piazza San Marco 121, San Marco ☎ 041 522 2105 🕐 Apr–end Oct daily 9am–11.30pm; Nov–end Mar Tue–Sun 9am–11.30pm 🚤 San Marco

CAMPO MANIN

There are very few squares in Venice where 20th-century architecture is the first thing that catches the eye, but yours is bound to be drawn inexorably to the monstrous, less-than-appealing bulk of the 1968 Cassa di Risparmio bank that looms over Campo Manin, designed by Pier Luigi Nervi.

A narrow street and a bridge lead into the square, and there's a real sense of space after the tiny alleys that surround it, an effect due to the enlargement of the *campo* in 1871 to make room for the monument to Daniele Manin, the leader of the 1848 uprising of Venice's citizens against the Austrian occupation. The bronze statue in the middle portrays the Venetian hero facing his own house, which still stands beside the left-hand bridge. The uprising was initially successful, a provisional government being set up and new currency printed. But resistance was short-lived, and in 1849, worn down by hunger and disease and bombed from the air by explosives attached to balloons, the Venetians surrendered. Manin died in 1857 in exile in France.

Calle de la Vida, on the left side of the *campo,* leads to the Palazzo Contarini del Bovolo (▷ 63).

➕ 58 G9 ✉ Campo Manin, San Marco 🚤 Rialto, Sant'Angelo

CAMPO SANT'ANGELO

Lying directly on the route from Campo Santo Stefano (▷ this page) to the Rialto, Campo Sant'Angelo is a wide, airy expanse that makes a good place to pause. Its size is due to the demolition, in 1837, of the church of the Angelo Michele, Sant'Angelo, which stood near the *rio* at the southwest side of the square. The *campo* has two late 15th-century well-heads and is surrounded by patrician houses. The isolated building in the middle of the square is the Oratorio dell'Annunziata, a chapel first built in the 10th century. The present building is one of a series of rebuilds; the interior contains a fine 15th-century Crucifixion. Be sure to take in the view of the campanile of Santo Stefano, the most steeply leaning tower in the city.

🕀 58 F10 ✉ Campo Sant'Angelo, San Marco 🚤 Sant'Angelo

CAMPO SANTO STEFANO

San Marco's second most important square, Campo Santo Stefano is a fine, open, irregular space, enclosed at its north end by the church of the same name (▷ 84–85), while the southern side leads to the approach to the Accademia bridge. From the *campo* there's a choice of routes—south to Dorsoduro across the Grand Canal, east to the Piazza and north to the Rialto. It's a busy square, but big enough to absorb the crowds easily, with plenty of room to serve as a playground for local kids and a hangout for students and backpackers. There's an impressive choice of cafés, but connoisseurs head straight for Gelateria Paolin (▷ 93), which serves some of the city's most delectable ices, while designer-name fans can browse through the fake bags on offer from the African street traders who normally congregate here. It's hard to imagine that this square was one of the main 18th-century bullfighting arenas, a role which was abandoned in 1802 when a bank of seats collapsed, killing a number of spectators. The

Above *Relaxing in the sunshine in Campo Santo Stefano*

central statue is of Nicolò Tommaseo (1802–74), a philosopher whose theories were important during the Risorgimento, the Italian movement of unification, and behind is the entrance to the Puntolaguna (▷ 63). At the Canal Grande end you'll see the 17th-century Palazzo Morosini, home to Francesco Morosini, the last doge to serve as the Republic's military commander (1688–94). He's probably better remembered by non-Italians for blowing up the Turkish gunpowder store in the Parthenon, doing more damage in 20 minutes than the wear and tear of the preceding centuries.

🕀 58 F10 ✉ Campo Santo Stefano, San Marco 🚤 San Samuele, Accademia

GIARDINI EX REALI

About the only patch of green in the vicinity of the Piazza San Marco is the Giardini ex Reali, a waterfront oasis of trees behind the Procuratie Nuove. It was created during the Napoleonic occupation, when Eugène Bonaparte, son of Napoléon III, demolished the old state granaries which stood here as part of his scheme to improve the area. He was also responsible for the elegant neoclassical pavilion at the west end, the Casino del Caffè, now home to the excellent main tourist office. Benches are shaded by trees and the view over the Bacino di San Marco is superb, but the

downsides are the constant crowds and serried rows of souvenir stalls. It's popular with artists, who sell their watercolours, oils and charcoal sketches. Despite this, the gardens have a certain allure.

🕀 59 H10 ✉ Giardini ex Reali, San Marco 🖐 Free 🚤 San Marco, Vallaresso

MUSEO CORRER

▷ 64–65.

MUSEO FORTUNY

www.museicivicivenezioni.it
In 1899 the Spanish-born painter, photographer and fabric designer Mariano Fortuny y Madrazo purchased one of the Pesaro family's *palazzi* in San Marco. It dates from the end of the 15th century and is a wonderful example of decorated Gothic, with two inner courtyards and an exterior stair leading to balconies that open into the *piano nobile*. This contains a huge *portego*, the quintessential Venetian central hall. Fortuny decorated the *portego* with textiles and hangings, setting up a workshop to pursue his interest in theatre and design. The two came together in his textiles—both in the pleated silk dresses known as Delphos, which liberated women's bodies, and in the stencilled brocades and velvets he used for interior decoration. Fortuny also produced silk lampshades in his own inimitable and instantly recognizable

style. He set up a factory in Venice and his fabrics and clothes were sold all over the world—a small factory on the Giudecca continued production up to the 1980s. Today, Fortuny-style silks and velvets are manufactured by Venetia Studium, with shops all over the city (▷ 91). The Palazzo Fortuny was left to the city in 1956 by the designer's widow and is now used for exhibitions and cultural events. Though in need of restoration, it's one of the most evocative of all *palazzi*, whose dimly lit interior, pricked with light from pierced lamps and hung with sumptuous textiles, embodies the voluptuousness of Fortuny's art.
🚹 58 F10 ✉ Rio Terrà della Mandorla, San Marco 3780 (round corner from main facade) ☎ 041 520 0995 🕐 Varies with exhibitions, but normally Tue–Sun 10–6 👋 €9 🚤 Sant'Angelo

PALAZZO CONTARINI DEL BOVOLO

The Gothic Palazzo Contarini del Bovolo is best known for its sinuous exterior staircase. You'll find it in the courtyard of the palace, where it was erected in around 1499 to link the loggias built on each floor when the owner, Pietro Contarini, enlarged his home. Such staircases are called *scale a chiocciola* (snail stairs) in Italian—the Venetian dialect for snail is *bovolo*. The beautiful red-brick and Istrian stone stair gives access on five different levels to graceful loggias curving around inside a tower that's said to be reminiscent of the tower of Pisa.
🚹 58 G10 ✉ Calle dei Risi, San Marco 4299 ☎ 041 270 2464 🕐 Interior closed to visitors 🚤 Rialto

PALAZZO DUCALE
▷ 66–71.

PALAZZO GRASSI

www.palazzograssi.it
The superbly symmetrical Palazzo Grassi is on the right-hand side of the Grand Canal, coming from San Marco, between the San Samuele and the San Tomà *vaporetto* stops. Outside, nothing could be more traditionally 18th-century classical than this palace. Inside, it's another story; the interior was converted in the 1980s by Gianni Agnelli of Fiat to become Venice's most high-profile exhibition venue. The *palazzo* was designed by Giorgio Massari (1687–1766) for a newly rich family, and was built between 1748 and 1772. The interior has neoclassical elements, with a monumental staircase rising to the frescoed *portego* on the *piano nobile*, from which richly stuccoed and decorated rooms lead off. These spaces were used under Fiat ownership to stage a series of world-class exhibitions throughout the 1990s. Following the death of Gianni Agnelli, the *palazzo* was bought by François Pinault, the French millionaire, collector and owner of Gucci, Yves Saint Laurent and Christie's. In 2007, the Grassi reopened as a venue for a series of cutting-edge art shows, centred around Pinault's collection of 20th-century and contemporary art.
🚹 58 E10 ✉ Campo San Samuele, San Marco 3231 ☎ 041 523 1680 🕐 Daily 10–7 👋 Adult €15, child (12–18) €10, under 12 free; combined ticket with Punta della Dogana adult €20, child €14 🚤 San Samuele

PUNTOLAGUNA

www.salve.it
Puntolaguna is a state-of-the-art multimedia information centre run by the Magistrato alle Acque, Venice's water authority. Workstations allow you access to a huge variety of information via CD-ROM, animations and internet sites, and there's a library of videos devoted to the lagoon and its ecosystem. You can pick up information about suggested itineraries for exploring the lagoon, learn more about the MoSE project (▷ 16), consult maps and talk to the enthusiastic and knowledgeable staff. This is a good place to bring children, and the staff run excellent workshops aimed at them, sometimes in English.
🚹 58 F10 ✉ Campo Santo Stefano, San Marco 2949 ☎ 041 529 3582 🕐 Mon–Fri 2.30–5.30. Closed Jul, Aug 👋 Free 🚤 Accademia

Below *Palazzo Grassi's classical lines seen from the Grand Canal*

INFORMATION

www.museicivicivenezian.it

🕂 59 G10 ✉ Ala Napoleonica, Piazza
San Marco 52, San Marco ☎ 041
240 5211 🕓 Apr–end Oct daily 9–7;
Nov–end Mar daily 9–5 🎟 Museum
Card (valid for Museo Correr, Museo
Archeologico, Biblioteca Marciana,
Palazzo Ducale) adult €12, child (6–14) €3;
holders of Rolling Venice card €7.50. No
single tickets for the Correr 🚤 Vallaresso
🎫 Guidebooks at bookstall; guided tours
of Biblioteca Marciana Sat–Sun 10–12,
2–3 🛍 🏛 Guidebooks, art books,
posters and museum gifts

Above *The entrance to the Correr is in the*
arcade of the Ala Napoleonica

INTRODUCTION

Overlooking the Piazza di San Marco, the Museo Correr traces the history of
the city of Venice. Its huge range of sculpture, paintings and historical objects
provides an insight into city life in the great days of the Republic.

The Museo Correr occupies the buildings around the Piazza which served
as Venice's 19th-century royal residence. Until the Napoleonic invasion the
west end of the Piazza was occupied by a church which stood between
the Procuratie Vecchie and the Procuratie Nuove. This was demolished, and
between 1806 and 1814 work started on the Ala Napoleonica. This was finally
completed in the mid-19th century, when Venice was under Austrian rule. It
served as the royal residence for the Habsburgs when they visited the city,
incorporating a complex that stretched the full length of the Procuratie Nuove
as far as the Biblioteca Nazionale Marciana. In 1923, this huge space was
opened as the Museo Correr, whose core comprises the 16th-, 17th- and
18th-century collections of Teodoro Correr, who gifted them to the city in
1830. The city's archaeological collections were housed in the same complex
as a separate museum, and there was public access to the magnificent
Libreria Sansoviniana. In the 1960s the third-floor rooms containing the picture
collection were revamped and in the late 1990s everything was linked as a
single entity, creating one of Venice's biggest museums.

The Museo Correr occupies the upper floors of the Ala Napoleonica, the
Procuratie Nuove and Sansovino's library building, and is housed in a series of
grand and elaborate rooms, many overlooking the Piazza. It's approached up a
monumental stairway, which is tucked under the arcade of the Ala Napoleonica
at the west end of the Piazza San Marco. The Correr is now directly linked
with the Museo Archeologico and the Biblioteca Nazionale Marciana, so you
can explore the whole complex on a single ticket. The top floor is home to the
Quadreria, a gallery tracing the development of Venetian painting. This is a big
museum and you need a whole morning to see everything. You may also find

that this is one to leave for the end of your visit, when what you have already learned about the city will help you make sense of many of the displays. If time is short, head for the highlights, leaving time to visit the sumptuous library.

WHAT TO SEE

THE CANOVA SCULPTURES

The neoclassical rooms of the first floor make the ideal setting for the slickly impressive sculptures by Antonio Canova (1757–1822), considered to be the finest sculptor of his age. He was a poised and technically outstanding sculptor, and you can trace his work process through the *maquettes*, or clay models, that he used as the first drafts for his highly polished works. The focal point of the display is his *Daedalus and Icarus*, created when he was just 22, in which the older man fixes a pair of wings onto the would-be aviator. The collection also includes casts of his work; the black studs on *Paris* were guidelines made by apprentices preparing the marble for the artist.

THE VENETIAN ROOMS

Many of the rooms (6–18) in the Procuratie Nuove are devoted to collections that document Venetian history, covering everything from daily life and local festivals to the workings of the State, the Arsenale, the ducal elections and the great commercial and naval achievements. Don't miss the bird's-eye view of Venice, a huge woodcut that was produced by Jacopo de' Barbari between 1497 and 1500 and is one of the most seminal images of the city. At the far end of the museum, past the picture gallery, there are more enjoyable Venetian displays, with cases devoted to games, pastimes and festivals and a whole exhibit of *zoccoli*, the famous elevated clogs worn by Venetian ladies of leisure. These first appeared in the early 15th century, and by the 17th had reached astounding heights, with women wobbling along supported by two attendants in order to keep their balance.

THE QUADRERIA

Apart from the Accademia (▷ 206–211) Venice has no better and more comprehensive painting collection than the Correr. The great Venetians, such as the Bellinis, are well represented—don't miss the *Portrait of the Doge Giovanni Mocenigo* (1480s) by Gentile Bellini, or the lovely *Madonna and Child* (1470–75) by Giovanni Bellini. Pride of the collection is Vittore Carpaccio's famous *Two Venetian Noblewomen* (1507), which shows two finely dressed ladies sitting on a balcony. For years this picture was known as *The Courtesans*, but it emerged that the sitters had been maligned when the top half of the picture, showing a hunting scene with men and dogs, was traced to the Getty Museum in California. Far from being courtesans awaiting trade, these eminently respectable ladies are merely terminally bored while the boys play. Other treasures include Antonello da Messina's *Pietà* (1475), an early oil painting, and a tranquil and lovely *Madonna* (1525) by Lorenzo Lotto.

BIBLIOTECA NAZIONALE MARCIANA

One of the most outstanding buildings of the ensemble around the Piazzetta (▷ 79–80), the Biblioteca Nazionale Marciana was designed by Sansovino (1486–1570) and completed in 1591. The main hall, among the most beautiful rooms in Venice, is richly decorated with carved and gilded wood, its ceilings covered with allegorical paintings by Veronese, Tintoretto and their followers, while a fresco of *Wisdom* by Titian adorns the anteroom. This grandeur is approached up a magnificent staircase; all gilt and stucco, it's a fitting entrance to one of the Republic's most prestigious buildings. Changing exhibitions of the library's treasures are often held, and there are permanent displays of illuminated manuscripts, early printed books from Venetian presses and historic maps.

Above *Decorative ceiling in the entrance hall of the museum*
Below *Madonna and Child by Giovanni Bellini*

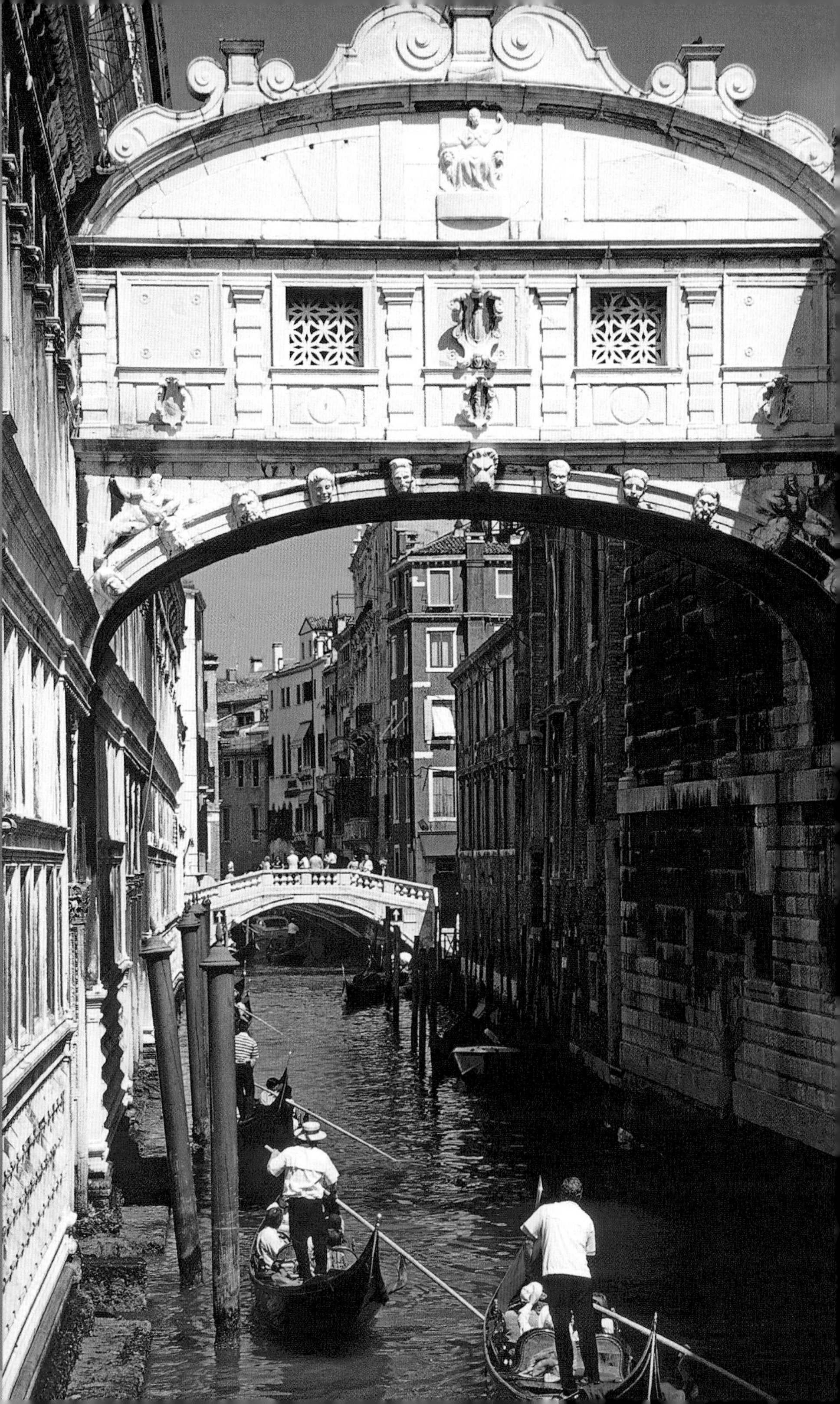

INTRODUCTION

Once the political and judicial hub of the Venetian Empire and home to the doge, the Palazzo Ducale is one of the world's most beautiful buildings. It's the grandest of all Venetian *palazzi* and one of the finest secular buildings of its era.

The Palazzo Ducale incorporated both a residence for the doge—the Venetian Republic's head of state—and the offices that housed the machinery of state. Here, in one building, were combined all the offices of government—councils, committee rooms, assembly chambers, diplomatic and foreign offices and the judiciary, as well as the state prisons. From the 14th century, government was in the hands of members of those patrician families whose names were inscribed in the so-called Libro d'Oro (Golden Book), and the building reflects their power, wealth and prestige, as well as that of the Republic itself. The first governmental building was erected on the site in the ninth century, but it was not until 1340 that the Palazzo began to assume its present shape. In this year work started on a new hall for the Maggior Consiglio (Great Council); it was completed in 1362, the start of a construction process that resulted in much of what we see today.

A serious fire in 1483 caused extensive damage, necessitating rebuilding, but it was decided to repair the damage, rather than build something new, a decision which left the magical fairy-tale Veneto-Gothic facade unaltered and was repeated after the further devastating fires of 1574 and 1577. The block across the Canale della Paglia, approached via the Ponte dei Sospiri (Bridge of Sighs) is the exception, being built in the late High Renaissance classical style. Since the fall of the Republic in 1797, the Palazzo Ducale has had many different functions, but still retains a role in the civil administrative life of Venice; as well as being open to the public it houses various city offices.

Built at a time when the rest of Europe cowered behind fortified walls, the fairy-tale facade of the Palazzo Ducale, light, airy and confident, embraces the outside world. It adjoins the Basilica di San Marco at the east end of the Piazza San Marco and overlooks the Piazzetta and the waters of the Bacino di San Marco. It's reached by taking the *vaporetto* from the railway station, a beautiful trip down the Grand Canal of about 35 minutes, or by approaching on foot from wherever you're based; walking from the station takes around 45 minutes. To see it thoroughly you should allow plenty of time, perhaps deciding in advance where you want to linger. The audioguide tour takes around two to three hours. There are information boards in Italian and English in many of the rooms; if you don't have a guidebook these are well worth reading. There's no ideal time to come, as the Palazzo Ducale is the number-one sight for every visitor to Venice.

WHAT TO SEE

THE EXTERIOR, THE PORTA DELLA CARTA AND THE COURTYARD

The beautiful pink-and-white facade of the Palazzo Ducale, one of the world's finest examples of Gothic architecture, runs along the Piazzetta and the water's edge. The waterfront facade, finished in 1404, is the older, and its design is echoed by the 15th-century Piazzetta side. Both facades have a ground-floor arcade topped by a gallery supporting the mass of the upper floors, the masonry closing in on the open space as the building heightens. The play of light and shade over solid form and through space adds to the impression of harmony, enhanced by the regularity of the arches and ground-floor columns and pillars, copies of the 14th- and 15th-century originals, which are now housed in the ground-floor Museo dell'Opera.

The main entrance is through the Porta della Carta. This monumental gateway, a superb example of Decorated Gothic at its most ornate, was

INFORMATION

www.museiciviveneziani.it
✚ 59 H10 ✉ Piazza San Marco (entrance on Riva degli Schiavoni)
☎ 041 271 5911 or call centre 041 520 9070 (Mon–Fri 9–6, Sat 9–2)
🕐 Apr–end Oct daily 9–7; Nov–end Mar daily 9–5 🎟 Museum Card (valid for Palazzo Ducale, Museo Correr, Museo Archeologico, Biblioteca Marciana) adult €12, child (6–14) €3; holders of Rolling Venice card €7.50. No single tickets for the Palazzo Ducale ⛴ Vallaresso, San Zaccaria 📖 Guidebooks in Italian, English, French, German, Spanish and Japanese €12.50 📞 Call 041 520 9070 for details; audioguides in Italian, English, French, German and Spanish €3. Guided tours of *itinerari segreti* (secret itineraries) daily; book 2 days in advance (tel 041 520 9070), price €16 🍴 🏛

Opposite Gondolas sail on the Canale della Paglia beneath Ponte dei Sospiri

TIPS

» The visitors' entrance is on the Bacino side.

» Expect parts of the Palazzo Ducale to be closed; a building this age is under constant restoration.

» Winter visitors should dress very warmly; there's no heating in the Palazzo Ducale and it can be extremely cold.

» The Museum Card for the Musei di Piazza San Marco covers entrance to all the museums in the Piazza (Palazzo Ducale, Museo Correr, Museo Archeologico Nazionale and Biblioteca Nazionale Marciana) plus one other civic museum. It costs €12 for adults and €7 for children, and is valid for three months.

» The Museum Pass covers entrance to all the Civic Museums (Musei di Piazza San Marco, Ca' Rezzonico, Palazzo Mocenigo, Museo Casa Carlo Goldoni, Museo del Vetro on Murano and Museo del Merletto on Burano). It is valid for six months and costs €18.

Above *The magnificent facade of the Palazzo Ducale*

designed by Bartolomeo and Giovanni Bon in 1438. It was completed during the dogeship of Francesco Foscari (1423–57), who is portrayed kneeling in front of the Lion of St. Mark over the doorway. From here, a portico leads through to the central courtyard, whose arcade and first-floor gallery echoes the exterior design. Access to the first floor is via the Scala dei Giganti (Giants' Stairway), begun in 1483 by Antonio Rizzo (c1440–99). It was named for the giant statues of Mars and Neptune, designed in 1566 by Jacopo Sansovino, at the top. Sansovino was also responsible for the grandiose Scala d'Oro (Golden Stair), encrusted with dazzling gilt and stucco work, which links this level with the *primo piano nobile*, home to the doge.

THE DOGE'S APARTMENTS

Elected from among the patrician families, the doge held office for life, sitting on all the major councils, a position of such potential power that it was tied up with endless restrictions to prevent its abuse. The rooms are both magnificent and austere, with superb ceilings and huge fireplaces. The finest chamber is the Sala delle Mappe (Map Room), decorated with maps showing the whole of the 16th-century known world, with Venice firmly as the central focus. This leads to the Sala delle Quattro Porte (Room of the Four Doors), a magnificent antechamber with ceiling frescoes by Tintoretto (1518–94), where foreign officials waited to meet the doge and councils.

THE ANTICOLLEGIO, COLLEGIO AND SALA DEL SENATO

The interconnecting trio of rooms known as the Anticollegio, the Collegio and the Sala del Senato are among the most interesting, and certainly the most lavish, in the *palazzo*. The Anticollegio, designed by Palladio (1508–80), richly stuccoed and decorated with canvases by Tintoretto, served as an inner waiting room for foreign delegations. From here, visitors entered the Collegio, the meeting place of Venice's Cabinet, which, chaired by the doge, presided over the Senate. The latter met in the Sala del Senato, a magnificent room large enough to accommodate this 300-strong body. The decoration of these three chambers was intended to illustrate the story of Venice, while at the same time impressing on foreign emissaries the city's might, power and riches. The panels are in praise of Venice herself, propaganda pieces showing the Serenissima triumphing over all and sundry. Nothing better illustrates this approach than the ceiling panels in the Collegio, where *Justice* and *Peace* are mere side-kicks to Venice, or the ceiling painting in the Sala del Senato, which shows *Venice Triumphant* in a suitably over-the-top gilded, carved surround.

THE SALA DEL MAGGIOR CONSIGLIO
By far the largest room in the *palazzo*, and indeed in the entire city, is the first-floor Sala del Maggior Consiglio, the meeting place for the Great Council—the lower house, made up of more than 2,500 aristocratic members. It stretches almost the entire length of the waterfront and is one of the earliest parts of the building. Badly damaged by fire in 1577, its present decorative scheme is the work of Tintoretto, who devised the complicated iconographical plan, devoted, as elsewhere, to the concept of Venice's prestige. Only the artist's mind-blowing *Paradiso* (1588–92), on the east wall, departs from this theme. The largest oil painting in the world (140sq m/1,500sq ft), it shows the blessed in heaven, as described by Dante in his *Paradiso*. Tintoretto was also responsible for the frieze around the walls, containing portraits of Venice's first 76 doges, best known for the black veil marking Marin Falier's spot; he was executed for conspiring against the State in 1355. The ceiling panels, by Veronese (1528–88) and Palma il Giovane (1548–1628), are further apotheoses of Venice, showing a personification of the city triumphantly crowned while her subjugated enemies struggle beneath her feet.

PONTE DEI SOSPIRI AND THE PRIGIONI NUOVE
Until the 16th century, prisoners of the State served their sentences either in the dreaded *pozzi*, underground cells beneath the palace, or in the attics. This changed after the construction of the Prigioni Nuove (new prisons) in 1598, where even petty criminals enjoyed the comforts of what was acknowledged to be Europe's most sophisticated prison accommodation. Access to the new block is across the Rio della Paglia, spanned by the famous Ponte dei Sospiri

Below *The imposing and magnificent Sala del Maggior Consiglio*

(Bridge of Sighs), designed by Antonio da Ponte and completed in 1614. By the 19th century the romantic legend was firmly established that, once across, no prisoner ever returned, hence the sighs. In the cell block, dark, narrow corridors and steep stairways link the warren of cells, many of which have their number and capacity painted over the door. Things can't have been too tough; the ground floor's small exercise yard once contained a tavern for the benefit of the inmates.

MORE TO SEE

ITINERARI SEGRETI
You'll have to book in advance for the Itinerari Segreti, a behind-the-scenes guided tour of the Palazzo that takes in the warren of small offices that link the public rooms. These modest chambers were the workplaces of the hundreds of clerks and other pen-pushers who put everything down on paper. This huge archive of the Venetian Republic, one of the world's largest, is now stored in the Archivio di Stato (▷ 159). The tour includes fascinating glimpses of the construction of the Palazzo, the torture room where criminals were persuaded to confess, and the roof-level prisons from where Casanova escaped.

MUSEO DELL'OPERA
A ground-floor museum off the courtyard where more than 40 original capitals from the outer loggia are preserved. Twelve date from the middle of the 14th century and are outstanding examples of sculpture, probably the work of Filippo Calendario. The scene showing the *Creation of Adam and Eve* is probably the finest, but don't miss those from the inner loggia, dating from 1340 to 1450.

ARCO DEI FOSCARI
This late Gothic arch stands opposite the Porta della Carta in the courtyard. The arch was commissioned by Doge Francesco Foscari in 1438, and designed and built by Antonio Bregno and Antonio Rizzo. Its style bridges the gap between Gothic and early Renaissance art.

SALA DEL MAGISTRATO
In this small room on the first floor, disturbingly bizarre works by Flemish painters, including Hieronymous Bosch, are displayed. They were probably

Below *Sansovino's ornate Scala d'Oro*
Right *Statues adorn the exterior of the palace*

commissioned from the artists in Flanders by Venetian merchants and later came into the collections by the Grimani family.

THE ARMOURY
The armoury holds a collection of almost 2,000 weapons, instruments of war and suits of armour. The displays are fascinating, but dauntingly large.

SALA DEL CONSIGLIO DEI DIECI AND SALA DELLA BUSSOLA
The Council of Ten was a highly secretive government magistracy that concentrated on investigating threats to the state. Its meeting room is magnificent, with a ceiling packed with allegorical paintings enclosed in gilded wooden surrounds. Tellingly, it lies next door to the Sala della Bussola, an intimate, wood-panelled chamber with a strange semi-circular door in one corner. This is the entrance to a passage leading directly to a secret chamber, where the Council of Ten met the inquisitors. Their prisoners were held in cells on the floor above.

BOCCHE DI LEONE
'Post-boxes' in the shape of grotesque masks and lions' heads are scattered throughout the *palazzo*, particularly in the loggia, the Sala della Bussola and the Sala della Quarantia Civil Vecchia. These were used for delivering anonymous accusations from one citizen against a to the Council of Ten, the much feared state inquisition.

PALAZZO DUCALE FLOORPLAN

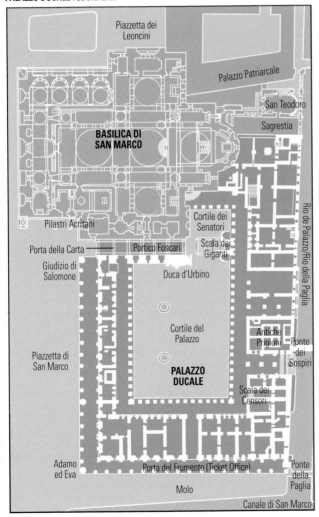

59 H10 ✉ Riva degli Schiavoni, San Marco 🚊 San Zaccaria 🚻 Wide choice

INTRODUCTION

This broad quayside with its procession of *palazzi*, historic hotels, stalls and cafés has some of the best, and most familiar, views in Venice. It is an ideal place for an evening stroll.

The Riva degli Schiavoni gets its name from the Italian word for Slav, *schiavone*, which, in Venice, was synonymous with slave. In the early days of the city's history slave trafficking was common, and most of the slaves were Slavs from the Dalmatian coast. By the 11th century the Slavs themselves were Christians and no longer fair game for slave traders, and over the years the Riva became the base for merchants from the east coast of the Adriatic who traded with Venice. The quayside they used has one of the city's most glorious locations, and it was targeted by the Senate in the 18th century for a makeover. Between 1780 and 1782 the architect Tommaso Temanza was responsible for widening what had been a typically narrow *fondamenta* into today's broad promenade, paved with Istrian stone. The Riva has had many illustrious visitors. As early as 1362 the poet Petrarch lived here, but it was the 19th century that saw an influx of famous foreigners. Henry James stayed at No. 4161, and Charles Dickens, Marcel Proust, John Ruskin and Richard Wagner all stayed at the Danieli hotel. The Riva today is still among the classiest addresses in the city, with an array of top-end hotels.

The wide waterfront of the Riva degli Schiavoni stretches beside the Bacino di San Marco from the Palazzo Ducale to the Rio Ca' di Dio, crossing several canals along the way. The promenade continues all the way to Sant'Elena, changing its name as it heads east to become the Riva Ca' di Dio, the Riva di San Biagio and the Riva dei Sette Martiri. The eastern end is very quiet, and this is the section to pause for a drink and take in the superb views. Nearer the Palazzo Ducale, crowds can be so thick you have to queue to cross the bridges, while the souvenir stalls block the panorama across to San Giorgio Maggiore. Stroll in whichever direction appeals, bearing in mind the west end is at its best early or late in the day.

Above *View along the waterfront*
Opposite *The distinctive Danieli is one of Venice's top hotels*

WHAT TO SEE

PONTE DELLA PAGLIA

The Ponte della Paglia, *the* place for that obligatory shot of the Ponte dei Sospiri (▷ 69–70), was built in 1360, and enlarged in 1847. Its name probably derives from the straw *(paglia)* which was delivered here as bedding for the prisoners. It is made of Istrian stone, and on the outside of the pillar at the top of the treads there's a charming shrine, dating from 1580, with a carving of the Virgin (1583), known as the Madonna dei Gondolieri. On either side of the bridge, this stretch of the Riva is crammed with souvenir stalls; if you're into kitsch and cheap goods, this has to be one of the best selections in all Venice.

SANTA MARIA DELLA VISITAZIONE (LA PIETÀ)

The 18th-century church of Santa Maria della Visitazione (▷ 111) is best known for its associations with Antonio Vivaldi (1678–1741), Venice's most popular composer.

GRAND HOTEL DANIELI

Few hotels in the world are better known than the Danieli (▷ 123), named after its first proprietor, Dal Niel. The building was once the Palazzo Dandolo and dates from the 15th century, an era when the Republic was encouraging the aristocrats to erect *palazzi* that would demonstrate Venice's ever-growing power and wealth. Its lovely ochre facade is typical of the period, with pointed Gothic windows and arches on all floors. In the 16th century it was the French embassy and by the fall of the Republic it had changed hands many times, finally being divided into flats occupied by several families. It was first rented in 1822 by Dal Niel, who turned it into an hotel. The interior retains many of the original features, cunningly combined with decoration of an overwhelming opulence, which makes full use of the richest of furnishings, fabrics and lighting. In 1948 an annexe was constructed to the west. The *calle* running down the east side of the hotel is Calle delle Rasse, its name a link with the Riva's Slav history. Rasse derives from *rascia*, a woollen fabric from Raska in Croatia, which was used to cover the *felze* (cabins) on gondolas.

A SPOONFUL OF SALT

Salt, that vital commodity essential for health and food preservation, was the catalyst that kick-started the Venetian economy and underpinned it for centuries to come. Salt was '*il vero fondamento del nostro stato*' (the true foundation of our state), with a mark-up hovering around 80 per cent and a monopoly on all trade throughout the Adriatic and the inland towns. The Romans' main salt-making centre was Comacchio, a coastal town south of the lagoon, but the Venetians established their own salt works by 523 and in 923 destroyed Comacchio, burning the citadel and massacring the inhabitants. Venice then concentrated on trading salt, which they bought up and shipped through the city. Within a few years, no salt could move on a ship in the Adriatic unless it was a Venetian ship bound to or from Venice.

TIPS
» Have a drink in the Danieli to see the interior.
» It makes sense to come to the Riva early or late, as this is an area that's heaving with daytrippers throughout the day.
» Many *vaporetto* lines leave from the San Zaccaria stops on the Riva; check numbers and directions carefully if you're catching a boat here.

REGIONS SAN MARCO AND SAN GIORGIO MAGGIORE • SIGHTS

INTRODUCTION

One of Palladio's greatest churches provides the perfect backdrop to the Bacino di San Marco; few other buildings could look as right as San Giorgio does from the Piazzetta. The best city views in Venice are from its campanile.

The island site of San Giorgio may have been inhabited in Roman times, and certainly became the site of a church as early as AD790. In 982 the Benedictines arrived, adding a monastery to the church; both were destroyed by an earthquake in 1223. The monastery was rebuilt in 1443, but it wasn't until 1565 that Palladio was commissioned to design a new church. Building was slow; the church was finally completed in 1610, and a new campanile finished in 1791. During Renaissance times, the monastery had close links with its sister house in Florence, and it was to San Giorgio that Cosimo de' Medici, head of the powerful banking family that controlled the city, fled when he was banished from Florence in 1433. He brought with him the architect Michelozzo, whose designs had immense influence on Venetian civic architecture. The monastery complex was again augmented, by a cloister and refectory, both designed by Palladio, in 1561. After the fall of the Republic in 1797, Napoleon dissolved the monastery and declared the island a 'free port'. In 1951 the monastery and island were acquired by Count Vittorio Cini, who established the Fondazione Cini in memory of his son, Giorgio, who had been killed in an air accident. New buildings were erected and major restoration carried out. The internationally renowned Foundation organizes conferences and stages exhibitions, concerts, dance and occasional opera.

The open waters of St. Mark's Basin frame the great Palladian church of San Giorgio Maggiore. Visiting here takes a bit of planning; although just a short hop across the water from San Marco, it's served by only one *vaporetto*, No. 2, leaving at 10-minute intervals from San Zaccaria. Start at the church before taking the elevator up the campanile for wonderful views over the city and the lagoon—a great way to get a bird's-eye view and, if you're new to Venice, your bearings. If you want to visit the monastery, home to the Cini Foundation, you'll need to come at the weekend, as during the week the complex is only open to groups.

Above *The campanile gives some of the best views of Venice*
Opposite *The monastery complex with its two cloisters viewed from the campanile*

WHAT TO SEE
THE CHURCH
San Giorgio Maggiore presents the final solution to the great Renaissance architectural puzzle: how to impose classical design onto a building that has no classical precedent. Andrea Palladio (1508–80) solved this by uniting two temple fronts on the facade, the giant Composite columns of the nave rising above the Corinthian columns marking the height of the lower aisles, an arrangement echoed in the luminous interior and emphasized by the use of white marble and stucco. This is a triumphantly light and airy building, full of soaring space from the high windows inspired by Roman bath design.
The choir is hung with two fine pictures by Tintoretto, *The Fall of Manna* and *The Last Supper* (1592–94). Just off the choir to the right, the Cappella dei Morti contains what may well be Tintoretto's last work, a haunting *Deposition* (1594). The superb wooden choir stalls, carved with scenes from the life of St. Benedict, date from the 1590s.

THE MONASTERY
Adjoining the church is the monastery complex, one of Venice's great delights and now home to the Fondazione Cini (tel 041 520 5558; www.cini.it; tel 041 524 0119 for tour bookings; guided tours Sat–Sun). Two cloisters lie at its heart: the Cloister of the Bay Trees, planned by Giovanni Buora between 1520 and 1540, and the Cloister of the Cypresses, designed in 1579 by Palladio. Around these harmonious spaces lie a dormitory designed by Buora, a double stairway and library by Baldassare Longhena and Palladio's magnificent refectory, reached through two anterooms. The buildings are surrounded by beautiful, verdant gardens, with an outdoor theatre, the Teatro Verde, in one corner.

MORE TO SEE
THE CAMPANILE
Take the elevator up the campanile for the best vantage point in Venice. From the top, both city and lagoon are spread before you. There's no better place to appreciate the lie of the city, the lagoon islands and the open sea beyond.

INTRODUCTION

Originally a marshy island known as the Morso, the area of the Piazza San Marco stands at one of the lowest points in Venice, and until the ninth century was an orchard for the nearby convent of San Zaccaria (▷ 114). There were two churches here, dedicated to San Teodoro—the city's first patron—and San Geminiano, and a lighthouse, the precursor of the Campanile. In 829 the first Basilica was built to house the remains of St. Mark, brought to Venice from Alexandria. This was replaced in 976 by a bigger sanctuary, and a hundred years later work began on the present Basilica, built between 1063 and 1094 and the third to occupy this site. In the 12th century Doge Sebastiano Ziani transformed the area in front of the Basilica into a public space, whose general shape remains today. The buildings, with the exception of the Basilica and the Campanile, date mainly from the period of urban renewal at the end of the 15th century. This continued for more than a hundred years, and saw the construction of the Procuratie, the Zecca (Mint), the Libreria Sansoviniana and the Loggetta at the foot of the Campanile. Napoleon's occupation in the early 19th century signalled the destruction of San Geminiano to make way for the Ala Napoleonica, which links the two Procuratie at the west end of the Piazza. The whole area still floods easily, and between 2004 and 2007 an ambitious project raised the *fondamenta* and installed a state-of-the-art drainage and pumping system on the water side of the Piazzetta.

The Piazza San Marco is a showcase for some of the finest Byzantine, Gothic and Renaissance architecture in Venice. Dominated by the glittering bulk of the Basilica di San Marco and its soaring Campanile (bell tower), and flanked by the Palazzo Ducale (▷ 66–71), it's home to compelling buildings and museums, trendy shops and a clutch of historic cafés. The Piazza is best seen in deep midwinter, daybreak or at dead of night, and a summer daytime visit may prove something of an endurance test, but it nevertheless remains an unmissable sight. The best approach is by foot from the west end of the Piazza; *vaporetto* No. 1 will drop you at Vallaresso/San Marco, just a couple of minutes' walk. Take time to look around the Piazza with its arcades and the Torre dell'Orologio, before going up the Campanile for the great cityscape and an overview of the Piazza. Then head for the interior of the Basilica, being sure to ascend to the loggia before you enter the church itself—once inside, you can't backtrack. After this, stroll through the Piazzetta down to the water's edge to take in the panorama over the Bacino di San Marco to San Giorgio Maggiore (▷ 74–75) and the mouth of the Grand Canal, before settling at a café table for an unforgettable, if pricey, drink in one of the world's greatest urban settings. For a plan of the area see the map, ▷ 296.

WHAT TO SEE

THE BASILICA

Eleventh-century Venice still looked culturally east to Byzantium, and this explains the decision to construct a church that is completely oriental in style. San Marco, with its centralized Greek-cross plan and multiple domes, is modelled on two basilicas in Constantinople, and the interior, with its raised choir and gold-ground mosaics, also owes much to the east. The north facade (fronting the Piazzetta dei Leoncini) was among the last areas to be completed, and is pierced with the Porta dei Fiori, built in the 13th century and incorporating an eighth-century Byzantine relief (in the first arch) of the Twelve Apostles. The main facade has five arched entrances and was considerably changed between the 11th and 15th centuries by the addition of marble columns and carved stonework in the Gothic style. The Sant'Alippio

INFORMATION
➕ 59 H10 ✉ San Marco 30124
🚤 Vallaresso, San Zaccaria

THE BASILICA
www.basilicasanmarco.it
➕ 61 H10 ✉ Piazza San Marco, San Marco ☎ 041 270 8311 🕐 Easter–end Oct Mon–Sat 9.45–5, Sun 2–5; Nov–Easter Mon–Sat 9.45–5, Sun 2–4; also Pala d'Oro, Tesoro, Gallery and Museum 💷 Basilica free, Pala d'Oro €2.50, Tesoro €3, Gallery and Museum €4 🚤 Vallaresso, San Zaccaria 📖 Electa guide at bookstalls in major museums, postcards, general guides and religious souvenirs at basilica 🎫 Tours available through various travel agencies; must be booked in advance; further details in the *APT Eventi e Manifestazione* information booklet (▷ 266)

Opposite *The Campanile dominates the Basilica di San Marco*

doorway, on the left, is the only one on the facade to preserve its 13th-century mosaic, which shows both the earliest known representation of St. Mark and that of the Basilica itself. The central door is adorned with Romanesque carvings dating from the 13th century. Considered to be the exterior's greatest treasures, these show the earth, the seas and animals on the underside, with the virtues and beatitudes on the outer face and the zodiac and labours of the months on the inner face. The outer arch shows Christ and the Prophets and dates from around 1260.

Behind the arches of the facade lies the narthex (atrium), a transitional space between the light of day and the semi-darkness of the interior that's totally Byzantine in conception. From here, steep steps rise to the gallery, where you'll find yourself at eye-level with the mosaics in the interior. This level gives access out onto the Loggia, once used by the doge as a vantage point during religious and civic festivals. You'll share the view with replicas of the famous bronze horses, the Quadriga, whose originals are inside. These evocative creatures were looted from Constantinople in 1204. They were probably made for the Hippodrome there in the third century, but could be as much as 500 years older, the only four-horse chariot group to survive from antiquity. Apart from a brief spell in Paris during the Napoleonic years, the horses have stood at San Marco for 800 years, as much a symbol of Venice as the winged lion of St. Mark.

Descending the stairs, you enter the Basilica proper, where the first impression is of dully glittering darkness, illuminated by shafts of light as the mosaics are struck by slanting sunbeams. The walls and domes are entirely covered with over 4,000sq m (43,055sq ft) of these mosaics, executed over six centuries and telling stories from the Bible. The finest are the early Veneto-Byzantine examples, which include the *Pentecost* dome over the nave, the central dome, at the crossing, showing the *Ascension*, and *Christ Emmanuel*, above the main altar. Old as it looks, the huge *Christ Pantocrator* above the apse is in fact a faithful 16th-century copy of the 11th-century original. Mosaics changed after the 15th century and the later examples are in a more painterly style, as craftsmen followed cartoons by contemporary artists, thus introducing perspective and relief. Both Titian and Tintoretto had a hand in these.

Below *The Byzantine Basilica di San Marco, Venice's most famous building*

The focal point of the interior, with its undulating 12th-century marble floor, is the iconostasis, a carved marble screen that's Byzantine and hides the chancel and high altar. The remains of St. Mark lie beneath the altar, which is backed by the Pala d'Oro, a 14th-century opulent gold altarpiece. It's covered with over 3,000 precious stones and decorated with 80 enamel plaques, many from Constantinople and dating from the 10th to 12th centuries, and was made by a Sienese master in 1342. To the left is the Chapel of the Madonna Nicopeia, a much-revered 12th-century Byzantine icon, and there's more Byzantine work in the Tesoro (Treasury). The 12th-century incense censer in the shape of a domed church and two 11th-century icons of the Archangel Michael are worth looking for here.

THE CAMPANILE

The Campanile (Bell-tower), the great punctuation point on the Venetian skyline, stands almost opposite the Basilica entrance at the east end of the Piazza; at 99m (325ft) it's the city's tallest building. The original structure, dating from the early 10th century, functioned as a combined bell-tower and lighthouse—the harbour occupied what is now the Piazzetta. Over the centuries it was constantly modified, the most extensive alterations being made by Bartolomeo Bon between 1511 and 1514, when the spire and gilded angel were added. Today's Campanile is just over a century old; on 14 July 1902 at 9.52am disaster struck, when the entire tower, weakened over the centuries, subsided into a tidy heap of bricks and debris. No other building was damaged and the only casualty was the custodian's cat. It was rebuilt *Com'era, dov'era* (Like it was, where it was) in 1912, Sansovino's little Loggetta (1537–49) at the foot of the tower being pieced together from its fragments found in the rubble.

✉ Piazza San Marco, San Marco ☎ 041 522 4064 🕐 Jul, Aug daily 9–9; Apr–end Jun, Sep, Oct daily 9–7; Nov–end Mar daily 9.30–3.45. Sometimes closed for maintenance from Sun after 6 Jan till end of Jan ✋ €8 🚤 Vallaresso, San Zaccaria 📖 Leaflet available

THE PIAZZA AND THE PIAZZETTA

Emerging from the narrow surrounding streets, the sheer scale of the Piazza is breathtaking. At the east end of its wide expanse rears the Basilica di San Marco, with the Palazzo Ducale, overlooking the Piazzetta, to the south. Arcaded buildings run down the long sides of the Piazza; these are the Procuratie Vecchie to the north, and the Procuratie Nuove opposite.

TIPS

» Don't start your Venetian sightseeing in San Marco; it's so overwhelming that it makes sense to save it until you've got a handle on the rest of the city.

» Remember the Basilica is a church, so cover your arms and shoulders when visiting; miniskirts and skimpy shorts are also unsuitable.

» If you have time, attend a service in the Basilica and see it in its real role as a functioning church.

» The queue to enter the Basilica starts to build around 9.15 and the wait can be as long as an hour, so come early or late in the afternoon when the day-trippers have gone.

» You'll have to move steadily through the Basilica, so read up on what you'll see before you go.

» Try and visit the Piazza at night, when you'll see it without crowds.

» Choose a clear day to go up the Campanile; heat or mist will obscure visibility.

Above *The Piazza San Marco, lined with arcaded buildings, looking east towards the Basilica di San Marco and the Campanile*

SANSOVINO'S BIG MISTAKE

In 1537, Jacopo Sansovino was appointed architect for the city library, to be constructed in the Piazzetta to house the state collection of Latin and Greek manuscripts and precious books. Successful and visionary, he was the obvious choice, and he designed a groundbreaking building that combined Roman High Renaissance ideas with the Venetian love of ornament, creating a building described by Palladio as 'the richest and most ornate since antiquity'. Things went badly wrong when the barrel vaulting of the ceiling collapsed shortly after its construction. Sansovino was thrown in jail, and only released on the pleadings of his friend, the painter Titian. He was forced to redesign the vault and pay for the repairs out of his own pocket, losing his position as Venice's favourite architect to the up and coming Palladio.

They housed the offices of the Procuratie, the officials who ran the government offices, oversaw the upkeep of the Basilica and supervised its finances. The original Procuratie Vecchie was built in the 12th century, and first rebuilt in 1500 by Mauro Codussi, the work being completed by Bartolomeo Bon and Sansovino in 1512. Scamozzi and Sansovino were responsible for the Procuratie Nuove; built between 1582 and 1640, its design echoes the older buildings. After the fall of Venice in 1797, the two wings were linked by the arcaded Ala Napoleonica, now home to the Museo Correr (▷ 64–65).

The Piazzetta runs down to the water's edge and is flanked by the Palazzo Ducale to the west (left) and the Biblioteca Nazionale Marciana (▷ 65) and the Zecca (Mint), designed by Sansovino between 1527 and 1537, to the right. Its two granite columns are topped by a winged lion, symbol of Venice, and St. Theodore, the city's first patron saint, complete with his symbolic crocodile. Both statues and columns were brought back from Tyre (in modern-day Lebanon) in 1170, and the space between them was declared a public execution area; many modern Venetians refuse to walk between the two. The Zecca, erected between 1537 and 1545, was moved here from its ninth-century home on the Rialto. It was Sansovino's first big commission and the first building in the city to be built entirely of stone, rather than having a wooden frame with a stone facade. On the other side of the Basilica, the tiny space fronted by marble lions is known as the Piazzetta dei Leoncini.

TORRE DELL'OROLOGIO

San Marco's clock tower was built between 1496 and 1506, and Mauro Codussi was responsible for the overall design. Its legend runs *Horas non numero nisi serenas* (I number only peaceful hours) and the exterior stone dial shows the 24 hours in Roman numerals, with the interior face showing the signs of the zodiac and phases of the moon. It's topped by two bronze 'moors', so-called for their dark patina, which were cast in the Arsenale in 1497.
☎ 041 520 9070 ⊕ Guided pre-booked tours in Italian daily 12 and 4; in English Mon–Wed 10 and 11, Thu–Sat 1, 2 and 3; in French Mon–Wed 1, 2 and 3, Thu–Sat 10 and 11 ✋ €12

Opposite *The Piazzetta, overlooked by the Palazzo Ducale*
Right *The Basilica's distinctive domes and beautiful decoration*
Below *View towards Murano from the Campanile*

Above *Statues of angels adorn the baroque interior of the church of San Moisè*

SANTA MARIA DELLA FAVA

The church of Santa Maria della Fava (Our Lady of the Bean) takes its name from a special cake traditionally eaten on All Souls' Day (1 November) and produced by a local baker. The church dates from the 18th century and contains two wonderfully contrasting paintings by two great 18th-century artists. Above the first altar on the right hangs Giambattista Tiepolo's early *Education of the Virgin*, a touching composition imbued with light and colour. In contrast you'll find Giambattista Piazzetta's *Madonna and Child with St. Philip Neri* (on the left), a far more sombre picture, redolent of the gravitas of the Counter-Reformation. The statues lining the nave are by Torretto (c1694–1774), best known, perhaps, as the master of Canova.

✚ 59 H9 ✉ Campo Rubbi, San Marco ☎ 041 522 4601 🕐 Mon–Sat 8.30–12, 4.30–6.30, Sun 8.30–12 ✋ Free 🚮 Rialto

SANTA MARIA DEL GIGLIO

www.chorusvenezia.org

Santa Maria del Giglio, founded in the ninth century by the Jubanico family, is also known as Santa Maria Zobenigo, a name derived from its first patrons. The church was rebuilt in the 1680s by the Barbaro family,

and few other Venetian facades are such an in-your-face case of self-aggrandizement. Pause to marvel at the total lack of religious symbolism among the crowded statues and reliefs, all extolling the virtues and triumphs of the Barbaros. The family, in fact, had a much greater opinion of themselves than that held by their fellow citizens. Admiral Antonio Barbaro, who paid for much of the church's rebuilding, was actually dismissed from the fleet for incompetence. He is one of the five heroic statues on the facade; the others represent his brothers. Above them hover the allegorical figures of Venice, Virtue, Wisdom, Honour and Fame and below are relief maps of the places associated with the clan's glorious triumphs. Inside there's a profusion of mainly undistinguished religious art, though some relief is available in the shape of two Evangelists by Tintoretto (1518–94) behind the altar, and there's a disputed Rubens—the only work by the master in Venice—in a side chapel.

✚ 58 F10 ✉ Campo Santa Maria del Giglio, San Marco 2542 ☎ 041 275 0462 🕐 Mon–Sat 10–5. Closed 1 Jan, Easter, 15 Aug, 25 Dec ✋ Chorus Pass (for all churches in Chorus group) €9, single ticket €3 🚮 Giglio

SAN MAURIZIO

Rebuilt in the early 19th century and hardly used in the 20th, San Maurizio found a new role in 2004 when it opened as a Vivaldi exhibition centre. The Greek-cross interior is now home to a series of exhibits of the life and times of Venice's most popular 18th-century composer, with excellent information panels in English and Italian. The chief draw is the fine collection of old musical instruments, whose sound provides the music that's a constant backdrop to your visit. You can buy CDs and DVDs and book concert tickets for events at La Pietà and the ex-church of San Vidal, just off Campo Santo Stefano.

✚ 58 F10 ✉ Campo San Maurizio, San Marco ☎ 041 241 1840 🕐 Daily 9.30–8.30 ✋ Free 🚮 Giglio

SAN MOISÈ

Walking from San Marco to the Accademia you'll pass the church of San Moisè, an over-the-top baroque extravaganza that's a hot contender for the award for the worst building in Venice. Take it in as a glorious example of the fact that lavish does not equal lovely. It's named after Moses, another illustration of the Venetian tendency to canonize Old Testament figures, a habit borrowed from the Byzantines. The 1668 facade is a riot of flora and fauna, including a very strange looking camel. The high altar by Arrigo Meyring, dating from around 1670, shows not only Moses receiving the tablets of the law on Mount Sinai, but the mountain itself. San Moisè is home to one of the city's fine 18th-century organs, and there are occasional recitals.

✚ 59 G10 ✉ Campo San Moisè, San Marco 1456 ☎ 041 528 5840 🕐 Mon–Sat 9.30–12.30 ✋ Free 🚮 Vallaresso

SAN SALVADOR

The luminous interior of San Salvador is a Tuscan symphony in cool grey and white. The design spans well over 30 years and Giorgio Spavento (died 1509), Tullio Lombardo (c1455–1532)

and Sansovino (1486–1570) were all involved in the planning. The 17th-century facade is nothing special, it's the interior that fires the imagination. The key to the design is three interlocking Greek crosses which pay homage to San Marco and Byzantium while simultaneously giving the church the basilical length required by religious orders. There's some fine Veneto-Tuscan sculpture, including Sansovino's monument to Doge Francesco Venier on the right wall. Farther down is the tomb of Caterina Cornaro, who was briefly the Queen of Cyprus (▷ 32). Caterina, who died in 1510, was a helpless pawn in the diplomatic dealings that led to Venice's annexation of the island after the death of her Cypriot husband.

San Salvador has two paintings by Titian (c1478–1576). *The Annunciation* at the end of the right-hand aisle is clearly autographed, *Tizianus, fecit, fecit*—did someone doubt it, or was it just a reminder to his fans of his genius? His other painting, *The Transfiguration*, hangs over the high altar, screening a magnificent silver reredos.

✚ 59 G9 ✉ Campo San Salvador, San Marco 4826 ☎ 041 523 6717 🕐 Mon–Fri 3–7 🖐 Free 🚢 Rialto

SANTO STEFANO
▷ 84–85.

SAN ZULIAN
The streets making up the Mercerie are more associated with conspicuous consumerism in most people's minds than with religion, and the church of San Zulian (San Giuliano), set right in this busy thoroughfare, is the exception that proves the rule. It's one of only two Venetian churches you can walk right around (the other is Angelo Raffaele, ▷ 201), and is a monument to the wealth of one man, Tommaso Rangone, who paid for its construction in the 1550s. He had no qualms about reminding worshippers who paid and there's a large monument to him right in the middle of Sansovino's harmonious facade. Rangone made his fortune from a treatment for syphilis—a scourge in this maritime city—and prided himself on his scholarship. The interior has a ceiling painting by Palma il Giovane (1548–1628), and there's a late Veronese *Pietà* over the first altar on the right.

✚ 59 H9 ✉ Campo San Zulian, San Marco 605 ☎ 041 523 5383 🕐 Mon–Sat 8.30–12, Sun 5–8 🖐 Free 🚢 San Zaccaria, Rialto

TEATRO LA FENICE
www.teatrolafenice.it
Fenice is the Italian word for phoenix, and in true phoenix tradition, Venice's opera house, designed by Giannantonio Selva in 1792, rose from the ashes of the disastrous fire of 1996 to reopen for the 2004–05 season. Fire has struck the building more than once, notably in 1836, when it had to be virtually rebuilt. Following this, it became one of Italy's foremost opera houses, staging the premieres of both *Rigoletto* and *La Traviata*, and functioning as a focal point for protests against the Austrian occupation. Audiences were known to bombard the stage with bouquets in the national colours of red, green and white and to shout repeatedly 'Viva Verdi', the composer's name being an acronym for Vittorio Emanuele, Re d'Italia (Vittorio Emanuele, King of Italy). The 1996 conflagration is shrouded in mystery, occurring when the nearest canal, which would have provided water for the pumps, was undergoing cleaning and was thus dry. The rebuilding dragged on for years, but it's generally agreed it was worth the wait. The new theatre has a glittering gilt and stucco auditorium, marble-clad foyer and glistening chandeliers that includes state-of-the-art systems and equipment. Book well in advance for performances or join one of the regular tours.

✚ 58 F10 ✉ Campo San Fantin, San Marco 1965 ☎ 041 786 511 🖐 €12 🚢 Giglio 🎧 Audioguides available daily from the box office, or contact HelloVenezia (041 2424; www.hellovenezia.com); guided tours daily via HelloVenezia

Below *Detail of the ceiling of San Zulian*

INFORMATION

www.chorusvenezia.org

➕ 58 F10 ✉ Campo Santo Stefano,
San Marco 2774 ☎ 041 275 0462
🕐 Mon–Sat 10–5. Closed 1 Jan, Easter,
15 Aug, 25 Dec ✋ Chorus Pass (for
all churches in Chorus group) €9, single
ticket €3 🚤 Accademia, San Samuele
🚌 Guided tours organized by Chorus
(tel 041 275 0462); information sheets
and audioguides in Italian, English, French
and German

Above *The quiet beauty of Santo Stefano
belies its bloody past*
Opposite *Decorative detail on one of the
arches in the nave*

SANTO STEFANO

The historic church of Santo Stefano, overlooking its lovely *campo*, is among
the finest examples of Venetian high Gothic. Standing at the north end of the
campo of the same name (▷ 62), it's the only church in Venice to be built
directly over a canal—you can see it passing under the apse if you stand on the
first bridge in the *calle* leading towards San Marco. This Augustinian church,
founded in the 13th century and rebuilt in the 14th and 15th centuries, had to
be re-consecrated no fewer than six times because of repeated murders that
were perpetrated within its walls.

You enter through a magnificent Gothic doorway, decorated with carved
stone ropework, leaves and vegetation, and surmounted by a typically Gothic
arch and side pinnacles. Inside, the superb ship's keel roof immediately catches
the eye, as do the diamond-patterned red-and-white brickwork, painted intarsi
and parade of marble columns separating nave and aisles. As in so many
Venetian churches, these are often hung with rich brocade, a reminder of
Venice's ancient Byzantine links—a common practice in eastern churches.
The bronze plaque in the middle of the nave floor marks the tomb of Doge
Francesco Morosini (in office 1688–94). He is best known for blowing up the
Parthenon in Athens, but was also responsible for looting the lions that now
stand outside the gates of the Arsenale (▷ 105). Look out, too, for the lovely
Lombardo monument to Giacomo Surian (1493), a physician from Rimini, to
the left of the door. The baptistery contains Pietro Canova's monument to
Giovanni Falier (1808).

THE SACRISTY PAINTINGS

Santo Stefano's best paintings are in the sacristy at the bottom of the right
aisle; among them are four shadowy late works by Tintoretto (1518–94), which
include the *Agony in the Garden*, the *Washing of the Disciples' Feet* and
the *Last Supper*. The composition of all three is typical of Tintoretto's highly
theatrical late style—note the lack of a central balance and the astonishing
perspective. These paintings are all illuminated by brilliant shafts of light against
dark and brooding backgrounds.

AROUND SAN MARCO

San Marco is the heart of Venice. This *sestiere* is much smaller than the others, but it's packed with narrow alleys, light-filled squares, magnificent patrician *palazzi*, churches, artisan workshops and mouth-watering stores. This walk winds its way through the maze and gives you an insight into the area's many facets.

THE WALK

Distance: 2.5km (1.5 miles)
Time: 1.5–2 hours
Start at: Ponte di Rialto
End at: Rialto *vaporetto* stop (Riva del Ferro)

HOW TO GET THERE

Take *vaporetto* No. 1 or 2 to Rialto.

★ With your back to the Rialto bridge, walk past the souvenir stalls and into Campo San Bartolomeo.

❶ This lively square was once part of the market, and it's still a popular rendezvous for Venetians. The church, remodelled in the 18th century, is used for temporary exhibitions. The bronze statue in the middle portrays Carlo Goldoni, Venice's most popular playwright.

Swing right along Via 2 Aprile, which widens out in front of the church of San Salvador (▷ 82–83). With the church on your left, continue along

Calle dell'Ovo and turn left into Calle dei Fabbri, one of the city's major shopping streets. Take the first right, which leads into Campo San Luca.

❷ The marble plinth in the square supposedly marks the exact centre of the city, and the church is the burial place of the writer Pietro Aretino. He is said to have died of a laughter attack in 1556, brought on by an obscene remark made about his sister.

Follow the crowds straight across the square and through to Campo Manin (▷ 61). Take the narrow *calle* halfway along the left-hand side of the *campo*, following the signs to the Palazzo Contarini del Bovolo and its famous stair (▷ 63). Backtrack into Campo Manin, turning left into the square, and cross the left-hand bridge, Ponte della Cortesia, to walk along Calle della Mandola. Take the first left, Calle dei Assassini. This

continues into Calle Verona, crosses a bridge and emerges into Campo San Fantin. The church of San Fantin faces the Teatro La Fenice (▷ 83) across the *campo*.

❸ San Fantin was founded in the ninth century; the present church, with its graceful domed apse, was built in the 16th century by Sansovino (1486–1570). San Fantin had its own *scuola*, devoted to comforting those condemned to death, which became the Ateneo Veneto (Academy of Letters and Sciences) in 1812.

Walk down the right-hand side of the Fenice and turn left along the back of the theatre to cross a small bridge on your right to follow Fondamenta Santo Cristoforo for about 15m (16 yards), then turn right over the bridge into Calle Caortorta, which leads into Campo Sant'Angelo (S. Anzolo, ▷ 62). On your left, across the canal, is the ex-Convento di Santo Stefano.

④ The Convent was founded at the end of the 13th century by the Augustinians, who built the beautiful Gothic church (▷ 84–85). The convent buildings are now government offices, but you can walk round the Renaissance cloister.

Take the left-hand exit, over the bridge, from Campo Sant'Angelo and walk through to Campo Santo Stefano (▷ 62) and its church. Follow Calle Spezier left out of Campo Santo Stefano (there's a *farmacia* on the corner of this narrow street), then walk through Campo San Maurizio.

⑤ The present church of San Maurizio (▷ 82) was built in 1806, contrasting with the lovely Palazzo Bellavite opposite. This *campo* really comes to life during the antique markets that are held here at intervals throughout the year. Keep going straight ahead through the *campo*, along Calle Zaguri, following the main route to San Marco. The next open space is the Campo Santa Maria Zobenigo, also known as Santa Maria del Giglio (▷ 82).

Follow the route towards San Marco, walking along Calle Larga 22 Marzo and over the bridge towards the church of San Moisè (▷ 82). Continue past the church then turn left. You are now in the smart Frezzeria, where arrows *(frezze)* were once manufactured. Take the second right (Calle Salvadego) and walk through to the Bacino Orseolo.

⑥ This is a 'dead-end' canal, and the nearest point to the Piazza San Marco reachable by gondola. Until 1869 only a narrow canal penetrated here and the congestion was immense, so the area was widened to allow more space for delivering passengers and turning gondolas. It is still among the busiest of the gondola stations.

From here, a right turn will lead you under the arcade of the Procuratie Vecchie and into the expanse of Piazza San Marco (▷ 76–81). Walk down the Piazza and turn left under the Torre dell'Orologio and up the crowded Mercerie, taking the third right to San Zulian (▷ 83). Walk left along the side of the church and turn left opposite the Mondadori bookstore, taking the second right into the Merceria San Zulian. Follow the yellow sign to the Rialto underneath the Sotoportego delle Acque to emerge onto the Mercerie. Walk straight on, across Via 2 Aprile and down to the Riva del Ferro.

⑦ This is one of the few stretches of *fondamenta* beside the Grand Canal, and runs into the Riva del Carbon. The words 'ferro' and 'carbon' mean iron and charcoal; this quayside was once the unloading place for these materials.

PLACE TO VISIT
EX-CONVENTO DI SANTO STEFANO
✉ Campo Santo Stefano
🕐 Tue, Thu 9–1

Above *Gondolas alongside Campo Manin*
Opposite *The Piazzetta adjoins the Piazza San Marco*

WHERE TO EAT
You'll be spoiled for choice on this walk, but Campo Santo Stefano is a great place for a break, or you could wait until you reach Piazza San Marco and splash out at Caffè Florian or Caffè Quadri (▷ 61).

WHEN TO GO
Morning, when the area is really bustling, is a good time for this walk, but be prepared for some of the narrower *calli* to be very crowded.

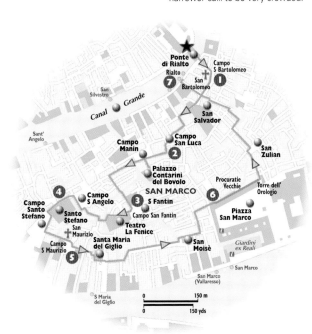

SHOPPING

BATA
www.bata.it
Deep in San Marco's bustling, sprawling Mercerie district, this modern, stylish Italian emporium offers top-quality leather items, from shoes to stylish, understated jackets. There is also an excellent women's section with lots of accessories. Staff are always attentive and there are plenty of places to sit down and take a breather.

✚ 99 G9 ✉ Mercerie, San Marco 4979A ☎ 041 522 9766 ⏰ Mon–Sat 9.30–7.30, Sun 10.30–7 🚤 Rialto

BEVILACQUA
www.luigi-bevilacqua.com
The big Italian fashion houses, like Dolce & Gabbana, come to Bevilacqua for their marvellous traditionally made Venetian brocades, velvets, taffetas and damasks, still produced on 17th-century looms. The curtain ties, swags and key tassels make wonderful souvenirs.

✚ 98 F10 ✉ Fondamenta della Canonica, San Marco 337B and Campo Santa Maria del Giglio, San Marco 2520 ☎ 041 528 7581 and 041 241 0662 ⏰ Mon–Fri 9.30–7, Sat 10–4.30 🚤 San Zaccaria, Santa Maria del Giglio

BLACK WATCH
Italian men take their appearance extremely seriously and this classy store caters for those looking for the highest-quality ready-to-wear fashion. The style is predominantly classic, distinguished by fine tailoring and beautiful natural fabrics such as wool, cashmere, linen and sea cotton. They also sell shoes and accessories and serve as the Venetian agents for Barbour.

✚ 98 G9 ✉ Calle del Forno, San Marco 4594 ☎ 041 523 1945 ⏰ Mon–Sat 10–7 🚤 Rialto

BOTTEGA VENETA
www.bottegaveneta.com
This elegant shop is famed throughout the world for its superior leather goods. Take the opportunity to get your hands on the new lines while staying in the Veneto region or indulge yourself with a belt, bag or wallet in super-soft leather. Bottega Veneta is a great place to buy classic gifts that are practical and enduring.

✚ 99 G10 ✉ Calle Vallaresso, San Marco 1337 ☎ 041 522 8489 ⏰ Mon–Sat 10–7.30, Sun 11–7 🚤 Vallaresso

BUOSI
Discerning Venetian professionals come here for fine tailoring and ready-to-wear clothes by Italy's

top men's designers. Everything here is classic in style and high quality, ranging from fine lawn and cotton shirts through cashmere and lambswool sweaters to suits and overcoats for both winter and summer. Alterations are done in two to three days.

✚ 99 G9 ✉ Campo San Bartolomeo, San Marco 5382 ☎ 041 520 8567 ⏰ Mon–Sat 9–7.30, Sun 10–7 🚤 Rialto

CALZATURE CASELLA
In the world of shoes, this is a Venetian institution, which is particularly popular with Japanese visitors. The emphasis is on classic styles, although the occasional twist on the old appears each season.

✚ 99 G9 ✉ Campo San Salvador, San Marco 5048 ☎ 041 522 8848 ⏰ Mon–Sat 10–7 🚤 Rialto

CALZOLERIA LA PARIGINA
Funky footwear fills this attractive outlet in the Mercerie shopping district. Leading brands represented include Clarks, Camper and Timberland. Lesser-known makes such as Husky, John Lobb and Vicini are well worth checking out. Another branch is located near the Scala di Bovolo at San Marco 4336.

✚ 99 H9 ✉ Merceria San Zulian, San Marco 727 ☎ 041 523 1555 ⏰ Mon–Sat

Opposite Campo San Bartolomeo, at the foot of the Rialto bridge, is a lively square

9.30–7.30, Sun 11–1, 1.30–6.30
🚤 San Marco

CAMICERIA SAN MARCO
www.shirtvenice.com
This wonderful shop specializes in all manner of shirts. Top-name brands are well represented, and there's a good range of accessories, including ties. If you fancy something original, then choose from the colourful array of natural fibre fabrics, or have a shirt, pyjamas or bathrobe tailored for you.
🚻 99 G10 ✉ Calle Vallaresso, San Marco 1340 ☎ 041 522 1432 🕐 Mon–Sat 9.30–7. Closed Sun 🚤 Vallaresso

CAMPO MARZIO
www.campomarziodesign.it
If you like fine desk accessories, come here for leather-bound notebooks, writing cases, files and folders, all in vibrant, radiant colours and softest leather. They also have a large range of elegant pens, pencils and other desk paraphernalia.
🚻 98 F10 ✉ Calle della Mandola, San Marco 3654/A ☎ 041 812 2697 🕐 Mon–Sat 10–7 🚤 Sant'Angelo

CIOCCA
Northern Italy is renowned for its stylish knitwear, and Ciocca has a superb range, with sweaters, cardigans, jackets and accessories in yarns that range from ultra-fine merino through cashmere to chunky thick wool ideal for outerwear. Styles encompass everything from utterly classic to seasonal specials based on hot new trends in fashion.
🚻 99 G10 ✉ Calle dei Fabbri, San Marco 1066 ☎ 041 522 7156 🕐 Daily 10–7.30 🚤 Rialto

EBRÙ
www.albertovalese-ebru.com
Alberto Valese was a front-runner in the reinvention of beautiful paper marbling in Venice, and his products are still the best—dozens of shapes and sizes of notebooks, folders, photo frames, boxes and albums

come in a choice of marbled or stamped paper in a huge variety of colours. Superb value for top-quality products.
🚻 98 F10 ✉ Campo Santo Stefano, San Marco 3471 ☎ 041 523 8830 🕐 Mon–Sat 10–1.30, 2.30–7.30, Sun 11–6 🚤 Accademia

FARMACIA DI SANTA MARIA NOVELLA
Step into this peaceful store and you'll be assailed by scent—from soaps, oils, candles, essences and perfumes. This gorgeous shop is a branch of the famous Florentine pharmacy and all its products are handmade using natural ingredients—and lovely packaging.
🚻 98 E10 ✉ Salizzada San Samuele, San Marco 3149 ☎ 041 522 0184 🕐 Mon–Sat 10–7 🚤 San Samuele

LA FENICE ATELIER
If you're looking for beautiful lingerie and table linen, this is a good place to start. Cristina Linassi has nightgowns and dressing gowns in gossamer fine cotton and smooth linens, all exquisitely finished with lace or embroidery, while table linens come in rich damasks.
🚻 98 F10 ✉ Calle dei Frati, San Marco 3537 ☎ 041 523 0578 🕐 Daily 10.30–7.30 🚤 Sant'Angelo

FURLA
Unusual leather bags for women are the lifeblood of this alluring shop. Exotic colours and designs give the goods a unique, vibrant character. There is also a good selection of gloves, belts and other leather accessories for women.
🚻 99 G9 ✉ Mercerie del Capitello, San Marco 4954 ☎ 041 523 0611 🕐 Mon–Sat 9.30–7.30, Sun 10.30–7 🚤 Rialto

GAGGIO
www.gaggio.it
Sumptuous hand-printed silk velvets and lush fabrics are used for wall-hangings and cushions and incorporated into bags, hats and scarves, renowned among dressmakers and designers. Gaggio's wares are obviously

expensive, but off-cuts or small lengths are also available—expect to pay around €150 a metre.
🚻 98 F10 ✉ Calle delle Botteghe, San Marco 3441–51 ☎ 041 522 8574 🕐 Mon–Fri 10.30–1, 4–7, Sat 10.30–1. Closed Sun 🚤 San Samuele

ITALOSPORT
The superb selection of quality sportswear includes fashionista-friendly labels such as Di Kappa and Fila. Pick up the latest official Juve, Milan, Roma, Venezia and Internazionale *calcio* (soccer) kits here.
🚻 98 G10 ✉ Campo Manin, San Marco 4254 ☎ 041 520 0696 🕐 Mon–Sat 9.15–7.30. Closed Sun 🚤 Rialto, Sant'Angelo

LANTERNA MAGICA
This is Venice's best traditional toyshop, which specializes in educational and exciting toys and games for all ages from all over the world, as well as distinctive teddy bears by Steiff and beautiful porcelain dolls.
🚻 99 H9 ✉ Calle delle Bande, Castello 5379 ☎ 041 528 1902 🕐 Mon 3–7, Tue–Sat 10–1, 3–7 🚤 Rialto, San Zaccaria

LELLABELLA
www.yarnshopinvenice.com
Lellabella has everything the avid knitter could need, from 2- and 4-ply to the most luxurious angora, cashmere and silks. Quirky yarns with fur trim, spangles and lurex thread are also on offer, along with embroidery silks, knitting needles and patterns.
🚻 98 G10 ✉ Calle della Mandola, San Marco 3718 ☎ 041 522 5152 🕐 Daily 9.30–7.30. Closed Sun Jul, Aug 🚤 Sant'Angelo

LIBRERIA STUDIUM
In addition to its wide selection of works on Venice, travel books and English-language paperbacks, this shop stocks the ultimate Venetian street index *Calli, Campielli e Canali* (published by Edizioni Helvetia), a street-map guide that shows every *sestiere* number. Fittingly, for a shop just behind San Marco, the back

room is crammed with religious works and icons.

✚ 99 H10 ✉ Calle Canonica, San Marco 337C ☎ 041 522 2382 ◷ Mon–Sat 9–7.30, Sun 10–2 🚊 San Zaccaria

LIVIO DE MARCHI

Wooden sculpture for the 21st century is showcased at Livio de Marchi. Here you will find immensely tactile carvings of everything from crumpled jeans and creased shirts to books, paintbrushes and tableware. Items in this shop are expensive, unique and beautiful.

✚ 98 E10 ✉ Salizzada San Samuele, San Marco 3157A ☎ 041 528 5694 ◷ Mon–Fri 9–12.30, 1.30–6; Sat by appointment 🚊 San Samuele

MANEKI–NEKO

Crisp cottons and linens are used here to make beautiful, easy-to-wear shirts and blouses, ranging from strictly tailored classic designs to casual, ideal for dressing up or down. It also stocks pretty nightgowns and bathrobes. Every item of clothing on sale in this delightful shop is designed and made by the owner, who has been supplying well-heeled Venetians for more than 20 years.

✚ 98 F10 ✉ Campo Sant'Angelo, San Marco 3820 ☎ 041 520 3340 ◷ Mon–Sat 10–7.30, Sun 11–7 🚊 Sant'Angelo

MARCHINI

www.golosessi.com
Many Venetians rate this as the best *pasticceria* in the city, and the selection of exquisitely decorated cakes, pastries and confectionery, all made with the highest-quality ingredients, takes most visitors' breath away. Pop in for a sugary mouthful, or buy a whole tray to take away—making sure to include a couple of *baute veneziane*, chocolates in the form of carnival masks. Delicious treats can also be made to order.

✚ 99 H10 ✉ Calle Spadaria, San Marco 676 ☎ 041 522 9109 ◷ Wed–Mon 9–8 🚊 San Marco

NOMINATION

www.nomination.it
Founded some 20 years ago, Nomination is an Italian firm, with branches all over the country, which makes distinctive, modern, well-designed jewellery at affordable prices. Hinged bracelets in silver and chrome set with semi-precious stones are the hallmark pieces, but the range has expanded and you'll find plenty to tempt you that's a bit out of the ordinary.

✚ 99 G9 ✉ Calle Goldoni, San Marco 4609 ☎ 041 520 1344 ◷ Daily 10–8 🚊 Rialto

OTTICA URBANI

www.otticaurbani.com
If you're looking for a pair of spectacles without a designer label but still chic and stylish, Ottica Urbani has its own range which includes a pair designed by Le Corbusier and some styles that fold up into a smart little box. Excellent value, and it can fill orders in a day or so.

✚ 99 G10 ✉ Frezzeria, San Marco 1280 ☎ 041 522 4140 ◷ Mon–Sat 9.30–1.30, 3.30–7.30 🚊 Vallaresso

PAUL & SHARK

Paul & Shark is one of Italy's big names for casual menswear, and you'll find an excellent choice of stylish, laid-back classic clothing here. This outlet is particularly noted for its range of well-tailored, comfortable trousers (pants) and sports clothes.

✚ 99 H9 ✉ Mercerie, San Marco 4844 ☎ 041 523 7733 ◷ Mon–Sat 10–7.30, Sun 11–7 🚊 Rialto

PAULY

www.paulyglassfactory.com
Pauly is one of the best city-centre outlets for Murano glass, with the accent on modern design, clean lines and vivid colours. It also sells glass jewellery and some more traditional pieces.

✚ 99 G10 ✉ Calle Larga San Marco, San Marco 4391A ☎ 041 520 9899 ◷ Mon–Fri 9.30–6, Sat–Sun 10–6 🚊 Vallaresso

LA PERLA

www.laperla.com
If Venice is the most romantic city in the world, make sure you are wearing the most romantic lingerie. The name speaks for itself: exquisite pieces made from the most sumptuous materials. Some night- and swimwear are also available, and the staff are helpful and discreet.

✚ 99 G9 ✉ Campo San Salvador, San Marco 4828 ☎ 041 522 6459 ◷ Mon–Sat 10–7.30 🚊 Rialto

PERLE E DINTORNI

It's easy to spend hours in this shop, choosing beads for a necklace. However, the staff are on hand to help you combine colours and effects which a novice would never have dreamed of. There is also ready-made jewellery in a range of prices.

✚ 98 F10 ✉ Calle della Mandola (Della Cortesia), San Marco 3740 ☎ 041 520 5068 ◷ Mon–Sat 9.30–7.30, Sun 12–7 🚊 Sant'Angelo

POT POURRI

www.potpourri.it
The layout of this shop is just like a house, with clothes strewn across seats and hangers on the backs of doors. The luxuriously feminine clothes are beautifully made, and women of most ages will find them very wearable. Visit their website before you come and arrange a 10 per cent discount.

✚ 99 G10 ✉ Ramo dei Fuseri, San Marco 1810 ☎ 041 241 0990 ◷ Mon–Sat 10–1, 3.30–7.30 🚊 Vallaresso

RIGATTIERI

This place stocks the very best of Italian ceramics. Wonderful decorative plates, vases and umbrella stands, fabulous pyramids of fruit and vegetables, elegant piece-work baskets and tureens are all for sale. There are also several tiny and affordable items, if you are looking for take-home gifts.

✚ 98 F10 ✉ Calle dei Frati, San Marco 3532–36 ☎ 041 523 1081 ◷ Mon–Sat 9–1, 3–8 🚊 Sant'Angelo

RIZZO REGALI

If you're looking for confectionery, chocolate or biscuits to take home, come here for one of the best selections in Venice. Biscuits come in attractive souvenir tins, there are specialities such as cookies from Burano, marzipan sweets masquerading as fruit and vegetables, and delicious chocolates sold loose or prettily packaged.

➕ 99 G9 ✉ Calle dei Fabbri, San Marco 4739 ☎ 041 522 5811 🕐 Mon–Sat 10–7, Sun 10.30–6.30 🚤 Rialto

ROLANDO SEGALIN

Since its foundation more than 50 years ago, this quirky little store has been creating made-to-order shoes and carrying out repairs. To see what Venetian style can be all about, take your time window-shopping even if you don't buy.

➕ 98 G9 ✉ Calle dei Fuseri, San Marco 4365 ☎ 041 522 2115 🕐 Mon–Fri 10–12.30, 3.30–7.30, Sat 10–12.30 🚤 Rialto

SERGIO ROSSI

www.sergiorossi.com

If it's leather shoes you're after, this is the place to gauge the latest trends, with the help of the exceptionally friendly and welcoming staff. Men's and women's ranges are extensive and cater for most tastes.

➕ 99 H9 ✉ Mercerie San Zulian, San Marco 705 ☎ 041 241 3615 🕐 Mon–Thu 10–1, 2–7, Fri–Sat 10–7, Sun 2–6.30 🚤 San Marco

TASSOTTI

www.tassotti.it

In this lovely paper and stationery store designs, unlike most paper in Venice, are based on flora and fauna, imagery, old maps and prints. Choose from wrapping paper and bookmarks, postcards or greetings cards or splash out on desk accessories.

➕ 99 H9 ✉ Calle della Bissa, San Marco 5471 ☎ 041 528 1881 🕐 Mon–Sat 10–1, 3.30–7 🚤 Rialto

VENETIA STUDIUM

Fortuny-style pleated silk and figured velvet scarves, pillows and bags in

a huge range of heavenly tones are available at this far-from-cheap and very tempting Venetian speciality store. They also make Fortuny-style lamps and have branches throughout the city.

➕ 98 G10 ✉ Calle Larga XXII Marzo, San Marco 2403; Calle delle Ostreghe, San Marco 2428; Merceria San Zulian, San Marco 723 ☎ 041 522 9281, 041 520 0505, 041 522 9859 🕐 Mon–Sat 9.30–7.40, Sun 10.30–6 🚤 Vallaresso

VIVALDI STORE

You'll find every example of 18th-century Venetian music in this stylish store, with the accent on the city's most popular composer, Antonio Vivaldi. CDs and tapes are the main draw, but you will also find sheet-music and scores, T-shirts, videos and other music-orientated souvenirs such as mouse mats, mugs, trays and table mats.

➕ 99 H8 ✉ Fontego dei Tedeschi, San Marco 5537 ☎ 041 522 1343 🕐 Daily 10–7 🚤 Rialto

ENTERTAINMENT AND NIGHTLIFE
ATENEO VENETO

www.ateneoveneto.org

Occasional classical concerts are held at this cultural institute, right next to the Teatro La Fenice (▷ 92). You are more likely to hear Chopin and Debussy than the Venetian favourite Vivaldi in the fresco-filled Aula Magna hall. Credit cards are not accepted.

➕ 98 G10 ✉ Campo San Fantin, San Marco 1897 ☎ 041 522 4459 🕐 Telephone for latest details 💶 Often free: telephone for latest details 🚤 Rialto, San Marco

BACARO JAZZ

The fabulous Cuban *barista* (barman) here does his utmost to make you feel welcome, and perhaps more importantly mixes a mean mojito. Expect plenty of jazz music and *gondolieri* out enjoying themselves. There is good food, too.

➕ 99 H8 ✉ Salizzada del Fontego dei Tedeschi, San Marco 5546 ☎ 041 528 5249 🕐 Thu–Tue 11am–2am 🚤 Rialto

CENTRALE

Right on the direct route from the Fenice to Piazza San Marco, the super-hip Centrale has been pulling in the crowds since its 2003 opening. Venice's most stylish late-night restaurant and lounge has its own water entrance leading directly into the beautifully lit minimal space, where tables are elegantly set with glass and service comes with flair. Come for a drink, a meal or entertainment, and experience an ambience that's distinctly special in this early-to-bed city.

➕ 99 G10 ✉ Piscina Frezzeria, San Marco 1569 ☎ 041 296 0664 🕐 Tue–Sun 6.30pm–2am 🚤 San Marco

EX-CHIESA DI SAN VIDAL

www.interpretivenezian.it

Chamber music by the likes of Bazzini, Bach, Schubert and Vivaldi is played year-round against the backdrop of Gaspari, Tirali and Carpaccio's 17th-century church interiors. Credit cards are not accepted.

➕ 98 E10 ✉ Campo San Vidal, San Marco 2862B ☎ 041 277 0561 🕐 Telephone for latest details 💶 €17–€22 🚤 Accademia

FONDAZIONE CINI

www.cini.it

The Giorgio Cini foundation, inaugurated in 1951, is based on the tranquil island of San Giorgio Maggiore. Among its cultural initiatives are concerts and recitals; in summer, some take place in the outdoor Teatro Verde (▷ 92). Credit cards are not accepted.

➕ 99 J12 ✉ Ísola San Giorgio Maggiore ☎ 041 524 0119 🕐 Telephone for latest details 💶 Telephone for latest details 🚤 San Giorgio

HAIG'S BAR

Haig's is an American-style piano bar, popular with visiting Americans and young locals—and those locals who wish they were younger! It serves very good but slightly pricey Venetian fare.

➕ 98 F11 ✉ Campo Santa Maria del Giglio, San Marco 5277 ☎ 041 528 9456

🕐 Daily 11.30–3, 7–2 🚤 Santa Maria del Giglio

INISHARK

Inishark serves Guinness and shows soccer on wide-screen TV. Owners Alberto and Maria extend a warm welcome and are always an entertainment in themselves.
✚ 99 H9 ✉ Calle del Mondo Novo, Castello 5787 ☎ 041 717 999 🕐 Daily 5pm–1am 🚤 Rialto

L'OLANDESE VOLANTE

With outside seating, this is a great place to meet in the warmer months, especially during the university term.
✚ 99 H9 ✉ Campo San Lio, Castello 5658 ☎ 041 528 9349 🕐 Mon–Fri 10am–1am, Sat 10am–2am, Sun 5pm–2am 🚤 Rialto

SCUOLA GRANDE DI SAN TEODORO

www.imusiciveneziani.com
Baroque and operatic concerts are performed at this magnificent building from May to November. Vivaldi's *Le Quattro Stagioni* (Four Seasons) features often, as does music from Mozart, Donizetti and Verdi. The orchestra and singers dress in 18th-century costume. Credit cards are not accepted.
✚ 99 G9 ✉ Salizzada San Teodoro, San Marco 4810 ☎ 041 521 0294 🕐 Telephone for latest details ✋ €23–€33 🚤 Rialto

TEATRO LA FENICE

www.teatrolafenice.it
Venice's beautifully rebuilt, world-famous opera house (▷ 83), ravaged by a catastrophic fire in 1996, opened for business once more for the 2004–05 winter season. The theatre, whose interior is one of the most dramatic venues in the world, is primarily an opera house, but also stages ballet and occasional concerts.
✚ 98 F10 ✉ Campo San Fantin, San Marco 1965 ☎ 041 786 511 🎧 Audioguides available daily from box office or contact HelloVenezia (tel 041 2424; www.hellovenezia.com); guided tours

available daily via HelloVenezia ✋ Tickets €20–€180 🚤 Santa Maria del Giglio

TEATRO GOLDONI

This famous, beautiful theatre, named for the Venetian playwright Carlo Goldoni (1707–93), stages plays from the 18th to 20th centuries, using big contemporary names and leading Italian directors. The Goldoni also puts on poetry readings, youth theatre and the occasional musical performance.
✚ 99 G9 ✉ Calle Goldoni, San Marco 4650B ☎ 041 240 2011 🕐 Telephone for latest details ✋ €25–€35 🚤 Rialto

TEATRO VERDE

www.cini.it
This open-air theatre is set in wonderful parkland on the island of San Giorgio Maggiore. The theatre was inaugurated in 1954 and renovated in the late 1990s. Since its reopening in 1999, it has concentrated on staging contemporary dance productions during the summer months.
✚ Off map 99 J12 ✉ Ísola di San Giorgio Maggiore ☎ 041 528 990 🕐 Telephone for latest details ✋ Telephone for latest details 🚤 San Giorgio

TORINO@NOTTE

www.torinonotte.tv
Live jazz, beer, spritz and toasted sandwiches attract the fun-loving crowd here. The action spills out onto the *campo* during the summer and at carnival time.
✚ 99 G9 ✉ Campo San Luca, San Marco 4597 ☎ 041 522 3914 🕐 Tue–Sat 7pm–1am 🚤 Rialto

VINO VINO

This lovely little wine bar also serves food, and the crowd is as diverse as the wine list. It's not really a place to ask for a beer.
✚ 98 G10 ✉ Calle delle Veste, San Marco 2007A ☎ 041 2417688 🕐 Wed–Mon 10.30am–midnight 🚤 San Marco

VITAE

For a beer, spritz or a Cuba libre, join the upwardly mobile in this trendy designer bar. Staff can be a little

over-exuberant, and like to put their favourite tracks on repeat, but the atmosphere is convivial.
✚ 98 G9 ✉ Calle Sant'Antonio, San Marco 4118 ☎ 041 520 5205 🕐 Mon–Sat 9pm–1am 🚤 Rialto

SPORTS AND ACTIVITIES

CARNIVAL – THE SHOW

www.venice-carnival-show.com
If you're fascinated by Carnival but not able to visit Venice during February, you can have a taste of it at this evening entertainment. Guests are welcomed with a huge buffet of hot and cold dishes, served with complementary wines, before entering the auditorium where a combination of live acts, digital projection, lighting and sound re-create the essence of Carnival and its history. It's unashamedly aimed at tourists but immensely popular, and for many people it's an unforgettable insight into Venice and its biggest winter festival.
✚ 99 G10 ✉ Teatro San Gallo, Campiello San Gallo, San Marco 1098 ☎ 041 241 1943 🕐 Telephone for latest details or reserve online ✋ €80 🚤 Vallaresso/ San Marco

VENICE EVENTS

www.veniceevents.com
You can have the wedding of your dreams expertly tailor-made by this friendly Anglo-Italian company which will organize everything from the paperwork and civil ceremony to the flowers, reception and that indispensable gondola journey. The service from this highly competent company is professional in the extreme, giving you a magical day to remember, arranged by a team that really understands every wedding is unique and special.
✚ 99 G10 ✉ Frezzeria, San Marco 1827 ☎ 041 523 9979 🕐 Mon–Fri 9–1, 3–6 ✋ Tailor-made 🚤 Vallaresso

HEALTH AND BEAUTY

MARIE ROSE BEAUTY SALON

www.starwood.com/grittipalace
For ultimate pampering in the beautiful surroundings of one of Venice's greatest hotels, book via

the concierge for a treatment in the Gritti's beauty salon (on the ground floor), where facials, body treatments, manicures, pedicures and hairdressing are all available.
🕂 98 F11 ✉ Hotel Gritti Palace, Campo Santa Maria del Giglio, San Marco 2467 ☎ 041 794 611 🕐 Tue, Fri–Sat 9–12, 3.15–7.30; rest of week 9–6.30
👋 Manicure from €35; facial from €65; waxing from €25 ⛴ Santa Maria del Giglio

SAN CLEMENTE BEAUTY AND WELLNESS CLUB
www.thi.it
Head across the lagoon on the private hotel launch from San Marco to the island of San Clemente, whose Beauty and Wellness Club offers a full range of beauty treatments, including massage, facials and body training. After your session, enjoy the hotel's swimming pool or stroll around the gardens.
🕂 Off map 99 H12 ✉ Ísola di San Clemente 1, San Marco ☎ 041 244 5001 🕐 Mon–Sat 9.30–7 👋 Manicure from €60; facial from €65

FOR CHILDREN
BOUTIQUE DEL GELATO
Be prepared to wait to be served at this busy, tiny *gelateria,* on the main drag from the Rialto to Santa Maria Formosa. Locals head here to find what many people consider to be some of the best ice cream in the city.
🕂 99 H9 ✉ Salizzada San Lio, Castello 5727 ☎ 041 522 3283 🕐 Feb–end Nov daily 10–8.30 👋 Cone €3–€4.50
⛴ Rialto

GELATERIA PAOLIN
The selection of ice cream here is endless and every choice fulfils its promise—what you'd expect from one of Venice's longest-established *gelaterie.* The old-fashioned varieties such as vanilla, chocolate, coffee, *stracciatella* (chocolate chip) and *nocciola* (hazelnut) are among the best in the city.
🕂 98 F10 ✉ Campo Santo Stefano, San Marco 296A ☎ 041 522 5576 🕐 Late Jun–end Aug daily 7.30am–11.30pm; closes 9.30pm rest of year 👋 Cone €3 ⛴ San Samuele

IGLOO
This is a wonderful ice-cream shop where the creamy chocolate, vanilla and other traditional flavours vie with summertime fresh fruit tastes. Take a card and get your tenth ice free.
🕂 98 F10 ✉ Calle della Mandola, San Marco 4819 ☎ 041 522 3003 🕐 May–end Sep daily 10.30–9; Oct, Nov, Feb–end Apr daily 11.30–7.30. Closed Dec and Jan
👋 Cone €3–€5 ⛴ Sant'Angelo

PUNTOLAGUNA
www.salve.it
Puntolaguna is a state-of-the-art, multimedia space devoted to the ecology and safeguarding of the lagoon. It runs workshops for children and there are also videos and CD-ROMs to keep them happy (▷ 63).
🕂 98 F10 ✉ Campo Santo Stefano, San Marco 2949 ☎ 041 529 3582 🕐 Mon–Fri 2.30–5.30 👋 Free ⛴ Accademia

Above *Italian ice cream—a real treat in an amazing variety of flavours*

PRICES AND SYMBOLS

The prices given are the average for a two-course lunch (L) and a three-course dinner (D) for one person, without drinks. The wine price is for the least expensive bottle.

For a key to the symbols, ▷ 2.

ACQUAPAZZA

www.venicemasaniello.com

You can sit outside overlooking one of San Marco's nicer *campi* and watch the world go by if you eat at this attractive, modern restaurant, where the accent is firmly on fish. Starters include prawns and rocket (arugula) with a balsamic vinegar dressing, a simple, lemon-drizzled seafood platter and fresh anchovies. Follow this with the catch of the day or a delicate fish risotto and round it off with a choice of home-made desserts. Acquapazza also serves good, crisp pizza if you're watching the budget.

➕ 98 F10 ✉ Campo Sant'Angelo, San Marco 3808 ☎ 041 277 0688 🕐 Tue–Sun 12–2.30, 7.30–9.30. Closed Jan 🖐 L €30, D €40, Wine €10 🚤 Sant'Angelo

ALLE TESTIERE

This tiny restaurant has a sky-high reputation for innovative and creative cooking, with local seafood and fish prepared with spice and herbs, a well-chosen cheeseboard and small, excellent, wine list. There are two sittings nightly; choose the later one (at 9pm) for a more relaxed meal.

➕ 99 H9 ✉ Calle del Mondo Nuovo, Castello 5801 ☎ 041 522 7220 🕐 Tue–Sat 12–2, 7–10.30. Closed last week Dec, 2 weeks Jan, last week Jul, 3 weeks Aug 🖐 L €45, D €70, Wine €8 🚤 Rialto

BISTROT DE VENISE

www.bistrotdevenise.com

This restaurant is popular with local poets and artists who do readings and exhibit their works here, as well as those visitors in the know, especially the French. The cooking can be variable, but good use is made of the freshest ingredients. The wine list boasts the richest pickings of the Veneto.

➕ 99 G9 ✉ Calle dei Fabbri, San Marco 4685 ☎ 041 523 6651 🕐 Daily 9am–1am 🖐 L €45, D €75, Wine €8 🚤 Rialto

CAFFÈ FLORIAN

www.caffeflorian.com

The sumptuous surroundings of Caffè Florian (▷ 61) have attracted well-heeled big names since 1720, and still draw numerous visitors to the city who are willing to pay €10 for a cappuccino and a table in the Piazza San Marco. You can also indulge in light lunches, sandwiches and elegant afternoon tea, beautifully served by impeccably trained staff—a quintessentially Venetian experience.

➕ 99 H10 ✉ Piazza San Marco, San Marco 56–59 ☎ 041 520 5641 🕐 May–end Oct daily 9.30am–12am; Nov–end Apr Thu–Tue 9.30am–12am 🖐 Coffee €10, spritz €9 🚤 San Marco

CAFFÈ QUADRI

www.quadrivenice.com

For something really special, book a table at the upstairs restaurant at Caffè Quadri (▷ 61), the great Piazza San Marco coffee house. The setting can't be bettered, and the surroundings, all neoclassical design, chandeliers and mirrors, are stunning. The food is good, too, with some Venetian staples served with a twist and vegetarian options—rare indeed in Venice. Alternatively, sit at one of the outside tables and enjoy the views of the Piazza.

🕂 99 H10 ✉ Piazza San Marco, San Marco 120–24 ☎ 041 522 2105 🕓 Apr–end Oct daily 9am–11.30pm; Nov–end Mar Tue–Sun 9am–11.30pm 🍴 Coffee €10, spritz from €10 🚤 San Marco

DA BRUNO

Whether it's a little *cicchetti,* some roasted meat or a big plate of something fishy, Da Bruno caters for all tastes and appetites. This small but excellent restaurant features very reasonably priced dishes, which means you can try almost everything. If you're adventurous but your partner has a rather more conservative palette, you will both be pleased by what the menu—and indeed the wine list—has to offer.

🕂 99 H9 ✉ Calle del Paradiso, Castello 5731 ☎ 041 522 1480 🕓 Daily 12–3, 6.30–10 🍴 L €35, D €55, Wine €7 🚤 San Zaccaria

DO FORNI

The two dining rooms here offer completely different experiences. One is all starched tablecloths and Murano glass chandeliers, while the other is like an English pub, with wooden tables and exposed beams. The food is classic Italian with a twist; the scampi in champagne served with egg noodles is a perfect example of the house style.

🕂 99 H9 ✉ Calle dei Specchieri, San Marco 468 ☎ 041 523 2148 🕓 Daily 12–3, 6–11 🍴 L €60, D €85, Wine €9 🚤 San Marco

HARRY'S BAR

If you are going to push the boat out in Venice, you'll get your money's worth at the world-famous Harry's Bar. This stylish and restrained restaurant has long been popular with visiting celebrities, including plentiful Americans. Harry's Bar is

famous for its Bellinis (prosecco with white peach juice) and its carpaccio of beef (razor-thin slices of raw sirloin). Both are worth the hype.

🕂 99 G11 ✉ Calle Vallaresso, San Marco 1323 ☎ 041 528 5777 🕓 Daily 9.30am–11pm 🍴 L €80, D €130, Wine €13 🚤 San Marco

OSTERIA AI RUSTEGHI

Venice is famous for its panini and *tramezzini* (filled rolls and sandwiches) and this tiny place offers well in excess of 30 varieties, which you can enjoy with a glass or bottle of wine from the extensive list. Sit in or outside on the *campo* and debate the merits of delights ranging from scampi and rocket (arugula) through egg and asparagus to full-flavoured porcini mushrooms and succulent beef.

🕂 99 H8 ✉ Campiello del Tintor, 5513 San Marco ☎ 041 523 2205 🕓 May–end Sep Mon–Fri 10–9.30; Oct–end Apr Mon–Sat 10–9 🍴 L €5, D €10, Wine €9 🚤 Rialto

TEAMO

This streamlined wine bar and café, with its clean modern lines and melange of modern and old

materials, is a good place to relax with a drink and a snack if you're looking for a lunchtime pause or early-evening aperitif. At lunchtime you can choose from *cicchetti* (nibbles) or simply sample a plate of mixed smoked meats and local cheeses.

🕂 98 F10 ✉ Ria Terà della Mandola, San Marco 30124 ☎ 041 277 0850 🕓 Daily 8am–10pm 🍴 L €17, Wine €12 🚤 Sant'Angelo/Giglio

VINI DA ARTURO

Tucked away near the Fenice theatre, this tiny restaurant is a well-kept secret among Venetians seeking a change from their traditionally fish-based menus. Here you'll find superb steaks, veal cutlets and escalopes, well-hung and cooked to perfection, which go down well after one of the imaginative salads served as antipasti. Desserts such as chocolate mousse and tiramisù are well above average and all made in-house. Credit cards are not accepted.

🕂 98 F10 ✉ Calle degli Assassini, San Marco 3656 ☎ 041 528 6974 🕓 Mon–Sat 12.30–2.30, 7.30–10.30. Closed last 2 weeks of Feb and Aug 🍴 L €50, D €80, Wine €9 🚤 Sant'Angelo

Below *The perfect spot for a romantic dinner date*

Above *The elegant Gritti Palace hotel fronts
the Grand Canal*
Opposite *The Noemi is great value*

PRICES AND SYMBOLS

Prices are the lowest and highest for
a double room for one night in high
season. Breakfast is included unless
noted otherwise.

For a key to the symbols, ▷ 2.

DO POZZI

www.hoteldopozzi.it

This friendly little hotel is tucked
away in an alley in the heart of San
Marco. Tables spill outside onto a
terrace from the small reception
areas. Bedrooms vary in size; all
are traditionally furnished. The
owners are helpful and there's great
attention to detail in the service
provided.

➕ 98 G10 ✉ Via XXII Marzo, San Marco
2373 ☎ 041 520 7855 🖐 €98–€280
🛈 29 🔄 🚢 Giglio

EUROPA & REGINA

www.westin.com

This Westin hotel occupies two
adjoining and magnificent *palazzi*,
overlooking the Grand Canal. The
public rooms are full of marble,
rich hues and sumptuous fabrics,

with a wonderful terrace for drinks
and dining right on the Grand
Canal. The bedrooms are simpler,
well furnished and equipped, but
somewhat bland. All have marble
bathrooms, minibar and 24-hour
room service. Access to the Lido
beach and sports facilities are
included.

➕ 98 G11 ✉ Off Calle Larga XXII
Marzo, San Marco 2159 ☎ 041 240 0001
🖐 €270–€1,800 🛈 185 rooms, 17 suites
🔄 🚢 San Marco

LA FENICE ET DES ARTISTES

www.fenicehotels.it

The old-established La Fenice et
des Artistes, close to the Fenice
and popular with musicians and
opera aficionados, is a true Venetian
institution with a loyal clientele.
Expect exposed beams, marble
and antiques in the public areas,
a theatre-style bar and bedrooms
of varying size and style—the
best have balconies, and all have
telephone, TV, private bathroom,
hairdryer and safe. La Taverna
restaurant serves classic Venetian
dishes, and you can breakfast
outside on sunny mornings in the
central courtyard.

➕ 98 F10 ✉ Campiello della Fenice,
San Marco 1936 ☎ 041 523

2333 🖐 €140–€310 🛈 67
🔄 🚢 Sant'Angelo, San Marco

FLORA

www.hotelflora.it

Hidden down a narrow *calle* a few
minutes' walk from the Piazza, the
Flora—family-run and brimming
with character—is a wonderfully
tranquil hotel, with a pretty garden
and sense of peace. Room sizes
vary greatly; some are extremely
pokey, and the quietest look onto
gardens. They have smallish private
bathrooms, and TV and phone are
included. The multilingual staff are
friendly and helpful and can arrange
baby-sitting.

➕ 98 G11 ✉ Calle dei Bergamaschi,
San Marco 2283A ☎ 041 520 5844
🖐 €180–€250 🛈 44 rooms 🔄
🚢 San Marco

GRITTI PALACE

www.starwood.com/grittipalace

One of Venice's great hotels,
the Gritti was chosen by Queen
Elizabeth II as her Venetian base.
This is a beautiful, old-fashioned
hotel, with elegance, style and
service to match. There's a huge
range of rooms, each uniquely
decorated and some overlooking the
Grand Canal, while the dining room,

bar and public areas are furnished with antiques and adorned with exquisite flowers; a drink on the terrace is one of the great Venetian experiences. A courtesy launch takes guests to the sports facilities, beach and pool of the Starwood group on the Lido.

✚ 98 F11 ✉ Campo Santa Maria del Giglio, San Marco 2467 ☎ 041 794 611 💶 €450–€1,500 🛈 91 rooms and suites ♿ ⛴ Santa Maria del Giglio

LOCANDA ART DÉCO

www.locandaartdeco.com

Sited near the Ponte dell'Accademia (Accademia Bridge), the Locanda will appeal to lovers of the belle époque, with both public rooms and bedrooms filled with assorted art deco antiques. Each attractive guest room has an orthopaedic mattress, private bathroom, kettle, TV, hairdryer and phone. The buffet breakfast is served in the charming breakfast room.

✚ 98 F10 ✉ Calle delle Botteghe, San Marco 2966 ☎ 041 277 0558 💶 €100–€170 🛈 6 ♿ ⛴ Accademia

NOEMI

www.hotelnoemi.com

This attractive and well-managed hotel is found in the long, straight, tourist-filled Calle dei Fabbri, near Piazza San Marco. Step inside and you're in one of the best-value lodgings in this expensive area, complete with marble floors and bright fabrics in the public areas and well-appointed, traditionally beamed bedrooms. Not all have bathrooms; enquire when you book. All have satellite TV, telephone and safe, and air-conditioning available on request for an extra fee. Credit cards are not accepted.

✚ 99 G10 ✉ Calle dei Fabbri, San Marco 909 ☎ 041 523 8144 💶 €50–€150 🛈 20 ♿ ⛴ San Marco, Vallaresso

NOVECENTO

www.novecento.biz

The Novecento is another stunning boutique hotel that's right up with the best of Venice's new-wave designer lodgings. The interior design pays homage to Fortuny, using rich colours and textures with a multi-ethnic twist as the backdrop to fine old furniture. There's a tiny courtyard, a breakfast room and honesty bar, and rooms are equipped with every comfort, including Philippe Starck bathrooms.

✚ 98 F10 ✉ Calle delle Dose, Campo San Maurizio, San Marco 2683 ☎ 041 241 3765 💶 €130–€240, excluding breakfast 🛈 9 ♿ ⛴ Giglio

SAN CLEMENTE PALACE

www.thi.it

Venice's five-star island hotel lies a 10-minute courtesy launch trip away from San Marco, on San Clemente. First settled in 1131, when the church was built, its buildings have been converted into a luxury hotel set among 1.6ha (4 acres) of park and gardens. Rooms and suites are themed and equipped with everything imaginable; there are three restaurants, bars, terraces, a swimming pool, tennis courts, a spa and beauty centre and a three-hole practice golf course. With this level of facilities and service to match, you may well never make it as far as the city centre.

✚ Off map 99 H12 ✉ Ísola di San Clemente 1, San Marco ☎ 041 244 5001 💶 €190–€1,000, excluding breakfast 🛈 205 ♿ 🏊 ⛴ Private launch

SAN SAMUELE

This above average one-star hotel is blessed with a wonderful location near the San Samuele *vaporetto* stop. A lounge area has the usual Venetian trappings: patterned wallpaper, marble floors, antiques and chandeliers. For this price, the rooms are nothing special, but in contrast to the competition they are clean and comfortable. Most have shared bathrooms and basic facilities. Credit cards are not accepted.

✚ 98 E10 ✉ Salizzada San Samuele, San Marco 3358 ☎ 041 522 8045 💶 €70–€110 🛈 10 ♿ ⛴ San Samuele

TORINO

www.hoteltorino.com

Good-sized rooms, solid furnishings and luxurious fabrics are the order of the day in this attractive hotel in the heart of San Marco. The main building occupies a 16th-century *palazzo*, and there are suites on offer in the two adjacent annexes. Elegant and substantial breakfasts are served in a pretty dining room, and there's even a tiny courtyard for relaxing; all together, it's excellent value for money in this area.

✚ 98 G11 ✉ Calle delle Ostreghe, San Marco 2356 ☎ 041 520 5222 💶 €95–€200 🛈 37 ♿ ⛴ Giglio

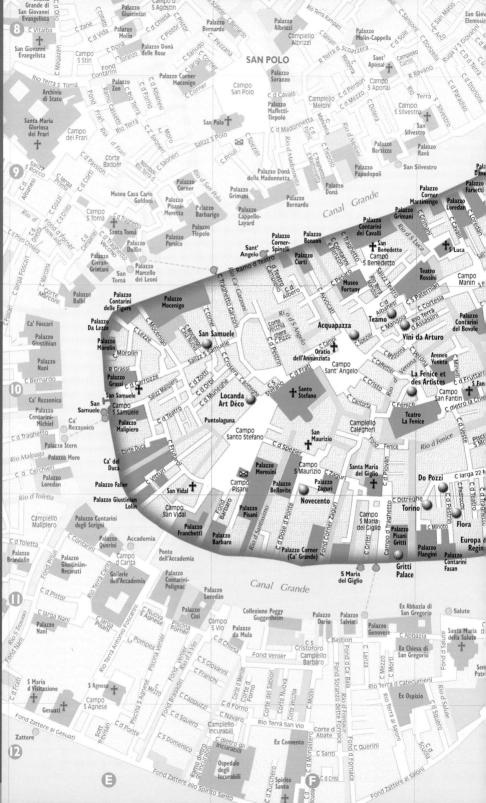

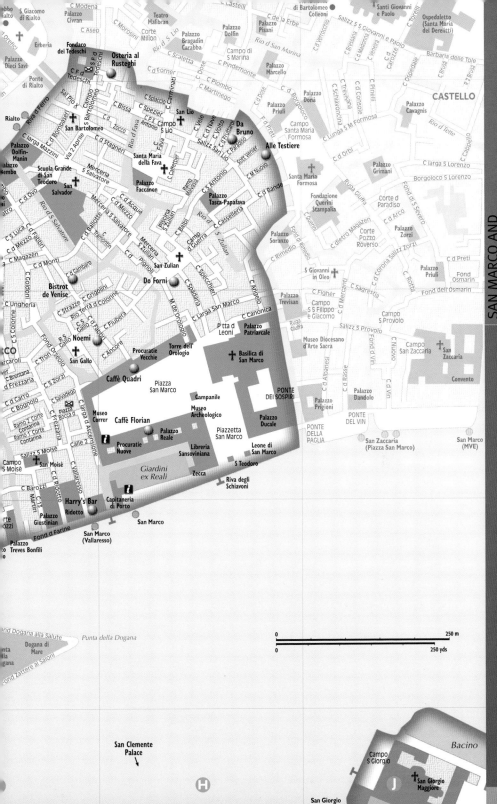

CASTELLO

Rialto

San Bartolomeo

Osteria al
Rusteghi

Fondaco
dei Tedeschi

San Lio

Da
Bruno

Alle Testiere

Santa Maria
della Fava

Santa Maria
Formosa

Palazzo
Grimani

Scuola Grande
di San
Teodoro

San
Salvador

Palazzo
Faccanon

Palazzo
Tasca-Papafava

Bistrot
de Venise

San Zulian

Do Forni

Noemi

San Gallo

Procuratie
Vecchie

Torre dell'
Orologio

Basilica di
San Marco

Caffè Quadri

Piazza
San Marco

Campanile

PONTE
DEI SOSPIRI

Museo
Correr

Museo
Archeologico

Palazzo
Dandolo

Caffè Florian

Palazzo
Reale

Piazzetta
San Marco

Palazzo
Ducale

PONTE
DELLA
PAGLIA

PONTE
DEL VIN

Procuratie
Nuove

Libreria
Sansoviniana

Leone di
San Marco

San Zaccaria
(Piazza San Marco)

San Marco
(MVE)

Giardini
ex Reali

S Teodoro

Zecca

Riva degli
Schiavoni

San Moisè

Harry's Bar

Ridotto

Capitaneria
di Porto

San Marco

San Marco
(Vallaresso)

Palazzo
Giustinian

Palazzo
Treves Bonfili

Punta della Dogana

Dogana di
Mare

San Clemente
Palace

Bacino

Campo
S Giorgio

San Giorgio
Maggiore

San Giorgio

0 ——————————————— 250 m
0 ——————————————— 250 yds

Ⓗ

Ⓙ

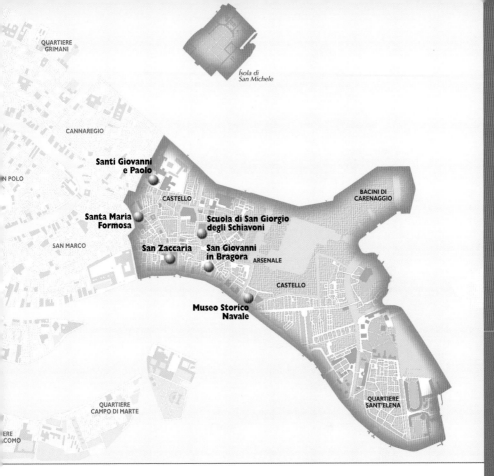

CASTELLO

Castello, which gets its name from the fortress *(castello)* that once stood here, is the biggest Venetian *sestiere* (ward), stretching from San Marco in the west to encompass the islands of San Pietro and Sant'Elena in the east. Historically, it was both the city's industrial powerhouse, with the Arsenale producing fleets of ships on the world's first production lines, and home to Venice's religious heart, the island of San Pietro, whose ancient church served as the city's cathedral until 1807. Its cityscape is varied, with a long southern waterfront, the Riva degli Schiavoni, overlooking St Mark's Basin and a northern quayside that looks towards the main lagoon islands and the distant Alps. To the east lies the Arsenale and Venice's most vibrant working-class district, centred around the wide Via Garibaldi; beyond are the quiet residential areas of Sant'Elena.

Given its size, it's no surprise that the *sestiere* is rich in interest, its attractions ranging from some of Venice's finest churches, through museums, *palazzi,* such as Renaissance Palazzo Grimani, to green spaces. To the north, reached via Campo San Zaccaria and its church, stands Santi Giovanni e Paolo, a huge Gothic edifice on a lovely square, that's the burial place of doges and heroes. En route too, lies spacious Campo Santa Maria Formosa, with its 15th-century church and beguiling Museo della Fondazione Querini Stampalia. From here, narrow streets, lined with quirky stores and artisan workshops, lead east to the Scuola di San Giorgio degli Schiavoni, a jewel of a building containing works by Vittore Carpaccio. There's open space around the Museo Storico Navale, Venice's maritime museum, and the Arsenale itself, a vast dock area that's now used as a venue for the Biennale, which runs every year, alternately focusing on either art or architecture. Farther east, it also occupies the Giardini Pubblici, the green space first laid out during the Napoleonic occupation.

San Michele

7

Palazzo
Seriman

Campiello
d'Pietà

Corte
Rimer

Corte
Carità

†Santa Lázzaro
del Mendicanti

Ospedale

Santa Maria
del Pianto

Santa Maria
del Pianto

Palazzo
Widman

Ospedale
Civile

Scuola Grande
di San Marco

8

Santa Maria
dei Miracoli †

Campo Santi
Giovanni
e Paolo

Santi Giovanni
e Paolo

Palazzo
Sanudo

Teatro
Malibran

Palazzo
Dolfin

Palazzo
Pisani

Monumento
di Bartolomeo
Colleoni

Ospedaletto
(Santa Maria
dei Derelitti)

Palazzo
Bragadin
Carabba

Palazzo
di S Marina

Palazzo
Marcello

Barbaria delle Tole

San Francesco
della Vigna

Celestia

†San Lio

Palazzo
Priuli

Palazzo
Donà

CASTELLO

Ex Chiesa
di S Giustina

Palazzo
Gritti o della
Nunziatura

Santa Maria
della Fava †

Campo Santa
Maria Formosa

Palazzo
Cavagnis

Campo
S Giustina

Palazzo
Gradenigo

Palazzo
Contarini

9

Santa Maria
Formosa

Palazzo
Grimani

Ex Ospizio

San Lorenzo

Palazzo
Tasca-Papafava
Querini
Stampalia

Fondazione
Querini
Stampalia

Campo
San Lorenzo

Ex Convento

Palazzo
Soranzo

Corte
del'Olio

San Zulian †

Palazzo
Zorzi

Scuola di
San Giorgio
degli Schiavoni

S Giovanni
dei Cavalieri
di Malta

Palazzo
Magno

S Giovanni
in Oleo

Palazzo
Priuli

Palazzo
Zorzi

†S Antonino

Torre dell'
Orologio

Palazzo
Trevisan

Museo di Dipinti
Sacri Bizantini

San Giorgio
degli Greci

Palazzo
Patriarcale

Museo Diocesano
d'Arte Sacra

Campo
San Zaccaria

Torri
del'Arsenale

ARSENALE

10

Basilica di
San Marco

Palazzo
Prigioni

Palazzo
Dandolo

Santa
Zaccaria

San
Martino

Campanile

Piazza
San Marco

Museo
Archeologico

Palazzo
Ducale

Convento

San Giovanni
in Bragora

Palazzo
Reale

PONTE
DEI SOSPIRI

PONTE
DEL VIN

Santa Maria
della Visitazione

Palazzo
Navagero

CASTE

Libreria
Sansoviniana

Piazzetta
San Marco

Leone di
San Marco

S Teodoro

Ca' di Dio

Zecca

Riva degli
Schiavoni

San Zaccaria
(Piazza San Marco)

San Marco
(MVE)

Riva degli Schiavoni

Ex Forni

Museo
Storico
Navale

Palazzetto
dello Sport

11

Arsenale

Riva dei Sette Martiri

†San Biagio

Via Giuseppe Garibaldi

CASTE

Canale di San Marco

12

Campo
S Giorgio

Bacino

San Giorgio

San Giorgio
Maggiore

Fondazione
Cini

Campo Nani
e Barbaro

Bacino di
San Giorgio

Isola di San
Giorgio Maggiore

13

†Zitelle

Teatro
Verde

QUARTIERE
CAMPO DI MARTE

H   J   K   L

BACINI DI
CARENAGGIO

Bacini

0   250 m
0   250 yds

Canale di Porta Nuova

San Pietro

Ísola di
San Pietro

Campo
S Daniele

Rio San Daniele

C. larga S Pietro

Campo di
San Pietro

C d Terco

San Pietro
di Castello

C S Giovanni

Campiello
Filigaretto

Campo
di Ruga

C. Marsani

C d De

Ex Palazzo
Patriarcale

Ísola della
Certosa

S Sforza

C Ruello

C d Salamon

ancesco
aolo

C d Blanco

C S Anna

Campiello
Vigna

Fond della Tana

Fond San Gioacchino

C Quintavalle

Campiello dei
Pomeri

onumento
Garibaldi

Fond S Anna

Ex Chiesa
di S Anna

Rio di Quintavalle

Giardini
Garibaldi

Secco Marina

Corte
Martin
Novello

Fond San Giuseppe

San Giuseppe
di Castello

Camdo
San
Giuseppe

Rio terra San Giuseppe

Paludo S Antonio

Biennale
Internazionale
d'Arte

Via XXIV Maggio

Darsena
di Sant'Elena

Giardini
Pubblici

Via 1V Novembre

Viale Trento

Rio di Giardini

C dentro il Giardino

C Nervesa

Ramo d
Montello

C d Asiago

C d
Pozzo

Viale Piave

Giardini

C del Pasubio

C d Congregazione

C del Pasubio

C Duca d'Aosta

Campo
d'Grappa

C Montesanto

Fond Darsena

C del Carso

Viale Piave

C Podgora

Fond S Elena

Campo
Sportivo

C Gen Chinotto

Campo d'
Independenza

Rio S Elena

Sant'Elena

Ísola di
Sant'Elena

QUARTIERE
SANT'ELENA

C Duca d'Aosta

C del Carnaro

Viale S Elena

Campo
d Chiesa

Parco delle
Rimembranze

N   P   Q   R

REGIONS   CASTELLO • SIGHTS MAP

103

ARSENALE

The Arsenale, whose name derives from the Arabic 'Dar Sina'a', the place of industry, was Venice's industrial powerhouse, an ultra-efficient shipbuilding production line that built the galleys that made Venetian seapower a reality. The wealth of the city, its *palazzi*, churches, sumptuous art and sculpture all derived from the profits of its trade and empire—profits dependent on its merchant and war fleets. For a taste of what made the Republic tick, there's nowhere better than this huge, and now virtually deserted, complex. Shipbuilding started here in the 12th century; by the 15th more than 16,000 people were employed here and the workers were capable of assembling a galley in just a few hours, using the world's first production line. The interior of the Arsenale is still occupied by the Italian Navy, and is off-limits as a military zone, but it's worth heading to the main gates to see as much as you can. The gateway, designed by Antonio Gambello in 1460, is the first example of Renaissance classical architecture in the city. The capitals on its columns are Veneto-Byzantine; the lions guarding it a mixed bunch. Two were looted from Athens in 1687—one of them has runic inscriptions on its side, probably carved by a Norse mercenary in service with the Byzantine empire. Just off the Campo della Tana, on the other side of the canal, is the huge building which once housed the rope works, the Corderia. It's used during the Biennale (▷ 21) as an overflow exhibition space, and there are plans for further development of the area as a cultural centre.

✚ 102 L10 ✉ Campo dell'Arsenale, Castello 🚢 Arsenale

BIENNALE INTERNAZIONALE D'ARTE

www.labiennale.org

Founded in 1895 by the mayor of Venice, Riccardo Selvatico, the Esposizione Internazionale di Arte della Biennale di Venezia is a showcase for the best in modern art, alternating in odd-numbered years with the Architectural Biennale, which takes place in even years.

Though spin-off exhibitions take place all over the city, notably in the Corderia (▷ this page; part of the Arsenale complex), the main focus is in the series of permanent pavilions in the Giardini Pubblici (▷ 106). Each pavilion was built and is funded by the exhibiting countries; some are works of art in their own right. Best are Alvar Aalto's 1956 Finnish design and the 1961 Scandinavian pavilion by Sverre Fehn.

Criticized in the late 1980s and early 1990s for having lost its edge, the Biennale is now right back with the heavy players on the international contemporary arts scene, and attracts huge crowds during its mid-June to mid-November season. The organization that runs it is also responsible for the city's annual Film Festival (▷ 21) and the architecture, music and dance festivals.

✚ 103 N12 ✉ Giardini di Castello ☎ 041 521 8711 🕐 Daily 10–6 during the Biennale 💶 €18 🚢 Giardini, Arsenale

CAMPO SANTI GIOVANNI E PAOLO

If you're looking for a monumental open space, Campo Santi Giovanni e Paolo, wrapped around three sides of the church (▷ 112) with its west side bordered by a busy *rio*, is the richest in Venice after the Piazza. Standing triumphantly above the square is the bronze statue of the *condottiere* Bartolomeo Colleoni (1400–76), a mercenary who left his wealth to the Republic on condition that a monument was erected to him 'outside the Basilica di San Marco'. The city fathers, to whom the cult of anonymity was everything, were horrified. With true Venetian guile they solved the problem by placing the statue outside the Scuola Grande di San Marco, not the Basilica.

The Florentine sculptor Andrea Verrocchio won the commission for the statue in 1481, which was eventually completed after his death in 1488. It's a superb piece, epitomizing the ideal of the commercial soldier's military prowess. Look at Colleoni's coat-of-arms on the pedestal, which feature some pear-shaped objects. These are a play on the soldier's name; Colleoni sounds very like the word *coglioni* (testicles), a fine example of 15th-century humour.

To the west of the *campo*, flanking the church, is the facade of the Scuola itself, decorated with exquisite marble perspectival panels by brothers Tullio (*c*1455–1532) and Antonio Lombardo (*c*1458–1516). The interior is now home to Venice's major hospital, part of which is attached to the church of the Ospedaletto by Baldassare Longhena (1598–1682) at the east end of the square.

✚ 102 J8 ✉ Campo Santi Giovanni e Paolo, Castello 🚢 Fondamente Nuove

Opposite *Statue of Bartolomeo Colleoni in Campo Santi Giovanni e Paolo*
Below *The German pavilion in the Giardini Biennale*

CAMPO SANTA MARIA FORMOSA

Every *sestiere* has its own central square, and Campo Santa Maria Formosa is definitely the hub of this part of Castello. Heading from San Marco to the Rialto, or north to Santi Giovanni e Paolo, you're bound to pass through it, so pause and take in the local life. It has a good morning market where stalls groan with fruit and vegetables, a couple of bars and an eclectic mix of both ordinary and palatial buildings. The most noticeable is the Palazzo Priuli on the northeast side, built in the late 16th century. The Veneto-Byzantine Palazzo Vitturi is another stunner—look out for its Byzantine carvings. The *campo* is dominated by the church of Santa Maria Formosa (▷ 113), and has the usual selection of elderly ladies on the benches and screaming small children. It's an irregular shape, with *rii* on two sides crossed by a variety of bridges, one leading to the Fondazione Querini Stampalia (▷ 107).

✚ 102 H9 ✉ Campo Santa Maria Formosa, Castello 🚏 San Zaccaria, Rialto

CAMPO SAN ZACCARIA

The best way into Campo San Zaccaria, a quietly elegant square, is by turning off the Riva degli Schiavoni, past some tempting shops and into this wide, open space. The brick facade to the right of the church of San Zaccaria (▷ 114) is that of the 13th-century church that stood here; the next building along was a convent, considered to be the most debauched in Venice, with elegantly dressed nuns entertaining their lovers in the parlour and officiating at some of the city's most fashionable salons. Given that girls were often abandoned in convents by fathers with old titles but no money for dowries, there may be some excuse for their behaviour. The building is now Venice's main *carabinieri* station. San Zaccaria was the scene of the murder of two doges, Pietro Tradonico in 864 and Vitale Michiel II in 1172. The latter brought

disgrace to the Republic by failing in his peace negotiations with the Byzantines. Coming home empty-handed, he added insult to injury by bringing the plague with him, and was assassinated as he fled to the church for sanctuary. His killers were never caught, but, hedging their bets, the Senate later decreed that only wooden buildings could be constructed between the *campo* and the Palazzo Ducale, making it easier to flush out would-be murderers. Wooden buildings, seen in many old paintings, remained here for the next 800 years, until the law was rescinded in 1948. These were then replaced by the modern annexe to the Danieli hotel; it remains a moot point whether this constitutes an architectural improvement on the wooden structures.

✚ 102 J10 ✉ Campo San Zaccaria, Castello 🚏 San Zaccaria

GIARDINI PUBBLICI

After an overdose of architectural grandeur the Giardini Pubblici provide a good antidote. Stretching back from the east end of the Riva in Castello, the gardens were created by Napoleon in the early 19th century. If you've got children who need some exercise, or want a cool place for a picnic, head here. Much of the area is occupied by the pavilions used during the Biennale (▷ 105); you can see the various buildings partly hidden in the trees, though the area is closed except during the Biennale. The rest of the grassy space is dotted with pine trees and benches and there are wide views over the lagoon. Until the beginning of the 20th century, when the Riva was extended this far east, the only access was from Via Giuseppe Garibaldi through the Giardini Garibaldi. On the waterfront the Riva dei Sette Martiri stretches to the west; cross the first bridge to see the *Donna Partigiana*, a bronze waterside memorial figure to the partisans executed here in 1944. There's more green space to the east, where the Parco delle Rimembranze extends along

the waterfront of the Quartiere Sant'Elena, a separate island.

✚ 103 M12 ✉ Riva dei Partigiani, Castello ✋ Free 🚏 Giardini

MUSEO DIOCESANO D'ARTE SACRA

www.veneziaubc.org

Many Venetian churches have closed or been deconsecrated over the years, and the Museum of Sacred Diocesan Art is the repository for many of the treasures they once contained. This quirky little museum, tucked off the main route from San Zaccaria to the Piazza, displays an eclectic collection of religious objects and paintings, along with temporary exhibits stored here while restoration is undertaken. Its chief treasure, however, is not its art, but the exquisite cloister of Sant'Apollonia in whose buildings it's housed. This superb, tranquil spot is Venice's only example of Romanesque architecture and dates from the 12th to 13th centuries. Rounded arches, supported by an Istrian stone colonnade, surround the central space, beautifully paved with herring-bone brickwork.

✚ 102 H10 ✉ Chiostro di Sant'Apollonia, Sant'Apollonia, Castello 4312 ☎ 041 277 0561 🕐 Daily 10–6 ✋ Cloister and museum €4, cloister only €1 🚏 San Zaccaria

Below *The cloister of Sant'Apollonia*

MUSEO DELLA FONDAZIONE QUERINI STAMPALIA

www.querinistampalia.it

The Fondazione Querini Stampalia was founded in the 19th century by the aristocrat Giovanni Querini, who bequeathed his *palazzo*, his art collection and considerable funds to the city. His will specified that the money was to be used to open a reading room and library and to promote 'evening assemblies'. The Foundation has kept the faith in every way, and the Renaissance *palazzo* is busy through the day and into the evenings with students using its excellent facilities, while baroque concerts are a regular weekend feature. Between 1959 and 1963 the ground floor and garden were imaginatively redesigned by Carlo Scarpa to become one of Venice's few truly first-rate examples of modern architecture. This is the perfect foil for the palace's second-floor museum, spread through a series of delightful period rooms. Among the pictures there's a *Presentation in the Temple* by Giovanni Bellini (1430–1516) and two portraits by Palma il Vecchio (1548–1628) of 16th-century members of the Querini family. But the museum's main delight has to be the series of 67 pictures of Venetian festivals, customs and ceremonies by the 18th-century artist Gabriele Bella (active in Venice 1760) and the series of genre paintings of bourgeois life by Pietro Longhi (1702–85). These give charming glimpses into Venetian life, with interior scenes involving hairdressers and tailors and portrayals of outdoor pursuits, including a precarious boatload of sportsmen hunting duck.

✚ 102 J9 ✉ Campiello Querini Stampalia, Castello 5252 ☎ 041 271 1411 ◷ Tue–Sat 10–8, Sun 10–7 ✋ Adult €8; child (under 11) free; Rolling Venice and Venice Pass holders €6. Includes entrance to the concerts for museum visitors every Fri and Sat at 5 and 7 🚤 San Zaccaria

MUSEO STORICO NAVALE

▷ 108.

Above *The classical frontage of the Renaissance Palazzo Grimani displays Roman and Tuscan elements, unusual in Venice*

PALAZZO GRIMANI

www.palazzogrimani.org

In a city whose domestic architectural keynotes are Venetian-Gothic or baroque, the stunning Palazzo Grimani shines as a Renaissance jewel. Built in the early 1500s by Doge Antonio Grimani, it passed to his heirs, Vittore, *procuratore generale* of Venice, and Giovanni, Patriarch of Aquileia, a passionate collector of antiquities. Between 1532 and 1569 the brothers completed Antonio's work, incorporating Roman and Tuscan decorative elements that are extremely rare in Venice. These classically inspired motifs were intended to make the architecture a fitting backdrop for Giovanni's antiquities, which were displayed in a series of splendid rooms around a three-sided courtyard decorated with exceptional stucco detail. Artists from central Italy, particularly Francesco Salviato and Federico Zuccari, were responsible for the frescoed and decorated chambers, rich in marble and gilded stucco, and illuminated by light streaming in from the courtyard and adjoining *rio*. After its completion, the *palazzo* rapidly became one of the most famous buildings in Venice, and Henry III of France put a visit to it at the top of his wish list when he came to the city in 1574.

A grand staircase, modelled on the Scala d'Oro of the Doge's Palace, leads up to the *piano nobile*, whose rooms, with their rational design and multi-coloured marble flooring, are more reminiscent of what you might find in Florence than anything of that date in Venice. Highlights include the polychrome marble Tribuna, a showpiece gallery for the most important pieces of sculpture, and the beautiful Sala ai Fogliami, its ceiling a naturalistic mass of interwoven frescoed trees and flowers, rich in identifiable birds and animals. Look too, for the frescoed Sala di Psiche, and the intricate gilded plasterwork throughout the *palazzo*. Neglected and decaying for decades, the palace was purchased by the Italian State in 1981, and finally re-opened after 27 years of restoration in late 2008; it's considered Venice's most important new restoration and museum.

✚ 102 J9 ✉ Ramo Grimani, Castello 4858 ☎ 041 520 0345 ◷ Guided tours in Italian only, which must be pre-booked: Tue–Sun 10, 12 and 3. Closed 1 Jan and 25 Dec ✋ Adult €8 (+ €1 reservation fee); EU residents under 18 free (but with €1 reservation fee) 🚤 Rialto, San Zaccaria

INFORMATION

MUSEO STORICO NAVALE

This superb collection of ships, models and nautical ephemera that places Venice's relationship with the sea in a clear historical context is housed a stone's throw from the Arsenale in an incomparable waterside position.

So entwined were Venetian fortunes with ships and the sea that the Republic established a ship museum as early as the 17th century, when the Casa dei Modelli was set up to display models of ships that were built in the Arsenale. Many of these disappeared during the Napoleonic occupation, but those remaining formed the nucleus of the present museum, set up during the Austrian administration in an old granary building. It came under the directorship of the Italian navy in 1919, and presents a complete overview of Venetian and Italian naval history. Don't expect modern presentation or interactive exhibits; this is an old-fashioned gem that will appeal to adults and children alike; with more than 25,000 exhibits there's something for everyone.

THE COLLECTION'S HIGHLIGHTS

The museum covers every aspect of maritime life, with models and fragments of ships through the ages, nautical and navigational instruments, uniforms, medals, charts and maps, maritime paintings, guns and artillery, Far Eastern vessels, model cruise ships and liners and a huge shell collection. Inevitably, the most interesting exhibits are those that major on Venice itself, particularly the city's traditional and ceremonial vessels. You can admire a scale model of the *Bucintoro*, the gilded barge used by the Doge in the Ascension Day ceremony of the marriage to the sea, and two *cortele*, decorated galley sides, dating from the 16th century; both on the first floor. On the third floor there's an excellent room devoted to the gondola, where you can learn about the boat's history and construction. Here you'll see a 19th-century gondola with the traditional cover, or *felze*, and one of the last privately owned gondolas in Venice, which belonged to Peggy Guggenheim. There's a series of naïf ex voto paintings, mainly from Naples, showing dramatic scenes of shipwrecks and storms at sea. These were commissioned in thanksgiving for deliverance by those rescued from peril on the sea, and were hung in parish churches, normally near the image to which the donor was devoted. There's an annexe, the Padiglione delle Navi (Ships' Pavilion), in an old oar-makers' shed down the *fondamenta* near the entrance to the Arsenale. Here, if it's open, you can see painted fishing boats, a funeral barge and ceremonial galleys.

Above *A 19th-century gondola is one of many vessels on display at Museo Storico Navale*

SANT'ELENA

Until the 19th century, Sant'Elena was a separate island as the city ended at the site of the Biennale (▷ 105). The occupying Austrians needed space to house and exercise their troops, and they reclaimed land from the lagoon and connected this new quarter to the city by bridges. It was later given over to apartment blocks, leaving the original island of Sant'Elena as the home of a naval college, Venice's football ground and an ancient church. The original church was founded here in the second half of the 12th century to house the body of Sant'Elena (c257–336), mother of the Roman emperor Constantine. First an Augustinian monastery, it was ceded by Pope Gregory II to the Benedictines in the 1430s, who rebuilt the church in the Gothic style. The doorway, moved here from Sant'Aponal near the Rialto in 1929, has a lovely lunette showing Vittore Cappello, a Venetian admiral who died fighting the Turks in 1467, kneeling before the Virgin. Sant'Elena lies in a chapel to the right of the entrance, though this is a moot point, as the Aracoeli church in Rome also claims to house the saint's body.

✚ 103 Q13 ✉ Campo Chiesa, Castello ☎ 041 205 155 🕐 Mon–Sat 5–7, Sun 9–12.30 ✋ Free ⛴ Sant'Elena

SAN FRANCESCO DELLA VIGNA

The superb Palladian church of San Francesco della Vigna in the northeast of Castello is one of Venice's best-kept secrets. It's a bit of a hike through a shabby area of Venice near the old gasworks to reach San Francesco della Vigna, a church standing in one of the most historic areas of the city. It was here, according to legend, that an angel appeared to St. Mark and told him that the lagoon islands were to be his final home. Later, the area was planted with vines, and when the Franciscans were given the land in 1253 they commemorated this in the name of their church.

Their first structure was demolished in the late 15th century and in 1534 work began on a new building, masterminded by Sansovino (1486–1570), a Renaissance architect from Tuscany. Some 30 years later, in 1568, Andrea Palladio was brought in to design the facade, a monumental stunner in pure white Istrian stone that's the first of his trademark superimposed temple fronts. It follows the design of Greek temples and is worth a few minutes' study to appreciate the perfect proportions of each element. Inside, there are further treats among the rational, humanistic design, with its broad nave and side chapels, dreamed up by the scholar monk Francesco Zorzi. As a Franciscan, he held to the tenets of modesty and restraint, a notion that disappears in the side chapels, decorated by the families who paid for them. To the left of the chancel is the Cappella Giustiniani, whose walls are adorned with marvellous sculptured reliefs by the Lombardo family. Off here, a door leads to the Cappella Santa, with a serene *Madonna and Child* by Giovanni Bellini (1430–1516). From here, you can access the peaceful cloisters. Back in the church, head for the right transept where you'll find a *Madonna and Child Enthroned* (c1460) by the Greek Antonio da Negroponte, a synthesis of Renaissance style and Gothic imagery that shows the Virgin surrounded by fruit and flowers. Elsewhere there are two Veronese canvases; the *Holy Family with Saints* (c1551) in the fifth chapel on the left was his first commissioned work in Venice.

✚ 102 K9 ✉ Campo di San Francesco, Castello 2786 ☎ 041 520 6102 🕐 Daily 8–12.30, 3–7 ✋ Free ⛴ Ospedale, Celestina

Below Resurrection, *attributed to Veronese, in a chapel of San Francesco della Vigna*

INFORMATION

✚ 102 K10 ✉ Campo San Giovanni in Bragora, Castello 2464 ☎ 041 520 5906
🕐 Mon–Sat 9–11, 3.30–5.30 🎟 Free
🚇 Arsenale

SAN GIOVANNI IN BRAGORA

The historic church of San Giovanni in Bragora is set in a quiet and spacious square with strong Vivaldi connections. Popular legend puts the foundation of San Giovanni in Bragora in the early eighth century, making it one of the oldest churches in the lagoon, though there's no proof for this whatsoever, as the earliest written records of its existence date from 1090. The curious name is shrouded in mystery and explanations range from a derivation of the dialect word *brago*, meaning mud, through *bragolare*, to fish, to *agora*, the Greek word for an important public square. The patron saint is St. John the Baptist, whose body the Venetians claimed to have brought to Venice from the East. Construction started on the present church in 1475, making it one of the last Gothic churches in the city—it was built around the same time as the Renaissance San Michele (▷ 111). The interior does show some drift towards Renaissance architecture, which you can see best by comparing the Gothic nave with the chancel. There was once a choir in the nave, which was demolished in the 18th century; look for the slightly raised floor under the last span of the nave to see where it once stood.

THE PAINTINGS

The Gothic interior houses three splendid pictures. Over the high altar there's a *Baptism of Christ* (1492) by Cima da Conegliano, a calm, perfectly balanced scene with a landscape background that's reminiscent of the countryside around the artist's home town of Conegliano, which also figures in the scene. Cima is also responsible for the painting to the right of the sacristy door, depicting *St. Helen and St. Constantine* (1501). On the left of the sacristy door is a 1498 *Resurrection* by Alvise Vivarini, where the figure of Christ is based on a classical statue of Apollo, still to be seen in the Museo Archeologico.

THE VIVALDI CONNECTION

Vivaldi's music is inexorably entwined with Venice, and his life with this church. He was born in one of the houses on the *campo* and baptized in the ornate red marble font, which started life as the capital of a Gothic column. On the wall to the right of the font are copies of the original baptismal registration, dated 6 May 1678. There's a plaque on the outside wall recording that the *Prete Rosso* (Red Priest) was baptized in San Giovanni. Vivaldi is often known by this nickname, which refers either to his red hair or the red cassock he often wore.

Above *Above the high altar is* The Baptism of Christ *by Cima da Conegliano*

SAN GIORGIO DEGLI GRECI

Greeks first came to Venice in the 11th century, and their numbers increased hugely after the fall of Constantinople to the Turks in 1453. In the heady atmosphere of the Renaissance they were particularly welcome as scholars, artists, scribes and publishers, while the goods shipped in by Greek merchants sold well throughout Venice. They became the largest ethnic group after Jewish people, their presence greatly enriching the cultural life of the city. The community was soon confident enough to apply for its own church in which to celebrate Mass according to the Orthodox rites, and in 1470 permission came for the establishment of a church, college and Scuola.

In 1526 the Greeks purchased land and commissioned Sante Lombardo to design a church, most of which was constructed between 1539 and 1561. The cupola and splendidly leaning campanile were added later. A century later, in 1678, Baldassare Longhena designed the Collegio Flanghini and the Scuola di San Nicolò dei Greci; the college now houses the Hellenic Centre for Byzantine and Post-Byzantine Studies and the Greek archives (www.istitutoellenico.org), while the Scuola is home to the Museo dei Dipinti Sacri Bizantini (Museum of Greek Sacred Paintings, tel 041 522 6581; daily 9–5). The interior of the church is Greek Orthodox in style, with a *matroneo* (women's gallery) and iconostasis, a solid, richly ornamented screen blocking off the main altar from the body of the church and behind which most of the celebration of the Mass takes place. Some of the icons (sacred paintings) date from the 12th century, but many are 16th-century examples by Michael Danaskinàs, a friend and contemporary of Domenikos Theotokopoulos, another Greek artist living in Venice, and better known as El Greco. There are more icons, as well as other religious objects, in the adjacent museum. Most date from the

15th to 18th centuries and form one of Europe's most important icon collections.

➕ 102 J10 ✉ Fondamenta dei Greci, Castello 3412 ☎ 041 523 9569 🕐 Wed–Mon 9–11, 2.30–4.30 💰 Free 🚤 San Zaccaria

SAN GIOVANNI IN BRAGORA
▷ 110.

SANTI GIOVANNI E PAOLO
▷ 112.

SANTA MARIA FORMOSA
▷ 113.

SANTA MARIA DELLA VISITAZIONE

The white facade of Santa Maria della Visitazione, also known as La Pietà, punctuates the eastern stretch of the Riva degli Schiavoni (▷ 72–73). It is linked with the Venetian composer Antonio Vivaldi, who was choirmaster at the adjoining orphanage. He wrote many of his finest pieces to be performed by the orphanage musicians, so renowned for their musical prowess that often parents tried to pass their children off as orphans to get them into the orchestra or choir.

The church's rebuilding started in 1745, and Vivaldi probably advised the architect, Giorgio Massari (1687–1766), for few other churches have such fine acoustics. For years it has been one of the major venues for Venice's series of baroque concerts. In 2007 the church closed for restoration, with no date, as yet, given for its re-opening, and its resident orchestra now performs elsewhere (▷ 119). The small Vivaldi museum behind the church remains open; simply walk down the *calle* to No. 4701.

➕ 102 K10 ✉ Riva degli Schiavoni, Castello ☎ 041 523 1096 🕐 Open occasionally during music festivals. Piccolo Museo de la Pietà Mon, Wed 11–4 🚤 San Zaccaria

SAN MICHELE

It's a short hop on the *vaporetto* to Venice's wonderfully atmospheric

cemetery island. Most of Ísola di San Michele is covered by the cemetery, where Venetians are buried in tiers of stone drawers or rest under monuments. The cemetery was established in 1807 during the Napoleonic era when city burials were forbidden, but bodies only lie here for 10 years before being removed to ossuaries on other lagoon islands. A sleek and minimal extension, to the island's east, was designed by British architect David Chipperfield. To enter the cemetery you will pass Mauro Codussi's beautiful church of San Michele in Ísola (1469), beautifully restored by UK-based Venice in Peril. The first truly Renaissance church in Venice, it bears an Istrian stone facing that inspired every gleaming white facade in the city.

➕ Off map 102 K7 ✉ Ísola di San Michele ☎ 041 729 2811 🕐 Apr–end Sep daily 7.30–6; Oct–end Mar daily 7.30–4; 25 Dec, 1 Jan 7.30–noon 💰 Free 🚤 Cimitero

SAN PIETRO DI CASTELLO

www.chorusvenezia.org
At the far eastern end of Castello stands the island of San Pietro, reached by two long bridges. Its church is one of oldest foundations in Venice and, until 1807, it was the city's cathedral. The still stately, but ramshackle old *palazzo* to the right of the church was once the Bishop's Palace. The present church was designed by Palladio (1508–80). The interior is high and bare, with the atmosphere of a humble parish church. Look for St. Peter's Throne in the right-hand aisle, a carved marble seat from Antioch that incorporates an Arabic funerary stele inscribed with verses from the Koran. The splendidly baroque high altar was designed by Baldassare Longhena in 1649 as a setting for the funerary urn of San Lorenzo Giustiniani, the first patriarch of Venice.

➕ 103 P10 ✉ Campo San Pietro di Castello, Castello 70 ☎ 041 275 0462 🕐 Mon–Sat 10–5. Closed 1 Jan, Easter, 15 Aug, 25 Dec 💰 Chorus Pass (for all churches in Chorus group) €9, single ticket €3 🚤 Giardini

INFORMATION

✚ 102 J8 ✉ Campo Santi Giovanni e Paolo, Castello ☎ 041 523 5913 🕒 Mon–Sat 9–6.30, Sun 3–6.30 💶 €2.50 🚤 Fondamente Nuove, Ospedale 📗 Guidebooks in Italian, English, French and German €3.60; audioguides in Italian, English and French €1

SANTI GIOVANNI E PAOLO

The Gothic church of Santi Giovanni e Paolo, known in the Venetian dialect as San Zanipolo, lies in one of the city's most spacious squares, complete with a splendid equestrian statue and the magnificent facade of what was once one of the grandest of all Venice's *scuole*. Try to choose a sunny day to come as the interior of the church can be very dark if it's gloomy outside.

Santi Giovanni e Paolo is a huge church, typical of all churches constructed by mendicant orders, who needed space to accommodate many people. The church is built of red brick with stone ornamentation, complete with a soaring facade. The main doorway, flanked by the tomb of Doge Tiepolo, who donated the land for the church, is surrounded by Byzantine reliefs and marble columns. The Cappella di Sant'Orsola (closed) is the burial place of Gentile (1429–1507) and Giovanni Bellini (1430–1516), two of Venice's finest painters.

THE MOCENIGO MONUMENTS

The west wall is devoted entirely to the glorification of the Mocenigo dynasty, one of Venice's most prominent families. They secured the services of the Lombardo family, the city's best sculptors, and all three—Pietro, Tullio and Antonio—have works here. The superb tomb on the left of the entrance commemorates Doge Pietro Mocenigo, whose sarcophagus, decorated with episodes from the his life, is supported by warriors representing the three Ages of Man and crowned with a statue of Mocenigo himself. The reliefs depict the labours of Hercules, and the Latin inscription suggests that his enemies' money paid for it all. The central monument, around the door, commemorates Alvise Mocenigo, and that on the right, Giovanni.

SAINTS VINCENT FERRER, CHRISTOPHER AND SEBASTIAN (GIOVANNI BELLINI)

The second altar on the right displays Giovanni Bellini's beautiful polyptych *Saints Vincent Ferrer, Christopher and Sebastian*. Painted in 1465, it is among the artist's earlier works, but already shows his innovative handling of light. St. Vincent, the central figure, was a fiery preacher. On the left, St. Christopher crosses the river carrying the Christ Child, while St. Sebastian, liberally punctured by the arrows of his martyrdom, is on the right. The panels above the saints show the annunciation on either side of a *Pietà*, and the *predella* panels, below the saints, depict miracles performed by St. Vincent.

Above *The spacious nave was designed to accommodate the crowds that flocked to this preaching church*

SANTA MARIA FORMOSA

The Renaissance church of Santa Maria Formosa stands in a rambling and lovely *campo* in Castello. The irregular space of the Campo Santa Maria Formosa (▷ 106) is edged with fine *palazzi*, but dominated by the church itself, the first of eight sanctuaries founded on the lagoon in the seventh century by St. Magno, Bishop of Oderzo. The Virgin appeared to him as a buxom and shapely matron—*formosa*—and instructed him to follow a white cloud and build a church wherever it settled. St. Magno built a now-vanished church, which was replaced in the 11th century by a typically Byzantine Greek-cross plan structure. Once a year, it was visited by the doge in commemoration of the rescue by the parishioners of some young women who had been abducted. For reasons lost in time, a straw hat was traditionally presented to the doge to commemorate his visit.

THE CHURCH

The present church of Santa Maria Formosa was the first in Venice to be revamped according to Renaissance ideals, an architectural *tour de force* given the retention of the original Byzantine plan. It was designed by Mauro Codussi in 1492, when the earlier church was beginning to show signs of deterioration. The church has two facades, one on the canal (1542) and one on the *campo* (1604), both added after Codussi's death; the campanile is baroque. The canalside frontage was financed by the Cappello family, though the little relief of a mortar to the right of the door is much later. This commemorates the destruction of the dome in 1916 by an Austrian incendiary bomb; it was rebuilt in 1921.

The interior has a Renaissance Latin-cross plan superimposed on the Greek, giving an overwhelming impression of space and balance. The three naves are almost the same length as the barrel-vaulted side chapels, which they intersect at domed cross vaults, producing an interior where the space is as central to the architecture as the solid stone—a key aspect of Renaissance design.

Two paintings are worth tracking down. One, in the first chapel on the south (right) side, is a triptych (1473) by Bartolomeo Vivarini showing the *Madonna della Misericordia*—the Virgin sheltering the faithful beneath her cloak; it was paid for by parishioners, and some of the kneeling figures are believed to be portraits of the donors. The other, near the main altar, is Palma il Vecchio's *Santa Barbara* (1522–24), an early martyr put to death by her own father.

INFORMATION

www.chorusvenezia.org

✚ 102 J9 ✉ Campo Santa Maria Formosa, Castello 5263 ☎ 041 275 0462 🕐 Mon–Sat 10–5. Closed 1 Jan, Easter, 15 Aug, 25 Dec 🎟 Chorus Pass (for all churches in Chorus group) €9, single ticket €3 🚤 San Zaccaria

Above Santa Barbara and Saints *by Palma il Vecchio*

INFORMATION

➕ 102 J10 ✉ Campo San Zaccaria, Castello 4693 ☎ 041 522 1257
🕐 Mon–Sat 10–12, 4–6, Sun 11–12, 4–6 💵 Free; chapels of St. Tarasius and St. Athanasius, sacristy and crypt €1.50
🚤 San Zaccaria

THE PRICE OF COLOUR

Venetian Renaissance artists relied on natural pigments, brought in from all over Europe and beyond. Browns and greys were easily obtainable—brown umber from Umbria, burnt Siena from Tuscany, Naples yellow from the slopes of Vesuvius. It was the reds, blues and golds that pushed the price of paintings up. In the 16th century Venice was the world's most important trading centre for red paints, made from the South American cochineal insect. The heavenly azure of the Virgin's robe in Bellini's *Madonna and Child with Saints* in San Zaccaria is painted with ultramarine, an intense blue pigment obtained from the mineral lapis lazuli and worth more than its weight in gold.

Below *San Zaccaria is a mix of architectural styles*

SAN ZACCARIA

The lovely church of San Zaccaria is a beguiling blend of Gothic and Renaissance architecture, with works spanning the development of Venetian painting. San Zaccaria, dedicated to the father of John the Baptist, who is said to be buried in the church, is the only Venetian church with an ambulatory and a crypt. It's set on Campo San Zaccaria (▷ 106), not far from San Marco, and had strong medieval links with the basilica—the doge came here annually for Easter Mass. The first Byzantine church was founded here in the ninth century and altered in the 10th, before receiving another overhaul between 1170 and 1174, when the campanile was added. The 14th century saw yet another update, this time in the Gothic style, but no sooner was the work complete than the Benedictines, who owned it, decided on a complete rebuild. Work started in 1458 and continued for more than a century, resulting in a building that incorporates both Gothic and Renaissance styles. You can see this best in the facade, the work of Antonio Gambello (c1460–1537) and Mauro Codussi (c1440–1504): Gothic as far as door level, and firmly Renaissance in the upper portion. To the right of this, the brick facade of the older church is still visible behind a little garden.

THE TREASURES

Inside, you'll notice the rib-vaulted ambulatory at once, an elegant ring of elliptical cupolas around the high altar, lit by long windows, the only ones in Venice so reminiscent of northern European Gothic. Looking around, the church is filled with 17th- and 18th-century paintings of distinctly variable quality. Standing artistically apart from the majority is Giovanni Bellini's luminously stunning *Madonna and Child with Saints* in the second chapel on the left. Painted in 1505, it's one of the city's great paintings, perfectly set in a contemporary frame whose design echoes the architectural elements of the work. It's worth visiting the Chapels of St. Athanasius and St. Tarasius in the right aisle. St. Tarasius' chapel was once part of the original church and houses three ornate *ancone*—wonderfully hieratic pictures in sumptuous gold Gothic frames—by Antonio Vivarini (c1415–76/84) and Giovanni d'Alemagna (died 1450). This chapel also gives access to the permanently waterlogged crypt, burial place of eight early doges.

SCUOLA DI SAN GIORGIO DEGLI SCHIAVONI

This intimate little building contains one of the most accurately observed and charming of all picture cycles, full of vivid detail. The Slavs, inhabitants of the Dalmatian (modern Croatia) coast on the Adriatic, first came to Venice as slaves but, by the 15th century, were sufficiently established as merchants and sailors to set up a *scuola* to protect their interests. Around 1500 a purpose-built *scuola* was created and in 1502 Vittore Carpaccio was commissioned to decorate the walls of the upper meeting chamber with episodes from the lives of Dalmatia's three patrons, St. George, St. Tryphon and St. Jerome. The work was completed between 1507 and 1509, and the paintings were subsequently moved to the ground floor when the building was enlarged in 1551. They are still here today, the only one of Carpaccio's cycles to remain in the *scuola* for which it was painted.

THE PAINTINGS

The Carpaccio cycle occupies the upper part of the walls of the *scuola*'s ground-floor hall, a dimly lit, wood-panelled chamber that's entered straight from the street. The narrative starts on the left-hand wall with the story of *St. George and the Dragon*, with the saint thrusting his lance into the creature's throat while the princess, surrounded by half-dismembered corpses, looks on. In the next picture, the *Triumph of St. George*, the dragon is finished off and the entire town converted to Christianity, with baptisms taking place in the next panel, *St. George Baptizing the Gentiles*. St. Tryphon, an obscure saint from Asia Minor, appears next, exorcizing a devil from the Roman Emperor's daughter—the demon appearing as a remarkably innocuous looking basilisk. The following two pictures show the *Agony in the Garden* and the *Calling of St. Matthew*, and the right-hand wall has three episodes from the *Life of St. Jerome*, an early father of the church, who, as we see in the first panel, earned a lion's undying devotion when he removed a thorn from its paw. The second picture shows the funeral of the saint, complete with the lion mourning in the background, while the third shows *St. Augustine in his Study* at the moment he had a vision of Jerome's death. This last is among Venice's best-loved paintings, a meticulously observed depiction of a 16th-century study that includes one of the most appealing little dogs ever painted.

INFORMATION

✚ 102 K9 ✉ Fondamenta dei Furlani, Castello 3259A ☎ 041 520 8446
🕐 Mon 2.45–6, Tue–Sat 9.15–1, 2.45–6, Sun 9.15–1. Closed 1 May, 15 Aug, 21 Nov ✋ €4 🚢 Arsenale, San Zaccaria
📖 Leaflet in Italian, English and French

TIP

» Allow time for your eyes to accustom to the dim light, and take time to pick out the wealth of detail in the paintings.

Below *The Scuola di San Giorgio degli Schiavoni lies tucked away in a little alley*

SAN MARCO TO THE ARSENALE AND CASTELLO

This walk takes you through Castello, a wonderfully varied *sestiere*, which includes some of the city's great churches and monuments. These contrast admirably with the everyday life of the local area, with its quiet residential streets, shops, markets and green spaces.

THE WALK

Distance: 3.2km (2 miles)
Time: 1.5–2 hours
Start at: San Zaccaria *vaporetto* stop
End at: Giardini *vaporetto* stop

HOW TO GET THERE

Take *vaporetto* No. 1, 2, 41, 42, 51 or 52 to San Zaccaria.

★ With your back to the water, turn right and cross the Ponte del Vin, taking the second left turn (yellow sign to San Zaccaria) into Campo San Zaccaria (▷ 106), home to one of Venice's most interesting churches (▷ 114). Leave the *campo* in the left-hand corner along Salizzada San Provolo. This widens out into Campo Santi Filippo e Giacomo. Walk on to the next bridge. Just before this on the left is the entrance to the Museo

Diocesano d'Arte Sacra (▷ 106). At the bridge, look left for a wonderful view of the Ponte di Sospiri.

❶ This is one of best, and least crowded, places from which to photograph the Bridge of Sighs, with the canal in the foreground and the Riva degli Schiavoni behind.

Walk on, bear right, then take the first right up Rama Va in Canonica, which crosses a busy street into Calle dell'Angelo. Cross the bridge at the end and turn right to walk briefly beside a canal, then turn left. Take the first right, then a left, and then a right onto Calle Ponte de la Guerra, which becomes Calle de la Banda. Cross another bridge to arrive in Campo Santa Maria Formosa (▷ 106). After visiting the

church (▷ 113), head right down Calle Lunga Santa Maria Formosa, and take the third left (blue sign for Ospedale, yellow sign for Santi Giovanni e Paolo), up to cross a bridge. Continue up Calle Bressana to emerge into Campo Santi Giovanni e Paolo (▷ 105). To the left of the church's main door is the former Scuola Grande di San Marco, now Venice's main hospital.

❷ The hospital's facade was started by Pietro Lombardo and Giovanni Buora in 1487, and completed in 1495 by Mauro Codussi. Its chief glories are the *trompe-l'oeil* panels by Tullio and Antonio Lombardi, showing episodes from the life of St. Mark and his lion.

Above *The pediment of the Arsenale*

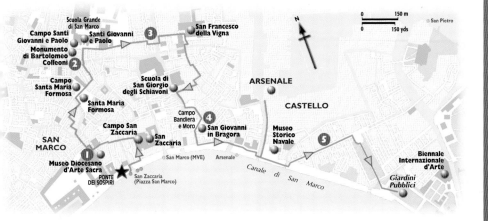

If you're not visiting the church
(▷ 112), turn immediately right and
head along Salizzada Santi Giovanni
e Paolo (Zanipolo). This stretch of
alleyway changes names several
times, but keeps its direction and
will lead you to a T-junction and the
Campiello Santa Giustina. Take the
diagonally right turning ahead
down Calle Zen, crossing the Rio di
Santa Giustina.

❸ The Rio di Santa Giustina is one
of Castello's main arteries, cutting
through from the lagoon to the
Bacino di San Marco. From the
bridge, there's a fine view onto the
lagoon and the cemetery island of
San Michele.

Across the bridge, turn left, then
right onto Calle San Francesco.
Ahead looms the facade of the
Franciscan church of San Francesco
della Vigna (▷ 109). Turn right and
cross the *campo* to pass under the
colonnade. Cross the bridge and
keep straight on, then bear left into
Calle delle Gatte. Follow this to
Campo delle Gatte and bear right
through the square into Calle Riello.
Take the first right onto Calle dei
Furlani, which brings you to the
Scuola di San Giorgio degli Schiavoni
(▷ 115). Turn left and walk beside
the canal, then left at the next bridge
into Salizzada San Antonin. At the

bottom don't miss the tiny alley to
the right, which leads into Campo
Bandiera e Moro.

❹ This quiet square houses the
church of San Giovanni in Bragora
(▷ 110) and the lovely Palazzo Gritti-
Badoer.

Cross the square diagonally right and
down Calle de Dose to the Riva degli
Schiavoni. Turn left and walk along
the Riva, crossing two bridges to
arrive at the Museo Storico Navale
(▷ 108). From here you can detour
along the right-hand side of the
canal to the entrance to the Arsenale
(▷ 105), retracing your steps to
continue along the waterfront
towards the heart of working-class
Castello, based around vibrant Via
Giuseppe Garibaldi.

❺ Via Giuseppe Garibaldi is the
widest street in Venice. Look for the
plaque on the wall of a house on
the right, which commemorates the
explorers John and Sebastian Cabot,
who once lived here.

Walk down past the market stalls
and turn right into tree-lined Viale
Garibaldi, which leads to the Giardini
Pubblici (▷ 106), home to the
Biennale (▷ 105) and a peaceful
green spot to relax.

WHEN TO GO
Morning is a good time for this walk;
churches and museums are open
and the streets are at their liveliest
with locals doing the daily shopping.

WHERE TO EAT
You could have a break at one of
the bars in Campo Santi Giovanni e
Paolo, or in Via Garibaldi. There are
numerous down-to-earth bars and
restaurants here, or you could pick
up a picnic at the market.

Below *View towards Ponte dei Sospiri*

REGIONS CASTELLO • WALK

SHOPPING

AL CAMPANIL

www.artigianatovenezianobeadsandglass.it
Come here for really unusual and pretty glass jewellery, the design imaginative, very fine and uncluttered. You'll find strings of tiny beads on chain and cord, dainty strings to wind several times round wrists or throat, huge single beads on knotted silk and twisted ropes of multi-coloured strings of beads.
✚ 124 J9 ✉ Calle Lunga Santa Maria Formosa, Castello 5184 ☎ 041 523 5734 ⏰ Mon–Sat 10–1, 3.30–7
🚊 San Zaccaria

ANTICLEA ANTIQUARIATO

This tiny treasure house overflows with cabinets and drawers full of antique beads, and is hung with quirky antiques. You can buy ready-made pieces or wait while they fashion beads of your choice into earrings, bracelets and necklaces.
✚ 124 J10 ✉ Calle San Provolo, Castello 4719A ☎ 041 528 6946 ⏰ Daily 10–7.15
🚊 San Zaccaria

ARABESQUE BARBIERI

Elegant little Arabesque Barbieri sells nothing but scarves, stoles and pashminas in silk, wool, cashmere and a wonderful range of colours and styles; all tracked down by the English-speaking owner, who has excellent contacts in the silk-weaving towns around Lake Garda.
✚ 124 J9 ✉ Ponte dei Greci, Castello 3403 ☎ 041 522 8177 ⏰ Mon–Sat 10–1, 3.30–7.30 🚊 San Zaccaria

AZIMUTS

This wonderful little treasure trove of a shop is crammed with nautical ephemera—everything from model yachts, fishing boats and gondolas, to china, charts and maps, as well as sea-faring books, photographs, and a few special pieces of jewellery with a maritime theme—look for the lovely silver sea shells and coral.
✚ 124 J8 ✉ Calle dell'Ospitaletto, Castello 6400 ☎ 041 523 4240 ⏰ Mon–Sat 10–1, 3.30–7 🚊 San Zaccaria

LIBRERIA ACQUA ALTA

This immensely browsable shop is a one-off, with its cluttered interior dominated by a gondola serving as a book display stand, and its walls stacked high with new and second-hand books. The multi-lingual owner is an enthusiast, who will go to great trouble to find something of interest. The accent of the stock is on Venice, and you'll also find photographs, posters and a selection of gifts.
✚ 124 J9 ✉ Calle Lunga Santa Maria Formosa, Castello 5176 ☎ 041 296 0841 ⏰ Mon–Sat 10–1, 3–7.30
🚊 San Zaccaria

MARCO POLO

Bruno Tagliapietra is renowned for his sumptuous and exquisite hand-blocked and figured damask velvets, made in the traditional Venetian style. Richly coloured fabric is made up into cushions, bedspreads, stoles and scarves of voluptuous beauty—not cheap, but a souvenir to hand on to the next generation.
✚ 124 L11 ✉ Via Garibaldi, Castello 1696 ☎ 041 523 2716 ⏰ Mon–Sat 10–12.30, 4–7.45. If closed ask at Castello 1764 for access 🚊 Arsenale

LA PADOVANA

This leather store has been pulling in locals and visitors for years, for their classic, middle-range shoes, and accessories, such as belts and purses. Not cutting edge

fashion-wise but well-made.
⊞ 124 J10 ⊠ Campo SS Filippo e Giacomo, Castello 4272 ☎ 041 522 4106 🕓 Mon 3–7, Tue–Sat 10–1, 3–7 🚤 San Zaccaria

ENTERTAINMENT AND NIGHTLIFE
FLORIDITA
Down in deepest Via Garibaldi, hot and steamy Floridita throbs to the sounds of salsa and merengue. Dancing is almost compulsory. Credit cards are not accepted.
⊞ 124 M11 ⊠ Via Garibaldi, Castello 68 ☎ 041 419 6963 🕓 Fri 9pm–4am 💷 €10 🚤 Arsenale

FONDAZIONE QUERINI STAMPALIA
www.querinistampalia.it
This cultural institution organizes artistic events, with regular Friday and Saturday classical concerts held in the opulent surroundings of a 15th-century *palazzo salone*. Credit cards are not accepted.
⊞ 124 J9 ⊠ Campiello Querini Stampalia, Castello 5252 ☎ 041 271 1411 🕓 Fri–Sat 5 and 8.30pm 💷 Adult €8, child €6, (including museum and exhibition admission) 🚤 Rialto, San Zaccaria

GIORGIONE
Venetians flock to this *trattoria*-cum-pizzeria for the quality food, Friulian wines and Venetian folk music. The owner, Lucio Bisutto, is one of the art's leading exponents and frequently performs his all-singing and a little dancing 'fisherman's tales from the *osterie*'.
⊞ 124 M11 ⊠ Via Giuseppe Garibaldi, Castello 1533 ☎ 041 522 8727 🕓 Thu–Tue 8pm–11pm 🚤 Giardini

MELOGRANO
On Saturday nights local jazz bands appear at this popular bar near the Giardini. It's also a great place to try *cicchetti* and some decent tipples,

away from the crowds.
⊞ 124 L11 ⊠ Riva VII Martiri, Castello 1643 ☎ 041 241 4196 🕓 Tue–Sun 8am–1am 🚤 Giardini

SANTA MARIA FORMOSA
www.collegiumducale.com
The 15th-century church of Santa Maria Formosa in Castello plays host to the Collegium Ducale orchestra. As well as baroque chamber music, there's a good smattering of favourite operatic pieces, from Albinoni to Rossini. Credit cards are not accepted.
⊞ 124 J9 ⊠ Campo Santa Maria Formosa, Castello 2542 ☎ 041 984 2542 🕓 Telephone for latest details 💷 €20–€25 🚤 San Zaccaria

SANTA MARIA DELLA VISITAZIONE (LA PIETÀ)
The celebrated Venetian composer Vivaldi (1678–1741) had a life-long connection with the church of Santa Maria della Visitazione, the Pietà (▷ 111). While the church is undergoing restoration, the three groups that normally perform here (all in 18th-century costume), the Virtuosi di Venezia, Le Venexiane and le Putte di Vivaldi, are staging their concerts at the Palazzo Papafava in Cannaregio. The building dates from the 14th to the 18th centuries and the concerts—of music by Vivaldi and his contemporaries—are given in the main room of the *piano nobile*.
⊞ 124 J10 ⊠ Performances at Palazzo Papafava, Calle Racheta, Cannaregio 3764 ☎ 041 520 8767 🕓 Telephone for latest details 💷 €15–€25 🚤 Ca' d'Oro

ZENEVIA
This bar is popular for its intimate nooks inside and its seating outside on Campo Santa Maria Formosa. Giant spritz and glasses of Guinness are consumed by an up-for-it crowd who come for the live jazz, blues and rock sounds each Thursday.
⊞ 124 H9 ⊠ Campo Santa Maria Formosa, Castello 5548 ☎ 041 520 6266 🕓 Wed–Mon 9pm–2am 🚤 Zattere, Rialto

SPORTS AND ACTIVITIES
PALESTRA ATHENA
Well-patronized by locals, this fitness centre offers both equipment, including weights, static bikes and rowing machines, and exercise classes (in Italian). Opening times may vary, so it's best to call ahead.
⊞ 125 M11 ⊠ Calle delle Ancore, Castello 1017 ☎ 041 523 2203 🕓 Mon–Thu 8–1, 4–8.30, Fri–Sun 9–1, 4–9 🚤 Arsenale

FOR CHILDREN
LA LUNA NEL POZZO
Venice city council runs this place, which is aimed at local children up to the age of 14, but also welcomes visitors. There are plenty of games, toys and activities, and the centre organizes workshops where older children can try everything from painting and weaving to puppetry, mask-making and paper marbling. The Lilliput play area is for children under 6 accompanied by an adult.
⊞ 125 N11 ⊠ Ex-Scuola Calvi, Fondamenta Sant'Iseppo, Castello 785 ☎ 041 520 4616 💷 Enrolment €8; then €8 per workshop, €1 per toy or game loan 🚤 Giardini

MUSEO STORICO NAVALE
▷ 108.

IL PINGUINO
The 'Penguin' is reputedly the best *gelateria* in this part of town; all ices are made on the premises and you'll find all the usual favourites, made using the purest ingredients. Flavours vary according to season in the fruit ice range, but they make the renowned *panna gelato*, a simple block of frozen, vanilla-flavoured fresh cream, year round. The best place to enjoy it is strolling along the Riva.
⊞ 124 L11 ⊠ Riva San Biagio, Castello 2141 ☎ 041 241 1395 🕓 Daily 10–10 💷 Cone €1.50–€3 🚤 Arsenale

Above Spaghetti alla arrigosta *(lobster)* is a
staple of seafood restaurants

PRICES AND SYMBOLS

The prices given are the average for a two-course lunch (L) and a three-course dinner (D) for one person, without drinks. The wine price is for the least expensive bottle.

For a key to the symbols, ▷ 2.

AL COVO

They really know their fish at Al Covo, and it's best to rely on the waiter's guidance to enjoy the best of Venetian cooking—whatever ends up on your plate will be super-fresh and expertly cooked. The menu changes depending on the catch, but look out for *dorada* (bream) and *seppie nero con polenta* (squid cooked in its ink with polenta). This is a serious restaurant with a deservedly high reputation.
✚ 124 K10 ✉ Campiello della Pescaria, Castello 3968 ☎ 041 522 3812 🕙 Fri–Tue 12–3, 6.30–10 ✋ L €40, D €65, Wine €12 🚤 Arsenale

AL MASCARON

Don't be put off by the paper tablecloths and having to share a table with locals—the food is worth it. There are no airs and graces about Al Mascaron, just great *cicchetti* and an anything-goes atmosphere. It also has a menu for pasta, risotto and salads if you fancy something more substantial. Credit cards are not accepted.
✚ 124 J9 ✉ Calle Lunga Santa Maria Formosa, Castello 5225 ☎ 041 522 5995 🕙 Mon–Sat 11–3, 6.30pm–12.30am. Closed Sun ✋ *Cicchetti* for two €12, Wine/beer from €1.50 🚤 San Zaccaria

CORTE SCONTA

The understated interior belies the Corte Sconta's reputation as one of Venice's finest, and most famous, restaurants, where the ethos is firmly based on high quality and fresh fish—from lagoon to pan to plate. A procession of superbly imaginative antipasti is the highlight of any meal, followed by light fish dishes, home-made pasta and traditional puddings. Service is laid-back, friendly and expert and the wine list admirably matched with the cuisine. Reserving ahead is essential; ask for an outside table in summer.
✚ 124 K10 ✉ Calle del Pestrin, Castello 3886 ☎ 041 522 7024 🕙 Daily 12–3, 6–10. Closed early Jan–early Feb, mid-Jul to mid-Aug ✋ L €60, D €90, Wine €9 🚤 Arsenale

DAL PAMPO (OSTERIA SANT'ELENA)

The sheer exuberance of the owner, Pampo himself, makes for a great evening out, as do the hearty cooking and robust wines. You may be the only visitors in the place but you're bound to feel at home.
✚ 125 P13 ✉ Calle Generale Chinotto, Castello 24 ☎ 041 520 8419 🕙 Thu–Tue 12–2.30, 7.30–9. Closed Christmas, May and Aug ✋ L €45, D €70, Wine €8 🚤 Sant'Elena

DA REMIGIO

Remigio's is a true local restaurant in traditional style serving excellent food at good prices. Enjoy the splendid antipasti and fish so fresh it's sticky. It gets very busy, so reserve ahead.

124 K10 ✉ Salizzada dei Greci, Castello 3416 ☎ 041 523 0089 ⏰ Mon 12.30–2.30, Wed–Sun 12.30–2.30, 7.30–10. Closed Christmas–end Jan, 2 weeks Jul and Aug 🖐 L €35, D €45, Wine €6 🚤 San Zaccaria

HOSTARIA ALL'OMBRA

The menu may be in several languages but the food at this restaurant-cum-*bacaro* is truly Venetian, with home-made pasta, super-fresh fish and a splendid range of *cicchetti*, the tapas-like starters so loved by locals. Inside this wonderfully typical family restaurant the decoration is simple and the lighting less than atmospheric, so it's best to grab a table outside in summer and watch the world go by.
124 L11 ✉ Via Garibaldi, Castello 1252/A ☎ 041 523 1179 ⏰ Tue–Sun 12–3, 7–10.30 🖐 L €20, D €35, Wine €8 🚤 Arsenale, Giardini

OSTERIA ALE DO MARIE

It may attract foreign visitors, but this remains a true Venetian neighbourhood restaurant, where the food is fresh, simple and seasonal. Fish is bought daily and the changing menu reflects this—though classics such as *sarde in saor* and spaghetti *alle vongole* are staples. They serve a particularly good tourist menu at lunchtime, excellent value at €18 including wine.
124 K9 ✉ Calle de l'Ogio, Castello 3129 ☎ 041 296 0424 ⏰ Tue–Sun 12.30–3, 7.30–10 🖐 L €25, D €40, Wine €9 🚤 Celestia

OSTERIA ALLA RIVETTA

You'll have to squeeze past the bridge steps to enter this little restaurant, where dishes of *cicchetti* are laid out on the counter to enjoy if it's too early for lunch. The accent is on fish, with all the local favourites and a daily choice of what's best in the market, simply grilled or fried with a light hand. Vegetables are delicious and varied, making it a good choice if you eat neither meat nor fish.
124 J10 ✉ Ponte San Provolo, Castello 4625 ☎ 041 528 7302 ⏰ Tue–Sun

12.30–3, 7.30–10 🖐 L €35, D €40, Wine €10 🚤 San Zaccaria

OSTERIA OLIVA NERA

Oliva Nera is one of a new breed challenging the old school of Venetian restaurateurs. Its menu, full of interesting quirks, yet executed confidently, shows that Venetian cooking can be given a contemporary edge. Delicious examples include scallops with wild mushrooms, octopus salad, and lamb cooked in thyme. The beautifully presented dessert menu includes pannacotta with wild fruits and a wonderfully rich mascarpone cheesecake. The uncomplicated interior provides comfortable surroundings, and the unpretentious staff make lunch or dinner here a refreshing change.
124 K10 ✉ Calle della Madonna, Castello 3417–18 ☎ 041 522 2170 ⏰ Fri–Tue 12–2.30, 6.30–10 🖐 L €50, D €85, Wine €9 🚤 San Zaccaria

PIZZERIA 84

This very basic pizzeria is run by an amiable, moustached Sardinian. It has no airs or graces, but serves pizza as good as you'll get in Venice, where fire restrictions prevent the use of wood-burning ovens. It's very popular so you may have to hang about at the bar, or outside, until a table is free. Take the children to watch the skilful chef prepare your pizza before your very eyes. Credit cards are not accepted.
124 K9 ✉ Salizzada Santa Giustina, Castello 2907A ☎ 041 520 4198 ⏰ Fri–Tue 5–9.30 🖐 D €18, Wine €6 🚤 Celestia

IL RIDOTTO

Clean-looking and modern styling, featuring warm brick, stainless steel and blond wood; are the keynotes of this light and airy restaurant, five minutes from San Marco. The food is straightforward Venetian, with plenty of fish specialities and a fine wine list; the same owners also run Aciugheta on the opposite corner, which has a superb selection of *cicchetti* from mid-morning onwards and also serves pizzas.
124 J10 ✉ Campo SS Filippo e Giacomo, Castello 4509 ☎ 041 520 8280 ⏰ Thu 7.30–10, Fri–Tue 12.30–3, 7.30–10 🖐 L €25, D €35, Wine €9 🚤 San Zaccaria

Below *You'll find pizzas aplenty in Venice*

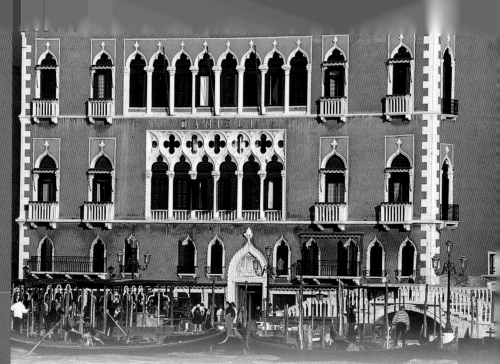

PRICES AND SYMBOLS

Prices are the lowest and highest for a double room for one night in high season. Breakfast is included unless noted otherwise.

For a key to the symbols, ▷ 2.

BISANZIO

www.bisanzio.com

The Busetti family has run this restored 16th-century *palazzo* hotel, near Vivaldi's church of La Pietà, since 1969. Guest rooms, some of which have balconies with rooftop views, have wooden floors, beamed ceilings and unfussy Venetian decoration. All have satellite TV, hairdryer and minibar. The Brown Lounge, bar and breakfast room all share an understated appearance. The continental breakfast may be taken in the old courtyard.

➕ 124 K10 ✉ Calle della Pietà, Castello 3651 ☎ 041 520 3100 💶 €110–€290 ⓘ 40 ♿ 🚤 San Zaccaria

BUCINTORO

www.hotelbucintoro.com

With wide views over the Bacino and set on just about the quietest stretch of the Riva, this four-star hotel is themed around its name; the Bucintoro was the Doge's state galley during the days of the Republic. Every room is named after an historic sailing vessel and the design features nautical details in restrained good taste. Most rooms are a good size, those at the front have superb views, as does the breakfast room and terraced tables outside. WiFi access is available in all rooms.

➕ 124 L10 ✉ Riva San Biagio, Castello 2135/A ☎ 041 528 9909 💶 €110–€250 ⓘ 20 ♿ 🚤 Arsenale

CAMPIELLO

www.hcampiello.it

This hotel, owned by the Bianchini sisters, is near the most popular San Marco sites. The bright and cheery hall, breakfast room and bar have marble floors and elegant furnishings. Bedrooms are comfortable and functional, with private bathroom, safe, TV, internet point and telephone, and some attractive Venetian antique pieces.

➕ 124 J10 ✉ Campiello del Vin, Castello 4647 ☎ 041 520 5764 🕐 Closed Jan 💶 €115–€180 ⓘ 17 🚤 San Zaccaria

LA COLOMBINA

www.hotelcolombina.com

This well-run hotel, named after the Carnival character, has superb views of San Marco and the Ponte dei Sospiri (Bridge of Sighs). Public rooms are filled with baroque decorative touches and furnishings, while guest rooms are typically Venetian, but not too over-powering—expect pastel patterned wallpaper, marble floors, dark wood antiques and chandeliers.

➕ 124 H9 ✉ Calle del Rimedio, Castello 4416 ☎ 041 277 0525 💶 €170–€395 ⓘ 32 ♿ 🚤 San Zaccaria

Above *The magnificent oldest building of the famous hotel Danieli*

DANIELI

www.danieli.hotelinvenice.com

This former home of Doge Dandolo ranks among the best of Italian hotels, with an ambience that's hard to beat. The Danieli (▷ 73) occupies three *palazzi* dating from the 14th, 19th and 20th centuries. Public rooms are sumptuous in every way, with marble floors, antique furnishings, sparkling glass and rich fabrics, while bedrooms and suites, though varying enormously in style and size, are equally well appointed. Restaurants and bars offer exceptional food, drink and service, uniting to give the ultimate Venetian experience. You will need to reserve well in advance for a room in the oldest building.

✚ 124 J10 ✉ Riva degli Schiavoni, Castello 4196 ☎ 041 522 6480 👋 €390–€2,400 🛈 233 rooms and suites 🔽 🚢 San Zaccaria

LOCANDA LA CORTE

www.locandalacorte.it

This pleasant hotel is set in a quiet corner of Castello, near the huge bulk of Santi Giovanni e Paolo church. Guest rooms have typically elegant Venetian furnishings, high ceilings and exposed beams. The secluded courtyard is a great place to relax and take the buffet breakfast.

✚ 124 J8 ✉ Calle Bressana, Castello 6317 ☎ 041 241 1300 👋 €115–€180 🛈 15 🔽 🚢 San Zaccaria, Fondamente Nuove

LOCANDA SANT'ANNA

www.locandasantanna.com

This out of the way hotel, near Via Garibaldi and San Pietro, is basic but comfortable. It is in the spacious, verdant and less touristy margins of the Castello *sestiere*, where most Venetians would prefer to live. The public rooms are functional and tidy, while the guest rooms are quite small. Air-conditioning is available on request. Credit cards are not accepted.

✚ 125 N11 ✉ Corte del Bianco, Castello 269 ☎ 041 528 6466 🌑 Closed Jan 👋 €70–€130 🛈 10 🔽 🚢 Giardini

LOCANDA SILVA

www.locandasilva.it

The Silva is in the bustling *calle* between Santa Maria Formosa and San Marco. The public areas, including the breakfast room, are clean, with modern furniture and fittings, and vibrant artwork on the walls. Guest rooms have light wood furniture, basic amenities and a functional modern character. Some have pleasant canal views and the cheapest share a bathroom.

✚ 124 H9 ✉ Fondamenta di Rimedio, Castello 4423 ☎ 041 523 7892 👋 €90–€130 🛈 23 🔽 🚢 San Zaccaria

METROPOLE

www.hotelmetropole.com

It may be right on the Riva, but the Metropole feels like an oasis of calm, largely thanks to its cool, spacious reading and sitting rooms, furnished with antiques from the owner's collection, and its wonderfully secluded garden. Bedrooms are elegantly furnished in the Venetian style, with touches like heated bathroom floors and the occasional canopied bed. Many have views: choose from the lagoon, the canal behind or the garden. A buffet breakfast is included and you can eat in the courtyard restaurant in the evening.

✚ 124 K10 ✉ Riva degli Schiavoni, Castello 4149 ☎ 041 520 5044 👋 €220–€750 🛈 56 rooms, 14 suites 🔽 🚢 San Zaccaria

PAGANELLI

www.hotelpaganelli.com

American novelist Henry James used the Paganelli as the setting for his *Portrait of a Lady,* and it remains a superbly sited hotel, offering good-value accommodation in this busy area. Rooms come in two types: large and luminous facing the lagoon, and tiny, cheaper rooms in the annexe, looking onto the Campo San Zaccaria. Most rooms have private bathrooms and hairdryers, telephones, TVs and safes. The public areas are grand in the Venetian style—*terrazzo* floors, traditional furnishings and more than

a touch of Murano glass. Breakfast is served in a functional 1970s-style room in the annexe.

✚ 124 J10 ✉ Campo San Zaccaria–Riva degli Schiavoni, Castello 4687 ☎ 041 522 4324 👋 €105–€195 🛈 22 🔽 🚢 San Zaccaria

LA RESIDENZA

www.venicelaresidenza.com

La Residenza, a short walk from San Marco and overlooking the tranquil Campo Bandiera e Moro, is a good choice for both location and price. It's housed in a handsome old *palazzo,* complete with stuccoed reading room, where breakfast is served, and furnished with some elegant pieces. The bedrooms have all been refurbished and facilities include private bathroom with shower, TV, safe and minibar.

✚ 124 K10 ✉ Campo Bandiera e Moro, Castello 3608 ☎ 041 528 5315 👋 €100–€155 🛈 15 🔽 🚢 Arsenale

RUZZINI PALACE

www.ruzzinipalace.com

Built in the 16th century, the Palazzo Loredan Ruzzini was empty for 20 years until a lengthy restoration saw it re-open as one of Venice's most luxurious hotels. The style combines modern good looks and great comfort with the building's original frescoed ceilings, exposed beams and stately proportions. Rooms at the front overlook the *campo* and there is WiFi access in all rooms. Good rates and offers are available online.

✚ 124 H9 ✉ Campo Santa Maria Formosa, Castello 5866 ☎ 041 241 0447 👋 €180–€250 🛈 28 🔽 🚢 Rialto

VILLA IGEA

www.hotelvillaigea.it

Beautifully set right on Campo San Zaccaria, the Igea had a complete overhaul in 2005, when all its rooms were upgraded and refurbished with light, cool colours and elegant fabrics. Half of these overlook the *campo;* specify when you book.

✚ 124 J10 ✉ Campo San Zaccaria, Castello 4684 ☎ 041 241 0956 👋 €155–€280 🛈 30 🔽 🚢 San Zaccaria

BACINI DI
CARENAGGIO

Bacini

Canale di Porta Nuova

0   250 m
0   250 yds

San Pietro

Ísola di
San Pietro

Campo
S Daniele

C larga S Pietro

Campo di
San Pietro

San Pietro
di Castello

Rio San Daniele

C d Terco

Campiello
Figaretto

C S Giovanni

Ex Palazzo
Patriarcale

Campo
di Ruga

C Marafani
C d Die

C d Bianco

C Sborca
C Sión

Locanda
Sant'Anna

Ísola della
Certosa

Fond della Tana

San Giovachino

C d'Anna

ancesco
aolo

C S Anna

Campiello de
Pomeri

Fond San Gioacchino

Fond S Anna

Campiello
del Pomeri

Rio di Quintavalle

C Quintavalle

numento
Garibaldi

Ex Chiesa
di S Anna

Giardini
Garibaldi

C d Forno
C d Trebbio

Correra

Corte
Martin
Novello

Secco Marina

Darsena
di Sant'Elena

Fond San Giuseppe

San Giuseppe
di Castello

Campo
San
Giuseppe

Rio terra San Giuseppe

Paludo S Antonio

Biennale
Internazionale
d'Arte

C Contro il Giardino

Via XXIV Maggio
Rame d
C Asiago

Montello
C d
Pozzo

Giardini
Pubblici

C Nervesa

C Paludo

C d Congressazion

Giardini

Viale Trento

C del Pasubio

Campo d
Grappa

C Montesanto

Fond Darsena

C del
Carso

C Montesanto

C Hermada

Campo
Sportivo

C Poddora

Campo d
Indipendenza

C Gen Chinotto

Dal Pampo
(Osteria Sant'Elena)

QUARTIERE
SANT'ELENA

Sant'Elena

Ísola di
Sant'Elena

Parco delle
Rimembranze

N   P   Q   R

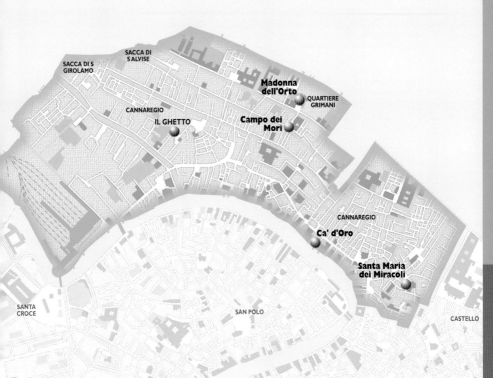

CANNAREGIO

Venice's northwest *sestiere* (ward), Cannaregio, was one of the earliest areas to be developed, when the sandbanks and marshlands were stabilized around a wide channel cutting south. This channel became the Canale di Cannaregio, the *sestiere's* main waterway, which, until the railway link with the mainland was built in 1846, was the entrance to Venice. Every arrival swept down this wide canal, which runs through the heart of Cannaregio to join the Canal Grande, the southern boundary. West of here is the railway station, still the arrival point for thousands of visitors, while to the east, the oldest settled part of Cannaregio, a warren of narrow streets with superb buildings sprawls as far as the Rialto and the boundary with San Marco. Northwards, wide *fondamente* (quaysides), lined with low-key buildings, ancient *palazzi* and workshops, run beside a trio of parallel canals lying to the south of the open waters of the lagoon.

A chain of mid-market shopping streets, known as the Strada Nova, which run from the San Marco boundary through to Santa Lucia station, dissects the whole *sestiere*. En route, the *campo* and church of Santi Apostoli is the main hub; to the north and east lie the luminous Renaissance church of Santa Maria dei Miracoli and the exuberant baroque excesses of the Gesuiti, right up near the lagoon.

Following the Strada Nova, the route leads past the Ca' d'Oro, Venice's most perfect example of medieval Venetian-Gothic architecture beautifully set on the Grand Canal, to the Cannaregio canal. From here, porticoes and narrow alleys run through to the Ghetto, the original inspiration for every sad ghetto of the world, to the three northern canals. Their sundrenched quaysides, busy with local life, lead first to Sant'Alvise, with its Tiepolo paintings, then past the charming Campo dei Mori, to the beautiful church of the Madonna dell'Orto with its mind-blowing canvases by Tintoretto.

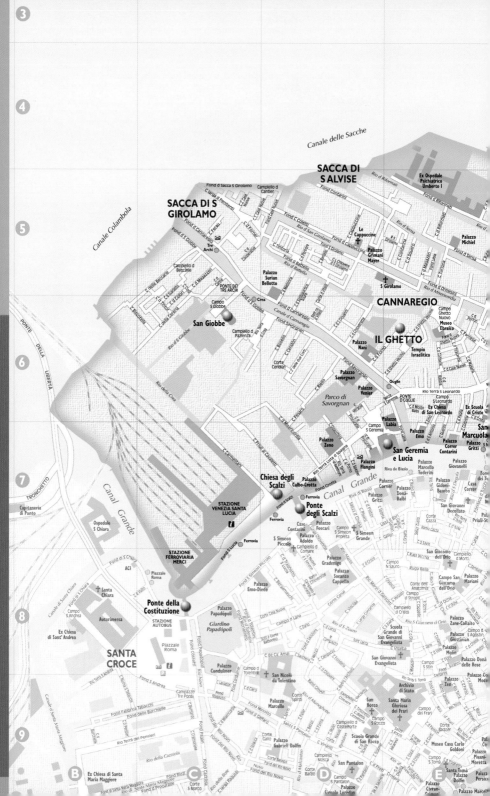

Canale delle Sacche

SACCA DI S ALVISE

Ex Ospedale Psichiatrico Umberto I

SACCA DI S GIROLAMO

Campiello d Cantier

Fond Contarini

Rio d Riformati

Fond d Riformati

Fond d Sacca S Girolamo

Le Cappuccine

Palazzo Michiel

Canale Colombola

C Feria d Pentieri

C d Cannaregio

C d Ferau

Fond d S Girolamo

Crea

C Crea

C d Colon

C Chiovere

Rio di San Girolamo

Rio d Orio

C d Caboato

Palazzo Grimani Mayer

S Girolamo

Fond d Sensa

Palazzo Surian Bellotto

Rio d Battello

Rio di Battello

Fond d Ormesini

Rio di Misericordia

Campiello d Beccarie

Palazzo Nani

CANNAREGIO

Campo Ghetto Nuovo Museo Ebraico

PONTE DEI TRE ARCHI

Campo S Giobbe

Fond d S Giobbe

Crea

Canale di Cannaregio

Fond Savorgnan

IL GHETTO

Tempio Israelitico

San Giobbe

Campiello d Pazienza

Corte Ceridon

Palazzo Savorgnan

Guglie

Rio della Crea

Parco di Savorgnan

Palazzo Venier

Ponte d Guglie

Rio Terra S Leonardo

Rio d S Leonardo

Ex Chiesa di San Leonardo

Ex Scuola di Cristo

Canal Grande

Palazzo Zeno

Campo S Geremia

Palazzo Labia

San Marcuola

Palazzo Correr Contarini

Palazzo Gritti

STAZIONE VENEZIA SANTA LUCIA

Chiesa degli Scalzi

Palazzo Calbo-Crotta

Palazzo Flangini

Palazzo Emo

San Geremia e Lucia

Riva de Biasio

Palazzo Giovanelli

Ponte degli Scalzi

Fond d Scalzi

Ferrovia

Palazzo Corner

Palazzo Dona-Balbi

Palazzo Gidoni-Bembo

Casa Correr

TRONCHETTO

Canal Grande

Capitaneria di Ponto

STAZIONE FERROVIARIA MERCI

Case Contarini

Palazzo Foscari

Campo S Simeon Profeta

S Simeon Grande

San Giovanni Decollato

Ospedale S Chiara

ACI

Piazzale Roma

S Simeon Piccolo

Palazzo Adolfo

Campiello d Comare

Palazzo Gradenigo

Campo N Sauro

Ponte della Costituzione

STAZIONE AUTOBUS

Piazzale Roma

Palazzo Emo-Diedo

Palazzo Soranzo Cappello

Scuola Grande di San Giovanni Evangelista

Campo San Giacomo dell'Orio

Palazzo Mariani

Santa Chiara

Campo S Andrea

Ex Chiesa di Sant'Andrea

Autorimessa

Palazzo Papadopoli

Giardino Papadopoli

Palazzo Condulmer

San Giovanni Evangelista

Palazzo Giustinian

Palazzo Molin

Palazzo Donà delle Rose

SANTA CROCE

Palazzo Tolentino

San Nicolò da Tolentino

San Rocco

Santa Maria Gloriosa dei Frari

Scuola Grande di San Rocco

Palazzo Zen

Palazzo Corner Moce

Palazzo Marcello

Archivio di Stato

Museo Casa Carlo Goldoni

Ex Chiesa di Santa Maria Maggiore

Fond Fabbrica Tabacchi

Fond delle Burchielle

Palazzo Gabrieli Bolfin

Campo S Pantalon

Santa Tomà

Campo S Pantalon

Canale delle Navi

nt'Alvise

t'Alvise

Ospedale
Fatebenefratelli

Madonna dell'Orto

Convento

Campiello
Piave

Madonna
dell'Orto

Scuola dei
Mercanti

QUARTIERE
GRIMANI

Casin
degli Spiriti

Corte
Cavallo

Fond Madonna dell'Orto

Corte Loredan

Palazzo
Minelli
Spada

Palazzo
Mastelli

Palazzo
Contarini
dal Zaffo

Sacca della
Misericordia

Campo
dei Mori

Casa
Tintoretto

Palazzo
Longo

Ex Convento
dei Servi di Maria

Fond d'Mori

Fond d Misericordia

Corte Vecchia

Palazzo
Diedo

Cappella del
Volto Santo

S Marziale

Campo
S Marziale

S Maria
Valverde

Scuola Vecchia
della Misericordia

Scuola Nuova
della Misericordia

Fond S Caterina

Canale della Misericordia

Fondamente Nuove

La Maddalena

S Fosca

Palazzo
Lezze

Palazzo
Vendramin

Palazzo
Molin

Palazzo
Papafava

Ex Chiesa
di Santa Caterina

Oratorio
dei Crociferi

Gesuiti

Palazzo
Donà

Fondamente
Nuove

Palazzo
Correr
Contarini

Palazzo
Soranzo

Palazzo
Giovanelli

Corte
Squero
Vecchio

Palazzo
Zen

Campo
dei Gesuiti

Canale delle Fondamente Nuove

Palazzo
Emo

Palazzo
Molin

Palazzo
Barbarigo

Palazzo
Zulian

S Felice

Campo
S Felice

Palazzo Gussoni-
Grimani della Vida

Ex Convento

Palazzo
Seriman

Campiello
d Pietà

Corte
Carità

Museo del
Tessuto e
del Costume

Palazzo
Pesaro

Palazzo
Donà

CANNAREGIO

Palazzo
Boldù

Campiello di
Testori

Strada Nova

Palazzo
Fontana

S Sofia

Santa Làzzaro
dei Mendicanti

Ospedale

Palazzo Corner
della Regina

Palazzo
Foscari

Ca' d'Oro

Campo
S Sofia

Ca' d'Oro

Palazzo
Sagredo

Santi
Apostoli

Palazzo
Widman

Campiello
Widman

Palazzo
Brandolin

Scuola
dell'Angelo
Custode

Campo
Santi Apostoli

Palazzo
Michiel
delle Colonne

Campiello
Cason

San
Canciano

Ospedale
Civile

Scuola Grande
di San Marco

Pescheria

Ca' da
Mosto

Campiello
Selvatico

Campiello
Corner

Santa Maria
dei Miracoli

Fabbriche
Nuove

Palazzo
Lion-Morosini

Palazzo
Bembo
e Boldù

Palazzo
Sanudo

Campo Santi
Giovanni
e Paolo

Campo
S M del
Domini

Gobbo
di Rialto

San Giovanni
Elemosinario

Fabbriche
Vecchie

S Giacomo
di Rialto

San Giovanni
Crisostomo

Teatro
Malibran

Palazzo
Dolfin

Palazzo
Pisani

Monumento
di Bartolomeo
Colleoni

Santi Giovanni
e Paolo

Ospedaletto
(Santa Maria
dei Derelitti)

Erberia

Palazzo
Bragadin
Carabba

Corte di
San Marina

Ponte
di Rialto

Campo
Rialto
Nuovo

Fondaco
dei Tedeschi

Rialto
Dieci Savi

Palazzo
Marcello

Barbaria delle Tole

POLO

Palazzo
Soranzo

Sant'
Aponal

Palazzo
Dolfin-Manin

Palazzo
Dandolo

San
Bartolomeo

Santa Maria
della Fava

San Lio

Campo
Santa Maria
Formosa

Palazzo
Donà

Palazzo
Priuli

CASTELLO

Palazzo
Cavagnis

Palazzo
Albrizzi

Campiello
Albrizzi

Sant'
Aponal

Palazzo
Bembo

Scuola Grande
di San
Teodoro

San
Salvador

Santa Maria
Formosa

Ex Ospizio

Palazzo
Gozzi

San
Cassiano

Campo
S Cassiano

Palazzo
Farsetti

Palazzo
Corner
Martinengo

Teatro
Goldoni

Santa Maria
della Fava

Palazzo
Faccanon

Santa Maria
Formosa

Fondazione
Querini
Stampalia

Campo
San Lorenzo

Palazzo
Muti-Baglioni

Palazzo
Loredan

San Salvador

Palazzo
Corner
Spinelli

Palazzo
Albrizzi

Palazzo
Malin-Cappella

Palazzo
Papadopoli

Palazzo
Barzizza

San Silvestro

Palazzo
Ravà

Palazzo
Grimani

Palazzo
Tasca-Papafava

Corte di
Paradiso

Borgoloco S Lorenzo

Palazzo
Donà
donnetta

Palazzo
Bernardo

Campiello
Meloni

Campo
S Silvestro

San
Silvestro

Campo
S Aponal

Terra de
d'Aponal

Palazzo
Corner
Contarini
dei Cavalli

Campo
San Benedetto

Teatro
Rossini

S Luca

Campo
S Luca

Teatro
Goldoni

Campo
S Angelo

San Zulian

S Giovanni in
Oleo

Palazzo
Zorzi

Canal
Grande

Canal
Grande

Grand
Canal

Palazzo
Corner
Mocenigo
Tiepolo

Palazzo
Maffetti-
Tiepolo

Museo del
Tessuto e
del Costume
Palazzo
Mocenigo

Sant'
Agnus Dio

0   250 m
0   250 yds

F   G   H   J

CAMPO DEI MORI

This attractive and historic square, in a tranquil part of Cannaregio, is just a stone's throw from two fine churches—Sant'Alvise and the Madonna dell'Orto. The Campo dei Mori lies on the route south from the church of the Madonna dell'Orto (▷ 138–139) towards the city centre. It's in an outlying area of great charm, well away from the main through-routes and sights, so it's better to combine a visit here with other sights in the vicinity. The best way to explore the area might be to follow the walk, ▷ 144–145.

THE MOORS AND THEIR CAMPO

There are several explanations for the name Campo dei Mori; it may refer to the proximity of the now extinct Fondaco degli Arabi, the trading warehouse run by the Arabs which stood nearby, or more likely to the four 13th-century statues of Moors standing around the square. These wonderfully naïve pieces show turbaned Moors, popularly associated with the Mastelli family, who used to live in the *palazzo* where two of the figures are embedded. They were a Greek trading family who originated in the Morea (the Peloponnese), and were known in the city as the Mori.

Three of the statues are said to represent brothers from the family—Rioba, Sandi and Afiani—who arrived in Venice in 1112 and settled; later family members participated in the Fourth Crusade and were probably present at the Sack of Constantinople in 1204. The Venetians have long had a fondness for the statues, particularly the one on the corner house, known as Sior Antonio Rioba, which was in need of a nose job and now sports a replacement iron one. The statue was used as a repository for denunciatory letters destined for the powers-that-be, which were left pinned at his feet, and his name was often used to sign vindictive verses. The fourth Moor, round the corner on the *fondamenta*, is set into the facade of No. 3399, Tintoretto's house. The statue was restored by the British Venice in Peril fund, and was found to have a local 15th-century version of a Roman altar as a column, while a recycled capital from the top of a column had been used as his turban.

INFORMATION

✚ 129 F6 ✉ Campo dei Mori, Cannaregio 🚤 Orto

Opposite *Tintoretto's house on the Fondamenta dei Mori*
Above *Detail of the facade of Tintoretto's house*

CA' D'ORO

INFORMATION

www.cadoro.org
www.polomuseale.venezia.beniculturali.it
✚ 129 G7 ✉ Calle Ca' d'Oro,
Cannaregio 3932 ☎ 041 520 0345
🕐 Mon 8.15–2, Tue–Sun 8.15–7.15.
Closed 1 Jan, 1 May, 25 Dec 🚤 Ca'
d'Oro 🚶 Adult €11 (combined ticket for
C'a d'Oro, Accademia and Museo d'Arte
Orientale); EU citizens under 18 free
🛈 Guidebook (€8.50) and audiotour (€6)
available in Italian, English, French and
German 📷

INTRODUCTION

Among the finest and most flamboyant of all Gothic *palazzi* in a splendid position on the Grand Canal, this is the perfect place to appreciate how medieval merchant businesses functioned. The Ca' d'Oro, Golden House, was built between 1420 and 1434 by Bartolomeo Bon and his associates for the Procurator Marino Contarini, and was intended, like all Venetian domestic buildings, to take the name of its owner. From the moment it was finished it was clear that Ca' Contarini was far too pedestrian a name for this glittering building, whose exterior was adorned with vermilion, ultramarine and gold leaf. Quickly dubbed Ca' d'Oro, the name remains, though the gold leaf has long since disappeared. Over the centuries the interior was drastically altered by successive owners, though the exterior remains the finest Veneto-Byzantine Gothic monument after San Marco. By the mid-19th century, the building was almost in ruins, and the Russian Prince Troubetskoy was able to acquire it cheaply as a gift for his mistress, the famous ballerina Maria Taglioni. Her talents did not extend as far as interior design and her 'restorations' invoked the wrath of English writer John Ruskin, in Venice writing his seminal *Stones of Venice*. In 1894 the building was bought by Baron Franchetti, who reinstalled the stair and well-head in the courtyard and filled the *palazzo* with his collections of paintings, sculpture and coins. In 1916 he left both building and collection to the state and the Ca' d'Oro opened to the public in 1927. There was another lengthy restoration between 1969 and 1984.

For an excellent view of the facade of the Ca' d'Oro, head for the Pescheria (fish market) on the opposite side of the Grand Canal. Once you've had a good look at the exterior, take the *traghetto* Santa Sofia across the water to the building itself. Allow time inside, working your way up from the ground floor, and be sure to linger on the exterior loggias, great places to watch the water traffic. The best time for this is during the morning, when delivery barges and service boats are constantly coming and going. The top floor contains an extensive coin, medal and miniature collection, which is probably only of limited interest to most visitors.

Above *The Ca' d'Oro's sparkling facade is a Grand Canal landmark*

THE INTERIOR OF THE CA D'ORO

Medieval Venetian merchants' houses were also their business premises, with goods stored in warehouses on the ground floor and offices leading off the *portego*, a huge reception room running the full depth of the *piano nobile*, the first floor. Today, the Ca' d'Oro's ground floor still reflects this layout, with the main door opening onto the water, warehouse space behind and a tiny pleasure garden and courtyard from where an exterior staircase leads to the upper floors. The rose marble well-head in the courtyard was carved by Bartolomeo Bon in 1472. The upper floors were completely reconstructed during the 1970s restoration, but they retain their open Gothic loggias overlooking the Grand Canal. The galleries contain works of art by Venetian artists such as Gentile Bellini (1429–1507) and Titian (c1487–1576), Florentine and Sienese paintings, Flemish tapestries and ghostly fresco fragments by Titian and Giorgione (c1476/8–1510).

SAN SEBASTIANO

Andrea Mantegna started painting *San Sebastiano* in 1506; it was his last work and remained unfinished at his death. The saint, patron of the sick, was a popular figure in plague-ridden Venice and a subject dear to artists, who used his martyrdom as an opportunity to depict a virtually naked figure—a subject normally tabooed by the ecclesiastical powers. San Sebastiano is seen riddled with arrows, while a guttering candle in the picture's right-hand corner alludes to the fleeting nature of life. The Latin inscription also refers to man's mortality; it reads 'Only the Divine is eternal, all else is but smoke'.

THE *ANNUNCIATION* AND THE *DEATH OF THE VIRGIN*

Two panels from Vittore Carpaccio's picture cycle for the Scuola degli Albanesi are now in the Ca' d'Oro, the *Annunciation* and the *Death of the Virgin*, part of a series that told stories from the life of the Virgin. Both painted in 1504, they are beautifully observed, charming paintings. The *Annunciation* is exquisitely rendered, with the Virgin half-turned away from the angel, as if lost in her own reaction to the momentous news that she is to be the mother of the Saviour.

Below *The courtyard of Ca' d'Oro*

CAMPO DEI GESUITI

If you're walking from the Rialto to the Fondamente Nuove to catch a boat to the islands, you'll find yourself in the Campo dei Gesuiti, a real 'neighbourhood' square used, as it's always been, by local people as a meeting place and somewhere for their children to play.

Unusually long and relatively narrow, it's busy all day with pedestrians hurrying to and from the boats, housewives laden with shopping, and grandmothers supervising noisy children and dogs from the shady benches dotted around. The canal on its south side is exceptionally busy and a great place to watch the variety of goods that arrive in the city and the expertise of the bargemen. Heading north, the big *palazzo* you see on the left is the Palazzo Zen, a Gothic-Renaissance building once decorated with frescoes by Tintoretto (1518–94). Tall, secretive houses line the east side, and at the end, where the *campo* narrows, surges the massive bulk of the church of the Gesuiti.

On the left of the *campo* is the Oratorio dei Crociferi (open Apr–end Oct Fri–Sat 3.30–6.30; Nov–end Mar Fri–Sat 3–6, €2), a 13th-century foundation similar to a *scuola* (literally 'school'), which was richly frescoed in the late 16th century by Palma il Giovane (1544–1628) with scenes from the history of the Crociferi, a religious order dedicated to the Holy Cross. The paintings, restored by the British charity Venice in Peril, were begun in 1581 and finished in 1591 and show the founding of the Order by Pope Anacletus to provide for pilgrims and the sick, the construction of an almshouse for 12 poor women in the 13th century, and the 1581 gift which led to the founding of the Oratory, the present building. The artist included portraits of his contemporaries, along with the commissioner, Father Priamo Balbi, and some of the local housewives who came to pray at the oratory.

➕ 129 H7 ✉ Campo dei Gesuiti, Cannaregio 🚏 Fondamente Nuove

CAMPO DEI MORI

▷ 131.

CAMPO SANTI APOSTOLI

The wide thoroughfare of the 19th-century Strada Nova, whose creation cut a wide swath through the old streets in this part of Cannaregio, finishes at Campo Santi Apostoli, where the route to the Rialto swings right and back into typically narrow *calli* once more. The *campo* marks a turning point; right to the Rialto, left towards the Fondamente Nuove. It's a busy place, dominated by its church (▷ 140), and very much a crossroads and the hub of a lively district. There are plenty of interesting local shops, a good corner bar and some shady trees. Pause here to admire the church facade; the campanile was built in 1672 and an old story tells of a sacristan falling from it but being miraculously caught on the minute hand of the clock. As it reached 6, it placed the sacristan gently on a convenient parapet.

➕ 129 G8 ✉ Campo Santi Apostoli, Cannaregio 🚏 Ca' d'Oro

GESUITI

The Jesuit church of Santa Maria Assunta, known as the Gesuiti, lies on the direct route from the Rialto to the Fondamente Nuove. The Jesuits, with their close ties to the Papacy, were never popular in republican Venice, falling out badly with the Serenissima, as the Venetian republic was known, in 1606, when they were expelled from the city in retaliation for Venice's excommunication by the papacy. By 1700 they were once more established and looking round for a new site for a church. The Order purchased an old church, knocked it down and erected a new one, built to a plan by Domenico Rossi between 1715 and 1729. The result was a vast construction of maximum impact, whose mind-bogglingly ornate interior epitomizes the dazzling richness preferred by the Order.

The interior space soars into dim heights, with towering pilasters and a baldachin over the altar modelled on Bernini's version in St. Peter's, while virtually every inch of wall space is festooned with billowing swags of drapery and richly figured damasks. But these swags and drapes, tassels and brocades are actually intricately carved and polished green and white marble, one of the most astounding sights to be found in any Venetian church. Hidden among this are two fine paintings: a night scene by Titian (1478–1576), the *Martyrdom of St. Lawrence*, over the first altar on the left, and the *Assumption of the Virgin* by Tintoretto (1518–94) in the left transept. The former, badly lit and hard to discern, shows the saint being roasted on a gridiron amid the taunts of his executioners.

➕ 129 H7 ✉ Campo dei Gesuiti, Cannaregio ☎ 041 528 6579 🕐 Daily 10–12, 3–6 ✋ Free 🚏 Fondamente Nuove

Opposite *Exterior detail of the monolithic Gesuiti church*

Below *See local life in Campo dei Gesuiti*

INFORMATION

Museo Ebraico and Synagogues
www.ghetto.it

✚ 128 E6 ✉ Campo Ghetto Nuovo,
Cannaregio 2902B ☎ 041 715 359 or
041 723 007 🕐 Jun–end Sep Sun–Fri
10–7; Oct–end May Sun–Fri 10–4.30.
May close early on Fri. Closed 1 May and
Jewish feast days. Guided tours half-
hourly ✋ Adult €8.50; child (under 12)
€7 🚤 Guglie, San Marcuola 🚩 Guided
tours in Italian, English, French and
Spanish 🚻 📖 Selection of books
on the Ghetto and the Jewish religion,
Jewish religious artefacts and gifts

INTRODUCTION

The world's first Jewish ghetto was established in Venice in 1516, and is set on
its own island in Cannaregio. In this fascinating and thought-provoking enclave
you can visit ancient synagogues set in and around a beautiful *campo*.

Jewish people first arrived in Venice in the 1390s and settled in an area of
Cannaregio with a foundry, or *geto*, a word that was to give its name to Jewish
forced settlement areas throughout the centuries. Jewish people were at
first only permitted to reside in Venice for periods of up to 15 days, and their
activities were restricted to medicine, money lending—a practice forbidden by
the church—and second-hand dealing. They won the right to live full time in
the city in 1516, when the Republic instituted the area of the Ghetto as their
compulsory place of residence in gratitude for their financial help following
the War of the League of Cambrai. Gates, controlled by Christian guards paid
for by the Jewish community, were shut between sunset and dawn at the
entrance to the Ghetto. Jewish people were compelled to wear distinctive
badges or caps, had limited property rights and were subject to a range of
financial penalties. Drastic as this sounds, they were probably safer in Venice
than elsewhere in Europe and the community was periodically augmented
by influxes from more oppressive countries such as Spain and Portugal. They
continued their traditional professions of usury and medicine—doctors being
the only people allowed to leave at night.

The gates were eventually torn down by Napoleon in 1797, and Jewish
people finally achieved full rights as Venetian citizens after the Unification of
Italy in 1866. By World War II their position was under threat from Fascism
and during 1942 and 1943 many were deported—around 200 died in the death
camps. The Jewish population today is small, but the Ghetto is still very much
the heart of the community and a place of pilgrimage for Jewish people from
many countries, who come to experience the first sad Ghetto in the world.

The main approach to the Ghetto is through a narrow alley leading off the
Fondamenta di Cannaregio. This brings you to the Ghetto Vecchio and over a
bridge to the Campo Ghetto Nuovo. Here you'll find the Holocaust Memorial
and Museo Ebraico (Jewish Museum), from where the Ghetto tours depart.
These leave half-hourly throughout the day and guides will fill you in on the
history of the Ghetto while you visit three synagogues. You can then visit the

Above *The occupants of the world's
original ghetto were forced to live in
cramped conditions*

museum and go on to explore the rest of the area, with its fascinating Jewish shops, at your leisure.

WHAT TO SEE

CAMPO GHETTO NUOVO AND THE HOLOCAUST MEMORIAL

The open space of the Campo Ghetto Nuovo is surrounded by what, for Venice, are extremely tall buildings. Overcrowding was a problem throughout the Ghetto's history, and the authorities only permitted construction of houses one-third higher than in the rest of the city, resulting in as many as seven floors crammed into the available space. These tightly packed buildings surround the *campo* on two sides; the north side is occupied by a purpose-built old people's home. To the left of this is the Holocaust Memorial, a series of seven reliefs by Arbit Blatas (1977), with a poem by André Tranc, commemorating the deportation and extermination of the city's Jewish people.

THE SYNAGOGUES

As successive waves of immigrants arrived in the Ghetto from other countries, they built their own synagogues, mainly incorporated into existing buildings, to maintain their individual rites. The Schola Tedesca was founded in 1528 by German Jews, the Schola Canton in 1531 by Ashkenazi French, the Schola Levantina by Jews from the eastern Mediterranean in 1538, the Schola Spagnola followed a Spanish Sephardic settlement in the late 16th century, and the Schola Italiana was established in 1575. As Jewish people were forbidden to work as architects, Christian designers were employed, resulting in strangely Christian-like interiors, with painted wood, stucco and gilt, though there are no figurative images as these are forbidden by Judaism. The synagogues were funded by prosperous members of the community, and the wealth of the different national groups is reflected in the design, with the Schola Levantina and the Schola Spagnola being the most lavish.

MORE TO SEE

MUSEO EBRAICO

The Jewish Museum was opened in 1955 to display a rich collection of silverware, religious ceremonial objects, textiles, prayer books and documents, dating mainly from the 16th to 19th centuries. The textiles and silverware are particularly impressive, and look for the ornately decorated marriage contracts.

TIP

» The excellent guided tours (booked at the museum) are the best way to see the Ghetto.

Below *A memorial plaque to the victims of the Holocaust*

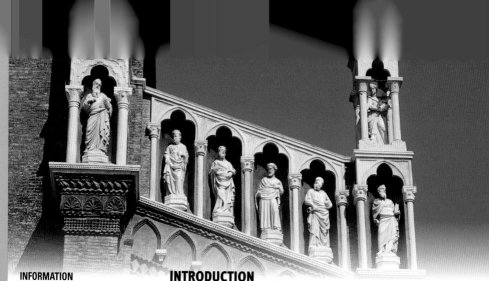

INFORMATION

www.chorusvenezia.org

✛ 129 G5 ✉ Campo Madonna dell'Orto, Cannaregio ☎ 041 275 0462 ⌚ Mon–Sat 10–5. Closed 1 Jan, Easter, 15 Aug, 25 Dec ✋ Chorus Pass (for all churches in Chorus group) €9, single ticket €3 🚤 Orto ⬤ Information sheet and audioguides in Italian, English, French and German 📷 Postcards

INTRODUCTION

This unspoiled and tranquil Gothic church, the burial place of the artist Tintoretto and home to some of his most compelling work, is tucked away in Cannaregio. The original church was founded around 1350 and dedicated to St. Christopher, the patron saint of travellers, in the hope he would keep an eye on the ferry service to the northern islands and the gondoliers who ran it from a nearby jetty. Some years later, a statue of the Madonna and Child started to attract attention as a miracle-worker in a nearby vegetable garden (orto). In 1377, St. Christopher was demoted and the Madonna was moved from the orto to the church. The statue is still there and can be seen in the Cappella di San Mauro, off the end of the right aisle near the main altar, while St. Christopher now presides over the central door of the facade. The church was rebuilt between 1399 and 1473; Tintoretto's paintings for the choir, apse and side walls cover 30 years of the 16th century.

In 1874 the church was badly restored, with its pavement tombs ripped up, its priceless organ demolished and the Greek marble columns in the nave overpainted. Things were put back to their near-original state and Madonna dell'Orto became the first major restoration to be funded after the 1966 floods by the British Venice in Peril Fund. This was founded by Sir Ashley Clarke, who became its first chairman and was made a freeman of Venice; he is commemorated by a plaque in the chapel to the right of the main altar.

Spend a few minutes admiring the facade of Madonna dell'Orto before you enter the church. The simple, airy interior repays a few minutes' appreciation before you move on to take in Tintoretto's frescoes; these are found above the entrance to the Cappella di San Mauro, in the choir and behind the high altar, in the apse and in the Cappella Contarini off the left aisle. Tintoretto is buried in the chapel on the right of the high altar, together with his children. You'll notice a photograph and an empty frame in the first chapel on the left; a superb Madonna and Child (1480) by Giovanni Bellini hung here until it was stolen in 1993.

WHAT TO SEE

THE FACADE

The beautiful, predominantly Gothic facade, overlooking its own campo and a canal, is built of the same red brick and Istrian stone as Venice's two other major Gothic churches, the Frari and Santi Giovanni e Paolo. Construction here, though, was long drawn out, with the result that the facade is a hybrid, incorporating both Gothic and Renaissance elements. The windows,

Above The statues in the niches on the facade of the church represent the twelve Apostles

with their filigree tracery, are clearly Gothic, while the onion-shaped dome of the campanile echoes the earlier Byzantine style. The elegant doorway by Bartolomeo Bon, with its columns and symmetrical lines, is resolutely Renaissance, as is the statue of St. Christopher by Nicolò di Giovanni above. Bridging the stylistic gap are the statues of the Apostles in the false gallery at the top of the aisle wings, thought to be carved by the Tuscan Dalle Masegne workshop.

THE INTERIOR

The interior is laid out in basilica form, the central nave and its side aisles drawing the eye forwards to the choir and chancel. The overwhelming impression is of space and light, the pointed Gothic arches adding to the feeling of soaring height. The decoration is simple, with Greek marble columns dividing the aisles from the nave, a plain wooden coffered ceiling and a red-and-white *terrazza* tiled floor, the perfect backdrop for the power of the church's stupendous artwork.

THE PAINTINGS

The Madonna dell'Orto was Tintoretto's parish church and the incredible paintings he created for it over a period of some 30 years were his gift to the church; he asked only for money for his materials. On either side of the high altar are the *Making of the Golden Calf* (on the left), and the *Last Judgement* (on the right), dating from 1562 to 1563, while four of the figures of the Virtues, set high behind the altar, are also by the artist. Imbued with religious passion and sincerity, they're full of movement, light and drama. The four carriers of the calf in the *Making of the Golden Calf* have been tentatively identified as Giorgione, Titian, Veronese and Tintoretto (fourth from the left).

In the apse the *Beheading of St. Paul* and *St. Peter's Vision of the Cross* (1566) are again full of movement—look out for the swirling, swooping angels—and provide a marked contrast with the sublimely mystical *Presentation of the Virgin in the Temple* (1552–53) over the entrance to the Cappella di San Mauro.

Tintoretto's final work here, *St. Agnes* (1577), shimmers with radiant blues, and there's another artistic treat in the form of Cima da Conegliano's *St. John the Baptist* (1493) in the first chapel on the right.

Above *Madonna dell'Orto's Gothic facade*
Below *The vaulted apse is decorated with works by Tintoretto, who is buried in the church*

PONTE DELLA COSTITUZIONE

In 2008, after years of delay, a new bridge opened to span the Canal Grande between Piazzale Roma and Santa Lucia railway station. Designed by Spanish architect Santiago Calatrava, the bridge is a sleek arc of Istrian stone, steel and glass whose prefabricated sections were floated into place up the Grand Canal. Despite the controversies which dogged its construction and its huge expense—more than €10 million—this elegant bridge will doubtless grow to be as useful and treasured as the other three.

✚ 128 C8 ✉ Ponte della Costituzione, Cannaregio 🚢 Ferrovia

PONTE DEGLI SCALZI

Until the beginning of the 21st century, the Ponte degli Scalzi, right by the railway station, was the most westerly bridge across the Grand Canal. It was named after the church on the left and built in 1934 to replace the original cast-iron one erected by the Austrians in 1858–60. The bridge's approach is right outside the railway station, next to the *vaporetto* stops and souvenir stalls. You may have to fight your way through, but from the bridge you'll get your first 'proper' view down the Grand Canal, and once on the other side, you lose the crowds and can plunge into the warren of streets and *campi* of the *sestiere* of Santa Croce.

✚ 128 D7 ✉ Ponte degli Scalzi, Cannaregio 🚢 Ferrovia

SANT'ALVISE

www.chorusvenezia.org

Sant'Alvise, dedicated to St. Louis, stands near the northern edge of Cannaregio in a low-key residential area. It was founded in 1388 by the noblewoman Antonia Venier, to whom Sant'Alvise had appeared in a dream, and stands isolated on its own island, accessible only from the south across the *rio* of the same name. The exterior facade is pure Gothic, with a flat brick surface divided by brick pilasters and broken only by an *oeil-de-boeuf* (ox-eye

Above *Santi Apostoli's campanile rises above its square*

shaped) window and Istrian stone doorway. Inside, little remains of the original, single-nave, basilical form. Above the entrance, Venice's first example of a hanging choir was added in the 15th century for the nuns from the adjoining convent to use for attending Mass. There were other alterations, including a charming *trompe l'oeil* ceiling in the 17th century, and in the 18th the church acquired its main treasures, three stunning canvases by Giambattista Tiepolo (1696–1770). These show scenes from Christ's passion: *The Crowning with Thorns* and the *Flagellation* in the nave, and *Christ's Ascent to Calvary* in the chancel. Under the hanging choir are the eight tempera panels known as the 'Baby Carpaccios', naively charming biblical scenes which English writer John Ruskin attributed to Vittore Carpaccio as a young child—they certainly date from around the time of the painter's childhood (1470), but are now attributed to Lazzaro Bastiani or a follower of his.

✚ 129 F5 ✉ Campo Sant'Alvise, Cannaregio ☎ 041 275 0462 🕐 Mon–Sat 10–5. Closed 1 Jan, Easter, 15 Aug, 25 Dec 🎟 Chorus Pass (for all churches in Chorus group) €9, single ticket €3 🚢 Sant'Alvise

SANTI APOSTOLI

The church of Santi Apostoli lies at the eastern end of the Strada Nova, at the crossroads between the main route to the railway station and the narrow streets leading north to the Fondamente Nuove. A church was first founded here in the ninth century and today's incorporates some parts of this early building, but dates principally from 1575, with later additions. Santi Apostoli's interior appearance is pure 18th century; only the Cappella Corner remains discernibly 16th century. It was probably designed by Mauro Codussi (1440–1504) and has a splendid altarpiece, the *Communion of St. Lucy*, by Giambattista Tiepolo. Caterina Cornaro (▷ 32), Queen of Cyprus, was once buried here. Santi Apostoli's campanile, finished in 1672, is one of the tallest in Venice. An old story relates how an elderly sacristan fell from the top but, miraculously, was caught by the minute hand which, slowly turning, eventually deposited him safely on the parapet.

✚ 129 G8 ✉ Campo Santi Apostoli, Cannaregio ☎ 041 523 8297 🕐 Mon–Sat 7.30–11.30, 5–7, Sun 8.30–12, 4.15–6.30 🎟 Free 🚢 Ca' d'Oro

SAN GEREMIA E LUCIA

Until the mid-19th century San Geremia could count this church his own, but since the destruction of the church of Santa Lucia, to make way for the railway station, he's had to share it with St. Lucia, whose mummified corpse is preserved in the church. This is a big, plain 18th-century building, dominated by a dome, whose austere grey-and-white interior is high and echoing. Despite this lack of inherent appeal, it's a great deal busier than many Venetian churches, due to a constant stream of devotees of the martyred St. Lucia. She was put to death in Syracuse in 304, after which her body went to Constantinople, from where she was brought home in triumph by the Venetians after the Fourth Crusade in 1204. Such was her modesty that, when praised by a would-be suitor for the beauty of her eyes, she promptly plucked them out, hence her role as patron of the shortsighted. There's a remarkable devotional painting of the saint holding her eyes—looking horribly like fried eggs—on a plate, or you can inspect her glass-encased, mummified corpse, decently covered by a red robe with just her little mummified feet sticking out.

➕ 128 E7 ✉ Campo San Geremia, Cannaregio 🕓 Mon–Fri 8.30–12, 3.30–6.30, Sun 9.30–12, 5.30–6.30 🖐 Free 🚊 San Marcuola, Ferrovia

SAN GIOBBE

For something with a distinctly Florentine taste, head for the church of San Giobbe, dedicated to an Old Testament figure, Job, who has been raised to sainthood. This is a Renaissance church, rational and airy in design and spirit, and it's the only place in Venice where you can see the terracotta work of the Florentine della Robbia family. San Giobbe was built around 1463 to commemorate the visit of San Bernardino of Siena, a fiery preacher and evangelist.

The lovely Renaissance doorway and chancel are the work of Pietro Lombardo (1435–1515). The Lombardo family were also responsible for the sculpture in the sanctuary and on the arch between it and the nave. Doge Cristoforo Moro (in office 1462–71), who paid for the construction of the church, is buried beneath the chancel floor, his tomb decorated with yet more Lombardo work. You'll find the della Robbia tiles and roundels in the Cappella Martini (second on left).

➕ 128 C6 ✉ Campo San Giobbe, Cannaregio 🕓 041 524 1889 🕓 Mon–Sat 10–12, 3–6 🖐 Free 🚊 Ponte Tre Archi

SAN GIOVANNI CRISOSTOMO

If you want to see an example of Renaissance architecture at its intimate best, head for San Giovanni Crisostomo—literally, St. John the Golden-Tongued—a few minutes' walk north from the Rialto. Its patron was the Archbishop of Constantinople, where churches followed a Greek cross floor plan, so it's fitting that its architect, Renaissance master Mauro Codussi (1440–1504), should have based his design on this layout. Inside there are two fine paintings. On the right-hand altar is Giovanni Bellini's outstanding last work, painted in 1513 when the artist was over 80, showing Saints Jerome, Christopher and Louis of Toulouse. It's awash with atmospheric colour, which owes much to the then upcoming Giorgione (c1478–1510), a perfect example of an old master learning right to the end of his career. On the high altar hangs *Saints John the Baptist, Liberale, Mary Magdalen and Catherine* by Sebastiano del Piombo, painted in 1509. There's an added bonus in the marble relief of the Coronation of the Virgin by Tullio Lombardo (c1455–1532).

➕ 129 H8 ✉ Fondamenta San Giovanni Crisostomo, Cannaregio 🕓 041 522 7155 🕓 Mon–Sat 8.30–12. 3.30–5, Sun 3.30–5.30 🖐 Free 🚊 Rialto

SAN MARCUOLA

You'll notice San Marcuola, one of the city's few churches lacking the usual grand marble facade, looming up next to the *vaporetto* stop of the same name. The builders never got round to putting on the stone facings, and you can still see the sockets and ledges on the brickwork which would have supported the marble. It's an interesting example of what lies behind every grandiose facade. This rather pedestrian church, whose name is a Venetian corruption of St. Ermagora and St. Fortunato, was designed by Giorgio Massari (1687–1766) and built between 1728 and 1736; the interior has statues of the church's patron saints and an early Tintoretto interpretation of the *Last Supper*. There's a ghost story connected with the church, which tells of a priest who proclaimed his total disbelief in ghosts from the pulpit. That night every corpse buried in the church rose up and beat the unfortunate cleric.

➕ 128 E7 ✉ Campo San Marcuola, Cannaregio 🕓 041 713 872 🕓 Mon–Sat 10–12, 5–7, Sun 8–1, 4.30–8 🖐 Free 🚊 San Marcuola

SANTA MARIA DEI MIRACOLI
▷ 142–143.

SCALZI, CHIESA DEGLI

Properly known as Santa Maria di Nazaretta, the Scalzi is so-called after its owners, the Carmelitani Scalzi, the barefoot Carmelites who in fact wear the sandals worn by many religious orders. They arrived in Venice in 1633 and 12 years later purchased land for a church, whose funding was hotly contended by the patrician class. Gerolamo Cavazza put up 70,000 ducats, most of which went on the facade, designed by Giuseppe Sardi. The church was consecrated in 1680. It was noted for its Tiepolo ceiling, destroyed in 1915 by an Austrian bomb destined for the nearby railway station, though even without this, the interior remains a riot of multicoloured baroque excess. Venice's last doge, Lodovico Manin, is buried in the second chapel on the left.

➕ 128 D7 ✉ Fondamenta degli Scalzi, Cannaregio 🕓 041 715 115 🕓 Daily 7–11.50, 4–6.50 🖐 Free 🚊 Ferrovia

INFORMATION

www.chorusvenezia.org

➕ 129 H8 ✉ Campo Santa Maria Nova, Cannaregio 6075 ☎ 041 275 0462 🕐 Mon–Sat 10–5. Closed 1 Jan, Easter, 15 Aug, 25 Dec 💵 Chorus Pass (for all churches in Chorus group) €9, single ticket €3 🚌 Ca' d'Oro, Rialto ⏺ Guided tours organized by Chorus (tel 041 275 0462); information sheets and audioguides in Italian, English, French and German

INTRODUCTION

The little canalside church of Santa Maria dei Miracoli, with its exuberant marble-clad facade, is Venice's most exquisite example of Renaissance architecture. This little gem is one of the most popular wedding churches in Venice.

In 1408 the Amadi family commissioned a *Virgin and Child* from the artist Nicolò di Pietro, which they placed in a street shrine. The Virgin soon became the object of popular adoration, credited with miraculous powers, which included reviving a man who had spent nearly an hour under the waters of Giudecca Canal. In time, a wooden chapel was built to house the Virgin, which was later extended as a church, lavishly funded by devout families. The commission was given to the Lombardo family, Renaissance stoneworkers who fused design, decoration and sculpture into a unique whole, and produced a homogeneous building covered both inside and out with polychrome marbles, put together with a great sensitivity to texture and colour. Work started in 1481 and the entire building was finished by 1489. Apart from the painted ceiling panels, installed in 1528, the church has remained untouched since it was built, though the adjoining convent was almost destroyed in 1810.

The exterior of Santa Maria is as lovely as the interior, so spend time walking around the church before you go in. The bridge overlooking the left-hand side is a good vantage point to admire the design. Inside, take your time, and if you have a Chorus Pass, be sure to pick up an audioguide, an excellent introduction to the church. Your visit will take anything from 10 minutes to half an hour or so.

WHAT TO SEE

THE EXTERIOR

Santa Maria dei Miracoli is one of the few Venetian churches wholly visible from the outside. The north side runs along a canal and the other three walls rise up from the pavement. For this reason, the designer, Pietro Lombardo (1435–1515), gave as much emphasis to the sides and rear as to the facade, decorating all four walls with columns, pilasters and inlaid polychrome

Above *The elegant exterior of the church of Santa Maria dei Miracoli*

marble. Unlike most classically based Renaissance buildings, the columns are Corinthian at the lower level—you'll notice that their capitals are ornately carved, while the next level are much plainer. These are Ionic, normally used at ground level. It's a small point, but indicative of the subtleties employed throughout the design, hardly noticeable details which contribute to the overall harmony of the church. Notice also the number of pillars down the side, far more than necessary, but making the church appear longer and its site not as cramped as the reality. Look, too, at the canalside wall, where the water reflects the columns, giving a quite deliberate illusion that the whole structure is rising from the water. All the walls are faced with different coloured marble and adorned with crosses, circles and octagons in darker contrasting stone. Tradition says some of these were surplus marbles from the decoration of San Marco itself.

THE INTERIOR

The interior has a single nave with a barrel-vaulted roof. At the west end is the raised nuns' choir, once reached by a private corridor that ran from the adjoining convent, supported by square carved columns. The main altar and apse, approached up a flight of steps topped by a delicately carved balustrade, still display the miraculous Madonna for whom the church was built. The entire interior is faced with multicoloured marble and contains some of the richest and most intricate and delicate carving to be found in Venice, seen at its best when the sun streams in, illuminating the rose, white, gold and silver-grey marbles. The altar steps and balustrade leading to the raised choir are beautifully carved with half-size figures of saints and an *Annunciation*, thought to be by Tullio Lombardo (*c*1455–1532), Pietro's son. All three family members worked on the rest of the carving, seen at its best at the base of the pillars in the choir and the columns below the nuns' choir at the back of the church. The ceiling of the choir is carved and decorated with 16th-century panels by the school of Titian, representing St. Francis, St. Clare and the Virgin, and the vault was decorated in 1528 with paintings of the Prophets by Pier Maria Pennacchi.

Left *The church's single nave is light and airy*
Below *The* Madonna and Child *on the exterior of the church*

THROUGH THE BACKSTREETS OF CANNAREGIO

The quiet, spacious canals and sun-drenched *fondamente* of northern Cannaregio are some of the least known, and loveliest, parts of Venice. Modest houses and low-key *palazzi* line the canals, there's plenty of local life and the area is scattered with a handful of superb and contrasting churches. This walk threads through narrow *calle*, along busy quaysides and across tree-shaded squares to show you the best of the *sestieri*, well away fom the crowds.

THE WALK

Distance: 4km (2.5 miles)
Time: 2 hours
Start at: Tre Archi *vaporetto* stop
End at: Ca' d'Oro *vaporetto* stop

HOW TO GET THERE

Take *vaporetto* No. 51 or 52 to Tre Archi.

★ Walk off the Tre Archi landing stage and turn right down the Fondamenta di Cannaregio, passing the graceful Ponte dei Tre Archi on your right.

❶ This is the only bridge in Venice with more than a single span; it's name means 'three arches'. The Canale di Cannaregio is one of the three waterways in Venice to be classified as a *canale* (the others are the Canal Grande and the Giudecca); all the rest are *rii*.

Take the seventh turn-off to your left, ducking under a *sotoportego* into the Soto de Ghetto Vecchio. This widens out and passes through two small *campi* to a bridge that crosses the Rio di Ghetto Nuovo, the canal that surrounds the Ghetto (▷ 136–137). Walk across the bridge to the Campo Ghetto Nuovo. Cross the *campo* diagonally to the right and take the bridge with the cast-iron balustrade over the Rio della Misericordia, turning right on the other side along the Fondamenta dei Ormesini.

❷ You are now well into an area that barely sees a tourist, with long, regular canals and *fondamente* lined with shops.

Take the second left up Calle della Malvasia and continue straight on to the next canal. Cross the bridge; the little-known church of Sant'Alvise (▷ 140) is on the right. Backtrack down Calle Capitello and turn left at the end into the Rio della Sensa. Walk left along the *fondamenta* and cross a bridge, then take the next turning left (blue sign to Fatebenefratelli) up Calle Loredan. This leads through to the third of the three parallel canals in this part

Above *A pretty balcony in Cannaregio*

of the *sestiere*, the Rio Madonna dell'Orto. Cross the bridge and turn right along the *fondamenta* to Madonna dell'Orto (▷ 138–139). With the church behind you, bear left for a short distance and cross the bridge to the Palazzo Mastelli.

❸ The facade of this picturesque Byzantine-Gothic *palazzo* has a relief of a man leading a heavily loaded camel. Legend says this refers to the builder of the house, an Eastern merchant who, having made his fortune, sent home for a beautiful wife. 'How will I find your house in such a vast and strange city?' wrote the girl, to which he replied 'Just look for a house with a reminder of home.' More prosaically, the camel probably refers to the trading links of the Mastelli family.

Walk through into the Campo dei Mori (▷ 131), and detour a few steps left to Tintoretto's house at No. 3399.

❹ This 15th-century house was occupied by the artist from 1574 until his death in 1594, when he lived here with his daughter, Marietta, also a painter.

Cross the canal and continue down Calle Larga to the next canal. Turn left along the Fondamenta della Misericordia; the building on the left at the far end, dominating

the Campo della Misericordia, is the defunct Scuola Nuova della Misericordia.

❺ The *scuola* was designed by Sansovino in 1532 when the Misericordia became a Scuola Grande; it was never finished. The old *scuola*, across the Rio della Sensa to the north, lies a short distance from Tintoretto's house and was used by the artist as a studio, where he worked on the *Paradiso* for the Palazzo Ducale (▷ 66–71).

Cross the bridge, turn right, then take the second bridge on the right and walk under two *sotoporteghi* (arches) to emerge on the Calle Rachette and take a left turn. Walk on, cross another wide canal and head right along the Fondamenta Santa Caterina. This leads into the Campo dei Gesuiti (▷ 134), with the over-the-top marvels of the church (▷ 134) at the far end on the right.

With your back to the church and the *carabinieri* station on your left, cross the bridge and walk down Salizzada Seriman. Bear left into Salizzada Spezier, then right into Rio Terrà Santi Apostoli, passing the Co-op on the right. Turn right along Rio Terrà dei Franceschi (past the cinema) and left onto Salizzada Pistor; this will lead you down into the Campo Santi Apostoli.

Follow the yellow signs to the Rialto, turning left up the narrow

Salizzada San Canciano immediately before the next bridge. This leads through Campo San Canciano into lovely Campo Santa Maria Nova, with its trees, benches and gossiping locals. The beautiful Renaissance church of Santa Maria dei Miracoli (▷ 142–143) stands at the far end. Turn right as you leave the church, cross a canal, then take the third turning left back onto Salizzada San Canciano. This leads to the main Rialto–Ferrovia route, so turn right and join the crowds through Santi Apostoli and along the Strada Nova. You'll pass pretty Campo Santa Sofia, fronting the Grand Canal, on your left. Take the narrow *calle* straight after the campo, which leads past the Ca' d'Oro (▷ 132–133), and on to the *vaporetto* stop.

WHEN TO GO

This is a good walk for either the morning or afternoon, though avoid the middle of the day when things will be very quiet and some churches are shut.

WHERE TO EAT

The cafés in and around Campo Santi Apostoli are a good place to pause and take a break. Alternatively, you could make a short detour to the Algiubagio (▷ 149) on the Fondamente Nuove near the Gesuiti, which is great for sandwiches, pizza and ice cream.

WHAT TO DO

SHOPPING

AL PUPO
Shopping tends to be good value in this part of town, and this children's and babies' outfitters on the main stretch from the railway station has a good range of delectable clothes at affordable prices. There's a big selection of babywear and clothes for children up to 7 or 8.
✚ 153 F7 ✉ Vittorio Emanuele Santa Fosca, Cannaregio 2212 ☎ 041 719 922 ⏰ Mon 3–7.30, Tue–Sat 9.30–1, 3–7.30 🚤 Ca' d'Oro, San Marcuola

BALLARIN
This excellent *pasticceria* has a fine range of cakes and pastries, ideal to sample with a cup of coffee or take away. It also makes delicious chocolates and sweets—look for the chocolate-coated orange peel, candied fruit and delectable fresh cream chocolate truffles.
✚ 153 H8 ✉ Salizzada San Giovanni Crisostomo, Cannaregio 5794 ☎ 041 528 5273 ⏰ Daily from 8.30 🚤 Rialto

CAMICISSIMA
There are bargain prices here on men's shirts, beautifully tailored in pure cotton and poplin. Here you will find great Italian style in a huge range of fabric designs and colours—buy two and get one practically free.
✚ 153 F6 ✉ Rio Terrà della Maddalena, Cannaregio 1367 ☎ 041 275 0925 ⏰ Mon–Sat 10–7 🚤 San Marcuola

CAMILLO MARCHI
The enticing aroma of freshly ground coffee beans wafts out of this little shop on the bustling route to the station. *Tostatura giornaliera*, daily roasting, is the motto, and the machines seem busy whatever time you visit. Enjoy a cup of coffee at the bar while you browse the varieties and roasts on offer.
✚ 152 E6 ✉ Strada Nova, Cannaregio 1337 ☎ 041 716 371 ⏰ Mon–Sat 8.30–8 🚤 Ca' d'Oro, San Marcuola

COIN
Coin, one of Italy's best department store chains, has everything a woman could possibly want in the shape of separates, suits, coats, jackets and accessories at great prices, and also sells tasteful homewares and linen. The staff win the prize for being among the most engaging shop assistants in Venice. Visit Coin Beauty at Campo Santa Luca for tempting beauty bargains.
✚ 153 H8 ✉ Salizzada San Giovanni Crisostomo, Cannaregio 5787 ☎ 041 520 3581 ⏰ Mon–Sat 9.30–7.30, Sun 11–7.30 🚤 Rialto

LA COMPAGNIA DELLE PERLE
There's a huge range of Venetian beads of every shape, style, hue and size in this pretty shop, where the staff will make up necklaces, earrings and bracelets on the spot once you have made your selection. They have ready-to-wear pieces as well, and prices range from practically pocket money to serious spending.
✚ 153 H8 ✉ Calle Dolfin, Cannaregio 5622 ☎ 041 520 6969 ⏰ Mon–Sat 10–7 🚤 Rialto, Ca' d'Oro

JB GUANTI
www.jbgloves.com
Leather gloves by the hundreds are found in this smart and helpful little store a few hundred metres from the Rialto bridge. They come in a kaleidoscope of colours and every type imaginable—kidskin, suede, sheepskin, calf and wonderful winter gloves with snug rabbit fur linings.

Opposite A tempting display of Venetian cakes and confectionery in Il Ghetto

➕ 153 H8 ✉ Salizzada San Giovanni Crisostomo, San Marco 4821 ☎ 041 522 8633 🕐 Mon–Sat 10–7.30 🚤 Rialto

OLD WORLD BOOKS
Right on the edge of the Ghetto is this English-owned bookshop specializing in second-hand, antiquarian and modern books about Venice—they also publish their own titles. This is a find for enthusiasts of the city, stocking out-of-print titles, lovingly tracked down by the owner.
➕ 152 E6 ✉ Calle del Ghetto Vecchio, Cannaregio 1190 ☎ 041 275 9456 🕐 Mon–Sat 10–1, 3.30–7 🚤 Guglie, San Marcuola

PANIFICIO VOLPE
Panificio Volpe specializes in traditional unleavened Jewish bread and delicious pastries and confections, in a city not particularly renowned for its bread. This is one of the few really good Venetian bakeries, and its reputation is such that you'll have to get there really early if you want to see what's on offer. Credit cards are not accepted.
➕ 152 E6 ✉ Calle del Ghetto Vecchio, Cannaregio 1143 ☎ 041 715 178 🕐 Mon–Sat 7–1.15, 4.30–7.30 🚤 Guglie

PAPILLON
If you're looking for something a bit quirky, head here, to Venice's only outfitter to the service industry. You can browse for cotton trousers, well-cut chef's and waiter's jackets, sturdy aprons and delicious little cotton maid's dresses, beautifully cut and made from finest Italian-woven cotton in checks, floral prints and plain colours.
➕ 153 G7 ✉ Salizzada del Pistor, Cannaregio 4555 (SS. Apostoli) ☎ 041 523 9318 🕐 Mon–Sat 10–1, 4–7 🚤 Ca' d'Oro

PERLIER E KELEMATA
With an ever-growing emphasis on organics, Italy's foremost manufacturer of natural beauty products is constantly expanding its lines. This branch carries the full

range of their honey-based products, as well as their other wares, just about everything for body, face and hair for men and women.
➕ 153 G7 ✉ Strada Nova, Cannaregio 4317 ☎ 041 241 1102 🕐 Mon–Sat 10–7.30, Sun 11–5 🚤 Ca' d'Oro

PETER'S TEAHOUSE
www.peters-teahouse.it
This very special shop is dedicated to teas—every type of leaf tea from India, China and Sri Lanka, herbal infusions from all over Europe and beyond, bush teas from Africa and *maté* from South America—along with every conceivable bit of tea-making paraphernalia to help you achieve the perfect brew.
➕ 153 G7 ✉ Salizzada del Pistor, Cannaregio 4553/A (SS. Apostoli) ☎ 041 528 9776 🕐 Mon–Sat 10–1, 3.30–7 🚤 Ca' d'Oro

ENTERTAINMENT AND NIGHTLIFE
AL PARLAMENTO
If you're up in Cannaregio, head for this popular bar, generally packed with locals enjoying Venice's most refreshing spritz, with outside tables overlooking the Canale di Cannaregio.
➕ 152 C6 ✉ Fondamenta San Giobbe, Cannaregio 511 ☎ 041 244 0214 🕐 Daily 8am–2am 🚤 Tre Archi

LA CANTINA
There are a number of bars on the Strada Nova but this is by far the best. It serves beer *alla spina* (on tap) and reasonable wines, and is a good place to pop into if you're passing.
➕ 153 G7 ✉ Campo San Felice, Cannaregio 3689 ☎ 041 522 8258 🕐 Tue–Sat 11–11 🚤 Ca' d'Oro

CASANOVA
Near the station, this internet café-cum-disco, Venice's only real nightclub, attracts a diverse crowd: students, tourists and the gay and lesbian scene. In the early evening Casanova shows live televised football *partite* (matches). Credit cards are not accepted.

➕ 152 D7 ✉ Lista di Spagna, Cannaregio 158A ☎ 041 275 0199 🕐 Wed–Sat 6pm–3am 💶 €10 🚤 Ferrovia

CASINÒ MUNICIPALE DI VENEZIA AND VENICE CASINO CA' NOGHERA
www.casinovenezia.it
If you want to place a bet in the opulent surroundings of a *palazzo* on the Grand Canal, Ca' Vendramin is the place to come, though the the Casinò at Ca' Noghera near Mestre is busier, flashier and more popular. Both offer the usual table games, such as roulette, baccarat and blackjack, and banks of slot-machines and electronic games. Male patrons will be expected to wear a jacket and tie at the Ca' Vendramin Calergi.
➕ 153 F7 ✉ Ca' Vendramin Calergi, Palazzo Vendramin Calergi, Calle Larga Vendramin, Cannaregio 2040 ☎ 041 529 7111 ✉ Ca' Noghera, Via Pagliaga 2, near Mestre ☎ 041529 7111 🕐 Casinò Municipale slot machines Sun–Thu 2.45pm–2.30am, Fri–Sat 2.45–3; tables Sun–Thu 3.30–2.30, Fri–Sat 3.30–3; Ca' Noghera slot machines Sun–Thu 11am–2.30am, Fri–Sat 11am–3am; tables Sun–Thu 3.30–2.30, Fri–Sat 3.30–3 💶 €5 entry or €10 for entry, including complimentary €10 token 🚤 Casinó Municipale: free shuttle from Piazzale Roma every 10 min from 2.50pm; Ca' Noghera: free shuttle from Piazzale Roma at 2.50pm and every hour from 4pm

GIORGIONE MOVIE D'ESSAI
www.comune.venezia.it/cinema
A good selection of art-house films is shown at this two-screen Cannaregio theatre, halfway down Rio Terrà on the Rialto side. Hollywood films are often dubbed into Italian, but shown in English on Tuesdays from October to May. Childrens' films are shown at 3pm on Saturdays and Sundays. Credit cards are not accepted and advance reservations are recommended, otherwise try to turn up 30 minutes before a show.
➕ 153 H7 ✉ Rio Terrà dei Franceschi, Cannaregio 4612 ☎ 041 522 6298 🕐 Telephone for latest details 💶 €6–€9 🚤 Ca' d'Oro

IGUANA

This Mexican bar/restaurant draws a crowd seeking sangria and song. Happy hour is from 6pm to 7.30pm, but it's best to come later when the staff have warmed up. The burritos and fajitas are good too.

➕ 153 G6 ✉ Fondamenta della Misericordia, Cannaregio 2515 ☎ 041 713 561 🕐 Tue–Sun 8am–2am 🚤 Madonna dell'Orto

PARADISO PERDUTO

The atmosphere at this renowned nightspot makes up for the fairly average food. Cheap wine and eclectic music attract a diverse, alternative crowd. Its legendary all-night themed parties have ruffled many locals' feathers over the years.

➕ 153 F6 ✉ Fondamenta della Misericordia, Cannaregio 2640 ☎ 041 720 581 🕐 Tue–Sun 7.45pm–midnight 🚤 Madonna dell'Orto

QUADRIFOGLIO

This bar near the station showcases live local bands every Friday evening. There's also the chance to munch on the excellent *taglieri* (meats and cheese slices) and panini, sip a cocktail and watch the nightly *passeggiata* on the Strada Nova. Credit cards are not accepted.

➕ 153 F6 ✉ Campiello dell'Anconeta, Cannaregio 1974–5 🕐 Daily 8am–2am 🚤 San Marcuola

TEATRINO GROGGIA

www.comune.venezia.it/teatrinogroggia
This small and very intimate venue in far-flung Sant'Alvise is renowned for its modern and contemporary theatre productions and concerts. As well as showcasing plays by emerging Italian writers, it also puts on the occasional productions in English. The music ranges from traditional American folk to minimal avant-garde. Credit cards are not accepted.

➕ 152 E5 ✉ Calle del Capitello, Cannaregio 3161 ☎ 041 524 4665 🕐 Telephone for latest details ✋ €5–€8 🚤 Sant'Alvise

TEATRO FONDAMENTA NUOVE

www.teatrofondamentanuove.it
Venice's premier avant-garde venue, wonderfully set on the northern lagoon in remote Cannaregio, was founded in 1993 in an old joiners' shop. It stages contemporary dance and organizes performances, film festivals, workshops and exhibitions as part of its innovative Art and Technology project, which explores the relationship between artistic creativity and technology.

➕ 153 H6 ✉ Fondamente Nuove, Cannaregio 5013 ☎ 041 522 4498 🕐 Telephone for latest details ✋ €20–€25 🚤 Fondamente Nuove

TEATRO MALIBRAN

A theatre has stood on this site since 1677, and the Teatro Malibran was Venice's most élite performance venue throughout the 18th century; this wonderful building re-opened in 2002 after extensive renovation. Formerly known as the Teatro di San Giovanni, it is now named after Maria Garcia Malibran, a famous 19th-century singer who performed here free of charge, and stages well-known operas such as *La Traviata* and more modern works, as well as classical concerts and ballet productions.

➕ 153 H8 ✉ Calle dei Milion, Cannaregio 5873 ☎ 041 786 603; box office 041 899 909 090 🕐 Telephone for latest details ✋ €25–€75 🚤 Rialto

SPORTS AND ACTIVITIES

PISCINA COMUNALE SANT'ALVISE

Venice's newest swimming pool is set in peaceful Cannaregio and offers lessons and swimming sessions; there's a warm mini-pool for smaller children. Note the opening hours for non-course swimming sessions, and remember you will have to wear a swimming cap in the water and flip-flops to walk from the changing rooms to the pool. Credit cards are not accepted.

➕ 152 E5 ✉ Calle del Capitello, Cannaregio 3163 ☎ 041 713 567 🕐 Mon, Wed, Fri 1–2.30. 9.30–10.15; Tue, Thu 3–4; Sat 5.45–7; Sun 10–12 ✋ €4.50 per session 🚤 Sant'Alvise

REMIERA CANOTTIERI CANNAREGIO

www.remieracanottiericannaregio.it
This friendly club, around the back of the station, will arrange courses in *voga all veneta*, the traditional Venetian rowing technique, with expert instructors. Credit cards are not accepted.

➕ 152 C6 ✉ Calle delle Cereria, Cannaregio 732 ☎ 041 720 539 🕐 Mon–Sat 3–7, Sun 8.30–12.30 ✋ Enrolment €30, membership €10 per month, lesson prices by arrangement 🚤 Tre Archi

Below *Take a cooling dip in Sant'Alvise swimming pool in Cannaregio*

PRICES AND SYMBOLS
The prices given are the average for a two-course lunch (L) and a three-course dinner (D) for one person, without drinks. The wine price is for the least expensive bottle.

For a key to the symbols, ▷ 2.

AL BACCO
A fine evening is the time to head for this wonderfully typical *osteria* in the depths of Cannaregio, where you can eat in a charmingly old-fashioned panelled interior, or the pretty courtyard garden at the back. Seafood and fish are the keynotes here, simply and beautifully cooked. Expect plenty of locals exchanging banter with the ebullient owner and his staff.
➕ 152 E5 ✉ Fondamenta Capuzine, Cannaregio 3054 ☎ 041 717 493 🕐 Tue–Sun 12–3, 7–10 🍴 L €35, D €56, Wine €8 🛳 San Marcuola

ALGIUBAGIO
This café with a small terrace has a striking view of the watery graveyard, San Michele. Right on the *fondamenta*, it gets much of its business from locals and visitors awaiting *vaporetti*. Its three adjoining outlets do tasty pastries for breakfast and quick snacks and

pizzas throughout the day. It also has a *gelateria* so, on a summer's evening, you can sit with an ice cream and dangle your legs over the lagoon. Credit cards are not accepted.
➕ 153 H7 ✉ Fondamente Nuove, Cannaregio 5039 ☎ 041 523 6084 🕐 Wed–Mon 6.30–6.30 🍴 Pastries €1, cone €2.50 🛳 Fondamente Nuove

ANICE STELLATO
The lovely 'Star Anise' effortlessly combines its role as a down-to-earth neighbourhood *bacaro* with that of a rustically elegant *trattoria* serving interesting and traditional Venetian food. You may find the bar area packed with locals, but, once at table, you can enjoy a meal, its makeup entirely dependant on the season and what looked good in the market. For a light lunch, choose a few saucers of *cicchetti* from the array, and enjoy them with an *ombra*, a glass of local white wine.
➕ 152 E5 ✉ Fondamenta della Sensa, Cannaregio 3272 ☎ 041 720 740 🕐 Wed–Sun 12.30–3, 7.30–10 🍴 L €25, D €35, Wine €10 🛳 Sant'Alvise

DA ALBERTO
Perfect for lunch, this inexpensive but utterly authentic Venetian bar

restaurant is run by three young men who, despite their years, make it all seem so effortless. Their array of *cicchetti* includes wonderful *sarde in saor* (sweet and sour sardines), *granseola* (spider crab) and *seppie in umido* (stewed cuttlefish). Booking is recommended.
➕ 153 H8 ✉ Calle Giacinto Gallina, Cannaregio 5401 ☎ 041 523 8153 🕐 Mon–Sat 12–3, 7–10. Closed mid-Jul to mid-Aug 🍴 L €30, D €55, Wine €7 🛳 Fondamente Nuove

FIASCHETTERIA TOSCANA
One of Venice's finest restaurants in an old merchant's wine store, this has shown consistent quality over the years. Enjoy classic Venetian dishes of seafood (of course), meat and game, all well prepared and presented. The extensive wine list includes robust Tuscan reds and whites, an interesting contrast to the fresher wines from the Veneto and Friuli. The professional service makes eating here a real pleasure.
➕ 153 G8 ✉ Salizzada San Giovanni Crisostomo, Cannaregio 5719 ☎ 041 528 5281 🕐 Wed–Sun 12.30–2.30, 7.30–10.30, Mon 12.30–2.30 🍴 L €65, D €105, Wine €9 🛳 Rialto

Above *A quiet corner of Cannaregio*

GAM GAM

For some really authentic Venetian Jewish cuisine try Gam Gam (meaning 'more! more!'), the famous kosher restaurant in the Ghetto. After washing your hands in the fountain, you sit in pleasant, pastel surroundings and enjoy some excellent *cholent*, couscous and *bourekas*. The wine list is kosher too, and includes Carmel and Golan.

➕ 152 D6 ✉ Fondamenta Cannaregio, Cannaregio 1122 ☎ 041 715 284 🕐 Sun–Fri 12.30–10 ✋ L €45, D €75, Wine €9 🚊 Guglie

OSTERIA BOCCADORO

Osteria Boccadoro is where savvy, well-to-do Venetians come to eat. As with all good fish restaurants the menu changes daily, but expect the likes of polenta with shrimp, squid with inky pasta, tagliatelle with clams and scampi, or go for the raw fish dishes. The astute waiters pay you just enough attention and there are wines from the Veneto and Friuli regions, plus some Sardinian whites.

➕ 153 H8 ✉ Campo Widman, Cannaregio 5405A ☎ 041 521 1021 🕐 Tue–Sun 12–3, 7–10 ✋ L €45, D €75, Wine €18 🚊 Fondamente Nuove

OSTERIA AL BOMBA

www.osteriaalbomba.it

This genuine neighbourhood *osteria* can be busy with gondoliers at lunchtimes, who take advantage of the value and range of delicious *cicchetti* that make up for the somewhat lack-lustre surroundings. Main dishes are mostly fish-based and there are vegetables cooked in a variety of ways, making it a good vegetarian choice. Credit cards are not accepted.

➕ 153 G7 ✉ Calle del Oca, Cannaregio 4297–98 ☎ 041 520 5175 🕐 Daily 10.30–2, 5.30–10.30 ✋ L €35, D €60, Wine €8 🚊 Ca' d'Oro

TRATTORIA CEA

This truly Venetian local eating house, and there aren't many left, has been satisfying the neighbourhood for many years and you could easily find yourself the only foreigner in the place. There's a good-value set menu at lunch, or go à la carte and choose from the short menu of mainly fish dishes. If you want to sample *baccalà mantecato* (creamed, dried salt cod), this is the place to try the real thing.

➕ 153 H7 ✉ Campiello Widmann, Cannaregio 5422/A ☎ 041 523 7540 🕐 Mon–Sat 12.30–3, 7.30–9.30 ✋ L €25, D €35, Wine €9 🚊 Fondamente Nuove

VINI DA GIGIO

www.vinidagigio.com

This increasingly well-known restaurant is excellent value, recommended for its superlative fresh fish and meat and game. In season, try the *masorini alla buranella* (wild duck from Burano), and the superb and varied antipasti. The wines come from all over the world, and include an excellent range served by the glass. Booking is essential and service can only be described as leisurely.

➕ 153 G7 ✉ Fondamenta San Felice, Cannaregio 3628A ☎ 041 528 5140 🕐 Tue–Sun 12–2.30, 7.30–10.30. Closed 3 weeks Jan–Feb, 3 weeks Aug–Sep ✋ L €40, D €60, Wine €6 🚊 Ca' d'Oro

Below *Inside Osteria al Bomba*

PRICES AND SYMBOLS

Prices are the lowest and highest for a double room for one night in high season. Breakfast is included unless noted otherwise.

For a key to the symbols, ▷ 2.

AI MORI D'ORIENTE

www.morihotel.com

Tucked away on one of Cannaregio's most tranquil canals, the Mori is housed in a converted Veneto-Gothic *palazzo*. Inside, public spaces are wood-panelled, with opulent fittings and intense colours, and the bedrooms are all furnished with a nod to Gothic design Some standard rooms are on the small side, so an upgarde is a worthwhile investment. The hotel offers up to 35 per cent reductions for internet bookings.

🕂 153 F5 ✉ Fondamenta della Sensa, Cannaregio 3319 ☎ 041 711 001 ✋ €410–€550 🛈 20 🎴 🚋 Madonna dell'Orto, San Marcuola

AL PONTE ANTICO

www.alponteantico.com

For the ultimate room with a view, you could book the main suite, complete with a terrace overlooking the Rialto Bridge, at this lovely hotel in a recently restored 16th-century *palazzo*. The comfortable, well-sized rooms have traditional fabrics and furnishings, and the public areas are decorated with frescoes and Venetian *terrazzo* flooring. Friendly staff and a splendid buffet breakfast add to the pleasures.

🕂 153 G8 ✉ Calle dell'Aseo, Cannaregio 5768 ☎ 041 241 1944 ✋ €190–€550 🛈 7 🎴 🚋 Rialto

CA'DOGARESSA

www.cadogaressa.com

This is a good bet in Cannaregio. The Antenori family's hotel is right on the Canale di Cannaregio, and front rooms have waterside views. The style, as you would expect in this 18th-century *palazzo*, is traditionally Venetian, with beamed ceilings, brocade, Murano glass chandeliers and rooftop *altana* (Venetian terrace). The owners go out of their way to help guests enjoy Venice, finding babysitters and booking restaurants. Free WiFi access is available.

🕂 152 C5 ✉ Fondamenta di Cannaregio, Cannaregio 1018 ☎ 041 275 9441 ✋ €85–€140 🛈 19 🎴 🚋 Guglie

GIORGIONE

www.hotelgiorgione.com

This 15th-century *palazzo* is down a tranquil *calle* off the Campo Santi Apostoli, and spreads its rooms between the old *palazzo* and a newer building. There are some split-level rooms with terraces and rooftop views; all have minibars, satellite TV and internet connections. The public areas are welcoming, and you can eat breakfast in the courtyard with its lily pond. Buffet breakfast is included. The attached Giorgione pub/wine shop serves traditional Venetian cuisine.

🕂 153 H7 ✉ Campo Santi Apostoli, Cannaregio 4587 ☎ 041 522 5810 ✋ €130–€330 🛈 76 🎴 🚋 Ca' d'Oro, Fondamente Nuove

GRAND HOTEL DEI DOGI

www.deidogi.com

Well off the beaten track, in the depths of a quiet corner of northern Cannaregio, this former French embassy *palazzo* and convent provides a water taxi service to San Marco for its guests. The hotel offers everything you'd expect in the way of luxury, with palatial accommodation, grandiose 18th-century style in the public areas and a lush garden with sublime views across the water to Murano. The restaurant serves Venetian food.

🕂 153 F5 ✉ Fondamenta Madonna dell'Orto, Cannaregio 3500 ☎ 041 220 8111 ✋ €350–€522 🛈 68 rooms and 1 suite 🎴 🚋 Madonna dell'Orto

LOCANDA AI SANTI APOSTOLI

www.locandasantiapostoli.com

Two of this hotel's rooms overlook the Grand Canal; all are tastefully decorated, featuring beamed ceilings and pretty fabrics. Public areas have chintz and antiques, there are guidebooks to borrow and the hotel is approached through a courtyard.

🕂 153 G8 ✉ Campo Santi Apostoli, Cannaregio 4391 ☎ 041 521 2612 ✋ €140–€320 🛈 12 🎴 🚋 Ca' d'Oro

MINERVA E NETTUNO

www.minervaenettuno.it

The Minerva e Nettuno is more than a cut above many of its rivals in the railway station area, with wood-beamed ceilings, and traditional furnishings in the spotlessly clean and simple bedrooms. Not all rooms have private bathrooms.

🕂 152 D7 ✉ Lista di Spagna, Cannaregio 230 ☎ 041 715 968 ✋ €60–€110 🛈 30 🎴 🚋 Ferrovia

ROSSI

www.hotelrossi.net

Rossi is a good option near the train station and Piazzale Roma. It's tucked away in a quietish *calle,* away from the Lista di Spagna crowds. Public areas are unassuming yet tidy; guest rooms are compact, comfortable and clean. Some rooms look onto an adjacent garden. Credit cards are not accepted.

🕂 152 D6 ✉ Calle delle Procuratie, Cannaregio 263 ☎ 041 715 164 ✋ €70–€100 🛈 20 🚋 Ferrovia

VILLA ROSA

www.villarosahotel.com

By Venice's standards, this hotel is good value for money; it's also handy for the train station. A cheery lobby welcomes guests, and bedrooms have decent facilities. Some look onto a pleasant courtyard, where breakfast is served in summer.

🕂 152 D6 ✉ Calle della Misericordia, Cannaregio 389 ☎ 041 716 569 ✋ €60–€115 🛈 34 🎴 🚋 Ferrovia

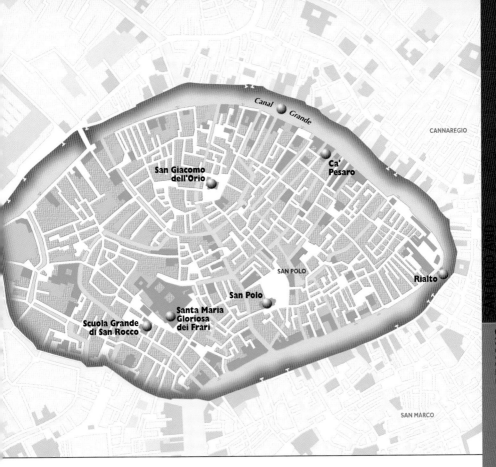

CANNAREGIO

Ca'
Pesaro

Rialto

SAN POLO

San Polo

Santa Maria
Gloriosa
dei Frari

San Giacomo
dell'Orio

Scuola Grande
di San Rocco

Canal Grande

SAN MARCO

REGIONS

SAN POLO AND
SANTA CROCE

SAN POLO AND SANTA CROCE

Enclosed by a loop of the upper stretches of the Grand Canal, the west-bank *sestieri* (wards) of San Polo and Santa Croce are densely populated, workaday districts, full of charm. There's a tangible sense here of Venice as a living city, where families work and live, school their children and do their shopping. Its focus is the Rialto, first settled around 1,500 years ago, and today still home to Venice's main, and most colourful, market. It gets its name from the Latin *Rivus Altus,* meaning high bank, where embryonic islands provided firm ground for the earliest lagoon settlers to build their houses. By the early Middle Ages it was the commercial heart of the city, home to merchants and bankers, and its history is reflected in the names of its maze of narrow streets and hidden squares.

The principal sights lie to the south of the area, along the route running from the Scuola Grande di San Rocco, with its superb picture cycle by Tintoretto, and the adjacent great Gothic church of Santa Maria Gloriosa dei Frari to the Rialto itself. From the Frari, direct routes run through the lovely *campo* of San Giacomo dell'Orio or via the serene Renaissance Scuola di San Giovanni Evangelista north towards the topmost point of the Grand Canal, where the road from the mainland reaches the city at the drab and noisy Piazzale Roma. Better to concentrate on the Rialto route, along which are to be found a clutch of contrasting churches, such as San Polo, set on a spacious *campo,* San Stae, a baroque extravaganza right on the Grand Canal, and ancient San Giovanni Decollato, a Byzantine-Venetian relic. Some fascinating museums, among them Ca' Pesaro and the Museo Carlo Goldoni, are housed in *palazzi,* but perhaps the main draw is the good shopping and great range of bars and restaurants.

6

Parco di
Savorgnan

PONTE
D'GUGLIE

Campo
S Leonardo

Ex Chiesa
di San Leonardo

C d Pasaro

C d Misericordia

C Prnuli al Cavaletti

C Carmelitani

Rio della Crea

C d Procuratie

C Gioranchina

C d vergola

Salizz S Geremia

Balbi
C d Mosto

E mo S Antonio

Palazzo
Labia

Fond Labia

Palazzo
Emo

Palazzo
Querini

Campo
S Geremia

Palazzo
Zeno

C d Procuratie

San Geremia
e Lucia

Palazzo
Flangini

7

250 m

250 yds

Chiesa degli
Scalzi

Riva de Biasio

Palazzo
Marcello
Toderini

Palazzo
Gidoni-
Bembo

Palazzo
Calbo-Crotta

Canal Grande

Palazzo
Corner

C Bembo

Ferrovia

Riva di Biasio

Ferrovia

STAZIONE
VENEZIA SANTA
LUCIA

Ponte
degli Scalzi

Ferrovia

Case
Contarini

Palazzo
Foscari

C Lunga Chioverette

Palazzo
Adoldo

Palazzo
Gritti

Palazzo
Donà-
Balbi

Palazzo
Zen

C d pistor

Salizz d Chiesa

S Sporca

Lista di Bari

Corte
Cazza

Ramo Cazza

San G
D

STAZIONE
FERROVIARIA
MERCI

S Lucia

Ferrovia

S Simeon
Piccolo

Fond S Lucia

Campiello d
Comare

Campo
S Simeon
Grande

Campo
S Simeon
Proféta

S Simeon
Grande

C Orsetti

Corte
Cazza

C d Savio

San Giacomo
dell'Orio

Fond S Simeon Piccolo

Palazzo
Emo-Diedo

C d Tolentini

C Nuova
d s Simeon

C Bergalmaschi

S Lucia

C d Tragheto

Campiello d
Muleghe

Ramo
Chioverette

Palazzo
Gradenigo

Palazzo
Soranzo
Cappello

Rio Marin

C d Croce

C d Cradisca

Ruga Vecchia

Campo
N Sauro

Corte dell'
Anatomia

Ruga Bella

Campo S
Giacom
dell'Ori

C d Oche

Ponte della
Costituzione

Palazzo
Papadópoli

Corte Casa Nuove

Campo d Lana

Fond d Tolentini

Fond di Monastero

Rio d Tolentini

Corte Canal

C d Dario

C Visciga

Rio Marin d Carzotti

Campo
d Strope

C Venzato

Campo
d Oche

C d Capello

Campiello
d Cristo

R Oche

C d Oro

STAZIONE
AUTOBUS

Giardino
Papadópoli

Sott e Corte
Battochio

C d Saccere

R
Campazzo

C d Lacca

C Larga Contarina

C S Zuane

Campiello
d Cristo

Rio S Giacomo d Orio

Palaz
Zane-

Piazzale
Roma

Campo d Lana

C d Mezzo

Campazzo

C d Fonderia

Scuola
Grande di
San Giovanni
Evangelista

C d Olio

Pa
Gi

C Vitalba

C d Vida

Palaz
Mol

Ponte della
Costituzione

Palazzo
Condulmer

Campo d
Tolentino

San Nicolò
da Tolentino

C d Chiovere

Campazzo

San Giovanni
Evangelista

C Zane

C d Dona

C Zane

Campazzo
Tre Ponti

C Lavadori

C d Clero

Ramo Cimesin

Campiello
Chiovere

Nicoletto

Rio Terra S Tomà

Campo
S Stin

Fond
Contarini

C sor

Palazze
Zen

Fond delle
Burchielle

Fond
Magazen

C d Clero

Corte
Spiriti

Rio d Muneghette

C d Archivio

Archivio
di Stato

Ramo Cassetti

Fond Pagan

C Bernardo

Fond del Rio Novo

Palazzo
Marcello

C Tintoretto

San
Rocco

Santa Maria
Gloriosa
dei Frari

Campo
dei Frari

C d Frari

Rio Terra dei Pensieri

Fond del Gaffaro

C d Clero
Castelforte

Campo
S Rocco

C Larga
Prima

Corte
Badoèr

Rio della Cazziola

C Cremonese

Salizz S Pantalon

C Spiriti

C Pasler

C Bezzo

Campiello d
Castelforte

Scuola Grande
di San Rocco

Salizz S
Rocco

C d Albanesi

C larga
Prima

C Galiazzi

Corte
Gallo

Palazzo
Gabrieli Dolfin

C Forno

C Molin

Campiello d
Castelforte

C d Scuola

C Scalater

Campo
S Tomà

Santa To

Fond Rizzi

C d Solacca

Rio d Malcanton

C Vinanti

Campiello
Mosca

C d Scuola

San
Tomà

Santa To
Vecchio

Fond d Procuratie

Corte
S Marco

C larga Raguséi

C d Bole

Corte
Basego

Corte
Barbo

San Pantalon

C Pantalon

C d Cristo

Campo
S Tomà

Palazzo
Civran-
Grimani

Fond d Ceren

Corte
Contarini

C Nova

Fond del Rio Novo

Fond del Rio Novo

Rio delle Bote

Campo
S Pantalon

Palazzo
Signolo
Loredan

C d Saoneria

Crosera

C d Frescada

San
Tomà

Palazzo
Balbi

Campo Santa
Margherita

Palazzo
Foscarini

Fond Foscarini

Rio S d Margherita

Santa
Margherita

C d Cafettier

C d Forno

Rio di Ca' Foscari

C larga Foscari

Corte
Marcona

Palaz
delle Figu

Rio della Crea

Palazzo
Foscarini

Fond Briati

Campo
d Carmini

Scuola Grande
dei Carmini

Scuola
dei Varotari

Rio Terrà di Scoazzera

C d Madonna

C Capeller

Ca' Foscari

Palazzo
Da Lezze

Palazzo
Giustinian

Palazzo
Morolin

Mor

C d Guardiani

Institutio Superiore
d'Arte Applicata

Rio Terrà Scoazzera

C d Soccorso

C Bernardo

Rio Terra Cani

Palazzo
Nani

Palazzo
Grassi

San Sam

Palazzo
Cicogna

Santa Maria
dei Carmini

Ca' Rezzonico

San
Samuele

REGIONS

8

9

10

ARCHIVIO DI STATO

www.archiviodistatovenezia.it

The smooth running of the Venetian state depended on an efficient bureaucratic administration. There were records of Council meetings to be kept, trade treaties to be made, ambassadors to be briefed, the Arsenale to run, spies' and informers' information to be collated, and an eye kept on suspicious characters at home and abroad. Everything was written down, and nothing was thrown away. This vast mountain of paperwork, going back to the ninth century, still exists; it's known as the Archivio di Stato (State Archive) and has been housed since the early 1800s in the monastery adjoining the Frari. Laid out, the paperwork would stretch more than 70km (43 miles). Much is of interest only to scholars, but the Archive occasionally stages exhibitions on aspects of Venetian history using its materials. If you want to look for something, you must request the files in the morning; a knowledge of Latin is useful and it helps to be able to decipher medieval and Renaissance handwriting.

🚩 156 E9 ⊠ Campo dei Frari, San Polo 3002 ☎ 041 522 2281 🕐 Mon–Thu 8.20–6, Fri–Sat 8.20–2 ♿ Free to students and academics; small variable charge for exhibitions 🚏 San Tomà

CAMPO DEI FRARI

The Campo dei Frari gets its name from the great church which dominates the square, Santa Maria Gloriosa dei Frari (▷ 176–179). If you're walking from the Accademia to the Rialto, it's right on the route and the perfect place to pause. Coming from the Accademia, duck under a *portego*, turn right and round the corner and you'll find yourself in the open space around the Frari. It's an oddly shaped *campo*, tucking itself round the sheltering walls of the basilica, and is constantly busy with locals and tourists.

Architectural fans can admire the exterior of the Frari, with its rose-red brick walls, lovely stone detailing and campanile soaring up above the paving, from different angles; for the best vantage point, cross the bridge opposite the main entrance and take it all in from the Fondamenta dei Frari.

The building on the right of the west, main door is the Archivio di Stato (▷ this page), home to the archives of the Republic.

🚩 156 E9 ⊠ Campo dei Frari, San Polo 🚏 San Tomà

CAMPO SAN GIACOMO DELL'ORIO

One of Venice's most appealing squares, Campo San Giacomo dell'Orio sprawls round the bulk of its church (▷ 174). Dotted with trees and benches, the *campo* is the focus of local life. The name is a subject of debate; St. James (San Giacomo) is clear enough, but dell'Orio could refer to a laurel tree *(lauro)* that once grew here, or the area might once have been known as San Giacomo dal Rio (St. James of the River). Typical houses surround the square, which stands at the heart of a densely populated residential district, but the church turns its back on these; like so many ancient Venetian churches, the main door faces the water.

🚩 156 E8 ⊠ Campo San Giacomo dell'Orio, Santa Croce 🚏 Biasio

CAMPO SAN POLO

The largest square on the west bank of the Grand Canal and the largest in the city after the Piazza, Campo San Polo is a a splendid open space, much loved by local kids as a place to practise soccer. Their parents and grandparents enjoy it too, and it's a great place to watch the crowds, sit in the sun and rest on your way from the Rialto to the Accademia. In past centuries it held weekly markets, parades and bull-fighting; today, it comes into its own in summer when it hosts an open-air film festival. Passersby tend to stick to the south side of the *campo*, the main route through to the Rialto, where you'll find the church of San Polo (▷ 181), leaving a huge area free.

Wander around to take in the beautiful *palazzi* that overlook the square. The most impressive has to be the double-facaded Palazzo Soranzo on the northeast side. Built in the 14th and 15th centuries, it is unusual in having its main facade on land rather than water. This wasn't always the case; there was originally a canal on this side of the *campo* in front of the *palazzo* and if you look carefully you can see where it was filled in. On the same side as the church stands the Palazzo Corner Mocenigo, designed in 1550 by Veronese Sanmicheli (1484–1559). It was home in 1909 to the disreputable writer Frederick Rolfe (Baron Corvo); he was thrown out when his hosts discovered that his work-in-progress, *The Desire and Pursuit of the Whole*, was a libellous satire on them and their friends.

🚩 157 F9 ⊠ Campo San Polo, San Polo 🚏 San Silvestro

Above *Beautiful Palazzo Soranzo in Campo San Polo*
Opposite *Relaxing in Campo San Polo, the second largest square in Venice*

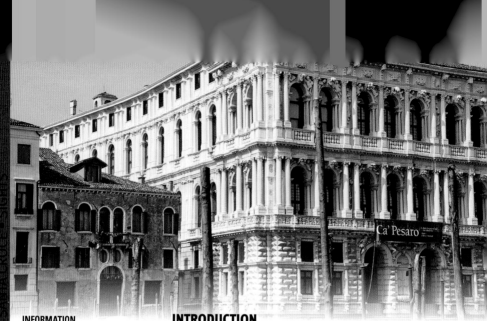

INFORMATION

www.museiciviciveneziani.it
➕ 157 F7 ✉ Santa Croce 2070–76
☎ 041 721 127 ⏱ Tue–Sun 10–5.
Closed 1 Jan, 1 May, 25 Dec ✋ €5.50,
Rolling Venice card holders €3, combined
ticket with Ca' d'Oro and Gallerie
dell'Accademia €11. Museum pass for
all civic museums adult €18, child (6–18)
€12 🚢 San Stae 📘 Guidebooks €6
💻 Café/bar selling drinks and light
snacks 🏛 Good book and giftshop
selling art books, museum souvenirs,
postcards and posters

INTRODUCTION

This magnificent 17th-century *palazzo* on the Grand Canal has been beautifully restored. It houses two important museums and holds paintings and sculpture covering the main Italian 20th-century movements.

The Ca' Pesaro was the home of the wealthy Pesaro family, who made their money from their monopoly of the transport links from the lagoon to the River Brenta. When bought by the family in 1628 it was three separate buildings, and in 1650 Leonardo Pesaro employed Baldassare Longhena to convert all three into one palatial whole. The work occupied the following 50 years and the result is one of the Grand Canal's greatest examples of Venetian baroque architecture, a fitting accompaniment to Longhena's other main Grand Canal buildings, the church of the Salute (▷ 216–217) and Ca' Rezzonico (▷ 202–203). Longhena died in 1682, by which time construction had barely reached the second floor, and Antonio Gaspari was called in to finish the job. He stuck closely to the original plans in most respects and was wholly responsible for the far less flamboyant side facade overlooking the Rio della Pergola.

By the 19th century the palace was the property of the ducal La Masa family from Verona, and in 1889 Felicità Bevilacqua La Masa, the dowager duchess, bequeathed the *palazzo* to the city. She visualized the foundation of an arts centre for struggling young artists, but the city fathers thought otherwise and in 1902 installed a modern art gallery to house works bought from the Biennale. This was joined, after World War I, by the Museo d'Arte Orientale, a vast and eclectic collection of Far Eastern art presented to Venice by Austria in reparation for the damage inflicted by incendiary bombs during the conflict.

The Ca' Pesaro lies a few minutes' walk from the *vaporetto* stop at San Stae; if you're approaching from San Marco you'll be able to get a look at the ornate facade from the boat; otherwise, to study it in detail, you'll need to position yourself on the other side of the Grand Canal. The best place to do this is at the end of Calle Traghetto on the left of the west end of the Strada Nova. Once inside, take time to walk through the entrance hall to the front of the building, with its superb view of the water traffic and buildings opposite. A grandiose staircase leads to the *piano nobile* (first-floor state rooms), where the Museo Galleria Internazionale d'Arte Moderna is situated. The Museo d'Arte Orientale is on the upper floor. If you're interested in Far Eastern art allow at least an hour to see this huge collection.

Above *Ca' Pesaro seen from the Grand Canal*

WHAT TO SEE

THE FACADE

It's worth studying the complex architecture of the Grand Canal frontage, a textbook example of baroque, where perfectly balanced basic architectural elements combine with flamboyant decoration. The lower plinth, at water level, is decorated with lions' faces and monstrous heads and is surmounted by a rusticated facade with two rows of windows, punctuated in the middle by twin doorways. These too are decorated with more statuary and carved swags. Above this, the first floor alternates deep-set arches and protruding columns, producing a superb chiaroscuro (light and shade) effect that's enhanced by the play of reflected light from the water. The second floor has more columns, though the windows are less deeply recessed, and rich stone ornamentation above the windows. Higher still, a wonderfully ornate frieze combines horizontal and upright decorative motifs to pull together the whole architectural ensemble triumphantly.

THE GROUND FLOOR

The land entrance to the *palazzo* is approached through a courtyard, whose focal point is a monumental well-head. This space is enclosed by a terrace and an arcade, which leads into the vast entrance hall. This runs along the axis of the entire building, a typical layout for Venetian *palazzi* since the 13th century. Off this were originally storerooms and offices; today these side spaces house the museum's café and shops, leaving the central space wonderfully uncluttered. At the canal end, shallow steps lead down to the water entrance, originally the main means of access.

MUSEO GALLERIA INTERNAZIONALE D'ARTE MODERNA

The *piano nobile* houses the Museo d'Arte Moderna, a well laid out series of interconnecting rooms (▷ 170).

MUSEO D'ARTE ORIENTALE

The second floor is home to the collections of the Museo d'Arte Orientale (▷ 170).

Left *Detail of the fine marble floor*
Below *A statue on the courtyard facade of Ca' Pesaro*

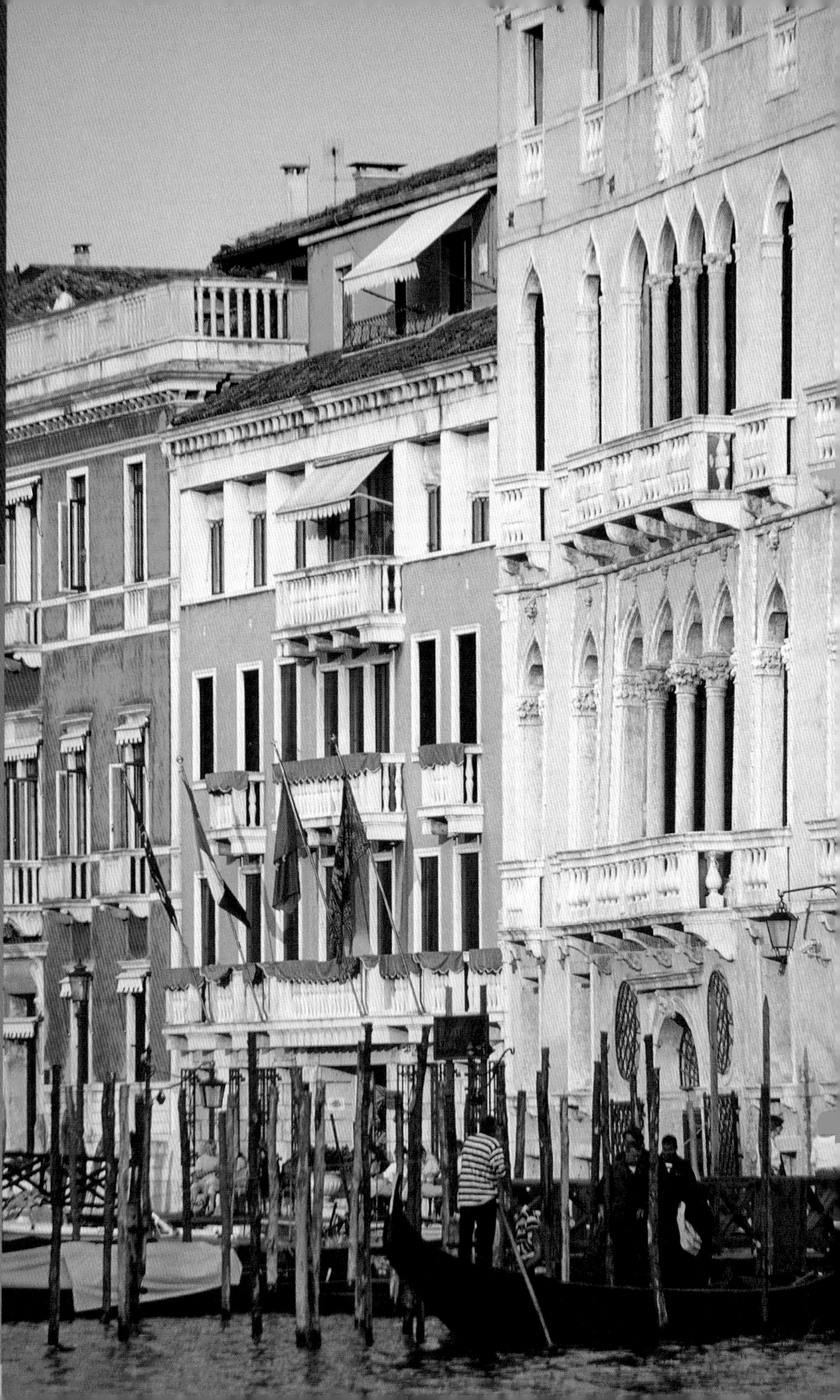

INTRODUCTION

Venice's ultimate must-see attraction is the Grand Canal, a magnificent waterway lined with *palazzi* and superb churches. The Grand Canal bisects the city and offers constantly changing vistas.

The earliest part of Venice to be settled and then developed for commercial purposes was the Rialto, the High Bank, where merchant vessels unloaded their wares. Ships approached it up a wide channel, which soon became the embryonic city's main thoroughfare, known as the Canal Grande. To the Venetians it's the *Canalozzo*, their high street, which divides the city in half, with three *sestieri*, San Marco, Castello and Cannaregio to the north and east, and three, Santa Croce, San Polo and Dorsoduro to the south and west. Along its length, the city's merchants, aristocracy and trading communities built their *palazzi*, headquarters and warehouses, each with its main facade on the water. These were erected and modified over five centuries, and their style covers the entire span of Venetian architectural development. Bridges were also built across the canal to link the city. The Rialto bridge, from the late 12th century, was the earliest; the Scalzi, by the railway station, and the Accademia were both first built in the 1850s during the Austrian occupation, while the new millennium saw the construction of a fourth bridge, the Costituzione, crossing the upper reaches of the Canal at Piazzale Roma, where the causeway from the mainland ends. *Traghetti*, gondola ferries, also operate at fixed points along the canal; these have been in operation throughout the city's history.

The Grand Canal is Venice's major thoroughfare, a wide waterway running northwest to southeast that was originally the main route for merchant vessels approaching the Rialto. It's almost 4km (2.5 miles) long and varies in width from 30m to 70m (100–230ft), with an average depth of around 5m (16ft). The best, and indeed, only way to see the whole thing is by water, travelling from Piazzale Roma or the Stazione Santa Lucia, all the way to the great set-piece of San Marco. Most visitors do this by taking either the No. 1 or 2 *vaporetto* from Piazzale Roma or Ferrovia as far as Vallaresso/San Marco or San Zaccaria. Other options are by water taxi or gondola; both are very expensive but worth considering, particularly if several people are sharing the cost. There are comparatively few places where you can sit or walk beside the Grand Canal; the best of these include the terrace in front of the station and the *fondamenta* on the opposite bank, the Riva di Biasio, San Marcuola and Santa Sofia, either side of the Rialto bridge, the Accademia and Campo San Vio, along the Salute *fondamenta* and at San Marco.

Bear in mind that the views from the Scalzi, the Rialto and the Accademia bridges are superlative, and that the windows and loggias of museums along the Canal are great vantage points; so if you're visiting the Ca' d'Oro, the Ca' Pesaro, the Collezione Peggy Guggenheim or the Ca' Rezzonico, don't forget to look out of the windows. Last but not least, for a truly watery bird's-eye view, do as the Venetians do and take one of the *traghetti* that ply back and forth across the canal at fixed points. These link crucial city through-routes, saving detours to bridges, and will give you glimpses of the Venetian palaces as they were designed to be seen, from water level. A *vaporetto* trip down the Grand Canal takes around 50 minutes, and you'll need to do it at least twice to see everything properly.

INFORMATION
➕ 157 F7 ✉ Venezia 🎬 Start at Piazzale Roma; end at San Marco
🎦 Included in some city tours. ▷ 252
🍴 Wide choice

WHAT TO SEE

PIAZZALE ROMA TO THE CA' D'ORO

Leaving the *vaporetto pontile*, you immediately pass under the Ponte della Costituzione (▷ 140), the newest of the four bridges across the Grand Canal,

Opposite Superb palazzi *line the Grand Canal, such as these at San Silvestre* traghetto *station*

REGIONS

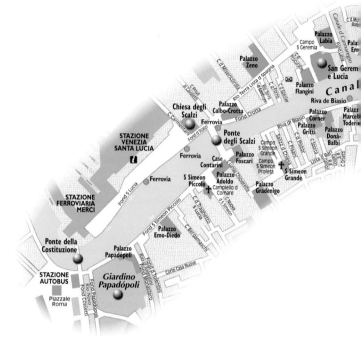

which opened in 2007. A very short hop takes you past the entrance of the Rio Nuovo, excavated in 1938, and the park of the Giardino Papadòpoli (▷ 170), both on the right, to the Stazione Ferroviaria Santa Lucia, first built by the Austrians in 1846 when the causeway was constructed. Today's structure dates from the 1930s, as does the Scalzi bridge (▷ 140). Opposite the station is the green-domed church of San Simeone Piccolo, built in 1738 in imitation of Rome's Pantheon. Almost opposite, on the left, is the ornate facade of the 1656 Chiesa degli Scalzi (▷ 141), a baroque architectural flourish by Baldassare Longhena, contrasting admirably with the first major palace, the Palazzo Calbo-Crotta, a Byzantine-Gothic structure that now houses a hotel.

Just past this, on the left, is the church of San Geremia e Lucia (▷ 141), right next to the Palazzo Labia, an 18th-century building whose main facade stretches along the Canale di Cannaregio, the gateway to the city before the causeway was built, which joins the Grand Canal at this point. The Palazzo Labia was the home of a family so rich and ostentatious that the host habitually ended the evenings by tossing the gold dinner plates into the canal—guests didn't realize that once they'd left, servants were despatched to fish them out again. Across the water, on the right, is the Riva di Biasio, named after a butcher executed for reputedly selling human flesh as pork. From here, a string of Gothic *palazzi* line both sides of the water until the San Marcuola *vaporetto* stop (on the left). The unfinished brick facade of the church of San Marcuola (▷ 141) is faced by the impressive, though badly restored, multi-arched Fondaco dei Turchi (▷ 171), trading headquarters for the Turks in Republican days, and the Deposito del Megio, once a granary.

Almost opposite this, on the left, is the Palazzo Vendramin-Calergi, designed at the end of the 15th century by Mauro Codussi, and the first Grand Canal *palazzo* to be influenced by the classically based principles of Andrea Palladio (1508–80). Its most famous resident was the composer Richard Wagner, who rented a suite of rooms and died here in 1883; today the palace is the winter home of Venice's Casino. Opposite this, is the Palazzo Belloni-Battagia,

TIPS

» The *vaporetto* is probably the best way of seeing the Grand Canal; gondolas and taxis are the far more expensive options.
» Start your trip at Piazzale Roma or the railway station, saving San Marco for the end.
» For the best views, head through the cabin to the outside seats at the stern.
» Avoid doing the trip during the morning and evening rush hours when *vaporetti* are extremely crowded.
» If time is short, take the No. 2, which has fewer stops than the No. 1.
» The *traghetti* crossings give you superb views from the water at different points along the Grand Canal.

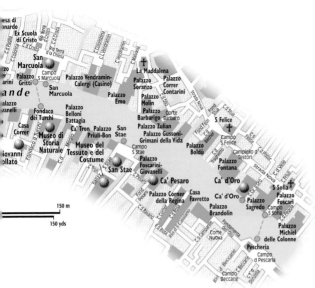

designed by Longhena for the Belloni family in 1647. The two *oculi* (obelisks) on the roofline denote the residence of a *capitan da mar,* an admiral in the Venetian fleet; you'll see other *palazzi* sporting these along the Canal. A little farther down, on the right, is the dazzling white baroque facade of the church of San Stae (▷ 185), with Longhena's 1652 Ca' Pesaro (▷ 160–161), now housing the Museo d'Arte Moderna, a couple of palaces down. It faces the Palazzo Gussoni-Grimani della Vida, a mid-16th-century late Gothic palace that, between 1614 and 1618, was the home to the English ambassador, Sir Henry Wotton. He had the benefit of the Tintoretto frescoes that once covered the facade, now long since faded to oblivion. The next important *palazzo* is on the same side, the beautiful Ca' d'Oro (▷ 132–133), Venice's Veneto-Byzantine Gothic palace *par excellence.*

Below *The view from the top of San Giorgio Maggiore*

CA D'ORO TO SAN TOMÀ

Across the water and a little farther down the Grand Canal from the Ca' d'Oro lie the Rialto markets (▷ 173), still occupying the same area they did more than 700 years ago. The open-arched building with the red awnings is the Pescheria, a neo-Gothic fish market built in 1907, and flanked by the bustling stalls of the fruit and vegetable vendors. The background to their wares is the long arcaded buildings of the Fabbriche Nuove and the Fabbriche Vecchie di Rialto, built in the 15th and 16th centuries by the Republic to house the trade ministry and other commercial administrative departments; the arched porticoes on the ground floor were originally occupied by shops. Just before the bridge, the Palazzo dei Camerlenghi curves around the waterside; built between 1523 and 1525, it was once the seat of the Venetian exchequer, with the ground floor reserved for those imprisoned for debt.

Opposite the Fabbriche Nuove and the Fabbriche Vecchie di Rialto, on the left, is one of Venice's oldest *palazzi*, the beguiling Ca' da Mosto, a 13th-century Veneto-Byzantine building with the typically rounded arches of this period. Down from here the canal swings a little, opening up views of the famous Ponte di Rialto (▷ 172–173). This is flanked by the grandiose Fondaco dei Tedeschi, built as a trade centre and warehouse by the Germans *(tedeschi)*, one of the most powerful and prosperous of all medieval foreign merchant groups in Venice. The present building dates from 1505 and replaced a 13th-century structure; today, it's the main post office. Past the bridge, there's an open *fondamenta* along the water's edge on either side of the Canal, a wharf once used for unloading vital supplies of charcoal, iron and wine and still named after those commodities.

The next stretch is packed with superb buildings, great Gothic and Renaissance palaces whose names trumpet the wealth and might of the aristocratic families. On the left, you'll see the adjoining Ca' Loredan and Ca' Farsetti, much-restored 13th-century *palazzi* that are now the offices of the Mayor of Venice, and the massive 16th-century Palazzo Grimani, seat of Venice's Appeal Court. This faces the Palazzo Papadòpoli, easy to spot with its roof obelisks, while farther down, on the same side, a row of Gothic palaces faces the Sant'Angelo *vaporetto* stop. Two of the finest here are the Palazzo Bernardo, whose delicate tracery was copied from the Palazzo Ducale, and the Palazzo Barbarigo della Terrazza, named after its much-envied roof terrace. On the left, opposite the San Tomà *traghetto* and *vaporetto pontile*, is the impressive Palazzo Mocenigo, home for two years to Lord Byron, assorted animals and his mistress from 1816. His many problems with this fiery lady, a local baker's wife, culminated in her throwing herself into the Grand Canal after Byron had remonstrated with her for attacking him with a table knife.

Above *Palazzo Grimani now houses offices of the judiciary*
Above right *Gondolas and* palazzi *on the Grand Canal—a typical scene*

SAN TOMÀ TO SAN MARCO

Past San Tomà, the Grand Canal makes a sweeping bend to the left; this is the Volta del Canal, with the Rio di Ca' Foscari running off to the right. Just before the *rio,* you'll see Palazzo Balbi, a splendid 16th-century palace that is now the seat of the regional council for the Veneto. Across the *rio* is the beautiful Gothic Ca' Foscari, part of the university buildings, commissioned in 1437 and stunningly restored in 2007. Next to it is the Palazzo Giustinian, another palace that was a temporary home to Richard Wagner (1813–83), who wrote part of his opera *Tristan and Isolde* here. Two doors down is the Ca' Rezzonico (▷ 202–203), which houses Venice's museum of 18th-century life. Facing it, on the opposite side of the canal, is the immaculate Palazzo Grassi (▷ 63), one of the city's most prestigious exhibition centres; there's usually an installation on the water outside to give you a taste of what's showing.

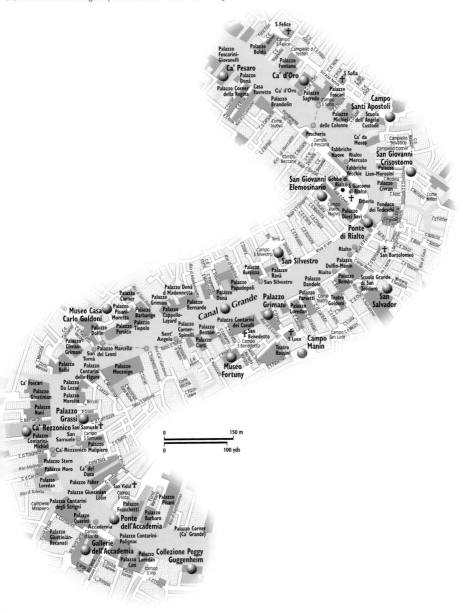

To break the journey, you could get off the *vaporetto* at Ca' d'Oro and take the nearby Santa Sofia *traghetto* across the canal to the Pescheria, walking down through the markets to the Rialto bridge, and across it to re-embark at the Rialto *vaporetto* stop.

The *campo* by San Samuele *vaporetto* stop is a good place to sit and observe canal life. Just past the *campo,* don't miss the tiny Palazzo Falier, a 13th-century charmer with two covered balconies, known as *liaghi.* Opposite Palazzo Falier stands Palazzo Loredan, built by the powerful Loredan clan, which became the Austrian ambassador's residence in 1582—the Austrians must have been keen to secure it as they were willing to pay the 29-years' rent demanded by the Venetian authorities in advance. Ahead now is the Ponte dell'Accademia (▷ 212), built in 1932 to provide a pedestrian link between San Marco and Dorsoduro, and one of the best vantage points for watching boat traffic on the Canal, to say nothing of the incomparable view down towards the Salute.

Immediately below the bridge on the left is the Palazzo Cavalli-Franchetti, a 15th-century building with lovely waterside gardens that was zealously restored in the 19th century. Next to it is the Gothic Palazzo Barbaro, purchased in 1885 by the Curtis family from Boston. They established a salon here, where guests included Henry James, Monet, Whistler, Robert Browning and the society portrait artist John Singer Sargent. Henry James wrote part of *The Aspern Papers* here and used the *palazzo* as a setting for *The Wings of a Dove.* On the right below the bridge is the magnificent Renaissance Palazzo Contarini-Polignac, another palace associated with 19th-century writers and artists, and the little *campo* fronting the water is Campo San Vio, home to Venice's Anglican church and a lovely place to relax by the canal. Past here is the Palazzo Barbarigo, decorated with garish 19th-century mosaics, and the unfinished Palazzo Venier dei Leoni, home to the Collezione Peggy Guggenheim (▷ 204–205). Opposite this, the massive facade of the Palazzo Corner della Ca' Grande, designed by Sansovino in 1545, dwarfs the tiny Casetta della Rose on its left. This pretty little palace, fronted by gardens, was home to the poet Gabriele d'Annunzio (1863–1938) during World War I, overlooked on the opposite bank by the home of his jealous mistress, the actress Eleanora Duse (1858–1924), who took lodgings from where she could keep an eye on his comings and goings.

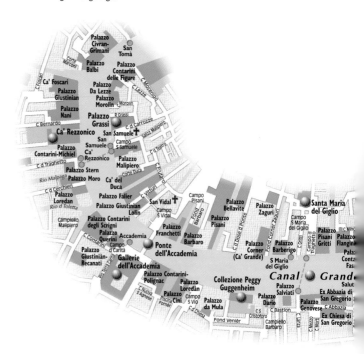

Back on the right bank, the eye is drawn to the drunkenly leaning Palazzo Dario, one of the canal's treasures. It was designed in the 1480s by Pietro Lombardo, also responsible for Santa Maria dei Miracoli (▷ 142–143), and you can see the similarities in the use of polychrome marble on the facade. The palace is said to be both haunted and cursed, a reputation that was bolstered by the suicide in the 1990s of its owner Raul Gardini, a businessman heavily implicated in the 1993 *tangentopoli* scandals of corruption in high places. Just past this is the technicolour glitter of the Palazzo Salviati, whose facade was created in 1924 by the glassmakers of the same name, who had a showroom in the building. Just down from here is the Ca' Genovese, built in 1892 and re-opened as a luxury hotel in 2009. There's more high-end accommodation on the opposite bank, where a string of Venice's grandest hotels lines the bank from the *vaporetto* stop of Santa Maria del Giglio onwards—the Gritti, the Europa, the Monaco and others. Look for the top-storey terraces at the Europa, used as a location for some of the Venetian scenes in the 1999 film *The Talented Mr Ripley*.

Across the water, the end of the Canal is dominated by the bulk of Longhena's plague church of Santa Maria della Salute (▷ 216–217), flanked on one side by the low Gothic ex-convent of San Gregorio, once home to the Woolworth millionairess, Barbara Hutton, and on the other by the row of buildings that culminates in the triumphant final flourish of the Dogana di Mare (▷ 214–215). After years of delay, these old customs warehouses, stunningly restored by the Japanese minimalist architect Tadao Ando, opened in 2009 as a contemporary art centre allied with the Palazzo Grassi. Opposite the point, the palaces give way to Harry's Bar and its surrounding glitzy stores, the Giardini ex Reali (▷ 62), with its charming pavilion, known as the Casino del Caffé, and pavement artists, the facade of the Zecca (Mint) and the glories of San Marco and the Palazzo Ducale (▷ 66–71).

Above *The Grand Canal by night*

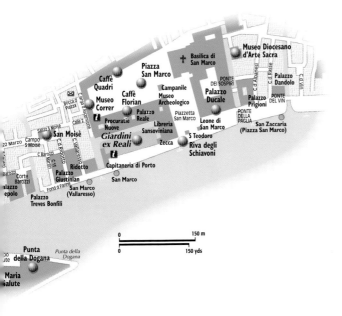

REGIONS

GIARDINO PAPADÓPOLI

At the west end of the Grand Canal, a stone's throw from Piazzale Roma with its buses and cars, is the Giardino Papadópoli, once one of the city's largest private gardens. It was created in 1810 with the demolition of a whole group of buildings standing at the junction of the Grand Canal with the Rio dei Tolentini. Among those destroyed were the church and monastery of Santa Croce, which gave the *sestiere* its name. The gardens are bounded on the western side by the Rio Nuovo. Today, the cool gardens are a good place to pause in this crowded urban area—worth bearing in mind if you're waiting for transport to the mainland.

✚ 156 C8 ✉ Giardino Papadópoli, Santa Croce ✋ Free 🚤 Piazzale Roma

MUSEO D'ARTE ORIENTALE

www.arteorientale.org

Venice's Museum of Oriental Art occupies the top floor of the Ca' Pesaro (▷ 160–161) and entry to the oriental art museum is included in the ticket for the Museo d'Arte Moderna (▷ this page). The vast collection of Japanese art is among the largest in the world and was amassed in the 19th century by the Conte de Bardi, who spent two years touring in the Far East. The collection was donated to Venice by the Austrians, as a peace offering for the damage their incendiary bombs had inflicted on the city during World War I. The layout of the museum has changed little since the original installation, and a visit is like stepping back in time, when museums were a positive jumble of apparently mismatched objects. Connoisseurs of Far Eastern art will find much to admire among the varied displays of arms, armour, paintings, screens, porcelain, sculpture and musical instruments. The lacquerwork, bronzes and porcelain are among the most interesting exhibits, and try not to miss the splendid photographs showing the noble collector posing in native dress.

✚ 157 F7 ✉ Ca' Pesaro, Santa Croce 2076 ☎ 041 524 1173 ⏰ Tue–Sun 10–5. Closed 1 Jan, 1 May, 25 Dec ✋ €5.50; holders of Rolling Venice card €3 (includes admission to Museo d'Arte Moderna) 🚤 San Stae

MUSEO CASA CARLO GOLDONI

www.museicivicivenziani.it

The playwright Carlo Goldoni (1707–93) was born in the Ca' Centanni, a 14th-century Venetian-Gothic *palazzo* with an internal courtyard whose stair leads to the *piano nobile*. The building's main role today is that of a theatrical study centre and archive, but it also houses a museum devoted to the life and times of the writer.

Goldoni transformed Venetian theatre by moving away from the much-loved, but narrow, format of the Commedia dell'Arte, which depended solely on the skills of the actor, to plays where the written text was all-important. His plays describe the daily life of the Venetians, satirizing the laziness of the aristocracy and the manners of the day. They were immensely successful, and Goldoni became one of the first authors to make a living from his writing. Three rooms on the *piano nobile* of the *palazzo* are dedicated to his work, prefaced by an informative, multilingual video presentation.

Don't miss the wonderful puppet theatre from the Palazzo Grimani, complete with all the beautifully dressed puppets used in this popular form of 18th-century entertainment.

✚ 157 E9 ✉ Calle dei Nomboli, San Polo 2794 ☎ 041 275 9325 ⏰ Wed–Tue 10–4. Closed 1 Jan, 1 May, 25 Dec ✋ €2.50; holders of Rolling Venice card €1.50 🚤 San Tomà

MUSEO GALLERIA INTERNAZIONALE D'ARTE MODERNA

www.museicivicivenziani.it

Housed in the stunning Ca' Pesaro (▷ 160–161), the Museum of Modern Art was founded in 1902 primarily to exhibit works purchased from the Biennale. Accordingly, much on display is alarmingly pedestrian late 19th- and early 20th-century Italian works by artists such as Filippo de Pisis, Giorgio Morandi and Guglielmo Ciardi. Their winsome lagoon scenes and run-of-the-mill landscapes are a salient reminder that, in its early days, the Biennale was far removed from its present role as a showcase for cutting-edge art. The museum has some foreign artists represented, with single works by Matisse, Klimt, Klee and Chagall and sculpture by Henry Moore. These are well-displayed in spacious first-floor interconnecting galleries, with some single pieces of sculpture on the ground floor.

✚ 157 F7 ✉ Ca' Pesaro, Santa Croce 2070–2076 ☎ 041 721 127 ⏰ Tue–Sun 10–5. Closed 1 Jan, 1 May, 25 Dec ✋ €5.50; holders of Rolling Venice card €3 (includes admission to Museo d'Arte Orientale) 🚤 San Stae

Right May Morning *by Guglielmo Ciardi (1842–1917), Museo d'Arte Moderna*

MUSEO DI STORIA NATURALE

www.museiciviciveneziani.it
www.msn.ve.it

Venice's Natural History Museum is in the old Fondaco dei Turchi, the Turks' Warehouse. From 1621 this 13th-century palace-cum-warehouse was rented by the Republic to Ottoman traders to serve as a warehouse, trade and social centre. As trade with the East declined, it fell into disrepair, and by 1880, when the municipality purchased it, was due for a complete overhaul. This 19th-century restoration has been much criticized, but the towers and long water-level arcade give some idea of the building's original appearance. From 1898 to 1922 the Fondaco housed the Correr Museum (▷ 64–65); since then it's been home to a small natural history collection. Downstairs there's an aquarium containing species that live in the Adriatic and some information on the ecology of the lagoon, but the main attraction lies through the inner courtyard. Here you'll find a state-of-the-art exhibition devoted to a hunt for fossilized dinosaurs in Saharan Africa. Huge fossils, known through Tuareg legends, were found during a 1973 expedition, as explained in an Italian-only video. Of more interest is the entire dinosaur fossil, rearing up impressively in the upstairs display area.

🗺 157 E7 ✉ Fondaco dei Turchi, Santa Croce 1730 ☎ 041 275 0206 🕐 Tue–Fri 9–1, Sat–Sun 9–4 👆 Free 🚤 San Stae

MUSEO DEL TESSUTO E DEL COSTUME

www.museiciviciveneziani.it

The Museum of Textiles and Costume occupies the Palazzo Mocenigo (▷ this page) and is both a museum and study centre, with an important library and large collection of fabrics and costumes. Some of these are displayed, along with shoes and fashion accessories, in the state rooms of the Palazzo. Venetian fashion was influenced, as elsewhere in Europe, by Paris, and embroidered fabrics, cascades of lace, tight-fitting bodices and

Above *The 13th-century Fondaco dei Turchi contains the Museo di Storia Naturale*

puffed skirts were the order of the day for women, while men dressed like peacocks in tailcoats, embroidered waistcoats, breeches, silk stockings and buckled shoes. The major fashion statement for women was the *andrienne*, a pleated tail at the back of the dress that ostensibly allowed greater freedom of movement, but was also a way of displaying expensive and rich decoration. There are good examples of these, along with fans, the typically Venetian lace scarves called *zendale*, purses, high-heeled shoes made from silk and alarmingly restrictive corsets.

🗺 157 F7 ✉ Salizzada San Stae, Santa Croce 1992 ☎ 041 721 798 🕐 Tue–Sun 10–4. Closed 1 Jan, 1 May, 25 Dec 👆 Adult €4; child (6–14) €2.50, Rolling Venice card holders €2.50 🚤 San Stae

PALAZZO MOCENIGO

www.museiciviciveneziani.it

The Palazzo Mocenigo near San Stae is one of several *palazzi* in the city built by the Mocenigo family, one of the grandest and oldest of the noble Venetian clans, who, between 1414 and 1778, provided the Republic with no fewer than seven doges. The family's grandest palace complex

is on the Grand Canal. Situated just behind San Stae, the palace now houses the Museo del Tessuto e del Costume (▷ this page) and, even if you're not particularly interested in the history of costume, is worth a visit for a fascinating glimpse of the style in which the 18th-century nobility lived. Set on a narrow *calle* a couple of blocks in from the Grand Canal, it was built in the 17th century, the interior being revamped in the 18th century and still retaining the decorations, fittings and furniture from that era. Many of the paintings, friezes and frescoes are by Jacopo Guarana (1720–1808). In typical Venetian style, the main *portego* runs the length of the building; the rooms off here show signs of the development of neoclassical decoration. They include several living-rooms, whose interior decoration and furnishing is colour-themed. A bedroom, dining room and library are all furnished with contemporary pieces and hung with paintings that complement the period detail.

🗺 157 F7 ✉ Salizzada San Stae, Santa Croce 1992 ☎ 041 721 798 🕐 Tue–Sun 10–4 👆 Adult €4, child (6–14) €2.50 🚤 San Stae

INFORMATION

✚ 157 G8 ✉ Rialto 🚤 Rialto, Rialto Mercato 🍴 Wide choice

INTRODUCTION

Venice's most famous bridge spans the Grand Canal at one of the city's longest-settled areas. It's the setting for the oldest and largest market, one of the most vibrant in Italy, and home to an ancient church.

The Rialto was one of the earliest parts of the lagoon to be settled and the word 'Rialto' is a corruption of Rivo Altus, the high bank, an area higher than anywhere else and thus less likely to flood. Settlements grew up on the marshy islets here and drainage was started, freeing space for the expanding city centre. By the 10th and 11th centuries the Rialto was the site of Venice's commercial heart, and in 1097 the market was permanently established here. A pontoon of boats linked the two banks in the 12th century and in the 13th the first of five wooden bridges was built across the canal. From the increasingly grand buildings on the Rialto, Venetian merchants controlled trade between Europe and the Far East, while Europe's major banks and international trading companies set up offices. In 1499 news of Portuguese explorer Vasco da Gama's voyage round the Cape of Good Hope to India reached the Rialto, the stock market crashed, and the good times were over as the merchants realized that Venice's overland monopoly to the East would cease. The Rialto's international role gradually declined, though, along with the Piazza, it remains the spiritual heart of the city to many Venetians today.

The Rialto bridge and its surrounding streets are one of Venice's major must-sees. The first view of the bridge, whether it's from the vantage point of a *vaporetto* on the Grand Canal or emerging from the maze of surrounding streets, is one of those quintessential Venetian moments where surprise and recognition combine. The bridge is the hub of the Rialto, so cross over it, taking in the view, then wander down the *fondamente* on either side to choose the perfect photo angle. Next, visit the church and head for the main fish, fruit and vegetable markets, before exploring the speciality food shops in the narrow streets behind the open market space.

Above *River traffic by the Rialto bridge*

WHAT TO SEE

PONTE DI RIALTO

The idea of a stone bridge at the Rialto was first broached in 1557 and the design was thrown open to competition, with big names such as Michelangelo, Palladio and Sansovino submitting plans. The prize was awarded to Antonio da Ponte, for his revolutionary single-span solution. Given the site's difficulties, the bridge went up in record time, and was opened in 1591. The portico now houses shops, and was a later addition. The *fondamente*, stretching below the bridge on either side of the water, are named for their original functions as unloading wharfs; the San Marco side is the Riva del Ferro, so called for the iron once unloaded here, while the Riva del Vin opposite recalls the thousands of wine barrels which once came ashore here.

THE MARKETS AND FOODSHOPS

There has been a fish market on the same site for more than a thousand years; today it's housed in and around the beautiful neo-Gothic Pescheria. Next to this are the fruit and vegetable stalls, brimming with seasonal produce at much lower prices than elsewhere in the city. The market *campi* and the streets behind here were where the original traders and merchants lived, and there are echoes of all this in the names—Ruga de' Orefici (Goldsmiths' Row), Ruga Speziali (Spicemakers Street) and Riva dell'Olio (Oil Quay). Today, they're lined with butchers' shops offering beautifully prepared meat, bakers selling traditional breads and biscuits, *alimentari* (general food stores), purveyors of fresh pasta, dried fruit and beans, cheese, teas, coffees and spices—making the area perfect for food souvenirs.

SAN GIACOMO DI RIALTO AND THE GOBBO DI RIALTO

The little church of San Giacomo, on the San Polo side of the bridge, is said to be Venice's oldest, founded, according to legend, on the same day as the city itself; 26 March 421. It dates from the 12th century, and retains its ancient Greek cross ground plan and portico, while the clock above the church is famous for its inaccuracy—and has been ever since its installation in the 15th century. Opposite the church is a statue of a kneeling figure supporting a staircase leading to a small column. This is the Gobbo di Rialto, the Rialto Hunchback, which, during the Middle Ages, marked the end of a route between the Piazza and the Rialto. Condemned wrongdoers could escape prison by running the course, naked, in a fixed time.

🕐 Mon–Sat 7–12, 3–6 ✋ Free

TIPS

» The fish market is closed on Mondays.
» Rialto shops are excellent for food specialities to take home.
» The clothes and shoe shops round here carry good, mid-range stock.
» To see the Rialto at its best come very early as the market is opening, but before the mass of tourists arrive.

REGIONS

Below left *Looking down the Grand Canal from the Rialto bridge*
Below *Barges filled with produce head for the Rialto markets*

173

INFORMATION

www.chorusvenezia.org

🕂 156 E8 ✉ Campo San Giacomo dell'Orio, Santa Croce 1456 ☎ 041 275 0462 🕐 Mon–Sat 10–5. Closed 1 Jan, Easter, 15 Aug, 25 Dec 🖐 Chorus Pass (for all churches in Chorus group) €9, single ticket €3 🚢 Riva di Biasio, San Stae 🚶 Guided tours organized by Chorus (tel 041 275 0462); information sheets and audioguides

SAN GIACOMO DELL'ORIO

The church of San Giacomo dell'Orio, with its fascinating mix of architectural and decorative styles, is the focus of a quintessentially Venetian *campo* and neighbourhood. San Giacomo dell'Orio was founded in the ninth century and rebuilt in 1225, when the square *campanile* was added. This rebuild incorporated some very old columns, a couple of which were brought from Constantinople on ships returning from the Fourth Crusade in 1204 and may well be Roman in origin. You can see these behind the pulpit and the right transept; the latter column is a solid mass of age-old green marble with an Ionic capital. The builders followed a Veneto-Byzantine plan, where the central apse is surrounded by arches delineating the side areas. Two hundred years later this all looked a bit old hat, and renovations at this time added a three-nave transept and an apse, making the whole church a mix of Byzantine and Gothic. At the same time, San Giacomo acquired its beautiful ship's keel roof, while later Renaissance additions provided the icing on the cake in the shape of sculpture, wood and gilding. Like that of so many old Venetian churches, the facade faces the water rather than its *campo*.

THE PAINTINGS

San Giacomo's biggest pictorial treasure is the cycle of paintings by Palma il Giovane (1548–1628) in the side chapel known as the Old Sacristy. These were commissioned in 1581, hot on the heels of the resolutions of the Council of Trent, which emphasized the central role of the Eucharist as both sacrifice and sacrament. From now on, artists would concentrate on a variety of scenes incorporating Christ's supreme sacrifice, rather than on the traditional, simpler, theme of the Last Supper. Palma's cycle shows episodes from both the Old and New Testaments, and includes subjects ranging from the *Fall of Manna* (bread from heaven to Moses' wandering people in the desert) to a candle-lit *Paschal Lamb*, which alludes to the altar table and its daily Sacrifice. The pictures radiate light and faith and, in their time, were the perfect means of communication between the church's teachings and the faithful. Back in the main church there are two further splendid works by Palma in the Chapel of the Holy Sacrament, a *Via Crucis* and *The Burial of Christ*. A far older image hangs in front of the main altar in the shape of a *Crucifix* (1350) by Paolo Veneziano (c1290–1362), while the altar is dominated by a glowing *Virgin and Saints* (1546) by Lorenzo Lotto.

Below *Solid architectural form and airy space give rhythm to the interior design of San Giacomo dell'Orio*

Above The Symbols of the Four Evangelists *in San Giovanni Decollato*

SAN CASSIANO

If you're wandering round the Rialto markets, make a detour to the church of San Cassiano. It's dedicated to an early martyr who was hacked to death by some particularly nasty children, a fate which destined him to become the patron saint of schoolteachers. His martyrdom is depicted in a painting opposite the altar. Tintoretto fans should seek out the church; it contains three major paintings by the artist. The barn-like exterior of San Cassiano is pretty dull, though it does have a pleasing 13th-century campanile. The interior, with its ceiling panel by Constantino Cedini, a Tiepolo fan, and a mass of heavy decoration, makes up for this. The Tintorettos are in the chancel. Note the *Crucifixion* (1565–68), with its startlingly low viewpoint, which makes you feel as if you're looking at the scene while lying on the grass. The other two paintings by the artist depict the *Resurrection* and the *Descent into Limbo*; both have been heavily restored.

➕ 157 F8 ✉ Campo San Cassiano, San Polo ☎ 041 721 408 🕐 Apr–end Sep daily 10–12, 5.30–7; Oct–end Mar daily 10–12, 4.30–6 🖐 Free 🚤 San Stae, Rialto

SAN GIACOMO DELL'ORIO

▷ 174.

SAN GIOVANNI DECOLLATO

Venetians refer to this church, dedicated to the decapitated St. John, by its dialect name of San Zan Degolà. Its origins are ancient indeed, probably as early as the seventh to eighth centuries, when an oratory was erected on an island in the small group that made up Santa Croce. In 1007, the Venier family built a parish church on the site, which was restored, but not much altered, by the Pesaros in 1213. With its triple-naved basilical interior and keel-vaulted ceiling, it's a perfect example of a Veneto-Byzantine church where little has changed over the centuries. Slender Greek marble columns, typically 11th century, separate the central nave from the aisles, and even the brick floor is contemporary—warm colours and soft light were designed to help contemplation. Once abandoned, the church was restored between 1983 and 1994 after the parishioners of nearby San Giacomo dell'Orio organized a protest at its dilapidated state. San Giovanni's chief treasures are its misty Veneto-Byzantine frescoes, rare in Venice, where many early ones have been victims of humidity. Those on the right-hand wall are the oldest, haunting images of *The Annunciation* and *St. Helena and Four Saints* dating from the 11th century. In the chapel to the right of the high altar is a superb 14th-century depiction of *St. Michael the Archangel,* showing the saint triumphant over Satan, while the ceiling frescoes, dating from the 13th and 15th centuries, show the *Symbols of the Four Evangelists* and *Christ Among the Evangelists.* This evocative early art is the perfect backdrop for the Orthodox rites held here; San Giovanni has recently become Venice's Russian church.

➕ 157 E7 ✉ Campo San Giovanni Decollato, Santa Croce ☎ 041 524 0672 🕐 Mon–Sat 10–12 🖐 Free 🚤 San Biagio

SAN GIOVANNI ELEMOSINARIO

www.chorusvenezia.org
It's easy to miss the entrance to the church of San Giovanni Elemosinario, tucked between the shops on the Ruga Vecchia near the Rialto. The church is so old it was traditionally under the protection of the doge, who attended Mass here weekly. The disastrous Rialto fire of 1514 totally destroyed the first building (1071), and the design for the replacement was entrusted to Antonio Abbondi, or Scarpagnino (active 1505–49), who was also involved in the reconstruction of the market area. He left the area in front as an open space, which was rented out by the clergy to stallholders and provided useful income. The work was finished by 1531, and resulted in a small church on a Greek cross plan with a vaulted, domed roof and plain, classical interior architectural features, which provided a good setting for the numerous works of art. The highlight is a superb painting by Titian of the church's patron, *St. John the Almsgiver* (1545), over the main altar, but don't miss the Cappella Corrieri on the right, where you'll find one of Pordenone's finest pictures showing *Saints Catherine, Sebastian and Roch* (c1530–35).

Back in the church, the organ shutters are the work of Titian's son, Marco Vecelli, and the central dome was decorated by Pordenone, with a depiction of *God the Father in Glory*.

Look for the piece of 12th-century sculptural relief in the left aisle, which shows a gentle ox reverently licking the Christ Child's face.

➕ 157 G8 ✉ Ruga Vecchia, San Polo 480 ☎ 041 275 0462 🕐 Mon–Sat 10–5. Closed 1 Jan, Easter, 15 Aug, 25 Dec 🖐 Chorus Pass (for all churches in Chorus group) €9, single ticket €3 🚤 San Silvestro, Rialto Mercato

INTRODUCTION

The Franciscans—*frari* in dialect—first came to Venice around 1222, and were granted a plot of land in 1250, not long after the death of their founder, St. Francis of Assisi. Work started on their first church on the site in the 1270s, but almost as soon as it was complete (1338) a larger one was needed to accommodate the crowds that flocked to hear the friars preach. Wealthy local families contributed enough money to enable the construction of a virtually new church, together with a new campanile, and work commenced in 1340. The bell-tower, the second highest in the city, was finished in 1396, but it was not until the 1430s that the church, together with the adjoining cloisters, chapter-house and convent (now housing the Archivio di Stato (▷ 159) was complete. The convent was suppressed under Napoleon, but the church remained in the care of the Franciscans, who today still administer to the needs of the surrounding parish.

The great Gothic church of Santa Maria Gloriosa dei Frari, the historical power base of the Franciscans, is one of the city's most compelling. It is the second-largest church in the city, rich in history, burial place of the famous, and contains some great paintings, monuments and sculpture. Unlike northern Gothic churches, but similar to Santi Giovanni e Paolo (▷ 112), it is built of brick, its plain exterior relieved by the stone detail round the entrances and windows and a few pieces of sculpture. Inside, it is huge, measuring 98m (320ft) long, 48m (158ft) wide and 28m (92ft) high, its size almost overwhelming the profusion of monuments, paintings and decoration. Rather than wandering about, it's best to make a methodical tour, starting at the right, just inside the main (west) entrance. The highlights below follow this route in an anticlockwise direction. To see it all thoroughly you should allow an hour to 90 minutes.

WHAT TO SEE

MAUSOLEO TIZIANO

The monument to the great artist Titian is distinguished by its size rather than its artistic merit, and was erected in the mid-19th century to designs by pupils of the sculptor Antonio Canova (1757–1822), who is buried opposite. A riot of figures and ornament, including a stone replica of the great *Assumption* painting farther down the church, the monument was erected as a gift from Ferdinand I of Austria, also ruler of the Veneto. Titian died, aged well over 90, during the major plague outbreak of 1576, and was one of the handful of victims to be properly buried in the city, rather than hastily interred on one of the lagoon islands, a measure of the huge fame he had achieved in his own city during his lifetime.

SACRESTIA AND THE *MADONNA AND CHILD*

The sacristy lies off the right transept of the church and contains one of the most beautiful of all Venetian paintings, Giovanni Bellini's triptych of the *Madonna and Child with Saints Nicholas, Peter, Mark and Benedict* (1488). The triptych was commissioned for the sacristy by Niccolò, Marco and Benedetto Pesaro in memory of their father Pietro, hence the inclusion of these four saints. It's a ravishing picture, imbued with soft light and warm colour, but it's also a technical masterpiece, with a staggering command of perspective and architectural detail, heightened by the painting's relationship to its original gold frame. The sacristy also contains a beautiful Renaissance tabernacle, attributed to Tullio Lombardo, which was designed to hold a reliquary containing a sample of Christ's blood.

INFORMATION

www.chorusvenezia.org
www.basilicadeifrari.it
✚ 156 E9 ✉ Campo dei Frari, San Polo 3072 ☎ 041 275 0462 ◷ Mon–Sat 9–6, Sun 1–6. Closed 1 Jan, Easter, 15 Aug, 25 Dec 💳 Chorus Pass (for all churches in Chorus group) €9, single ticket €3 🚢 San Tomà 📖 Information sheets in Italian, English, French and German 🎧 Guided tours organized by Chorus (tel 041 275 0462); information sheets and audioguides in Italian, English, French and German

Opposite *Wooden stalls of the Gothic-Renaissance* coro *(choir)*

TIPS

» Wrap up warmly if you're visiting during winter; the church is not heated.
» Look for details of the concerts held in the magnificent setting of the Frari.
» If you're in Venice between Christmas and the end of January don't miss the *presepio* (crib/crèche) here; one of the city's most charming, it comes complete with sound and light effects, running water and moving figures.

Above *Wooden beams emphasize the height of the Gothic ceiling*

CAPPELLA DI SAN GIOVANNI BATTISTA

This chapel, to the right of the high altar, contains Venice's only sculpture by the Florentine master Donatello (1386–1466). The attenuated, expressive wooden figure of the prophet, in polychrome and gilded wood, was commissioned by Florentine merchants in 1438 from their fellow countryman, working at that time in Padua.

THE HIGH ALTAR AND THE *ASSUMPTION*

Titian's great *Assumption* over the high altar dominates the church, the eye drawn magnetically towards it through the choir from the moment you enter. It was painted between 1516 and 1518 and attracted attention for its radical composition. No previous altarpiece had departed from vertical composition, the norm being gentle, static figures grouped around a central focus. Titian revolutionized this, dividing his painting into horizontal zones and filling every figure with energy and movement, as if buffeted by some celestial wind. To balance this, individual figures are used to stress the vertical within each group and so complement the thrusting height of the surrounding architecture. Colour, too, plays an important part in unifying the different elements, and the whole is suffused with a glorious light, the epitome of the Venetian gift to the development of 16th-century painting.

THE *CORO*

The simplicity of the Frari's interior makes the perfect foil for the sumptuousness of the *coro* (monks' choir), one of the most ornate pieces of woodcarving in the city. It dates from 1468 and is the work of Mauro Cozzi, who oversaw the incredible carving and superb intarsia (mosaic woodwork) decoration. It is one of the few choirs in Italy to occupy the centre of the nave.

THE *MADONNA DI CA' PESARO*

Another magnificent Titian hangs on the left-hand aisle. The *Madonna di Ca' Pesaro* was painted in 1526, eight years after the *Assumption*, and shows the Virgin with saints and members of the Pesaro family, the donors. Once more, Titian breaks ground compositionally, this time moving the figure of the Virgin—normally firmly at the centre—to the right, and bisecting the picture with two massive columns. The painting was commissioned by Bishop Pesaro, who is buried in the tomb to the right, and refers to his expedition against the Turks in 1502, hence the turbaned figure on the left. On the right, the figures are Pesaro portraits, kneeling as they wait to be introduced to the Madonna, while the Virgin is said to be modelled on Titian's wife, Celia, who died in childbirth. The movement, realism and strong sense of humanity make this a ground-breaking work, which was to influence the composition and spirit of many subsequent altarpieces painted in Venice.

CANOVA MONUMENT

It's impossible to miss the vast white pyramid in the left aisle, an over-the-top marble monument to the sculptor Canova. It was designed by the sculptor himself as a mausoleum for Titian and completed by his pupils in 1827, five years after his death. The sculptor's body is actually buried in his home town of Possagno, a tiny village in the foothills of the Alps north of Venice, but this huge monument does contain an urn preserving his heart. Mourning classical figures approach a half-open door, a trick copied from Roman tombs, but first prize has to go to the wonderfully soporific and deeply unintimidating lion.

TOMBS

The Frari has some superb tombs of members of prominent Venetian families. Highlights are the spectacularly bad-taste monument to Doge Giovanni Pesaro (1669), complete with Moors, rotting corpses and two griffins; the serene Renaissance tomb of Doge Niccolò Tron (1473); and that of Doge Francesco Foscari, who died, a few days after his son's execution for treason, in 1457, after 34 years as doge. The composer Claudio Monteverdi (1567–1643) is buried in the third chapel to the left of the high altar.

Below left *Santa Maria Gloriosa dei Frari ranks after Santi Giovanni e Paolo as the most important Veneto-Gothic structure in Venice*
Below *Statue by Jacopo Negretti, also known as Palma il Giovane*

SAN NICOLÒ DA TOLENTINO

The church of San Nicolò da Tolentino stands tucked away near Piazzale Roma, well off the beaten track, though fans of lavish baroque decoration should make a point of seeing it. It was built for the Theatine Order, established in Rome in the early 16th century, whose members fled north to Venice after the sack of Rome in 1527. They first settled in Dorsoduro, but moved to the present site in Santa Croce in 1590, commissioning Vicenzo Scamozzi to design a church and convent in 1591. There was a major fallout between the order and the architect, resulting in an unfinished facade when the church was consecrated in 1601. This was remedied between 1706 and 1714 when the massive classical Greek-Roman temple front was designed by Andrea Tirali. Restrained and sober, it's the perfect introduction for the decorative blast that greets you inside. San Nicolò is wedding cake baroque at its most exuberant, its interior swarming with putti, white stucco, coloured marble, gilding and frescoes. The paintings are mostly by non-Venetians, though the high altar and choir are the work of Baldassare Longhena. First prize in the decorative stakes goes to the tomb of Doge Francesco Morosini, which shows the great man reclining in ecstatic delight, while angels pull aside the surrounding drapes. The modern building on the left of the side of the church is the entrance to Venice's architectural faculty, one of the most prestigious in Italy, now housed in the ex-convent buildings.
✚ 156 D8 ✉ Campo dei Tolentini, Santa Croce 265 ☎ 041 522 2160 ◷ Daily 9–12, 4–6 🖑 Free 🚏 Piazzale Roma

SAN PANTALON

To see one of the most mind-boggling ceilings you'll ever come across, head for the church of San Pantalon, set on the fringes of the university district near Campo Santa Margherita. The saint, court physician to the Emperor Galerius in the fourth century, converted to Christianity and was put to death for his faith by Diocletian. As a doctor, Pantalon was well respected in plague-ridden Venice, and there was a church dedicated to him on the same site as early as the 11th century. This was demolished in the 17th century and rebuilt between 1668 and 1686 by Francesco Comino. The church contains some fine paintings, notably Veronese's last great work, *St. Pantalon Healing the Sick* (1587), and a serene *Coronation of the Virgin* (1444) by Antonio Vivarini in the Cappella del Sacro Chiodo, a side chapel where a nail from Christ's Cross was venerated. The church's chief draw, however, is the astounding ceiling, the world's largest area of painted canvas. It's the work of the little-known Gian Antonio Fumiani, who worked on the canvases telling the story of *The Miracles and Martyrdom of San Pantalon* between 1680 and 1704. The 60 panels were invisibly joined to make one entire, vertiginously foreshortened whole, where whirling saints are drawn up past mighty architecture to the golden light of heaven. Fumiani fell off the scaffold to his death during the final stages of its assembly.
✚ 156 D9 ✉ Campo San Pantalon, San Polo ☎ 041 523 5893 ◷ Daily 4–6 🖑 Free 🚏 San Tomà

SAN POLO

▷ 181.

SAN ROCCO

If you haven't already overdosed on paintings by Tintoretto (1518–94) in the adjoining Scuola Grande di San Rocco (▷ 182–184), it's worth going into the church of San Rocco to see the artist's take on the life of St. Roch. The church stands at right angles to the Scuola and makes a good architectural contrast. It was designed by Bartolomeo Bon and built between 1489 and 1508. The interior was extensively altered in the 18th century. There are paintings by Tintoretto and his school throughout the church; the major panels are those in the chancel, which show scenes from St. Roch's life. Be warned, the iconology is confusing and the pictures are hard to see whatever time of day you visit. Luckily, the lower ones are the best. They show *St. Roch Curing the Plague Victims* on the right, and *St. Roch Healing the Animals* opposite.
✚ 156 D9 ✉ Campo di San Rocco, San Polo ☎ 041 523 4864 ◷ Apr–end Oct daily 7.30 or 8–12.30, 3–5; Nov–end Mar daily 8–12.30, 2–5 🖑 Free 🚏 San Tomà

Below The Annunciation by Tintoretto in the church of San Rocco

SAN POLO

The historic church of San Polo, whose origins are rooted in the ninth century, occupies Venice's second-largest square. The *sestiere* of San Polo, the Venetian version of San Paolo (St. Paul), gets its name from this church. It was built facing the canal, away from the *campo*, though later buildings have blocked its water facade and entrance. The original Byzantine church was heavily altered in the 14th and 15th centuries with Gothic elements such as the side portal, the rose window and the wooden ceiling. In 1804 there were more alterations in an attempt to impose a neoclassical look; some of these were removed in the 1930s, but the interior remains a rather unsatisfactory jumble. The campanile, detached from the church across the *salizzada*, has suffered less since its construction in 1362; look out for the pair of stone lions at the base. Inside, paintings include a *Last Supper* by Tintoretto (1518–94) to the left of the entrance as you go in, and the *Marriage of the Virgin* by Veronese (1528–85) in the left apse chapel.

VIA CRUCIS

San Polo's main draw is the brilliant cycle of paintings by Giandomenico Tiepolo (1727–1804) in the Oratory of the Crucifix, which occupies the former narthex of the main church, now inaccessible from outside. Giandomenico was the son of the more famous Giambattista (1696–1770), who is represented in San Polo by a painting showing the *Virgin Appearing to St. John of Nepomuk* on an altar in the left aisle of the main church. Giandomenico was only 20 when he painted the *Via Crucis*, the 14 episodes from Christ's journey to Calvary, and the cycle is one of the rare examples of his work not stylistically dictated by his father, with whom he mostly collaborated. Here are none of the radiantly colour-filled, light-drenched works normally associated with the Tiepolos, but a series of surprisingly realistic paintings, with the emphasis firmly on everyday life and normal people. These are far darker paintings, whose characters are sharp portraits of contemporary Venetian society in the decades that preceded the fall of the Republic. To the left of the entrance Christ is shown carrying his cross in the hours before his death; to the right, the story continues immediately beside the door, while the paintings farther down show St. Vincent Ferrer, St. Helena and St. Philip Neri. The ceiling panels show *Angels in Glory* and the *Resurrection*.

INFORMATION

www.chorusvenezia.org

✚ 157 F9 ✉ Campo San Polo ☎ 041 275 0462 🕐 Mon–Sat 10–5. Closed 1 Jan, Easter, 15 Aug, 25 Dec 🖐 Chorus Pass (for all churches in Chorus group) €9, single ticket €3 🚊 San Silvestro, San Tomà 🚢 Guided tours organized by Chorus (tel 041 275 0462); information sheets and audioguides in Italian, English, French and German

Above *The exterior of the much-altered church of San Polo*

181

INFORMATION

www.scuolagrandesanrocco.it

✚ 156 D9 ✉ Campo San Rocco, San Polo 3052 ☎ 041 523 4864 🕓 Daily 9.30–5.30. Closed 1 Jan, Easter, 25 Dec ✋ Adult €7, under 26 €5. Entrance includes audioguide 🎧 San Tomà 📖 Leaflet and floor plan in Italian, English, French and German. Several guidebooks (€4.50–€15) in Italian, English, French, German and Spanish, all illustrated but with differing levels of information 📷 Guided tours in Italian, French and English; €5

INTRODUCTION

Tintoretto's powerful picture cycle in the Scuola Grande di San Rocco is a series of 54 staggering paintings, produced by the artist in three bursts of creativity over a period of 23 years. This colossal achievement covers the walls and ceilings of the sumptuous headquarters of the richest of the 15th-century *scuole*, dedicated to San Rocco (St. Roch).

St. Roch (1295–1327) was born in France but spent much of his life in Italy working with the plague-stricken. Soon after his death he became patron of plague sufferers, and was particularly revered in Venice, where his body was brought in 1485, becoming one of the city's co-patrons in 1576. The Scuola was founded in 1478 and, in 1515, Bartolomeo Bon started work on the Scuola building. During the years before its completion in 1549, other architects were involved in the design, but its interior decoration is almost entirely by Tintoretto, who worked here at three different times. In 1564 he won the commission by presenting a finished canvas rather than a sketch and volunteering to do the work for nothing more than the cost of his materials. Tintoretto completed the first phase, the Albergo, between 1564 and 1567, going on to decorate the Great Upper Hall between from 1575 to 1581 and working on the Ground Floor Hall from 1583 to 1587.

The Scuola is still the seat of the Archbrotherhood of St. Roch, the only confraternity to have been spared dissolution under Napoleon. Today, it has about 350 members of both sexes, who meet annually in Council and continue to function as an active charity.

The Scuola has three magnificent halls, the Ground Floor Hall being linked to the Great Upper Hall and the adjoining Albergo, both on the first floor, by a splendid and monumental staircase. Start your visit upstairs in the Albergo, the first to be decorated, then spend time in the Great Upper Hall before moving downstairs. You should allow 1 to 2 hours for a thorough visit.

Above *Detail of Tintoretto's monumental Crucifixion in the Sala dell'Albergo of the Scuola Grande di San Rocco*

CRUCIFIXION (SALA DELL'ALBERGO)

The *Crucifixion*, painted in 1565, is a powerful synthesis of narrative and passionate devotion, described by English writer John Ruskin (1819–1900) as 'beyond all analysis and above all praise'. This is one of the greatest paintings in the world, packed with detail and drama, and bathed in light. The composition is extraordinary, the figure of the crucified Christ dominating and forming the central axis from which radiating diagonals spread out to encompass the other elements of the narrative. Within this tight compositional frame, the scene is packed with diverse activity, the figures full of movement and the natural and architectural details further pulling the scene together. Tintoretto originally envisioned many of the figures as nudes, and only added clothing and decoration as the work progressed.

ADORATION OF THE SHEPHERDS (GREAT UPPER HALL)

This New Testament scene is a perfect example of just what sets Tintoretto apart from other artists of his day. His work defies conventional contemporary ideas of perspective, colour, form and light and always pursues a compositional scheme that heightens the inherent drama of the scene. Thus the Virgin and Child are here placed on the higher level of a two-floor stable, whose poverty is accentuated. There's no gentle light, no ordered calm, as in traditional Bethlehem scenes, but a livid sky and a tumbledown building where the very roof is collapsing through the rafters.

Below *The richly carved and decorated Renaissance facade of the Scuola*

GALLERY GUIDE
Albergo
» Scenes from the Passion of Christ and
the Crucifixion on the walls.
» Allegories of the seasons, guilds and
Virtues on the ceiling.

Great Upper Hall
» Scenes from the Old and New
Testaments on walls and ceiling.
» Panel paintings on easels by Tintoretto
(1518–94), Titian (1478–1576), Giorgione
(1476/8–1510), Giovanni Bellini
(1430–1516) and Tiepolo (1696–1770).
» 17th-century carved wooden stalls by
Francesco Pianta; many are caricatures
of trades including a Painter, said to be
Tintoretto complete with brushes.

Staircase
» Two large canvases painted by Antonio
Zanchi (1631–1722) and Pietro Negri
to commemorate the end on the 1630
plague.

Ground Floor Hall
» Scenes from the New Testament.

THE LAST SUPPER (GREAT UPPER HALL)
The Last Supper was a popular subject with Tintoretto, who departed, in almost
all his versions, from the horizontal table with the Apostles on either side of the
central figure of Christ. Here, the table is a diagonal arrowing up from the right
hand, with Christ leaning forward towards his followers. There's a strong sense
of darkness that forebodes the tragedy to come, emphasized by the servants
in the kitchen area, who carry out their work oblivious to the drama about to
unfold. We, the spectators, are drawn into the scene by the linking figures on
the steps that act as a lead into the heart of the painting.

THE ANNUNCIATION (GROUND FLOOR HALL)
The ground floor paintings were the last to be executed. In The Annunciation,
the angel, a whirling mass of wings and drapery that's attended by a swarm
of accompanying cherubs, crashes into the Virgin's chamber. She draws back
in astonishment and fear, while the mass of shattered beams and the broken
brickwork of the outside walls seem to stand for the spiritual chaos that will be
swept aside by the coming of the Redeemer.

FLIGHT INTO EGYPT (GROUND FLOOR HALL)
Tintoretto was born in the foothills of the Dolomites to the north of Venice
and it's tempting to believe that he used his memories of his birthplace as
the background for this picture, one of the few in San Rocco where landscape
plays a major part. The figures of the Virgin and Child and St. Joseph may be
fleeing danger, but they are surrounded by the beauty of God's creation, a
promise that good will prevail against evil. This is a fine painting in which to
take in the artist's late style; its fluid brushwork, off-centre composition and
dramatic light give an edge that was centuries ahead of its time.

Above *A bridge approaching the Scuola*

SAN SILVESTRO

You will walk past the church of San Silvestro if you approach the Rialto from the *vaporetto* stop of the same name. A big, plain building, tucked away off the main streets, San Silvestro was completely rebuilt in the neoclassical style between 1837 and 1843. There's little to admire in the interior with the exception of a stunningly simple *Baptism of Christ* by Tintoretto (1518–94), featuring Christ standing in what appears to be a mountain stream, over the first altar on the right. Across from the church is the Palazzo Velier (1022), where artist Giorgione died in 1510.
➕ 157 G9 ✉ Campo San Silvestro, San Marco ☎ 041 523 8090 🕓 Mon–Sat 7.30–11.30, 4–6 ✋ Free 🚤 San Silvestro

SAN STAE

www.chorusvenezia.org
San Stae is the Venetian version of Sant'Eustachio, a martyr who converted after seeing a vision of the crucified Christ between a stag's antlers. The church has a dramatic setting, on its own *campo* right on the Grand Canal. It was built in 1678 on the site of a Veneto-Byzantine church, but the facade, the sort of late baroque design where every gesticulating saint seems to be battling in some divine gale, postdates the church and was added in 1709 by Domenico Rossi.

Things are less turbulent inside, where there's the gleam of startling white *marmorino* (marble veneer) all around the single-nave, barrel-vaulted interior. In 1722, a legacy enabled the church to ask all the leading artists of the day to produce a painting of an apostle of their choice for San Stae; the results are still here, an anthology of the last burst of pictorial creativity before the end of the Republic. The finest paintings are Giambattista Tiepolo's *Martyrdom of St. Bartholomew* (left wall), a horribly realistic rendering of the saint being flayed alive, painted in 1722 when the artist was 26; *The Liberation of St. Peter* (right wall) by Sebastiano Ricci (c1659–1734); and Giambattista Piazzetta's *Martyrdom of St. James the Great* (1717), showing the saint as a confused old man, also on the left. The church is used for concerts and exhibitions.
➕ 157 F7 ✉ Campo San Stae, Santa Croce 1981 ☎ 041 275 0462 🕓 Mon–Sat 10–5. Closed 1 Jan, Easter, 15 Aug, 25 Dec ✋ Chorus Pass (for all churches in Chorus group) €9, single ticket €3 🚤 San Stae

SCUOLA GRANDE DI SAN GIOVANNI EVANGELISTA

www.scuolasangiovanni.it
San Giovanni Evangelista was one of the six *Scuole Grandi*, Venice's super players in the charitable guild field. In medieval times it was the

guardian of a relic of the True Cross, which made it among the richest of the guilds, with funds enough to commission the great *Miracles of the True Cross* cycle (▷ 209–210) that now hangs in the Accademia. Its headquarters, among the city's most beautiful Renaissance complexes, stand down a narrow *calle*, close to the Frari (▷ 176–179). The building was designed by Mauro Codussi in 1454 and stands on the right of a tiny *campo*, approached through a magnificent archway, designed by Pietro Lombardo (1481). This arch, with its delicate carving and classical lines, is surmounted by an eagle, the symbol of St. John the Evangelist. The *scuola* itself has a superb double stairway leading to the Albergo, the main committee room, which is hung with paintings depicting episodes from the life of St. John. Concerts are held in the *scuola*; the church is open on *scuola* opening days and by appointment.
➕ 156 E8 ✉ Calle della Scuola, San Polo 2454 ☎ 041 718 8234 🕓 Telephone to arrange visit or consult website for opening days ✋ Donation (€5) 🚤 San Tomà, Piazzale Roma

SCUOLA GRANDE DI SAN ROCCO

▷ 182–184.

Below *Statues and carved capitals on the facade of San Stae church*

EXPLORING SAN POLO AND SANTA CROCE

The *sestiere* of San Polo contains the Rialto, the Frari and San Rocco. Santa Croce has its share of delights too, from grand *palazzi* and ancient churches to a clutch of the city's most characteristic squares. For all that, big sights aside, these quarters of the city are comparatively little visited. This walk explores the off-the-beaten-track corners of the area, with some delightful discoveries along the way.

THE WALK

Distance: 3km (1.8 miles)
Time: 2 hours
Start at: San Rocco (nearest *vaporetto*: San Tomà)
End at: Frari (nearest *vaporetto*: San Tomà)

HOW TO GET THERE

Take *vaporetto* No. 1 or 2 to San Tomà.

★ With your back to the Scuola Grande di San Rocco (▷ 182–184) and the church of San Rocco (▷ 180) on your left, head right, then follow the curve of the street round the bulk of the Frari (▷ 176–179) and into Campo dei Frari (▷ 159). With the main door of the church behind you, cross the Ponte dei Frari, turn right along the canal, then left on to Rio Terrà. Take a right turn at the supermarket and walk along

to the T-junction, then turn left into Calle Saoneri. Cross a bridge and keep going until the street widens and you see the entrance to San Polo (▷ 181) on your left. The wide expanse of Campo San Polo (▷ 159) is at the far end of the church. Go under the Sotoportego de la Madonneta off the right-hand corner of Campo San Polo, and follow the yellow signs along to the Rialto. En route you'll walk past the de-consecrated church of Sant'Aponal.

❶ *The Crucifixion* and *Scenes from the Life of Christ* over the door of Sant'Aponal date from 1294; the church itself is an even older foundation, where Pope Alexander III is said to have taken refuge from Frederick Barbarossa's troops in 1177.

The route comes to a T-junction where the Ruga dei Orefici meets the Ruga degli Speziati.

❷ Both these names refer to the streets' medieval function when the Rialto area was the hub of the city's commerce and trade; Orefici gets its name from the goldsmiths who once worked here, and Venice's ancient spice trade is commemorated in the word *speziati*.

Walk straight ahead into Campo Cesare Battisti.

❸ The buildings around the *campo* are the Fabbriche Vecchie and Fabbriche Nuove, built after the great fire of 1514. This broke out in midwinter and, as the surrounding

Above *Buildings in Campo San Polo*

canals were frozen, raged unchecked for a whole day, destroying the entire Rialto area with the exception of the campanile of the church of San Giovanni Elemosinario (▷ 175). Both blocks and the arcades of the Fabbriche were completed by 1550; Sansovino was responsible for the design of the Nuove. The buildings once housed trade, navigation and food supply administration; until recently, they were the site of the city's law courts.

Turn left and walk along to the Rialto markets (▷ 172–173). Keeping the Pescheria and Grand Canal on your right, cross a bridge and continue along the Riva del Ogio (Riva dell'Olio) beside the water. At the end turn left and walk down Calle del Campanile into Campo San Cassiano (Cassan).

❹ This square was the site of the world's first purpose-built opera house, which opened during the lifetime of the composer Monteverdi in 1636.

Leave the square in the right-hand corner just past the church, walk over the canal and along to the junction with Calle Regina. Turn right, then first left into Calle del Ravano, over a bridge, then right again beside a canal; the entrance to the Ca' Pesaro, home to the Museo Galleria Internazionale d'Arte Moderna (▷ 170) is at the bottom on your right. Cross the canal and walk down Calle Pesaro, then turn right and emerge again on to the Grand Canal, overlooked by San Stae (▷ 185).

❺ The dazzling white baroque church of San Stae was built in 1709. To the left of it is the old Scuola dei Tiraoro e Battiloro, the headquarters of the goldsmiths' and silversmiths' guild, suppressed in 1876.

Turn left down Salizzada San Stae on the other side of the church and keep going till you see the entrance to the Museo del Tessuto, housed

in the grandiose Palazzo Mocenigo (▷ 171), on your left. Past here, take the first turning right down Calle del Tentor, following the yellow signs to Piazzale Roma. After the second bridge turn left into Calle Larga to emerge into Campo San Giacomo dell'Orio (▷ 159), a charming, busy square that's a focal point for locals in this part of the city.

Walk across the *campo* keeping the church on your right, then take the right-hand bridge which leads via the Ruga Bella into Campo Nauzario Sauro. Turn left and walk through Campo dei Tedeschi, with its trees and benches, to the oddly shaped Campiello delle Stroppe. Keeping the open space on your left, walk down Calle del Cristo into the triangular canalside Campiello del Cristo. Cross the Ponte del Cristo, turn left and walk beside Rio Marin, across a bridge and right into Calle del'Ogio.

About 50m (55 yards) down, look right and you'll see the beautiful complex of the Scuola Grande di San Giovanni Evangelista (▷ 185), while ahead looms the mass of the Archivio di Stato (▷ 159). At the end of this narrow street, opposite the Archivio, turn left, then right over the

bridge and you'll see the Campo dei Frari on the other side of the canal.

WHEN TO GO
For the Rialto market, make this a morning walk. Start early if you plan to visit the churches and museums.

WHERE TO EAT
There are good cafés and bars in Campo San Giacomo dell'Orio. Alternatively, head for Alla Madonna near the Rialto (▷ 191).

Below *Detail of a painting in San Cassiano*

SHOPPING

ALIANI GASTRONOMIA

This beautiful delicatessen will tempt anyone self-catering or putting together an elegant picnic. As well as a huge selection of cured meats, salami, sausages and ham, superb cheeses from all over Italy and farther afield, they have a mouth-watering selection of ready-made dishes ranging from starters to meat, fish and vegetables, all freshly made daily using the highest quality, seasonal ingredients.

✚ 195 G8 ✉ Ruga Rialto, San Polo 654 ☎ 041 522 4913 ⊙ Mon–Sat 8.30–7.30 🚤 San Silvestro/Rialto Mercato

ANA EMA

This quirky little shop near the Frari shop carries an excellent range of pretty silk scarves and pashminas in glowing hues. The speciality, though, is the selection of felt hats, bags and jewellery, stylish and unusual, all made using the season's most fashionable colours as inspiration.

✚ 194 E9 ✉ Rio Terrà Amalteo, San Polo 2603 ☎ 041 717 443 ⊙ Mon–Sat 10–1, 3–7.30 🚤 San Tomà

ANDREA BALDAN

All the shoes here are made in Italy—not always the case any more in larger stores—and there's something for everyone in the range of both classic and fashionable styles on offer. They have particularly pretty ladies' flat shoes—the ideal solution for stony Venice.

✚ 194 E9 ✉ San Rocco, San Polo 3047 ☎ 041 528 7501 ⊙ Mon 3.30–7.30, Tue–Sat 9.30–1, 3.30–7.30 🚤 San Tomà

BALOCOLOC

www.balocoloc.com

All the hats sold here are original and handmade by the owner, Silvana Martin, who changes her designs to suit the season. There are lovely brimmed hats, doge-like knitted hats in bright designs and some pretty berets. You can take your time and have a real rummage while Silvana sits making up her creations in the background. The shop also stocks costumes for the Carnevale at better prices than some of the more well-known shops.

✚ 195 F8 ✉ Calle Lunga, Santa Croce 2134 ☎ 041 524 0551 ⊙ Mon–Sat 9–7.30 🚤 San Silvestro

CASA DEL PARMIGIANO

www.aliani-casadelparmigiano.it

A stone's throw from the main Rialto markets, this little family-run shop sells superb cheese, *salumeria* (delicatessen) from all over Italy and light-as-a-feather home-made fresh pasta. Locals consider this one of the best shops in Venice, so be prepared to wait to be served. A number of cheeses and salamis are vacuum-packed, ideal for taking home.

✚ 195 G8 ✉ Erberia, San Polo 214–15 ☎ 041 520 6525 ⊙ Tue–Sat 8–1, 5–7.30, Mon 8–1 🚤 Rialto

COLORCASA

This shop is crammed with some of the most sumptuous decorating fabrics you can imagine—silks, brocades and figured velvets are for sale by the length or made up into cushions, drapes and bags. Silk key tassels and curtain swags are equally tempting, and ColorCasa stocks wonderfully warm *trapunti* (quilted bedcovers) in vivid fabrics.

✚ 195 F9 ✉ Campo San Polo, San Polo 1989–91 ☎ 041 523 6071 ⊙ Mon–Sat 9.30–1, 3–7.30 🚤 San Tomà

DROGHERIA MASCARI

On the 'street of spice merchants', this wonderful shop, crammed with interesting foods, spices, dried fruit and nuts, teas, coffees and sweets, also has nicely wrapped packets of dried mushrooms, jars of truffles, balsamic vinegar and beautiful biscuits. It's a great place to track down that take-home foodie souvenir, or even buy a jar of Frank Cooper's Oxford marmalade.

195 G8 ☒ Ruga Spezieri, San Polo 381–2 ☎ 041 522 9762 ⏰ Mon–Tue, Thu–Sat 8–1, 4–7.30, Wed 8–1 🚤 Rialto

FRANCIS MODEL

Tired of the mass-produced, generic designer goods on sale around the San Marco shopping district? This atmospheric shop, which has been in business for more than 40 years, might be just right. Family Artigiani produce wonderful handbags, briefcases and elegant portfolios, though limited edition, high-quality, hand-crafted goods come at a price.

195 G8 ☒ Ruga Rialto/del Ravano, San Polo 773A ☎ 041 521 2889 ⏰ Mon–Sat 9.30–7.30, Sun 10–6 🚤 Rialto

GILBERTO PENZO

www.veniceboats.com

Gilberto's academic yet still practical approach to re-creating Venetian boats in miniature is respected the world over. His crowded workshop is fascinating and you can buy models of classic Venetian vessels of all sizes, including inexpensive kits to build yourself when you get home.

195 E9 ☒ Calle Seconda dei Saoneri, San Polo 2681 ☎ 041 719 372 ⏰ Mon–Sat 10–1, 4–7.30 🚤 San Tomà

HIBISCUS

A rainbow of hot Indian colours shines in the great selection of ethnically inspired scarves, jackets, bags and jewellery in this tempting store, a wonderful, if expensive, contrast to the vast number of cheap glass and mask shops in this area. The clothes are well cut and the stock changes continually.

195 F9 ☒ Ruga Rialto, San Polo 1060–61 ☎ 041 520 8889 ⏰ Mon–Sat 9.30–7.30, Sun 11–7 🚤 San Silvestro

IDEAUOMO

Family-run Ideauomo is very popular with local men, who value its well-tailored, classic clothes. It sells everything from suits and overcoats through to casual wear

and sweaters, changing the stock regularly. Prices are good and alterations, if required, will be ready in two to three days.

194 E9 ☒ Campo San Tomà, San Polo 2817 ☎ 041 520 5030 ⏰ Mon–Sat 10–5.30 🚤 San Tomà

LEGATORIA POLLIERA

The old-style paper shops are no longer as common in Venice as they once were, and this lovely old shop, just opposite the Frari, is a real find if you're hunting for paper, prints and paper products. Here are agendas and notebooks, address books and desk paraphernalia, all printed using traditional methods.

194 E9 ☒ Campo dei Frari, San Polo 2995 ☎ 041 528 5130 ⏰ Mon 3–7, Tue–Sat 10–1, 3–7 🚤 San Tomà

MAGAGÈ

If your children are really fed up with sightseeing, a half hour here could give a welcome respite—this is a toy shop with something for everyone, from dolls, teddies and pull-along toys to state-of-the-art electronics. It's aimed at children aged between two and ten, and there's plenty on offer that won't break the bank.

195 G8 ☒ Ruga Spezieri, San Polo 383 ☎ 041 241 1503 ⏰ Mon–Sat 10–1, 3.30–7 🚤 Rialto Mercato

MERCATO DI RIALTO

Traders have been selling their fruit, vegetables and other produce here for a thousand years. While much is shipped over from the mainland, the colour, plumpness and taste of the goods still tends to be far superior to what many of us are used to in supermarkets back home. Look for the truly local produce from Sant'Erasmo, labelled 'San Rasmo' or *'nostrani'*. Credit cards are not accepted.

195 G8 ☒ Ruga dei Orefici, San Polo ⏰ Mon–Sat 8–1 🚤 Rialto

IL NIDO DELLE CICOGNE

Italians spend a fortune on their children's clothes in shops precisely like this one, which caters for every age from babies up to age 12. You'll

find everything from classics such as tweed coats to mini versions of the latest haute couture.

194 E9 ☒ Campiello San Tomà, San Polo 2806 ☎ 041 528 7497 ⏰ Mon–Sat 10–1, 4–7 🚤 San Tomà

PESCHERIA

A visit to a fish market may not at first sight appeal to everyone, but the produce, atmosphere and location, right on the Grand Canal, make this one special. There are some real characters among the fishmongers, but it's the strange fish, inky squid and still-scuttling crabs that are the real stars. If you're buying, all stall holders will readily gut, slice and prepare your purchases for you, so all you have to do is put them straight into the pan. Credit cards are not accepted.

195 G8 ☒ Fondamenta dell'Olio, San Polo ⏰ Tue–Sat 8–1 🚤 Rialto

SABBIE E NEBBIE

This elegant little shop specializes in contemporary Italian ceramics with clean, sleek and minimalist lines, influenced by Japanese designs— they also stock pieces from Japan in muted tones and wonderful glazes, as well as a great selection of unusual textiles made up as scarves and throws.

195 E9 ☒ Calle dei Nomboli, San Polo 2768A ☎ 041 719 073 ⏰ Mon 3–7, Tue–Sat 3–1, 3.30–7.30 🚤 San Tomà

TRAGICOMICA

www.tragicomica.it

Superb handmade masks, created by an artist trained at Venice's Accademia delle Belle Arti, echo the 18th-century heyday of Carnevale. Look for Harlequins, Columbines and pantaloons, the plague doctor and imaginative mythological masks.

195 E9 ☒ Calle dei Nomboli, San Polo 2800 ☎ 041 721 102 ⏰ Mon–Sat 10–7 🚤 San Tomà

ZAZÙ

You could wear the clothes from Zazù anywhere, anytime; fabrics are natural and soft and the cut is beautiful, with items such as

voluminous trousers tapering at the ankle, draped tops, and bias-cut skirts in softest jersey. Colours are deep, with lots of grey and black, or gentle tones of sand and off-white.
✚ 195 E9 ✉ Calle dei Saoneri, San Polo 2750 ☎ 041 715 426 🕐 Mon 4–8, Tue–Sat 10–1, 4–8 🚏 San Tomà

ENTERTAINMENT AND NIGHTLIFE

ARENA DI CAMPO SAN POLO
www.comune.venezia.it/cinema
From late July to early September this *campo* is transformed into an open-air cinema. The backdrop of flickering colours across crumbling Venetian buildings is sometimes more captivating than the films, generally repeats of first-run favourites from the previous season. Films are usually dubbed into Italian. Credit cards are not accepted.
✚ 195 F9 ✉ Campo San Polo, San Polo ☎ 041 524 1320 🕐 Telephone for latest details 💶 €6.50–€8.50 🚏 San Silvestro, San Tomà

BAGOLO
Oriental lanterns, clean architectural lines and bright colours characterize this contemporary bar, popular with Venetians and students. Live jazz pulls a loyal crowd each Thursday. It serves great snacks and has a choice of grappa and German beers.
✚ 194 E8 ✉ Campo San Giacomo dell'Orio, Santa Croce 1584 ☎ 0347 366506 🕐 Tue–Sun 6.30–11pm 🚏 San Stae

CAFÉ DEI FRARI
This is a great place for an aperitif, especially if you want to dine nearby. Many Venetians start their night with the house spritz or prosecco.
✚ 194 E9 ✉ Fondamenta dei Frari, San Polo 3564 ☎ 041 524 1877 🕐 Mon–Sat 9–9, Sun 5–9pm 🚏 San Tomà

CANTINA DO MORI
The house spritz here is one of the most drinkable you'll get and the *cicchetti* (or tapas) are the perfect accompaniment.
✚ 195 G8 ✉ Calle do Mori, San Polo 429 ☎ 041 522 5401 🕐 Mon–Sat 8.30–8.30 🚏 Rialto, San Silvestro

CHIESA DI SAN GIACOMETTO
www.prgroup.it
The intimate church of San Giacomo di Rialto, affectionately known as San Giacometto, is near the Rialto markets. The original building was erected in the fifth century. Concerts by the Ensemble Antonio Vivaldi and other guest orchestras are held in this evocative church interior. Credit cards are not accepted.
✚ 195 G8 ✉ Campo di San Giacometto, San Polo ☎ 041 426 6559 🕐 Telephone for latest details 💶 €17–€22 🚏 Rialto, San Silvestro

EASY BAR
Beams, bricks, stylish hi-tech touches and an adventurous menu give this bar and music venue a contemporary feel. On Wednesday nights and during the Carnival, Easy Bar hosts live rock and jazz bands—the action often takes place outside in the *campo*.
✚ 195 F8 ✉ Campo Santa Maria Mater Domini, Santa Croce 2119 ☎ 041 524 0321 🕐 Fri–Wed 7am–10pm 🚏 San Stae

PALAZZETTO BRU ZANE
www.bru-zane.com
Dedicated to French Romantic music of the 19th century, the Palazzetto Bru Zane opened in 2008 as the venue for around 100 concerts annually, themed to aspects of the French Romantic movement. Some concerts are given in the Scuola Grande di San Rocco (▷ this page).
✚ 194 E8 ✉ Calle dell'Ogio, San Polo 2368 ☎ 041 521 1005 🕐 Telephone or check website for times and programmes 💶 €25–€35 🚏 San Tomà, Piazzale Roma

SANTA MARIA GLORIOSA DEI FRARI
www.chorusvenezia.org, www.basilicadeifrari.it
The cavernous interior of the Frari church is the setting for quality concerts of sacred music. There are regular concert series in the spring and autumn, featuring orchestral ensembles or organ recitals. Credit cards are not accepted.
✚ 194 E9 ✉ Campo dei Frari, San Polo ☎ 041 522 2637 🕐 Telephone for

latest details 💶 €8–€12, sometimes free; telephone for latest details 🚏 San Tomà

SCUOLA GRANDE DI SAN GIOVANNI EVANGELISTA
www.orchestradivenezia.it
Classics by Vivaldi and other composers are played at this *scuola*, founded in the 13th century. Period costumes are worn by the dancers who perform to the music. Credit cards are not accepted.
✚ 194 E8 ✉ Campiello della Scuola, San Polo 2454 ☎ 041 718 2347 🕐 Telephone for latest details 💶 €21–€31 🚏 San Tomà

SCUOLA GRANDE DI SAN ROCCO
www.musicinvenice.com
This famous confraternity has a rich musical tradition stretching back over 500 years, and its magnificent interior is the splendid backdrop to baroque music concerts performed on period instruments, featuring works by Monteverdi (1567–1643) and Giovanni Gabrieli (c1553/4–1612), who was organist here for 27 years. Credit cards are not accepted.
✚ 194 D9 ✉ Campo San Rocco, Santa Croce ☎ 041 523 4864 🕐 Telephone for latest details 💶 Telephone for latest details 🚏 San Tomà

VIDEOTECA PASINETTI
www.comune.venezia.it/cinema
Although functioning primarily as a resource centre and archive, this cinema runs occasional film seasons, showing movies, videos, TV documentaries and newsreels from its vast collection. Credit cards are not accepted.
✚ 195 F7 ✉ Palazzo Mocenigo, Santa Croce 1991 ☎ 041 524 1320 🕐 Telephone for latest details 💶 €4–€6 🚏 San Stae

HEALTH AND BEAUTY
STEFANO E CLAUDIA
Join the city's fashion-conscious women for a stylish Italian cut and blow-dry, where a shampoo comes wth a view of the Grand Canal.
✚ 195 G9 ✉ Riva del Vin, San Polo 1098B ☎ 041 520 1913 🕐 Tue–Sat 9–5 💶 Shampoo and blow-dry €30; full cut and blow-dry €65 🚏 San Silvestro

EATING

PRICES AND SYMBOLS
The prices given are the average for a two-course lunch (L) and a three-course dinner (D) for one person, without drinks. The wine price is for the least expensive bottle.

For a key to the symbols, ▷ 2.

AE OCHE
In a city where wood-burning ovens are forbidden by law, it's hard to find a really good pizza, but you won't be disappointed at Ae Oche. This little pizzeria has the most amusing staff and the pizzas are reassuringly good. There's a host of European beers to help wash it down.
✚ 194 E8 ✉ Calle delle Oche, Santa Croce 1552A/B ☎ 041 524 1161 🕔 Daily 12–2.30, 7–10 ✋ L €25, D €40, Wine €7 🚤 San Stae

AL PONTE
Affectionately known as La Patatina, after its famous chunky chips, this busy place serves straightforward Venetian fare, such as *polpette* (meat balls), seafood risotto and *fritto misto*. Eating at the bar is excellent value; you'll pay more for table service.
✚ 195 E9 ✉ Ponte San Polo, San Polo 2741 ☎ 041 523 7238 🕔 Mon–Sat

9.30–2.30, 5–10 ✋ L €15, D €35, Wine €9 🚤 San Tomà

AL VECIO FRITOLIN
www.veciofritolin.it
Whatever was caught that morning will be marinated in a sweet and sour sauce, tossed in flour and fried or flame grilled at Al Vecio Fritolin. There's not a lot of choice, but whatever is served is always delicious. Fried fish with polenta, and pasta with beans are wholesome popular dishes. The selection of wines will help the *cicchetti* down. Credit cards are not accepted.
✚ 195 F8 ✉ Calle della Regina, Santa Croce 2262 ☎ 041 522 2881 🕔 Tue–Sat 12–2.30, 7–10, and lunch on Sun ✋ *Cicchetti* for two €12. Wine/beer from €1.50 🚤 San Stae

ALLA MADONNA
Popular with locals, this is a big bustling place, serving all the Venetian staples, with some run-of-the-mill dishes, such as *cotoletta alla Milanese*, you'll find all over Italy. The food is fairly simple but tasty, the service charming and the wine list small but well considered. However, you're not encouraged to linger over your meal.

Above *Canalside Da Fiore restaurant*

✚ 195 G8 ✉ Calle della Madonna, San Polo 594 ☎ 041 522 3824 (no reservations) 🕔 Thu–Tue 12–3, 7–10 ✋ L €50, D €80, Wine €10 🚤 Rialto

ALLA ZUCCA
In Venice, as in all Italy, pity the vegetarians. But not at La Zucca (The Pumpkin), where the mainly vegetarian cuisine is cooked with style and imagination. The dishes marry pumpkin, courgette (zucchini) flowers and fennel with an array of cheeses. It's great value for money and very popular, so book in advance.
✚ 195 E7 ✉ Ponte del Megio, Santa Croce 1762 ☎ 041 524 1570 🕔 Mon–Sat 12–2.30, 7–10.30 ✋ L €55, D €85, Wine €8 🚤 San Stae

ANTICA BESSETA
The interior of this established restaurant may be traditional Venetian, but the food is a happy combination of classic ingredients from the city given an elegant new twist. A procession of beautifully presented courses will give you the chance to try all the specials, with good wine and highly professional

service to add to the pleasure—reserve ahead to guarantee an outside table in the pretty courtyard.

✚ 194 E7 ✉ Salizzada de Ca' Zusto, Santa Croce 1395 ☎ 041 721 687 ⏰ Wed–Mon 12.30–3, 7.30–10 🖐 L €40, D €60, Wine €11 🚤 Riva de Biasio

ANTICA BIRRARIA LA CORTE
This converted warehouse is one of a small number of a new breed of Venetian eateries. The seating spills out into the evocative expanse of Campo San Polo, the inside is contemporary. The food nods to all the Venetian and Italian classics—it's good quality and won't break the bank. You can snack or go the whole hog here.

✚ 195 F8 ✉ Campo San Polo, San Polo 2168 ☎ 041 275 0570 ⏰ Daily 11–3, 6–10 🖐 L €35, D €50, Wine €8 🚤 San Silvestro

ANTICA OSTERIA AL PANTALON
On the main route to the Frari, this long, narrow restaurant tempts diners with its eye-catching display of fish and seafood. This, and the excellent pasta and rice dishes, are cooked to order with simple elegance at the plain wooden tables. It's wise to be guided by the staff and to reserve ahead during the busy months—it's extremely popular with students from the nearby university.

✚ 194 D9 ✉ Crosera San Pantalon, Dorsoduro 3958 ☎ 041 710 849 ⏰ Mon–Sat 12.30–3, 7–10 🖐 L €25, D €40, Wine €12 🚤 San Tomà

ANTICA OSTERIA RUGA RIALTO
Old blends with contemporary and utility here. The cicchetti are among the best in town and are served by staff who know their stuff. You can either stand at the bar or sit in the wooden salon around the back. Old characters mix with artists and musicians. Artwork is exhibited and rock and jazz gigs are staged. Credit cards are not accepted.

✚ 195 G8 ✉ Ruga Rialto, San Polo 692, 30125 Venezia ☎ 041 521 1243 ⏰ Daily 11–10 🖐 Cicchetti or tapas for two €10, Wine/beer from €2 🚤 Rialto

ANTICHE CARAMPANE
This off-the-beaten-track restaurant specializes in beautifully cooked, elegantly served seafood and fish. The style is a modern take on tradition, seen at its best in dishes such as spaghetti alla granseola (pasta with spider crab), cassopipa (spaghetti with a spicy fish sauce) or branzino in salsa di peperoni (sea bass in a sweet pepper sauce). The wine list is long and interesting and desserts light, elegant and imaginative. Booking is essential.

✚ 195 G8 ✉ Ponte delle Tette, San Polo 1911 ☎ 041 524 0165 ⏰ Mon 7.30–10.30, Tue–Sat 12.20–3, 7.30–10.30 🖐 L €35, D €55, Wine €12 🚤 San Silvestro

ANTICO GIARDINETTO
Tucked away on a quiet street, this long-established eating house has a pretty garden—hence the name. The food is classic Venetian, so expect fresh fish cooked with care and antipasti such as sarde in saor, risotto alle seppie (black risotto with cuttlefish) and a superlative tiramisù for pudding.

✚ 195 F8 ✉ Calle dei Morti, Santa Croce 2253 ☎ 041 722 882 ⏰ Tue–Sun 12–3, 7–10 🖐 L €30, D €45, Wine €12 🚤 Rialto/San Stae

BOTTEGA DEL CAFFÈ DERSUT
Huge windows allow a glimpse into the interior of this café, where you can stand at the bar or relax on one of the cosy sofas while you enjoy one of the speciality coffees—different flavours, different toppings, many laced with cream—or get a vitamin fix in the form of a blended veggie juice or mixed fruit smoothie made to order. There are mouth-watering pastries, tarts and cakes.

✚ 194 E9 ✉ Campo dei Frari, San Polo 3014 ☎ 041 303 2159 ⏰ Mon–Sat 6am–8pm, Sun 8–1 🖐 Coffee €1.10–€3, smoothies and shakes €3–€5, cakes €3 🚤 San Tomà

DA FIORE
Perhaps better known for its fine cellar, Da Fiore is considered one of the top restaurants in Venice. However, dining here may not incur as much damage to the bank balance as some of the other 'top' restaurants. The food takes an international approach to Venetian cooking. If you want to dine beside Venice's glitterati, it's best to book.

✚ 195 E8 ✉ Calle di Scaleter, San Polo 2202A ☎ 041 721 308 ⏰ Tue–Sat 12.30–2.30, 7.30–10.30 🖐 L €70, D €110, Wine €12 🚤 San Stae

DA PINTO
If you wonder how some of the strange marine creatures you saw at the Pescheria taste, this little restaurant is a good place to do some adventurous trying. It's famed for its baccalà mantecato (creamed salt cod). The wine list is mediocre, but the house wines are fine. You can sit inside, or out on the campo. Credit cards are not accepted.

✚ 195 G8 ✉ Campo delle Becarie, San Polo 367 ☎ 041 522 4599 ⏰ Tue–Sun 7.30–2.30, 6–9.30 🖐 L €50, D €80, Wine €7 🚤 San Silvestro

IMPRONTACAFE
The stretch from the Frari to Campo Santa Margherita is university territory and this lively, well-designed, modern bar and restaurant pulls in crowds of students and young visitors. You can come here for breakfast, a light lunch, full dinner or just a drink, and find a buzzy atmosphere and choice of simple dishes. There's a good range of wines by the glass.

✚ 194 D9 ✉ Calle dei Preti Crosera, Dorsoduro 3815 ☎ 041 275 0386 ⏰ Daily 6am–2am 🖐 L €22, D €30, Wine €10 🚤 San Tomà

IL REFOLO
A charming, trendy pizzeria, with tables set on one of Venice's prettiest campi, the 'Sea Breeze' serves excellent pizzas, creative salads and pasta dishes, dressed with the catch of the day. There's also veal and chicken for secondi. The house wines are both drinkable.

✚ 194 E7 ✉ Campo del Piovan, Santa Croce 1459 ☎ 041 524 0016 ⏰ Tue–Sun 12–2.30, 7–10; closed lunch Tue 🖐 L €35, D €55, Wine €8 🚤 San Stae

SAN POLO AND SANTA CROCE ▪ EATING

PRICES AND SYMBOLS

Prices are the lowest and highest for a double room for one night in high season. Breakfast is included unless noted otherwise.

For a key to the symbols, ▷ 2.

AI TOLENTINI

www.albergotolentini.it

If you're looking for a simple hotel, the Tolentini, a few minutes' walk from Piazzale Roma, is a good find. The immaculately clean rooms are on the small side, but the beds are comfortable and some rooms have canal views. There are bars close by, and the area is bustling with students from the university. Online booking rates are reduced, and prices plummet in winter.

➕ 194 D8 ✉ Calle Amai, Santa Croce 197 ☎ 041 275 9140 💷 €100–€150, excluding breakfast ⓘ 11
🚇 Piazzale Roma

AL PONTE MOCENIGO

www.alpontemocenigo.com

Cross the Mocenigo's private bridge and you'll find yourself in a peaceful courtyard, a lovely place in summer for breakfast or an evening drink. Inside, the theme is 18th-century Venice, and the high-ceilinged bedrooms come complete with painted armoires and Murano glass chandeliers.

➕ 195 F7 ✉ Calle Mocenigo, Santa Croce 2063 ☎ 041 520 5555
💷 €120–€190 ⓘ 10 🚭
🚇 San Stae

ALEX

www.hotelalexinvenice.com

If you're watching the budget, this traditional hotel, around the corner from the Frari, is a good bet. Family run, it offers clean, comfortable rooms in an ideal location.

➕ 194 E9 ✉ Rio Terrà dei Frari, San Polo 2606 ☎ 041 523 1341 💷 €60–€112
ⓘ 11 🚇 San Tomà

IRIS

www.irishotel.com

The Iris is in a quiet area near the Frari church. The guest rooms are light and simply furnished; not all have private bathrooms, but each has a TV, hairdryer and telephone. Il Giardinetto restaurant is deservedly popular for its fish dishes, pizzas and live piano and jazz music.

➕ 194 E9 ✉ Fondamenta dei Forner, Calle del Cristo, San Polo 2910A ☎ 041 522 2882
💷 €110–€180 ⓘ 30 🚭 🚇 San Tomà

LOCANDA ARMIZO

www.armizo.com

Tucked under a *sotoportego* in the corner of the *campo* lies the Armizo, a small hotel housed in a converted merchant's premises, that offers excellent value and comfortable accommodation. Four spacious rooms overlook the *campo,* and will sleep up to five. Giancarlo and Massimiliano take trouble to look after their guests and it shows in the friendly welcome and well-presented breakfasts served in the bedrooms.

➕ 195 G9 ✉ Campo San Silvestro, San Polo 1104 ☎ 041 520 6473 💷 €69–€249
ⓘ 7 🚭 🚇 San Silvestro

LOCANDA CA' FOSCARI

www.locandacafoscari.com

The Ca' Foscari is a great budget choice, near the Frari. Not all rooms have their own bathrooms, but the warm welcome, spotless rooms and fresh flowers make this superb value for money.

➕ 194 E9 ✉ Calle della Frescada, Dorsoduro 3887B ☎ 041 710 401
💷 €85–€100, excluding breakfast ⓘ 11
🚭 🚇 San Tomà

LOCANDA STURION

www.locandasturion.com

The convivial Italo-Scottish management welcomes visitors to this well-run hotel, originally founded in the late 1200s as an inn for visiting merchants. Most of the rooms face a quiet *calle* and each has a TV, safe, hairdryer, minibar and kettle. The luminous breakfast room and some bedrooms have views of the Rialto; many have rich Venetian interiors. There's no elevator.

➕ 195 G9 ✉ Calle del Sturion, San Polo 679 ☎ 041 523 6243 💷 €120–€240
ⓘ 11 🚭 🚇 San Silvestro, Rialto

MARCONI

www.hotelmarconi.it

Only two of the rooms at this well-priced hotel have that coveted Grand Canal view, but the bonus of the others is their tranquillity. Public rooms are traditionally decorated and furnished, and there are outdoor tables for morning coffee with a close-up view of the Rialto bridge.

➕ 195 G9 ✉ Riva del Vin, San Polo 729 ☎ 041 522 2068 💷 €70–€325, excluding breakfast ⓘ 26 🚭 🚇 Rialto

MARIN

www.albergohotelmarin.it

Nadia, Bruno and their family will give you a warm welcome at their hotel, near the station, but removed from the crowds. Rooms are clean and functional; not all have private bathrooms, so specify when you book. This is excellent value.

➕ 194 D8 ✉ Calle Muneghe, Santa Croce 670B ☎ 041 718 022 💷 €60–€100 ⓘ 17
🚭 🚇 Santa Lucia

SAN CASSIANO CA' FAVRETTO

www.sancassiano.it

A 14th-century Gothic *palazzo* houses the San Cassiano—difficult to find, but worth the journey. The elegant reception rooms and lovely veranda overlook the Grand Canal, and bedrooms are spacious and well-equipped. This is a quiet part of town, and the hotel is particularly appealing if you want something special away from the crowds.

➕ 195 F7 ✉ Calle de la Rosa, Santa Croce 2232 ☎ 041 524 1768
💷 €60–€310, excluding breakfast ⓘ 36
🚭 🚇 San Stae

6

Parco di
Savorgnan

Rio della Crea

C d Pesaro

C Priuli al Cavaletti

C d Misericordia

C Carmelitani

C Cinchina

C d Procuratie

C Vergola

Fond Labia

Campo
S Geremia

Palazzo
Labia

Palazzo
Zeno

Palazzo
Emo

Campo
S Leonardo

Ex Chiesa
di San Leonardo

C d Mosto

Salizz
S Geremia

PONTE
D GUGLIE

Balbi

C S Antonio

C Emio

C d Leatro

Pala
Cor
Cont-

San Geremia
e Lucia

Palazzo
Flangini

Rio Terra Lista d Spagna

C d Spezier

C d Forno

Fond d Forno

Fond Labia

C d Procuratie

STAZIONE
VENEZIA SANTA
LUCIA

250 m

250 yds

Chiesa degli
Scalzi

Fond di Scalzi

Ponte
degli Scalzi

Ferrovia

Ferrovia

Palazzo
Calbo-Crotta

Fond Crotta

Canal Grande

Riva de Biasio

Palazzo
Marcello
Todérini

Palazzo
Corner

C Rama Zen

Palazzo
Gidoni-
Bembo

Riva di Biasio

Palazzo
Donà-
Balbi

C d Pistor

Palazzo
Gritti

C S Pisani

Salizz d Chiesa

C d Pistor

Lista d Barl

Rio Terra

Rio Terra

C Bembo

C Bembo

C Orsetti

Antica
Besseta

Corte
Cazza

Ramo Cazza

Il Refolo

C d Savio

STAZIONE
FERROVIARIA
MERCI

S Lucia

Ferrovia

Fond

Fond S Simeon Piccolo

S Simeon
Piccolo

Case
Contarini

C Lunga Chioverette

Palazzo
Foscari

Palazzo
Adoldo

Campiello d
Comare

Campo
S Simeon
Grande

C d Pistor

Campo
S Simeon
Proféta

S Simeon
Grande

Gallion

Gallion

C Ruga Vecchia

San Giacomo
dell'Orio

Campo S
Giacom
dell'Ori

STAZIONE
AUTOBUS

Ponte della
Costituzione

Palazzo
Papadópoli

Palazzo
Emo-Diedo

C d Traghetto
S Lucia

C Bergamaschi

Marin

Campiello d
Malvasie

Ramo
Chioverette

C Nuova
d S Simeon

Palazzo
Gradenigo

Palazzo
Soranzo
Cappello

Rio Marin

Rio Marin d Garzotti

Ruga Bella

Corte dell'
Anatòmia

Campo
d Strope

Campiello
d Cristo

Campo
N Sauro

Gradisca

C d Croce

C Venzzo

R Ochre

C d Oche

Campo S
Giacom
dell'Ori

Ae Oche

Giardino
Papadópoli

Piazzale
Roma

Fond Cossetti

Fond Papadópoli

Fond Monastero

Rio d Tolentini

Corte Casa Nuove

Campo d Lana

C Dario

C Lacca

Corte Canal

C Visciga

Rio d S Zuane

C Larga Contarina

C d Croce

Campiello
d Cristo

C Cappello

Rio S Giacomo d Orio

C d Oche

C d Orio

Palaz
Zane-

Pa
Gi

Ponte della
Costituzione

Palazzo
Condulmer

Palazzo
Papadópoli

Campo d
Tolentini

Ai Tolentini

C de Ca' Amai

Sott e Corte
Battochio

C d Saccere

C d Mezo

Campazzo

R

Rio d S Zuane

Sott Lacca

C S Zuane

C d Ollo

Scuola
Grande di
San Giovanni
Evangelista

C Vitalba

San Giovanni
Evangelista

C Magazen

Campo
S Stin

C Zane

C d Vida

C d Dona

Palaz
Mol

Palaz
Sor

Rio Novo

C Lavadori

Fond Condulmer

C d Clero

San Nicolò
da Tolentino

C Sacchere

Campazzo

C d Chiovere

Ramo Crimesin

C Fonderia

Ramo
Chiovere

Campiello
Chiovere

C del Forno

Archivio
di Stato

C Chioveretto

Rio Terra S Tomà

Ramo
Zen

Palazz
Zen

Ale

Fond
Magazen

Corte
Spiriti

Palazzo
Marcello

C Spiriti

Corte
Castelforte

Campiello d
Castelforte

San
Rocco

San
Tintoretto

C Tintoretto

C d Tintoretto

Campo
d Frari

Santa Maria
Gloriosa
dei Frari

Fond Frari

Corte
Badoer

Fond delle
Burchielle

Campazzo
Tre Ponti

Fond d Procuratie

Fond Minotto

Fond d Gaffaro

Salizz S Pantalon

C Faller

C d Forno

C Molin

Scuola Grande
di San Rocco

Campo
S Rocco

Salizz
S Rocco

Bottega del
Caffè Dersut

C Cozzi

C d Corti

Campo
S Tomà

Fond Pisan

C Cremonese

C de Bernardo

Corte
Gallo

C d Solazza

Corte
Basego

Palazzo
Gabrieli Dolfin

C d Malcanton

Campiello d
Castelforte

C Nova

Corte

C Vinanti

Corte
Barbo

Scuola Grande
di San Rocco

C Nova

C S Scuola

C Scalater

C d Cristo

C Albanesi

Frescada

Corte
Prima

C d Corti

Iris

Campo
S Tomà

Santa To

Traghetto
Vecchio

Rio della Cazziola

Fond Rizzi

Fond d Procuratie

Corte
S Marco

Fond d Cereri

Rio Terrà del Pensieri

Corte
Contarini

C d Caffettier

Rio Terrà d Scoazzera

Campo Santa
Margherita

Santa
Margherita

C d Forno

Fond d Caffettier

Campiello
Mosca

San Pantalon

Antica Osteria
Al Pantalon

Improntacafe

Campo
S Pantalon

Palazzo
Signolo
Loredan

Salizz S Pantalon

Rio di Malcanton

Rio
Novo

C Pret croce

Locanda
Ca'Foscari

Palazzo
Civran-
Grimani

S Pantalon

C d Saoneria

C d Chiesa

C Larga Foscari

Corte
Marcon

Palazzo
Balbi

Rio di Ca' Foscari

Palazzo
Foscarini

Rio Rossa

Rio Briati

Fond d Guardiani

C d Guardiani

Campo
d Carmini

Scuola Grande
dei Carmini

Instituto Superiore
d'Arte Applicata

Santa Maria
dei Carmini

Fond Briati

Rio Terrà d Scoazzera

Rio d Carmini

C d Vida

C d Mardona

C Cappeller

C Bernardo

Fond Rezzonico

Ca' Foscari

Palazzo
Da Lezze

Palazzo
Giustinian

Palazzo
Morolin

Palazzo
Grassi

Palazz
delle Figu

Palazzo
Nani

Ca' Rezzonico

San
Samuele

Cam
S Sam

Mo

R Gras

San San

Salizz S Samuele

REGIONS

C

D

E

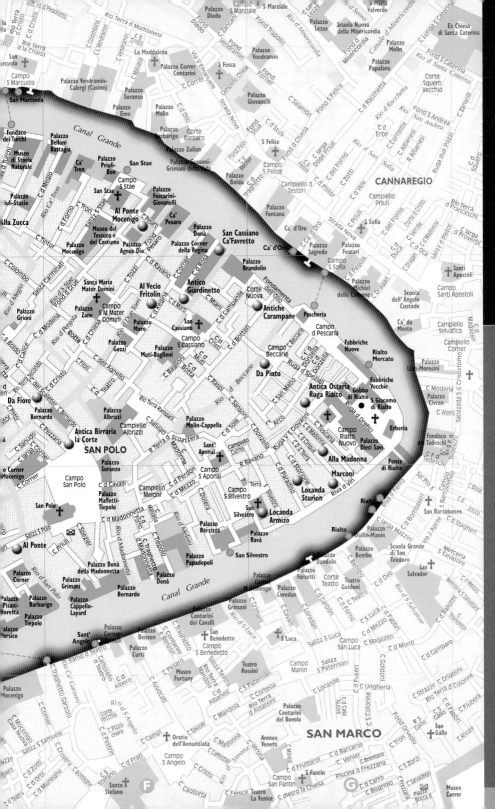

SIGHTS 198
WALK 222
WHAT TO DO 224
EATING 227
STAYING 230

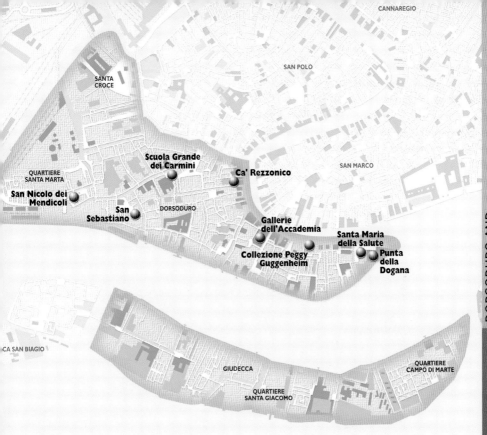

DORSODURO AND THE GIUDECCA

Dorsoduro, whose name comes from the firm land, the 'hard back', on which it stands, is one of Venice's most compelling areas, home to three important galleries and some superb art-filled churches. It's a *sestiere* (ward) of contrasts, workaday and low-key to the west, prosperous and chic—*the* place to live—to the east and north. Its boundaries are the Grand Canal to the north, San Polo and Santa Croce to the northwest and the Giudecca canal to the south, with the long, and separate, island of the Giudecca lying across this deep waterway. Campo Santa Margherita, one of Venice's liveliest and most attractive *campi*, is the hub, from where you can head east and parallel with the Grand Canal to the church of the Salute, set virtually at the end of this tapering stretch of land. South from here, the long waterfront known as the Zattere runs west; off it are fashionable residential streets, peaceful canals and picturesque squares. Dorsoduro's west end lies in one of the oldest parts of the city; here the shabby streets around San Nicolò dei Mendicoli contrast with bustle around the sprawl of Stazione Marittima, where the ferries and huge cruise liners dock.

To the east, a trio of galleries, the Accademia, the Collezione Peggy Guggenheim and the Punta della Dogana, cover just about the whole gamut of artistic development, and there's more to be found in Dorsoduro's churches and *palazzi*. You'll find architecture that spans the centuries and paintings by big-name artists such as Veronese, at San Sebastiano, and Tiepolo in the Ca' Rezzonico, a wonderful palace-museum that illustrates the hedonistic lifestyle of 18th-century Venice. The presence of the university lends a buzz to the whole area, with students filling the bars and restaurants and ensuring that shopping here has the edge on many other areas.

Ospedale
S Chiara

STAZIONE
VENEZIA SANTA
LUCIA

Ferrovia

STAZIONE
FERROVIARIA
MERCI

Ponte della
Costituzione

Fond di S Chiara
ACI

Piazzale
Roma

Santa
Chiara

STAZIONE
MARITTIMA
MERCI

Bacino della
Stazione Marittima

Ex Chiesa
di Sant'Andrea

Autorimessa

STAZIONE
AUTOBUS

Piazzale
Roma

**SANTA
CROCE**

Palazzo
Papadópoli

Giardino
Papadópoli

Palazzo
Condulmer

San Nicolò
da Tolentino

Archivio
di Stato

San
Rocco

Santa Maria
Gloriosa
dei Frari

Scuola Grande
di San Rocco

Ex Chiesa di Santa
Maria Maggiore

Ex Chiesa di Santa
Maria Maggiore

Rio della Cazziola

San Pantalon

Santa
Margherita

Campo Santa
Margherita

Scuola
dei Varoteri

Ca' Foscari

Palazzo
Giustinian

Palazzo
Balbi

Scuola Grande
dei Carmini

Istituto Superiore
d'Arte Applicata

Ca' Rezzon

Palazzo
Giustinian
Michiel

San Barnaba

**QUARTIERE
SANTA MARTA**

S Teresa

Santa Maria
dei Carmini

**Campo
San Barnaba**

San Nicolò
dei Mendicoli

Angelo
Raffaele

Collegio
Armeno

Magazzini Generali

**San
Sebastiano**

DORSODURO

Ospedale
G B Giustinian

Palazzo
Brandolin

San Trovaso

Banchina del Porto Commerciale

Palazzo
Molin

San Basilio

STAZIONE
MARITTIMA

STAZIONE
MARITTIMA

**Squero di
San Trovaso**

S Maria
d'Visitazione

Zattere

Zattere

Zattere

Zattere

Canale di Fusina

Sacca Fisola

Campiello d
Vaporetto

Canale della Giudecca

Campo
S Biagio

Mulino
Stucky

SACCA SAN BIAGIO

S Gerardo
Sagreda

Campo d
Lavraneri

San Biagio

Campiello
Priùli

Ex Convento
delle Convertite
(Penitenziario
Femminile)

S Eufemia

Campo
S Cosmo

Campo
delle
Rotonda

Ex Chiesa d
S Cosmo e
Damiano

GIUDE

Ísola della Giudecca

A   B   C   D

198

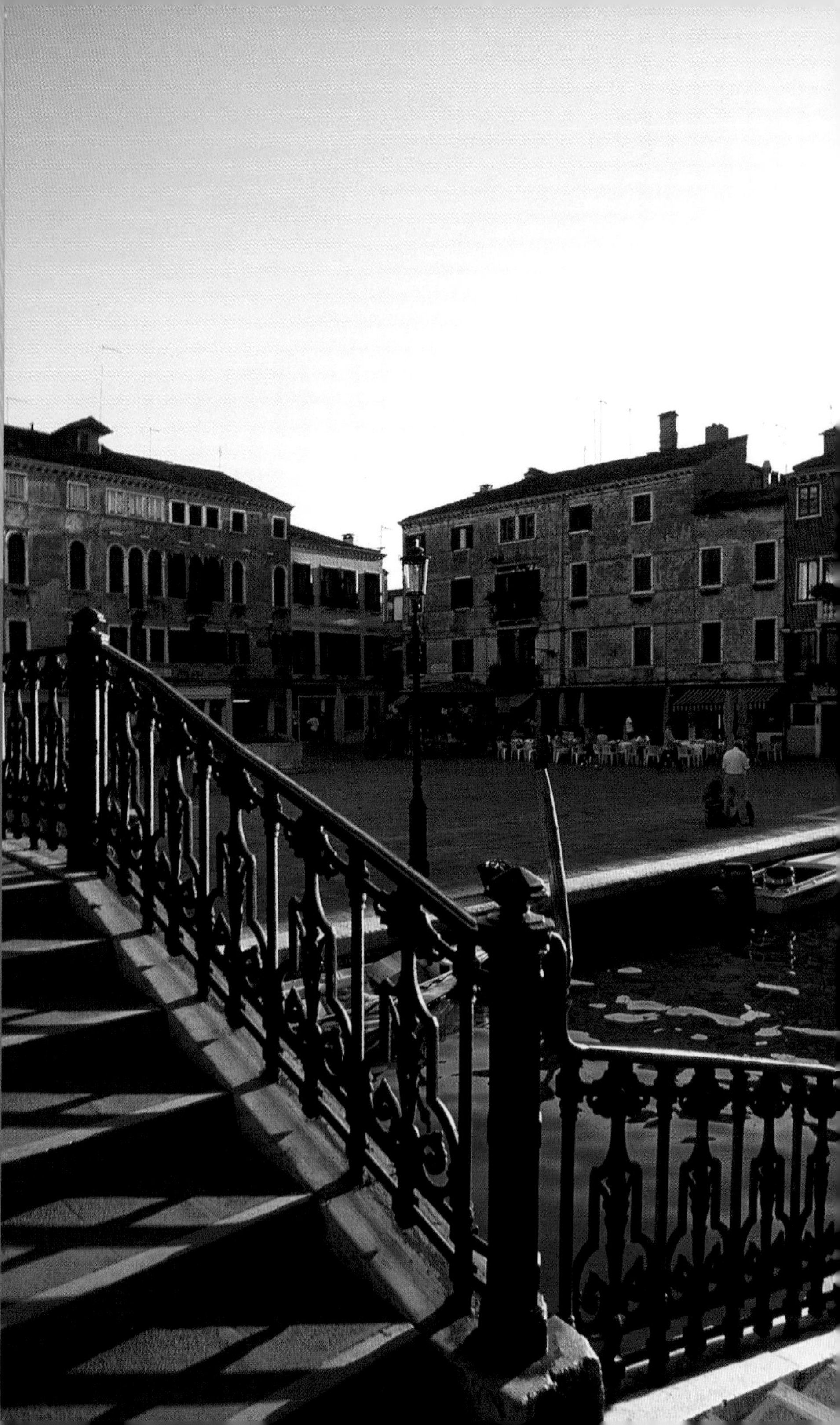

ANGELO RAFFAELE

The church of the Angelo Raffaele is one of the city's oldest foundations, traditionally established in the eighth century, though today's structure, in the shape of a Greek cross, dates from the 17th century. It's tucked away in a secluded part of Dorsoduro, standing in a spacious *campo* and fronted by a *rio*, and is one of only two Venetian churches that you can walk the whole way around outside. Visitor numbers have risen dramatically since the success of Salley Vickers' book *Miss Garnet's Angel* (published 2000); the church plays a starring role in the novel. The facade is flanked by two bell-towers, visible over much of eastern Dorsoduro, and above the main door is a statue of the Archangel Raphael, holding the hand of the boy Tobiolo and accompanied by a dog. Inside, the ceiling fresco by Gaspare Diziani shows *St. Michael Driving Out Lucifer*, but the real gems are on the organ loft. Five panels painted by Gianantonio Guardi (1699–1760) show scenes from the apocryphal story of *Tobias and the Angel*, miracles of liveliness, charm and luminosity. Elsewhere in the church are other sculptures and images of the Archangel with Tobias and his dog; Tobias is always pictured holding a fish, which plays a key role in the biblical story.

🕇 198 C10 ⊠ Campo Angelo Raffaele, Dorsoduro ☎ 041 522 8548 🕒 Daily 9–12, 3–5 ✋ Free 🚤 Ca' Rezzonico, San Basilio

CAMPO SAN BARNABA

Home to one of the world's most photographed vegetable shops—it's on a boat—cosy Campo San Barnaba is a bit of a route hub, with streets leading to many places you may be visiting. The *vaporetto* stop Ca' Rezzonico lies down a narrow alley to the east, and another *calle* heads west to the delights of San Sebastiano (▷ 219) and San Nicolò dei Mendicoli (▷ 218). Southwest lies the Accademia (▷ 206–211) and the spine of Dorsoduro, while the route north will bring you to Campo Santa Margherita (▷ this page),

Above *Detail from the carved relief on the pulpit of 17th-century Angelo Raffaele*
Opposite *Looking out across Campo San Barnaba from the bridge*

heart of the *sestiere*. There's a fine church, and a clutch of little shops and bars, a great place for watching Venice go by.

On the top of the bridge, neatly incised in the stone, are the imprints of two sets of footprints. These are reminders of the starting points of the officially sanctioned fights that were a means of allowing the working classes to let off steam and channel any aggression towards each other rather than the state. Venice had two main rival factions, the Nicolotti, based near the *campo*, and the Castellani. The rumpus normally started with individual fights between the designated champions on various bridges, with throngs of eager spectators lining the banks on either side. Once the initial brawl was over, the whole thing degenerated into a general free-for-all, the *frotta*. It was a normal occurrence for as many as 10 people to be killed in these punch-ups, either from the injuries they sustained or by falling from the bridge and drowning in the canal. The fights were finally halted in 1705 after a particularly vicious contest. San Barnaba's bridge is still known as the Ponte dei Pugni, the Bridge of Fists.

🕇 198 D10 ⊠ Campo San Barnaba, Dorsoduro 🚤 Ca' Rezzonico

CAMPO SANTA MARGHERITA

Campo Santa Margherita has to be one of Venice's most appealing, liveliest squares. Come here at different times of day to experience how the Venetian *campi* can be all things to the people who live around them—babies and grandmothers, shoppers and elderly men, students and tourists.

The square stretches out in an oddly shaped rectangle, around which are set lovely old Gothic houses, many dating back to the 14th century. At the north end stands the restored church of Santa Margherita, now part of the university. You can see St. Margaret's dragon on the campanile; she and the beast also feature on the facade of a house at the same end of the square, with the saint standing triumphantly on the monster. Market stalls, trees and benches are dotted around, while just off-centre stands a quirky little building, the Scuola dei Varoteri, once the headquarters of the tanners' guild. Left from here the street curves round towards San Barnaba, while to the right, past the fish stalls, the *campo* leads to the entrance to the Scuola Grande dei Carmini (▷ 221).

🕇 198 D10 ⊠ Campo Santa Margherita, Dorsoduro 🚤 Ca' Rezzonico

INFORMATION

www.museiciviciveneziani.it

✚ 198 E10 ✉ Fondamenta Rezzonico,
Dorsoduro 3136 ☎ 041 241 0100
🕐 Wed–Mon 10–5. Closed 1 Jan,
1 May, 25 Dec 💶 €6.50; 'Rolling Venice'
card holders €4.50; museum pass for all
civic museums adult €18, child (6–14) €12
🍴 Ca' Rezzonico 🎧 Audioguides (€3)
and guidebooks (€12) in Italian, English,
French and German 🖥 ♿ Excellent

INTRODUCTION

The sumptuous 17th- to 18th-century Ca' Rezzonico houses a museum of life
in the 18th century, Venice's most hedonistic era. Fine furniture, textiles, glass
and great paintings are beautifully set in its opulently decorated rooms.

In 1667, the Venetian Procurator Filippo Bon commissioned Baldassare
Longhena to design a major palace for his family on the Grand Canal. Work
was soon under way, and by the time of Longhena's death in 1682 the
structure was complete as far as the *piano nobile*. His death coincided with
a sharp downturn in the Bon family fortune and work on the *palazzo* ceased
for the following 70 years. It then came to the attention of the *nouveau riche*
Rezzonico clan, who bought the palace in 1751 and appointed Giorgio Massari,
one of Venice's most esteemed architects, to complete it. It was finished in
1756 and remained home to the Rezzonico family until the last member died
in 1812. A string of owners followed, among them Pen Browning, whose
father, the poet Robert Browning, died here in 1889. It eventually became the
property of Count de Minerbi, an Italian member of parliament, who sold it to
the Comune di Venezia in 1935. It became the city's museum of 18th-century
life, used to display furniture, paintings and *objets d'art* from all over Venice
in what became increasingly shabby surroundings. A major restoration was
carried out in the late 1990s, and in 2001 this stunningly revamped palace was
once more open to the public.

The water facade of the Ca' Rezzonico can be seen from Campo San
Samuele, on the opposite side of the Grand Canal, or take it in from the
vaporetto. If you're arriving by boat, you can normally enter the *palazzo* from
the water entrance, by crossing the bridge to the right of the *vaporetto pontile*.
On foot, the entrance is on the side of the building.

Start your visit by walking up the magnificent stairway to the *piano nobile*,
following the designated route; you'll find good information in each room. The
second floor contains some very fine pictures, and the third floor is home
to a huge, mediocre picture collection bequeathed by Count Egidio Martini
in the mid-20th century. This shouldn't detain you, though the 18th-century
apothecary's shop is worth a look. Leave time to relax in the pretty garden
behind the *palazzo*.

Above *View of the Ca' Rezzonico from the Grand Canal*

WHAT TO SEE

THE BALLROOM
The most original architectural feature is the ballroom, approached by a ceremonial stairway and occupying the height of two floors of the building. This design innovation, the brainchild of Giorgio Massari (c1686–1766), was unique in Venice and created an immense space that was the scene of some of the 18th century's grandest entertaining. The sense of grandeur is accentuated by the *trompe l'oeil* architecture painted on the walls, the dizzying ceiling frescoes, the dazzling gilding and stucco decoration, and the florid gilded wood and metal chandeliers, part of the original furnishings of the *palazzo*.

THE *PIANO NOBILE*
From the ballroom, a series of ornately decorated, interconnected rooms fans out, each furnished with fine contemporary pieces and decorated with rich fabrics and wallhangings. Highlights include the Tiepolo ceiling panels in the Throne Room and Nuptial Room, some stunning *ciocche* (ornate gilded locks and door furniture), Murano glass chandeliers, and the mind-blowing furniture designed by Andrea Brustolon (1662–1732). This furniture-maker worked almost exclusively in ebony and boxwood; look for the extraordinary console-cum-vase stand, all writhing forms, intricate carving and chinoiserie effects, that represents an *Allegory of Hercules*.

THE SECOND-FLOOR GALLERY
The central section of the second floor is occupied by the *portego*, a long room running the full depth of the building and used as a *quadreria*, picture gallery. Pride of place goes to two paintings by Canaletto, the only examples of his work in Venice itself; they show *A View of the Rio dei Mendicanti* and *The Grand Canal from Ca' Balbi*. Don't miss the series of pictures by Francesco Guardi (1712–93) and Pietro Longhi (1702–85), two of Venice's finest genre painters, who portayed scenes from everyday Venetian life—gambling rooms, bad behaviour in high society, carousing nuns and a charming rhinoceros, painted during a carnival visit to the city.

THE TIEPOLO FRESCOES
Also on the second floor is the beautifully restored cycle of frescoes painted by Giandomenico Tiepolo between 1759 and 1797 for his own villa on the mainland. These are intensely personal works, painted for pleasure, not as a commission, and encompass everything from delicate religious pictures for the chapel to the antics of Punchinello, an ancestor of the puppet Mr. Punch. The most striking work is the surreal *Mondo Novo* (New World) of 1791, showing a crowd, seen from behind, peering into a peepshow.

Below *Tiepolo's* Mondo Novo *(New World) fresco*

INFORMATION

www.guggenheim-venice.it

✚ 199 F11 ✉ Palazzo Venier dei Leoni, Calle San Cristoforo (entrance on Fondamenta Venier), Dorsoduro 704 ☎ 041 240 5411 🕐 Wed–Mon 10–6 ✋ Adult €12, child (10–18) €7, under 10 free ⛴ Accademia/Salute 📷 Audioguides and guidebooks available in Italian, English, French, German, Spanish and Japanese. For information on guided tours tel 041 240 5440 💻 🏛 Excellent

INTRODUCTION

The Palazzo Venier dei Leoni is one of the Grand Canal's most eccentric buildings, an unfinished palace known by Venetians as *il palazzo non finito*. What exists was constructed by the Venier family, one of the oldest Venetian noble clans. Work started on the building, designed by Lorenzo Boschetti, in 1748, but never progressed further than the first floor. Its distinctive appearance appealed to Peggy Guggenheim, who realized its potential as a showcase for her modern art collection and purchased it in 1948. She had started amassing contemporary art in the 1920s, buying from and dealing in the works of a whole generation of innovative abstract and Surrealist artists and marrying Max Ernst, one of the great exponents. In 1949 she staged the first exhibition in the garden of the *palazzo*, utilizing more of the interior as exhibition space over the years, though she continued to live in the palace. In 1969 she donated both the *palazzo* and her collection to her uncle's foundation, the Solomon R. Guggenheim Foundation, which, since her death in 1979, has administered and expanded the house and museum. Her ashes were interred in a corner of the garden, near the graves of her dogs.

The rooms in the gallery are fairly small, so viewing can be a problem; be prepared to wait to see some of the major pieces. The collection, one of the world's most important outside the US, covers all the main 20th-century movements and is beautifully presented. The garden is a delight, with its superb views up and down the Grand Canal. The light-drenched main rooms of the *palazzo* are approached through the garden court where sculpture by artists such as Giacometti (1901–66) and Henry Moore (1898–1986) are displayed. The interior rooms still combine Peggy Guggenheim's furniture and memorabilia with her collection; look especially for the magnificent silver bedhead by Alexander Calder. The art collection covers all the major names and movements of the early to mid-20th century: Cubism, Surrealism, Abstract Expressionism and Constructivism represented by Picasso, Chagall, Magritte, Dalí, Brancusi, Rothko, Jackson Pollock, Klee, Ernst, Calder, Cornell and Miró.

WHAT TO SEE

THE GARDEN

The garden is one of its chief pleasures, an oasis of green, cool light and shade, the perfect setting for the sculpture. You can see where Peggy's ashes were interred or walk out to the terrace above the water.

Above *The garden terrace of the Palazzo Venier dei Leoni*

RAIN (MARC CHAGALL)

Painted in 1911, this is a typical example of Chagall's naïve, folklore-based art, with its plant and animal symbolism, which nevertheless illustrates his awareness of avant-garde French painting, notably Cubism. The references to peasant country life have a dream-like quality.

THE RED TOWER (GIORGIO DE CHIRICO)

The Red Tower (1913) is one of the earliest paintings in what is called the Metaphysical style, where illogical perspective is used to create a sense of unreality. Such paintings were designed to provoke feelings of unease, loneliness and threat.

THE KISS (MAX ERNST)

This picture, which includes a man and woman embracing and two birds, was influenced by the composition of Leonardo da Vinci's *Madonna with St. Anne* to which Ernst (1891–1976) applied the erotic philosophy of Sigmund Freud, creating the synthesis of reality with instinct that was the hallmark of Surrealism.

MOBILE (ALEXANDER CALDER)

A fine example of Calder's wind-driven mobiles, which he created throughout his working life; this one dates from 1941.

THE ANGEL OF THE CITY (MARINO MARINI)

This bronze equestrian statue by Italy's leading post-war sculptor stands on the terrace of the museum and may have been influenced by ancient Etruscan sculpture.

MOON WOMAN (JACKSON POLLOCK)

Pollock was Peggy Guggenheim's discovery. This early painting (1942) shows stylistic elements which were to develop into his instantly recognizable drip painting, seen in the nearby *Alchemy*.

SACRIFICE (MARK ROTHKO)

This seminal watercolour (1946) shows Rothko moving from a Surrealist point of departure towards the use of large bands of 'floating' colour that typify his greatest work.

TIPS

» Be prepared for year-round crowds, with the summer months bringing the worst.

» The museum café is one of the best in Venice, so plan your visit to include lunch or tea time.

» There's a superb museum shop with a wide range of books and gifts.

Below *Admiring the bronze equestrian statue*, The Angel of the City, *by Marino Marini, on the terrace*

GALLERIE DELL'ACCADEMIA

INTRODUCTION

The Accademia contains a comprehensive and specialist collection of all that's best in Venetian painting. It's world-class, yet intimate, tracing the development of Venetian art from the 14th to the 18th century.

The Accademia delle Belle Arti, which houses the Gallerie dell'Accademia, was founded in 1750 as the city's art school. It moved to its present home in 1807 under Napoleon, who, having suppressed dozens of churches and monasteries, needed somewhere to put their artworks. It was envisioned that the paintings would be as much used by art students as admired by the public, and this was the Accademia's initial role. The art school still exists, but today the Accademia is primarily known as one of Europe's finest specialized collections. It is housed in three connected former religious buildings—the Scuola Grande di Santa Maria della Carità, its adjacent church of Santa Maria, and the Monastery of the Lateran Canons.

For an overview of the development of Venetian painting, head for the Gallerie dell'Accademia, the city's main gallery, a splendid collection where you can compare works by all the great masters and revel in the richness of colour and light that typifies Venetian painting. Five hundred years of Venetian painting are covered by the Accademia's 24 more or less chronologically arranged rooms, where you can trace the development of technical mastery of composition, perspective and anatomy.

A major plus is that the Gallery is surprisingly small, so there's little chance of mental indigestion or total exhaustion; allow a couple of hours for a thorough visit. Floor plans and guidebooks are available at the front desk, and enthusiasts can also pick up an audioguide here. The well-organized, well-lit rooms all have information boards in several languages. Venetian painting can be overwhelming in its richness and complexity, so if you're not a gallery fan at home, you may get little out of the Accademia.

WHAT TO SEE

CORONATION OF THE VIRGIN (ROOM 1)

Early Venetian painting bridged the gap between mosaics and true panel painting, and Paolo Veneziano (c1290–1362) was the prime exponent of this trend. His stylized and immobile figures reflect Byzantium, while the luminous colours of his work herald the future Venetian obsession with colour and light. No painting better illustrates this than *The Coronation of the Virgin*, dated around 1350, a huge gold-ground polyptych where the central scene of Christ, the Virgin and angels is surrounded by panels showing scenes from the lives of Christ and the saints, notably St. Francis of Assisi.

SAN GIOBBE ALTARPIECE (ROOM 2)

The dramatic advances in perspective and the handling of space, form and light that marked the Renaissance came later to Venice than elsewhere in Italy and developed highly individually. By the mid-15th century the Bellini family had developed the concept of the *sacra conversazione*, a unified composition of the Madonna and saints, of which the *San Giobbe Altarpiece* by Giovanni is a superb example. It was painted for the church of the same name in 1478, probably as a plague offering, the naked figure of St. Sebastian being normally associated with sickness. The background, with its coffered ceiling, originally corresponded exactly to the frame and the picture's original setting in the church. This monumental work contrasts with another *sacra conversazione* by the same artist in the next room, *The Madonna with Child with Saints Catherine and Magdalene*, a far more intimate and domestic picture.

INFORMATION

www.gallerieaccademia.org

199 E11 Campo della Carità, Dorsoduro 1050 041 520 0345

 Mon 8.15–2, Tue–Sun 8.15–7.15 (last entrance 6.30). Closed 1 Jan, 1 May, 25 Dec Adult €6.50, EU citizens 18–25 €3.25, EU citizens under 18 and over 65 free, non-EU citizens under 12 free. Combined ticket with Ca' d'Oro and Museo d'Arte Orientale €11. Advance booking Mon–Fri 9–6, Sat 9–2 (tel 041 520 0345) or book online (see above) Accademia Illustrated guides in Italian, English, French, Spanish, German and Japanese €15.50 and €8.20 Audioguides in English, Italian, French and German €4; guided tours in English and Italian, 11–1, 3.30–5, Sun 10–12 (tel 041 520 0345 for further details) Guidebooks, art books, postcards and gifts

Opposite Madonna with Child *by Giovanni Bellini*

DORSODURO AND THE GIUDECCA • SIGHTS

REGIONS

207

LA TEMPESTA (ROOM 5)

Art historians have written and argued about the meaning of *La Tempesta* for decades, interpreting Italy's most enigmatic picture, with its emphasis on landscape and extraordinary light, as myth, allegory or even political statement. Whatever the hidden meaning, if indeed there is one, this painting is one of few works that can be reliably attributed to Giorgione, who died in Venice in 1510 at the age of 32. His work has intense luminosity, and often relies on humanist principles, seen here in the harmony between the human figures and the natural world.

FEAST IN THE HOUSE OF LEVI (ROOM 10)

The huge *Feast in the House of Levi* by Veronese (*c*1530–88) is unmistakeable: a stupendous set piece where the figures are pictured against a background of classical architecture. The theatricality of the composition is typical of the artist, who was fascinated by the theatre, an interest seen at its height in his work in the church of San Sebastiano (▷ 219). The picture was painted in 1573 for the refectory of Santi Giovanni e Paolo (▷ 112) as a replacement for a *Last Supper* by Titian that had been lost in a fire. The theme was to be the same, but when Veronese delivered the finished work, the Inquisition came down hard, objecting to the inclusion of 'buffoons, drunkards, Germans, dwarves and similar indecencies'. Veronese, who appears in the work as the figure in green to the left of the centre, was ordered to make changes to render the sacred subject more pious; instead, he simply changed the picture's name.

THE MIRACLE OF ST. MARK FREEING THE SLAVE (ROOM 10)

The work of the towering figure of Tintoretto (1518–94) epitomizes the triumphalism of Venetian High Renaissance painting. The blasts of colour, dramatic light and the technical wizardry of his dizzying use of foreshortening is shown to its best advantage in *The Miracle of St. Mark Freeing the Slave*, painted in 1547 for the Scuola Grande di San Marco. It tells the story of a slave, sentenced to torture and blinding by his master for worshipping St. Mark's relics, being freed by the miraculous intervention of the saint. The warm flesh tones and minutely rendered fabrics are an admirable foil to the looser treatment of textiles in the artist's much later *Madonna dei Camerlenghi* (1567) in the next room.

Above *Waiting for the Accademia to open*
Above right *Detail of a ceiling painting by Marco Cozzi*

PIETÀ (ROOM 10)

Titian's deeply spiritual *Pietà*, painted in 1576 and intended for his own tomb in the Frari, is charged with religious intensity. The picture is imbued with his awareness of the immediacy of death, the paint scratched and scraped onto the canvas. He portrayed himself as Nicodemus, the figure to the right of Christ wearing a red cloak.

SCUOLA GRANDE DI SAN MARCO (ROOM 17)

Venice has few paintings by her great master of cityscapes, Canaletto, and the Accademia contains only one. Bernardo Bellotto was a pupil of the great man, and produced this view—unchanged today—of the facade of the Scuola Grande di San Marco in 1740. It shows afternoon light catching an everyday scene in this northern Venetian *campo*.

THE APOTHECARY (ROOM 17)

Genre painting—the illustration of scenes from everyday life—is a Venetian 18th-century speciality, and this is the most famous example of the work of one of its foremost exponents, Pietro Longhi (1702–85). Signed on the back by the artist, it shows the interior of a pharmacy, with the apothecary himself treating a girl for toothache. An apprentice tends to a cauldron of medicine in one corner and the shelves contain some of the blue-and-white containers for remedies that are still to be seen in the city's museums.

MIRACLES OF THE RELIC OF THE CROSS (ROOM 20)

This cycle of eight paintings by a group of artists that included Gentile Bellini and Vittore Carpaccio, was executed between 1494 and 1510 for the Scuola di San Giovanni Evangelista. The pictures illustrate miraculous episodes focused around a relic of Christ's cross, but the importance of the cycle lies in the pictorial representation of Venice and the wealth of anecdote and decorative detail. Three paintings stand out: the *Miracle of the Cross at the Rialto* (1494) by Vittore Carpaccio, and the *Miracle of the Cross at Ponte San Lorenzo* (1500) and the *Procession in Piazza San Marco* (1496) by Gentile Bellini. The latter

Below *Room 10 displays paintings by Tintoretto, Titian and Veronese*

shows an instantly recognizable Piazza, with a procession wending its way across the foreground and the Doge's entourage appearing from the Palazzo Ducale. Bellini exercised some licence by moving the Campanile over to the right so the whole facade of the Basilica is visible, while the buildings on the right have been replaced by the Procuratie Nuove. In contrast, the Rialto panel, still portraying the original wooden bridge with its movable central section, shows just how much the city has changed in the last 500 years.

ST. URSULA CYCLE (ROOM 21)

Between 1490 and 1494, Vittore Carpaccio painted a narrative cycle of nine pictures for the Scuola di Sant'Orsola. It tells the story of St. Ursula, a Breton princess, who, accompanied by her fiancé, Hereus, and an entourage of 11,000 virgins, attempted to cross Europe to Rome, only to be massacred by the Huns near Cologne, exactly as had been foretold in a dream. Like the True Cross cycle, it's packed with intricate detail, much of it a meticulous record of 15th-century costume and interior decoration. There are references to contemporary Venetian buildings and the Castel Sant'Angelo in Rome, and Carpaccio's trademark dogs and monkeys appear more than once. Some of the paintings contain several episodes of the story, and the audioguide is useful for sorting out the twists and turns of the tale.

PRESENTATION OF THE VIRGIN (ROOM 24)

Still hanging in its original site in the Scuola Grande di Santa Maria della Carità, now part of the Accademia, the *Presentation of the Virgin* by Titian was painted between 1534 and 1539. It draws heavily on the Venetian narrative tradition, but in a wholly 'modern' way, with landscape, architecture and figures perfectly balanced, while the small figure of the Virgin ascending the stairway is the focal point for the whole composition.

Below *Room 23, the nave of the former church of Santa Maria della Carità*
Opposite The Creation of the Animals *by Tintoretto, Room 6*

MORE TO SEE

La Pietà: Giovanni Bellini, Room 5
Adam and Eve: Tintoretto, Room 6
Discovery of the True Cross: Giambattista Tiepolo, Room 11
Madonna dei Camerlenghi: Tintoretto, Room 11
Translation of the the Body of St. Mark: Tintoretto, Room 11
The Family of the Procurator Luigi Pisani: Alessandro Longhi, Room 16
Views and genre paintings: Canaletto, Guardi and Pietro Longhi, Room 17

GALLERIE DELL'ACCADEMIA FLOORPLAN

GALLERY GUIDE

1: 14th–15th c. panel paintings
2: 15th–16th c. Venetian Renaissance altarpieces
3: 16th c. Venetian panel paintings, including G. Bellini
4: Mantegna, Piero della Francesca, Hans Memling
5: G. Bellini, Giorgione
6: 16th c. Venetian paintings, including Veronese, Tintoretto
7: Lorenzo Lotto, Bernardo Licinio
8: Palma il Vecchio, Romanino
9: School of Titian
10: 16th c. Venetian masters, including Veronese, Tintoretto, Titian
11: Tintoretto, Strozzi, Tiepolo
12: Corridor: 18th c. landscapes
13: Bassano, Tintoretto, Titian
14: Early 17th c.
15: Corridor: Tiepolo, Pellegrini Solimena
16: Early work by Tiepolo
16a: Alessandro Longhi, Piazzetta, Galgario
17: Canaletto, Guardi, Tiepolo, Pietro Longhi, Rosalba Carriera
18: 18th c. paintings
19: Bartolomeo Montagna, Giovanni Agostino da Loda, Boccaccino
20: Miracles of the Relic of the True Cross
21: Vittore Carpaccio's Legend of St. Ursula
22: Bookstand
23: Former monastery church: Giovanni Bellini, Antonio and Bartolomeo Vivarini
24: Former Hall of the Carità Brotherhood: Antonio Vivarini, Titian, Giovanni d'Alemagna

GESUATI

www.chorusvenezia.org

The church of the Gesuati makes a good stopping point on a walk along the Zattere. This wonderfully rococo church, also known as Santa Maria del Rosario, stands four-square on the waterfront, its facade designed by Giorgio Massari (1686–1766) and built for the Dominicans between 1726 and 1743. Massari worked frequently with the painter Giambattista Tiepolo (1696–1770), and the Gesuati is a good place to see Tiepolo's dizzyingly foreshortened ceiling frescoes in a setting designed specifically for them. The interior is an intriguing mix of classicism and the sugary elements of rococo, the lines of the columns leading the eye up to the three vertiginous Tiepolo ceiling panels depicting Scenes from the Life of St. Dominic (1737–39).

The first altarpiece on the right, showing the *Virgin with Saints Catherine of Siena, Rose of Lima and Agnes* is also by Tiepolo. The third altar has a magnificent and intense *Crucifixion* by Tintoretto (1518–94).

✚ 198 E12 ✉ Zattere ai Gesuati, Dorsoduro 917 ☎ 041 523 0625 ⏰ Mon–Sat 10–5. Closed 1 Jan, Easter, 15 Aug, 25 Dec 🎟 Chorus Pass (for all churches in Chorus group) €9, single ticket €3 🚤 Zattere, Accademia

GIUDECCA

The island of the Giudecca lies south of central Venice across the wide, deepwater Canale della Giudecca. It was once a chain of small islands, settled as early as the ninth century.

From the 13th century it was popular as a place of escape from the summertime heat, and wealthy aristocrats built sumptuous *palazzi* here, surrounded by gardens. Later, it became Venice's inner industrial zone, with shipbuilding and factories providing employment throughout the 19th and much of the 20th centuries. Over the past 50 years industry has declined, and the Giudecca today is a largely residential area.

A broad *fondamenta*, with superb views across to Dorsoduro, runs all along the north side of the island. Here stand the main sights—the churches of the Redentore (▷ this page), the Zitelle and Sant' Eufemia. The Zitelle, like the Redentore, was designed by Andrea Palladio in the 16th century, but Sant'Eufemia is far older, its foundation dating from the ninth century. The *fondamenta* is also home to the island's food shops, bars and restaurants, some modest houses and grand 14th-century *palazzi*, and, at the west end, the vast red-brick bulk of the Molino Stucky, a former flour mill built in the 1890s. This now houses one of Venice's most luxurious hotels (▷ 231). There's more accommodation at the opposite east end of the Giudecca in the shape of the Cipriani (▷ 230), one of the world's most famous hotels.

✚ 198 E13 ✉ Giudecca 🚤 Palanca, Redentore, Zitelle

PONTE DELL'ACCADEMIA

Of the bridges crossing the Canal Grande, the Accademia bridge, lying closest to San Marco, is the widest. The present wooden structure dates from 1984, and is an exact copy of the previous bridge, erected as a temporary measure in 1933. The first Accademia bridge, an ugly cast-iron affair, was built by English engineers in 1854. Never loved and, by the 1930s, too low for *vaporetti* to pass underneath, it was replaced by a design identical to that at the station. Unlike the Ponte degli Scalzi, though, the Accademia bridge was built temporarily of wood, stone being too expensive for construction across this far wider stretch of water. In the 1980s, the bridge, by this time much loved by Venetians, had reached the point of collapse. New designs were mooted in the face of outcry from the conservative citizens; they won the day, and today's bridge, with its superb views up and down the Canal Grande, is a replica of the last.

✚ 199 E11 ✉ Ponte dell'Accademia, Dorsoduro 🚤 Accademia

PUNTA DELLA DOGANA

▷ 214–215.

IL REDENTORE

www.chorusvenezia.org

Looking across the Giudecca Canal, the eye is immediately drawn to the harmonious facade of Palladio's great church of Il Redentore, with its classical frontage and airy dome. From 1575 to 1576 plague swept the city, eventually killing more than

Below *The Ponte dell'Accademia is a copy of the earlier bridge*

50,000 people. Once it had abated, the doge and Senate, as an act of thanksgiving, determined to build a church in a prominent site. Andrea Palladio (1508–80) was the obvious choice of architect. Work started in 1577 and was completed 12 years after his death. The exterior has a Greek-temple facade, approached by a flight of steps, with the dome rising behind. Inside, Palladio had to accommodate a choir for the monks, a tribune for the city dignitaries and a simple nave for the common people. He employed the style of architecture used for Roman baths as his solution, producing a sophisticated and harmonious design where the three elements are virtually fused. Paintings were commissioned by the Senate and follow an agreed pattern, including popular topics such as the *Nativity*, the *Baptism of Christ*, the *Deposition*, the *Resurrection* and the *Ascension*. There are two good examples in the sacristy on the right of the choir; a *Madonna and Child* by Alvise Vivarini (c1445–1505) and the *Baptism of Christ* by Veronese (1528–88). Once built, the church became the focus of the Festa del Redentore, still celebrated today (▷ 274).

✚ 199 F13 ✉ Campo del Redentore, Giudecca 195 ☎ 041 523 1415 🕐 Daily 10–7 💶 Adult €15, child (12–18) €10, under 12 free; combined ticket with Punta della Dogana adult €20, child €14 🚤 Redentore

SAN BARNABA

It's easy to hurry past the church of San Barnaba, the focal point of a waterside *campo* on the route between the Accademia (▷ 206–211) and Campo Santa Margherita (▷ 201). This is an ancient foundation, from the ninth century, and is the third church to be built on the site. It dates from 1749, and architecturally is a re-working of the Gesuati (▷ 212), with a classical facade punctuated with Corinthian columns and topped by a triangular pediment. Inside, the single nave has three side altars and a series of frescoes from the school of Tiepolo.

Above Flight of Angels *by Sebastiano Ricci in Santa Maria dei Carmini*

The square brick campanile was built in the year 1000 and is one of the oldest in Venice. The 18th-century inhabitants of the neighbourhood were known as Barnabotti and included many impoverished noblemen, drawn here by cheap rents. Visitors wrote home about the silk-clad beggars—the nobility were forbidden to work but obliged to wear silk, creating some interesting sartorial sights. San Barnaba has starred in two Hollywood movies; Katherine Hepburn fell into the adjoining canal in the classic *Summertime* (1955) and, years later, the church masqueraded as a library in *Indiana Jones and the Last Crusade* (1989). Today, it's used as a venue for temporary art- and history-related exhibitions.

✚ 198 D10 ✉ Campo San Barnaba, Dorsoduro 2771 ☎ 041 270 2464 🕐 Mon–Sat 9.30–12.30, 3.30–7, Sun 3.30–6.30 💶 Free 🚤 Ca' Rezzonico

SANTA MARIA DEI CARMINI

Most visitors associate the Carmini with Tiepolo (1696–1770), whose dizzying work decorates the Scuola of the same name. Santa Maria, now a parish church, was built originally as the Venetian heart of the Carmelite order—a statue of the Virgin of Carmelo perches on top of its campanile. The building is a wonderful mixture of styles, with a Renaissance facade fronting a predominantly Gothic interior, laid out on a basilica plan and dating from the 14th century. Twelve ancient columns support each side of the soaring vault, 97m (318ft) high, drawing the eye to the 14th-century Gothic apse. Large and very ordinary baroque paintings cover most of the interior walls, but there are a couple of gems, notably Cima da Conegliano's *Adoration of the Shepherds* (1509) in the right nave and Lorenzo Lotto's *St. George and the Dragon* (1529) on the left-hand side of the nave—look closely at the meticulously detailed landscape, complete with the tiny figures of St. George and the Dragon, considered by the art historian Bernard Berenson (1865–1959) to be one of the most beautiful in all Italian art. On your way out, don't miss the Gothic side door embedded with Byzantine stonework fragments.

✚ 198 D10 ✉ Campo dei Carmini, Dorsoduro 2617 ☎ 041 270 2464 🕐 Mon–Sat 2.30–5.30 💶 Free 🚤 San Basilio, Ca' Rezzonico

PUNTA DELLA DOGANA

INFORMATION

www.palazzograssi.it
199 G11 ⊠ Campo di Salute,
Dorsoduro 2 ☎ 041 523 1680 🕓 Daily
10–7 🖐 Adult €15, combined ticket
with Palazzo Grassi €20, child (12–18)
€10, combined ticket with Palazzo Grassi
€14, under 11 free 🛥 Salute 🚩 Guided
tours via Vivaticket (tel in Italy 100 139
139, from overseas +39 445 230 313);
audioguides in Italian, English and French
€5, audioguide to Punta della Dogana and
Palazzo Grassi €8 📖 Pocket guides and
full catalogues available at the bookshop
📕 Wide range of Electa guide books
and art books, also souvenirs, gifts, cards
and posters 🍹 Drinks and snacks, wines
at ground-floor café, also WiFi internet
access

INTRODUCTION

The buildings of the Dogana di Mare, Venice's historic customs house, stand at the tip of Dorsoduro, where the Giudecca Canal merges with the Grand Canal. This string of warehouses, culminating in a tower and portico, was designed by Giuseppe Benoni and built between 1677 and 1682. Neglected for years, in 2007 the buildings were leased by the city to François Pinhault, the millionaire collector and owner of the Palazzo Grassi (▷ 63). In June 2009, after a €20 million restoration, the 3,440sq m (37,000sq ft) space opened as a permanent contemporary art museum, its interior transformed by the Japanese minimalist architect Tadao Ando into a superb synthesis of old and new.

François Pinhault's artistic vision for the Dogana is that of a living collection which continues to evolve with the contributing artists. It is not fixed in terms of historical movement or a particular approach to art-making, an idea which possibly makes it unique. The works on display, which represent about 10 per cent of the Pinhault collection, are intended to be viewed in conjunction with the temporary shows staged at the Palazzo Grassi. The Dogana selection is partly dictated by the building itself, with its different scales, oddly-shaped spaces and natural light, and is partly a representation of Pinhault's own artistic passion. Some exhibits come from the existing collection and are by artists admired and collected by Pinhault for years, but he has also commissioned new works by young artists and will continue to do so, to illustrate the role of the Dogana as an ongoing project for the city and the Venetians. Some of the work is deeply disturbing, but it is undeniable that this exciting space has brought a new vibrancy to the Venetian art scene.

WHAT TO SEE
THE BUILDING

Tadao Ando's stunning conversion and restoration of the 17th-century buildings into a 21st-century art space was a project perfectly suited to the design philosophy of this self-taught architect, whose work has always been inspired as much by the vernacular architecture of Japan as by the masters of the 20th century. Here, the superb fusion of traditional Venetian elements such as brick and stone with steel, glass and concrete create a truly outstandingly beautiful building.

It is envisaged that the following works will form part of the permanent exhibition, though there may be occasional changes.

Above *An exhibition of artists from the François Pinhault collection in the Punta della Dogana*

CHARLES RAY — *BOY WITH FROG* (OUTSIDE)

Standing right at the point where the Grand Canal meets the open waters of the Bacino di San Marco is this enigmatic sculpture of a naked boy holding a frog, by a Los Angeles-based sculptor known for his ability to jar the spectator's perceptions.

RACHEL WHITEREAD — *UNTITLED (ONE HUNDRED SPACES),* 1995 (ROOM 1)

More than half the floor space of the first gallery is occupied by this work by one of Britain's best-regarded modern artists, a member of the Brit Art movement, who was responsible for the empty plinth in London's Trafalgar Square. Here, rows of iridescent glass cubes are made instantly comprehensible when viewed as what they actually are—casts of upturned chairs, delineating space.

JEFF KOONS — *BOURGEOIS BUST — JEFF AND ILONA,* 1991 (ROOM 4)

This slick double bust by one of the US's most accessible modern artists is surprisingly small compared with the scale normally used for his huge works, usually portraying banal objects. His best-known work is *Puppy*, a 12.4m (43ft) high topiary and flower sculpture outside the Guggenheim Museum in Bilbao, Spain.

CINDY SHERMAN — *UNTITLED,* 2007–2008 (ROOM 4)

This photographer is best known for her series of shots depicting herself in a variety of costumes and disguises, designed to amuse, stimulate and disturb the viewer as well as providing a commentary on present-day issues.

JAKE AND DINOS CHAPMAN — *F******* HELL,* 2008 (ROOM 2)

This seminal work is a re-make of the artists' 1999 tableau *Hell*, destroyed in the fire at the Momart warehouse in London in 2004. Featuring more than 30,000 inch-high figures, many in Nazi uniform, it has strong echoes of suffering and hell, and is typical of the brothers' apocalyptic, yet witty, take on modern times and themes.

RICHARD PRINCE — *RE-ART (GNX),* 2007, *DENIS WILSON (HOOD),* 2007 (ROOM 18)

Two works by this appropriation artist, who has caused furore over the years by his use of re-photography to produce controversial images.

TIPS

» Buy a joint ticket for the Punta della Dogana and the Palazzo Grassi as the two art spaces are designed to be seen as a single exhibition.
» The audioguide is highly recommended to help you make sense of it all.
» The Punta della Dogana is well worth visiting for the building alone, even if you are not interested in contemporary art.

Below left *Punta della Dogana entrance*
Below Boy with Frog *by Charles Ray*

INFORMATION

🕂 199 G11 ✉ Campo della Salute,
Dorsoduro ☎ 041 522 5558 ⏱ Church
and sacristy 9–12, 3–5.30 💶 Church
free, sacristy €2 🚢 Salute

Above *The silhouette of Santa Maria
della Salute, one of Venice's landmark
buildings, dominates the mouth of the
Grand Canal*

INTRODUCTION

The gleaming white bulk of Santa Maria della Salute looms over the San
Marco entrance to the Grand Canal. It is a superb example of Venetian baroque
architecture and is the city's most important 17th-century church. Approach it
through the labyrinthine streets of Dorsoduro or catch the No. 1 *vaporetto*
to Salute.

The 1629 outbreak of plague killed more than 45,000 people, a third of the
city's population, in 12 months. In October 1630 the Senate vowed to build
a church in honour of the Virgin if she would save the city; within weeks the
pestilence retreated, probably due as much to the onset of winter as divine
intervention. The Senate held a competition to find an architect worthy of the
commission, and it was awarded to Baldassare Longhena. Buildings were
razed to free up space and more than a million wooden piles were driven into
the subsoil to support the foundations. Work started on 1 April 1631 and was
completed in 1681, a year before the architect's death.

The church was dedicated to the Madonna della Salute, the Virgin of both
'health' and 'salvation'. The feast of the Salute remains an important day for all
Venetians (▷ panel opposite).

WHAT TO SEE
THE EXTERIOR

Revolutionary in design, the huge, domed, octagonal construction combined
prevailing trends and influences in a totally new fashion, creating a building
where traditional Veneto-Byzantine architectural elements go hand in hand
with new baroque ideas. Baldassare Longhena designed it in 1631 and the
plan owes much to Palladio. From the quayside, a flight of steps leads up
to the Palladian facade, distinguished from the other seven sides by huge
half-columns and the classically inspired main doorway. The main dome
is buttressed by circular volutes, or *orecchioni*, 'little ears', while behind it,
the smaller domes and twin campaniles echo the Byzantine style of earlier
buildings. More than 120 statues decorate the niches and pinnacles.

THE INTERIOR

In contrast to the exterior exuberance, the interior is austere, with six chapels clustered around the central space and the cupola, supported by eight enormous pillars, rising high overhead. This layout is loaded with Marian symbolism, and the shape of the church refers to the eight-pointed Marian star, the dome represents the Virgin's crown, and the central plan is a symbol of the womb. The inscription *Unde origo inde salus* (from the Origins came Salvation) in the middle of the beautiful marble floor is a reference to the story of Venice's foundation under the Virgin's protection, while the encircling roses allude to the rosary, the Virgin's own prayer. Another dome rises over the choir, and the high altar, also designed by Longhena, portrays the Virgin and Child rescuing Venice from the plague, while a serene Byzantine icon forms the focal point. Flemish artist Justin le Court (1627–79) was responsible for the sculpture, and Francesco Morosini brought the Byzantine painting back to Venice in 1672.

THE PAINTINGS

With the exception of an early Titian, the *Descent of the Holy Spirit* (1555), on the third altar on the left, the finest pictures are in the sacristy, whose entrance is to the left of the high altar. Here are no fewer than eight Titians, brought here from the suppressed church of San Spirito in 1656. The earliest (1510) commemorates the end of an earlier plague and shows *St. Mark Enthroned between Saints Cosmas, Damian, Roch and Sebastian*; St. Roch is invoked against infectious diseases and Cosmas and Damian were both doctors. The powerful ceiling panels show *Cain and Abel*, *David and Goliath* and the *Sacrifice of Abraham* and were painted between 1542 and 1544. Look for a tranquil *Madonna* by Palma il Vecchio (*c*1480–1528) and Tintoretto's superb *Marriage Feast at Cana* (1561), which contains a supposed self-portrait—the artist is the first Apostle on the left.

SALUTE

The feast of the Salute, when Venetians still come to give thanks for good health, takes place on 21 November. A week before the feast, a pontoon bridge is constructed over the Canal Grande, to give direct access to the church, and citizens cross it to hear Mass, light candles and meet their friends.

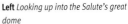

Left *Looking up into the Salute's great dome*
Below *The magnificent polychrome marble floor*

INFORMATION

✚ 198 B10 ✉ Campo San Nicolò dei Mendicoli, Dorsoduro 1907 ☎ 041 275 0382 🕐 Mon–Sat 10–12, 4–6, Sun 4–6 👜 €1 🚤 San Basilio, Ca' Rezzonico 📄 Information leaflets in Italian, English and French 📖 Postcards

TIP

» This corner of Dorsoduro also contains the churches of Angelo Raffaele (▷ 201) and San Sebastiano (▷ 219), within a five-minute walk

SAN NICOLÒ DEI MENDICOLI

The 13th-century Veneto-Byzantine church of San Nicolò dei Mendicoli is one of the oldest churches in Venice. This most ancient church was founded, like the cathedral in Torcello (▷ 247), in the seventh century, possibly by a group of Paduans fleeing the Lombard invasions. The original church was dedicated to San Niceta, a Serbian martyr, but was replaced in the 12th century by the present building. It has miraculously retained its original plan, with a partition screening the nave from the altar area. In the 15th century the portico was added to the front. Designed as a shelter for beggars and mendicants, it's one of only two remaining in Venice—the other fronts San Giacomo in the Rialto (▷ 174). The interior was reworked in the 16th century, and the church served as the parish church for this working-class area through to the 19th century. By 1900 its congregation had fallen away, and San Nicolò was closed between 1903 and 1924 for the first of a series of prolonged repairs. The next restoration took place from 1972 to 1977 by the British-based Venice in Peril fund, which re-roofed the church, raised and restored the floor, and conserved much of the interior decoration. The exterior featured in Nicolas Roeg's 1970s movie *Don't Look Now*, starring Donald Sutherland and Julie Christie.

THE CHURCH AND CAMPO

The interior of the church, much more than the sum of its parts, is a wonderful muddle of architectural elements, panelling, wooden sculpture, and bits and pieces. It epitomizes the long history of the building and gives an impression of comfortable charm. The basic plan is that of a 12th-century basilica, with two rows of 12th-century columns topped by 14th-century capitals. Above these, on either side of the nave, are gilded statues of the Apostles, and there's a fine 15th-century statue of the church's patron, St. Nicolas, above the high altar. Today this is separated from the nave by a pierced screen, topped with a Crucifixion, that echoes the original iconostasis. The ceiling has painted 16th-century panels depicting scenes from the life of St. Nicolas.

Outside, the ensemble of campanile, *campo*, *fondamenta* and bridges is a typical Veneto-Byzantine urban scheme. The bell-tower is 12th century, there's an ancient column topped by the lion of St. Mark, and a flagpole, once used by the Nicolotti, a working-class faction constantly at loggerheads with the Castellani from eastern Venice, who were based in this area.

Above *Detail of the ceiling tondo*

SAN SEBASTIANO

This Dorsoduro church is brilliantly and lavishly decorated by the late Renaissance genius Veronese. A church and monastery, dedicated to the Virgin, were first founded here in the 14th century, and rebuilt, with St. Sebastian as an additional patron, after a plague outbreak in 1464. In 1505, this was demolished and a new church, designed by Scarpagnino (1505–49), erected. In 1555 Veronese started work on the internal decoration of the church, completed in two bursts, from 1555 to 1559 and 1565 to 1570. The church was closed in 1810 and reopened in 1856. Restorations were carried out in the 1980s and 1990s, and 2009 saw the start of another major project.

THE DECORATIVE SCHEME

San Sebastiano's prior commissioned Paolo Caliari, a fellow native from Verona, also known as Veronese, while the artist was in his 20s, and the iconography of the cycle of paintings is probably the prelate's inspiration. It brought together the church's two patrons, the Virgin and St. Sebastian, using scenes from their lives and New and Old Testament incidents to illustrate the triumph of faith over heresy, and thus of the Resurrection over sin and its consequences, plague and death.

Veronese first painted the ceiling of the sacristy with a *Coronation of the Virgin* and the *Four Evangelists* in 1556, moving on to the body of the church the following year. The three great ceiling panels over the nave depict scenes of the *Life of Esther*, surrounded by sumptuous painted architectural illusionism. Veronese then worked on the monks' choir, running around the back and side walls of the church, the organ panels and surrounding decoration, between 1558 and 1559. In 1565 he returned to the church, completing the work around the high altar, which portrays the *Martyrdom of St. Sebastian* set against an imaginary Rome, in 1570.

San Sebastiano's decoration is a *tour de force*, full of visual tricks, dizzying perspectives and foreshortenings, and glowing with rich, jewel-like tones, a reminder of the artist's fascination with theatre design. Veronese's genius lies not only in his technical ability, but also in his gift to portray figures that are modelled on real people and scenes that appear as contemporary events, but are yet removed from the everyday world by the clear, transparent tones and unearthly light. *The Virgin and Child* above the high altar is also by Veronese, while there's a Titian, *St. Nicholas* (1563), on the left wall of the first chapel on the right. Veronese is buried in the chapel to the left of the chancel.

INFORMATION

www.chorusvenezia.org

✚ 199 C11 ✉ Campo San Sebastiano, Dorsoduro ☎ 041 275 0462 🕐 Mon–Sat 10–5. Closed 1 Jan, Easter, 15 Aug, 25 Dec 🎟 Chorus Pass (for all churches in Chorus group) €9, single ticket €3 🚤 San Basilio, Ca' Rezzonico ✇ Guided tours organized by Chorus (tel 041 275 0462); information sheets and audioguides in Italian, English, French and German

Below *Many of the architectural details of San Sebastiano are, in fact, trompe l'oeil paintings*

SAN TROVASO

The present San Trovaso, built between 1584 and 1657, is the fourth church on this site. Its puzzling name is another example of Venetian mangling of two distinct saints' names, in this case the martyrs St. Gervasio and St. Protasio. The church is remarkable for its two virtually identical facades, one at each end, and is clearly influenced by the design of the Palladian church of Zitelle on the Giudecca (▷ 212). According to the story, San Trovaso stood on the boundary between the two areas controlled by the rival gangs of the Nicolotti and the Castellani. Two entrances meant that each faction could arrive at religious ceremonies in style without the danger of confronting each other.

The main draw in the spacious, but bland, interior are the paintings. Works by Tintoretto (1518–94) and his son, Domenico (c1560–1635), are scattered around—the *Last Supper* in the left transept and the *Temptation of St. Anthony* in the chapel to the left of the high altar are by the master. On the side wall there's a charming contrast to the latter in the shape of an International Gothic gold-ground picture of *St. Chrisogonus* (c1450) by Michele Giambono. The Renaissance is represented by the marble reliefs in the Clary Chapel in the right transept. These show a procession of angels, some playing musical instruments, while the others hold the symbols of the Passion.

✚ 198 D11 ✉ Campo San Trovaso, Dorsoduro 1098 ☎ 041 296 0631 🕐 Mon–Sat 2.30–5.30 💲 Free 🚤 Accademia, Zattere

SCUOLA GRANDE DEI CARMINI

▷ 221.

SQUERO DI SAN TROVASO

Venice had more than 10,000 gondolas in the 16th century; today there are only a few hundred, built in a handful of specialist boatyards, called *squeri*. One of the most famous, and easiest to see, is the Squero di San Trovaso, on the waterfront of the Rio San Trovaso, just behind the Zattere. Construction sheds and workshops are set back from the *rio*, and there's generally activity of some sort, as gondolas are overhauled and repaired.

Venice's gondolas developed in a unique fashion to meet the conditions of the city and lagoon, with shallow keels and perfect manoeuvrability, ideal for the narrow city *rii*. Being asymmetrical along the central line gives them a slight list to the right, which compensates for the weight of the gondolier, who rows in the Venetian fashion, standing. Eight types of wood are used in the construction: oak, elm, fir, larch, lime, walnut, cherry and mahogany, with beech for the oars. These rest in the *forcola*, a sensuously carved rowlock, whose shape allows the oar to be used in eight different positions. The bow is decorated with the *ferro*, whose six front-facing prongs traditionally represent the six *sestieri* of Venice. Gondolas have been painted black since 1562, when laws were passed forbidding excessive ornamentation, and the traditional cabin, the *felze*, was abolished in the 19th century. Water conditions take a tremendous toll on the boats, which suffer from the backwash of motorboats, and they need to be cleaned and overhauled once a month. To get a real insight into the beauty of the craft and the expertise of the gondolier, take a *traghetto* across the Grand Canal and watch the oarsmen.

✚ 198 D11 ✉ Rio San Trovaso, Dorsoduro 🚤 Zattere

ZATTERE

The Zattere is the name given to the string of *fondamente* overlooking the Canale della Giudecca on the southern side of Dorsoduro. It runs from the Punta della Dogana (▷ 214–215), in the east, to the Stazione Marittima in the west, and gets its name from the quayside's original function as an unloading point for bulky goods, which were floated in on rafts known as *zattere*. Much of this cargo went to the huge Magazzini del Sale (salt warehouses) near the Dogana, now used as boathouses and exhibition space. Farther west are the churches of the Gesuati (▷ 212) and Santa Maria della Visitazione (▷ 111). The Zattere's sunny, sheltered position and wide promenade make it a popular place for the *passeggiata* evening stroll. There are benches, restaurants and cafés, and excellent ice cream, at Nico's (▷ 226).

✚ 198 D11 ✉ Zattere, Dorsoduro 🚤 Zattere, San Basilio

Below *The Zattere has the air of a sunny promenade with views to La Giudecca*

SCUOLA GRANDE DEI CARMINI

This uniquely preserved *scuola* is home to dazzling works by Giambattista Tiepolo. Of Venice's remaining charitable confraternity buildings the Scuola Grande dei Carmini was the only one to escape the maraudings of Napoleon's troops, and is the only surviving *scuola* that still retains its 18th-century appearance. Tucked away just off beguiling Campo Santa Margherita, in the *sestiere* of Dorsoduro, this Carmelite stronghold has some flamboyant interior decoration, as well as a series of nine superb Tiepolo panels, enough to convert even the most anti-baroque art lover. For a dizzying blast of *trompe-l'oeil* perspective this is the place to come.

THE *SCUOLA*

The Carmelites, founded in Palestine in 1235 as a women's order, are a religious confraternity especially devoted to the Virgin Mary. This is their Venetian headquarters from which they practise their charitable works, attending services in the nearby church of Santa Maria dei Carmini (▷ 213). They moved here in 1667 and commissioned Baldassare Longhena (1598–1682), designer of the Salute (▷ 216–217), to convert the existing building. He added the perfectly symmetrical facade, and planned the interior, which, like that of all *scuole*, includes a *salone* and *albergo*: meeting rooms for the members of the confraternity. In 1739 the Carmelites employed the artist Giambattista Tiepolo to decorate the upper hall containing the Salone, a task that occupied him until 1749. Access to this upper chamber is via a wonderfully ornate double staircase, all gilded stucco and well-fed *putti*, and the hall itself is dominated by Tiepolo's panels. Don't even attempt to understand the iconography—loosely based around the Carmelite emblem, the scapular—but just enjoy the swirling figures, the startling colours, the audacious off-centre composition and the mind-blowing accomplishment of the *trompe-l'oeil* perspective. The archive room next door contains a *Judith and Holofernes* by Giambattista Piazzetta (1683–1754), while the ground floor has 18th-century chiaroscuro (light and shade) works.

INFORMATION

www.scuolagrandecarmini.it

✚ 198 D10 ✉ Campo dei Carmini, Dorsoduro 2617 ☎ 041 528 9420
🕐 Daily 11–4 ✋ Adult €5, child (under 14) €2, Rolling Venice card holders €4
🚉 Ca' Rezzonico

Above *The facade of the* scuola *is adorned with busts and statues*

THROUGH DORSODURO

This walk takes you through the heart of Dorsoduro. En route you'll explore hidden corners, visit some of the city's most interesting churches and museums, and enjoy views that range from picturesque alleys to sweeping vistas encompassing some of Venice's great landmarks.

THE WALK

Distance: 3.7km (2.3 miles)
Time: 2–2.5 hours
Start at: Ca' Rezzonico *vaporetto* stop
End at: Accademia *vaporetto* stop

HOW TO GET THERE

Take *vaporetto* No. 1 to Ca' Rezzonico.

★ Alight at Ca' Rezzonico and walk down Calle Traghetto to Campo San Barnaba (▷ 201). Cross the square, walk past the vegetable boat and right over Ponte dei Pugni. Continue straight ahead down Rio Terrà Canal, bearing left to Campo Santa Margherita (▷ 201), the focal point of Dorsoduro. Turn right into the *campo*, then take the third turning left (yellow sign to Piazzale Roma/ P.le Roma Ferrovia) off the square, and cross the canal. Over the bridge,

turn left and follow the canal. Keep on this *fondamenta* as it passes the second church (Angelo Raffaele) on the other side of the canal, then turn right into Campiello Riello. Walk through to the next canal and turn left along Fondamenta Tron to reach San Nicolò dei Mendicoli (▷ 218) and its *campo*.

❶ This charming little square featured in Nicolas Roeg's cult 1970s movie *Don't Look Now*. Its earlier inhabitants were fishermen and salt-pan workers, and it gave its name to one of two rival factions, the Nicolotti. The big building across the canal to the west was once a cotton mill; it's now part of the university.

Retrace your steps back through Campiello Riello and turn right over the first bridge. Turn left on

the other side and walk along the Fondamenta de Pescheria to the church of Angelo Raffaele (▷ 201). Exiting the side door of the church, turn left and walk down the side of the church into the spacious Campo Angelo Raffaele (Campo de l'Anzolo Rafael), which leads into Campo San Sebastiano and Veronese's church of San Sebastiano (▷ 219). Cross the bridge in front of San Sebastiano and head down Calle Avogaria, which becomes Calle Lunga.

❷ This is a busy neighbourhood street, packed with little shops providing everyday necessities for locals, and interesting gift and antique shops, cafés and restaurants for visitors. Pause to admire the

Above *Strolling along the Fondamenta di Zattere*

breads and pastries on offer, or pop into the wine shop where empty bottles are filled from giant casks. Calle Lunga leads back to Campo San Barnaba, where you turn right under the *sotoportego* and follow this main route through Dorsoduro along Calle della Toletta to the Rio San Trovaso. Cross over Ponte delle Maravegie and turn right down the *fondamenta*, from where you'll see the facade of the church of San Trovaso (▷ 220) and the Squero di San Trovaso (▷ 220) across the water. At the bottom is the Fondamenta Zattere (▷ 220). Turn left and walk along beside the Canale della Giudecca until you come to the church of the Gesuati (▷ 212). Continue along the Zattere, cross a bridge and continue to pass the church of Spirito Santo.

❸ The church and convent of Spirito Santo were founded in 1483, though the present church dates from the 16th century. The convent was constantly rocked by scandal, the foundress being accused of squandering community funds to entertain her lover, the local priest.

Continue to the next bridge, cross it and turn left to walk beside the Rio de la Fornace (Fornasa), with the walls of the old Magazzini del Sale on your right.

❹ This was where Venice's only raw material was stored. Salt was produced in salt pans near Chioggia.

The warehouses, first built during the 14th century, could store up to 44,000 tonnes. Today, they're used as *cantiere* (boat sheds) and for exhibitions and events.

At the end of this street (T-junction), turn right and walk through a small *campo*, with the facade of the 15th-century ex-church of San Gregorio, a Benedictine foundation dating from the ninth century, ahead of you. Continue under the *sotoportego* (to the left), which once connected the church with its abbey, to cross the wooden bridge and reach the great church of Santa Maria della Salute (▷ 216–217).

After visiting the church, retrace your steps back to the T-junction and cross the bridge. Follow the street round to Campiello Barbaro, with its three acacia trees, across another bridge, and walk round to the Fondamenta Venier, where you'll find the entrance to the Collezione Peggy Guggenheim (▷ 204–205) on your right. Leaving the museum, turn right and follow the street along to emerge into Campo San Vio.

❺ This is one of only a handful of *campi* overlooking the Grand Canal and a good place to pause. The building on the right as you face the water is the Anglican church of St. George's; the first chaplain accompanied the English Ambassador to Venice in 1604 and the present building has been in use since 1889.

Above *Dorsoduro's famous vegetable boat at Campo San Barnaba*

Bear left and cross the bridge into the Piscina del Forner then Calle Nuova Sant'Agnese; walk along this, then turn right to the Ponte dell'Accademia (▷ 212).

WHEN TO GO
Try to avoid wet or windy weather as there's not much shelter in some areas and the Zattere can be very windy.

WHERE TO EAT
The Zattere makes a good stopping place; roughly halfway along the walk, it has a good choice of bars and cafés with outside tables and lovely views. Pick of the bunch is Al Chioschetto (Dorsoduro 1460A, Jun–Sep 7.30am–1am).

SHOPPING

ANNELIE

If you can't get to Burano, this shop has some lovely antique lace inlays. It also sells authentic little lace-trimmed tablecloths, sheets and bedclothes at affordable prices, along with very special baby clothes and dreamy nightwear.

✚ 232 D10 ✉ Calle Lunga Santa Barbara, Dorsoduro 2748 ☎ 041 520 3277 ⓧ Mon–Sat 9.30–12.30, 4–7.30 ⛴ Ca' Rezzonico

ANTICHITÀ

Beautiful antique beads and other jewellery, and a fine selection of small antiques, fabrics and lace can be found here. Choose your beads and have them made up on the spot, or bring beads for re-stringing.

✚ 232 E11 ✉ Calle Toletta, Dorsoduro 1195 ☎ 041 522 3159 ⓧ Mon–Sat 10–1, 3.30–7.30 ⛴ Accademia

ANTIQUARIATO OGGETISTICA CLAUDIA CANESTRELLI

Tucked away on one of Dorsoduro's prettiest *campi* is Claudia's little shop, selling old prints, lamps and ornaments, though the chief draw are the exquisite 18th-century style earrings which she makes. Each pair

is different, but most incorporate pearl drops, tiny emeralds and rubies and lustre beads, at surprisingly good prices. She gives a 10 per cent discount for cash.

✚ 233 F11 ✉ Campiello Barbaro, Dorsoduro 364A ☎ 041 522 7072 ⓧ Daily 10–12.30, 3–6 ⛴ Salute

BAC ART STUDIO

www.bacart.com

For some stunning photos of Venice to take home and prove to people that it really does look dreamlike, Bac Art Studio has an impressive range. There are also framed prints of original art, as well as stationery and calendars.

✚ 233 E11 ✉ San Vio, Dorsoduro 862 ☎ 041 522 8171 ⓧ Mon–Sat 9–1, 2.30–6 ⛴ Accademia

LIBRERIA TOLETTA E TOLETTA STUDIO

The Libreria is an excellent bookshop with a huge range of coffee-table books on Venice, guidebooks, Italian classics, art and cookery books—and they're all offered with a 20 to 40 per cent discount. Across the *calle,* the Studio has yet more art books, posters, T-shirts and small gifts suitable for souvenirs.

✚ 232 D11 ✉ Calle Toletta, Dorsoduro 1214 ☎ 041 523 2034 ⓧ Mon–Sat 9.30–1, 3–7.30; also Oct–end May Sun 3.30–7.30 ⛴ Ca' Rezzonico

MONDONOVO

Venice's most famous *mascheraio* has been setting an example to other mask makers for decades with its enormous variety of traditional and modern masks, handmade on the premises from papier-mâché and beautifully gilded and painted.

✚ 232 D10 ✉ Rio Terrà Canal, Dorsoduro 3063 ☎ 041 528 7344 ⓧ Mon–Sat 9.30–6.30 ⛴ Ca' Rezzonico

PANTAGRUELICA

Pantagruelica is arguably the finest food shop in Venice, offering the best produce from all over Italy, lovingly tracked down by the enthusiastic owner, who is happy to spend time talking about the food producers he patronizes. The emphasis is on quality, so expect to find organic produce heavily featured. It's highly recommended for its cheese, *salumeria,* oils, dried goods and fresh truffles in season.

✚ 232 D10 ✉ Campo San Barnaba, Dorsoduro 2844 ☎ 041 523 6766 ⓧ Mon–Sat 9–8 ⛴ Ca' Rezzonico

Opposite Lace handicrafts make beautiful souvenirs of Venice

RISUOLA TUTTO DI GIOVANNI DITTURA

One of Dorsoduro's last traditional neighbourhood shoe stores specializes in *friulani*—jewel-bright velvet and silk slippers with bicycle-tyre soles. Prices for these truly Venetian souvenirs are astonishingly cheap (from €15) for the quality. They also sell wellington boots and waders during the months of *acqua alta* (high water).

🔲 233 E11 ✉ Calle Nuova Sant'Agnese, Dorsoduro 871 ☎ 041 523 1163 🕐 Mon–Sat 9–7.30, Sun 10–6 🚤 Accademia

SIGNOR BLUM

www.signorblum.com
Generations of children have received Mr Blum's colourful pieces—wooden toys and sculptures that behave like three-dimensional jigsaws. There are gondolas and *vaporetti,* churches and palaces, even the Rialto Bridge; wonderful gifts for children to cherish. If you're watching the cash, they have mobiles, fridge magnets and bookmarks which all make ideal small presents.

🔲 232 D10 ✉ Campo San Barnaba, Dorsoduro 2840 ☎ 041 522 6367 🕐 Mon–Sat 10–1, 4–8 🚤 Ca' Rezzonico

STUDIO GENNINGER

Leslie Ann Genninger is grudgingly considered one of the master beadmakers in Venice—not bad for an American, and an American woman at that. She follows the rules in making her beads, but creates something altogether different.

🔲 232 E10 ✉ Calle del Traghetto, Dorsoduro 2793/A ☎ 041 522 5565 🕐 Mon–Sat 10.30–6.30 🚤 Ca' Rezzonico

SUSANNA & MARINA SENT

For a more contemporary take on Murano glass, Marina and Susanna Sent have funky vases, plates and jewellery that won't break the bank. They also have very interesting *lattimo* (milk glass) pebbles in a variety of hues that would look great just about anywhere.

🔲 233 E11 ✉ Campo San Vio, Dorsoduro 669 ☎ 041 520 8136 🕐 Daily 10–6. Closed Nov and Jan, Dec closed Sun and Tue, other days 11–6 🚤 Accademia

ENTERTAINMENT AND NIGHTLIFE

IL CAFFÈ

Campo Santa Margherita is one of Venice's loveliest spots, and Il Caffè is a superb place to sit with a drink in hand and enjoy it all. The coffee is great, the *piadine* (thin, flat bread sandwiches) plentiful and the staff are young, bright and cheery. This becomes one of the lively square's focal points in the evening. Credit cards are not accepted.

🔲 232 D10 ✉ Campo Santa Margherita, Dorsoduro 2963 ☎ 041 528 7998 🕐 Daily 7.30am–2am 🚤 Ca' Rezzonico

GREEN PUB

The name, as with many Venetian establishments, describes it accurately. The location, one of Venice's most vibrant areas by night, is what makes it so popular.

🔲 232 D10 ✉ Campo Santa Margherita, Dorsoduro 3053A ☎ 041 520 5976 🕐 Fri–Wed 7.30am–2am 🚤 San Tomà

PICCOLO MONDO (EL SUK)

This is a small 'elegant and intimate' club with a dash of 1970s-style decoration. It attracts a diverse crowd: from well-dressed Italians to student types from the nearby Università di Ca' Foscari. Credit cards are not accepted.

🔲 232 E11 ✉ Calle Contarini Corfu, Dorsoduro 1056 ☎ 041 520 0371 🕐 Daily 10pm–4am 🖐 €10 🚤 Accademia

ROUND MIDNIGHT

Round Midnight is a good bet if you can't get to Jesolo or the Lido for the dance clubs. This intimate club attracts all sorts for the mainstream house music. Credit cards are not accepted.

🔲 232 D10 ✉ Fondamenta del Squero, Dorsoduro 3102 ☎ 041 523 2056 🕐 Mon–Sat 9pm–2am 🖐 €10 🚤 Ca' Rezzonico

SUZIE CAFÉ

Popular with students in the day, this friendly bar transforms itself into a swinging bar at night. On Friday nights, live jazz, reggae or funk bands perform. During the summer, a host of other home-grown bands appears at weekends. Credit cards are not accepted.

🔲 232 C11 ✉ Campo San Basilio, Dorsoduro 1527A–B ☎ 041 522 7502 🕐 Telephone for latest details 🚤 Zattere

TEATRO DA L'AVOGARIA

This experimental theatre was founded in 1969 by the internationally renowned director Giovanni Poli. Since his death in 1979 it has continued to stage works by little-known 15th- to 19th-century playwrights.

🔲 232 C10 ✉ Corte Zappa, Dorsoduro 1617 ☎ 041 520 6130 🕐 Telephone for latest details 🖐 Entry by voluntary donation 🚤 San Basilio

SPORTS AND ACTIVITIES

CANOTTIERI GIUDECCA

www.canottierigiudecca.com
You can learn to row the Venetian way in the quiet waters behind the Giudecca under the instruction of expert rowers, or take the tiller of a sailboat. Credit cards are not accepted.

🔲 233 E13 ✉ Fondamenta Ponte Lungo, Giudecca 259 ☎ 041 528 7409 🕐 Mon, Sun 2.30–7.30, Tue–Sat 9–12.30, 2.30–7.30; hours may vary in winter 🖐 Enrolment €26; insurance €8, then €10 per lesson 🚤 Palanca

EUTONIA CLUB

www.eutoniaclub.it
This gym near Campo Santa Margherita has excellent facilities and a small garden. Its numerous fitness courses and activities include step, spinning, yoga and belly dancing, as well as salsa and merengue classes.

🔲 232 D9 ✉ Calle Renier, Dorsoduro 3656 ☎ 041 522 8618 🕐 Mon–Fri 8am–10pm, Sat 10–1 🖐 Annual enrolment €28, then 8 1-hour sessions €50; telephone for details of classes and prices for non-members 🚤 Ca' Rezzonico

PALESTRA CLUB DELFINO

www.palestraclubdelfino.com
State-of-the-art computerized
techno-gym fitness rooms are on
offer here, with a solarium and
massage services for post-exercise
wind-down. You will need a fitness
certificate signed by your doctor.
➕ 233 E12 ✉ Zattere, Dorsoduro 788A
☎ 041 523 2763 🕐 Mon–Fri 9am–10pm,
Sat 9am–midnight 🖐 €20 per day
🚤 Zattere

PISCINA COMUNALE DI SACCA FISOLA

This municipal pool, set amid the
modern council flats of the small
island at the west end of the
Giudecca, is for serious swimmers.
The times given are for non-course
swimming sessions, and remember
you will have to wear a swimming
cap in the water and flip-flops to
walk from the changing rooms to the
pool. Credit cards are not accepted.
➕ 232 A12 ✉ San Biagio–Sacca Fisola,
Giudecca ☎ 041 528 5430 🕐 Mon,
Thu 10.30–12, 1–2.30; Tue, Fri 1–2.30,
6.30–7.15; Wed 3.45–5; Sat 3.45–5, 6.30–8;
Sun 3–6 🖐 €4.50 per session
🚤 Sacca Fisola

REALE SOCIETÀ CANOTTIERI BUCINTORO

www.bucintoro.org
Experienced rowers and novices
are welcomed by the famous
Reale Società Canottieri Bucintoro,
based near La Punta della Dogana
and the Salute church. Try your
hand at voga alla veneta (Venetian
rowing), canotaggio (regular rowing),
canoeing, kayaking or sailing.
Lessons are available for children.
Credit cards are not accepted.
➕ 233 G12 ✉ Zattere, Dorsoduro 10, 15
and 261 ☎ 041 522 2055, 041 520 5630,
041 523 7933; for lessons call 3356 673851
🕐 Tue–Sat 9–6, Sun 9–1 🖐 Enrolment
€42, then €52 for 8 rowing lessons
🚤 Salute, Zattere

HEALTH AND BEAUTY
CIPRIANI CASANOVA SPA

www.hotelcipriani.it
The luxurious surroundings of the
Cipriani hotel on La Giudecca are
a wonderful place to enjoy some
serious pampering at the Casanova
Spa. Facial and body treatments,
massage, manicures, pedicures
and private training are all available,
or you could book a full day's
treatment, which includes use of the
steam and sauna rooms. The Cipriani
also has its own hairdressing salon,
Puccio e Franco, which cuts and
styles both men and women's hair,
and offers facials and manicures.
➕ 233 H13 ✉ Giudecca 10 ☎ 041
520 7744 🕐 Mon–Sat 10–7 🖐 Half-day
treatments from €300; other treatments from
€60 🚤 Zitelle

FOR CHILDREN
GELATERIA SQUERO

This relative newcomer on the
gelato scene is giving nearby Nico
a good run for its money with its
super-light sorbets and mousses—a
house speciality—and creamy ices.
➕ 232 E11 ✉ Fondamenta Nani,
Dorsoduro 989–90 ☎ 041 241 3601
🕐 Daily 11–8 🖐 Cone €3 🚤 Zattere

GROM

A nationwide chain, established
in the early years of this century,
GROM have made a big impact
with their excellent ices, made
from impeccably sourced and finest
ingredients. The range of flavours
changes monthly, and nothing is on
offer unless it's in season, so don't
expect strawberry ice cream in
December or mandarin in July. The
flavours are clear and true; coffee
and salted caramel are particularly
noteworthy.
➕ 232 D10 ✉ Campo San Barnaba,
Dorsoduro 2761 ☎ 041 099 1751 🕐 Daily
10–10 🖐 Cone €2.50–€4 🚤 Ca' Rezzonico

THE GREAT DRAGON HUNT

www.stgeorgesvenice.com
Older children might enjoy this
unique take on Venice, organized
by the chaplaincy of the Anglican
church in the city in aid of church
funds. The hunt involves tracking
down 24 images of St. George and
the Dragon, scattered all over the
city. Route and transport instructions
are given and each dragon has
to be verified by answering
one or two questions. The hunt
criss-crosses Venice, introducing
children (and parents) to hidden
corners they might otherwise miss;
allow approximately five hours to
complete the whole course.
➕ 233 F11 ✉ St. George's Anglican
Church, Campo San Vio, Dorsoduro ☎ 041
520 0571 🕐 All year, but telephone
or email for further details 🖐 €12 per
questionnaire 🚤 Accademia

NICO

In the summer, Fondamenta Zattere
is a perfect spot to sit and enjoy
an ice cream and look out over the
shimmering water to Giudecca.
The gelati and frozen yoghurts
are beautifully made; try the
gianduitto (chocolate and hazelnut
with mounds of whipped cream),
renowned throughout Venice. The
café here serves a good selection of
snacks and drinks.
➕ 232 E12 ✉ Zattere, Dorsoduro 958
☎ 041 522 5293 🕐 Daily 8am–10pm
🖐 Cone €3 🚤 Zattere

Below While away a leisurely day at a spa, or
sample body pampering treatments

EATING

PRICES AND SYMBOLS

The prices given are the average for a two-course lunch (L) and a three-course dinner (D) for one person, without drinks. The wine price is for the least expensive bottle.

For a key to the symbols, ▷ 2.

AI CUGNAI

This genuine neighbourhood restaurant lies on the route from the Accademia to the Guggenheim, and has been pleasing locals and tourists alike for many years. You'll find all the usual Venetian favourites on the relatively short menu, with specialities such as a good *sarde in saor* (sweet and sour sardines), grilled fish and calorie-laden desserts such as *zuppa inglese* (trifle); vegetables here are excellent.
✚ 233 E11 ✉ Piscina Forner, Dorsoduro 857 ☎ 041 528 9238 ◉ Tue–Sun 12.30–2.30, 7.30–9.30 🖐 L €25, D€40, Wine €9 ⛴ Accademia

AI GONDOLIERI

www.aigondolieri.com
The variety and quality of food and wine offered at this well-known gastronomic haven, one of Venice's finest restaurants, will surely please. The accent is firmly on meat, with well-sourced, well-hung cuts

beautifully cooked and served in elegant surroundings.
✚ 233 F11 ✉ Fondamenta Venier, Dorsoduro 366 ☎ 041 528 6396 ◉ Wed–Mon 12–3, 7–10 🖐 L €45, D €65, Wine €12 ⛴ Accademia

AL BOTTEGON (CANTINONE GIÀ SCHIAVO)

This wonderful *bacaro,* with its waterside setting and crowds spilling out onto the *fondamenta,* is a great place for lunch and has one of the best wine cellars in the city. You can even buy wine, ready chilled, to take away. Three generations of the same family work here, cheerfully churning out delicious *cicchetti* and bulging panini—a real Venetian institution.
✚ 232 E11 ✉ Fondamenta Nani, Dorsoduro 992 ☎ 041 523 0034 ◉ Mon–Sat 8–2.30, 4–9.30 🖐 L €12, D €20, Wine €5 ⛴ Zattere, Accademia

CASIN DEI NOBILI

Translated as 'little house of the noble people', this is a great place to eat if you are a couple, but the wait for bigger groups might be frustrating. It's basically a pizzeria popular with students, and you'll be able to eat cheaply and well if you stick to the pizza menu. The waiters are happy to suggest alternatives

from the usual range of Venetian-style *primi* and *secondi*. There's a nice garden for summer eating. Credit cards are not accepted.
✚ 232 D10 ✉ Campo San Barnaba, Dorsoduro 2765 ☎ 041 241 1841 ◉ Tue–Sun 12–2.30, 7–10 🖐 L €25, D €40, Wine €8 ⛴ Ca' Rezzonico

CIPRIANI RESTAURANT

www.hotelcipriani.com
If you book a table at the Cipriani Restaurant, its private launch will collect you from San Marco, then take you back again later. But the journey isn't the main reason for coming here—it's the exclusive location, the dining terraces, elegant interior and matchless regional Italian cuisine that have earned the Cipriani its reputation. The menu and wine list are very carefully thought out, the cooking and service superlative, making this an unforgettable experience.
✚ 233 H12 ✉ Hotel Cipriani, Giudecca 10 ☎ 041 520 7744 ◉ Daily 12–11. Closed early Nov–early Apr 🖐 L €80, D €140, Wine €16 ⛴ By way of the Cipriani's private launch, San Marco or 41, 42

Above *Outdoor tables at Locanda Montin are popular on warm days*

227

CODROMA

Codroma has been serving late-night *cicchetti* for more than a hundred years and offers live jazz, serious credentials for local and visiting barflies. The *cicchetti* are unbeatable and the house red is good. Credit cards are not accepted.

➕ 232 C11 ✉ Ponte del Soccorso, Dorsoduro 2540 ☎ 041 524 6789
🕐 Mon–Sat 8am–2am. Closed Sat in summer 🍴 *Cicchetti* for two €10, Wine/beer from €2 a glass 🚤 Ca' Rezzonico

DO FARAI

It's worth tracking down this restaurant, not far from Campo Santa Margherita, for a dining experience in one of Venice's oldest establishments, where the atmosphere and surroundings are genuinely warm and welcoming. Factor in high-quality, classic Venetian cooking with the accent on fish and you'll have a memorable evening; the *frittura* of mixed fish and the shell fish are recommended.

➕ 232 D10 ✉ Calle dei Ragusei, Dorsoduro 3278 ☎ 041 277 0369
🕐 Tue–Sun 12.30–3, 7.30–10 🍴 L €25, D €40, Wine €10 🚤 San Basilio, Ca' Rezzonico

LA FURATOLA

It's best to book for an evening table at this little restaurant just off Campo San Barnaba, where the accent is on seasonal, local produce and traditional Venetian cooking. Fish soups here are very good—try the scampi, followed perhaps by a plate of inky spaghetti *alle seppie nere* (pasta with cuttlefish in its own ink), or a plain grilled fish, served with tiny seasonal vegetables from Sant'Erasmo. There's a carefully chosen wine list of Veneto and Friulian wines.

➕ 232 D10 ✉ Calle Lunga di San Barnaba, Dorsoduro 2869 ☎ 041 520 8594
🕐 Tue–Sun 12.30–2.30, 7.30–10, Mon 7.30–10 🍴 L €45, D €55, Wine €12 🚤 Ca' Rezzonico

HARRY'S DOLCI

For summer dining, Harry's Dolci (Harry's Desserts) offers a little more than its counterpart at San Marco—and at more agreeable prices. It makes the most of its great location and fabulous views, with a beautiful dining terrace right beside the water. Especially recommended are the pasta dishes, but whatever you choose, make sure you leave room for the sublime puddings—the *tris di cioccolato,* a trio of chocolate concoctions, is stunningly good.

➕ 232 D12 ✉ Fondamenta San Biagio, Giudecca 773 ☎ 041 522 4844
🕐 Wed–Sun 12–2.30, 8–10.30. Closed Nov–end Apr 🍴 L €80, D €110, Wine €12 🚤 Palanca

L'INCONTRO

The Sardinian fare served here gives a real insight into the range of Italy's regional cuisine. The sturdier flavours and vivid colours typify the Sardinian character and cooking, exemplified by the rabbit with myrtle and the wholesome *pane frattau* (paper-thin bread). There are some good wines from the south and the classic *seadas:* fat, sweet ravioli covered in hot honey.

➕ 232 D10 ✉ Campo Santa Margherita, Dorsoduro 3062A ☎ 041 522 2404
🕐 Wed–Sun 12.30–2.30, 7.30–10.30, Tue 7.30–10.30 🍴 L €40, D €55, Wine €9 🚤 San Tomà

LOCANDA MONTIN

The Locanda, tucked away behind San Trovaso, has been a reliable choice for more than 50 years. It has its ups and downs, but the cooking can still be top-notch and the service and atmosphere is traditionally Venetian. Straightforward Venetian specials and other dishes are perfectly presented, there's a fine wine list and good house wines, and a garden for summer eating.

➕ 232 D11 ✉ Fondamenta di Borgo, Dorsoduro 1147 ☎ 041 522 7151
🕐 Thu–Mon 12–3, 7–10. Closed 2 weeks Jan and 2 weeks Aug 🍴 L €45, D €75, Wine €10 🚤 Accademia

MISTRÀ

Young and enthusiastic owners have converted part of an old warehouse overlooking the boatyards of the southern Giudecca into an airy and laid-back restaurant. Beautiful views over the lagoon are the backdrop to some competently cooked fresh fish and seafood. Off the beaten track, but Mistrà is well signed and packed with locals.

➕ 233 E14 ✉ Fondamenta San Giacomo, Giudecca 212/A ☎ 041 522 0743
🕐 Wed–Sun 12–3, 7.30–10.30, Mon 12–3 🍴 L €25, D €35, Wine €12 🚤 Redentore

OSTERIA 1518

Just off the west end of the Zattere, you'll find the 1518, whose tables spill outside in warm weather throughout the year. Straightforward and unassuming, it prides itself on traditional Venetian cuisine served at honest prices. Expect fish from the market, a few meat dishes and look for the set menus served at both lunch and dinner, which are considerably better than those served in busier parts of town.

➕ 232 C11 ✉ Calle del Vento, Dorsoduro 1518/A ☎ 041 520 5799 🕐 Tue–Sun 12–10 🍴 L €20, D €40, Wine €7 🚤 San Basilio

OSTERIA AE BOTTI

You can sit outside at this little restaurant on the Giudecca and drink in one of Venice's loveliest views while enjoying freshly prepared *cicchetti* and a good selection of daily specials. Inside, there are comfortable tables or you can just have a bite at the bar, choosing from a selection of fresh fish and local meat specials—this is a good-value and friendly choice in a sublime location.

➕ 232 E13 ✉ Fondamenta Sant'Eufemia, Giudecca 609 ☎ 041 724 1086
🕐 Mon–Sat 11–10 🍴 L €25, D €35, Wine €12 🚤 Palanca

PIZZERIA ALLE ZATTERE

The main draw here is the incomparable position, with tables set on a floating dock looking across to the Giudecca, perfect on summer evenings and sheltered for sunny winter lunches. The menu is straightforward Venetian, and includes pasta with mussels *(cozze)*

and clams *(vongole)*, *seppie con polenta* (black squid with polenta) and *fegato alla Veneziana* (liver with onions). They also serve fine pizzas and good-value set menus.

✚ 232 E12 ✉ Fondamenta delle Zattere, Dorsoduro 791/A ☎ 041 520 4224 🕐 Daily 11–10 🖐 L €25, €35, Wine €10 🚏 Zattere, Accademia

RIVIERA

Waterside tables overlook the Giudecca canal at this elegant restaurant set at the western end of the Zattere. The Venetian-inspired menu is firmly fish-based, but there are delicate antipasti such as *fiore di Zucche* (stuffed courgette flowers) or *granseola* (spider crab) drizzled with lemon and fruity olive oil.

✚ 232 C11 ✉ Fondamenta Ponte Lunga, Dorsoduro 1473 ☎ 041 522 7261 🕐 Tue 12.30–3, 7.30–10, Wed 12.30–3, Thu–Sun 12.30–3, 7.30–10 🖐 L €45, D €45, Wine €12 🚏 San Basilio

TAVERNA SAN TROVASO

Right on the route between the Accademia and Campo Santa Margherita, this bustling, cheerful restaurant has been popular for years for its excellent value and good home cooking. There's always fresh grilled fish on the menu; other specialities include tagliatelle *al ragù d'anitra* (pasta with duck sauce), fried mixed fish and *baccalà in umido* (creamy stewed salt cod). If you're penny counting, go for a pizza—huge, crisp and delicious, with toppings such as *rucola e grana* (rocket and parmesan), gorgonzola or the San Trovaso special—billed as 'pizza with a little bit of everything'.

✚ 232 E11 ✉ Fondamenta Priuli, Dorsoduro 1016 ☎ 041 523 4583 🕐 Tue–Sun 12.30–2.30, 7.30–10 🖐 L €25, D €35, Wine €10 🚏 Accademia

Below *A fresh salad of* frutti di mare *(seafood) makes a delicious lunch*

PRICES AND SYMBOLS

Prices are the lowest and highest for a double room for one night in high season. Breakfast is included unless noted otherwise.

For a key to the symbols, ▷ 2.

LA CALCINA

www.lacalcina.com

The excellent-value, classy Calcina, in its superb and secluded setting on the sunny Zattere looking across to the Giudecca, served in the 1870s as a lodging for the English writer John Ruskin and has been welcoming guests ever since. The airy, spacious rooms have parquet flooring and are simply furnished with attractive period touches. Each room has a private bathroom, telephone, hairdryer and safe. Breakfast is served inside or on a terrace above the water, and the roof terrace is another bonus.

🕂 233 E12 ✉ Fondamenta Zattere ai Gesuati, Dorsoduro 780–83 ☎ 041 520 6466 🖐 €120–€300 🛈 32 🌀 🛥 Zattere

CA' PISANI

www.capisanihotel.it

Ca' Pisani's stylish interiors are inspired by the 1930s and '40s—smooth lines, exposed beams and art deco furnishings mix with modern, minimalist decoration. Each room is individually designed and has a relaxing, sophisticated charm. Facilities are excellent and bathrooms the most contemporary in town. La Rivista restaurant continues this theme and serves simple, modern and classic Italian cuisine. There's a sauna and access to a nearby gym.

🕂 232 E11 ✉ Rio Terrà Antonio Foscarini, Dorsoduro 979A ☎ 041 240 1411 🖐 €190–€400 🛈 29 🌀 🛠 Gym access 🛥 Accademia

CENTURION PALACE

www.sinahotels.com

Five-star luxury came to Dorsoduro in October 2009, when the Palazzo Genovese opened, after a lengthy restoration. Set in a prime position where the Grand Canal opens out into the Bacino, the hotel fuses a sensitive reconstruction of an historic building with 21st-century taste and style. Rooms are superbly equipped and comfortable in a modern and individual fashion, while the bar, all-white restaurant and lounges overlook the Grand Canal. It's quiet, discreet and something special for visitors looking for a less-than-traditional type of hotel.

🕂 233 F11 ✉ Campo San Gregorio, Dorsoduro 173 ☎ 041 34281 🖐 €220–€440 🛈 50 🌀 🛥 Salute

CIPRIANI

www.hotelcipriani.com

One of the world's great hotels, the Cipriani, set at the east end of the Giudecca across the water from San Marco, offers luxury, privacy and superb service. The Palazzo Vendramin and Palazzetto Nani Barbaro suites come with waterside views and your own private butler; all other rooms and suites are individually furnished with superb facilities. Within the extensive grounds there's a heated swimming pool, gym and beauty centre, red clay tennis court and vineyards. Dining at the Cipriani Restaurant is a well-heeled event, while the Cips Club is a more informal experience on a floating platform, with no jacket required. The hotel runs a free shuttle boat service to and from San Marco.

🕂 233 H13 ✉ Giudecca 10 ☎ 041 520 7744 🕘 The main hotel building closes between November and early April. Palazzo Vendramin and Palazzetto Nani Barbaro stay open year round 🖐 €850–€1,300 🛈 103 rooms and suites 🌀 🛠 🛥 Outdoor Olympic size 🛥 Zitelle

DINESEN

www.hotelamerican.com

The balconies of the Dinesen, dripping with flowers, overhang the Rio di San Vio, one of the quietest and most attractive of Dorsoduro's canals. This refurbished hotel, formerly the American, has airy, spacious rooms, furnished and decorated in traditional Venetian style, a relaxing bar and pretty garden; the staff pride themselves on the level of service—booking tickets and tours and arranging baby-sitters—making this an excellent choice in a great part of town away from the crowds.

⊞ 233 E11 ☒ Fondamenta Bragadin, Dorsoduro 628 ☎ 041 520 4733 ✋ €100–€300 ① 30 ⑤ 🖴 Accademia

LOCANDA SAN BARNABA

www.locanda-sanbarnaba.com

Just a few steps from the Ca' Rezzonico *vaporetto* stop, the San Barnaba is acknowledged as one of the best hotels in this price range in this area. Every bedroom is different, but all are tastefully furnished with period pieces, lovely textiles and have parquet floors and exposed beams. Public areas are elegant, and there's a small courtyard and a rooftop terrace. The hotel has ground-floor rooms and there are no bridges between it and the *vaporetto,* making it a good option for visitors with disabilities.

⊞ 232 E10 ☒ Calle del Traghetto, Dorsoduro 2785-86 ☎ 041 241 1233 ✋ €120–€200 ① 13 ⑤ 🖴 Ca' Rezzonico

LOCANDA SAN TROVASO

www.locandasantrovaso.com

This friendly, family-run hotel near the Zattere waterfront is good value for Venice. A small *altana* (roof terrace) allows guests to enjoy fantastic views and soak up the sunshine. The spacious and simple rooms have Venetian decoration and fittings; their facilities include private bathroom with shower, though none has television. Air-conditioning is available on request, and there are some pretty rooms in the new

annexe across the alley, which are payable by cash only; you can use credit cards in the main hotel.

⊞ 232 D11 ☒ Fondamenta delle Eremite, Dorsoduro 1350–51 ☎ 041 277 1146 ✋ €110–€160 ① 7 ⑤ 🖴 Zattere

MOLINO STUCKY HILTON

www.hilton.com/venice

The Hilton Group have carried out a fabulous conversion on this 19th-century flour mill on the island of Giudecca, resulting in Venice's slickest and most international hotel. It's squarely aimed at Americans and business people, with wonderfully sybaritic rooms and superb conference facilities. There are two restaurants, terraces and bars, and non-residents should make a point of enjoying a drink in the Skyline Bar, with its rooftop pool and fabulous city and lagoon views.

⊞ 232 C12 ☒ Giudecca 810 ☎ 041 272 3311 ✋ €495–€3,200 ① 330 rooms, 50 suites ⑤ 🏊 🖴 Palanca; hotel has private launch service to San Marco

OSTELLO DI VENEZIA

www.ostellovenezia.it

Venice's youth hostel is on the Giudecca, a boat ride from San Marco, and has wonderful views across the water to Santa Maria della Salute and San Marco. Accommodation is cheap and basic, with dormitory beds and communal bathrooms. There is an 11pm curfew; checkout time is 9.30am. A small continental breakfast is included and cheap meals are available (€8) in the evening. It is essential to reserve well ahead in writing, particularly during the summer. Credit cards are not accepted.

⊞ 233 G13 ☒ Fondamenta Zitelle, Giudecca 86 ☎ 041 523 8211 ⊘ Closed 12 Dec–31 Dec ✋ €20 ① 260 beds 🖴 Zitelle

PALAZZO STERN

www.palazzostern.com

For a room with a view on the Grand Canal, you could check into the Stern, one of Venice's prettiest Gothic *palazzi.* Outside, the breakfast terrace is set right

on the canal; inside, a three-year overhaul has restored the interior to its extraordinary Gothic-Moorish appearance, the work of the 19th-century owner. Public areas and bedrooms are rich in colour, tiling and mosaics; there are carvings and elaborate plasterwork, columns and pillars, making a stay here more than a little out of the ordinary. All rooms have WiFi internet access.

⊞ 232 E10 ☒ Calle del Traghetto, Dorsoduro 2792/A ☎ 041 277 0869 ✋ €190–€500 ① 24 ⑤ 🖴 San Samuele

PAUSANIA

www.hotelpausania.it

This 14th-century *palazzo,* complete with quadruple lancet windows, stunning staircase and original well, has been tastefully refurbished. Public areas have marble floors, understated decoration, Murano glass chandeliers and frescoed ceilings. The similarly decorated bedrooms are spacious and well-equipped: all have bathroom, telephone, TV, radio and minibar. The buffet breakfast is served in a room overlooking the garden—a rarity in Venice. Reserve early as this is a real gem.

⊞ 232 D10 ☒ Fondamenta Gherardini, Dorsoduro 2824 ☎ 041 522 2083 ✋ €130–€250, excluding breakfast ① 26 ⑤ 🖴 Ca' Rezzonico

TIZIANO

www.hoteltizianovenezia.it

Well off the beaten track, near the historic church of San Nicolò dei Mendicoli, this friendly hotel offers utter tranquillity. The building dates from the 15th century, and period details such as exposed beams and warm brickwork have been retained, with plenty of 21st-century comforts grafted on. The bedrooms are low-key Venetian in style, with painted wardrobes and bed heads; the breakfast room is charming, and, in warm weather, tables spill outside.

⊞ 232 B10 ☒ Rielo, Dorsoduro 1873 ☎ 041 275 0071 ✋ €100–€350 ① 14 ⑤ 🖴 San Basilio

Opposite *The luxurious Cipriani hotel*

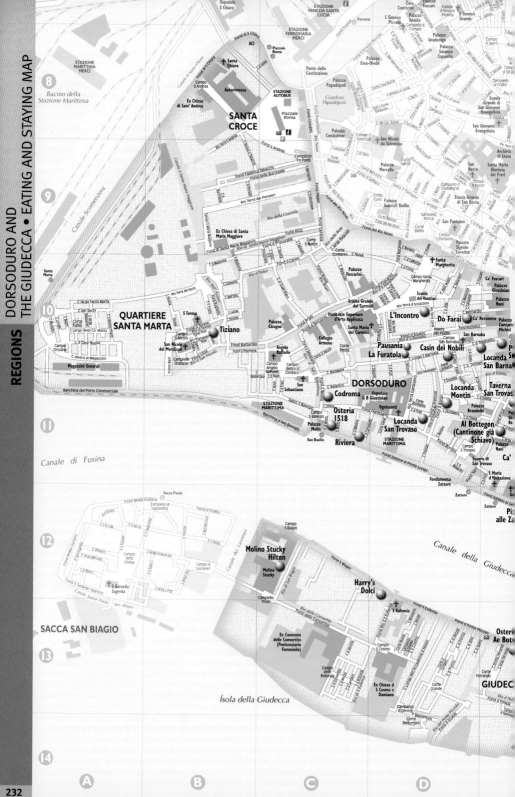

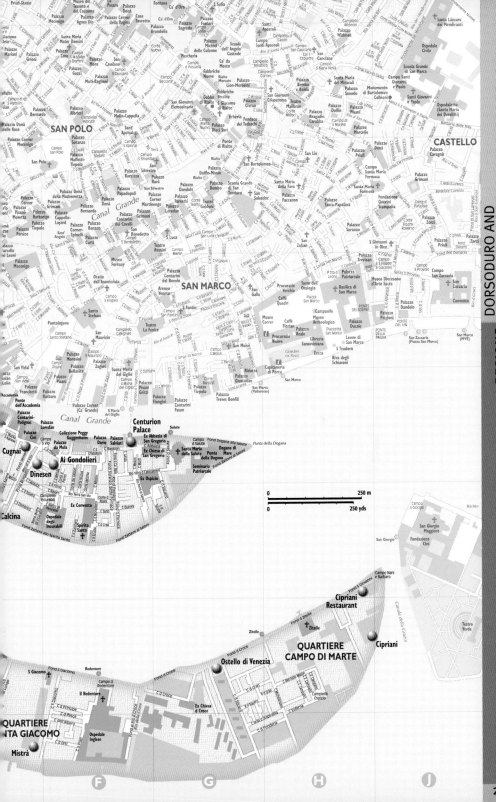

SAN POLO

CASTELLO

Canal Grande

SAN MARCO

Centurion
Palace

Cugnai

Ai Gondolieri

Dinesen

Calcina

Canal Grande

0   250 m

0   250 yds

San Giorgio
Maggiore

Fondazione
Cini

San Giorgio

Cipriani
Restaurant

Cipriani

Ostello di Venezia

QUARTIERE
CAMPO DI MARTE

Redentore

Il Redentore

QUARTIERE
NTA GIACOMO

Ex Chiesa
d Croce

Ospedale
Inglese

Mistrà

Teatro
Verde

F   G   H   J

EXCURSIONS

There's more to Venice than the compact historic centre, with its cramped alleys, canals and sunny *campi*, and most visitors spend at least half a day or so exploring the islands of the lagoon. These are scattered over the 50km (31-mile) length of this inland sea, so taking them in may require a bit of forward planning. The top three, in terms of visitor numbers, are Murano, Burano and Torcello, all lying in the northern lagoon. An organized excursion may be a good option if time is limited, but it's more fun to head to the Fondamenta Nova and take the *vaporetti* that connect them to the centre. Murano, famed for its glass-making, is the first stop, followed by Burano, famed for lace-making, and neighbouring Mazzorbo. From here, it's just a hop to dreaming Torcello and its superb and ancient basilica.

The southern lagoon contains the islands of Sant'Erasmo, where you can walk for miles through vegetable fields, peaceful Vignole and San Lazzaro degli Armeni, home to an Armenian monastery. Beyond these, the long sandy island of the Lido forms a bulwark against the open seas of the Adriatic. This is seaside Venice, complete with cars, and you can come here to enjoy the beaches, play golf, go horse-riding or simply bicycle for miles.

The time may come when these watery pleasures diminish and you need a change and a shot of something more modern. The region of the Veneto is rich in lovely cities, and the historic, contrasting and thriving centres of Padova (Padua), Vicenza and Verona all lie within easy reach. Though popular, none is as crowded as Venice itself, and an excursion will give a real taste of the Veneto, one of Italy's most dynamic regions.

Primolano

Riva del Garda

Arco

Rovereto

10 km

5 miles

Asiago

Torbole

Mori

SR249

SS240

Bassano del Grappa

TRENTINO-ALTO ADIGE

SS46

SP350

Àstico

SS47

Limone sul Garda

Ala

Ràossi

SS12

Malcésine

Marostica

Piovene-Rocchette

SS349

2218m
▲
M Baldo

Recoaro Terme

Schio

Thiene

Breganze

A22 E45

Malo

A31

Valdagno

SS46

Sandrigo

Cittade

Bolca

SS12

Chiampo

Orolo

SP246

Vicenza

Pia sul B

Arzignano

SP248

Brenta

Bussolengo

Montécchio Maggiore

SS3

Verona

Soave

A4 E70

VENETO

Grisignano di Zocco

SR11

San Martino Buon Albergo

SR11

Villafranca Veronese

San Bonifácio

SS500

Villafranca di Verona

San Giovanni Lupatoto

Lonigo

Abano Te

E45

Buttapietra

Montegro Ter

A22

Isola della Scala

Bovolone

SS434

Albaredo d'Adige

SS500

Cologna Véneta

Noventa Vicentina

SS247

SS12

Angiari

Montagnana

Monsélice

SS16

Nogara

Cerea

SR10

Este

Legnago

Merlara

Guá

A13

SP482

Villa Bartolomea

Ádige

Bagnolo San Vito

Ostiglia

SS434

Badia Polésine

Lendinara

SR88

Rov

San Benedetto Po

LOMBARDIA

Fratte Polesine

SP413

Póggio Rusco

SP496

Sérmide

Castelmassa

Móglia

Felonica

SR 482

Occhiobello

Polesella

SS12

Pilastri

Novi di Módena

Mirándola

EMÍLIA - ROMAGNA

Bondeno

SS16

Copparo

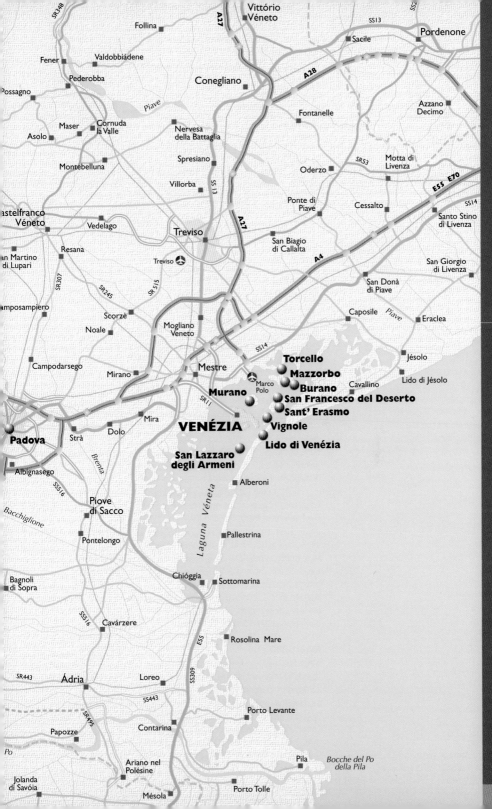

SS348

Vittório
Véneto

Follina

A27

SS13

Sacile

Pordenone

SS

Fener

Valdobbiádene

Pederobba

Conegliano

A28

Azzano
Decimo

Possagno

Piave

Fontanelle

Maser

Cornuda
la Valle

Nervesa
della Battaglia

Asolo

Cornuda
la Valle

SR53

Motta di
Livenza

Montebelluna

Spresiano

Oderzo

ESS E70

Castelfranco
Véneto

Villorba

SS 13

Ponte di
Piave

Cessalto

SS14

Santo Stino
di Livenza

Vedelago

A27

San Biagio
di Callalta

A4

San Giorgio
di Livenza

San Martino
di Lupari

Resana

Treviso

Treviso

San Donà
di Piave

SR307

SR245

SR515

Camposampiero

Caposile

Piave

Eraclea

Scorzè

Mogliano
Veneto

Noale

SS14

Jésolo

Campodarsego

Mestre

Marco
Polo

Torcello

Lido di Jésolo

Mirano

Murano

Mazzorbo

Cavallino

Mira

Murano

Burano

VENÉZIA

SR11

San Francesco del Deserto

Padova

Strà

Dolo

Sant' Erasmo

Vignole

Albignasego

SS16

San Lazzaro
degli Armeni

Lido di Venézia

Brenta

Alberoni

Bacchiglione

Piove
di Sacco

Laguna Véneta

Pontelongo

Pallestrina

Bagnoli
di Sopra

SS16

Chióggia

Sottomarina

Cavárzere

 E55

Rosolina Mare

SR443

Ádria

Loreo

SS309

SS443

Porto Levante

SR495

Papozze

Contarina

Po

Pila

Bocche del Po
della Pila

Jolanda
di Savóia

Ariano nel
Polésine

Porto Tolle

Mésola

INFORMATION

⊠ Ísola di Burano

🚢 Burano (LN) 🎫 Included in some tours. For details of the Musei delle Ísole pass, ▷ 265

TIPS

» Come to Burano on the ACTV service (▷ 50) rather than by expensive excursion boat—you'll have longer and will be able to go at your own pace.

» The trip from Murano to Burano takes 35 minutes.

» Combine Burano with Torcello for a day's outing.

BURANO AND MAZZORBO

These adjacent islands in the northern lagoon have a long tradition of fishing and lace-making.

BURANO

Burano was one of the first places in the lagoon to be settled, and even after the decline of nearby Torcello (▷ 247), it continued to prosper as a fishing community. With the men away on the boats, lace-making became the traditional occupation for the women, and gossamer-fine Burano lace was renowned all over Europe. Both traditions continue today, on a smaller scale, and Burano retains a sense of individuality and an atmosphere that's very different from that of Venice. Much of this is due to the almost impossible picturesqueness of the place, where the *rii* are still busy with boats, nets are hung out for mending and drying, and the *fondamente* are lined with vividly painted houses, a practice said to have originated to help the fishermen distinguish their own houses on the way home.

Walk from the *vaporetto pontile* towards Via Galuppi, the main street, and you'll pass houses in a rainbow of colours to find restaurants specializing in the freshest of fresh fish, and a wealth of lace shops. Much of the lace is now imported and machine-made, but some women still produce the real thing. You can trace the history of Burano lace in the Museo del Merletto (tel 041 730 034; Apr–end Oct Wed–Mon 10–5; Nov–end Mar Wed–Mon 10–4; €4). It stands on the *campo* at the end of Via Galuppi, named after Baldassare Galuppi, Burano's most famous son, a 17th-century composer who set many of Carlo Goldoni's plays to music. On the other side of the square is the church of San Martino (daily 8–12, 3–7; free), with a drunkenly tilting campanile and a fine *Crucifixion* by Tiepolo (1696–1770).

MAZZORBO

Mazzorbo was first settled in the 10th century and is linked to Burano by a wooden bridge, which has stupendous views across the lagoon to Venice. Walk across it from Burano and find yourself in yet another different world, one of small farms, pine trees and winding pathways. These lead to the 14th-century Gothic church of Santa Caterina, once the focal point of a thriving medieval community. Nothing remains of the early *palazzi*, which were dismantled by their owners, their stones shipped across to booming Venice. Between the bridge and the *vaporetto* stop there's a charming park, great for a picnic, and a good place for kids to run around and let off steam.

Above *Burano is known for its multi-hued buildings and its lace-making*

THE LIDO

The Lido is an island bulwark between the Adriatic and the lagoon, with hotels, beaches and outdoor pursuits.

LIDO GEOGRAPHY AND HISTORY

The island of the Lido is essentially a long, narrow sandbank. To the north, across the Porto di Lido, lies the mainland at Punta Sabbioni; to the south, the Porto di Malamocco, the busiest of the lagoon entrances, divides the Lido from the island of Pellestrina. Once a sparsely inhabited island of dunes and pinewoods, the Lido today combines its role as a residential suburb with that of seaside resort and overspill hotel area for Venice. It was 'discovered' by mid-19th-century Romantic writers, including Lord Byron and Robert Browning, and opened up as a resort in Edwardian times when the cult of the seaside first emerged. The grandiose hotels constructed for the leisured rich still survive.

WHAT TO DO AND SEE

If you're in Venice with children, or feel like a change, the Lido makes a pleasant respite. A 10-minute boat trip from the city will bring you to a different world, where cars, buses and supermarkets are the backdrop to lazy beach days. You could visit the ancient church of San Nicolò, founded in the 10th century. It was here that the Doge came on Ascension Day after the celebration of the city's marriage to the sea (▷ 274). The Lido is rich in art nouveau—a style known as Liberty in Italy—and art deco buildings. Look for the Hungaria Palace and the Villa Monplaisir (No. 14) on the Gran Viale, the main boulevard that links the lagoon with the sea, and don't miss the Hotel Excelsior, a neo-Moorish fantasy, complete with minaret. You can visit these on your way to the Lido's main attractions—the beaches, tennis courts, golf course, and walking and bicycling opportunities. If you need some exercise and a respite from stony streets, this is the place to come.

A DAY ON THE BEACH

Great strides have been made in improving the water quality of the Adriatic, making a beach day a more attractive prospect than it once was. All the grand hotels have their own *stabilimenti* (private beach establishments), with loungers, sunshades, changing cabins and restaurants; other privately run *stabilimenti*, much patronized by Venetians who come here on summer afternoons, offer similar facilities at lower prices. The *comune*, the local council, has free beaches, both on the Lido and the nearby island of Pellestrina.

INFORMATION

🚹 Gran Viale Santa Maria Elisabetta 6a, Lido di Venezia ☎ 041 526 5721 🕓 Jun–end Sep daily 9.30–4 🚆 Lido

Above *Walkway on a Lido beach overlooking the open Adriatic Sea*

INFORMATION

✉ Ísola di Murano

🚏 Colonna, Faro, Navagero, Museo, Venier 🛒 Wide choice

TIPS

» Bear in mind that the glass factories are closed on Saturday and Sunday.

» If you're buying, remember that the cheaper the glass, the less likely it is to have been made on Murano. All Murano glass is marked as such.

» The best production houses open to the public include Mazzega, where you can see demonstrations of chandelier production; CAM Vetri D'Arte, which specializes in mirrors and goblets; and Fratelli Barbini, one of the most innovative of all glass producers.

Above *A glassmaker at work on the Riva Longa*

INTRODUCTION

The lagoon island of Murano is a minature Venice, and has been the historic heart of Venetian glass production for more than 800 years, reaching its peak between the fifth and 16th centuries.

Murano was a Roman settlement, and later, one of the first lagoon islands to be permanently inhabited, becoming a prosperous trading community by the 11th century. In 1291, the Senate decided to transfer all glass furnaces to the island to avoid the constant danger of fire within the city. This had the bonus of keeping all the *maestri* (master glass-workers) and their trade secrets safely in one place, protecting Venice's monopoly on glass. In the 14th century every mirror in Europe was made in Venice. So possessive was Venice of the manufacturing process that any worker leaving the island was proclaimed a traitor, and even today skills are passed on solely by apprenticeship with a master. The industry declined during the 19th century with the advent of industrial glass-making, but has revived to become the main money-maker, with a profusion of small factories, many in the hands of families who have been involved in the business since the 13th century.

It's a 10-minute trip across the lagoon to Murano, a self-contained community with its own Grand Canal, fine churches, *palazzi* and glass-blowing industry. There are numerous privately run excursions from the city, but for good value and flexibility make the trip independently via the ACTV services (▷ 50). Allow two to three hours for a thorough visit. It's quite feasible, given an early start, to combine a visit to Murano with a trip to the northern islands of Burano and Torcello; study the *vaporetto* timetable with care as onward connections run half-hourly only.

WHAT TO SEE

THE GLASS FACTORIES

Away from the kitsch on offer in the shops along the Fondamenta dei Vetrai, superb glass is still produced on Murano. Venetian glass is made by the blowing and flamework process, whereby glass is repeatedly heated, stretched and blown to build up gradually the finished piece. The workers perform as a team, led by the chief blower, the *maestro* (master). Each workman's individual skills are an integral part of the process and each member of the team has a specific and highly specialized role. The work is intense, concentrated and very hot. For this reason, the most serious production houses are not open to the public, but plenty of others are (▷ Tips).

MUSEO DEL VETRO

www.museiciviveneziani.it

Italy's only glass museum is housed in the beautiful *palazzo* that was the former residence of the Bishop of Torcello. It traces the history of glass-making on Murano via a series of displays of glass right through from Roman times to the present day, with sections on the actual manufacturing process. One of the earliest of the ornate pieces is the 15th-century Barovier marriage cup, while other rooms are devoted to Venetian mirrors—a monopoly for centuries— and mind-blowing examples of 18th- and 19th-century polychrome glass chandeliers. Look for the examples of the different speciality glass for which Venice was famed: *milfiori* (thousand flowers), a technique where strands of coloured and transparent glass are fused; *stellaria*, where plain glass is shot with copper crystals; and *vetro latino*, with its porcelain-like finish. Note, too, the beautiful collections of *perle*, the intricate and delicate glass beads used all over the world as a form of currency.

✉ Fondamenta Giustinian 8, Murano ☎ 041 739 586 🕐 Apr–end Oct Thu–Tue 10–6; Nov–end Mar Thu–Tue 10–5 💶 €5.50, Rolling Venice card holders €3 🚏 Museo

SANTA MARIA E DONATO AND SAN PIETRO MARTIRE

Murano's greatest architectural treasure is the church of Santa Maria e Donato, a beautiful 12th-century basilica with a colonnaded exterior apse that's a classic of Veneto-Byzantine style. Inside, the mosaic marble paving, all geometric designs, flowers and animal motifs, dates from 1140 and is overlooked by a golden mosaic of the Madonna. The church of San Pietro has two superb pictures by Giovanni Bellini (1430–1516), *The Assumption* and a *Virgin and Child with Saints*.

✉ Campo San Donato, Murano 🕐 Apr–end Sep 9–12, 4–6.30; Oct–end Mar 9–12, 4–6 💶 Free 🚏 Museo

SHOPPING

LUIGI CAMOZZO

Luigi Camozzo is one of Murano's true *maestri*, renowned for his engraving. His pieces are heavily textured, the glass incised and etched to resemble stone and marble. The shapes are simple and his pieces are true works of art; the prices reflect this. He also runs courses in glass engraving.

✉ Fondamenta Venier 3, Murano ☎ 041 736 875 🕐 Mon–Fri 11–1.30, 2.30–6 🚏 Murano Venier

MAZZEGA

www.mazzega.it

This highly regarded and long-established glass manufacturer produces excellent Venetian glass of all types. Visit on a weekday to see the demonstrations of chandelier production and glass sculpture.

✉ Fondamenta da Mula 147, Murano ☎ 041 736 888 🕐 Daily 9–4 🚏 Museo, Venier

MURANO COLLEZIONI

www.muranocollezioni.com

If you're looking seriously for modern glass, it's worth a visit to browse the huge range on offer here and compare styles and prices. The outlet is run by three big names in the glass industry— Borovier e Toso, Carlo Moretti and Venini.

✉ Fondamenta Manin 1D, Murano ☎ 041 736 272 🕐 Daily 10.30–5.30. Closed Sun Nov–end Apr 🚏 Colonna

ROSSANA E ROSSANA

www.ro-e-ro.com

This glass-maker produces some high-quality, decorative pieces which combine centuries of tradition with graceful and clean, modern and classical lines, using many of the best Muranese techniques.

✉ Riva Longa 11, Murano ☎ 041 527 4076 🕐 Apr–end Oct daily 10–6; Nov–end Mar daily 10–5 🚏 Murano Venier

Left Mosaic floor in Santa Maria e Donato

AROUND MURANO WALK

Murano and its glassworks are high on most visitors' list, but there's more to the island than crystal. This is an independent community with its own churches, housing, shops and way of life that's remarkably self-contained. This walk takes you through the heart of the island and gives glimpses of everyday Murano life from the main *fondamente*.

THE WALK

Distance: 2.5 km (1.5 miles)
Time: 2 hours–half a day with visits
Start at: Colonna *vaporetto* stop
End at: Faro *vaporetto* stop

★ Take either the No. 42 from Piazzale Roma or the Fondamente Nuove or the DM from Piazzale Roma and disembark at Colonna. At the *pontile* turn right and walk up the Fondamenta dei Vetrai. Cross the canal at the first bridge on the right to the showrooms exhibiting modern Murano glass.

❶ The exhibits here are by the glass firms of Barovier e Toso, Carlo Moretti and Venini, three of Murano's best-known and most innovative large-scale producers.

Continue along this side of the canal, lined with primarily Gothic structures.

❷ These were built as homes for the glassworks' owners and doubled as warehouses for raw materials and workshops where the glass was blown.

Take the next bridge on your left back across the canal and walk along the Fondamenta dei Vetrai to the church of San Pietro Martire (▷ 241), one of Murano's only two functioning churches. Continue along the *fondamenta* (now Fondamenta da Mula), keeping an eye open for a narrow passage to your left just before the Ponte Vivarini, signed Formia.

❸ Formia is one of the best working *fornaci* (glass factories) to visit. Windows open into the busy workshops where teams of *maestri* and their helpers will be working flat out. Watch carefully and you'll be able to see how each member of the team has a very specific and skilled role in the manufacture of each finished piece (▷ 241).

Walk past the bridge to admire the Palazzo da Mula.

❹ This 15th-century Gothic *palazzo* was renovated in the 19th century, but still retains some lovely windows and Veneto-Byzantine motifs dating from the 12th and 13th centuries.

Cross the Ponte Vivarini and turn right along the Fondamenta Cavour, which becomes the Fondamenta Giustiniani at the canal junction.

❺ This is lined with glass shops, many selling cheap and unattractive foreign imports. If you want to buy, make sure the article comes from one of the main showrooms or boutiques and is guaranteed to be made on Murano.

Continue along the Fondamenta Giustinian to the entrance to the Museo del Vetro (▷ 241). As you leave the museum turn left and walk along to the Campo San Donato and the superb basilica of Santa Maria e Donato (▷ 241).
   Cross the the bridge outside the back of the basilica and turn left to walk along the Fondamenta Sebastiano Santi, lined with modest canalside houses. Cross the next bridge on your left, turn left on the other side, and walk back to the basilica. With your back to the basilica entrance, take Calle San Donato and follow it along to a T-junction where you turn left onto Calle Conterie.

❻ The run-down buildings here date mainly from the 19th century, a time of huge expansion on Murano. During the 17th and 18th centuries Murano, as well as being Europe's main glass supplier, was also a popular resort with Venetian noblemen, who built country retreats surrounded by gardens on the island. During the late 1800s the gardens were built over and two inlets were filled to create new residential areas.

Follow Calle Conterie to emerge into Campo San Bernardo, a lovely, low-key *campo* with trees and benches, that gives a taste of Murano's true life away from the tourists. Turn left down Calle de Mistero and walk back down to hit the Fondamenta Cavour. Turn right across Ponte Vivarini, then right again and left over the next bridge across the Rio dei Vetrai. Turn right over the bridge and along the Fondamenta Daniel Manin, taking the third left into the wide Viale Garibaldi which leads across to the Faro *vaporetto* stop. Take the No. 41 or DM back to the city.

WHERE TO EAT
Bar Ice on the Campo San Donato makes a good place to pause, and serves snacks all day (8.30am–10pm). For lunch, try the Antica Trattoria, Riva Longa 20.

Above *A mosaic shop sign*
Opposite *The arcaded facade of the 12th-century church of Santa Maria e Donato*

WHEN TO GO
Leave the city centre early and spend the morning exploring Murano, returning in the afternoon via San Michele (▷ 111).

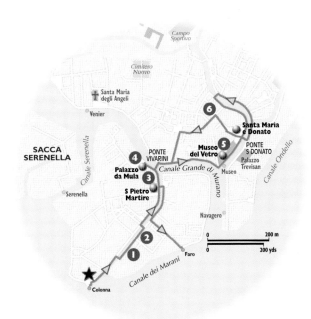

TOURIST INFORMATION OFFICES
Stazione Ferroviaria 36130
www.turismopadova.it
☎ 049 875 2077
🕐 Mon–Sat 9.15–7, Sun 9–noon

Galleria Pedrocchi 35130
www.turismopadova.it
☎ 049 876 7927
🕐 Mon–Sat 9–1.30, 3–7

HOW TO GET THERE
Padua is 32km (20 miles) west
of Venice. All southwest trains
from Venice on the Bologna
line stop at Padua; journey time
25–35 minutes; tel 041 892 021
for information. SITA buses from
Piazzale Roma run every
30 minutes, with a journey time
of 45 minutes; tel 049 820844 for
information.

Above *The Prato della Valle has statues
of local dignitaries and is surrounded
by a canal*

INTRODUCTION

Historic Padua, only a short train ride from Venice, is a university city and
the Veneto's most important economic centre, combining art, monuments,
churches and tempting shops, all scattered around a beguiling and compact
historic district.

WHAT TO SEE

CAPPELLA DEGLI SCROVEGNI

www.cappelladegliscrovegni.it

The chapel was built in 1300 by Enrico Scrovegni to atone for his father's
usury—Scrovegni senior died screaming 'give me the keys of my strong
box', and was nominated by Dante for a place in *Inferno*. Between 1303 and
1309 the walls were frescoed by Giotto with scenes from the life of Christ
and the Virgin, set against a background of radiant blue. Visitors are limited to
25 at a time, but you can fill in the wait in the multimedia room, an excellent
introduction to Giotto and his times.

✉ Piazza Eremitani 8 ☎ Book at least three days in advance (tel 049 201 0020) or book online.
If entry times are not fully booked some tickets may be available at the ticket desk for immediate
entry. Tickets may be collected 1 hour in advance 🕐 Mon 9–7, Tue–Sun 9am–10pm. Closed
1 Jan, 15 Aug, 25, 26 Dec 💶 Adult €12, child (6–17) €5, under 5 free; free with PadovaCard
(includes admission to the Musei Civici and Palazzo Zuckermann)

MUSEI CIVICI EREMITANI

Occupying adjoining buildings to the Cappella degli Scrovegni, the Musei Civici
Eremitani, Padua's main museum complex, focus on Venetian painting and
sculpture from the early 14th to 19th centuries. The big local names in painting
are all represented and include Giovanni Bellini, Titian, Tintoretto, Giorgione,
Veronese and Tiepolo, and there are works by Flemish and Dutch artists.
Sculptures date back to the 15th century, and the archaeological section is
particularly strong in Roman sculpture, busts and statues from the surrounding
area, as well as Egyptian, Greek and Etruscan antiquities.

The Palazzo Zuckermann, across the road, houses the applied and decorative
arts collections.

PALAZZO DELLA RAGIONE

The Palazzo della Ragione, medieval Padua's assembly hall and law courts, was built between 1218 and 1219. This vast building, altered repeatedly over the centuries, is remarkable today for the cycle of 15th-century astrological frescoes in the main hall, which also contains a huge wooden horse, constructed for a tournament in 1466. The ground floor has been home to food stalls for more than 800 years, while the Piazza della Frutta and Piazza delle Erbe, on each side of the palace, host a fine food and produce market.

✉ Piazza delle Erbe (entrance from Via VIII Febbraio) ☎ 049 820 5006 🕐 Tue–Sun 9–7. Closed 1 Jan, 1 May, 15 Aug, 25, 26 Dec ✋ Adult €4, child (6–17) €2

CAFFÈ PEDROCCHI

The splendidly eclectic Caffè Pedrocchi, built in the early 19th century, was once Padua's main intellectual salon; today, it doubles as a bar and restaurant. The upstairs rooms were restored and reopened in 1999, and present a succession of themed spaces whose decoration encompasses every style from Etruscan and Greek to Gothic and Renaissance—the Egyptian Room, with its starry ceiling and dog gods, is pick of the bunch.

✉ Via VIII Febbraio 15 (entrance from Piazzetta Pedrocchi) ☎ 049 878 1231 🕐 Tue–Sun 9.30–12.30, 3.30–6 ✋ Adult €4; child (6–17) €2.50

BASILICA DI SANT'ANTONIO

The Basilica di Sant'Antonio, Il Santo, is one of Italy's main pilgrim shrines, packed with supplicants, who come to pray to this Portuguese-born patron of Italy. The Basilica was built between the mid-13th and 14th centuries and its treasures include marble bas-reliefs showing scenes from St. Anthony's life in the Cappella dell'Arca, which contains his tomb. Donatello (1386–1466) created the bronze panels on the high altar; he was also responsible for the superb equestrian bronze dominating the surrounding square, which shows the mercenary Erasmo de Narni, also known as Gattamelata (Honey Cat).

✉ Piazza del Santo ☎ 049 878 9722 🕐 Mon–Fri 6.20am–7pm, Sat–Sun and holidays 6.30am–7.45pm ✋ Free

TIPS

» The PadovaCard is valid for 48 or 72 hours and gives free admission to all civic museums, free transport and reductions on other museums, guided tours, selected shops and accommodation. It costs €15 or €20 from tourist information offices.

» The train is by far the best way to get to Padua; you'll avoid most of the sprawling and unattractive outskirts and the station is an easy 15-minute walk from the historic heart of the city.

» Sightseeing Padova (www.city-sightseeing.it) is a hop on-and-off sightseeing bus, with multi-lingual commentary. It tours the main city sights daily from March until the end of October, departures at 10.30, 12, 2.45, 4 and 5.15. Tickets (valid for 24 hours) cost €13 for adults, €6 for children (5–16), and are free for under 5s.

PADOVA

0   200 m
0   200 yds

Below *The wooden horse in Palazzo della Ragione's main hall*

SANT'ERASMO

Bigger than Venice itself, Sant'Erasmo is one of the lagoon's best-kept secrets. It lies northeast of the city, a long, flat, sparsely inhabited island where sandy paths criss-cross well-kept fields and tiny vineyards. Sant'Erasmo produces huge quantities of vegetables for the city markets, and produce marked 'San Rasmo' or *'nostranno'* on market stalls will certainly have come from here. The major crop is artichokes, and the island produces some unique varieties, resulting in a long growing season—artichokes of various types are available in Venice practically year-round. The island is traversed by a single road, where rickety old unlicensed cars trundle up and down, there are no police here to worry about, and no doctor, pharmacy or secondary school either. The island does have a tiny store at the main settlement around the church, and a couple of *trattorie*. Its chief charm lies in its bucolic atmosphere and the beautiful countryside. Take *vaporetto* No. 13, alight at Capannone, and you can spend the whole day ambling through vineyards and past old farmhouses to the old Austrian stronghold of Forte Massimiliano— the perfect antidote to the stony streets of Venice.

✉ Ísola di Sant'Erasmo 🚢 Capannone, Chiesa, Punta Vela

SAN FRANCESCO DEL DESERTO

www.isola-sanfrancescodeldeserto.it
Legend and truth intermingle to tell how, in 1220, St. Francis of Assisi returned to Italy from the Holy Land. On his way he stopped at a lagoon island near Venice, where he planted his staff in the ground. It grew into a tree, and swallows flew in to perch in it and sing to the holy man. The island is today known as San Francesco del Deserto, a cypress-clad oasis of peace near Burano (▷ 238) that's home to a thriving Franciscan monastery. The monks have been here since soon after the death of St. Francis, when the island's owner, Jacopo Michiel, bequeathed it to the Order. The present church, dating from the 15th century, is surrounded by two cloisters, a refectory, offices and monks' cells, and is approached by a tree-lined avenue. Cypresses, deciduous trees, orchards and vegetable gardens cover the rest of the island; there's no other place in the lagoon as tranquil. If you want to visit, you can negotiate a price with Burano's water taxi owner, who runs occasional group tours to the island. The monks also run retreats and workshops.

✉ Ísola di San Francesco del Deserto 🕿 041 528 6863 🕐 Tue–Sun 9–11, 3–5. Guided visits by Franciscan monk ✋ Free but donation recommended 🚢 Access by taxi from Burano (to book tel 041 735 420, 041 730 001 or mobile 335 581 3731—Gianni Amadi & Figli)

SAN LAZZARO DEGLI ARMENI

Allow an afternoon to visit the Armenian monastery island of San Lazzaro, home to a small community of monks and one of the world's most important centres of Armenian culture and learning. This tiny island was gifted by the Doge in 1717 to an Armenian abbot called Mekhitar, who had fled north up the Adriatic to escape the Turks in the Peloponnese. Armenians had been in Venice since the 11th century, and with the establishment of the monastery, the Venetian Armenian community became the focus of Armenian Catholic culture throughout the world. It remains so today, and the monastery is supported and visited by Armenians from around the world.

The monastery tour takes in the immaculate cloister and the church, rebuilt after a fire in 1883, before heading upstairs to the museum and modern library, containing more than 40,000 priceless books and manuscripts. The museum is a jumble of objects and bits and pieces, ranging from an Egyptian mummy to fine antique porcelain and paintings donated by Armenian benefactors. The old library was once the haunt of Lord Byron, who used to row across from Venice three times a week to wrestle with the Armenian language, said to be among the world's most fiendishly difficult. The monks are proud of the Byron connection, the fact that they were the only monastery in the city to be spared the Napoleonic axe, and their long association with Venice, still occasionally referred to here as La Serenissima.

✉ Ísola di San Lazzaro degli Armeni 🕿 041 526 0104 🕐 One guided tour daily 3.25–5.15 (coincides with *vaporetto* No. 20 from San Zaccaria at 3.10) 👤 Adult €6; child (under 12) €3 🚢 San Lazzaro

VIGNOLE

Vignole, like Sant'Erasmo, is a market garden island, reached by *vaporetto* No. 13. It was once a popular summer resort for Venetians escaping the heat of the city, but, like its neighbour, is now dedicated to artichokes and asparagus rather than pleasure. It retains the ruins of a medieval chapel dedicated to Sant'Erosia, and is a popular weekend island with picnicking Venetians, who come here by boat.

✉ Ísola di Vignole 🚢 Vignole

Below *Vineyard on Sant'Erasmo, often called the garden of Venice*

TORCELLO

The evocative rural backwater of Torcello, dreaming in the past, is Venice's most ancient settlement and the site of a superb basilica, the oldest building in the lagoon. Torcello was founded in the fifth century by Roman citizens fleeing successive waves of invading barbarians on the mainland. It was the first serious lagoon settlement and, by the 14th century, was home to a prosperous community, whose population numbered more than 20,000. During the 1400s, when malaria was rife, the population fled to Venice, leaving the palaces to decay and the canals to silt up. Today, all that remains of past glories are a handful of scattered houses and restaurants, a hotel, a couple of bridges crossing a muddy canal, an 11th-century church and the great basilica of Santa Maria Assunta.

From the landing stage a path runs beside Torcello's canal, crossed by the simple stone span of the Ponte del Diavolo (Devil's Bridge), to the main piazza. Around here everything there is to see is grouped. You will also find the so-called Trono di Attila, a primitive stone chair once used by the bishop.

THE CHURCHES

The island has two wonderful churches—the Basilica di Santa Maria Assunta (open Mar–end Oct daily 10.30–6; Nov–end Feb daily10–5) and the church of Santa Fosca. The basilica dates from 638 and is the oldest building in Venice. It was altered in the ninth and again in the 11th century, but has remained virtually unchanged since. The lofty interior, bare and cool, has some superb mosaics from the ninth to 12th centuries on the vaults and walls. Wholly Byzantine in style, they represent *Christ and the Apostles* in the right-hand apsidal chapel, the *Virgin and Child* in the apse, and the finely detailed *Last Judgement* on the west rear wall.

Next to the basilica is the beautiful 11th-century church of Santa Fosca, another Byzantine-influenced construction with a Greek-cross plan and an external colonnade. Behind the basilica is the campanile, whose steep, twisting ramps lead to a panorama of water, sky, mudflats and marsh.

MUSEO DEL TORCELLO

The museum houses a low-key display of archaeological finds from Torcello and the lagoon (Mar–end Oct Tue–Sun 10.30–5.30; Nov–end Feb Tue–Sun 10–5).

INFORMATION

✉ Torcello 🚢 Torcello 🍴 Several bar/restaurants 🗓 Some souvenir stalls

Above *Santa Fosca and the campanile of the Basilica di Santa Maria Assunta*

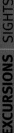

INFORMATION

www.tourism.verona.it

🛈 Via degli Alpini 9, off Piazza Brà

☎ 045 806 8680 🕑 Jun–end Sep daily 8–8; Oct–end May Mon–Sat 9–6, Sun 9–1

HOW TO GET THERE

Verona is 124km (77 miles) northwest of Venice. Trains run regularly between Venice and Verona, with a journey time of 90 minutes.

INTRODUCTION

Rose-red Verona, the setting for Shakespeare's *Romeo and Juliet,* is rich in Roman ruins, ancient churches, fine *palazzi* and monuments. One of northern Italy's most prosperous cities, with a thriving cultural life, it's an ideal place for a mix of sightseeing, excellent shopping and fine dining.

Verona was founded by the Romans in 89BC, and its history is a story of domination by exterior powers, ending with its annexation by Venice in 1402. Today it's among Italy's most prosperous provincial cities with a thriving economy, whose mainstays are manufacture, printing and pharmaceuticals. The city's historic core, still contained within massive 16th-century walls, has miraculously retained most of its Roman, medieval and Renaissance monuments, with the Piazza dell'Erbe still occupying the site of the Roman forum. The grid of streets round this area is within a loop of the River Adige, and it's here that virtually all the city's main monuments can be found.

WHAT TO SEE

PIAZZA BRÀ AND THE ARENA

Head first for Piazza Brà, a huge, irregular *piazza* fringed with cafés and dominated by one of the city's best-known monuments, the great Roman amphitheatre known as the Arena. Built in the first century AD, it's the third largest of the surviving Roman amphitheatres in Italy, an elliptical structure measuring 110m (360ft) by 139m (456ft) and capable of seating 25,000. In 1114 a serious earthquake destroyed all but four of the arches of the exterior arcade, but the interior is intact with steeply pitched tiers of pink marble seats and spectacular views from the top. Since 1913 it's been the venue for a popular summer opera season, with sets of gargantuan dimensions.

✉ Piazza Brà ☎ 045 800 3204 🕑 Tue–Sun 8.30–7.30, Mon 1.30–7.30 (subject to alteration during the opera season) 👆 €6

PIAZZA DELL'ERBE

Verona's focal square, the Piazza dell'Erbe, is connected with Piazza Brà by Via Mazzini, a pedestrianized thoroughfare that's home to the city's most tempting shops. At the far end, the Piazza, ringed by architecture spanning the centuries, is home to a plethora of market stalls firmly aimed at tourists. The finest buildings are at the northern end: the medieval Torre di Gardello, the beautifully frescoed late Renaissance Casa Mazzanti and the Palazzo Maffei, a highly decorated baroque palace. The tall buildings at the opposite end of the Piazza once marked the edge of the Jewish ghetto.

Above *View of Verona and the River Adige*

PIAZZA DEI SIGNORI

The Piazza dei Signori is linked with the Piazza dell'Erbe by the 12th-century Palazzo della Ragione and contains the elegant Loggia del Consiglio, built in the 15th century. A statue of the poet Dante (1265–1321) stands in the square, and, on its south side, a gateway leads into the Mercato Vecchio, a courtyard with Romanesque arches and exterior Gothic staircase. From here you can climb the 83m (272ft) Torre de' Lamberti (tel 045 927 3027; daily 8.30–7.30; €4), built in the 12th century. The east exit of Piazza dei Signori leads to the Scaligeri tombs, funerary monuments to the della Scala family. By the 1200s this clan were Verona's most powerful family, naming themselves after dogs—Mastino, 'the Mastiff', Cangrande, 'Big Dog' and Cansignorio, 'Lord Dog'. Railings around the tombs are decorated with ladder motifs (Scala means 'ladder').

CASA DI GIULIETTA

Verona's most popular tourist attraction, the Casa di Giulietta (Juliet's House), is besieged throughout its opening hours by visitors. The house has no connection with the Juliet story; the Montagu and Capulet families did exist, but they lived nearer Vicenza than Verona. The cult of Juliet was the inspiration of the Verona tourist board during the economically depressed 1920s. The house dates from the early 14th century and was probably originally an inn; the famous balcony, however, was erected by the city council in 1928.

✉ Via Cappello 23 ☎ 045 803 4303 🕔 Tue–Sun 8.30–7.30, Mon 1.30–7.30 ✋ €6

MUSEO CIVICO D'ARTE

The Scaligeri fortress, known as the Castelvecchio, is a splendid riverside structure which is home to the Museo Civico d'Arte. The restored interior, all steel walkways and gleaming glass, is a labyrinth of passages, stairs and lofty rooms where the museum's collections are displayed. As well as sculpture and goldwork, there are works by big names here—look for Mantegna's *Holy Family*, a serene *Madonna* by Giovanni Bellini (1430–1516), a *Nativity* by Tintoretto (1518–94) and *Sante Caterina e Veneranda* by Carpaccio (1460–1525).

✉ Corso Castelvecchio 2 ☎ 045 806 2611 🕔 Tue–Sun 8.30–7.30, Mon 1.30–7.30 ✋ €2.50

TIPS

» From outside the station, buses 11, 12, 13 (weekdays) and 91 and 92 (Sundays and holidays) leave from Marciapiedi A for Piazza Brà. Buy your ticket before you board from the machine at the stop or inside the station at the tobacconist.

» The VeronaCard gives free admission to all the main sites, museums and churches and all public transport within the city. It is available for either 1 or 3 days at €10 or €15 and is on sale at central museums, churches, galleries and tobacconists.

» A hop on-and-off sightseeing bus, with multi-lingual commentary, tours the main city sights daily, with a choice of two routes departing hourly (Jun–end Sep 9–7; Oct 9.30–6.30). Tickets (valid 24 hours) cost €15 for adults, €7.50 for children (5–16), and are free for under 5s.

» Verona's famous opera season, with performances held in the Arena, runs from June to end August. More information at www.arena.it.

VERONA'S CHURCHES

» Verona's main churches, with the exception of San Zeno, all lie in the *centro storico*.

» If you cross the River Adige over Ponte Garibaldi near the Duomo, you'll find yourself in 'Veronetta', with its two superb churches—15th-century San Giorgio in Braida and beautiful Santo Stefano, pieced together in the 12th century from earlier buildings. East lies the Teatro Romano, still used for a summer drama festival, while there are sunset views from the Castel San Pietro higher up the hill.

Sant'Anastasia

☎ 045 592 813 🕔 Mar–end Oct Mon–Sat 9–6, Sun 1–6; Nov–end Feb Tue–Sat 10–1, 1.30–4, Sun 1–5 ✋ €2

Duomo (Cathedral)

☎ 045 592 813 🕔 Mar–end Oct Mon–Sat 10–5.30, Sun 1–6; Nov–end Feb Tue–Sat 10–4 ✋ €2

San Zeno Maggiore

☎ 045 592 813 🕔 Mar–end Oct Mon–Sat 8.30–6, Sun 1–6; Nov–end Feb Tue–Sat 10–5, Sun 1–5 ✋ €2

INFORMATION

www.provincia.vicenza.it
ℹ Piazza Matteotti 12 ☎ 0444 320854
🕐 Mon–Sat 9–1, 2–6

HOW TO GET THERE

Vicenza is 74km (46 miles) northwest of Venice. All northwest trains from Venice on the Verona line stop at Vicenza. The journey time is 55 minutes.

Above *Vicenza stands in the gentle green Venetian plain*

INTRODUCTION

Beautiful Vicenza, ringed with green hills, is a prime example of a prosperous Veneto town, with excellent facilities and an easy-going lifestyle. Its artistic appeal lies in its superb *palazzi* and civic buildings.

All over the Western world, civic buildings and churches pay homage to Vicenza's architectural glories, the work of its most famous son, Andrea di Pietro della Gondola, also known as Palladio (1505–80). This pocket-sized city, a UNESCO World Heritage Site, contains some of his finest works, and with its laid-back atmosphere, smart shops, restaurants and green spaces it deserves to be one of the Veneto's must-sees. In 1404 Vicenza became a Venetian possession, adorned with Gothic palaces, but in the 16th century Palladio and his neoclassical style burst upon the scene. Though born in Padova (Padua), Palladio found his major patron, the humanist nobleman Trissino, in Vicenza and between 1540 and 1580 transformed the face of the city.

WHAT TO SEE
THE HISTORIC HEART

The heart of Vicenza is bisected by the Corso Palladio. It's lined with a stunning procession of grandiose mansions and *palazzi*, of which five were designed by Palladio. From the west end of the *corso* and the Porta Castello, these are the Palazzo Thiene Bonin Longare (1562) on the left, the altered Palazzo Capra (1540–45) at No. 45, which retains its Palladian facade and doorway, and the Palazzo Thiene at No. 47. This was probably first designed by Giulio Romano and later modified by Palladio. Palladio was also responsible for the Palazzo Pojana at No. 97, a double-block mansion which abuts the Palazzo Trissino, designed by Vincenzo Scamozzi (1552–1616), Palladio's most gifted pupil. At the far end of the *corso* stands Casa Cogollo (1560–70), thought to have been Palladio's own house. The *corso* opens into Piazza Matteotti, home to both the Teatro Olimpico and the Palazzo Chiericati (1550), one of Palladio's most triumphant buildings, now housing the Museo Civico (Jul–end Aug Tue–Sun 10–6; Sep–end Jun Tue–Sun 9–5; entry with Vicenza Card only €8).

South from here lies the Piazza dei Signori, the heart of the *centro storico*, dominated by Palladio's Basilica (closed for restoration until the end of 2010), started in 1549, and his Loggia del Capitaniato. The double-tiered loggia of the Basilica encloses the earlier Gothic Palazzo della Ragione, which suffered from subsidence until Palladio's intervention. The huge and elegant complex next to the Loggia is the Monte di Pietà, Vicenza's 16th-century pawn-shop. Behind the Basilica, the Piazza dell'Erbe sells fruit and vegetables as it has since medieval times. Scattered about central Vicenza, notably on Contrà Porti and Contrà Riale, are more Palladian palaces—Palazzo Barbaran (home to the Museo Palladiano), Palazzo Colleoni Porto and Palazzo Iseppo Porto. Corso Fogazzero has fine Gothic buildings and Palladio's Palazzo Valmarana-Braga (1566).

THE TEATRO OLIMPICO

The Teatro Olimpico, Europe's oldest indoor theatre, was designed by Palladio in 1579 and opened in 1585. The architect died before it was complete, though the astonishing *trompe l'oeil* stage set was inspired by his designs and executed after his death by Vincenzo Scamozzi. Five wood and stucco Renaissance street scenes radiate back from the front stage seemingly for several hundred metres. It's all illusion; the set is only 15m (40ft) deep and 2m (6.5ft) high. The auditorium is modelled on Greek and Roman theatres; 13 semicircular wooden steps, which double as seating, rise in front of the stage.
✉ Piazza Matteotti 11 ☎ 0444 222 800 🕐 Jun–end Aug Tue–Sun 9–7; Sep–end May Tue–Sun 9–4.45 🖐 Entry with Vicenza Card only: adult €8, under 14 free, family €12

THE MUSEUMS AND CHURCHES

Vicenza's main museum, Museo Civico (tel 0444 222811; Jul–end Aug Tue–Sun 10–6; Sep–end Jun Tue–Sun 9–5; entry with Vicenza card only: adult €8, under 14 free) occupies the Palladian Palazzo Chiericati, and gives an overview of local painters, as well as a fine collection from farther afield. This includes pictures by Giovanni Bellini (1430–1516), Tintoretto (1518–94), Veronese (1528–88) and Giambattista Tiepolo (1696–1770). The Venetian schools also figure strongly in the Palazzo Leoni Montanari, a baroque *palazzo* that contains 14 quirky genre paintings by Pietro Longhi (1702–85), as well as a large collection of Russian icons. Architecture fans should not miss the Museo Palladiano (tel 0444 323 014 or see www.cisapalladio.org for current opening times and prices), in a palace designed by the great man.

Vicenza's churches are lower key; they include Santa Maria Nova, designed by Palladio in 1575; the Duomo, an ancient foundation that was restored after extensive damage in World War II; and the Gothic Franciscan San Lorenzo. Pick of the bunch is Santa Corona (Tue–Sun 8.30–12, 3–5; free), a 13th-century Gothic church with a Palladio chapel and paintings by Bellini and Veronese.

VILLAS AND GREEN SPACES

The hill on Vicenza's southeastern edge is Monte Berico, an important plague shrine topped by a 17th-century basilica (May–end Sep 6–12.30, 2.30–7.30; Oct–end Apr 6–12.30, 2.30–6; €2). Close by are two villas; Villa Valmarana (10 Mar–8 Nov Tue–Sun 10–12, 3–6; 9 Nov–9 Mar Sat–Sun 10–12, 2–4.30; €8), nicknamed 'Ai Nani' after the stone dwarfs on its wall, contains astounding frescoes by Tiepolo father and son. Villa Capra Valmarana, or the Rotonda (13 Mar–3 Nov gardens: Tue–Sun 10–12, 3–6; interior: Wed 10–12, 3–6; gardens €5, house and gardens €10), is the only Palladian villa built purely for pleasure and one of the most imitated, with four symmetrical facades.

North of central Vicenza, across the River Bacchiglione, lies the Parco Querini, a lovely space with statues and cool green shade, while, to the south, the Parco Marzo is the perfect place to relax after all that sightseeing.

TIPS
» Visits to the Teatro Olimpico are only available by buying the full Vicenza Card combined ticket (€8), valid for 3 days, from the tourist office and all participating museums.
» The station is a 15-minute walk from Vicenza's historic heart.
» Before visiting Vicenza, you can download a walking tour (English and Italian) as a podcast for an MP3 player (visit www.provincia.vicenza.it).

EXCURSIONS SIGHTS

If time is short or you need a hand to unlock the hidden pleasures of Venice, there's plenty of choice on land or water to help you discover the city and the lagoon with local experts.

BOAT TOURS

IL BURCHIELLO
www.ilburchiello.it
Cruises along the Riviera del Brenta with stops at three important Palladian villas: Pisani, Barchessa Valmarana and Foscari Wildmann. Modern boats are used with commentary and catering facilities. ✉ Sita spa, Divisione Navigazione, Via Orlandini 3, Padova ☎ 0498 206 910 🕐 Mar–end Oct, departures from either Venice (La Pietà, Riva degli Schiavoni) or Padua, return by bus ✋ Adult €79, child (12–17) €52, (6–11) €37; optional lunch €28. Phone booking is recommended, as the website will not support credit card bookings. Book in Venice, and you can pay by credit card on boarding

EXCURSIONS TO MURANO, BURANO AND TORCELLO
Four-hour boat trip to the three northern lagoon islands with 35-minute stops at each. ✉ APT Venezia ☎ 041 529 8711 🕐 Apr–end Oct daily departures from Alilaguna *pontile* at the Giardinetti Reali at 9.30 and 2.30; Nov–end Mar departures from Alilaguna *pontile* at the Giardinetti Reali at 2. Minimum 4 people. Can be booked in advance at APT ✋ Adult €20; child (6–12) €10; under 6 free

GONDOLA SERENADE
A 40-minute gondola trip down quiet canals, which is accompanied by musicians and singers. ✉ APT Venezia ☎ 041 529 8711 🕐 Daily 6.30 and 7.30; meeting point: Santa Maria del Giglio station ✋ €40

GRAND CANAL TOUR
One-hour boat tour with commentary. Traverses the Grand Canal from the Giardinetti Reali to the rail station and returns via the Giudecca and the island of San Giorgio Maggiore.

✉ APT Venezia ☎ 041 529 8711 🕐 Daily departures from the Alilaguna *pontile* at the Giardinetti Reali daily 4.30 and 5.30. Minimum 4 people. Can be booked in advance at APT ✋ €30 (no reductions)

WALKING TOURS

AVVENTURE BELLISSIME
www.tours-italy.com
A range of theme-based tours on foot in Venice, offering a host of options including Art and Architecture, Photography, Children's Venice and Specialist Shopping. Also boat trips around the lagoon and to the islands. ✉ Calle dei Preti, San Marco 2442A ☎ 041 970 499 🕐 11 Mar–6 Nov ✋ €20–€70

VENICE EVENTS
www.tours-venice-italy.com
Anglo-Italian company offering themed tours of the city focusing on art and architecture, as well as bespoke tours on anything from museums to lagoon wildlife, and helicopter flights over the city and lagoon. ✉ Frezzeria, San Marco 1827 ☎ 041 523 9979 🕐 Daily 11.15, 4, 5.30 (depending on tour), contact office for details ✋ €30–€50 (depending on tour)

VENICE ON FOOT
Two-hour walking tour around the main monuments of San Marco. ✉ APT Venezia ☎ 041 529 8711 🕐 English daily 9.15; French daily 9.15; Spanish Tue–Thu, Sat–Sun 9.15; German Mon, Fri 9.15 ✋ Adult €38, child (6–14) €19, Palazzo Ducale ticket €28

VENICE ON FOOT AND BY GONDOLA
Combined city walking and gondola tours. ✉ APT Venezia ☎ 041 529 8711 🕐 English daily 3, French daily 3, Spanish Tue–Thu, Sat–Sun 3, German Mon, Fri 3 ✋ €39

SPECIAL INTEREST

APT VENEZIA
www.turismovenezia.it
The APT runs a wide range of specialized, themed tours around the city and lagoon. ☎ 041 529 8711

GIARDINI STORICI
www.giardini-venezia.it
Guided tours for small groups to visit private and historic gardens in Venice and the islands. ✉ Wigwam Club, Giardini Storici, Via Ca' Rossa 2B, Venezia Mestre ☎ 041 610 791 (booking essential) 🕐 Apr–end Nov ✋ Varies

NATURAVENEZIA
www.natura-venezia.it
Natural history excursions in Venice, the lagoon and the lagoon islands. ✉ Cooperativa Limosa, Via Toffoli 5, Venezia Marghera ☎ 041 932 003 🕐 By arrangement ✋ Varies

BESPOKE TOURS

ASSOCIAZIONE GUIDE TURISTICHE
The official tourist guide co-operative offers made-to-measure city tours in Italian, English, French, Spanish and German. Arrange in advance. ✉ Calle Cassellaria, Castello 5327 ☎ 041 521 0762 🕐 Mon–Fri 9–6, Sat 9–1 ✋ €200 for up to 30 people

PRACTICALITIES

Practicalities gives you all the important practical information you will need during your visit, from money matters to emergency phone numbers.

VENICE

TEMPERATURE

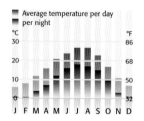

RAINFALL

WEATHER

Venice's position, surrounded by sea and virtually in the foothills of the Alps, has a major influence on the climate, which, apart from the summer months, has more in common with central Europe than the true Mediterranean.

Spring comes around March, with frequent rain showers up to the end of April. Temperatures continue to rise during May, with rain getting less frequent until, by the middle of June, the summer weather systems are established; these bring high temperatures, occasional high humidity and sunshine. During the summer months of June, July and August fixed hot, dry weather is the norm, though this breaks down into dramatic thunderstorms and heavy showers at two- to three-weekly intervals. Temperatures begin to fall in September and October, and by the end of the month there is increasing rainfall and the likelihood of *acqua alta* (▷ 47) soars. November is wet and brings mist, foggy days and more *acqua*

alta, and by December winter is setting in. The rain continues on and off up to Christmas, but there can be dry, crisp and sunny days. These are frequent in January and early February, accompanied by low temperatures and severe frost; snowfalls are not unknown. Late February and March see more rain, sunshine and rising temperatures as the Venetian spring starts.

WHEN TO GO

The best time to visit Venice is in the spring and autumn (fall), when the weather is pleasantly warm with frequent sunny days. The city is busy, but not too crowded, and away from the major sights you're likely to have places virtually to yourself. The height of summer sees Venice at its worst—hot and packed with day-trippers. August is the holiday month for Venetians, and it's not unusual for shops and restaurants to close for two to three weeks. If you are prepared to wrap warmly, January and February are good months to visit; there are few visitors and the city sparkles in the winter sun. The fortnight of Carnevale (▷ 21 and 274), generally in February, sees Venice as crowded as during high season.

WEATHER REPORTS

Weather reports are given during news bulletins on Italian TV, and the Italian local press has daily weather maps and forecasts. BBC World News and CNN news have websites (www.bbc.co.uk, www.CNN.com), and broadcast regular global weather updates in English, and The Weather Channel and the Met Office in the UK also have global weather websites (www.weather.com, www.metoffice.com).

WHAT TO TAKE

Locals dress well at all times. Skimpy T-shirts, vests, shorts and general scruffiness are not appreciated by the Venetians. You will need lightweight cottons and linens to wear during the summer, natural fabrics being more comfortable in hot and humid conditions. Remember, though, to bring clothes that cover your shoulders and knees for visiting churches; you won't be allowed in if you are improperly dressed. Spring and autumn call for heavier clothing, and layering makes sense, as temperatures can fluctuate considerably throughout the day. If you're visiting in winter you will need warm clothing and a winter coat, and don't forget gloves, scarves and a hat as the weather can be bitter.

Bear in mind that *acqua alta* can occur anytime from mid-September until December (and even outside these months), and you will need waterproof boots (which you can buy in Venice) for negotiating flooded streets.

Remember to pack:
» Waterproofs
» A folding umbrella
» A small bag for daily use
» Comfortable shoes
» Your address book, for emergency contacts or postcards
» Photocopies of all important documents: passport, insurance details, credit card, debit card and passport numbers and registration numbers for mobile (cell) phones, cameras and other expensive items
» A torch (flashlight) and binoculars—both are useful in dark churches and museums
» A first-aid kit and any prescribed medication
» An Italian phrasebook—any attempt at Italian is appreciated
» Earplugs if you are a light sleeper—Venice is surprisingly noisy around dawn and church bells may wake you early
» Toiletries and sunscreen in screw-top containers inside plastic bags to guard against leakage.

TIME ZONES

Italy is on Central European Time (CET), one hour ahead of GMT (Greenwich Mean Time) during the winter. In April, the clocks are put forward by one hour, and then put back again in October.

CITY	TIME DIFFERENCE	TIME AT NOON IN VENICE
Amsterdam	0	noon
Auckland	+11	11pm
Berlin	0	noon
Brussels	0	noon
Chicago	-7	5am
Dublin	-1	11am
Johannesburg	+1	1pm
London	-1	11am
Madrid	0	noon
Montreal	-6	6am
New York	-6	6am
Paris	0	noon
Perth, Australia	+7	7pm
San Francisco	-9	3am
Sydney	+9	9pm
Tokyo	+8	8pm

DOCUMENTS
PASSPORTS
Officially visitors from EU countries need only a national identity card to enter Italy. In practice, you will need a passport. All other foreign visitors to Italy will need a passport, which should be valid for at least another six months from the date of entry into Italy. If you lose your passport, contact your embassy (▷ 262).
» Keep a note of your passport number or carry a photocopy of the information page separately.
» Alternatively, scan the information pages of your passport and any other important documentation and email them as attachments to a web-based email account you can access from anywhere in the world.

CUSTOMS
Duty-paid guidelines for non-EU citizens
US citizens can bring home up to $800 of duty-paid goods, provided they have been out of the country for at least 48 hours and haven't made another international trip in the past 30 days. This limit applies to all members of the family, regardless of age, and exemptions may be pooled.

» 200 cigarettes; or
» 100 cigarillos; or
» 50 cigars; or
» 250g smoking tobacco
» 1 litre of spirits or strong liquors

» 2 litres of still table wine
» 2 litres of fortified wine, sparkling wine or other liquors
» 60cc/ml of perfume
» 250cc/ml of toilet water

Duty-paid guidelines for EU citizens
European Union citizens can take home unlimited amounts of duty-paid goods, as long as they are for personal use. In the UK, HM Revenue and Customs considers anything over the following guidelines as for commercial use:

» 3,200 cigarettes; or
» 400 cigarillos; or
» 200 cigars; or
» 3kg of tobacco
» 110 litres of beer

» 10 litres of spirits
» 90 litres of wine (of which only 60 litres can be sparkling wine)
» 20 litres of fortified wine (such as port or sherry)

VISAS
If you are an EU national, or from Australia, Canada, New Zealand or the US, you do not need a visa for stays of up to 90 days. To extend your visit you can, one time only, apply to any police station for an extension of a further 90 days. This extension cannot be used for studying or employment, and you will have to prove that you can support yourself financially.

Regulations can change at short notice, so check before making travel arrangements. If you are a citizen of a country other than those mentioned above, you should contact the Italian Embassy in your home country.

DUTY-FREE AND DUTY-PAID GUIDELINES
Anything that is clearly for personal use can be taken into Italy free of duty. Carry receipts for valuable items to prove on your return home that they haven't been bought in Italy. For up-to-date information, see the HM Revenue and Customs website (www.hmrc.gov.uk) or that of the US Customs and Border Protection (www.cbp.gov). You cannot buy goods duty-free if you are touring within the EU. You cannot bring home goods for payment, or payment in kind, or for resale. Such goods are considered for commercial use, and duty is payable.

TRAVEL INSURANCE
Take out travel insurance when you book your trip. Most policies cover cancellation, medical expenses, accident compensation, personal liability and loss of belongings (including money). They should also cover the cost of getting you home in case of medical emergency.

ITALIAN EMBASSIES ABROAD

COUNTRY	ADDRESS	WEBSITE
Australia	12 Grey Street, Deakin ACT 2600, tel 02 6273 3333	www.ambcanberra.esteri.it
Canada	275 Slater Street, 21st Floor, Ottawa (ON), KIP 5HP, tel 613 2322401	www.ambottawa.esteri.it
Ireland	63–65 Northumberland Road, Dublin 4, tel 1 6601744	www.ambdublino.esteri.it
New Zealand	34 Grant Road, PO Box 463, Thorndon, Wellington, tel 4 4735339	www.ambwellington.esteri.it
South Africa	796 George Avenue, Arcadia 0083 Pretoria, tel 012 4305541/2/4/4	www.ambpretoria.esteri.it
UK	No. 14 Three Kings Yard, London W1Y 2EH, tel 020 73122200	www.amblondra.esteri.it
US	3000 Whitehaven Street NW, Washington DC 20008, tel 202/612-4400	www.ambwashingtondc.esteri.it

MONEY

LOST/STOLEN CREDIT CARDS
American Express
44 1 273 696 933
Diners Club
44 1 252 513 500
CartaSí including
MasterCard and Visa
800 151 616
Visa
800 819 014

CREDIT AND DEBIT CARDS

» MasterCard, Diners Club, American Express and Visa credit cards *(carte di credito)* are widely accepted in Venice, though not for relatively small payments and purchases, and some smaller establishments still do not take them.

» Look for the credit card symbols in the shop window or on the restaurant door or check with the staff.

» You can also use your credit card to make cash withdrawals, although your credit card company will charge it as a cash advance. Contact your credit card company before you go to get a PIN number if you do not already have one.

» Credit cards are not accepted for food purchases, though debit cards can be used in some supermarkets, providing they are the chip and pin type.

» You must notify both your credit card company and your bank if you intend to use your cards in Venice; failure to do so will cause an automatic block.

TRAVELLERS' CHEQUES

» Travellers' cheques are accepted almost everywhere. To avoid additional exchange rate charges, take them in euros, pounds sterling or US dollars.

» You can exchange travellers' cheques without commission at American Express, Salizzada San Moisè, San Marco 1471 (tel 041 520 0844) and Travelex, Piazza San Marco, San Marco 142 (tel 041 277 5057), or at the Rialto branch at Riva del Ferro, San Marco 5126 (tel 041 528 7358).

LOST AND STOLEN CARDS AND TRAVELLERS' CHEQUES

» If your credit card or bank card is stolen, report it to the police and telephone the appropriate emergency number. All are open 24 hours a day and have English-speaking staff.

» If your travellers' cheques are stolen, notify the police, then follow the instructions given with the cheques. You can contact the Venice office of American Express or telephone the following toll-free numbers:
For American Express travellers' cheques, call 800 872 000
For Thomas Cook's travellers' cheques, call 800 872 050

CASH MACHINES/ATMS

» Cash machines, or Bancomats in Italy, are plentiful and many are accessible 24 hours a day.

» Most have instructions in English and other languages, as well as Italian.

» You avoid commission and the exchange rates are better when you withdraw cash with a debit card (Cirrus/Maestro/Delta) from ATMs rather than using a bureau de change.

» Check with your bank before leaving home that you will be able to take cash out with your card while in Venice.

CURRENCY EXCHANGE AND BANKS

Travellers' cheques, cheques and foreign money can be changed at banks, the railway station and the airport, and very often at major hotels (generally at a poorer rate). Many banks in your home country have differing exchange rates depending on the denominations of currency being bought or sold. Check with banks for details and shop around before you buy. Banks are listed in the *Pagine Gialle* (Yellow Pages) under *Banche e Istituti di Credito*. Banks offer a better rate of exchange than the numerous bureaux de change *(cambio)* in Venice, many of which advertise 'no commission' but offer poor exchange rates. If you are using a bank to change travellers' cheques or draw money on your credit card across the counter, you will need to produce your passport. Remember that bank transactions in Italy can be slow and cumbersome, so allow plenty of time.

CURRENCY RESTRICTIONS

The import and export of local and foreign currency is limited to €10,329.14, but check with your embassy before departure if you need to bring large sums into the country. Amounts greater than this should be declared and validated in Italy.

WIRING MONEY

» Wiring money is quite a lengthy process and the bureaucracy involved means that it is probably not worthwhile unless you are planning to spend quite a long time in Italy.
» Ask your bank at home for a list of affiliated banks. You can get money wired out to any bank from home, but if your bank is already in contact with certain banks in Italy it will make the process a lot easier. Always ask for a separate letter, telex or fax confirming that the money has been sent and ask that it be sent to Swift. It can take up to a week for the money to transfer.

» If you have a bank account in Italy and at home, you can transfer money directly if both the banks are part of the Swift system of international transfers. Again it takes about 5 to 7 days, if not longer.
» American Express, Moneygram and Western Union Money Tranfers are faster from the US, but more expensive.

TAX REFUNDS

All non-EU shoppers are entitled to an IVA (sales tax) refund on major purchases. Ask for an itemized *fattura* (invoice) when shopping, then present this at customs for stamping when leaving the EU. Return the stamped invoice to the store within four months of the date of purchase and the shop will refund the IVA direct.

DISCOUNTS

» Those over 65 can often get discounted admission charges to museums and galleries—use your passport as proof of age.
» Children's admission charges are usually available up to the age of 18, and reductions also exist for people between 18 and 26.
» If you are a student, you will qualify for some reductions; for details of specifically Venetian student and young people's cards, ▷ 265.

SOME EVERYDAY ITEMS AND HOW MUCH THEY COST	
Takeaway sandwich	€3
Bottle of water	€1–€2
Cup of coffee (at the bar/sitting)	€1/€2–€8
Beer—half a litre (at the bar/sitting)	€1.50/€3–€10
Glass of house wine (at the bar/sitting)	€1.50/€3–€12
Daily newspaper (Italian)	€1.80
20 cigarettes	€4
Ice cream (takeaway)	€2–€4
ACTV biglietti a tempo (24 hours)	€18

TIPPING
Italians do not tip heavily. Service is often included in your hotel or restaurant bill, although a little extra is appreciated if the service has been good. The following is a general guide:
Pizzerias/*trattorias*: round up to the nearest euro
Expensive restaurants: 10%
Bar service: up to 25¢, or 5–10% for table service
Taxis: round up to nearest 50¢
Porters: 50¢–€1 per bag
Chambermaids: 50¢–€1 per day
Cloakroom attendants: 50¢
Toilets: 25¢

HEALTH

BEFORE YOU GO

» No vaccinations are necessary for a trip to Italy, unless you are coming into the country from an infected area. If you have any doubts, contact your doctor before you leave. It is a good idea to check when you last had a tetanus injection, and, if more than 10 years ago, have a booster before you travel.

» You should always take out health insurance, and most people do so as part of their travel insurance. Ensure that it covers the cost of getting you home in a medical emergency. If you already have health insurance to cover treatment at home, check with your insurer before you leave home that you will be covered while abroad.

» In addition to health insurance, European citizens should carry an EHIC (European Health Insurance Card), which you should get before departure. This replaces the old E111, and is obtainable from post offices and travel agents. Italy has a reciprocal health agreement with the rest of the EU, Iceland, Liechtenstein and Norway, which allows reduced-cost dental and medical (including hospital) treatment on presentation of the EHIC. A fee must be paid, though, plus part of the cost of any

prescribed medicines. For specialist treatment you will need medical insurance.

» It is essential for non-EU visitors to carry health insurance.

» Visitors from the US and Canada may find that their existing health policy covers them while they are abroad. Check with your insurance company before you travel, and remember to bring your policy identification card.

» Check with your doctor or pharmacist for the chemical name for any prescription drugs you need, in case you need to replace them while you are away. Brand names often change from country to country.

» For up-to-date information, visit the Department of Health's website, www.doh.gov.uk (in the UK), or the National Center for Infectious Diseases, www.cdc.gov/travel, in the US.

» It is a good idea to take photocopies of all important documentation, which should be kept separate from the originals.

» Alternatively, you could scan the photocopies or the originals and send them to an email address that can be accessed anywhere in the world.

HOW TO GET A DOCTOR (UN MEDICO)

» To get in touch with a doctor, ask at your hotel or consult the Yellow Pages (Pagine Gialle) under Unità Sanitaria Locale.

» For an ambulance, call 118. Ambulance boats in Venice will come to the nearest fondamenta to your hotel; the number to call is 041 523 0000.

» If you need emergency treatment, go directly to the pronto soccorso (casualty department/emergency room) of the nearest hospital.

HOW TO GET TREATMENT WITH YOUR EHIC

» If you need medical treatment while you are away, take your EHIC to the USL (Unità Sanitaria Locale) office, which will give you a certificate of entitlement.

» Take this to any doctor or dentist on the USL list to receive free treatment. If they need to refer you to a hospital, they will give you a certificate that entitles you to free treatment.

» If you go to hospital without being referred by a doctor, you should give the EHIC to them.

» If you do not have a USL certificate, you will have to pay for treatment and it may be difficult to get the money back afterwards, and then you will probably only receive a partial refund.

» If you are charged in full for medicines, keep the receipts—you will not get a refund without them.

» Carry a photocopy of your EHIC, as some doctors and hospitals may keep it. If they do, you can pick up another form when you get home.

HOW TO GET TREATMENT WITH INSURANCE

» If you have health insurance at home it is likely that it will cover you for medical treatment abroad. Check your policy before you leave home.

» Take a copy of your insurance documents to the doctor or hospital—they may be able to bill your insurance company direct.

» If you have to pay for treatment, keep all of your receipts for your insurance claim.

PHARMACIES (FARMACIE)

» Pharmacies sell toiletries as well as a wide range of over-the-counter medicines.

» Pharmacists are well-trained and can deal with minor ailments and provide some medicines that are only available on prescription in the UK and US.

» Most pharmacies are open during normal shop hours (8.30–1 and 4–8), but a rota system operates outside opening hours in Venice so there is at least one open at all times—a copy of the rota is displayed in pharmacy windows.

DENTISTS (DENTISTI)

» If you have an EHIC, contact the USL, as above.

» If you do not have an EHIC, contact a private dentist (in the Yellow Pages under Dentista). Again, take a copy of your insurance details and keep your receipts.

OPTICIANS (OTTICHI)

» Opticians can usually carry out minor repairs to your glasses, such

as replacing screws on the spot for little or no charge.

» Lenses can often be replaced overnight.

» If you really cannot survive without your glasses or contact lenses, bring a copy of your prescription with you so that you can have replacements made up if necessary.

TAP WATER

» Venice's tap water in hotels and restaurants is safe to drink.

» You should be on the look out for signs (often on public fountains) that say acqua non potabile. This means that the water there is not safe to drink.

SUMMER HAZARDS

» From April to the end of September the sun is strong and you will need to wear a high-factor sunscreen (broad spectrum of factor 15 or above is recommended).

» Insect bites are irritating rather than dangerous. There are no malaria-carrying insects in Italy, but there is an ongoing and severe mosquito problem in Venice from April through to November.

» Do not open the bedroom window after dusk and ask your hotel for a plug-in electric mosquito repellent; tablets for these are available in supermarkets, alimentari and hardware stores.

HEALTHY FLYING

» Visitors to Italy from as far as the US, Australia or New Zealand may be concerned about the effect of long-haul flights on their health. The most widely publicized concern is deep vein thrombosis, or DVT. Misleadingly called 'economy class syndrome', DVT is the forming of a blood clot in the body's deep veins, particularly in the legs. The clot can move around the bloodstream and could be fatal.

» Those most at risk include the elderly, pregnant women and those using the contraceptive pill, smokers and the overweight. If you are at increased risk of DVT see your doctor before departing. Flying increases the likelihood of DVT because passengers are often seated in a cramped position for long periods of time and may become dehydrated.

To minimize risk:

Drink water (not alcohol)
Don't stay immobile for hours at a time
Stretch and exercise your legs periodically
Do wear elastic flight socks, which support veins and reduce the chances of a clot forming

Exercises

Other health hazards for flyers are airborne diseases and bugs spread by the plane's air-conditioning system. These are largely unavoidable, but if you have a serious medical condition seek advice from a doctor before flying.

1. Ankle Rotations	2. Calf Stretches	3. Knee Lifts
Lift feet off the floor. Draw a circle with the toes, moving one foot clockwise and the other counterclockwise.	Start with heel on the floor and point foot upward as high as you can. Then lift heels high, keeping balls of feet on the floor.	Lift leg with knee bent while contracting your thigh muscle. Then straighten leg, pressing foot flat to the floor.

FOR EMERGENCY TREATMENT

If you need emergency treatment you can go straight to the pronto soccorso (casualty department or emergency room) at the following hospitals:

Ospedale Civile (main hospital, English spoken), Campo Santi Giovanni e Paolo, Castello 6777, tel 041 529 4588 (information department), 041 529 4111 (main switchboard), 041 529 516 (casualty department).

Ospedale al Mare (subsidiary hospital, English spoken), Lungomare d'Annunzio 1, Lido, tel 041 529 4111 (main switchboard), 041 529 5400 (casualty).

BASICS

ELECTRICITY

The electricity supply in Italy is 240 volts. Plugs have two round pins. If your appliances operate on 240 volts, you just need a plug adaptor. If your voltage is different (such as in North America), you will need an adaptor and transformer; bring these with you as they are hard to find in Venice.

LAUNDRY

» Most visitors use the hotel laundry, where clothes are returned to your room and the (often high) charge added to your bill.
» Self-service launderettes (la lavandaria automatica) are few and far between in Venice. The best places to find one are in the university areas of San Polo and Santa Croce. A wash will cost around €7.
» Dry-cleaning (lavasecco) starts from around €4 for a shirt, up to €8.50 for larger items such as jackets and coats, but the quality of the service varies immensely.

MEASUREMENTS

Italy uses the metric system, with all foodstuffs sold by the kilogram or litre. Italians also use the

ettogrammo (100g or just under 4oz), usually abbreviated to etto.

LAVATORIES

» Venice has public lavatories at the railway station and in larger museums.
» There are public lavatories, marked with blue and green signs, throughout the city, with a flat rate of €1.50 entrance. They are clean and well run and the most useful ones are at:
Accademia—underneath the bridge on the Galleria side (open daily 8–8);
Rialto—Campo Rialto Nuovo (open daily 7–5);
Campo San Bartolomeo—Calle della Bissa (open daily 8.30–8);
San Marco—Giardinetti (open daily 9–8).
» You can also use lavatories in bars and cafés, which are legally obliged to let you use their facilities. However, it's considered good form to buy a coffee or glass of water at least before you use them. Sometimes there is only one lavatory for both men and women, and in some places there is a dish for gratuities—you should tip around 25¢. Where separate facilities exist, make sure you recognize the

difference between signori (men) and signore (women).

SMOKING

» Smoking is still common in Italy, but is no longer permitted indoors in any public places, on public transport, inside airport buildings and in most public offices and buildings.

CONVERSION CHART

FROM	TO	MULTIPLY BY
Inches	Centimetres	2.54
Centimetres	Inches	0.3937
Feet	Metres	0.3048
Metres	Feet	3.2810
Yards	Metres	0.9144
Metres	Yards	1.0940
Miles	Kilometres	1.6090
Kilometres	Miles	0.6214
Acres	Hectares	0.4047
Hectares	Acres	2.4710
Gallons	Litres	4.5460
Litres	Gallons	0.2200
Ounces	Grams	28.35
Grams	Ounces	0.0353
Pounds	Grams	453.6
Grams	Pounds	0.0022
Pounds	Kilograms	0.4536
Kilograms	Pounds	2.205
Tons	Tonnes	1.0160
Tonnes	Tons	0.9842

» Smoking is banned in all bars and restaurants.

» Cigarettes and other tobacco products can only legally be sold in *tabacchi* (tobacconists) to over 16s. Stand-alone *tabacchi* are open during normal shop hours (▷ 265). Those attached to bars stay open longer.

VISITING VENICE WITH CHILDREN

Venice is by no means a child-friendly city and the nature of the city makes travelling with very young children in pushchairs (strollers) difficult. If you're bringing your kids, it's worth booking accommodation on the Lido, from where sightseeing can be judiciously mixed with the pleasures of sea and sand. For further ideas and information, ▷ 239.

» Children are welcomed at most hotels and in almost all restaurants. Family-run and more modest restaurants will serve small portions, and will often produce simple meals such as pasta in tomato sauce, pizza or fish and chips. Hotels will provide extra beds in your room if asked; this normally adds another 33 per cent to the room price.

» Disposable nappies (diapers) and baby foods are available in many food shops *(alimentari* or *supermercati)*. If your child is still bottle-fed, bring the milk powder (formula) with you as you may not be able to find your preferred brand in Venice.

» Remember that the lack of public lavatories and changing facilities, most of which may not be as clean as you are used to, can make things difficult for people with very young children. Always carry tissues or wipes, as not all establishments will provide toilet paper.

» Italian children stay up late—if parents are eating out, the kids go too. This means that most hotels do not offer a baby-sitting/listening service.

» Put on high-factor sunscreen and keep children covered up until they acclimatize to the sun. If they're swimming or on the beach at the Lido, persuade them to cover up and swim in a T-shirt.

» Children are susceptible to heat stroke, so seek shade in the middle of the day and keep their heads and necks protected.

» Many Venetian hotels are unheated until the end of October.

» If you're planning an excursion out of the city, children between 4 and 12 qualify for a 50 per cent discount on trains; those under 4 go free.

» For ideas on how to keep children occupied, see the What to Do listings in the individual regions of this book or ask for suggestions at the tourist information offices.

» There is an excellent children's guide to Venice in English available at good book shops *(Viva Venice* by Paolo Zoffoli and Paola Scibilia, published by Elzeviro, 2002). Look, too, for *Venice for Kids* by Elisabetta Pasqualin (Fratelli Palombi 200), one of a series covering the major Italian cities.

VISITORS WITH DISABILITIES

» Venice presents unique problems to people with disabilities, but should not be crossed off the holiday list. For full information on visiting Venice, ▷ 54.

» The city council runs an information service for people with disabilities, which is available in English. Contact: Informahandicap, Piazzale Candiani 5, Mestre, tel 041 274 8144 (Venezia), 041 274 6144 (Mestre), www.comune. venezia.it/handicap.

PLACES OF WORSHIP

If you are Catholic you will have no problem finding somewhere to celebrate your faith in Venice. Mass times vary from church to church, but details of Sunday services can be found on all church doors. The Sunday 11am High Mass in the Basilica di San Marco is a superb occasion for Catholics and non-Catholics alike, and provides a chance to experience this unique building functioning as a living church. Sunday Mass is celebrated in English at 9.30am from May to September in San Zulian. Other denominational services are listed below.

ANGLICAN
St. George's, Campo San Vio, Dorsoduro 870, tel 041 520 0571. Eucharist Sunday 10.30am

GREEK ORTHODOX
San Giorgio dei Greci, Fondamenta dei Greci, Castello 3412, tel 041 522 5446. Services Sunday 9.30 and 10.30am

JEWISH
Services are held after sunset on Friday in different synagogues depending on the time of year. Contact the Museo Ebraico for further information:
Campo Ghetto Nuovo, Cannaregio 2902, tel 041 715 359

LUTHERAN
Campo Santi Apostoli, Cannaregio 4448, tel 041 522 7149. Morning service 10.30am on 2nd and 4th Sunday of the month

METHODIST (VALDESE)
Fondamenta Cavagnis, Castello 5170, tel 522 7549. Sunday service 11am

RUSSIAN ORTHODOX
San Giovanni Decollato, Campo San Giovanni Decollato, Santa Croce 1670, tel 041 524 0672. Morning service Sun 11am

USEFUL CONTACTS FOR DISABLED TRAVEL

TOURISM FOR ALL
c/o Vitalise, Shap Road Industrial Estate, Shap Road, Kendal, Cumbria LA9 6NZ, tel 0845 124 9971, www.tourismforall.org.uk
A UK-based company that produces publications and information on accessibility

RADAR
12 City Forum, 250 City Road, London EC1V 8AF, tel 020 7250 3222, www.radar.org.uk

SATH
347 5th Avenue, Suite 605, New York City, NY 10016, tel 212/447-7284, www.sath.org

FINDING HELP

PERSONAL SECURITY

Venice is one of Italy's safest cities, and serious crime against visitors is extremely rare. Be aware of pickpocketing, which can occur in the more crowded city areas, at the railway station or on crowded *vaporetti*. Taking a few sensible precautions will help prevent becoming a victim.

» Passports, credit cards, travel tickets and cash should not be carried together in handbags or pockets. Only carry what you need for the day and use the safety deposit facilities in hotels.

» Never carry money or valuables in your back pocket. Always keep them secure in a money belt or something similar.

» Do not flaunt your valuables. Leave expensive jewellery in hotel safes and, if you are a woman walking around on your own, consider turning any rings with stone settings around so that only the band is visible and not the jewels.

» Never put your camera or bag down on a café table or on the back of a chair, from where it could be snatched.

» Keep a close eye on your possessions in crowded areas.

» Wear handbags across your body, rather than just over your shoulder, from where they can be easily snatched.

REPORTING THEFT

Report thefts to a police station, where you will need to make a statement *(denuncia)*. It is unlikely that you will get your belongings back, but you need the statement to claim on your insurance.

» In Venice, you will need to go to the office in Campo San Zaccaria. The process may be time-consuming and the duty officer may not necessarily speak English, but it is essential as insurance companies will not consider a claim unless it is backed by a police report.

» If your passport is lost or stolen, report it to the police and your consulate. Getting a replacement

is easier if you have kept a copy of your passport number or a photocopy of the information page safe (▷ 255).

» If your credit card or bank card is stolen, report it to the police and phone the appropriate bank card/credit card emergency number to cancel your card. All are open 24 hours a day and have English-speaking staff (▷ 256).

» If your travellers' cheques are stolen, ▷ 256.

LOST PROPERTY

Venice has three main *uffici oggetti smarriti* (lost property offices). If you lose something try whichever seems the likeliest.

» ACTV: Ísola Nova del Tronchetto, tel 041 272 2179. Open daily 7.30–6. For items lost on *vaporetti* and buses.

» Comune (City Council): Fondamenta del Monastero, Santa Croce 250, tel 041 274 7070. Open Mon–Fri 8.30–12.30. For items lost in public places.

» Stazione Santa Lucia: Centro Accoglienza Clienti, Stazione Santa Lucia, tel 041 785 670. Open daily 7am–9pm. For items lost on trains and in the station.

POLICE

There are three branches of the police in Italy, any of which should be able to help you if you are in difficulty.

» The *carabinieri* are military police, easily recognizable by the white sash they wear across their bodies. They deal with general crime, including drug control.

» The *polizia* is the state police force, whose officers wear blue uniforms.

EMERGENCY PHONE NUMBERS

Police *(carabinieri* and local police) 112 or 041 271 5511	
Ambulance 118 or 041 523 0000	
Fire brigade 115 or 041 257 4700	
Coastguard 041 240 5711	

They also deal with general crime, and if you are unfortunate enough to be robbed (or worse) they are the ones you will need to see.

» The *vigili urbani*, the traffic police, wear dark blue uniforms and white hats. You will only need to deal with them if an incident occurs while you are away from Venice.

WHAT TO DO IF YOU ARE ARRESTED

If you are taken into custody by the police, you could be held for up to 48 hours without appearing before a magistrate. You can also be interviewed without a lawyer present. You do, however, have the right to contact your consul, who is based at your country's embassy, but you are still bound by Italian law. Your consul will not be able to get you out of prison, but will visit you and put you in touch with English-speaking lawyers and interpreters, offer advice and support and contact your family on your behalf. Try to keep hold of your passport and contact your travel insurance company, as your insurance may cover you for legal costs.

CONTACTING YOUR EMBASSY IN ROME

American Embassy	Via Vittorio Veneto 121, 00187, tel 06 46741	www.rome.usembassy.gov
Australian Embassy	Via Antonio Bosio 5, 00161, tel 06 852721	www.italy.embassy.gov.au
British Embassy	Via XX Settembre 80a, 00187, tel 06 4220 0001	www.fco.gov.uk
Canadian Embassy	Via Zara 30, 00198, tel 06 85444 2911/2912	www.canada international.gc.ca/italy-italie/
Irish Embassy	Piazza di Campitelli 3, 00186, tel 06 697 9121	www.embassyofireland.it
New Zealand Embassy	Via Clitunno 44, 00198, tel 06 853 7501	www.nzembassy.com

USEFUL NUMBERS

Operator 170	
Post/telegram enquiries 8031 60	
Time 4161	
Italian directory enquiries 12	
International directory enquiries 170	

COLLECT OR CREDIT CARD CALLS

To make collect calls go through the operator on 170. For credit card calls you will need to call the operator in the country you are calling:

Australia (OPTUS) 800 172 611	
Australia (TELSTRA) 800 172 601	
Canada 800 218 800	
Ireland 800 172 256	
New Zealand 800 172 641	
UK 800 172 442	
USA (AT&T) 800 172 444	
USA (MCI) 800 905 825	
USA (SPRINT) 800 172 405	

COMMUNICATION

COUNTRY CODES FROM ITALY

To call abroad from Italy, first dial 00, followed by your country code (see below), the area code (sometimes minus the first zero) and then the telephone number.

Australia	61
Belgium	32
Canada	1
France	33
Germany	49
Ireland	353
Netherlands	31
New Zealand	64
Spain	34
UK	44
USA	1

To call Italy from home, the country code is 39: You need to keep the zero of the code (but drop the zero for Italian mobiles).

CALL CHARGES

» There are several call bands for telephone charges. Peak time is between 8am and 1pm, off-peak between 1pm and midnight, and cheaper international rates between 6.30pm and 8am (in two price bands—up to midnight and after) and at weekends.

» Free phone numbers *(numeri verdi)* usually begin with 800 and national call rate numbers begin with 848 or 199.

» Hotels tend to overcharge for long-distance and international calls, so it is best to make calls from public phones, using telephone cards.

PAYING FOR CALLS
Public telephones and phone cards

» Public telephones can be found all over Venice, both in street booths and bars. You can also use these for text messages.

» Most public telephones now take phone cards *(carte telefoniche)* rather than cash. These are available in denominations of €2.50, €5 and €10 from *tabacchi*, newsstands and some bars. Public phones also take credit cards.

» Tear off the corner of the card and slide it in the appropriate slot to get a dialling tone. Dial the number. The display will show how much remaining credit you have on the card. After you hang up, the card is returned so you can use it until it runs out.

» If you are calling abroad it's cheaper to buy an international

rather than a Telecom Italia phone card. These operate like a scratch card with a hidden number you dial when you start using the card, and can be used with public, private and mobile phones.

» Interglobal Card 5, Planet, Welcome and Europa are some of the best-value cards.

Reverse-charge (collect) calls

You can place a direct call abroad from Venice by reversing the charges or by using a phone credit card number. To reverse the charges, call the International Operator on 170 or, for a cheaper alternative, dial the country's operator direct on one of the free numbers in the chart above.

MOBILE PHONES

» British, Australian and New Zealand mobile phones can be used in Italy without any problem. You may need to unbar your phone for overseas use; contact your service operator for details.

» Due to their different frequency, American cell phones can only be used if they are triband.

» It can be very expensive to use your mobile phone abroad and you will often be charged to receive calls as well as make them; check with your service provider before you leave.

» If you travel abroad frequently and intend to use your phone, consider swapping your SIM card to a card from an alternative provider—either a foreign network or a dedicated provider of international mobile phone services. You can buy these at mobile phone shops before you leave.

» Text messages are often a cheaper alternative to voice calls, but check the charges for making calls and text messages with your service provider. Italian mobile numbers begin with 330, 335, 347, 368, etc.

» If you are using your mobile without changing the SIM card you will need to dial the Italian international code (00 39) to call local Venetian numbers.

INTERNET CAFÉS

» These are relatively widespread in Venice and reasonably cheap—you can expect to pay around €5 an hour. The cafeecs.net website (www. cafeecs.net) has an impressive searchable directory of internet cafés in Italy.

» You do need a web-based email account if you want to send or receive email from abroad (hotmail, yahoo, etc.).

» Remember to log out once you have finished browsing or emailing at an internet café and close the browser completely to dump your session cookies (temporary files where your personal info is sometimes stored). These are shared computers and you don't want someone else reading your mail or accessing your personal files.

LAPTOPS

» If you intend to use your own laptop in Italy, remember to bring a power converter to recharge it and a plug socket adaptor. A surge protector is also a good idea. To connect to the internet you need an adaptor for the phone socket.

» If you use an international internet service provider, such as AOL or

Compuserve, it's cheaper to dial up a local node rather than the number in your home country.

» Wireless technology, such as Bluetooth or Blackberry, allows you to connect to the internet using a mobile phone.

» Dial-tone frequencies vary from country to country, so set your modem to ignore dial tones.

POST OFFICES

» Venice's main post office is at Salizzada del Fontego dei Tedeschi, San Marco 5554, tel 041 271 7111, open Mon–Sat 8.30–6.30. It provides a full range of post office services and operates a *fermo posta* (poste restante) service.

» Each city district also has its own post office. These are open Mon–Fri 8.10–1.30 and Sat 8.10–12.30.

POSTAL SERVICES

» You can buy stamps (*francobolli*), send letters and packages, faxes and telegrams from Venice's post offices. Italy's postal service, Poste Italiane (tel 803 160; www.poste.it), has improved considerably in recent years, and you can be sure your letters will arrive in reasonable time.

» Use the *posta prioritaria* service to ensure quick delivery. This promises delivery within 24 hours in Italy,

3 days for EU countries and 4 to 5 for the rest of the world. Stamps for this service cost 65¢–€1.70 for Italy and the EU and 85¢–€1.85 for the rest of the world.

» Stamps are also available from tobacconists, denoted with an official *tabacchi* sign, a large 'T'. If you need to send a heavy letter or a package, you are better off taking it to a post office, where it can be weighed.

» Post (mail) boxes are red and have two slots; *per la città* is for Venice, and *tutte le altre destinazioni* for everywhere else, including international destinations.

POSTCARDS

» These are classed as low-priority post, and even sent *prioritaria* they take up to two weeks to arrive at their destination.

SENDING ITEMS OF VALUE

» You can use the registered post (*raccomandato*) to send valuable items; add an extra €3.80 on top of the price of normal postage.

» The cost of insured mail (*assicurato*) depends on the value of the items (€8.50 for packages up to €50 in value).

» Insured mail services are not available to the US.

POSTAGE RATES			
The only postal service in Italy is now Posta Prioritaria			
Posta Prioritaria	Letter (under 20g)	Letter (50–100g)	Delivery time
Europe	65¢	€1.70	3 days
US and rest of World	85¢	€1.85	4–8 days

OPENING TIMES AND TICKETS

BANKS

Banks open Monday to Friday 8.30–1.30 and 3–4.30. Larger branches may open on Saturday.

POST OFFICES

Post offices open Monday to Friday 8.10–1.30 and Saturday 8.10–12.30.

PHARMACIES

Pharmacies are usually open the same hours as shops, but take turns to stay open in the afternoon and late in the evening. A list in the shop window shows other pharmacies in the area and their opening times.

MUSEUMS AND GALLERIES

Opening times for museums and galleries vary greatly. Many close one day a week, usually Monday.

CHURCHES

Some churches open around 7 for Mass, then close for the rest of the day, though some with important artworks may be open 10–12 and 4–6. Some only open on Sundays. Times are displayed on the main door. Churches in the Chorus group (see right) are open from 10 to 5 Monday to Saturday.

CAFÉS AND BARS

Some are open for breakfast, others open for lunch, and some are only open in the evenings. Wine bars usually close at midnight or later.

RESTAURANTS

Restaurants that serve lunch open from 11am and usually close in the afternoon. Those that only serve dinner open after 7pm and stay open late. Pizzerias usually open only in the evening. Many restaurants close for August (*Chiuso per ferie*).

SHOPS

Shops open between 8 and 9 and close for lunch at 1. They re-open in the afternoon at 3.30 or 4 and close at 8. Most are closed Sundays and Monday mornings, but some shops open all day (*Orario continuato*).

VENETIAN HOLIDAYS

1 Jan	New Year's Day
6 Jan	Epiphany
Mar/Apr	Easter Monday
25 Apr	Liberation Day
1 May	Labour Day
29 Jun	St. Peter and St. Paul Day
15 Aug	Assumption of the Virgin
1 Nov	All Saints' Day
8 Dec	Feast of the Immaculate Conception
25 Dec	Christmas Day
26 Dec	St. Stephen's Day

NATIONAL HOLIDAYS

Shops and banks close on national holidays. There is a limited public transport service on Labour Day and Christmas Day. However, apart from on Labour Day, Assumption and Christmas Day, most bars and restaurants remain open.

VENICE COMBINED MUSEUM TICKETS AND DISCOUNT CARDS

» The Museum Pass gives entrance to the Musei di San Marco (Palazzo Ducale, Museo Civico Correr, Museo Archeologico, Biblioteca Marciana), Musei del Settecento (Ca' Rezzonico, Palazzo Mocenigo, Casa Goldoni), Musei delle Ísole (Museo del Vetro on Murano, Museo del Merletto on Burano) and Ca' Pesaro (Galleria d'Arte Moderna and Museo d'Arte Orientale). Full price €18; students aged 15–29 and holders of Rolling Venice cards €12.
» Gallerie dell'Accademia has a combined ticket for the Accademia, Museo d'Arte Orientale and Ca' d'Oro; full price €11, reduced €5.50.
» The Chorus Pass allows entry to 15 of the city's most artistically important churches. Single ticket €2.50; full price €9, reduced €6. It is valid for a year. You can buy the pass at any Chorus church (tel 041 275 0462; www.chorusvenezia.org).

VENICE CARD

There are two types, the Blue Card and the Orange Card.
» The Blue Card is valid for all public transport, with free access to public toilets and baby-changing facilities. 3 days: full price €48, reduced (under 30) €47; 7 days: full price €68, reduced (under 30) €67.
» The Orange Card is valid for all public transport, entrance to Musei Civici (civic museums), all Chorus churches, Fondazione Querini Stampalia, Museo Ebraico, with free entrance to public lavatories; 3 days: full price €73, reduced (under 30) €66; 7 days: full price €96, reduced price (under 30) €87.
» The Venice Card can be purchased by telephone on 041 24 24, online at www.hellovenezia.com or in person at main ACTV offices, tourist information offices, Marco Polo and Treviso airports and Santa Lucia station. If booking by phone or online you will be given a reservation number and you can then pick up the card from any outlet on arrival.

ROLLING VENICE

A discount card for people aged 14–29, this gives discounts on hotels, restaurants, shops, museums, some cultural events and a 72-hour *vaporetto* pass (€18 rather than €31). It costs €4 and is valid for 1 year. It is obtainable from VeLa and APT offices; take two passport-size photos and an identity document.

VENICE CONNECTED

Launched in 2009, Venice Connected is an online, reduced-price, advance booking service for all city services, including transport, museum entrances, parking, WiFi access, public lavatory entrance fees and other facilities. The service is aimed at spreading visitor numbers more equally throughout the year, with considerable savings for tourists arriving during low-season weeks. All services on offer are optional, enabling you to build your own package. You will then be sent an email containing the code enabling you to access your bookings, which you should take with you to Venice. Once there, take the code to one of the Venice Connected offices, where you will be issued with all the documentation you need. Book seven days in advance at www. veniceconnected.com.

TOURIST OFFICES

Venice's main tourist office is underneath the arcade in the southwest corner of Piazza San Marco (San Marco 71f; tel 041 529 8711; open daily 9.30–3.30). The staff have city maps and the APT also publishes *Eventi e Manifestazioni*, an invaluable pamphlet, every three months, which details useful numbers, museum and church opening times, exhibitions, lectures and guided tours, and includes a day-by-day cultural What's On. The tourist office can also give you information on sightseeing, guided tours, travel and accommodation. The staff speak good English and, if things are fairly quiet, are extremely helpful. There are other APT offices around the city, the best of which is in the Palazzina del Santi by the Giardini ex-Reali. This office also doubles as a ticket agency for concerts, opera and theatrical performances, and has an excellent bookshop with a good range of English-language guidebooks, picture books, Venice-related literature and souvenirs. There are APT offices at the following addresses:

» Aeroporto Marco Polo (arrivals hall)
» Stazione Ferrovia Santa Lucia
» Piazzale Roma (Garage ASM)
» Gran Viale 6a, Lido di Venezia (May–Sep)
» Cavallini Treporti, Punta Sabbioni (May–Sep).

ITALIAN GOVERNMENT TOURIST OFFICES ABROAD

AUSTRALIA	CANADA	UK	USA
Level 26	175 Bloor Street East,	1 Princes Street	630 Fifth Avenue, Suite 1565
44 Market Street	Suite 907 South Tower	London W1B 2AY	New York NY 10111
NSW 2000 Sydney	Toronto, Ontario M4W 3R8	tel 020 7489 1254/020 7355 1557	tel 212 245-5618/245-4822
tel 92 621666	tel 416 925-4882	www.italiantouristboard.co.uk	www.italiantourism.com
www.italiantourism.com.au	www.italiantourism.com		Also in Chicago and LA

USEFUL WEBSITES

GENERAL WEBSITES

www.turismovenezia.it
The APT official site includes details of accommodation, transport, eating and drinking, and sightseeing.

www.comune.venezia.it
The official Venice city council site gives comprehensive transport, accommodation and cultural listings. The FAQ section is useful for first visits, but the site is in Italian only.

www.hellovenezia.com
Comprehensive site run by VeLa covering every aspect of ACTV city transport and current events.

www.veniceconnected.com
Advance, reduced-price booking; official site for transport, sightseeing and everything you'll need (▷ 265).

www.museicivicivenezia ni.it
Excellent site covering all the civic museums.

www.chorusvenezia.org
Comprehensive information on churches in the Chorus group.

www.veniceguide.net
Tourist information and listings, and some quirky articles on aspects of Venetian life. Italian only.

www.venezia.net
Another good independent site that offers interesting snippets of history, news and culture, as well as the usual listings. Good shopping links.

www.venetia.it
This site is worth a glance for its history and articles.

www.carnevale.venezia.it
Everything you need to know about the Carnival, and a photo library.

MISCELLANEOUS

www.weather.com
www.bbc.co.uk/weather
Weather for Venice and elsewhere.

www.paginegialle.it
Italian Yellow Pages.

www.comune.venezia.it/flex/ cm/pages/ServeBLOB.php/L/EN/ IDPagina/1339
Full list of public lavatories in Venice.

NEWS

La Repubblica
www.repubblica.it
Il Messaggero
www.ilmessaggero.it
Corriere della Sera
www.corriere.it
Il Gazzettino
www.gazzettino.it

TRANSPORT

www.veniceairport.it
Full details of both Marco Polo and Treviso airports.

www.actv.it
The official site of ACTV gives full timetables, routes and prices for *vaporetti* and mainland bus services.

www.trenitalia.it
Train information and online booking.

KEY SIGHTS QUICK WEBSITE FINDER

SIGHT	PAGE	WEBSITE
Ca' d'Oro	132–133	www.cadoro.org
Ca' Pesaro	160–161	www.museicivicivenezia ni.it
Ca' Rezzonico	202–203	www.museicivicivenezia ni.it
Collezione Peggy Guggenheim	204–205	www.guggenheim-venice.it
Gallerie dell'Accademia	206–211	www.galleriaccademia.org
Museo Correr	64–65	www.museicivicivenezia ni.it
Palazzo Ducale	66–71	www.museicivicivenezia ni.it
Santa Maria Gloriosa dei Frari	176–179	www.basilicadeifrari.it

MEDIA, BOOKS AND FILMS

TELEVISION

» Italy has three state-run television stations (RAI-1, -2 and -3); three stations run by Berlusconi's Mediaset group (Italia Uno, Rete Quattro and Canale Cinque); and a number of local channels. RAI-3 has international news broadcasts, including an English-language section. It starts at 1.15am.

» Italian television usually comprises a mixture of soaps, chat shows and American imports dubbed into Italian.

» Most hotels, from mid-range upwards, have satellite television, so you can keep up to date with the news and sport on BBC World, CNN and Eurosport.

RADIO

» RAI Radio 1, 2 and 3 (89.7FM, 91.7FM and 93.7FM), the state-run stations, have a mixture of light music, chat shows and news—all in Italian.

» Radio Italia Network (90–108FM) is the best national radio station for dance music and Radio Deejay (99.7–107FM) plays a variety of popular music and chat shows.

» You can pick up three local radio stations in Venice. Radio Venezia (100.95 and 92.4 FM) offers pop music and light news; Radio Capital (98.5 FM) alternates local news and advertising with 1980s and '90s hits; and Radio Padova (103.9 and 88.4 FM) plays non-stop popular chart music.

» You can get BBC radio stations including Radio 1, 2, 5 Live and 6 Music on the internet via www. bbc.co.uk. The BBC World Service frequencies in Italy are MHz 12.10, 9.410, 6.195 and 0.648.

» Visit www.radio-locator.com to find US radio stations online.

MAGAZINES

» *Amica* is a stylish Italian read with articles on all that is fashionable and cutting edge in Italy, and there are also Italian-language versions of popular glossies such as *Vogue* and *Marie Claire*.

» English-language magazines are few and far between; if you read Italian, magazines such as *Panorama* and *L'Espresso* are good for news.

» *Casa Bella* showcases the best of Italian homestyle, while *Bell'Italia*, a beautiful travel magazine in the National Geographic style, has regular features on different parts of Italy.

NEWSPAPERS
English-language

» The *Financial Times*, the *Wall Street Journal*, *USA Today*, the *International Herald Tribune* and most British and European dailies are available in Venice from about 2pm on their day of publication.

» The best places to find them are at the airport, the railway station, the *Rialto*, the newsstand just outside the west end of Piazza San Marco and the one at the foot of the Accademia Bridge.

Italian-language

» *La Repubblica*, *Corriere della Sera* and *La Stampa* are the main national newspapers.

» Venice has two daily newspapers: *Il Gazzettino* and *La Nuova Venezia*.

» There are two daily sports papers—*La Gazzetta dello Sport* (pink paper) and the *Corriere dello Sport*. *La Gazetta* also publishes a supplement on Saturday called *Sport Week*.

BOOKS

For more Venetian background than your guidebook can provide, there's a choice of books on both the art and history of the city. *Venice: A Maritime Republic* by Frederick C. Lane is a scholarly, in-depth history; for something lighter, but no less thorough, try John Julius Norwich's *A History of Venice* or Jan Morris' seminal and impressionistic *Venice*.

The best companion guide to Venice is J. G. Links' *Venice for Pleasure*, a series of city walks annotated with fascinating and idiosyncratic information. If the city as a fictional protagonist appeals,

you'll find it wonderfully evoked in *The Wings of the Dove* by Henry James, while the edgy corruption of 20th-century Venice is marvellously portrayed in *Death in Venice* by Thomas Mann.

Other 20th-century writers who've featured the city include Ian McEwan, whose *The Comfort of Strangers* employs Venice as the backdrop to a disturbing tale of a dysfunctional marriage. The sinister undertones induced by the city's atmosphere contribute to the tension in Barry Unsworth's *The Stone Virgin*, an art history romance spreading across the centuries, and there's a touch of the same in Sally Vicker's *Miss Garnett's Angel*, the story of the effect of Venice on a staid English spinster.

On a lighter note, two crime writers capture the very essence of everyday Venice and its inhabitants. Michael Dibdin's *Aurelio Zen* is a world-weary and all too human detective from an old Venetian family, while Donna Leon's series of detective stories starring Commissario Guido Brunetti draw the reader into the city behind the tourist face.

FILMS

Venice has provided the perfect stage set for a series of romantic and historical movies. Among the best known are David Lean's *Summertime*, starring Katherine Hepburn, *Death in Venice* with Dirk Bogarde, the sumptuously filmed *Wings of the Dove* with Helena Bonham Carter, and Nicholas Roeg's atmospheric yet disturbing 1973 *Don't Look Now*.

In the 21st century *The Talented Mr. Ripley* included an evocative portrait of Venice in the 1950s, while *Casanova* (2005) conjured the hedonism of the 18th century (▷ 35), contrasting with 1920s Venice portrayed in *Brideshead Revisited* (▷ 19).

MAPS
▷ 47.

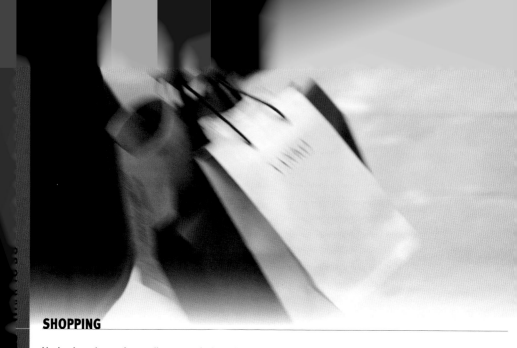

SHOPPING

Venice is a shopper's paradise, an entirely pedestrianized city where everything from haute couture to the most outrageous kitsch is on offer, including some uniquely Venetian products. Many stores are open all day, operating an *orario continuato* from around 10am until 7.30pm. Increasingly, shops are open on Sundays, lifting their shutters around 11am and staying open until 7 or 7.30pm.

Mornings are the time to visit the city's markets at the Rialto, along the Via Garibaldi, the Strada Nova and in many of the key neighbourhood *campi*—though there are no fish markets on Mondays. Markets operate from around 8am until 1pm, while smaller food shops are open from 8am to 7pm, closing at 1pm until 4pm for lunch. Supermarkets are open all day from 8am to 8pm, with reduced opening hours on Sundays.

Other shops normally open at 10am; some smaller, family-run businesses close for lunch between 1pm and 4pm. In August many smaller shops shut for the traditional two-week break, revolving round Ferragosto, the public holiday on 15 August. Apart from food shops, many shops are closed on Monday mornings, while food shops shut from Saturday lunchtime until Monday morning, though *pasticcerie* are usually open on Sundays for

people to buy cakes and pastries for Sunday lunch.

SHOPPING AREAS

Each of the six *sestieri* has its own shopping area, with the majority of stores in San Marco. Here you'll find international retailers, the big names in fashion, leather goods and jewellery, mainly along the stretch from the Piazza di San Marco towards the Accademia. Running north towards the Rialto, the string of streets known as the Mercerie has myriad shops, good trawling ground for clothes, leather goods, antiques and speciality shops selling beads, paper and masks. Eastwards, Castello is lower key, its draw the little artisan stores found tucked away in minor *calli*. Both sides of the Rialto bridge are good shopping areas; the west side, in San Polo, rich in mid-price fashion and leather shops as well as some of Venice's best food speciality

stores. Head down through San Polo to Dorsoduro, where the accent is on art galleries, bookstores and jewellers, or into Santa Croce, where the student population ensures great shopping for books and artisan products of all kinds. On the San Marco side of the Rialto, streets run west into Cannaregio and the joys of the Strada Nova, home to some of the city's best value and popular outlets.

SPECIALITY SHOPPING

Foremost among uniquely Venetian products is Murano glass, clearly labelled with its trademark, Vetro Artistico Murano. Prices reflect this—if there's no trademark and it doesn't cost much, it's not true Venetian. The same applies to Carnival masks, sold everywhere, and often made in the Far East. You'll find the real thing in artisan shops with integral workshops out the back, where a high-quality papier

ITALIAN DESIGNER SHOPS IN SAN MARCO

Bottega Veneta
Bruno Magli
Emporio Armani
Fendi
Fratelli Rossetti
Giorgio Armani
Gucci
Laura Biagiotti
Max Mara
Missoni
Prada
Valentino
Versace

mâché mask will cost anything from €80 to €200.

Sumptuous textiles are another speciality, and you can buy printed velvet and damask throws, shawls and scarves, delicately pleated, vibrantly coloured Fortuny-style silks, and all manner of home accessories such as tassels, tie-backs, cushions and runners. They're light to carry home, as are Venetian paper products. Handmade paper is either block-printed or marbled and then crafted into notebooks, albums, photograph frames and desk items. You'll probably also be tempted by the beautiful glass bead shops—choose from made-up pieces or have something designed and created on the spot.

It must be said too, that Venice has some of Italy's best kitsch.

Head for the stalls along the Riva degli Schiavoni, near the Piazza San Marco or outside the railway station, to find a wondrous array of paintings of gondolas and sunset scenes, gondoliers' hats and shirts, plastic gondolas, gondolas in snowstorms and a mind-boggling selection of some of the best of the worst glass trinkets and ornaments.

CREDIT CARDS, SALES TAX AND RECEIPTS

Credit cards are widely accepted in Venice for amounts over €20. Food shops and markets remain the exception, though some other stores, particularly small, family-run businesses, still offer a good discount for cash. Non-Italian debit cards are not normally accepted.

The Duty Free scheme operates in many Venetian shops; this ensures a rebate of sales tax to visitors from outside the EU; ask at individual stores for details and the necessary paperwork.

You should always get a *ricevuta fiscale* (official receipt) which will include the IVA (VAT) details, as Italian law requires all shopkeepers and restaurateurs to provide this. You must keep the receipt, even for small purchases, as the authorities have tightened up on cash trading to cut down on tax abuse, and you could be stopped by the Guardia di Finanza, who can ask to see your receipts to prove the shop has declared the sale. Failure to produce a receipt can result in a fine of up to €155.

SUPERMARKETS IN VENICE

If you're cooking for yourself, or just want to pick up picnic supplies or a drink, it may be easier to head for a supermarket rather than struggle with non-English speakers in a traditional *alimentari* (general food store). Venice's supermarkets are hard to spot; the list below covers most city areas.

BILLA	CO-OP	SMA
Zattere	**Santa Croce**	**Dorsoduro**
Dorsoduro 1491, tel 041 5226187	Campo San Giacomo dell'Orio, Santa Croce	Campo Santa Margherita, Dorsoduro 3112,
Strada Nova	1493, tel 041 275 0218	tel 041 522 6934
Cannaregio 3659, tel 041 523 8046	**Santa Croce**	
Cannaregio	Fondamenta Santa Chiara (Piazzale Roma),	**SU VE (SUPERMARCATO VENEZIANO)**
Fondamenta Contarini, Cannaregio 3027,	tel 041 527 6639	**Castello**
tel 041 524 4786	**Castello**	Calle del Mondo Novo, Castello 5811,
Lido	Calle del Pistor, Castello 5989, tel 041 522 3415	tel 041 522 9138
Gran Viale, tel 041 526 2898	**Giudecca**	
	Campiello Ferrando, Giudecca, tel 041 528 7625	
	Murano	
	Riva Longa 27, Murano, tel 041 527461	

ENTERTAINMENT AND NIGHTLIFE

Venice draws heavily on its musical legacy to provide visitors with unique opportunities to enjoy Venetian music in unforgettable settings. An evening at the opera or a concert of 18th-century music is one of the best ways to enjoy the city's beautiful buildings. Nightlife in Venice is decidedly low-key. Late-night possibilities are really limited to bars and live-music cafés, where you can hear jazz, blues or reggae, with an occasional Latino or rock session. The main party areas are Campo Santa Margherita in Dorsoduro, the heart of student nightlife, and Fondamenta della Misericordia in Cannaregio, where a string of waterfront bars and tiny clubs transforms the whole quayside into one long nightspot. If you can't live without serious clubbing, it's best to head for Mestre, a short bus or train ride across the causeway, or, in summer, the throbbing house and techno scene at the resort of Lido di Jesolo.

CINEMA

The 12 days of the Venice Film Festival are atypical as far as movie-going in Venice is concerned. The Festival apart, the only year-round cinema is the Giorgione Movie d'Essai (▷ 147). From July to September you can catch mainstream films at the open-air screenings in Campo San Polo, while the Videoteca Pasinetti (▷ 190) runs short film seasons. Check the local press for screening details.

CLASSICAL MUSIC, OPERA AND BALLET

The Fenice orchestra divides its energies between opera, classical music and ballet, and its time between the Fenice and the Teatro Malibran (▷ 148). The opera season runs from September to June, but classical concerts are performed throughout the year in the churches and *scuole*. The dance season theoretically matches that of the opera, but there's normally little on offer. The summer dance schedule organized during the Biennale (▷ 274) has live dance performances.

MUSIC IN CHURCHES AND *SCUOLE*

Concerts of 18th-century music in churches and *scuole* are a big draw.

Standards of performance vary, but the venues are magical, often enhanced by musicians playing in 18th-century costume. The main venues are the churches of Santa Maria Formosa and the Frari and the *scuole* of San Giovanni Evangelista, San Rocco and San Teodoro (▷ 92, 190). The ex-church of San Vidal also stages regular performances.

THEATRE

Venice's main theatres are the Teatro Goldoni and the Teatro Malibran (▷ 92, 148). Both offer a varied schedule of plays, and the Malibran also acts as a concert and dance venue. The Goldoni is strong on Venetian classics, but is also noted for contemporary productions. Smaller, more avantgarde city theatres include the Teatro Fondamenta Nuove, which also offers dance and film, the Teatrino Groggia, and the Teatro da l'Avogaria (▷ 148, 225), an experimental theatre. The season runs from November to June, when the Biennale takes over. Note that performances are in Italian.

WHAT'S ON

For concerts, theatre and opera, there are comprehensive day-by-day listings in *Eventi e Manifestazioni*, an information-packed listings guide obtainable free from the tourist information offices. Performance is also listed in the *Venezia News* (€2.20), a monthly bilingual listings magazine, and the two local daily papers, *Il Gazzettino* and *La Nuova Venezia*; all are available from newsstands. Posters also advertise cultural events, and the staff at the tourist office in the Giardini ex-Reali (▷ 62) has full listings and will also book tickets for some venues.

TICKETS

For performances at the Fenice, Goldoni and Malibran, book in advance, either at the venues or via the theatres' websites. Otherwise, tickets can be bought at the box offices just before the performances. VeLa sells performance tickets at the *vaporetto* stops at Piazzale Roma, the Rialto, Ferrovia, San Zaccaria and the Rialto. The APT office at the Giardini ex-Reali also books and sells tickets, and many hotels will provide tickets for classical music concerts.

SMOKING

Smoking is prohibited in all public places.

NIGHTLIFE

In Venice itself, late-night bars generally get going around 10.30–11pm and will stay open until around 2am, with later hours at the weekends, particularly those popular with students. Dress code is relaxed, so wear what you like, remembering that Venetian bars can get very hot and crowded. Most places do not charge an entry fee, so you can hear live music for just the cost of your drink; details of what's on are listed in the monthly listings magazine, *Venezia News*, available at newsstands, and in the free *Venezia da Vivere* leaflet that you'll find in some bars and restaurants.

If you're heading across the causeway for some serious mainland clubbing at Mestre or Jesolo, bear in mind that although most venues open at 11pm, nothing much gets going until 1am and will rock on till dawn. If you're going to Mestre, take the bus from Piazzale Roma (2, 3, 4 or 6); in summer, the nicest way to get to Jesolo is to take the No. 12 or 14 *vaporetto* from San Zaccaria to Punta Sabbioni, from where regular buses connect with Jesolo. Return boats run thoughout the night, though you may have to change at the Lido. All mainland clubs charge an admission fee, which ranges from €15–€20, and usually includes one drink.

GAY AND LESBIAN VENICE

Venice's gay scene is very low-key, with no bars or clubs that are specifically gay, though there is the almost exclusively gay Alberoni Beach on the Lido, and Il Muro (The Wall), by the Giardinetti Reali on the St. Mark's Basin side of Piazza San Marco.

There's more action in Padova (Padua), a 20-minute train ride away on the mainland, but Venice itself is a small town, with all the drawbacks that implies for gay locals and visitors. For evening eating, drinking and relaxation, it's best to head for Campo Santa Margherita, with its bars and cafés; Fondamenta della Misericordia in Cannaregio is also worth exploring.

For more information, pick up a copy of *Babilonia*, a monthly gay magazine that has listings for all Italy, or log onto www.arcigay.it, the official site of Italy's foremost gay and lesbian network. The nearest branch to Venice is in Padova (Via Garibaldi 41, tel 049 990 0827), or contact them via the website: www.tralaltro.it.

SPORTS AND ACTIVITIES

At first glance, sporting opportunites would seem distinctly lacking in crowded, urban Venice, but those with energy to spare will find plenty to do. Most Venetians are more than happy to spend their leisure time simply enjoying the atmosphere and beauty of their surroundings, relaxing and doing nothing—the art of *dolce far niente*. But many are strong supporters of the city's two main spectator sports, soccer, the grand Italian passion, and rowing, Venice's own great obsession. At weekends, the streets of the Lido are filled with cyclists, and it's quite common to see joggers pounding the streets of Venice.

SOCCER

AC Venezia football team was founded in 1907 and has a passionate local following. Fortunes fluctuate, and in 2009 they were forced to declare bankruptcy and were relegated to Serie D, from where they can only dream of the golden days of 1999, when they rose to the giddy heights of Serie A. Home matches take place on Saturdays and Sundays between September and June, and visiting fans are herded straight off the trains onto special *vaporetti*, which take them directly to the stadium, on Sant'Elena in the far east of the city. Tickets cost between €20 and €50 and are on sale at the ground, at main ACTV and VeLa offices (▷ 50), or from two branches of the Banca Antoniana Popolare Veneta (Campo San Bartolomeo, San Marco 5400 and Strada Nuova, San Marco 5400).

You can find out more by checking www.aqvaalta.com

ROWING

The main festivals all have a watery theme, and locals follow the fortunes of their rowing clubs eagerly, with young people participating at every level in preparation for the city's 120-plus annual regattas. Visitors can sign up for tuition, or rent boats to explore the lagoon under their own steam. Venetian rowing, *voga alla venetia*, is unique in that the rower stands up, facing the direction of travel.

There are various styles of rowing, the gondoliers' *voga ad un solo remo* (one-oar rowing) being the most famous and difficult. But with good tuition, it's perfectly possible to learn the other types in a few lessons, and it is very satisfying to master this elegant sport.

OTHER ACTIVITIES

The early morning is the best time for jogging in Venice, where you can combine flat running through uncrowded streets with the bursts of energy needed to get you over the bridges at a good rate. Popular places include the wide *fondamenta* of the Zattere, along the Riva degli Schiavoni towards the Giardini Pubblici, or the quiet, tree-shaded green areas of Sant'Elena. Alternatively, you could hop on a boat and pound the well-paved roads and the beaches of the Lido.

If you feel the need for more strenuous activity, you can head out of town to the *terra firma*, the hills and some splendid walking, or cross the lagoon to the Lido, with its beaches, bicycle rental, golf course, tennis courts and riding club.

HEALTH AND BEAUTY

Venice may not be the obvious place for pampering, but it could prove a real treat after days walking around the city. Venice's top spas (see below) have the advantage of being sited in the city's most sybaritic surroundings, well away from the crowded centre, where you can indulge yourself with the full range of treatments for face and body. If salt wind and spray have wreaked havoc with your hair, the city is well served with hairdressers to suit all tastes; appointments are often not necessary, but be warned that Italian hairdressers are all à la carte with regards to pricing, and every drop of conditioner or pat of mousse will be added to your bill. For the ultimate well-being treatment, you could consider heading out of town to the peaceful, and still rural, Euganean Hills, where thermal springs provide healing waters at various spa resorts.

CIPRIANI CASANOVA SPA
www.hotelcipriani.it
The luxurious surroundings of the Cipriani hotel on La Giudecca are a wonderful place to enjoy some serious pampering at the Casanova Spa. Facial and body treatments, massage, manicures, pedicures and private training are all available, or you could book a full day's treatment, which includes use of the steam and sauna rooms. The Cipriani also has its own hairdressing salon, Puccio e Franco, which cuts and styles both men's and women's hair, and offers facials and manicures.
✉ Giudecca 10 ☎ 041 520 7744
🕐 Mon–Sat 10–7 ✋ Half-day treatments from €300; other treatments from €60
🚤 Zitelle

HOTEL TERME MIRAMONTI
www.relilax.com
Some of Italy's best-known thermal waters are found in the Euganean Hills, south of Padova (Padua) and an easy journey from Venice. The healing properties of the hot springs and mud have been recognized since Roman times, and the Miramonti is among the best of the

spa hotels, offering a range of full beauty and therapeutic treatments using both thermal waters and hot and cold mud. Set in rolling green surroundings, ideal for walking, the hotel has its own golf course and swimming pool.
✉ Piazza Roma 19, Montegrotto Terme, Padova ☎ 049 891 1755 🕐 1 Mar to mid-Jan; telephone for further details ✋ Full details on request 🚤 Train to Padua, then local service to Montegrotto; by car take A13 motorway towards Padua and exit at Padova Sud for Abano and Montegrotto

MARIE ROSE BEAUTY SALON
www.starwood.com/grittipalace
For ultimate pampering in the beautiful surroundings of one of Venice's greatest hotels, book via the concierge for a treatment in the Gritti's beauty salon, where facials, body treatments, manicures, pedicures and hairdressing are all available. It's on the ground floor.
✉ Hotel Gritti Palace, Campo Santa Maria del Giglio, San Marco 2467 ☎ 041 794 611 🕐 Tue, Fri–Sat 9–12, 3.15–7.30; rest of week 9–6.30 ✋ Manicure from €35; facial from €65; waxing from €25 🚤 Santa Maria del Giglio

SAN CLEMENTE BEAUTY AND WELLNESS CLUB
www.thi.it
Head across the lagoon on the private hotel launch from San Marco to the island of San Clemente, whose Beauty and Wellness Club offers a full range of beauty treatments, including massage, facials and body training. After your session, enjoy the hotel's swimming pool or stroll around the gardens.
✉ Ísola di San Clemente 1, San Marco ☎ 041 244 5001 🕐 Mon–Sat 9.30–7 ✋ Manicure from €60; facial from €65

STEFANO E CLAUDIA
Join the city's most fashion-conscious women for a stylish Italian cut and blow-dry at Venice's smartest hairdressers, where a shampoo comes wth a view of the Grand Canal.
✉ Riva del Vin, San Polo 1098B ☎ 041 520 1913 🕐 Tue–Sat 9–5 ✋ Shampoo and blow-dry €30; full cut and blow-dry €65 🚤 San Silvestro

FOR CHILDREN

Venice is not a children's city, and parents still at the toddler stage should think twice before tackling it encumbered with kids' paraphernalia. There are few attractions aimed specifically at children, but, equally, there are few more fascinating destinations for older kids. The actuality of the

city—the boats, the daily life—will keep children enthralled and, as throughout Italy, locals will welcome them with open arms. Simply crossing bridges, taking the vaporetti and walking down streets without cars will be a major adventure. Aim to punctuate the sightseeing with boat rides, scoops

of gelati—Venetians are master ice-cream makers—and trips to the beach or outer islands. Facilities such as children's menus or baby-changing tables don't really exist, but most children love pasta and pizza, all readily obtainable, and you can take a break from restaurant food by organizing a picnic.

Venice's great festivals have long been an integral part of the city's life. The roots of many of today's festivals lie centuries deep, processions and celebrations commemorating key events in the city's history. Others are revivals or relatively modern.

For practical details, look on the websites for the various events. The tourist offices have details, which are clearly listed in their publication *Eventi e Manifestazioni* (▷ 271), and there are posters all over the city for big festivities such as the Redentore and the Regata Storica. These two, and the Vogalonga, will affect city transport, so check the posters at the *vaporetto* stops for details of curtailed services.

FEBRUARY/MARCH
CARNEVALE
www.carnivalofvenice.com
www.comune.venezia.it
Carnevale (▷ 21) is a stunningly successful modern take on Venice's pre-Lenten Carnival, revived in 1980. Events and entertainment are held all over the city every day; big days are the first Sunday and the Thursday before Shrove Tuesday (Mardi Gras).
✉ Throughout city ⊕ 10 days ending on Shrove Tuesday

SU E ZO PER I PONTI
www.comune.venezia.it
The name means 'Up and Down the Bridges' and this fun trawl around Venice involves orienteering yourself between specific points throughout the city—with plenty of chances to pause for refreshment.
✉ Throughout city ⊕ 4th Sunday of Lent
☎ 041 590 4717 🚢 San Marco for start

APRIL
FESTA DI SAN MARCO
The feast day of St. Mark, Venice's patron saint, is celebrated by a morning Mass in the basilica and an afternoon gondola regatta between Sant'Elena and the Punta della Dogana at the entrance to the Grand Canal.

✉ Bacino di San Marco ⊕ 25 April
🚢 Vallaresso, San Zaccaria

MAY
FESTA E REGATA DELLA SENSA
A re-enactment of the Marriage to the Sea (▷ 27) takes place off San Nicolò, when the mayor sails across St. Mark's Basin on a decorated boat to throw a laurel wreath into the sea, followed by a regatta.
✉ San Nicolò del Lido ☎ 041 529 8711, 041 274 7737 ⊕ 1st Sunday after the feast of the Ascension 🚢 Lido

VOGALONGA
www.vogalonga.com
This is a 33km (20-mile) row from the Canale della Giudecca through the lagoon and back down the Canale di Cannaregio and the Canal Grande to St. Mark's. Canale di Cannaregio is the place to see boats re-enter the city (▷ 20).
⊕ 1st Sunday after the feast of the Ascension

JUNE
VENEZIA SUONA
www.veneziasuona.it
Hundreds of bands and musicians play rock, jazz, folk and reggae from about 4pm in *campi* all over the city.
☎ 041 275 0049 ⊕ Late June/early July

FESTA DI SAN PIETRO
Venice's liveliest local festival celebrates the feast of St. Peter and is based around his church in Castello. Events include concerts, food stands, dancing and entertainment.
✉ San Pietro di Castello ⊕ Week of 29 June 🚢 Giardini

JUNE/NOVEMBER
BIENNALE D'ARTE CONTEMPORANEA E ARCHITETTURA
www.labiennale.org
The Biennale, established in 1895, is one of Europe's most prestigious contemporary art festivals (▷ 21), drawing huge international crowds; its younger brother, the architectural Biennale, was founded in 1980 and is proving to be an equal crowd-puller.
✉ Arsenale and Giardini Pubblici ☎ 041 521 8711 ⊕ Art (odd years) mid-Jun to Nov; architecture (even years) Sep–Oct 🚢 Arsenale, Giardini

JULY
FESTA DEL REDENTORE
Venice's oldest continuously celebrated festival started in 1576 to give thanks for deliverance from plague (▷ 21). A pontoon bridge spans the Canale della Giudecca from near Salute to Redentore throughout the week, across which Venetians process to Il Redentore on La Giudecca.
✉ Bacino di San Marco, Canale della Giudecca ⊕ 3rd weekend in July

AUGUST
FERRAGOSTO
During the feast of the Assumption of the Virgin most Venetians leave the city for this bank holiday weekend and head for the beach. There's a concert on Torcello and the tourist office has details of other events.
✉ Torcello ⊕ 15 August 🚢 Torcello

MOSTRA INTERNAZIONALE D'ARTE CINEMATOGRAFICA
www.labiennale.org
This high-profile, international Film Festival (▷ 21) has daily screenings

and boasts an increasing influx of big-name stars.

✉ Palazzo del Cinema, Lungomare Marconi, Lido ☎ 041 272 6501, 041 521 8878 🕐 12 days, starting during the last week in August 🚢 Lido

SEPTEMBER
REGATA STORICA
A day's celebration of rowing kicks off with a spectacular historical procession down the Grand Canal of ornate boats rowed by locals in 16th-century costume (▷ 20). Four races follow, and the finishing line is at the Volta, the sharp curve on the Grand Canal, where the judges sit and the prizes are presented.

✉ Canal Grande 🕐 1st Sunday in September

SAGRA DEL PESCE
Burano's big day sees outdoor stands selling fried fish and vast quantities of white wine. The festivities are followed by the last regatta of the season.

✉ Burano 🕐 3rd Sunday in September 🚢 Burano

OCTOBER
SAGRA DEL MOSTA
A wonderfully bucolic festival takes place on the farming island of Sant'Erasmo to celebrate the first pressing of the local wine. The sampling is accompanied by side-shows, foodstalls and the chance to see the locals letting their hair down.

✉ Sant'Erasmo 🕐 1st weekend in October 🚢 Sant'Erasmo

VENICE MARATHON
www.venicemarathon.it
This marathon runs from the Riviera del Brenta, on the mainland, across to Venice and through the city to finish in Castello. The Zattere is a good vantage point.

✉ Finish at Riva dei Sette Martiri ☎ 041 940 644 🕐 Last Sun in October

NOVEMBER
FESTA DI SAN MARTINO
The Festa di San Martino is Venice's answer to 'trick or treat', when swarms of children, armed with their

mothers' pots and pans, dart around making a noise in praise of St. Martin, and earning treats to go and bang somewhere else. *Pasticcerie* sell horse-and-rider-shaped cakes, lavishly decorated with chocolate, icing and silver balls in honour of the feast.

✉ Throughout city 🕐 11 November

FESTA DELLA MADONNA DELLA SALUTE
This feast celebrates another plague deliverance (see Festa del Redentore) with a pontoon bridge across the Grand Canal from Campo Santa Maria del Giglio to just west of the church of the Salute. Locals process across to light candles and hear Mass, before sampling cakes and goodies on sale at stalls set up for the feast.

✉ Santa Maria della Salute 🕐 21 November 🚢 Salute, Giglio

DECEMBER/JANUARY
LA BEFANA
The tourist board is making a real effort to make more of the traditionally low-key Christmas festivities, with Christmas markets at different venues, Christmas trees

in the *campi* and lights twinkling down the main *calli*. Roasted chestnut stalls appear and 6 January sees the Regata delle Befane down the Grand Canal, a race with the rowers dressed as the Befana, the old woman who takes the place of Father Christmas in Italian life. Many churches have wonderfully ornate *presepi* (Christmas cribs/crèches), complete with sound-and-light effects, and often including moving figures and running water.

✉ Throughout the city 🕐 Christmas, New Year and Epiphany

COSTUME RENTAL
ATELIER PIETRO LONGHI
✉ Campiello de Ca' Zen, San Polo 2580
☎ 041 714 478
🕐 Mon–Sat 10–1, 2.30–7.30
🚢 San Tomà

BALOCOLOC
▷ 188.

NICOLAO ATELIER
✉ Calle Lungo, Cannaregio 2590
☎ 041 520 7051
🕐 Mon–Fri by appointment only 9–1, 2–6
🚢 Rialto

Food in Venice can be glorious, but it can also be dire, so, if you want to eat well, steer away from places offering a *menù turistico* and be prepared to pay more than you might expect. Venetian cooking is based on fish, game and vegetables, with the accent on the fish and seafood. As everywhere in Italy, food is local and seasonal, and the year brings a delicious procession of specialities.

LA CUCINA VENEZIANA

One of the great joys of Venice is its *cicchetti*, tiny tapas-style dishes of fish, seafood, vegetables and meat, that are eaten either at a *bacaro* (see opposite) or as part of the *antipasti* (starters) of a meal. Unlike much of Italy, the *antipasti* in Venice are an important part of eating, and can appear in such abundance you may have no room for much else. Don't worry, it's perfectly acceptable to finish with just a risotto or plate of pasta, or even move straight on to dessert.

Fish, eaten all year in Venice, reigns supreme, and it's worth wandering through the fish stalls of the Rialto market to see what will be on offer in the restaurants. Many of the crustaceans and smaller fish appear as *antipasti* or crisply fried in a *fritto misto* (mixed fried seafood), while larger fish are most commonly served freshly grilled *(alla griglia)*, the skin crisp and salty, with a wedge of lemon. The main exception is *baccalà mantecato*, a creamy paste made with dried salt cod, olive oil and garlic.

Meat, on the whole, is not as popular; though chicken and veal escalopes are common. The great local meat dish is *fegato alla veneziana*, veal liver slow-cooked with onions, but Venetians also enjoy *polpette*, spicy little meatballs made of minced beef, pork and turkey.

Vegetables are eaten in huge amounts by Venetians, and most restaurants will have a more than adequate choice. The great local vegetable is a variety of *carciofo* (artichoke), grown on the island of Sant'Erasmo, provider of much of the best fresh produce in the Venetian markets. They are violet in colour, and the first young ones, known as *castrauri*, are thinly sliced and eaten raw in April; later, mature globes are boiled and eaten leaf by leaf, or have the leaves discarded, leaving just the delicate choke. Another local vegetable is *radicchio di Treviso*, a long-leafed variety of the more familiar round red one. It appears from November to February and is always cooked, usually on the grill, a process that accentuates the contrast between the bitter leaves and sweet stalk. Vegetables also appear in soups and *risotti*—look out for *pasta e fagioli*, a bean and pasta broth, and *risotto di zucca*, a delicious golden rice dish made with pumpkin.

WHEN TO EAT

Hotels generally serve a buffet breakfast of fruit juice, cereal, yoghurt and cold meats and cheeses from around 8am to 9.30/10am.

Locals often pop into a bar on their way to work for a cappuccino and a freshly baked *brioche* (sweet pastry). Late morning sees Venetians pouring into the bars and *bacari* for an *ombra*, a small glass of wine and a couple of *cicchetti* (tiny snacks) before lunch. Both lunch and dinner operate in Venice on two different timescales—one for locals and one for tourists. *Trattorie* and *bacari* patronized by locals follow workers' rhythms, with lunch served from midday to about 2pm and dinner from 6.30pm to 9pm, while smarter restaurants follow Italian standard practice, with lunch from around 1pm to 3pm and dinner from 7.30pm to 10pm. Eating earlier, like the locals, will probably prove cheaper, though there's no guarantee that smaller places will charge you the same price as their regular patrons.

WHERE TO EAT

Venice, like many Italian cities, has a confusing array of differently named eating places. A *ristorante* tends to be expensive, with polished service, immaculate tables and shining cutlery and glass. The *trattoria* is less formal, less expensive, and often family-run. Such places may not have a printed menu, and the waiter will simply reel off a list of what's on offer; many speak enough English to help you choose. *Osterie* were originally pretty basic, and some still are, but the appellation has also been adopted by some very trendy establishments and can be synonymous with excellent food and rustic elegance. *Pizzerie* in Venice tend to open all day rather than just in the evenings; though be aware that wood-fired ovens are forbidden in the city due to the fire risk, and a Venetian pizza won't come near those served south of Rome. For fast, inexpensive food, your best bet is a *bacaro*, Venice's great contribution to Italian eating. *Bacari* serve wine and *cicchetti*. Often hidden down side-streets, they are frequently very old, with blackened beams and a few rickety tables; some have long tables

in a room behind the bar, where more substantial meals are served at lunchtime. Order a drink, and choose what you want to eat from the counter; the barman will keep a rough count of what you've had and you pay as you leave. Many close in the evenings, and few accept credit cards, but they are the best place to sample real Venetian cooking at excellent prices.

Venice's better restaurants lie in those parts of the city where there are still significant numbers of resident Venetians: northern Cannaregio, eastern Castello, Santa Croce, western Dorsoduro and the Giudecca. San Marco, on the whole, is over-priced; it's here that waiters lurk in doorways to persuade passing tourists to come in and eat—the wise visitor will realize this is the quickest route to mediocre food and rip-off prices.

WHAT TO EAT

A full Venetian meal is gargantuan—*antipasti*, a *primo* (first course) of soup, rice or pasta, a *secondo* (main course) of fish with vegetable *contorni* (side dishes), then *formaggi* (cheese) and *dolce* (pudding). Do as the locals do and pick and mix. *Antipasti* are so good that if the waiter suggests a selection and you overindulge, just skip the *primo* or *secondo*, or miss the *antipasti* and start with a *primo*. Few Venetians eat either cheese or pudding in restaurants, preferring to head for a *pasticceria* or choose a *gelato* if they want something sweet to round off the meal. Some of the city's best restaurants offer a *menù degustazione*, a tasting menu that will include small portions of the house specials—a great way to experience the best. Note that the price of fish on the menu is often quoted by weight, usually per 100g (*un etto*).

IL CONTO (THE BILL)

Most restaurants still charge for *pane e coperto* (cover charge), and may automatically bring bottled water with your order. Check the bill,

and ask for a *ricevuta fiscale* (official receipt), which, by law, restaurants must provide. Normally, service is not included; if it is, it will appear as *servizio compreso*. Otherwise, 5 to to 10 per cent is the rule, depending on the restaurant and level of service. Most accept credit cards, though they cannot be used in *bacari* and most bars.

BARS AND CAFÉS

Sitting with a drink in a sunny *campo* or a bar will certainly double the price, and send it sky-high in the famous bars that ring the Piazza San Marco. Locals use bars for that essential shot of caffeine, the espresso—known simply as *un caffè*. They also drop in throughout the day for cold drinks, beer and snacks. Specialities of Venetian bars include rich, smooth *cioccolato* (hot chocolate), and Venice's own apéritif, the *spritz*, an alarmingly potent mix of white wine, Campari bitter or Aperol and soda, and *prosecco*, a light, dry, sparkling white wine from the Veneto. *Prosecco* is used to make the Bellini, a delicious summertime blend of white peach juice with sparkling wine, sampled at its best at Harry's Bar, its place of origin. Bars also serve sandwiches and rolls, the most typical being the *tramezzino*, a half-round of soft white bread, whose fillings include delicacies such as crabmeat, *bresaola* (cured dried meat) with cheese, or prawns with rocket and mayonnaise. Some bars and cafés also double as *gelaterie*, serving a fantastic range of ice creams. As a rule of thumb, buy from those outlets marked *produzione propria* or *artigianale* to ensure you're getting the best freshly made, home-produced ices.

SMOKING

All restaurants in Italy are now non-smoking indoors, though you can smoke if you're eating at outside tables in warm weather. Some smaller establishments do, however, permit smoking and these are mentioned.

Venice is justly renowned for its fish and seafood. Although many restaurants provide English menus, to taste the best of Venetian cuisine, you may need to get away from tourist-orientated restaurants, so some Italian words may be useful—and a sense of adventure and willingness to try something new will add enormously to your eating experience. This menu reader includes key words to help you work out what's on offer, and help familiarize you with some of Venice's most famous dishes.

PIATTI (COURSES)

antipasto	starter
cicchetti	starter served as tapas-style snack
contorni	vegetable/side dishes
dolci	desserts
formaggio	cheese
menu à prezzo fisso	fixed-price menu
panino	filled roll
primo piatto	first course
secondo piatto	second/main course

PESCE (FISH) AND FRUTTI DI MARE (SEAFOOD)

acciughe	anchovy
aragosta	lobster
baccalà	dried salt cod
branzino	sea bass
calamari	squid
canocie mantis	shrimp
caparozzoli	Venus clams
capelunghe	razor-shell clams
capesante/canestrelli	scallops

coda di rospe	monkfish
cozze/peoci	mussels
dentice	dentex (like sea bass)
dorate	sea bream
fritto misto	mixed fried fish
gamberi	shrimp
granceola	spider crab
granchio	crab
merluzzo	cod
moeche/moleche	soft-shell crab
molloschi	shellfish
ostriche	oyster
pesce spada	swordfish
polipi	octopus
salmone	salmon
sampietro	John Dory
sarde	sardines
scampi	prawns
schie/cance	baby prawns
seppie	cuttlefish
sgombro	mackerel
sogliola	sole
tonno	tuna
triglie	mullet
trota	trout
vongole	clams

CARNE (MEAT)

agnello	lamb
anatra	duck
bistecca	steak
braciola	pork chop
cacciagione	game
cavel/cavallo	horse meat
cervo	venison
cinghiale	boar
coniglio	rabbit
faraona	guinea fowl
fegato	liver
maiale	pork
manzo	beef
pancetta	cured pork (similar to bacon)
pollo	chicken
polpette	spicy meatballs
prosciutto cotto	cooked ham
prosciutto crudo	Parma ham
salsiccia	sausage
tacchino	turkey

CONTORNI (VEGETABLES AND SIDE DISHES)

asparagi	asparagus

carciofo .... artichoke
carota .... carrot
castrauri baby artichokes served raw
cavolfiore .... cauliflower
cavolo .... cabbage
ceci .... chickpeas
cetriolino .... gherkin (pickle)
cetriolo .... cucumber
cicoria .... chicory
cipolla .... onion
fagioli dried beans (borlotti, canellini)
fagiolini .... green beans
fave .... broad beans
finocchio .... fennel
funghi .... mushrooms
insalata (verde/mista) .... green/
mixed salad
insalatina .... baby salad leaves
latuga .... lettuce
melanzana .... aubergine (eggplant)
patata .... potato
peperone .... (bell) pepper
piselli .... peas
pomodoro .... tomato
porro .... leek
radicchio .... bitter red 'lettuce'
rucola .... rocket (arugula)
sedano .... celery
spinaci .... spinach
verdure .... green leaf vegetables
zucca .... pumpkin
zucchina .... courgette (zucchini)

SPECIALITÀ
(LOCAL SPECIALITIES)
abbacchio ....roast lamb baked in a
casserole, sometimes flavoured with
anchovies
agnolotti ...... crescent shaped pasta
stuffed with chopped meat, spices,
vegetables and cheese
anguille alla veneziana ..... eels with
tuna and lemon
baccalà alla vicentina .... dried cod
poached in milk
baccalà mantecato .... dried cod
creamed with oil and milk
bagna cauda ..... hot sauce flavoured
with anchovies for
dipping vegatables
bigoli all buranese ... fat spaghetti in
anchovy and onion sauce
bistecca alla fiorentina ....
Florentine-style steak
bocconcini .... fried layered veal
and ham
bollito misto .... meat platter

bovoleti ...... baby snails cooked with
parsley and garlic
bresaola .... air-dried spiced beef
brodetto .... classic mixed fish soup
broèto .... eel soup
cacciucco alla livornese ...... seafood
stew
calzone .... pizza dough rolled
with the chef's choice, usually
combining sausage, cheese and
tomatoes, and baked
castradina ... lamb and cabbage stew
castrauri .... raw baby artichokes
cervello al burro nero ..... calf brains
in black-butter sauce
cima alla genovese ..... rolled fillet of
veal with eggs,
mushrooms and sausages
costoletta alla milanese ... fried veal
with breadcrumbs,
sometimes with cheese
fegato alla veneziana .... braised
liver with onions
gnocchi ...... dumplings usually made
from potatoes
insalata di frutti di mare .. garnished
seafood salad
osso buco .... tender beef or veal
knuckle served with a strong sauce
pancetta .. herb-flavoured sliced pork
pasta e ceci .... pasta and
chickpea soup
pasta e fagioli .... dried bean
and pasta soup
pasticcio .... lasagne
piselli al prosciutto peas with strips
of ham
pizzaiola .... tomato and oregano
sauce, usually with beef
polenta .... maize meal, served as a
primo or *contorno*
polenta de uccelli ...... roasted small
birds served with polenta
pollo alla cacciatore .... chicken
with mushrooms and
tomatoes cooked in wine
radicchio di Treviso al ferro .... long
radicchio leaves cooked on the grill
ragù .... meat sauce
ravioli .... stuffed squares
of pasta
risi e bisi .... risotto with peas
risi e luganega .... rice and pork
sausages
risotto ai funghi .. mushroom risotto
risotto alla milanese .... rice with
saffron and wine

risotto alla seppie .... cuttlefish
black risotto
risotto del mare .... seafood risotto
risotto di radicchio .... risotto
with radicchio
risotto di zucca .... pumpkin risotto
sarde in saor .... sweet-sour sardines
schie e polenta .... tiny shrimps
with polenta
seppie in nero ...... cuttlefish cooked
in its own ink
stufato .... beef braised in white
wine and vegetable
spaghetti all vongole veraci ....
spaghetti with clams
trenette .... thin noodles served
with pesto sauce and potatoes
vitello tonnato .... cold veal and
tuna fish sauce

DOLCI (CAKES AND DESSERTS)
bigne .... chocolate, coffee or
liqueur cream-filled profiteroles
bussolai, baicoli, esse .... hard,
sweet biscuits from Burano
flavoured with lemon and vanilla
cassatta alla siciliana .... sponge,
sweet ricotta cheese, candied fruit
and chocolate butter cream icing
fregolotta .... traditional Venetian
plain cake flavoured with almonds
fritelle deep-fried sweet dough fritter
gelato .... ice cream
macedonia .... fruit salad
semifreddo .... soft iced pudding
flavoured with liqueur
tiramisù ..... chocolate/coffee sponge
and mascarpone pudding
zabaglione .... whipped egg, sugar
and sweet wine froth, a
traditional pick-me-up
zuccotto .... sponge cake soaked
in liqueur with chocolate,
nuts and whipped cream

FRUTTA (FRUIT)
ananas .... pineapple
arancia .... orange
banana .... banana
cedro .... lime
ciliegia .... cherry
fico .... fig
fragola .... strawberry
lampone .... raspberry
limone .... lemon
mela .... apple
melone .... melon

nespola	loquat
pera	pear
pesca	peach
pesca noci	nectarine
pompelmo	grapefruit
susina	plum
uva	grape

LATTICINI E PASTICCERIA (DAIRY AND BAKERY)

bruschetta ....toasted bread with oil, garlic and tomatoes
burro ....butter
dolcelatte..........creamy blue cheese
focaccia............... oil-enriched dough left to rise slowly and usually topped with olive oil, and sometimes rosemary and onions
fontina ....smooth, dense cheese from northern Italy
gorgonzola ....strong blue-veined cheese
mozzarella ....fresh milk cheese
pane ....bread
panettone ....sweet yeast cake with dried fruit
panna ....heavy cream
parmigiano ....parmesan cheese
ricotta.................... fresh milk cheese
toast................ toasted cheese and ham sandwich
tramezzino .... generously filled white bread sandwich
uove ....eggs

BEVANDE (DRINKS)

acqua minerale, frizzante/naturale .... sparkling/flat mineral water
amaretto .... sweet almond-based drink
amaro..........................bitter digestif
aperitivo......... before dinner apéritif
Bellini................prosecco with fresh white peach juice
birra.. beer
birra alla spina............ draught beer (beer on tap)
caffè Americano ....weak coffee
caffè corretto ......coffee with a dash of *grappa* or brandy
caffè espresso ....coffee
caffè Hag..........decaffeinated coffee
caffè latte..................... milky coffee
caffè macchiato......... strong coffee with a drop of milk
cappuccino ...milky coffee with froth
digestivo .... after dinner liqueur

frappé............milkshake made with ice cream
frullato ....milkshake
ghiaccio ....ice
granita ....crushed ice covered in syrup (usually coffee)
prosecco .... sparkling white wine from the Veneto
sambuca ...aniseed-flavoured liqueur
secco, brut .... dry
spremuta di arancia............freshly squeezed orange juice
spritz .... white wine, Campari bitter and soda
succo di arancia, pesca/pera/ albicocchi ....orange/ peach/pear/apricot juice
tè ....tea
tè al latte freddo ....tea with milk
tè al limone ....tea with lemon
vini della casa .... house wines
vini locali ....local wines
vini pregiati .... quality wines
vino bianco.....................white wine
vino rosato ....rosé wine
vino rosso ....red wine
vino sfuso .... house wine (draught/on tap)

CONDIMENTI (SEASONINGS)

aceto ....vinegar
aglio ....garlic
basilico...................................... basil
capperi ....capers
erbe aromatiche.....................herbs
olio ....oil
pepe .... pepper
peperoncino ....chilli pepper
pesto .... green sauce made from basil leaves, cheese, garlic, marjoram and pine nuts

prezzemolo.......................... parsley
rosmarino .... rosemary
sale...salt
senape .... mustard
zucchero ....sugar

IL CONTO (THE BILL)

coperto .... cover charge
IVA.................. VAT value added tax
ricevuta fiscale ....official receipt
servizio compreso ....service included
servizio non compreso........service not included

UTENSILI (UTENSILS)

bicchiere .... glass
bottiglia ....bottle
cotello .... knife
cucchiaio................................spoon
forchetta .... fork
piatto ....plate
tazza..cup

METODI DI CUCINA (COOKING METHODS)

affumicato ....smoked
al ferro/alla griglia ....grilled
al forno....................................baked
arrosto..................................roasted
al sangue .... rare
al vapore ....steamed
ben cotto ....well-done
bollito....................................boiled
cotto.....................................cooked
crudo...raw
fritto .... fried
spiedini .... meat grilled over an open flame
stufato..................................stewed
tostato ....toasted

RESTAURANTS BY CUISINE

As everywhere in Italy, locals in Venice firmly believe their own cuisine is unrivalled, and the concept of restaurants featuring cuisine from other parts of the world is alien. There are, accordingly, virtually no restaurants serving 'foreign' food, though more innovative establishments are experimenting with a lighter take on traditional Venetian cooking. The restaurants below are listed by cuisine and by area, and it's worth considering how long it will take you to get from your hotel to dinner after a long day's sightseeing—and perhaps choosing something local.

CAFÉ/BAR

Algiubagio ....Cannaregio
Bottega del Caffè Dersut San Polo
Caffè Florian ....San Marco
Caffè Quadri ....San Marco
Harry's Bar ....San Marco
Harry's Dolci ....Giudecca
Improntacafé .... Santa Croce
Osteria ai Rusteghi ......San Marco
Teamo ....San Marco

CICCHETTI/SNACKS

Al Bottegon .... Dorsoduro
Al Mascaron ....Castello
Antica Osteria Ruga Rialto............
.... San Polo
Codroma ....Dorsoduro
Da Alberto....................Cannaregio
Hostaria all'Ombra ....Castello
Osteria Ae Botti..............Giudecca

CLASSIC ITALIAN/VENETIAN

Ai Gondolieri ....Dorsoduro
Antico Giardinetto ..... Santa Croce
Bistrot de Venise ....San Marco
Cipriani Restaurant.........Giudecca
Da Fiore............................San Polo
Do Forni ....San Marco
Fiaschetteria Toscana...Cannaregio

Trattoria Cea ....Cannaregio
Vini da Gigio ....Cannaregio

CONTEMPORARY VENETIAN

Antica Besseta .... Santa Croce
Antica Birraria la Corte .... San Polo
Mistrà ....Giudecca
Osteria Oliva Nera ....Castello

FISH AND SEAFOOD

Acquapazza ....San Marco
Al Bacco........................Cannaregio
Al Covo ....Castello
Al Vecio Fritolin .... Santa Croce
Alle Testiere ....San Marco
Antica Osteria al Panatalon ....
.... San Polo
Antiche Carampane   San Polo
Corte Sconta ....Castello
Da Pinto ....San Polo
Da Remigio ....Castello
Osteria Ale Do Marie.........Castello
Osteria alla Rivetta ....Castello
Osteria Boccadoro ....Cannaregio
Osteria al Bomba ....Cannaregio
Riviera.............................Giudecca

KOSHER

Gam Gam ....Cannaregio

PIZZA

Ae Oche .... Santa Croce
Casin dei Nobili............Dorsoduro
Il Refolo...................... Santa Croce
Pizzeria 84.........................Castello
Pizzeria alle Zattere ......Dorsoduro

SARDINIAN

L'Incontro.....................Dorsoduro

TRADITIONAL VENETIAN

Ai Cugnai......................Dorsoduro
Alla Madonna....................San Polo
Al Ponte ....San Polo
Anice Stellato...............Cannaregio
Da Bruno.......................San Marco
Dal Pampo ....Castello
Do Farai.........................Dorsoduro
La Furatola.....................Dorsoduro
Il Ridotto ....Castello
Locanda Montin............Dorsoduro
Osteria 1518 ....Dorsoduro
Taverna San Trovaso .....Dorsoduro
Vini da Arturo...............San Marco

VEGETARIAN

Alla Zucca .... Santa Croce

Compared with its population, Venice has more tourist accommodation than any other Italian city. This ranges from the five-star luxury of some of the world's greatest hotels to the rather bland modern chain hotels and simple, low-key *pensioni*. Despite this, the city remains a seller's market, popular at all times of year, and this is reflected in the high prices of all its accommodation.

WHERE TO STAY

There's little to be found in the way of special offers on any sort of room, and value for money is a relative concept. Given this, it's worth thinking hard about the location of your hotel, as this will make a huge difference to your enjoyment of the city.

San Marco has a large number of places to stay and is right in the heart of the action, but it's also constantly crowded and noisy, elements which could cost you sleep and might be hard to endure in the heat of summer. To the west, Cannaregio is a good bet for its range of relatively cheaper accommodation, particularly around the railway station, though again, this area can be extremely busy

as it's on the main route to San Marco for day-trippers. East of San Marco, Castello has much to offer; it's more remote, quieter and you'll pay far less for a room with a view than in the San Marco area. Across the Grand Canal, Santa Croce and San Polo have plenty of choice, particularly around the Rialto. Hotels here tend to be family-run, smallish places, with traditional Venetian-style rooms. Dorsoduro is another good choice, its quiet canals and residential streets providing peaceful nights, with the bonus of two major museums on the doorstep. For true peace and ultimate luxury, leave the city and head for the lagoon; two of Venice's most sybaritic hotels, the Cipriani and the San Clemente, are a boat-ride away from San Marco.

Wherever you choose, it's worth bearing in mind that this is a small city, so getting about from what seems a far-flung location may not prove too bothersome in reality—and travelling by boat is half the fun. When choosing your accommodation, think about your arrival, remembering you'll have to carry your luggage over bridges from the nearest water arrival point, making the proximity of the closest *vaporetto* stop another factor which may influence you.

Venice is very hot during the summer, so a courtyard or garden is a bonus, as are rooms away from the street. Bear in mind that noise bounces off water and narrow streets, especially if they are major thoroughfares.

WHAT YOUR MONEY BUYS

A star system operates in Venice, with five stars denoting the highest standards of comfort, luxury and convenience. Rooms at this level cost from around €350 for a single to €700–€2,000 for a double or suite per night. Four-star options range from around €280 to €400, three-star from €170 to €300, while two-star cost €150 to €220. At the low end of hotels proper, expect to pay between €50 and €150 for a simple room, which may well not have its own bathroom.

The last few years have seen a burgeoning number of boutique hotels and trendy bed-and-breakfast establishments opening in Venice, which are often housed in lovely old buildings tucked away from the main streets. They charge anything between €150 and €400 for a double and are extremely popular, with visitors returning time after time.

Most Venetian hotels include breakfast in the cost of the room; in smaller places, this may be served in your room. You can expect television (often satellite), telephone, a mini-bar and air-conditioning in three-star hotels; you may have to pay extra for the air-conditioning in cheaper places. If you want a room with a view, find out in advance how much of a view you'll be getting for your hefty surcharge; you could end up forking out a huge supplement for a glimpse of the Grand Canal from the bathroom window.

MAKING RESERVATIONS

It pays to reserve accommodation well in advance, especially if you're planning a visit during peak periods. The city is especially packed during Carnevale, and you should reserve six months or more ahead to ensure plenty of choice, and at least two months ahead for much of the rest of the year. Venice's least busy month is January, virtually the only time when you could safely arrive without a confirmed reservation, though the choice will be limited, as many hotels close from after Christmas until Carnevale.

Do consult hotel websites for details of any special deals, or consider taking a package break to Venice. Tour operators usually have a fixed room allocation in some of the best hotels and their packages, which include flights and transfers, may be very competitively priced. If you haven't reserved ahead, ask to see the room before you commit yourself; this is perfectly acceptable in Italy. If you're making a reservation in advance from home, be sure to get written confirmation and take it with you, or you may turn up and find all knowledge of your booking denied.

It's a good idea to make sure your hotel has sent you directions for your arrival before you leave home, which should include a locator map, details of the nearest *vaporetto* stop and a local landmark such as a *campo* or church. Venice is a confusing city for first-time visitors and you don't want to have to carry your luggage farther than you have to or get lost before you've even started your visit.

If you don't have a reservation, go to the accommodation desks run by the Associazione Veneziani Albergatori (Venetian Hoteliers' Association), who will do their best to help. These are at Santa Lucia railway station (tel 041 715 288); the arrivals hall at Marco Polo airport (tel 041 541 5017) and the Comunale parking area at Piazzale Roma (tel 041 522 8640). You can also telephone them on 041 523 8032 or 041 522 2264.

OTHER OPTIONS

If you're watching the budget, bear in mind that mainland hotels are cheaper than those in the city proper, though the Venetian experience won't be the same. Mestre, a 10-minute hop by bus or train across the water, has plenty of hotel accommodation, much of which provides parking. Padova (Padua), half an hour or so by train from Venice, has a lovely historic area, with a style of its own that's a good contrast to Venice itself.

If you're interested in the increasingly popular self-catering option see below.

ONLINE HOTEL BOOKING

www.venicehotel.org
www.veneziasi.it
www.venicehotel.com
www.alfabookings.com/venice
www.invenicehotels.com
www.hotelinvenice.com
www.veniceby.com
www.veniceclick.net

SELF-CATERING

An increasing number of visitors rent apartments when visiting Venice. The benefits are obvious: more space, independence, the flexibility of doing what you want, when you want, the chance to buy and cook your own food and really feel part of the city, and for many people the prime consideration, far lower prices.

There are a number of both Venetian-based and international companies offering places in Venice, as well as numerous private owners renting their own holiday flats out while they're away from the city. If you're considering the rental option, there are a few points worth considering:

» Choose the location carefully, making sure there are food shops within easy reach—everything you buy has to be carried home.

» Check that linen, heating, air-conditioning, lighting, gas and end-of-stay cleaning is included in the rent.

» Check that there's an on-the-spot agent in case of emergencies—this is particularly important in the case of private rentals.

» If the rentals are on the third or fourth floors, bear in mind it's unlikely there will be access by elevator.

» Remember that Venetian buildings are old, and be prepared to trade state-of-the-art decoration, furnishing and facilities for the chance to stay in a historic house in a unique city.

Once you have mastered a few basic rules, Italian is an easy language to speak. It is phonetic and, unlike English, particular combinations of letters are always pronounced the same way. The stress is usually on the penultimate syllable, but if the word has an accent, this is where the stress falls.

Vowels are pronounced as follows:

a	casa	as in mat short 'a'
e	vero closed	as in base
e	sette open	as in vet short 'e'
i	vino	as in mean
o	dove closed	as in bowl
o	otto open	as in not
u	uva	as in book

Consonants as in English except:
c before i or e becomes ch as in church
ch before i or e becomes c as in cat
g before i or e becomes j as in Julia
gh before i or e becomes g as in good
gn as in onion
gli as in million
h is rare in Italian words, and is always silent
r usually rolled
z is pronounced tz when it falls in the middle of a word

All Italian nouns are either masculine (usually ending in o when singular or i when plural) or feminine (usually ending in a when singular or e when plural). Some nouns, which may be masculine or feminine, end in e (which changes to i when plural). An adjective's ending changes to match the ending of the noun.

SHOPPING
Could you help me, please?
Può aiutarmi, per favore?

How much is this/that?
Quanto costa questo/quello?

I'm looking for…
Cerco…

Where can I buy…?
Dove posso comprare…?

I'll take this
Prendo questo

Are the instructions included?
Ci sono anche le istruzioni?

Do you have a bag for this?
Può darmi un sacco?

Can you gift wrap this please?
Può farmi un pacco regalo?

Do you accept credit cards?
Accettate carte di credito?

I'd like a kilo of…
Vorrei un chilo di…

When does the shop open/close?
Quando apre/chiude il negozio?

GETTING AROUND
Where is the train/bus station?
Dov'è la stazione ferroviaria/ degli autobus (dei pullman—long distance)?

Does this train/bus go to…?
È questo il treno/l'autobus (il pullman—long distance) per…?

Where are we?
Dove siamo?

When is the first/last bus/ vaporetto to…?
Quando c'è il primo/l'ultimo autobus/ vaporetto per…?

Do you have a vaporetto map?
Ha una piantina dei vaporetti?

Do I have to get off here?
Devo scendere qui?

Please can I have a single/return ticket to…
Un biglietto di andata/ andata e ritorno per…

I would like a standard/first class ticket to…
Un biglietto di seconda/ prima classe per…

Where is the timetable?
Dov'è l'orario?

Where can I find a taxi?
Dove sono i tassì?

Please take me to…
Per favore, mi porti a…

How much is the journey?
Quanto costerà il viaggio?

I'd like to get out here please
Vorrei scendere qui, per favore

Is this the way to…?
È questa la strada per…?

IN TROUBLE
Help!
Aiuto!

Stop, thief!
Al ladro!

Can you help me, please?
Può aiutarmi, per favore?

Call the fire brigade/police/an ambulance
Chiami i pompieri/la polizia/ un'ambulanza

I have lost my passport/wallet
Ho perso il passaporto/il portafoglio

Where is the police station/ hospital?
Dov'è il commissariato/l'ospedale?

I have been robbed
Sono stato derubato

I need to see a doctor/dentist
Ho bisogno di un medico/ dentista

Excuse me, I think I am lost
Mi scusi, penso di essermi perduto

MONEY
Is there a bank/currency exchange office nearby?
C'è una banca/un ufficio di cambio qui vicino?

Can I cash this here?
Posso incassare questo?

I'd like to change sterling/dollars into euros
Vorrei cambiare sterline/dollari in euro

Can I use my credit card to withdraw cash?
Posso usare la mia carta di credito per prelevare contanti?

HOTEL
I have made a reservation for... nights
Ho prenotato per...notti

Do you have a room?
Avete camere libere?

How much per night?
Quanto costa una notte?

Double/single room/twin room
Camera doppia/singola/
Camera a due letti

With bath/shower
Con bagno/doccia

May I see the room?
Posso vedere la camera?

I'll take this room
Prendo questa camera

Could I have another room?
Vorrei cambiare camera

Is there an elevator in the hotel?
C'è un ascensore nell'albergo?

Is the room air-conditioned/ heated?
C'è aria condizionata/riscaldamento nella camera?

Is breakfast included in the price?
La colazione è compreso?

When is breakfast served?
A che ora è servita la colazione?

The room is too hot/too cold/ dirty
La camera è troppo calda/ troppo fredda/sporca

I am leaving this morning
Parto stamattina

Please can I pay my bill?
Posso pagare il conto?

TOURIST INFORMATION
Where is the tourist information office, please?
Dov'è l'ufficio turistico, per favore?

Do you have a city map?
Avete una cartina della città?

Can you give me some information about...?
Puo darmi delle informazioni su...?

What sights/hotels/restaurants can you recommend?
Quali monumenti/alberghi/ristoranti mi consiglia?

What is the admission price?
Quant'è il biglietto d'ingresso?

Is there an English-speaking guide?
C'è una guida di lingua inglese?

Do you have a brochure in English?
Avete un dépliant in inglese?

Could you reserve tickets for me?
Mi può prenotare dei biglietti?

RESTAURANT
Waiter/waitress
Cameriere/cameriera

I'd like to reserve a table for... people at ...
Vorrei prenotare un tavolo per... persone a...

A table for..., please
Un tavolo per..., per favore

Could we sit there?
Possiamo sederci qui?

Are there tables outside?
Ci sono tavoli all'aperto?

We would like to wait for a table
Aspettiamo che si liberi un tavolo

Could we see the menu/wine list?
Possiamo vedere il menù/la lista dei vini?

Do you have a menu/wine list in English?
Avete un menù/una lista dei vini in inglese?

What do you recommend?
Cosa consiglia?

What is the house special?
Qual è la specialità della casa?

I can't eat wheat/sugar/salt/ pork/beef/dairy
Non posso mangiare grano/ zucchero/sale/maiale/manzo/latticini

I am a vegetarian
Sono vegetariano/a

I'd like...
Vorrei...

May I have an ashtray?
Può portare un portacenere?

I ordered...
Ho ordinato...

Could we have some salt and pepper?
Può portare del sale e del pepe?

The food is cold
Il cibo è freddo

This is not what I ordered
Non ho ordinato questo

Can I have the bill, please?
Il conto, per favore?

Is service included?
Il servizio è compreso?

The bill is not right
Il conto è sbagliato

We didn't have this
Non abbiamo avuto questo

AROUND THE TOWN
on/to the right
a destra

on/to the left
a sinistra

around the corner
all'angolo

opposite
di fronte a...

straight on
sempre dritto

near
vicino a

Where do you live?
Dove abita?

I live in...
Vivo in...

cross over
attraversi

in front of/behind
davanti/dietro

north/south/east/west
nord/sud/est/ovest

free
gratis

open/closed
aperto/chiuso

cathedral/church
cattedrale/chiesa

castle/palace
castello/palazzo

museum/gallery
museo/galleria

monument
monumento

town
città

old town
centro storico

square
piazza/campo

bridge
ponte

canal
rio

island
ísola

river/lake
fiume/lago

street/avenue
via/viale

no entry
vietato

entrance/exit
ingresso/uscita

CONVERSATION
What is the time?
Che ore sono?

I don't speak Italian
Non parlo italiano

Do you speak English?
Parla inglese?

I don't understand
Non capisco

Please repeat that
Può ripetere?

My name is
Mi chiamo

What's your name?
Come si chiama?

Hello, pleased to meet you
Piacere

Good morning
Buongiorno

Good afternoon/evening
Buonasera

Goodbye
Arrivederci

How are you?
Come sta?

Fine, thank you
Bene, grazie

I'm sorry
Mi dispiace

TIMES, DAYS, MONTHS

Monday	lunedì
Tuesday	martedì
Wednesday	mercoledì
Thursday	giovedì
Friday	venerdì
Saturday	sabato
Sunday	domenica
day	giorno
week	settimana
today	oggi
yesterday	ieri
tomorrow	domani
January	gennaio
February	febbraio
March	marzo
April	aprile
May	maggio
June	giugno

July	luglio
August	agosto
September	settembre
October	ottobre
November	novembre
December	dicembre

NUMBERS

0	zero
1	uno
2	due
3	tre
4	quattro
5	cinque
6	sei
7	sette
8	otto
9	nove
10	dieci
11	undici
12	dodici
13	tredici
14	quattordici
15	quindici
16	sedici
17	diciassette
18	diciotto
19	diciannove
20	venti
21	ventuno
22	ventidue
30	trenta
40	quaranta
50	cinquanta
60	sessanta
70	settanta
80	ottanta
90	novanta
100	cento
1000	mille
million	milione
quarter	quarto
half	mezza
three quarters	tre quarti

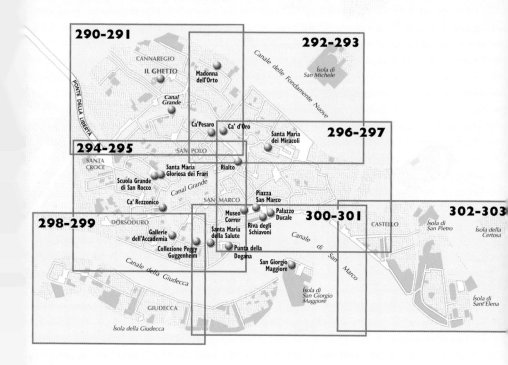

290-291

CANNAREGIO

IL GHETTO

Madonna dell'Orto

PONTE DELLA LIBERTÀ

Canal Grande

Ca'Pesaro

Ca' d'Oro

292-293

Canale delle Fondamente Nuove

Ísola di San Michele

Santa Maria dei Miracoli

296-297

294-295

SAN POLO

SANTA CROCE

Santa Maria Gloriosa dei Frari

Rialto

Scuola Grande di San Rocco

Canal Grande

Ca' Rezzonico

SAN MARCO

Piazza San Marco

Museo Correr

Palazzo Ducale

300-301

CASTELLO

Ísola di San Pietro

302-303

Ísola della Certosa

298-299

DORSODURO

Gallerie dell'Accademia

Santa Maria della Salute

Riva degli Schiavoni

Collezione Peggy Guggenheim

Punta della Dogana

Canale di San Marco

San Giorgio Maggiore

Canale della Giudecca

Ísola di San Giorgio Maggiore

Ísola di Sant'Elena

GIUDECCA

Ísola della Giudecca

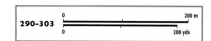

290-303

| 0 | | 200 m |
| 0 | | 200 yds |

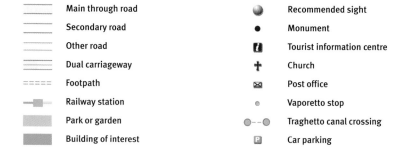

———	Main through road	⬤ Recommended sight
———	Secondary road	● Monument
⋯⋯	Other road	🛈 Tourist information centre
═══	Dual carriageway	✝ Church
-----	Footpath	✉ Post office
⊷	Railway station	○ Vaporetto stop
	Park or garden	⦿--⊙ Traghetto canal crossing
	Building of interest	🅿 Car parking

MAPS

Map references for the sights refer to the individual locator maps within
the regional chapters. For example, San Marco has the reference ✚ 59 H10,
indicating the locator map page number (59) and the grid square in which
San Marco sits (H10). These same grid references can also be used to locate
the sights in this section. For example, San Marco appears again in grid
square H10 within the atlas, on page 296.

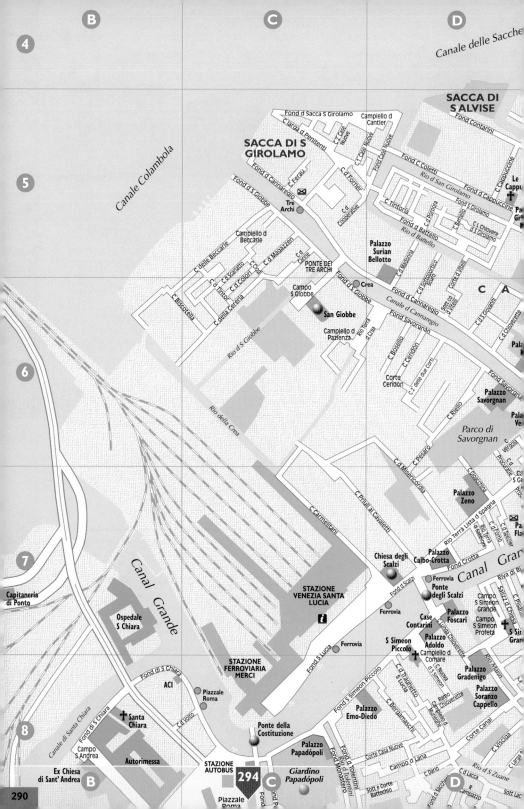

4

Canale delle Sacche

**SACCA DI
S ALVISE**

Fond Contarini

Canale Colambola

Fond d Sacca S Girolamo

Campiello d
Cantier

**SACCA DI
S GIROLAMO**

C larga d Penitenti

C Case Nuove

C Case Nuove

Fond Casa Nuove

Fond C Coletti

Rio d San Girolamo

Fond d Capuccine

Le Cappu

C Cappuccine

5

Fond d S Giobbe

Fond d Cannaregio

C Ferau

C d Former

C d
Cooperativa

C d Borgo

Fond S Girolamo

C L Chiovere
d S Girolamo

Tre
Archi

PONTE DEI
TRE ARCHI

Campiello d
Beccarie

C delle Beccarie

C d Magazzen

C d Canne

Rio d Battello

Fond d Battello

Palazzo
Surian
Bellotto

C Madonna

C d Sottoportico
Scuro

Corte d Vitelli

C A

C

Crea

C d Scarlato

C d Colonn

Campo
S Giobbe

Fond d S Giobbe

Canale d Cannaregio

C d Vitelli

C S Giovanni

C d Chiovere

Pal

C della Cereria

C d Tintor

San Giobbe

Fond Savorgnan

C Tintoria

d Crea

Rio Terra

Campiello d
Pazienza

C Bosello

C d Cendon

Fond Savorgna

C Biscotella

Rio d S Giobbe

C-t delle due Corti

6

Rio della Crea

Corte
Cendon

C Pesaro

C Riello

Palazzo
Savorgnan

Pala
Ve

Parco di
Savorgnan

C d Misericordia

C Giacomina

Palazzo
Zeno

C
S Ge

Canal Grande

C Friuli al Cavaletti

C Carmelitani

Rio Terra Lista d Spagna

Palazzo
Flai

C d Spezier

Capitaneria
di Ponto

7

Chiesa degli
Scalzi

Rio Terra
d Stabilimti

C d Crotta

Fond Crotta

Canal Gran

Ospedale
S Chiara

**STAZIONE
VENEZIA SANTA
LUCIA**

Fond d Scalzi

Palazzo
Calbo-Crotta

Ponte
degli Scalzi

Riva di

Campo
S Simeon
Grande

Salizz d Chiesa

Ferrovia

Ferrovia

Case
Contarini

Palazzo
Foscari

Campo
S Simeon
Profeta

S
Gran

Santa
Chiara

ACI

Fond di S Chiara

Fond di S Chiara

C d Volto

**STAZIONE
FERROVIARIA
MERCI**

Ferrovia

Fond S Lucia

S Siméon
Piccolo

Palazzo
Adoldo

Campiello d
Comare

C d Chiovere

S Lucia

C Cuova

Rio Marin

Palazzo
Gradenigo

Piazzale
Roma

Fond S Simeon Piccolo

C Traghetto

C d s simeon

Ramo
Chiovere
te

Palazzo
Soranzo
Cappello

Campo
S Andrea

Canale di Santa Chiara

8

Ex Chiesa
di Sant' Andrea

Autorimessa

**STAZIONE
AUTOBUS**

Ponte della
Costituzione

Palazzo
Papadópoli

Palazzo
Emo-Diedo

Giardino
Papadópoli

C Berталmaschi

Corte Casa Nuove

Fond Tolentini

Fond di Tolentini

Fond Monastero

Campo d Lana

C Dario

Rio d S Zuane

Corte Canal

Corte
Battochio

Sott e Corte

Sott Lac

C Visciga

C Lacca

Piazzale
Roma

J K L

4

Cimitero ○ San
Michele

5

Cimitero

Ísola di
San Michele

6

Canale delle Fondamente Nuove

7

Fondamente Nuove

Santa Lázzaro
dei Mendicanti

Ospedale ○

Ospedale
Civile

297

uola Grande
a San Marco

Santa Maria
del Pianto

8

Santi Giovanni
e Paolo

Ospedaletto
(Santa Maria
dei Derelitti)

J K L Celestia

293

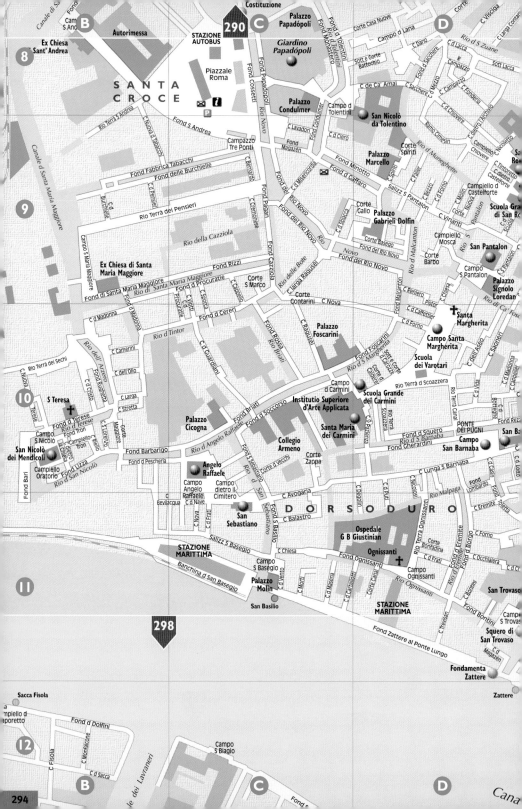

B

8 Ex Chiesa
'Sant' Andrea

Autorimessa

290 C

STAZIONE
AUTOBUS

Palazzo
Papadópoli

D

C. Viscila

Corte Casa Nuove

Campo d Lana

C. d Saccere

C. d Lacca

C. d'Chiovere

C. d Fonderia

Ramo Cimesin

Campazzo

Campiello Lucchese

Sott. Lacca

S A N T A
C R O C E

Piazzale
Roma

Giardino
Papadópoli

Fond S Andrea

Campazzo
Tre Ponti

Rio Nuovo

Fond Cossetti

Fond Papadópoli

Fond Monastero

Palazzo
Condulmer

Campo d
Tolentini

San Nicolò
da Tolentino

C de Ca' Amai

Sott. e Corte
Battochio

9

Canale di Santa Maria Maggiore

Fond Fabbrica Tabacchi

Fond delle Burchielle

Rio Terra dei Pensieri

Rio della Cazziola

Fond S Andrea

Fond Pagan

Rio Novo

Fond del Rio Novo

Palazzo
Marcello

Corte
Spiriti

Rio d Mungheitte

Palazzo
Gabrieli Dolfin

Corte
Gallo

Campiello o
di Castelforte

Scuola Gra
di San N

C d Clero

Fond
Magazèn

Fond Minotto

Fond d Caffaro

Salizz S Pantalòn

San Pantalon

Palazzo
Signolo
Loredan

10 S Teresa

Ex Chiesa di Santa
Maria Maggiore

Campo S Maria Maggiore

Fond di Santa Maria Maggiore

Rio di Santa Maria Maggiore

Fond di Santa Maria Maggiore

Corte
S Marco

C Larga Ragusèi

Corte
Contarini

C Nova

Palazzo
Foscarini

Campo Santa
Margherita

Santa
Margherita

Scuola
dei Varotari

Rio d Tintor

Palazzo
Cicogna

Campo
d Carmini

Scuola Grande
dei Carmini

Rio Terrà di Scoazzera

PONTE
DEI PUGNI

San Ba

San Nicolò
dei Mendicoli

Collegio
Armeno

Santa Maria
dei Carmini

Institutio Superiore
d'Arte Applicata

Campo
S Barnaba

Campo
San Barnaba

11 STAZIONE
MARITTIMA

Angelo
Raffaele

San
Sebastiano

D O R S O D U R O

Ospedale
G B Giustinian

Ognissanti

San Trovaso

298

Banchina d San Basegio

Palazzo
Molin

San Basilio

STAZIONE
MARITTIMA

Squero di
San Trovaso

Fond Zattere al Ponte Lungo

Fondamenta
Zattere

12 Sacca Fisola

Fond d Dolfini

Campo
S Biagio

Zattere

B

C

D

Cana

Ospedale

8

293

ta Maria
l Pianto

Celestia

9

R. Moschette
C. delle Capuccine
Rio di Santa Giustina
Fondamenta di Santa Giustina

d Mezzo
d Forno
etier

C Zen
L
C Cavalli

Ex Chiesa
di S Giustina

C S Francesco
C del Teuem

Palazzo
Gritti o della
Nunziatura

San Francesco
della Vigna

C Orti
C d Pieta

C Assisi
C Sagredo
C 2

Campo
S Giustina

Campo della
Confraternita

C d Cimitero

C d
C Oratorio

Corte del
Muneghe

aterano

spizio

San
Lorenzo
po
enzo

C S Agostin

Palazzo
Gradenigo

Palazzo
Contarini

Rio d S Francesco

Campo
d Celestia

Campo
S Ternità

Darsena
Grande

Canale delle Galeazze

Salizzada S Giustina

Ramo S Francesco

C Morion

Corte
d Vida

C d Vida

C S Lorenzo

Salizz S Francesco

C Nuova

C dell'Olio

Caffettier

Campo
S Ternità

C Dona

Rio d Celestia

10

Ex Convento

S Giovanni
dei Cavalieri
di Malta

Salizz
d Gatte

C Cruzzi

Rio d S Ternità

C Magno

Fond S Giorgio
d Schiavoni

C d Furlani

Campo
d Gatte

C Scudi

C Angelo

Palazzo
Magno

C Caigri

Scuola di
San Giorgio
egli Schiavoni

C d Magazen

eo di Dipinti
i Bizantini

S Antonino

Rio di Furlani

C d Arco

Corte
Soranzo

C Meneghette

Campiello
due Pozzi

Corte
d Angelo

C Boselio

Salizz S Antonin

Corte
Venier

C Morte
Rio d Corre

Corte
ollani

etro la Pieta

C Terrazera

Salizz d Pignater

Piscina S Martin

C Venier

Rio S Martino

Palazzo
Navagero

Campo
Bandiera
e Moro

C d Dose

C d Pestrin

San Giovanni
in Bragora

Campiello
Piovan

C Gritti

C dietro
Erizzo

C Crosera

C d Fonte

C Canoletto

C Crandiben

Chiodista

San
Martino

Fond di Fronte

C Arsenale

Torri
dell'Arsenale

Campo
Arsenale

ARSENALE

Darsena Arsenale Vecchio

Fond di Madonna

Ca' di Dio

Ex Forni

Riva degli Schiavoni

C dei Forni

C d Vida

C Malvasia
Vecchia

C Pegola

C Teglia

C Pegola

C A S T E L L O

Arsenale

Riva Ca' di Dio

Fondamenta dell'Arsenale

Rio dell'Arsenale

Museo
Storico
Navale

Campo della Tana

Rio della Tana

Fond della Tana

Palazzetto
dello Sport

Corte
della
Tana

Corte
Nuova

C d Preti

S Francesco
di Paolo

S Francesco
di Paolo

C Frisiera
C Bassa

301

Campo
S Biagio

Riva S Biagio

San Biagio

Corte
Forment

C Grimana

Fond
della
Tana

302

Via Giuseppe Garibaldi

C Sartin
C Squero
C Sartin
C Pistor
Sodoco
C Caboto
C Vecchia
euavicchia C
te sartin
C angelo
C d Istor
Monumento
a Garibaldi

Riva dei Sette Martiri

C Pedrocchi

C Colonne
Corte Colonne
C Schiavona

C San Domenico

Giardini
Garibaldi

Viale Garib

11

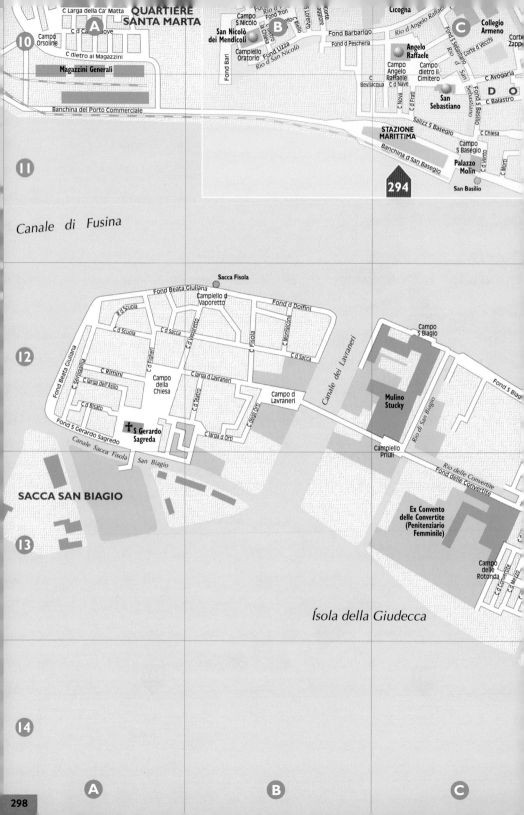

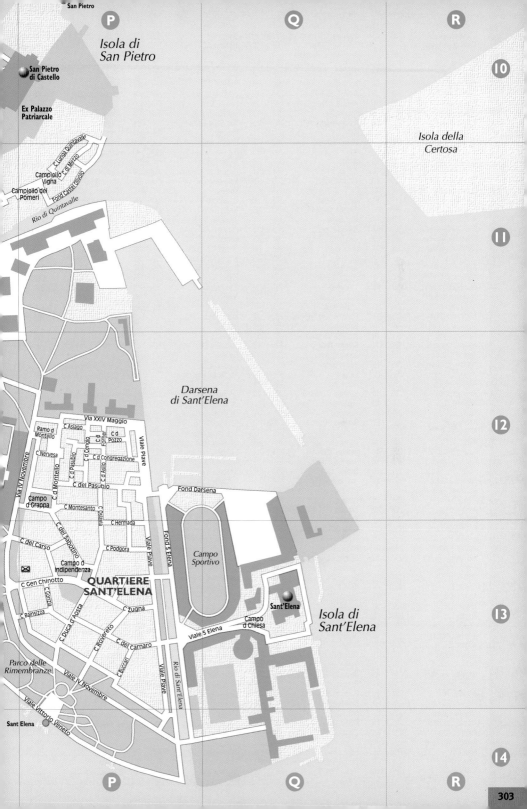

San Pietro

10

Isola di
San Pietro

San Pietro
di Castello

Ex Palazzo
Patriarcale

*Isola della
Certosa*

C.Lunga Quintavalle

C Dil Mezzo

Campiello
Vigna

Campiello dei
Pomeri

Fond Cazze Quinod

Rio di Quintavalle

11

*Darsena
di Sant'Elena*

12

Via XXIV Maggio

Ramo d
Montello

C Asiago

C d
Forner

C d
Pozzo

C Nervesa

C d Cengio

C Pasubio

C d Aslio

C d Congregazione

Viale Piave

C del Pasubio

Campo
d Grappa

C d Montello

C Montesanto

C Hermada

Fond Darsena

Fond S Elena

Via IV Novembre

C del Carso

C del Sabotino

Ostaria

C Podgora

Viale Piave

*Campo
Sportivo*

13

Campo d
Indipendenza

**QUARTIERE
SANT'ELENA**

Sant'Elena

*Isola di
Sant'Elena*

C Gen Chinotto

C Gorilla

C Zugna

Campo
d Chiesa

C Bainsizza

C Duca d'Aosta

C Rovereto

C del Carnaro

C Buccati

Viale S Elena

*Parco delle
Rimembranze*

Viale IV Novembre

Viale Piave

Rio di Sant'Elena

Viale Vittorio Veneto

Sant'Elena

14

PICTURES

The Automobile Association would like to thank the following photographers and companies for their assistance in the preparation of this book.

Abbreviations for the picture credits are as follows:
(t) top; (b) bottom; (l) left; (r) right; (c) centre (AA) AA World Travel Library.

166tl AA/A Mockford & N Bonetti;
169tr AA/R Newton;
170 Museo d'Arte Moderna, Venice, Italy/Bridgeman Art Library;
171 AA/A Mockford & N Bonetti;
172 AA/S McBride;
173bl AA/A Mockford & N Bonetti;
173br AA/C Sawyer;
174 AA/A Mockford & N Bonetti;
175 AA/A Mockford & N Bonetti;
176 AA/C Sawyer;
178 AA/D Miterdiri;
179bl AA/S McBride;
179br AA/S McBride;
180 AA/A Mockford & N Bonetti;
181 AA/A Mockford & N Bonetti;
182 AA/C Sawyer;
183 AA/A Mockford & N Bonetti;
184 AA/A Mockford & N Bonetti;
185 AA/S McBride;
186 AA/S McBride;
187 AA/A Mockford & N Bonetti;
188 AA/S McBride;
190 AA/A Mockford & N Bonetti;
196 AA/A Mockford & N Bonetti;
200 AA/S McBride;
201 AA/A Mockford & N Bonetti;
202 AA/A Mockford & N Bonetti;
203 AA/C Sawyer;
204 AA/S McBride;
205 AA/S McBride;
206 AA/A Mockford & N Bonetti;
208tl AA/A Mockford & N Bonetti;
208tr AA/A Mockford & N Bonetti;
209 AA/A Mockford & N Bonetti;
210 AA/A Mockford & N Bonetti;
211 AA/A Mockford & N Bonetti;
212 AA/A Mockford & N Bonetti;
213 AA/A Mockford & N Bonetti;
214 AGF/Scala, Florence;
215bl directphoto.bz/Alamy;
215br Imagebroker/Alamy;
216 AA/C Sawyer;
217bl AA/A Mockford & N Bonetti;
217br AA/A Mockford & N Bonetti;
218 AA/C Sawyer;
219 AA/A Mockford & N Bonetti;
220 AA/S McBride;
221 AA/A Mockford & N Bonetti;
222 AA/S McBride;
224 Images Etc Ltd/Alamy;
226 Image 100
227 AA/A Mockford & N Bonetti;
229 AA/N Setchfield;

230 AA/A Mockford & N Bonetti;
234 AA/A Mockford & N Bonetti;
238 AA/C Sawyer;
239 AA/A Mockford & N Bonetti;
240 AA/S McBride;
241 AA/C Sawyer;
242 AA/C Sawyer;
243 AA/S McBride;
244 ImageState/Alamy;
245br CuboImages srl/Alamy;
246 AA/A Mockford & N Bonetti;
247 AA/A Mockford & N Bonetti;
248 AA/A Mockford & N Bonetti;
250 De Agostini/Getty Images;
252 AA/A Mockford & N Bonetti;
253 AA/A Mockford & N Bonetti;
256 AA/T Harris;
257 AA/A Mockford & N Bonetti;
258 AA/C Sawyer;
260 AA/A Mockford & N Bonetti;
263 AA/A Mockford & N Bonetti;
264 AA/A Mockford & N Bonetti;
268 AA/C Sawyer;
269 AA/A Mockford & N Bonetti;
270 AA/C Sawyer;
271 maurice joseph/Alamy;
272 AA/A Mockford & N Bonetti;
275 AA/A Mockford & N Bonetti;
276 AA/A Mockford & N Bonetti;
278 AA/C Sawyer;
280 AA/A Mockford & N Bonetti;
281 AA/C Sawyer;
282 AA/A Mockford & N Bonetti;
289 AA/A Mockford & N Bonetti.

CREDITS

Managing editor
Marie-Claire Jefferies

Project editor
Lodestone Publishing Ltd

Design
Drew Jones

Picture research
Carol Walker

Image retouching and repro
Jackie Street

Mapping
Maps produced by the Mapping Services Department of
AA Publishing

Main contributors
Sally Roy, The Content Works, Tim Jepson

Updater
Sally Roy

Indexer
Marie Lorimer

Production
Lorraine Taylor

Published by AA Publishing, a trading name of AA Media Limited, whose registered office is
Fanum House, Basing View, Basingstoke, RG21 4EA. Registered number 06112600.
A CIP catalogue record for this book is available from the British Library.

ISBN 978-0-7495-6761-3

KeyGuide is a registered trademark in Australia and is used under licence.
Colour separation by AA Digital Department
Printed and bound by Leo Paper Products, China

The content of this book is believed to be accurate at the time of printing. Due to its nature the content is likely to vary or change and
the publisher is not responsible for such change and accordingly is not responsible for the consequences of any reliance by the reader on
information that has changed. Any rights that are given to consumers under applicable law are not affected. Opinions expressed are for
guidance only and are those of the assessor based on their experience at the time of review and may differ from the reader's opinions based
on their subsequent experience.

We have tried to ensure accuracy in this guide, but things do change, so please let us know if you have any comments at
travelguides@theAA.com.

A04823
Mapping produced from map data © New Holland Publishing (South Africa) (Pty) Ltd 2009
Weather chart statistics supplied by Weatherbase © Copyright (2005) Canty and Associates, LLC
Transport map © Communicarta Ltd, UK

Find out more about AA Publishing and the wide range of travel publications and services the AA provides by visiting our website at
theAA.com/shop

Thank you for buying this KeyGuide. Your comments and opinions are very important to us, so please help us to improve our travel guides by taking a few minutes to complete this questionnaire.

You do not need a stamp (unless posted outside the UK). If you do not want to cut this page from your guide, then photocopy it or write your answers on a plain sheet of paper.

Send to: **KeyGuide Editor, AA World Travel Guides**
FREEPOST SCE 4598, Basingstoke RG21 4GY
Email: **travelguides@theaa.com**

Find out more about AA Publishing and the wide range of travel publications the AA provides by visiting our website at theAA.com/shop

ABOUT THIS GUIDE

Which KeyGuide did you buy? ....

Where did you buy it? ....

When? ....month .... year

Why did you choose this AA KeyGuide?
☐ Price ☐ AA Publication
☐ Used this series before; title
☐ Cover ☐ Other (please state)

Please let us know how helpful the following features of the guide were to you by circling the appropriate category: very helpful (VH), helpful (H) or little help (LH)

Size	VH	H	LH
Layout	VH	H	LH
Photos	VH	H	LH
Excursions	VH	H	LH
Entertainment	VH	H	LH
Hotels	VH	H	LH
Maps	VH	H	LH
Practical info	VH	H	LH
Restaurants	VH	H	LH
Shopping	VH	H	LH
Walks	VH	H	LH
Sights	VH	H	LH
Transport info	VH	H	LH

What was your favourite sight, attraction or feature listed in the guide?

Page.................Please give your reason ....
....

Which features in the guide could be changed or improved? Or are there any other comments you would like to make?

....

ABOUT YOU

Name (Mr/Mrs/Ms)..

Address ....

....

....

Postcode... Daytime tel nos...

Email...
Please only give us your mobile phone number/email if you wish to hear from us about other products and services
from the AA and partners by text or mms.

Which age group are you in?
Under 25 ☐   25–34 ☐   35–44 ☐   45–54 ☐   55+ ☐

How many trips do you make a year?
Less than1 ☐   1 ☐   2 ☐   3 or more ☐

ABOUT YOUR TRIP

Are you an AA member?   Yes ☐ No ☐

When did you book?.............. month................. year

When did you travel?............. month................. year

Reason for your trip?   Business ☐   Leisure ☐

How many nights did you stay? ....

How did you travel?   Individual ☐   Couple ☐   Family ☐   Group ☐

Did you buy any other travel guides for your trip? ....

If yes, which ones?..

Thank you for taking the time to complete this questionnaire. Please send it to us as soon as possible, and
remember, you do not need a stamp (unless posted outside the UK).
AA Travel Insurance call 0800 072 4168 or visit www.theaa.com

VENICEs in the KeyGuide series:
Australia, Barcelona, Berlin, Britain, Brittany, Canada, China, Costa Rica, Croatia, Florence and Tuscany, France,
Germany, Ireland, Italy, London, Mallorca, Mexico, New York, New Zealand, Normandy, Paris, Portugal,
Prague, Provence and the Côte d'Azur, Rome, Scotland, South Africa, Spain, Thailand, Venice, Vietnam,
Western European Cities.

The information we hold about you will be used to provide the products and services requested and for identification, account administration,
analysis, and fraud/loss prevention purposes. More details about how that information is used is in our privacy statement, which you'll find
under the heading "Personal Information" in our terms and conditions and on our website: www.theAA.com. Copies are also available from us
by post, by contacting the Data Protection Manager at AA, Fanum House, Basing View, Basingstoke, Hampshire RG21 4EA.

We may want to contact you about other products and services provided by us, or our partners (by mail, telephone, email) but please tick the
box if you DO NOT wish to hear about such products and services from us. ☐

AA Travel Insurance call 0800 072 4168 or visit www.theaa.com

Contents

Preface to the Sixth Edition

Since the last edition of this book was published in 1991 there has been a greater range of changes in the NHS in the UK than at any other time since its inception in 1948. In addition, for the first time the Government published a strategy document which discussed the main preventive health aims of the next decade – the White Paper *The Health of the Nation*. This important initiative is essentially preventive in its concept – it concentrates on how to reduce the incidence and mortality of those diseases and accidents which, in the last 20–25 years, have become the most serious and threatening.

The changes in the structure and functioning of the NHS have also been widespread and now affect every professional in the health services, and especially nurses. All changes inevitably result in much uncertainty which quickly can reduce staff morale.

The aim of this new sixth edition is to provide all nurses working in the NHS and in training with a readable and up-to-date description of the changing preventive health problems in the UK and internationally and to give, at the same time, a detailed description of the more important recent advances in preventive health. In this context, special attention has been given to illustrating how altering the lifestyles of people can be equally effective as therapeutic and nursing advances. Such changes are crucial if the increase of some conditions like ischaemic heart disease, many cancers, mental illness, suicide and HIV infections and AIDS are to be reduced or halted.

As the complexity (and cost) of investigation, treatment and care continues to rise dramatically in hospitals, it is becoming clear that more care in future will have to be carried out within the community while the patient remains at home. Such a development will be bound to affect all primary health teams in general practice. The preventive role of practice nurses, health visitors and district nurses in such teams is becoming pre-eminent and this trend will increase. Most GPs are now concentrating upon clinical work in their surgeries with patients being encouraged to come there for advice. As this trend develops, less home visits will be carried out by GPs and it will fall to the practice nurses and their colleagues to carry out home visits. *This means that nurses in the future will influence the prevention of illnesses and accidents to a greater extent than ever before.* At the same time, many practice nurses will be appointed who have, in the past, had limited training in preventive health methods. One of the main aims of this edition is to help by providing practice nurses and their colleages with a clear description of the new structure and functioning of the NHS and of the principles of preventing illnesses and accidents.

Any nurse involved in preventive work in the community also needs to know the role of the local personal social services who provide so much help and support to children in need and their families, to those who have to care for mentally disordered relatives at home, to those who support and help chronically disabled persons and their families and also to give assistance to the ever increasing numbers of elderly people in the community.

The format of the book remains the same – Chapters 1–14 cover the health services and 15–22 the social services. There are 2 new chapters on 'Health Audit' (Chapter 2) and on 'Strategy for Health' based on the White Paper '*The Nation's Health*' (Chapter 11).

It is now certain that in the next 30–35 years the problems facing the NHS will intensify. There are two reasons for this:

- demographic changes which are rapidly occurring in the population and especially the rapidly increasing proportion of very old people (those over 85). In 1994 this figure is 1 in 59 but this will rise to 1 in 49 by year 2000, to 1 in 42 by year 2011, to 1 in 38 by 2021 and to the dramatic level of 1 in 29 by 2031. These figures were published by the OPCS in early 1994. This change will inevitably produce massive extra problems for the NHS as persons over 85 will always require some support and surveillance however fit or prosperous they might be. Most of these problems will have to be solved within the community and in the person's own home. It is here that the role of the *practice nurse, district nurse and health visitor* will become so important together with other members of the primary health care team;
- the dramatic improvements in the treatment and prognosis of many serious diseases which means that more people who previously died quickly from such diseases will now survive. However many of these will still require a great deal of continuing care and support which the NHS and social services will have to provide.

Chapter 1 on the structure of the NHS describes in detail the new approach which within the NHS differentiates between the 'providers of health care' (hospitals and community health services) and the 'purchasers' of such health services (GPs who are fundholders and the DHAs for the smaller practices). DHAs now concentrate more on defining the detailed health needs of their area and each DHA now has a Director of Public Health who leads such studies.

Every health service should analyse carefully its results and then lay down exact criteria by which all types of health care can be judged and measured (health audit). The new Chapter 2 describes in detail how this should be done. There is a natural scepticism that it is almost impossible to measure and compare the results of health care in different areas fairly. There are pitfalls but such questioning is essential if a health service is to remain up to date and effective. It is the only way that it is possible to be certain that the service is still concentrating upon important current issues. Health audit can never be effective if carried out only by specialist statisticians: *it must involve all health professionals (especially nurses and doctors)*. Hopefully this new chapter will help nurses to understand and enjoy carrying out health audits.

Chapter 3, dealing with the measurement of health, contains much new material. Two special approaches have been introduced, illustrating the importance of:

• recognising trends;
• the effect of lifestyles on certain diseases especially ischaemic heart disease.

An interesting table is introduced showing the trends in 'avoidable deaths' which, in children, almost halved between 1979 and 1992 and have fallen to three-quarters in those aged 15–64 over the same period. Ischaemic heart disease is still very high in the UK but a slow decline has begun. Full details are given of the important effect 'lifestyles' can have on the incidence of this condition.

One of the most dramatic recent falls in mortality has been recorded in *sudden infant death syndrome* – from 1190 deaths in 1989 to 456 in 1992. Full details of this advance are given in Chapters 3 and 5. The steady fall in infant mortality continues but unfortunately there is still great inequality throughout the country. The best areas show a level of 4.1 per 1000 but the worst are double that – in the central areas of the cities of Manchester, Bradford and Birmingham. Social class differences are still marked, with Classes I and II having the lowest mortality.

The chapter on maternity services includes a note on the recent research which demonstrated the importance of folic acid intake by pregnant mothers in preventing the subsequent development of a neural tube defect in the baby. Full details are given in Chapters 4 and 14. Details are also included of the latest Confidential Report into Maternal Deaths for the years 1988–90. Although such deaths have now reached a very low level, still almost half would never have occurred if some mistake had not taken place. The study again showed that errors were connected with lack of adequate antenatal care. However a special further problem was a lack of experience – junior staff rather than consultants being left to deal with emergencies. In particular, five deaths from haemorrhage occurred after elective Caesarian sections for placenta praevia compared with none in the previous 3 years (1985–7). This report recommended that at all such future operations, a consultant should always be present and that written protocols for the management of massive haemorrhage should always be available.

Chapter 5 now includes more details about *child health surveillance (CHS)*, which is increasingly being carried out in general practice. All nurses working with children should keep up to date with new CHS techniques for they represent some of the more important preventive health initiatives. In addition, this chapter gives details of the dramatic reduction in the levels of sudden infant deaths in the UK.

Immunisation still remains one of the most effective ways to prevent certain serious diseases. Target payments introduced in 1990 have raised the percentages of children protected to over 90% in most instances. In 1992, Hib vaccination was introduced and full details of this procedure are given in Chapter 7.

Chapter 8 reviews the current position of communicable diseases. MMR vaccination has already shown that measles may eventually become very rare. But as one group of communicable diseases recede others increase. This is happening for example with tuberculosis where from 1987 to 1992 the numbers of cases in the UK increased by 10%. The relationship between AIDS and higher tuberculosis levels is now unmistakeable. For instance in some areas in Africa there is now an epidemic of tuberculosis. This emphasises the importance of all nursing and medical staff in the UK making certain that they have BCG vaccination if sensitive, and that they check their own health by having periodic chest X-rays.

This chapter also contains more on listeriosis with full details of the foods which vulnerable persons (pregnant women and immunosuppressed adults) should avoid eating.

In Chapter 9, it is pointed out that HIV infection is becoming an increasing threat in the UK and the world. It is essential for *all nurses (and doctors) to understand the trends of this infection* (which in most cases is the precursor of AIDS).

Three very serious features are now becoming clear:

- women are being infected as much as men;
- infection is spreading from the high risk groups (i.e. homosexuals) to the general population;
- the proportion of people now acquiring HIV infections through heterosexual sex is rising rapidly – by 1994 in the UK it is at least 50% and by 2000 is expected to be 85%.

Because of the very long incubation period between HIV infection and the development of clinical AIDS, similar increases in AIDS are likely to follow.

Also in this chapter, it is pointed out that hepatitis B is becoming very serious for all nurses (and doctors) as, if they become carriers, their jobs will be at risk. Such staff, *if they become a carrier, now have an absolute duty to report this fact to their employer. Failure to do so is likely to lead to them being accused of serious professional misconduct.* Note that while the carrier rate of hepatitis B in the UK is only about 0.1% (1 in 1000), in Africa and the Far East it is already 20% (1 in 5). Any nurse who is visiting such countries (even for a holiday) *should always be immunised against hepatitis B before they leave the UK.*

The section on ischaemic heart disease in Chapter 10 has been extended to emphasise the importance of an individual's lifestyle in the prevention of this disease. Reference is also made to the recent evidence showing how effective emergency treatment given by ambulance personnel and paramedics can be. It is now clear that skilled use of defibrillators and modern resuscitation methods can reduce immediate mortality considerably.

Many WHO advances are described in Chapter 13. These include efforts to reduce maternal mortality in the Third World and to concentrate on improving health services for the mentally disordered. Malaria still remains a major problem, particularly because of the development of drug resistance. Oral rehydration has proved to be an effective practical method to reduce mortality from diarrhoeal diseases. As mentioned above, tuberculosis is increasing rapidly in Africa because of the large numbers of AIDS patients. In Europe, the experimental oral vaccination of foxes against rabies has proved so successful that it has been extended to many countries.

Since 1991, many changes in social services (see Chapter 15) have mirrored those in the NHS. Community care social services now have a high priority while quality assurance units have been set up in social services departments to ensure that all social care is effective – these checks cover social services provided by local authorities, voluntary bodies and the private sector.

There is now a division within social services into the 'providers' who are mainly those providing residential services for children, physically disabled persons, mentally disabled people and elderly persons as well as day centres of all types, home helps and meals and transport services, and the 'purchasers' who are mainly the social workers and other professional staff who assess the needs of individuals, sort out priorities and then arrange for help to be provided. More and more of the providers are now in the voluntary and private sectors, particularly in the residential fields for children (see chapter 16), care of mentally disordered persons (Chapter 19) and especially in the care of elderly persons (Chapter 20). The degree of change is dramatically illustrated in Table 20.2 which indicates who now provides residential places for elderly people – in 1992 only 30.3% were provided by local authorities compared with 60.2% in 1983 whereas the private sector is now responsible for 56.4% compared with 24.5% in 1983. These changes are complex and this means that *there is now a greater need for close and effective liaison between the social services and the NHS.*

In Chapters 16–22, many new features are included. In 1992 the Disabled Living Allowance replaced the Attendance and Mobility Allowances for those under the age of 65. It has two parts – a care element and a mobility element. A new third group may now qualify and a medical examination is usually not required.

The individual can now receive financial help after 3 months (formerly 6 months) but if the qualifying cause is a terminal illness, help can be obtained immediately. It is crucial for nurses to understand that any patient who may qualify and is around the age of 65 *must make a claim immediately* If they delay it may be too late and if they would have qualified for the mobility element, they may have lost this for the rest of their life. Any person developing a qualifying disability after the age of 65 can still claim the Attendance Allowance.

Chapter 19 on the care of mentally disabled persons has been completely rewritten with much new information including details of the extended community care services and of the new Supervised Discharge introduced in 1993 which is intended to make the discharge of potentially dangerous patients from mental hospitals safer.

The chapter on care of elderly persons contains many new topics of special interest to nurses including firstly the findings of a research study by Taylor and Ford in Aberdeen which showed that the groups of old people at greatest risk were those who:

● were over the age of 80;
● had been recently discharged from hospital;
● had recently moved home.

The first two of these groups will continue to increase during the next decades because of the demographic changes already mentioned and because of the growing need to reduce the pressure on hospital beds. This trend will further add to the problems of nurses working in the community.

Secondly there is an extended section on dementia in elderly persons. Recently some fascinating studies on dementia have been published showing that 5–7% of persons aged 65 and over suffer from some dementia. The incidence of Alzheimer's disease rises rapidly after age 60 and may be up to 20 times greater over the age of 80. Such an incidence emphasises the future problems to be faced as the proportion of persons aged 85 and over doubles in the next 35 years. The fundamental differences between Alzheimer's disease and the acute confusional states are explained in detail. It is becoming more important for nurses (and especially for those working in the community) to understand the diverse causes of acute confusional states which are usually found in persons over the age of 80. Many of these have relatively simple cases (such as dehydration, certain medicines and drugs which at this age need their doses to be reduced, common infections, hypoxia, etc.). Once the cause is remedied the confusional state immediately clears up – this is in contrast to Alzheimer's disease which is slowly progressive and for which at present there is no effective treatment. The correct diagnosis of an acute confusional state depends more on the acute observation by professionals caring for the patient, and nurses therefore are in one of the best positions to make the correct diagnosis at an early stage and thus to remedy the problem promptly.

Once again I would like to thank my wife for all her constant encouragement and patient help at so many stages of this edition – with the typing of the script and proof reading.

Brian Meredith Davies

1 The structure of the health services in the United Kingdom

Before discussing the various parts of the hospital, community and preventive health services, it is important that the structure of the health services in the United Kingdom is fully understood.

The National Health Service (NHS) was first introduced in 1948. Since then there have been many major and minor changes made in the way the NHS is organised. The general principles however have remained the same – a fully comprehensive health care service should be available to all the UK population *with no large extra cost at the time such care is required*. There are a number of small financial contributions required for prescriptions, eye testing, provision of spectacles, dental care, etc. but these are not required for certain age groups or for those in social need.

Organisation of the NHS

The latest large-scale organisational changes followed the passing of the National Health and Community Care Act 1990 which became fully operational in 1992 when also, for the first time in the history of the NHS, the Government published a 'strategy for health' in a White Paper called *The Nation's Health*. As it is easiest to appreciate the main reasons for this strategy after a full description of the NHS and public health and preventive medicine has been given in this book, the White Paper *The Nation's Health* is described in full detail in Chapter 11.

The main changes introduced by the National Health and Community Care Act 1990 included the following:

- *financial changes* which enabled the health services to make new contracts which are aimed at a better matching of money resources and the provision of health care. These changes also introduced the concept of a clear division between the 'providers' of health services (the hospitals, and community units) and the 'purchasers' of health care, usually GPs either acting as a General Practice Fund Holder or through the District Health Authority (DHA).

The objective of this change apart from hoping to provide a better match between 'providers' and 'purchasers', is to make the health services more competitive. This has often been referred to as 'the internal market' within the NHS;

- the establishment of *self-governing NHS hospital trusts* (see p. 12);
- the setting up of *General Practice Fund Holders* for the largest general practices;
- more control over prescribing in general practice by introducing *annual indicative budgets* for all GPs (see p. 25):
- an extension of the management principles originally introduced by the Griffiths report. This is mainly within the Regional and District Health Authorities;
- large-scale changes in the organisation of the Regional Health Authorities (RHAs) and DHAs (see pp. 9, 10). At the same time a new body – the Family Health Service Authority (FHSA) – was created which is now accountable to the RHA and which replaced the former Family Practitioner Committee which had reported directly to the Department of Health;
- *short-term contracts* for some senior staff;
- changes in general practice including *compulsory retirement of GP principals at age 70* (see p. 20) and allowing part-time doctors to act as principals (see p. 20).

Functions of the Secretary of State for Health

The Secretary of State for Health has full responsibility for the health and personal social services, is a member of the Cabinet, and is directly responsible to Parliament. The duties of the Secretary of State for the local authority social services are described in Chapter 15.

In the health field, the Secretary of State for Health must provide, to the extent which he or she considers necessary, the following services.

- hospital accommodation;
- medical, nursing and ambulance services;
- dental services;
- facilities for the care of expectant and nursing mothers;
- facilities for the prevention of illness and aftercare of persons either recovering from various illnesses or still suffering from some chronic condition. These include vaccination and immunisation and physiotherapy and occupational therapy services;
- such other services which are required for the diagnosis and treatment of illness including full pathological, bacteriological and blood transfusion services;
- school health services in conjunction with Local Education Authorities;

- family planning services;
- health education;
- advising and cooperating with other Government departments such as the Home Office, Department of Education and Science and the Ministry of Agriculture, Fisheries and Food.

There are a number of Standing Advisory Committees (such as the Standing Advisory Committee on the Prevention of Disease by Immunisation) to which the Secretary of State may refer various specific problems. There is also a Select Committee of Parliament to look into health matters and which reports to the Secretary of State and Parliament. Recent examples of such reports include those issued on community care for the mentally ill and those with learning disabilities (formerly called mental handicap), misuse of drugs, and primary health care funding in the NHS. The Public Accounts Committee of Parliament also examines all expenditure incurred in the NHS to ensure that proper use is being made of resources.

The Secretary of State also periodically sets up an Expert Committee or Inquiry to advise on a specific health or social service topic which may have caused national concern. An example of this was the Inquiry into child sexual abuse in Cleveland in 1987–8 under Lord Justice Butler-Sloss. This type of Committee or Inquiry collects evidence from various sources, studies that evidence and recommends a course of action. In the Lord Justice Butler-Sloss Inquiry its recommendations were later enacted in the Children Act 1989 (see p. 306).

In addition to these expert committees, the Secretary of State has a large staff of experts to advise him or her, based at the Department of Health in London and locally in various regional offices. Centrally such civil servants work under *the NHS Policy Board* which *advises on strategy and policy in the NHS*, and *the NHS Management Executive*, which is a committee of nine professional experts who are concerned with the efficient running and control of the NHS.

Parliamentary control

Because the Secretary of State is answerable to Parliament for the conduct of the NHS, it is always open to any Member of Parliament to raise a question, however detailed, and this must be answered by the Secretary of State either verbally, at question time, or in writing.

In very serious instances, the Secretary of State can set up an Inquiry or Committee which then considers all aspects of the query and later reports to the Secretary of State who then presents that report to Parliament. A further method of control was introduced in 1975 by the creation of a Health Commissioner for England and a separate one for Wales (see p. 29).

Administration of the NHS

The simplest way to understand the functioning of the NHS is to examine the plan of its administration, as shown in Fig. 1.1.

The main organisation of the NHS was radically altered in 1991. Before this, there was a hierarchical management structure from Department of Health (DH) → RHAs → DHAs for all hospital services and community health services, with the local control being at DHA level. GP services, dental services, pharmaceutical and optical services were then organised by Family Practitioner Committees which reported directly to the DH. Figure 1.1 shows the latest organisation, which is based on an entirely different approach in which there are two main arms to the NHS: the 'providers', who in the main *provide hospital and community care*; and the 'purchasers', who are the services which use the hospital and community health services (the GPs and the Primary Health Care teams), who need these services for

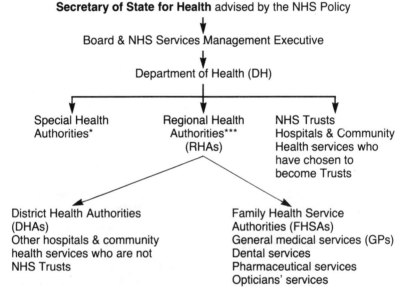

Secretary of State for Health advised by the NHS Policy
Board & NHS Services Management Executive
Department of Health (DH)

Special Health Authorities*

Regional Health Authorities*** (RHAs)

NHS Trusts Hospitals & Community Health services who have chosen to become Trusts

District Health Authorities (DHAs) Other hospitals & community health services who are not NHS Trusts

Family Health Service Authorities (FHSAs) General medical services (GPs) Dental services Pharmaceutical services Opticians' services

* Special Health Authorities include the Health Education Council, Postgraduate Teaching Hospitals in London, NHS Training Authority, Special Hospital Authority (Ashworth Hospitals North and South, Broadmoor and Rampton Hospitals)
*** RHAs
Note Community health services include ambulances, district nursing, midwifery, health visiting, family planning, chiropody and dietetics.

Fig. 1.1   The organisation of the NHS following recent reforms introduced by the National Health and Community Care Act 1990.

their patients, for it is to GPs and Primary Health Care teams that the general public first turn in the NHS.

There are many reasons for these radical reforms, but the main ones are to improve the efficiency and effectiveness of the hospital and community health services to enable them to meet the ever-increasing demand for health care, which results from the following:

- the demographic changes which are likely to occur in the UK in the next 30 years, and especially the expected rapid rise in the proportion of the population over the age of 85 (see p. 372);
- the considerable improvements in the treatment and outlook of many serious diseases such as cancers, heart and vascular conditions which formerly in many instances resulted in early death of the patient. This has meant that there is now a higher proportion of people who are living longer and many of these will make heavier demands on the hospital and especially on the community health services in the future;
- the complexity of many hospital treatments and their increasing costs also makes it more important that in future they should always be used effectively and in the closest conjunction with the community and GP services.

The new type of organisation is also designed to be less restricted by geographical barriers (the GP fund holders are free to send their patients to any hospital) and this will give doctors and nurses more freedom and hopefully stimulate more initiatives and reduce bureaucracy.

The 'providers'

One of the more important and crucial changes in the organisation of the hospital services within the NHS has been the creation of the *new NHS Trusts* which, in future, will increasingly run and develop NHS hospitals and some of the community health services. These bodies are completely independent of the RHAs and DHAs and are accountable directly to the DH (see Fig. 1.1). They are self-governing and have a number of new freedoms. Each Trust is run by a Board of Directors who determine their own management structure, employ all their own staff and set their own terms and conditions of service. These Trusts can own and sell their assets, retain any surpluses and can borrow money within annual limits agreed by the DH.

NHS Trusts have been created for:

- hospitals;
- community health services including district nursing, health

visiting, midwifery, family planning, chiropody, dietetics and nursing home registration;
- ambulance services.

The first NHS Trusts were created in 1991 with a second wave in 1992 and a third in 1993. They have proved popular with staff mainly because they provide more freedom, specialisation and more flexibility. Now the majority of large hospitals are run by a single NHS Trust. They are far less encumbered by geographical constraints and are in a better positon to meet local needs.

Note that it is important to understand that until the transfer of all hospitals to NHS Trusts is completed (and this is not likely until 1996–7) DHAs will still have to manage directly any hospitals or community health services which have not yet changed from DHA control to NHS Trust control. In this respect, DHAs will still, for the time being, have to act as both the 'providers' and the 'purchasers', but generally, their responsibility as 'providers' of hospital services will be a diminishing one.

The 'purchasers'

GPs in the NHS represent the main group of 'purchasers'. The 1990 Act created a new and relatively independent group of GPs – the General Practitioner Fund Holders (GPFHs). Any practice with at least 9000 patients can apply to become a fund holder. If accepted, such a practice is then able to purchase much of its hospital care from specific hospitals. Acute emergencies are excluded from the arrangements. This scheme has proved popular with GPs and already three waves of fund holders have been appointed, in 1991, 1992 and 1993. Doctors who work in small practices still have to depend on DHAs to provide their hospital care but it is likely they will join together, with other small practices to become fund holders (see p. 25).

Interim period

The interim period during which more and more fund holders are being appointed is likely to be confusing to nurses and other staff. As the number of NHS Trusts appointed and the numbers of GPFHs rises, the DHA's role as a 'provider' will diminish.

Family Health Service Authorities (FHSAs)

FHSAs, who manage the contracts of GPs, dentists, pharmacists and opticians, are the third group of NHS authorities who have had their duties and responsibilities changed by the NHS and Community Care

Act 1990. Not only do they have a new name (formerly they were called the Family Practitioner Committee), but they are now *accountable to the RHA directly and not to the DH.*

FHSAs now have the following additional duties to carry out:

- to assess the health needs of the local population and to develop GP, dental, pharmaceutical and optical services to meet those needs identified. In carrying out this assessment FHSAs must work closely with the local DHAs who are also checking the health needs of the district;
- to plan and to provide GP, dental, pharmaceutical and optical services for the district;
- to assist RHAs to introduce the Fund Holding scheme.

Hospital and community health services

Regional Health Authorities

Up to April 1994 there were 14 RHAs in England, but from that date these were reduced to eight following a radical merger of many of the former RHAs. The geographical distribution of the new RHAs is shown in Fig. 1.2. These RHAs are:

- **North West** incorporating the former North Western and Mersey – population 6.42 million;
- **North East and Yorkshire** made up of the former North and Yorkshire – population 6.78 million;
- **South Thames** consisting of the former South West Thames and South East Thames – population 6.74 million;
- **North Thames** incorporating the former North West Thames and North East Thames – population 7.36 million;
- **East Anglia and Oxford** made up of the former East Anglia and the Bedfordshire DHAs – population 5.09 million;
- **South West** consisting of the former South Western and Wessex – population 6.28 million;
- **Trent** (unchanged) – population 4.72 million;
- **West Midlands** (unchanged) – population 5.27 million.

This alteration in the make up of the RHAs is the first change in moves to reduce bureaucracy in the NHS, with the Secretary of State announcing that the money saved will be used to improve patient care. The second stage will be in 1996 when the new RHAs will be abolished and will become *regional offices of the NHS Management Executive.* Further details about the second stage have not yet been announced.
The main responsibilities of the RHAs include:

- planning and monitoring the functioning and performance of the DHAs and the FHSAs;
- implementing the reforms of the NHS and especially the creation

Fig. 1.2   National Health Service Regions in England (in 1996 will become regional offices of the NHS Management Executive). **1** North West, **2** North East and Yorkshire, **3** South Thames, **4** North Thames, **5** East Anglia and Oxford, **6** South West, **7** Trent, **8** West Midlands.

of the NHS Trusts and the General Practitioner Fund Holders in conjunction with the FHSAs;
- the development and control of the contracts between 'providers' and 'purchasers' including reconciliation in disputes over such contracts;
- the allocation of resources to each DHA and FHSAs;
- the development of a regional plan for specialist services and especially deciding the best location for the rarer specialities within the region (such as chest surgery, radiotherapy, neurosurgery, etc.);
- ensuring, together with the DHAs and NHS Trusts, that there are adequate medical and dental teaching and research facilities within the region, including postgraduate teaching;
- the siting of blood transfusion units;
- the funding and training of non-medical staff, assessing the demand for training and generally ensuring that there is an adequate supply of staff;
- making certain that the new competitive approach in contracts between 'providers' and 'purchasers' does not disturb priorities for the provision of essential amd emergency health services or the availability of such essential care throughout the whole region
- for the time being, the RHAs will continue to manage the capital building programme for the DHAs which still manage some hospitals and community health services (i.e. those which are outside the control of the NHS Trusts); however as more and more Trusts are formed, RHAs will mainly concentrate upon *strategic planning and the monitoring of the provider/purchaser reforms.*

The structure of each RHA

Each RHA consists of:

- a chairman who is appointed by the Secretary of State;
- five non-executive members one of whom must be a chairman of one of the FHSAs in the region and someone from a medical or dental school in the region;
- up to five executive members including the Regional General Manager and the Director of Finance of the RHA.

Note that including the chairman there will always be a majority of members outside the health professions on the RHA. Doctors, nurses and other health care staff usually form the executive members.

Senior staff of the RHA

There is a Regional Team of Officers headed by a Regional General Manager (RGM) and including a Director of Finance, Regional Medical Officer (RMO), Regional Nursing Officer (RNO) and Regional Works Officer. Each RGM is responsible for the development of strategic plans and priorities for the region and for the allocation of financial resources to the DHAs and FHSAs. The RGM is also responsible for the NHS building programme (although the detailed control will increasingly be undertaken by the NHS Trusts). The RGM must set out clear objectives for each of the District General Managers (DGMs) and monitor their performance.

District Health Authorities

There are 192 DHAs in England. The arrangements in Scotland, Wales and Northern Ireland differ and are described separately (see pp. 27–29). DHAs eventually will be affected by the reforms introduced in 1991 more than any other organisation within the NHS. Before 1991, DHAs were the main providers and managers of hospitals and community health services, but by 1994 much of this work has been taken over by the developing NHS Trusts. DHAs continue to manage some hospitals and community services outside the Trusts, but this work is likely to diminish in the future.

The future main task of the DHAs will be to act as purchasers for GPs who are not GPFHs. In addition DHAs will:

- assess the local district population's need for hospital and community health services;
- monitor the effectiveness of the health care which hospitals and community health services provide;
- negotiate contracts for hospitals for GPs who are not GPFHs to use;
- monitor the functioning of such contracts;
- assess and evaluate the services provided by hospitals, define and refine the standards of such care by which these can effectively be measured; every effort should be made to develop *numerate output measurements* – in other words to test the results of local hospital and community services by numerical methods rather than just by measuring the amount of work undertaken.

In carrying out all these duties, DHAs should always work closely with local authorities, and especially with those large local authorities which provide personal social services, for these bodies are in charge of widespread community-based social services for elderly persons, those who are mentally disordered and for people who suffer from chronic physical disabilities.

Community health services

The community health services which are either under the control of DHAs or the developing NHS Trusts include:

- maternity and child health services;
- health visiting;
- vaccination and immunisation (although the majority of these are now undertaken directly by GPs in their own practices);
- prevention of disease, care and after care – these include health education, chiropody, some occupational therapy in the community, tuberculosis after care and some types of convalescence;
- school health services (in conjunction with the corresponding Local Education Authority – see Chapter 6).

Structure of each DHA

Since 1991, the numbers of members in a DHA have been reduced to a maximum of 11, including:

- a chairman;
- five non-executive members;
- five executive members who must include the DGM and the Director of Finance.

Officers of the DHA

The most senior officer in a DHA is the DGM; he or she is assisted by Unit General Managers (UGMs) for those hospitals and community health services which are still run directly by a DHA (i.e. those that have not yet been taken over by an NHS Trust). There is also a District Director of Finance, a District Medical Officer, a Director of Public Health and two clinicians and hospital consultant and one GP).

Director of Public Health

This post was created in 1988; its main duties include:

- the provision of epidemiological advice to the DGM and DHA to enable them to plan preventive health services and to evaluate their effectiveness;

- to develop policies with special reference to the prevention of illness, health promotion and health education;
- the surveillance, of the levels of non-communicable diseases in the district and its environmental health problems;
- the surveillance, prevention, treatment and control of communicable diseases in the district;
- the publication of an annual report for the DHA which is a public document and is available to the public generally.

NHS Trusts

NHS Trusts are self-governing and are run by a Board of Directors who are accountable to the Department of Health (see Fig. 1.1). Each Trust has the responsibility of managing and running hospitals and/or community health services locally. These Trusts have wide freedoms. However each Trust must prepare an annual plan which outlines their proposals for developing the hospital and community health services as well as their plans for capital development. The Department of Health must either accept them or, by agreement, modify them. Every NHS Trust must *prepare an Annual Report and generally work within the framework of the NHS*. All NHS Trusts are also accountable to the Secretary of State whose eventual control in the event of a serious dispute would be to dismiss the Trust and appoint a new chairman and members.

Each NHS Trust has a chairman and up to 10 other members. The main responsibilities of the Trust are:

- to determine the overall policies of the Trust;
- to monitor the carrying out of those policies;
- to maintain financial responsibility for the health services under their control.

All NHS Trusts receive their income from the 'purchasers', who are either GPFHs or the DHAs.

Aims and objectives of the NHS Trusts

The main aim in setting up the NHS Trusts was that, with their greater freedom, the Trusts should be in a better position to improve standards in the hospital and/or community health services locally. It should be easier for them to introduce innovations within the local health services as the NHS Trusts will no longer be constrained by the need to obtain agreement from the DHA and RHA before any radical changes could be decided and implemented.

The NHS Trusts are still accountable to the Secretary of State so that limitations on their decisions and actions can still be maintained. Whether or not this new opportunity to improve the health services locally succeeds will largely depend on the ingenuity and drive of the professional staff in the hospitals and community services. The doctors, nurses and managers will all have a particular role to play in developing and improving services as they will be in an excellent position to suggest innovations and then to persuade the NHS Trust Directors to support their introduction.

Joint care planning

Many of the personal social services run by large local authorities can have an important impact on the local health services, and vice versa. Generally these social services provide much of the supporting community care for very vulnerable groups. The success of the present trend to develop more effective community care for elderly persons (and especially for those over the age of 80 years), for many of the mentally disordered people and for those who are seriously disabled and handicapped depends to a large extent on the local social services developing comprehensive supportive care. These supporting services include day centres, workshops, homes and hostels and all other forms of community care such as home helps and meals-on-wheels. To make certain that the balance of both the health and social services complement each other, the Department of Health has decided that there should be a number of effective local *Joint Care Planning Teams* drawn from officers of the DHA and officers from the local Social Services Department.

These teams are made up of professionals from both services – doctors, nurses and managers from the hospitals, GPs from the primary health care services, health visitors from the community health services and social workers and managers from the local authority social services. The recommendations of these Joint Care Planning Teams are then discussed by the Joint Consultative Committee (see below) and their decisions are sent to the DHA and local authority Social Services Committee and eventually to the Department of Health. In this way, it is expected that there should be a more balanced and coordinated development locally.

Two types of these Joint Care Planning Teams have been developed:

- *permanent teams* who deal with
  — children
  — maternity services
  — mentally ill persons
  — those with learning disabilities
  — elderly persons;

- *'ad hoc'* teams set up to study a special subject and then make recommendations; such teams cover a wide field and recent examples include:
  - a review of primary health care;
  - day surgeries in local hospitals;
  - establishment of day centres for mentally ill persons;
  - local drug and alcohol problems;
  - diagnosis, treatment and prevention of child abuse.

Joint finance

Because many community care problems can only be solved if extra finance is made available, a system of 'joint financing' has been introduced by the Department of Health. In this scheme, finance from the health service has been transferred from the local health budget to enable selected social services to be funded. This is usually arranged over a 7 year period but with some mentally ill persons being discharged from hospital finance is provided in this way for a longer period. The justification for this scheme is that it benefits the health services in the long term because the need for long-term hospital care is reduced. An equally useful and valuable feature is that it is usually a much more satisfactory solution for the patient.

Joint Consultative Committees

Every DHA and the matching local authorities must set up a Joint Consultative Committee (JCC) which has the responsibility of advising on the planning and operation of the health services and the social, environmental and education services run by the local authority. The aim of these committees is to improve coordination between the various services.

Community Health Councils

There is approximately one *Community Health Council* for each area of a DHA. Their main functions are to represent the local consumers' interests and to ensure that the development of the local health services takes regard of local opinion and concerns. Each Community Health Council contains 18–30 members, one third of whom are drawn from voluntary bodies that are active within the district. About half the members are appointed by the corresponding local authority and one-sixth by the RHA which provides the permanent staff. No member of the RHA, DHA or FHSA, nor any doctor or nurse or other NHS employee may serve on a Community Health Council. The Community Health Council can investigate the following matters:

- the effectiveness of the health services in that district;
- the planning of the health services locally;
- variations in local health services and the closure of hospitals or specific hospital departments;
- collaboration between the health services and local authority environmental education and social services;
- standards of service including the number of hospital beds in the district and the average numbers of patients on GP lists;
- patient facilities including out-patients, open visiting of children, waiting times, amenities for hospital patients and arrangements for rehabilitation of patients;
- waiting periods for in-patient and out-patient treatments and for domiciliary services;
- quality of catering in hospitals;
- general complaints from patients only.
- advice to individual members of the public on how and where they should lodge a complaint and the facts that should be provided.

Each Community Health Council must issue an annual report which is sent to the RHA, DHA and FHSA and also to the local public libraries to provide an opportunity for the local people to maintain a careful watch over the health services in the district.

General practitioner services

A special authority called the Family Health Service Authority (FHSA) is responsible for all matters concerning GPs, the pharmaceutical services and general ophthalmic services (local opticians). The FHSA is accountable to the RHA (see Fig. 1.3). All these professionals (including the GPs) are independent contractors and hold contracts with the FHSA. Each FHSA consists of a Chairman and 10 members all appointed by the Secretary of State. The General Manager of the FHSA is automatically a voting member and there are also four professional members – a GP, a dentist, a pharmacist and a community nurse.

There are 100 FHSAs in England, 15 in Scotland, eight in Wales and three in Northern Ireland. Their duties include:

- administering locally the GP, pharmaceutical and general ophthalmic services;
- supervising the registers for GPs choosing to undertake additional services (maternity services, child health surveillance, minor surgery and contraception services);
- monitoring and auditing the behaviour of GPs;
- allocating funds to GPs and supervising indicative prescribing budgets (see p. 25);

- setting up a Medical Audit Advisory Group for the area to support and monitor the health audits of the local practices;
- inspecting practice premises;
- holding the contracts of the GPs who are GP Fund Holders and checking their budget expenditure;
- assisting practices in the introduction of information technology (including the installation of computers in practices) – there can be up to a 50% grant paid towards the cost;
- informing the public of the GP services available locally;
- dealing with complaints from patients.

Medical list

Each FHSA must keep a list of all GPs in the area, and this must indicate those who undertake maternity services, child health surveillance, minor surgery and contraceptive services. This list is readily

Fig. 1.3 Organisation of the Regional Health Authority and Family Health Services Authority.

available to the public at the local FHSA headquarters and at main post offices.

The public have a completely free choice of doctor and the doctor can decide whether or not to accept any patient on his/her list. Once a patient has been accepted, the doctor is required to render all proper and necessary treatment. If the doctor had agreed also to supply any of the additional medical services outlined above, then the treatment to be given will include all such services and the doctor will receive additional remuneration for that extra work. Every GP is responsible for ensuring adequate medical cover during the doctor's absence on holiday or sickness.

If any patient has difficulty in finding a doctor to accept him or her, an application can be made to the *Allocation Committee*, a subcommittee of the FHSA, which will then allocate the patient to a convenient doctor. There are facilities for a patient to change their doctor if they so wish or for a doctor to indicate that he/she no longer wishes to look after a particular patient.

Information to patients

The FHSA must provide within its Medical List (see above) the following information to patients about each practice and doctors:

- the date of first registration of the doctor;
- the sex of the doctor;
- details of the medical qualifications of the doctor;
- the nature of any clinic provided by the doctor for the patients;
- the number of assistants and trainees employed by the doctor;
- the number of persons employed or available at the practice;
- the average hours worked by each person;
- if the doctor so desires, details of any language other than English spoken by the doctor or other person employed in the practice.

Practice leaflet

All GPs must publish a *practice leaflet* which should provide the following information for patients:

- names and addresses of the doctors in the practice, their sex and the date of their first registration;
- the times when the doctors are available for consultation and how appointments can be made;
- how to obtain an urgent or non-urgent visit;
- the method of repeat prescriptions;
- details of staff and their roles at the practice premises;

- whether practice nurses/nurse are employed;
- how to contact the community nurse, midwife and health visitor;
- details of other health services available in the practice such as immunisation sessions, ante-natal clinics, maternity services, cervical smear tests and how these can be arranged, child health surveillance and minor surgery (if these are undertaken);
- arrangements for the staff to receive patients' comments on the provision of services undertaken in the practice;
- an indication of the practice areas normally covered. Usually the doctor will only agree to provide medical services for those persons living within the practice area but may accept patients from outside in certain circumstances;
- details of the surgery premises and whether they provide access for handicapped persons and for wheelchairs;
- whether teaching of GP trainees and/or students takes place.

Additional medical services provided by some GPs since 1990

Child health surveillance (CHS)

Provided the GP has certain qualifications or has substantial experience of the running of a CHS clinic or has recently worked in a paediatric department and is prepared to undertake at least 2 half-day training sessions every 3 years, he/she can apply to the FHSA to be recognised as qualified to undertake regular CHS sessions in the practice (this is controlled by special DH regulations). CHS involves a monitoring process on children under the age of 5 years. This is carried out by a series of examinations of the child at a number of sessions at spaced intervals to check that the progress of the child is normal (see p. 97).

Minor surgery procedures

GPs who are likewise trained in this work and have had experience in minor surgical procedures can apply to the FHSA to be recognised to undertake the following:

- injections
    - intra-articular
    - peri-articular
    - varicose veins
    - haemorrhoids
- aspirations
    - joints
    - cysts

- bursae
- hydrocoele
- incisions
  - abscesses
  - cysts
  - thrombosed piles.

Extra fees are paid by the FHSA for all these services.

Medical examinations of newly registered patients

GPs are expected to undertake a medical examination of all newly registered patients (aged 4 years and over) within 3 months of registration. A full medical history should be carried out, and other factors that should be discussed are the lifestyle of the individual including the use of tobacco, diet, exercise, consumption of alcohol, etc. Other family and social circumstances such as employment, housing, etc. should also be touched upon as well as enquiring from the person whether there are any particular worries at the time.

The offer of a physical examination should also be made and, if carried out, a record made of the findings, including weight, blood pressure and urine testing and the results entered into the patient's records. Any significant findings should of course be discussed with the patient as well as any particular problems raised.

Subsequent regular medical examinations

These are always useful, especially for patients aged 75 and over. Practice nurses can often carry out the initial visit, especially in very old people for a visit to the patient's home can often be very useful as an indicator of how such an individual is managing. This is especially important in very old persons living alone. In people over the age of 85 years it is helpful to check the following:

- sensory functions;
- mobility;
- mental condition;
- physical state including any incontinence;
- social environment – the state of the home gives a good indication as to how well the individual is managing;
- use of medicines; in particular, it is always essential to check certain medications that are permanently being used as *in patients over the age of 75–80* some can easily produce acute confusionary states unless the dosage is reduced (see p. 379).

Distribution of GPs and size of doctors' lists

Special arrangements have operated within the NHS since its inception to ensure that generally there is a fairly even distribution of GPs throughout the UK. A *Medical Practices Committee*, set up by the Secretary of State nationally, is constantly assessing the numbers of GPs in different areas. It then classifies each area into one of four types.

- *Designated area* – this is an area in which there is a shortage of GPs. Doctors are encouraged to practise in such an area and will receive a special inducement payment.
- *Open area* – this is a district with a fair number of GPs where the doctor: patient ratio is between 1: 2100 and 1: 2400. Permission will always be granted to practise in such an area.
- Intermediate area – This is an area where the doctor: patient ratio is between 1:1700 and 1:2100. Applications to practise in such a district will never be granted automatically. Each application is considered on its merits with special reference to the trends in the area.
- *Restricted area* – this is an over-doctored area where the number of patients per doctor is less than 1700. Permission is never granted to start a practice in such an area and entry can only be granted by applying for a vacancy or partnership or assistantship.

Any doctor wishing to start a new practice must first apply to the FHSA.

Age limit for all GPs

Since 1991, all GP principals whether working full time or part time have to retire from NHS practice when they reach the age of 70.

From 1991, for the first time, GPs who only work part time in general practice can act as principals in the NHS. Three groups can be included:

- those doctors working 26 hours a week or more but less than full time;
- those working 19–26 hours a week;
- those working 13–26 hours a week.

It is hoped that this change will encourage women with families to return to general practice once their families have grown up, thus strengthening the services.

Vocational training

Every GP principal must now have completed a 3 year approved training scheme in which the trainee undertakes suitable hospital posts including general medicine, paediatrics, obstetrics and gynaecology, geriatrics, psychiatry and accident and emergency. There is also a compulsory 1 year training in general practice, usually spread between different types of practice.

Methods of controlling general practice

The main local method of controlling general practice is through the *Local Medical Committee*. This consists of a committee of doctors which acts as the local medical advisory committee to the FHSA. Any difficulties with a particular practice or with local policies are first referred to the Local Medical Committee who then advises the FHSA. If a doctor is considered by the Secretary of State to be prescribing excessive drugs and appliances for his or her patients, the Local Medical Committee has the task of carrying out an investigation. If, as a result of their inquiry, the committee comes to the conclusion that there has been excessive prescribing, then they must report the case to the FHSA which may then recommend the Secretary of State to withhold a certain sum from the remuneration of the doctor as a penalty. Such action is rarely taken without a warning first being given to the doctor.

Other similar expert committees help with the administration of the other services, for example:

- Dental Services Committee;
- Area Chemists Contractors Committee for the pharmaceutical services;
- Ophthalmic Services Committee.

Investigations of serious complaints raised by patients about the services provided by GPs

A special *Medical Services Committee is appointed by the FHSA* to investigate any serious complaint raised by a patient about the services provided by his or her GP. This consists of the Chairman of the FHSA plus six other members, three of whom must be from the Local Medical Committee. There is a set procedure laid down for the investigation of such complaints. Minor complaints are first investigated by the General Manager of the FHSA and major complaints by the Medical Services Committee. The hearing is always in private and the doctor's name is never made public. The Medical Services Committee reports its findings to the FHSA which then sends its decisions on to the Secretary of State. The doctor may also appeal to the Secretary of State. In the case of a proved complaint, the doctor may be warned, have a special limit as to the number of patients on his or her list imposed, or have a sum withheld from his or her remuneration. There is no appeal beyond the Secretary of State, whose decision is final.

In very serious cases, the FHSA can refer the case to a central *Tribunal* set up by the Secretary of State with a Chairman who is a barrister or solicitor of at least 10 years standing. The Tribunal holds an inquiry and, if satisfied that the case is serious enough, can order the removal of the doctor from general practice in the NHS. In such a case, there is an appeal to the Secretary of State. This is quite different from action by the *General Medical Council* which can determine the fitness *of any doctor to practise in any field.*

Charges to patients

There is no additional cost to the individual patient in obtaining medical care from hospitals or from the GP. However for some patients there are *prescription charges*. Over 80% of all prescriptions are free either because of the age of the patient or because of their medical or social condition. The following groups receive free prescriptions:

- children aged 16 years or under and young persons under the age of 19 in full-time education;
- women aged 60 years and over and men aged 65 years and over;
- expectant and nursing mothers who have had a baby during the past 12 months;
- those in receipt of Income Support or Family Credit;
- patients suffering from certain medical conditions including epilepsy, diabetes (which is either being treated with insulin or drugs), diabetes insipidus, myxoedema, hypoadrenalism (Addison's disease), myasthenia gravis, permanent fistulas and any physical condition that prevents the patient from leaving their home.

Recent changes which are designed to encourage more effective preventive medicine in general practice

Since 1990, special payments for cervical cytology, childhood immunisations and for booster immunisations at age 5 have been *linked to a minimum percentage achieved within the practice.* No payments are made below the minimum value and a higher payment is made if the top level is reached. The childhood immunisation target payments are made for all children aged 2 years on the first day of each quarter. To qualify, the child must be fully immunised (three doses for diphtheria, tetanus, poliomyelitis and pertussis, and one dose for measles, mumps and rubella or for measles alone). Any child who has been immunised at a local clinic outside the practice will count towards the target but not for payment of the immunisation. This method of encouraging high immunisation rates is based on the finding that to achieve any effective prevention, at least 70% of the child population must be immunised. However almost complete eradication of the disease will only follow if over 90% of children are immunised.

A similar principle is also used to encourage GPs to increase their numbers of cervical smears undertaken – no fees unless 50% of the 25–64 year old women in the practice (21–64 in Scotland) have an adequate smear test within the previous 5.5 years. Smears taken outside the practice count towards the target but not towards payment. The higher rate of payment is paid if at least 80% of women within the practice have had a smear test.

Target payments

	Higher	Lower
Cervical cytology	80%	50%
Child immunisations	90%	70%
Pre-school booster	90%	70%

Health Promotion Clinics and Chronic Disease Management Programmes

In the White Paper *Health of the Nation* which was published in 1992, the concept of *key strategies* and *preventive health targets* for the UK was introduced (see Chapter 11).

The Department of Health has indicated that it hopes to achieve these improvements gradually in a number of ways but especially by encouraging GPs and their primary health care teams to do more preventive health work. Health Promotion Clinics were first introduced in a few pilot schemes and, in 1993, a contract was agreed between the Department of Health and the BMA to start nationwide *Health Promotion Clinics* and *Chronic Disease Management Programmes*.

General practices have been invited to start this preventive work. The main aim is to develop this preventive work gradually and a flexible programme has been agreed. The system devised has three bands and this will enable practices to start their health promotional work at whatever level is appropriate to their practice and their area. As any practice develops its programmes, it will, in future, be able to progress from one band to the next. The three bands initially introduced in 1993 are:

- Band 1 – programmes to reduce smoking prevalence in the practice population.

- Band 2 – programmes to minimise mortality and incidence in individuals who are at risk of hypertension or who already have established heart disease.
- Band 3 – programmes offering a full range of primary prevention of coronary disease and stroke including those at special risk. These factors are discussed in detail in Chapters 9 and 10 (see pp. 184 and 211). Also under Band 3, Chronic Disease Management Programmes have been agreed for diabetes and asthma.

National criteria for this work have been published by the Department of Health and practices wishing to undertake this preventive work must first apply to the FHSA and, if approved, will qualify for the payment of a special fee.

It is expected that as this preventive drive is established in general practice, the range of health promotional work will be extended to include other key health prevention targets as outlined in the White Paper.

Deprivation area payments

Since 1990, because research has consistently shown higher levels of preventable disease among areas of population which suffer from many social problems, special extra *deprivation area* payments have been paid to practices which work in such districts. It was hoped that such payments would stimulate more preventive work in these 'at risk' groups. The system is based on local political wards (postcode sectors) and was devised by Prof. Barry Jarman. It considers eight different variables:

- old people living alone
- children aged under 5 years
- single parent households
- unskilled people
- unemployed persons
- overcrowded houses
- persons who have recently moved households
- ethnic minority households.

Using these eight variables, a '*Jarman Index*' has been defined and a score in excess of 30 qualifies an area to be classified as a '*Deprivation Area*' and the doctors practising in it to receive an extra payment.

It is interesting to note that 9.1% of the population in England and Wales live in such areas but in Scotland 11.4% of the population qualify. This confirms the finding that the degree of social deprivation is higher in Scotland.

Any nurse working in a community which mainly serves such areas should realise that there is a greater need for more preventive health work there than in better off districts to counter the detrimental effects of the living conditions in such areas.

Practice budgets for GPs

One of the more interesting innovations introduced in 1990 has been that the largest practices (those with more than 9000 patients) can become *General Practice Fund Holders (GPFHs)*. Such practices are then given their own budgets to manage which are expected to cover the cost of:

- *hospital services* – to cover the cost of all hospital treatments, (except emergency work) including in-patient care, out-patient investigations, diagnostic tests and day care;
- *prescribing costs* – to cover the costs of all drugs and appliances prescribed for patients in the practice;
- *community nursing services* used by the practice patients;
- some of the *practice staff costs*.

This revolutionary scheme has been gradually introduced since 1991–2 for large practices which wish to become GPFHs. Grants have been made available to cover the management and preparation costs. This includes the total cost of introducing computers into all such practices (whose use in such a scheme is essential and 75% of the software costs).

To become a GPFH, an application must first be made to the FHSA who administers the scheme. Once agreed, each practice is allocated a budget which it is expected to keep within. An overspend of up to 5% is permissible but this amount will be deducted from the next year's budget. Any overspend in excess of 5% will be investigated and may result in the practice ceasing to be a GPFH.

Indicative drug budgets

In an attempt to reduce prescribing costs, a new system of control has been introduced. The FHSA provides each practice with a computerised breakdown of their prescribing costs. For GPFHs these must be met from their budgets. For other practices, doctors are appointed by the FHSA to oversee the prescribing and to visit those practices which do not hold their own budgets. In all practices, unusual treatments which cost more than £5000 are exempted and adjustments made – for GPFHs additional costs above £5000 per year are paid by the RHA and for other practices are accepted as reasonable. If however a practice continues to prescibe excessively and inappropriately, the FHSA still has the right (as has always existed) to withhold some of the doctor's remuneration. Such action is rarely taken, a warning first being given to the doctor.

General nature of medical services offered

A general practitioner working in the NHS must render to his or her patient all necessary and appropriate services of the type usually provided by family doctors. These include:

* giving advice where appropriate in connection with the patient's general health, and in particular about the significance of diet, exercise, the use of tobacco, the consumption of alcohol and the misuse of drugs;
* offering consultations to patients and, where appropriate, physical examinations for the purpose of identifying, or reducing the risk of injury or disease;
* offering to patients, where appropriate, vaccinations and immunisations against measles, mumps, rubella, pertussis, poliomyelitis, diphtheria and tetanus;
* arranging for the referral of patients, as appropriate, for the provision of any other services under the National Health Service Act 1977;
* giving advice, as appropriate, to enable patients to avail themselves of services provided by the local authority social services.

A doctor is not required to provide to any person contraceptive services, child health surveillance or minor surgery services unless the GP has agreed to undertake and has been accepted by the FHSA to provide such services.

A part-time principal (see p. 20) is only required to provide those medical services which he or she has agreed to undertake.

Annual reports

Since 1991, each practice must submit an annual report to the FHSA by the end of June each year. Such a report must include reference to the following:

* details of all non-medical staff within the practice, their qualifications and training in the previous 5 years;
* any changes in the practice premises since the last annual report;
* details of all referrals to hospital specialists classifying them as either in-patients or out-patients and their clinical specialty;

- the number of patients who reported directly to hospital (mainly to Accident and Emergency departments);
- details of the doctors' medical commitments outside the NHS practice plus the number of hours taken up by such work annually;
- arrangements made for patients to make comments (which are recorded) to the doctors or to other practice staff on the provision of general medical services;
- information about orders for drugs and appliances and details of the arrangements made for repeat prescriptions.

Health audit in general practice

Since 1990, as in all other branches of the NHS, GPs and their practices are expected to carry out continuous health audits to identify various problems, to set priorities and standards of medical care and later to check whether these standards have been reached. Chapter 2 deals in detail with all types of health audit.

NHS in Scotland, Wales and Northern Ireland

Generally the same principles apply to all NHS services in Scotland, Wales and Northern Ireland. There are however small differences and these are now described.

Scotland

The Scottish Home and Health Department is responsible to the Secretary of State for Scotland for the administration of the NHS in Scotland. Its head office is at New St Andrews House, Edinburgh.

There are 15 local Health Boards in Scotland which administer on behalf of the Secretary of State for Health Services in Scotland (other than those carried out by the Common Services Agency – see below). These Boards take major policy decisions such as the allocation of resources and the long-term planning of the services.

A Board General Manager (BGM) is in executive charge of each Board. Their responsibilities are roughly similar to those of the District General Managers in England but the BGM has more specific authority for public accounting. Unit General Managers have been appointed in Scotland but many of these posts are part-time. Each Board also has a Chief Administrative Medical Officer whose main task is the identification, measurement and coordination of medical care.

The Secretary of State for Scotland is responsible to Parliament and there is a Scottish Health Service Planning Council set up to advise the Secretary of State on:

- the identification of health priorities in relation to the resources available and the necessary measures to meet them;
- the implementation, review and evaluation of health planning in Scotland's national health services;
- the integration of health care with other kinds of care to ensure a coordinated policy for the treatment of people in need.

To assist the Council in these tasks, it has set up a number of advisory groups.

An interesting difference in Scotland is that a central body – the Common Services Agency – has been set up to provide on behalf of the Secretary of State and the Health Boards a range of specialised services which are more effectively organised on a national basis, including the ambulance and blood transfusion services, the buying of all equipment and other supplies, the planning and design of all health buildings, legal services and health education. Responsibility for the administration of these services in Scotland rests with the Common Services Agency (appointed by the Secretary of State) whose head-quarters are at Trinity Park House, Edinburgh and which also has a number of separate units including the Scottish Health Services Council, the Scottish Health Education Unit, the Communicable Diseases (Scotland) Unit, the Central Legal Office of the Health Services in Scotland and the Information Services Division.

In addition there are the following:

- A series of *local area consultative committees* to advise the Health Boards on the provision of services in their area. These represent doctors, dentists, pharmacists and ophthalmic and dispensing opticians and advise on all professional matters.
- *University liaison committees* which advise on undergraduate and postgraduate teaching and on research.
- A series of 48 *local health councils* which represent the 'consumer' interests of patients.

In the Scottish health services, much emphasis has been placed on integration of services for patients and not only at senior management level. Services are planned mainly to meet the needs of patients and to make the best possible use of the staff, money and physical resources. Teamwork in all aspects of the health services is stressed as well as the involvement of doctors and clinical workers in management matters.

Wales

One of the main differences in the health services between England and Wales is that there is no regional tier of health authorities in

Wales. The Secretary of State for Wales has overall responsibility for the health services in Wales, is accountable to Parliament, and has four main duties:

- to determine the health policies for Wales;
- to allocate resources between the nine DHAs in Wales;
- to ensure that the objectives of the services are achieved;
- to make certain that the standards of the health services in Wales are satisfactory.

There are nine DHAs in Wales: Dyfed, Clwyd, Gwent, Gwynedd, Mid Glamorgan, Powys, South Glamorgan, West Glamorgan and West Dyfed. These DHAs are responsible to the Secretary of State for Wales for all the day-to-day health services (with the exception of those carried out by the Welsh Health Technical Services Organisation – see below).

District and Unit General Managers operate in Wales and have similar responsibilities to their counterparts in England.

The *Welsh Health Technical Services Organisation* is directly accountable to the Secretary of State for Wales and has three main functions:

- the designing and building of all major hospitals and other capital works for the health services in Wales;
- the control and running of a central computer service for the health services in Wales;
- the negotiation of all central supply contracts in Wales.

Northern Ireland

A unified structure exists in Northern Ireland which is outside local political control and deals with all the health services and social services. At provincial level, the Department of Health acts as a government agency and is responsible for the policies and the allocation of resources. There are four Boards and each has a General Manager who is personally accountable to the Board for the effective and efficient use of services for patients and clients. There is also an Area Executive Team of chief officers and clinicians which includes a consultant and a GP.

Health Service Commissioners

Health Service Commissioners for England and Wales were introduced in 1973 to investigate complaints against the relevant health authorities. Both these Commissioners are only removable on an address to both Houses of Parliament and their salaries are paid directly by the Treasury (out of the Consolidated Fund). They are therefore in the same independent position as High Court Judges. The main function of these Health Service Commissioners is to investigate the following:

- an alleged failure in a service provided by a relevant health authority such as the RHA, DHA, FHSA, Public Health Laboratory Service Board or any special body appointed before and after 1 April 1974;
- an alleged failure of a relevant body to provide a service which it was a function of that body to provide;
- any other act taken by or on behalf of a relevant body in a case where it is alleged any person has sustained an injustice or hardship in consequence of the failure or of maladministration.

It is most important to note that the Health Commissioners are specifically excluded from dealing with the following:

- professional complaints against decisions of individual doctors or nurses in regard to individual patients;
- any action which is dealt with by the Tribunal (see p. 22);
- any complaint which is subject to an action in a court of law.

2 Health audit

An important new concept within the NHS which was introduced with the passing of the National Health Service and Community Care Act 1990 is that all professional staff in the NHS should regularly carry out health audit.

Health audit has been defined as a *continuous and formal method of studying and assessing the results of health care with the objective of constantly improving the quality of population and individual patient care*. All nursing and medical staff have of course been concerned with assessing their treatments and with keeping them up to date so that the best and most effective patient care can always be given. From time to time, such staff have gone on special postgraduate training courses with this in mind. Indeed some nurses such as midwives can only legally practise if they have attended such a course in the last 5 years.

These praiseworthy efforts to keep up to date and to improve health care are however quite different from formal health audit, which attempts the following:

- *to lay down explicit criteria by which patient care can be judged and measured*. A simple example might be the waiting time patients on average have to spend before they can obtain an operation. It is known that such times vary widely throughout the NHS. What are the reasons for this? If one hospital can arrange a hip replacement operation within 2 months how can it be justifiable for other patients to have to wait 1½–2 years?
- *to study all aspects of health care and to develop wherever possible numerical measurements of patient care so that fair and accurate comparisons can be made*. This entails very careful analysis of many factors which can affect health care and to measure them in precise and carefully defined terms. For instance, it is of very little value to compare the mortality after certain operations unless it is clear that *the same type of cases are being compared*. Therefore in all cancer treatments an important factor is *the stage of the disease when treatment started*. Generally the earlier the diagnosis was made and treatment commenced the better the results are likely to be. Such an audit might suggest that it would be worthwhile investigating why one hospital generally diagnoses and starts

treatment earlier than another hospital. The next crucial question which follows is what can be done to remedy this inequality of health care? The correct answer can only be found after considering many quite different factors including some that are outside the hospital completely and even outside the remit and management of the NHS.

Health audit, which is now being carried out throughout the NHS, should emphasise such local differences and help persuade staff of the need to be flexible and to be prepared to change patterns of health treatments and care to meet local needs. In the past, most such studies and investigations have been carried out in specialist departments (such as those dealing with nursing or medical teaching and research). It is hoped that in future all branches of the NHS will become involved through the health audits which they will be undertaking and as a consequence there will eventually be a significant improvement in the health of the nation.

All health audits should include a clear statement of the action required to remedy the various health problems identified.

Health audit should be a regular commitment and carried out annually in every hospital, community health care services and general practice. Different aspects of health audit should be undertaken each year as such a programme enables a good assessment to be made of whether earlier changes introduced have resulted in a real improvement. If not, then the question arises – what further alterations are required? In this way health audit can become a continuous reappraisal process aimed at steadily introducing various improvements into the services and then assessing their value.

How to measure the results of patient care in all health services

All health audit soon comes up against many difficulties but one that is constantly found is how to evaluate the medical and nursing services. So often one hears that all that is needed are more financial resources and/or trained staff. This may be true but it certainly does not follow that just providing these services will cure all the problems. The real test is whether the changes actually introduced result in:

- less incidence of the disease in question;
- less mortality;
- help for those sections of the community who are at greatest risk.
  In the preventive field, it is of course a truism that often those at greatest risk are the least likely to take advantage of the preventive procedure because they either do not understand what should be

done (i.e. come forward to take part in some screening preventive method such as cervical cytology) or because they are too forgetful.

In the past, the main basis for improving the health services has been to recruit more staff and/or to provide better equipment. Then success has been measured by demonstrating that more operations have been carried out or more diagnostic procedures undertaken, etc. But this is really only demonstrating an increase in the work that has been carried out and although that may well be very helpful it does not necessarily lead to better patient care. It may be that the extra work is not helping to solve the problem first identified. A true advance will only follow if the new and improved methods *lead to an improvement in the health of the person or of the community being looked after locally.*

'Outcome' and 'input' measurements

To make certain that all NHS staff realise how important it is to *measure the results of medical care in terms of true improvements in health* rather than just demonstrating that more health work has been undertaken, *health audit has concentrated upon differentiating between 'outcome' measurements and 'input' ones.*

An 'outcome' measurement is a clear indication that the health of an individual or a group of persons or community has been improved in some way. This can mean that the disease in question has had its incidence clearly reduced or that the treatment results are obviously much better because the mortality and chronic invalidism from the condition have significantly fallen over a period of time. Occasionally this is very obvious – when poliomyelitis vaccination was widely introduced in the late 1950s, the number of poliomyelitis cases fell dramatically from many hundreds annually (in an epidemic year from many thousands) to single figures for the UK with epidemics completely disappearing. Obviously with such an effective preventive measure it then follows that the greater numbers of persons immunised, the fewer cases are likely to result. But it is still important to check that the numbers of cases of poliomyelitis remain at a tiny level (an 'outcome' measurement), for if a series of batches of vaccine were used which were ineffective the number of immunisations carried out (an 'input' measurement) would cease to be a useful indicator of the prevention of this disease.

Another example was the introduction of hip replacement for serious degenerative arthritis of the hip. Before this had been developed persons with such a condition lost their mobility and were in constant pain. After the procedure for hip replacement had become widespread such patients' prospects were completely changed – they lost their pain and maintained their mobility. As judged by the 'outcome' measurement of pain and mobility the introduction of hip replacement was correctly accepted as a great advance.

A further example is given by an ophthalmic surgeon carrying out a programme of lens replacement operations for cataract. If the surgeon reported that he/she had replaced the lens in 50 patients in 2 months, then that statement is strictly an 'input' measurement. If however the report stated that the sight of 50 persons had been greatly improved by carrying out lens replacement operations on 50 persons, then that statement is a 'outcome' measurement. Although superficially the two statements may seem to be the same, they are not because the first is just a record of what work had been carried out while the second also indicates that *the results had been extremely successful* and had clearly achieved the main objectives of the work.

In the past, most health services have been routinely assessed using a series of 'input' measurements, such as:

- how many hospital beds are there?
- how many consultants and nurses are working in certain specialties?
- how much is being spent on the NHS?

Although these statistics are important, it is essential to concentrate more on *the effect of the various health services*. As soon as this becomes accepted, another advantage is likely to follow – it becomes clearer that *more emphasis must be given in the future to all forms of preventive health*. A good example is ischaemic heart disease, the incidence and mortality of which rose rapidly in UK and many developed countries from 1950 to 1980 (see p. 51). Many treatment improvements including more intensive care units were introduced during this period but the incidence continued to rise although the rate of increase in the mortality had slowed down. It was only when *the causes of this increase in incidence and mortality* were finally worked out and more emphasis was placed on how to prevent ischaemic heart disease that a significant decline started. This advance involved persuading more members of the general public to change certain features of their lifestyles (see p. 184), and therefore to avoid factors that are likely to increase the incidence of ischaemic heart disease.

Priorities among NHS services

Within the NHS, one of the more difficult problems that health audit has highlighted is not deciding what improvements are needed but *which should be given priority*. It is never easy to work out a logical system of priorities, mainly because there are so many conflicting needs. Another problem is connected with the fact that the composition of the population requiring health care is constantly changing. The most important demographic change now occurring in the UK is that the proportion of very old persons aged 85 and over is expected to rise dramatically from the present time until at least the year 2031. All health and social services are bound to come under much more pressure just because anyone of that age requires more health and social care, and a further factor is that at least a third of this age group live on their own.

The development of effective 'outcome' measurements in the NHS will undoubtedly help to determine priorities on a logical basis, and this is especially important because *the main aim of the NHS should be to make certain that health care is freely available to those in greatest need.* If any section is failing to obtain health care then the NHS is failing in one of its most important objectives. Because of this aim, the NHS has a special responsibility to ensure steps are taken to correct any inequalities of health care and effective health audit will always emphasise this point and tend to develop health care services more logically.

An excellent example is cancer of the cervix uteri in women and smear testing. When it was first demonstrated that these tests were of great value as they *identify those women who are at high risk* (the test shows a pre-cancerous stage enabling immediate treatment to be given *before the cancer develops*), great steps were taken to increase the smear testing nationwide. A 'league table' style of results of the number of smear tests carried out was published to stimulate backward areas to increase their testing (an 'input' measurement). As these rose all seemed well, and the numbers of cases of cervical cancer slowly fell until further research demonstrated that this fall in mortality of cancer of the cervix uteri was very unequal throughout the community; deaths from this condition were 6.5 times less common in Social Class I than in Social Class V (see p. 63). This difference was partly due to different lifestyles in these social classes, but made far worse by the fact that far fewer women in Social Class V have cervical smear testing. This meant that just concentrating on counting the number of smear tests did not give an accurate measure of the preventive work being undertaken. What was required was special work to persuade women in Social Class V to come forward for smear testing. When this was carried out, mortality began to fall more quickly.

Structure of health audit

To carry out health audit successfully, there are a number of stages which always should be undertaken. This is usually illustrated as a cycle which starts by carefully *analysing all aspects of the health work being examined.* The next stage is to agree the *standards of service* which should be aimed at. Then a decision must be made on the *changes and improvements required to reach the new standards.* The final stage is the *carrying out of these changes and then observing and analysing their effect* to see if the various problems and deficiencies originally found have been rectified. This cycle is illustrated in Fig. 2.1.

Ideally *all health audits should be a continuous process* with these stages being repeated annually. Because in practice most improvements rely on being able to finance them as well as recruiting and training any necessary extra staff, it is convenient to complete each stage at a set time each year. Then the whole audit programme can conveniently fit in with the annual estimates and with training schedules. In many instances, the implementation of changes may have to be spread over a number of years to enable the resources such as finance, staff and possibly new capital equipment and buildings to be arranged.

Setting of standards

The setting of standards is undoubtedly the most difficult part of any cycle of health audit. It should be a continuous process as standards of health care are always changing: what was accepted 10–15 years ago may today be totally inappropriate. Again it is usual to go through a cycle of stages in the setting of standards. These are illustrated in Fig. 2.2.

In an attempt to encourage the setting of standards, the Department of Health in the recent NHS changes has, for the first time, introduced numerical standards to be aimed at in some services. An example is the *target payments* for immunisations in young children and for cervical

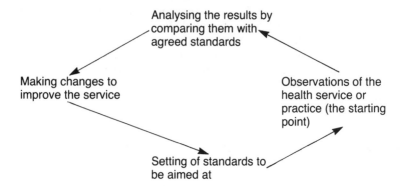

Fig. 2.1 Cycle of health audit.

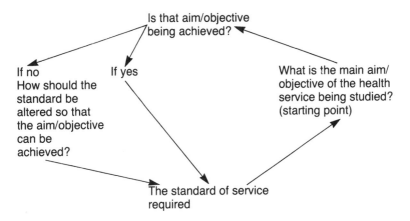

Fig. 2.2 The cycle used to set standards in any health audit.

smear testing in women carried out in general practice. The fees paid for such services are now linked to defined national standards as an incentive to improve these essential services (see p. 22).

The setting of standards will never be easy and most professionals tend to defer making them. Yet they are important for another reason: they force nurses and doctors to ask the vital question – *from whose point of view are the standards being considered*? The only correct answer must be that *the interests of any patient should always be paramount, although a balance must be held between the interests of the staff and the overall NHS.* The setting of standards always raises further difficult questions such as what should be the priorities between different types of patients, between the preventive and the therapeutic services, between emergency health services and those for acutely and chronically ill patients and between the various different age groups of patients.

It soon becomes obvious to anyone who understands the demographic changes rapidly occurring in the UK and especially the increasing proportion of very old people over 85 years of age in the population (see p. 372) that *the NHS will never have sufficient resources of finance, equipment and staff to meet every health demand.* Therefore priorities become very important to ensure that the available resources are used in the most effective way. This is where health audit is so valuable and one of the main reasons why, in 1991, it was introduced throughout the NHS.

Health audit in its very processes tests the health needs of the population and how effective the various health services in the NHS are at meeting them. Nurses and all other staff should realise that health audit is not just a complicated technical study which academic experts alone can understand and carry out. Audit has become *a crucial part of the daily life of all nurses wherever they work*. If patient care is to meet all its changing requirements, then those staff who are always closest to patients, such as most nurses, will be in the ideal position to see and appreciate what is going wrong and to suggest how practical improvements could be made.

Another important feature of health audit is that, in many instances, it is best if carried out in *multiprofessional teams or groups*, whether audit is taking place in general practice, in the community health services or in hospitals. In all these three areas of the NHS, nurses have a significant and vital role to play in developing effective ongoing audit.

Organisation of health audit in the NHS

The following have an active role in all health audit carried out within the NHS:

- all professional and managerial staff working in the NHS at all levels and parts of the service;
- the Royal Colleges and especially the Royal College of Nursing, the Royal College of Physicians, the Royal College of Surgeons and the Royal College of Obstetricians and Gynaecologists.
- the King's Fund who, since 1988, have specialised in this field (especially in the hospital services), and have published many useful reports and handbooks on different aspects of health audit;
- central Government, especially through the Audit Commission Health Advisory Service, and also the Joint Policy Advisory Group/Management Executive Unit within the Department of Health, who work on the development and application of health outcome assessment;
- many professional organisations including the specialist nursing bodies and the British Medical Association.

Types of health audit

The following are the main types of health audit constantly being carried out within the NHS:

- the *analysis and review of random selected medical and nursing records*. In all these, *complete confidentiality is essential*. In many instances, a short pilot study was first carried out and the results of this were used to determine the full audit that followed. Difficulties which have commonly arisen are often concerned with definition which must be precise and as specific as possible and always relevant to the agreed aim and objective of the audit. Wherever possible a *numerical scale of assessment* should be used to narrow down definitions and to make later comparisons more accurate;

- *detailed study of any health topic.* Such audits can either be *prospective or retrospective.* Both can be useful. The retrospective audit can be set up more quickly but is more limited in its scope as it has to rely on the form and quality of the nursing or medical records available for analysis. The prospective audit has one important advantage – it can make certain that the records are devised in such a way that they cover exactly what is being audited;

- *analysis of different nursing or medical statistics in different areas of the UK and in different socio-economic groups of the population.* Many of these have been kept in standardised forms for many years and therefore are useful *to study trends in the incidence of diseases or mortality.* Chapter 3 gives many examples of the types of statistics that have been recorded to date;

- *specific audits aimed at testing the effectiveness of the NHS services locally.* These types of audit are constantly being carried out throughout all sections of the NHS generally. They fall into three types.

  — *Those undertaken in hospitals.* These cover both in-patient and out-patient services as well as studies of waiting times. All possible health services undertaken in hospitals have had audits which have checked on all aspects from 1988 to 1994, so any nurse wishing to start such an audit should be able to find many helpful published reports which are likely to be very useful in the planning of the audit.

  — *Those undertaken in general practice.* The range of nursing and health audits already being undertaken covers all aspects of primary health care. Recent examples have included studies of clinical treatment and care for heart and stroke conditions, hypertension, anaemias, diabetes, thyroid problems, mental illness and many others. Prescribing costs have been extensively audited as have various *preventive measures* now being widely carried out in primary health care. These have included audits on immunisation and vaccination, cervical cytology, well person screening, breast feeding and screening for urological diseases. Much of this valuable audit work in general practice is undertaken by the *increasing numbers of nurses now working there either as practice nurses, health visitors or district/community nurses.* Many audits have already been carried out by nurses working in the community health services as health visitors, district nurses, etc., although today these nurses are usually attached to general practices and therefore it is convenient to classify most of their audit work under 'general practice'. The subjects covered by these audits are widespread and include child health, non-communicable disease control, maternity services and care of physically disabled persons and mentally disordered persons living in the community. Nurses still carry out much of the day-to-day audit work in the community care services and are therefore at the centre of all such audits.

— *Studies in 'patient satisfaction'.* This type of audit is relatively new, as originally most nurses and doctors expressed the view that any patient's individual comments on health care are bound to be biased and therefore should not be used as an outcome measurement. However later studies have shown this is not the case and that particularly in hospitals, relatively simple problems, such as excessive waiting times for appointments or in clinics and especially poor information being given to patients and relatives, can be the cause of much dissatisfaction. *Undoubtedly many professional staff, particularly doctors, suffer from a weakness in their communication with patients and relatives.* Recent audits have shown up some of these problems and, in many hospitals, steps have now been taken to remedy this. Certainly nurses should never forget that the absence of good communication can easily add to any patient's and family's anxiety and can impede recovery. Within general practice the development of the team approach has done much to improve communication and it is often the practice nurse who can play an important part in improving this problem. Certainly nurses in primary health care teams are often in an ideal position to assess whether patient satisfaction is at a high level and, if not, exactly why this is not so. Any good practice nurse will then bring this matter of patient dissatisfaction up at a primary health care team meeting, and this can often then be traced to lack of communication which, if quickly remedied, will certainly lead to a better quality of health care.

Educational elements of health audit

In most instances nurses and other professionals have found that the very process of carrying out health audit can soon become a learning process. This is true wherever the audit takes place – whether in hospitals, in the community or in general practice. Another benefit is that all records tend to improve, as in carrying out the audit nurses soon realise the value of good records.

Because audits usually involve to some extent a team approach, they often bring to the surface vigorous differences of opinion – even in senior staff – about the best ways of treating and managing certain medical and surgical conditions. The debate which then always follows is in itself an educational process, particularly for the more junior staff. This debate can provide a stimulating educational exercise within any NHS service and has proved very useful to staff at all levels, even the most senior.

Another advantage, particularly in a large hospital, is that many nurses work in highly specialised departments and in relative isolation from the mainstream work of the hospital. Most audits involve a team approach and this can become a powerful influence in improving the liaison between the different hospital departments and the nurses working within them.

Family Health Service Authority and health audits

So far much of the discussion in this chapter has focused on audits carried out in hospitals, community health services and general practices. There is however another aspect – audits undertaken by the Family Health Service Authority (FHSA). It is important that there is full coordination between different practices undertaking audit so that each can learn from the other and widen their own audits. A statutory committee which is called the *Medical Audit Advisory Group* (MAAG) is responsible for audits in the FHSA. It consists of 12 doctors most of whom are GPs plus a local consultant who is very active in audit work within the local hospitals. There should also be in the group a representative involved in local postgraduate education.

The main duties of the MAAG include:

- making certain that there are proper measures to ensure complete confidentiality in all local medical audits carried out in primary health care;
- providing a forum for discussion on any special problems which an audit in any individual practice may reveal;
- reporting to the FHSA at regular intervals on the general progress of health audit in these local practices.

In addition, the local MAAG may arrange for audits to be undertaken which *involve all doctors within the area of the FHSA*. Examples of such general audits that have been carried out include those calculating:

- the proportion of GPs in the area who have already established age and sex registers of all the patients in their practices;

- the numbers of practices that have set up disease management policies;
- the numbers of practices which have a computer operating;
- which practices have prescribing policies and general details about such arrangements.

The MAAG also provides the ideal forum for confidential discussions of the findings of audits already carried out in primary health care in the district and the consequential implications for all local general practices. The MAAG can also decide how best to arrange, if need be, for a skilled health audit coordinator to be appointed to assist general practices in their individual efforts to set up new health audits.

Role of nurses in health audit in general practice

All nurses in or attached to general practices have a very important role in much of the audit that is carried out there, and especially in the following:

- the *identification of problems*. These are varied; some of the commonest are connected with *accessibility* (whether patients can easily obtain help from the GP or nurse), the non-attendance after initial immunisations or follow-up examinations and why certain patients never seem able to understand their treatment instructions and therefore fail to carry out their treatments properly. Most of this audit work will be carried out by *practice nurses* (see pp. 97, 217), health visitors (see pp. 88, 97) or district nurses;
- *the setting of priorities*;
- *collecting information:* nurses have been very helpful in sorting out the best methods of collecting information about patients and then making certain that these methods are later used in various audits within their practices. This is important because the better the method of finding potential problems, at an early stage, the easier it is for any practice to sort them out;
- *the checking of standards.* This is always a very time-consuming and difficult part of any audit in general practice and a good practice nurse, health visitor or district nurse can be invaluable. A particular advantage which these nurses have is that they are more likely, in a modern practice, to be the staff who mainly undertake home visiting, and this is often the place where it is possible to see more easily the practical problems many patients and their families have to face;
- *checking that patients in disease management programmes carry out instructions correctly.* For instance, some practices have a programme which aims at ensuring that all hypertensive patients

have a medical check-up annually. In many such practices it is the nurse who usually follows up non-attenders;

- helping to make certain *that various preventive health targets are reached.* These include immunisations for children, cervical cytology testing, and also checking up that all women aged 50–65 years, if possible, have a mammography test regularly. Practice nurses and health visitors are ideally placed in their home visiting to check that women are taking advantage of these valuable screening tests;

- ensuring that *family planning is available* to those who need it. This is especially important in those practices with a high proportion of their patients in Social Classes IV and V. In many cases the only certain way to ensure that family planning techniques are properly understood is for a nurse to visit the home to discuss with the mother or person at risk of an unwanted pregnancy. In the relative privacy of their home, this is often more effective than trying to explain these matters in a busy clinic or surgery.

A well organised and intelligently planned series of health audits in general practice can soon become an effective way to introduce preventive health work into a busy general practice. *In this respect, the role of the nurses working in the primary health care team in the practice is paramount.*

3 The measurement of health

The measurement or assessment of the health of a community is an important part of any preventive health programme. Rarely is it possible to attempt to carry out all the desirable preventive health work at once. Therefore it is essential to be able to determine the *top priorities* which should be the first health problems to be tackled. It is also very useful to be able to compare the health of, say, one city or country with another. Often in this way, marked variations will be shown to occur in different places and then a search can be started to discover, if possible, the reasons for these differences.

The determination or assessment of the health of any group of individuals may occasionally be possible by carrying out a series of medical examinations of all the persons in, say, a factory or school. But this is never possible or practical in a large district, city or country. The measurement of trends in the health of such populations is only possible by indirect methods and the study of various facts such as mortality of the population from different diseases and examination of the incidence of illness over a period of time. The collection, analysis and interpretation of such information is called *vital statistics*.

Most of these studies are concerned either with the incidence of diseases (*morbidity*) or with the proportion of people within the community dying from diseases (*mortality*). Although accurate records of the incidence of diseases are the more valuable, it is rarely possible to rely on such figures as there is no method of ensuring that all or even a fixed proportion of cases are reported. It is, however, necessary and essential to know the cause of all deaths (for legal purposes) and therefore mortality statistics are usually very complete and certainly more reliable when dealing with large communities. But even with mortality statistics, difficulties may arise from different standards of diagnosis or when new forms of treatment completely alter the risks of dying from a particular disease. For example, the mortality from typhoid fever during the last 40 years has fallen from over 10% to well under 1% because of the introduction of antibiotics such as ampicillin. Thus the present mortality rate no longer can be used as a reliable indicator of the incidence of this disease. Equally mortality statistics are clearly of no use at all to indicate the levels of diseases that are never fatal. For these reasons the measurement of health is only indicated by a wide variety of recorded facts collected by many methods and occasionally necessitating special research projects and studies.

Whatever methods are used, it is obviously desirable to refer to all health statistics in a form that is comparable in all areas of the community. Normally the unit of population is either per 1000 or 100 000 persons. Thus the *birth rate* is the number of babies who are born per year per 1000 people. The *infant mortality rate* is the number of infants under the age of 1 year who die per 1000 births per year. However the *maternal mortality rate* is now calculated as the number of women who die from causes associated with childbirth and pregnancy per 100 000 total births. This is because the number who now die from these reasons is so small that it is more convenient to refer to their incidence in this way.

Obviously to be able to do this, it is essential to know or to calculate accurately the exact number of persons in any community – either a district or country. A *census* – when the population is counted – is undertaken every 10 years and was last carried out in the UK in April 1991. The Office of Population Censuses and Surveys (OPCS) then publishes the results of the census, analyses them in great detail and in the intermediate years until the next census calculates the estimated population of all areas. Already preparatory studies have been started by the OPCS for the next census in 2001.

Age distribution of the population

The distribution of the various age groups within the population is important in assessing the health needs and the trends which are developing (such as the steady increase in the proportion of very old persons over the age of 85 years). Unless these figures are accurately known the various health services required cannot be planned for and developed. Table 3.1 shows the age and sex structure of Great Britain population in 1993. Note that there are larger numbers of males in the youngest age groups but after the early fifties there are more women than men in the population. The reason for this is because for every 1000 girls born there are approximately 1050 boys born. However, the mortality of boys and men is greater than for girls and women so that after the early fifties there are more women in the community. This becomes very marked in very old age, after the age of 85 years.

Birth Rate

The birth rate is the number of children born per 1000 of the population. In 1992, the birth rate of the UK was 13.6. Figure 3.1 illustrates the variations in the birth rate that have occurred in the UK

Table 3.1   Age and sex structure of the population of Great Britain 1993 (thousands).

Age group (years)	Persons	Males	Females
0–4	3759 (6.6%)	1926	1833
5–14	7152 (12.7%)	3672	3480
15–24	7473 (13.2%)	3836	3637
25–34	9044 (16.0%)	4599	4445
35–44	7582 (13.4%)	3801	3780
45–59	9818 (17.4%)	4893	4925
60–64	2769 (4.9%)	1341	1428
65–74	5046 (8.9%)	2279	2768
75–84	2953 (5.2%)	1093	1860
85+	964 (1.7%)	237	727
Total	56 560	27 677	28 883

(From Population Trends, 1994.)

this century. Note that there were marked peaks in the birth rate in 1920 and in 1947, this coincided with the immediate post-war period of the two World Wars when families were reunited. The birth rate of any community can be affected by many factors:

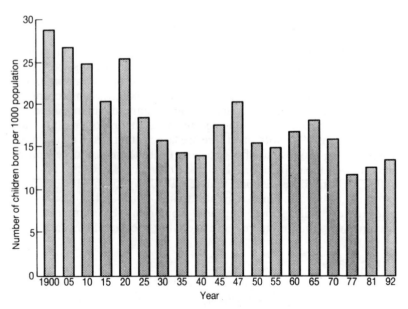

Fig. 3.1   Birth rate, UK, 1990–92.

- the numbers of persons of reproductive age in the community: the higher that proportion then the higher is likely to be the birth rate and vice versa. A rapidly developing township which has largely been created by young rehoused families will therefore have a high rate while a retirement area will have a relatively low rate;
- whether there is widespread use of family planning. Generally a predominantly Roman Catholic country will show a high rate but there are exceptions – at present Italy has the lowest rate in Europe;
- rapidly developing countries usually show a high rate – for instance Israel has a rate of 23.1 (1988);
- primitive countries with a high infant mortality rate usually also show a high birth rate. This is true of many Third World countries; it was also true of the UK before 1910.

During the decade 1981–91 there was a marked rise in the number of first births within marriage to women aged 30 years and over. Whereas in 1981 32 500 women had their first child when aged 30 years and over (5.4% of all births in that year), by 1991 the figure had risen to 49 100 (7.4% of all births). This is an increase of 51%. Over the same period, there was also a trend for the mean age of women when they had their first birth to rise (see Table 3.2). The table also shows that the mean age of first births within marriage are highest in Social Classes I and II compared with Social Classes IV and V.

Various death rates

The *crude death rate* (the number of persons dying per 1000 population) is of very little value as the age distribution of the population in different districts and areas is never known accurately. When a large number of the residents are aged, the number of deaths

Table 3.2 Mean age of women at their first birth within marriage by social class of their husband (England, 1981 and 1991)

Social class of husband	Mean age of women at first birth		
	1981	1991	1992
All social classes	25.5	27.5	27.8
I and II	27.6	29.0	29.2
III Non-manual	26.1	27.7	28.0
III Manual	24.5	26.7	27.1
IV and V	23.4	25.8	26.1

(From the Chief Medical Officer's Report, *On the State of the Public Health, England 1992*, Department of Health.)

in that community is bound to be high irrespective of the living conditions in that area. Much more important are the *standardised mortality ratios* (SMRs) and other specialist death rates such as the *infant mortality rate* (IMR) – see below.

Standardised mortality ratio

This is a valuable simple method used to compare the mortality from various diseases. The SMR is the percentage ratio of the number of deaths observed in a particular year or group of the population to the number expected. Adjustments are made for the sex/age differences in the years or groups being compared. The SMR is especially useful to compare the mortality of different:

- causes (see Table 3.3)
- years (see Table 3.4)
- social classes (see Table 3.15)
- occupations (see Table 3.16).

Table 3.3 is a good example and compares the mortality for different diseases in 1990 with those in 1980. The rate in 1980 is called the *index rate* and by convention this SMR is called 100. Note that Table 3.3 shows that by 1991 the SMR for 'All causes of death' had fallen to 83 for men and to 86 in women. This indicates that the mortality from all causes in males was 83% for men and 86% for women of the index year (1980). Table 3.3 shows many fascinating changes. Generally the mortality of most diseases fell during this period but there were exceptions. With diabetes for instance, the mortality increased by approximately 50.5 in both sexes. There was also a large increase in deaths from meningococcal infections which was due to a large localised outbreak in Gloucestershire in the 1980s. Cancer of the lung showed a marked difference in the trends of its mortality in men and women – deaths in men fell by 1991 to 80% of the 1980 rate but increased in women to 123%. This finding is associated with the increased incidence of smoking in women in the 1970s and 1980s compared with a steady reduction in men over this period.

Trends in 'avoidable deaths'

In the last few years, the concept of 'avoidable deaths' has been introduced. These are deaths which could have been prevented if either the diagnosis had been made early enough and the correct treatment started or if the patient had not chosen to lead a certain lifestyle (such as smoking) which is known to be a major factor in the development of certain diseases (see Table 3.4).

Table 3.3   Standardised Mortality Ratios (SMRs) in selected causes. England 1992 (SMR 1980 = 100), Department of Health.

Males		Females	
All causes	81	All causes	83
Bronchitis	17	Bronchitis	29
Pneumonia	33	Nephritis/nephrosis	40
Nephritis/nephrosis	36	Ulcer of stomach	40
Hyperplasia of prostate	37	Pneumonia	41
Tuberculosis (respiratory)	48	Hypertensive disease	51
Hypertensive disease	48	Suicide	51
Chronic rheumatic heart		Pregnancy, childbirth	
disease	56	and abortion	59
Motor vehicle accidents	68	Other accidents	59
Ulcer of stomach	69	Chronic rheumatic heart	
Cancer of stomach	70	disease	63
Ulcer of duodenum	73	Motor vehicle accidents	66
Other accidents	75	Cancer of stomach	67
Cerebrovascular disease	76	Tuberculosis (respiratory)	67
Cancer of lung	77	Cancer of cervix uteri	76
Congenital malformations	79	Cerebrovascular disease	77
Ischaemic heart disease	79	Congenital malformations	78
Leukaemia	95	Ischaemic heart disease	88
Cancer of breast	105	Leukaemia	99
Suicide	106	Ulcer of duodenum	99
Diabetes	155	Cancer of breast	105
Meningococcal infection	291	Cancer of lung	125
		Diabetes	145
		Meningococcal infection	192

(From Health and Personal Social Services Statistics, Department of Health, 1994.)

Note that in 1992, the percentage of all 'avoidable deaths' was 44.5% of those that occurred in 1979. There was however a wide variation in the causes of death. The largest fall recorded was in the number of deaths from chronic rheumatic heart disease, the 1992 figure being 14% of that in 1979. The least fall was in asthma and cervical cancers where the deaths were 68% of those that were reported in 1979.

Causes of death

In 1992 in England and Wales there were 558 313 deaths (271 732 men and 256 561 women). The vast majority of these deaths (nearly 95%) fell into nine main groups, as shown in Table 3.5.

Table 3.4   Trends in 'avoidable deaths', England and Wales 1982–92 (SMR 1970 = 100).

	Standardised Mortality Ratios (SMRs)					Actual deaths[1]	
	1979	1982	1985	1988	1992	1979	1992
Hypertension[2]	100	84	76	63	52	9482	5181
Perinatal mortality[3]	100	77	67	60	51	9400	5213
Cervical cancer[2]	100	90	91	84	68	1142	785
Hodgkin's disease[2]	100	86	75	74	59	365	229
Respiratory diseases[4]	100	87	50	40	28	329	93
Surgical diseases[5]	100	77	66	69	60	262	155
Asthma[2]	100	105	113	106	68	250	183
Tuberculosis[2]	100	91	65	55	47	222	106
Chronic rheumatic heart disease[2]	100	52	35	18	14	133	22
Total avoidable deaths	100	81	72	62	54	21 585	11 967
All causes (ages 0–14)	100	82	74	71	54	11 132	6450
All causes (ages 15–64)	100	92	88	82	74	127 194	94 491
All causes (all ages)	100	94	92	85	824	591 039	558 313

[1] Excluding deaths from visitors to the UK.
[2] Ages 15–64 years.
[3] Stillbirths are included in perinatal mortality and in total avoidable deaths but not in deaths from all causes.
[4] Ages 1–14 years.
[5] Appendicitis, abdominal hernia, cholelithiasis and cholecystitis.
(From Report of CMO Department of Health, 1993, published 1994.)

Table 3.5   Main causes of death in England and Wales, 1992

Cause of death	Males	Females	Total	%
All causes	271 732	256 561	558 313	100
Diseases of circulatory system	122 381	132 302	254 683	45.6
Neoplasms (cancers)	76 248	69 715	145 963	26.1
Diseases of respiratory system	29 554	30 854	60 388	10.8
Diseases of digestive system	7911	10 831	18 742	3.4
Injury and poisoning	10 738	5958	16 638	3.0
Diseases of nervous system and sense organs	5553	6024	11 577	2.1
Endocrine, nutritional and metabolic diseases and immunity disorders	4732	5906	10 638	1.9
Diseases of musculo-skeletal system	1187	4189	5376	1.0
Diseases of urinary system	2322	2984	5306	0.9

(From OPCS Monitor, 93/2.)

Note that 45.6% of all deaths were caused by diseases of the circulatory system; this classification includes 155 904 deaths from ischaemic heart disease and 84 834 deaths from acute myocardial infarction – a grand total of 240 738 deaths from heart disease (43.3% of all deaths in England and Wales). The next commonest cause of death is neoplasm or cancer which is responsible for 145 963 deaths (26.1% of all deaths). These figures clearly demonstrate why so much research and study is concentrated upon these two major causes of death.

Ischaemic heart disease

Death due to ischaemic heart disease began to increase rapidly in 1950 and from 1971 continued its rise but at a slower rate in men until the mid 1970s and in women until 1986. Since that time the numbers of deaths have fallen slightly (see Table 3.6).

Table 3.6 Deaths from ischaemic heart disease, England and Wales (rates per 100 000 population, 1961–92).

Year	Males	Females
1961	297.5	210.1
1966	323.2	222.3
1971	347.5	237.9
1976	371.1	266.6
1981	368.8	259.4
1986	365.0	271.4
1991	327.8	262.7
1992	315.5	254.9

(From various OPCS Monitors in the DH2 series.)

Within the UK, there are marked variations in the incidence of ischaemic heart disease in different areas. The lowest rates are in East Anglia where there is an SMR of 86 for men and 89 for women. The highest rates in the UK are in Scotland where there is an SMR of 126 for men and 118 for women. Further details about ischaemic heart disease are given in Chapter 10, dealing with the epidemiology and prevention of this disease.

There are wide variations in the mortality of ischaemic heart disease in different countries of the world (see Table 3.7).

Social class differences have an effect on the mortality (and incidence) of ischaemic heart disease in the UK with the greatest number of deaths in Social Classes IV and V and the smallest in Social Classes I and II (See Fig. 3.2).

Table 3.7 Deaths from ischaemic heart disease and acute myocardial infarction in various countries. Rates for men per 100 000 population, 1989 (unless otherwise stated).

Japan	43.2	Austria	218.2
Portugal	99.8	Germany (Federal)	227.4
France	103.4 (1988)	Australia	260.9
Netherlands	140.4 (1987)	New Zealand	267.2 (1987)
Israel	168.6 (1987)	Ireland	287.0 (1988)
Canada	208.1 (1988)	England and Wales	335.8
USA	220.9 (1988)	Scotland	391.5

(From World Health Organisation Annual Statistics, 1991.)

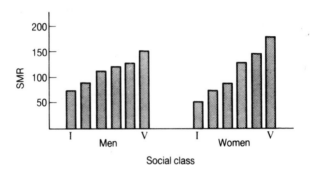

Fig. 3.2 Mortality from ischaemic heart disease, England and Wales, 1979–80, 1981–2. (From *Occupational Mortality*, OPCS, 1987.)

All these statistical findings suggest there are certain factors connected with the incidence of ischaemic heart disease. Much research has been carried out and it is now known that there are at least *eight different factors* which have been identified as causing ischaemic heart disease:

● hypertension;
● cigarette smoking;
● genetic factors – there are some families with a higher incidence;
● physical activity – the more active a person is the lower the chances are of developing ischaemic heart disease;
● a diet high in vegetable fibre seems to have a protective effect;
● a diet low in fat (especially animal fats) is associated with reduced risks;
● obesity should be avoided;
● diabetes is associated with greater risks.

When so many different factors are identified, complicated combinations of factors can produce curious results. For instance, the occupational group which has the lowest level of ischaemic heart disease is farmers and farm workers, yet their intake of dairy products (cream, butter and animal fats, etc.) is among the highest in the UK. In this case, the multifactorial effect of the various factors is clear – the consumption of large amounts of dairy products is more than compensated by the high intake of fibre in their diet and the high level of physical activity in these workers.

Hypertensive disease

One of the most dramatic falls in the mortality of any non-communicable disease since 1961 has been seen in hypertensive disease (see Table 3.8).

Table 3.8 Deaths from hypertensive disease, England and Wales, 1961–92. Rates per 100 000 population.

Year	Males	Females
1961	31.7	40.5
1966	21.6	27.7
1971	17.6	20.4
1976	14.2	16.8
1980	10.6	12.0
1985	7.9	10.1
1991	5.9	7.1
1992	5.4	6.7

(From various OPCS Monitors DH2 Series.)

Cancer

Cancers are the second commonest cause of death in the UK (see Table 3.5). The 11 principal causes of cancer deaths are shown in Table 3.9, which also illustrates the trend of these deaths during the period 1971–92.

Note that although there was an overall increase of 10.0% in these deaths in the period 1971–92, there was much variation between the different cancers and between the sexes. The largest percentage increases occurred in *cancer of the lung in women – 93.8% and a massive 116.9% in cancer of the prostate in men*. There were also substantial increases in *cancer of the bladder in women (45.5%)* and in *cancer of the colon in men (31.9%)*. The outstanding decreases occurred in *cancer of the stomach* in both sexes (a reduction of 31.8% in men and 45.5% in women) and in *cancer of the cervix in women (28.8%)*.

Table 3.9   Principal causes of cancer deaths in England and Wales, 1971–92.

Site		1971	1980	1992	Change by 1992 compared with 1971
Lung	Males	25 142	26 738	22 668	−2474 (−9.8%)
	Females	5672	8385	10 994	+5322 (+93.8%)
Stomach	Males	7233	6403	4994	−2339 (−30.9%)
	Females	5174	4497	3291	−1883 (−36.4%)
Breast	Females	11 182	12 167	13 663	+2481 (+22.2%)
Colon	Males	4195	4287	5531	+1336 (+31.8%)
	Females	6041	6027	6103	+62 (+1.0%)
Rectum	Males	3142	3014	3218	+76 (+2.4%)
	Females	2642	2566	2404	−242 (−9.0%)
Pancreas	Males	2757	3027	2926	+169 (+6.1%)
	Females	2442	2837	3108	+666 (+27.3%)
Prostate	Males	4027	5038	8735	+4708 (+116.9%)
Ovary	Females	3667	3711	3880	+213 (+5.8%)
Cervix uteri	Females	2394	2068	1647	−668 (−28.2%)
Leukaemia	Males	1675	1800[1]	1969	+294 (+17.6%)
	Females	1394	1549[1]	1647	−252 (+18.1%)
Total*		92 570	98 819	101 872	+9302 (+10.0%)

[1] 1981.
* Total includes other sites not mentioned here.
(From various OPCS Monitors.)

It is interesting to see a completely different trend in deaths from cancer of the lung – *a 9.8% decrease in men but an 93.8% increase in women.* There are of course still many more deaths in men due entirely to the fact that the numbers of men smoking in the past greatly exceeded women. But whereas now men are giving up smoking more quickly the numbers of young women starting to smoke are greater than young men.

Because of the demographic changes occurring in the population over the 21 years, with a marked increase in people over the age of 45 (an age when the chance of anyone developing cancer starts to increase steadily), the recorded 110% increase in total cancers is not a 'real' increase. In fact, but for the remarkable improvements in cancer treatment over this period, the increase would have been much greater. This is an example of how difficult it often is to interpret correctly vital statistics over a period of time.

Most cancers show a similar social class gradient, with the lowest incidence and mortality in Social Classes I and II and the highest in Social Classes IV and V (see Fig. 10.1 in Chapter 10 and Table 3.16). The one exception is *cancer of the breast in women* where there is an inverse social class gradient with the highest levels in Social Classes I and II and the lowest in Social Classes IV and V. The reason for this is not clear.

Infant mortality rate

The IMR is a most useful death rate as it gives a good indication of the living conditions in any area. It is defined as the number of infants who die under one year of age per 1000 live related births. In the UK in 1992 the IMR was the lowest ever recorded (6.6). This means that 0.66% of infants who had been born alive died before reaching their first birthday. The improvement in IMR this century is shown graphically in Fig. 3.3. The fall in IMR has been dramatic – in 1900 the IMR was 150; since then there has been an improvement of 22.7 times. This also gives a good indication of the improvements in living conditions over this period. Generally the rate has fallen steadily although there have been periods such as the depression in the 1930s when the rate of improvement stopped.

In Table 3.10 the IMRs of many District Health Authorities in England and Wales are compared. It will be seen that over the 3 year period 1990–92 (chosen to overcome the problem of small numbers distorting the results, the IMR varied from 4.1 and 4.2 in mid-Surrey and north-west Hertfordshire to 10.4 in central Manchester, 10.4 in Bradford and 11.6 in west Birmingham.

Many people find it difficult to believe that the excellent paediatric services available in most large cities do not improve matters. They do play a useful part in keeping the deaths lower than they would be otherwise, but *the main factors affecting any infant's life are the conditions in the infant's home.*

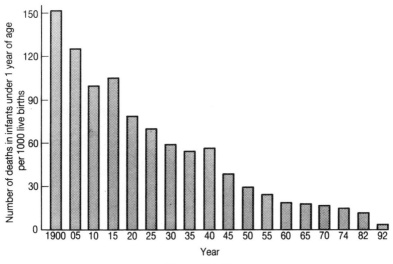

Fig. 3.3   Infant mortality rate, UK, 1900–92.

Table 3.10   Infant mortality rates of District Health Authorities in England and Wales, 1990–92 (England and Wales IMR = 7.3).

Mid-Surrey	4.1	Plymouth	6.5	Pembrokeshire	8.2
North-west Hertfordshire	4.2	South Glamorgan	6.5	Leeds	8.6
Cambridge	4.6	Bath	6.9	Newcastle	8.6
Winchester	5.1	Mid-Glamorgan	6.9	Northampton	8.9
East Dyfed (Wales)	5.4	Tower Hamlets	7.0	Bloomsbury	9.1
Dorset	5.4	Brighton	7.2	Preston	9.5
East Suffolk	5.5	Hull	7.6	Bolton	9.8
Bristol and District	5.9	Leicestershire	7.9	Sandwell	9.9
Oxfordshire	6.1	Nottingham	8.1	Central Manchester	10.2
Eastbourne	6.3	Darlington	8.1	Bradford	10.4
Liverpool	6.4	Milton Keynes	8.2	West Birmingham	11.6

(From OPCS Monitor DH3/1.)

The level of infant mortality is always lowest in Social Classes I and II and highest in Social Class V. This is clearly seen in Table 3.11, which also indicates that the perinatal mortality rate (see p. 57) and the stillbirth rate also vary in a similar way with the Social Class of the family. As might be expected, there are wide variations in the infant mortality rates of different countries of the world (see Table 3.12).

Neonatal mortality rate

Most of the first-year infant deaths occur within the first 28 days of an infant's life, and these deaths are called the *neonatal mortality rate*. In the UK in 1992 the neonatal mortality rate was 4.3. Thus the infant mortality rate of 6.6 in that year was made up as follows:

- neonatal mortality rate, 4.3
- post-neonatal mortality rate, 2.3
- infant mortality rate, 6.6.

Table 3.11   Infant mortality rate, perinatal mortality rate and stillbirth rate by social class, England and Wales, 1991.

	Social Class					
	I	II	III N	III M	IV	V
Infant mortality rate (all classes 6.6)	5.6	5.3	6.1	6.2	7.1	8.2
Perinatal mortality rate (all classes 7.7)	6.0	6.2	7.3	7.3	8.3	10.6
Stillbirth rate (all classes 4.6)	3.4	3.4	4.0	4.4	4.9	6.9

(From OPCS Report DH3 No. 25 1993.)

Table 3.12 Infant mortality in different countries, 1989 (unless otherwise stated).

Japan	4.5 (1990)	USA	9.1
Sweden	5.6	Israel	9.6 (1990)
Netherlands	6.8	New Zealand	10.2
Canada	7.2	Greece	11.0
France	7.4	Portugal	13.1 (1988)
Germany (Federal)	7.4	Former USSR	23.0
United Kingdom	7.9 (1990)	Nicaragua	62.0 (1988)
Australia	8.0	India	75.0
Italy	8.8	Guatemala	97.0 (1988)

(From *Demographic Year Book United Nations 1990*, published 1992.)

The year 1992 saw a dramatic fall in the post-neonatal mortality rate due almost entirely to the marked reduction in the number of deaths due to sudden infant death syndrome (cot deaths). This was due to the implementation of expert advice that babies should not be placed prone but laid with their face down or on their sides when sleeping (see p. 103). Table 3.13 shows the reduction in sudden infant death syndrome in the period 1989–92 for England and Wales.

Table 3.13 Deaths due to sudden infant death syndrome occurring from age 28 days to 1 year of age, England and Wales, 1989–92.

1989	1190
1990	1079
1991	912
1992	456

(Source OPCS.)

Perinatal death rate

The *perinatal death rate* is a useful rate as it is a good indicator of the hazards facing any baby immediately before and after birth. It is defined as the *combination of stillbirths and infant deaths that occur in the first week of life*. In 1992 in the UK the perinatal mortality rate was 7.7. There are four main factors which influence the perinatal mortality rate:

- *maternal age* – perinatal mortality tends to be high in very young mothers and in mothers over the age of 35 years;
- *parity* – the rate is lowest for mothers who already have one child and highest for mothers having their first baby or with three or more children;

- *legitimacy* – the rate is consistently higher in unmarried mothers and especially in very young mothers not living with the father and no longer living at home;
- *social class* – the lowest perinatal mortality rates are in Social Classes I and II and the highest in Social Class V (see Table 3.13).

Maternal mortality rate

The *maternal mortality rate* is the number of women who die from causes associated with childbirth per 100 000 births. Although the maternal mortality rate has fallen dramatically in the UK this century, from a figure of 481 in 1900 to 7.0 in 1988–90, the fall has been quite different from that seen in the infant mortality rate (see Fig. 3.3). The maternal mortality rate hardly fell at all up to 1937. It then fell rapidly when two great advances were introduced – the first was the introduction of chemotherapy and then antibiotics to combat dangerous bacterial infections that caused many deaths at that time from puerperal sepsis. This was then followed in 1940 by the start of widespread blood transfusion, the introduction and development of which was accelerated by World War II (as a life-saving procedure in many seriously wounded servicemen) but which also helped to reduce the impact of the complication of post-partum haemorrhage which is another important cause of maternal mortality. A further advance in the treatment and care of toxaemia of pregnancy followed next. In the

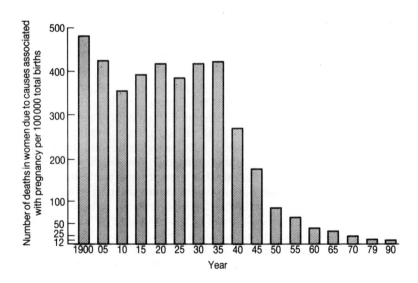

Fig. 3.4   Maternal mortality, England and Wales, 1900–90.

last 25 years the improvements have continued – another great advance was the encouragement that the NHS gave to women to have their delivery in hospital where the best facilities are available to deal with any emergency that might occur. So successful was this policy that now 99% of babies are delivered in hospital, even though some may stay there only a short time after delivery (see Chapter 4).

The maternal mortality rate is mainly affected *by the quality of obstetric care, and thus tends to be lower in large cities than in isolated country areas* (in other words the complete opposite to the infant mortality rate).

Because so few cases of maternal deaths now occur, it is best to use a 3 year period to study their incidence. In the UK since 1952, every 3 years a report has been published by the Department of Health on the Confidential Enquiries into Maternal Deaths – the latest report was published in early 1994 and covered the period 1988–90 and its findings are reported in Chapter 4 (p. 79).

Morbidity

Morbidity is the study and measurement of the incidence of disease and is very important to make certain that any health service keeps pace with the changing patterns of illness. In only a few instances such as serious communicable diseases (with the exception of AIDS and sexually transmitted diseases) are diseases reported compulsorily through a system of *statutory notification*. Table 3.14 gives these notifications for England and Wales in 1992.

It should be noted that AIDS and HIV infections and sexually transmitted diseases such as syphilis and gonorrhoea have *not* been made notifiable. This is because to do so would be counter-productive as it would be likely to lead to some concealment and reticence of patients going to see a doctor or going to a hospital clinic. Indirect methods are therefore used to estimate the numbers of patients with these conditions.

In the case of AIDS and HIV infections a confidential system of voluntary reporting by all doctors to the Communicable Disease Surveillance Centre at Colindale, London has been introduced. Results are then published by the Department of Health each year. The government has funded the Medical Reseach Council to institute a programme of anonymous surveys of HIV infection in certain antenatal clinics and in genitourinary medical clinics in hospitals mainly in the London area. It is hoped this system will enable a watch to be maintained on the general incidence of HIV infection in the community.

In the case of sexually transmitted diseases complete secrecy surrounds all patients at hospital clinics – no names are used (only

Table 3.14   Communicable diseases notified in England and Wales 1992.

Food poisoning	63 347
Dysentery	16 960
Measles	10 267
Viral hepatitis	8993
Rubella	6261
Scarlet fever	4645
Tuberculosis (respiratory)	4205
Meningitis	2571
Mumps	2412
Whooping cough	2309
Other forms of tuberculosis	1513
Malaria	1189
Ophthalmia neonatorum	424
Meningococcal septicaemia	277
Typhoid fever	193
Paratyphoid fever	81
Acute encephalitis	34
Leptospirosis	28
Cholera	25
Diphtheria	8
Tetanus	6
Typhus	6
Viral haemorrhagic fever	4
Acute poliomyelitis	3
Anthrax	1
Rabies	0

(From OPCS Monitor MB2 94/3 1994.)

numbers) – and the overall results are reported by the hospitals to the Department of Health which then publishes them annually.

Congenital malformations

Special arrangements have been made for there to be notifications of all congenital malformations to the OPCS. This was introduced following the thalidomide tragedy. This enables a watching brief to be constantly maintained on any possible connection between the incidence of congenital malformations and any new drugs taken by the mother during her pregnancy or any infections which the mother may have suffered from early in her pregnancy (see Chapter 5, p. 95). Already some significant changes have been observed in the occurrence of congenital malformations during the 1980s including *a marked reduction in central nervous system anomalies, which have fallen by 74% for live births and by 91% for stillbirths.*

Cancer registrations

Special arrangements have also been made for the *registration of all cancer cases*. These are reported from all hospitals treating such cases to the OPCS. The latest figures published by the OPCS cover 1989 and are given in Table 3.15.

General Household Survey

Another interesting source of morbidity statistics published each year is the General Household Survey (GHS). This is a general survey on all features to do with households in Great Britain including data on a *self-reporting basis of illness* in the residents. It is based on a sample of about 10 000. It especially reports on long-standing illnesses and disability (defined as that limiting any individual's activity permanently) and on acute illness (which limits a person's activity in the 2 weeks prior to the survey). Data from the 1992 survey showed that 1% of adults reported that cancers were the cause of their long-standing illness. Although care must be taken in the interpretation of these results because they are based upon an individual's assessment of their health, certain trends have been recognised such as *an increase generally in long-standing illness*. Medical consultations with a GP within the 14 days prior to the survey are also recorded and show that the consultation rate for females is higher than males. This is especially the case for ages 16–44 years where 17% of females had visited their doctor compared with 9% in males.

Table 3.15 Cancer registrations (England and Wales, 1989) by sex and proportion. Total 205 734; males 101 242 and females 104 492.

Males		Females	
Lung	25%	Breast	27%
Other	16%	Other	13%
Large intestine/rectum	13%	Large intestine/rectum	13%
Prostate	10%	Lung	10%
Bladder	8%	Leukaemia	7%
Leukaemia	8%	Ovary	5%
Stomach	7%	Cervix uteri	4%
Pancreas	3%	Stomach	4%
Oesophagus	3%	Other uterus	4%
Brain, eye and other CNS	2%	Bladder	3%
Mouth and pharynx	2%	Pancreas	3%
Skin (melanoma)	1%	Skin (melanoma)	2%
		Oesophagus	2%
		Brain, eye and other CNS	2%
		Mouth and pharynx	1%

(From Report of the CMO *On the State of the Public Health*, Department of Health 1993, published 1994.)

Special studies and research projects

Self-reporting of illness is useful, as recorded in the GHS, but may not accurately indicate the prevalence of certain mental illnesses because the patient may not have enough insight to recognise how their behaviour is changing. Special studies can help, and the Royal College of Physicians in 1988 reviewed several studies of dementia. These indicated that *some form of dementia may be present in 5–7% of persons aged 65 and over*. The incidence of *Alzheimer's disease* rises rapidly after the age of 60 and may be up to 20 times commoner at 80 than at 60. Such studies also confirm that such illnesses can create major problems for the relatives caring for the patient at home especially when they are deteriorating rapidly.

Rates of *psychotic depression* also increase in older people, and studies have reported that the levels of such illnesses in people over the age of 65 were 5.8% in surveys in Liverpool (1987), 4.3% in Nottingham (1987) and 15.9% in London (1990). When residents in local authority homes were included the levels reached 18.5% in London. Another consistent finding was that psychotic depression was much more common in people not currently married and in those living alone.

Two important national studies of morbidity in general practice have already been undertaken, in 1971–2 and in 1981–2, and a further study was completed in 1991–2. The results have been published by the OPCS. These studies are large, involving 50 general practices in all parts of the UK and over 330 000 patients. The value of such a succession of similar planned studies is that they provide the *ideal opportunity to examine trends in morbidity*. This is very important as it allows the NHS to check whether their provision is still completely relevant to the present needs of the population and to adjust the provision of specialist and other services to meet the ever-changing needs. This is especially true at present when the proportion of very old persons in the country (over the age of 85 years) is rising rapidly (see p. 372).

Social factors in disease

A further method that can be used to study disease is to compare the mortality of illness by grouping the family by occupation. The population of the UK is divided into six social classes based on the occupation of the chief wage earner in the family as follows:

Non-manual
Social Class I   Professional occupations (lawyers, doctors, clergymen, accountants, etc.)

Social Class II	Managerial and other professional occupations (teacher, nurse, sales managers, etc.)
Social Class III N	Non-manual skilled occupations (clerks, shop assistants, etc.)
Manual	
Social Class III M	Skilled manual occupations (bricklayers, underground coal miners, etc.)
Social Class IV	Partly skilled occupations (bus drivers, postmen, etc.)
Social Class V	Unskilled occupations (labourers, porters, etc.)

This social class classification can be used to compare the relative mortality of various groups in the community. These results are published by the OPCS every 10 years in a report entitled *Occupational Mortality*, usually published about 6 years after the census – the last report came out in 1987. Many of the results are given in the format of the Standardised Mortality Ratio (SMR) (see p. 48). Any group experiencing exactly the national average mortality would have an SMR of 100. If the SMR was 75, then it would indicate that the group has 75/100 or three-quarters of the expected mortality (it is enjoying less mortality than expected). If a group has an SMR of 150, this means that it suffers from a mortality of 150/100 or one and a half times the expected mortality (i.e. a mortality 50% greater than average).

Table 3.16 demonstrates the usual wide range of variations found in different social classes.

Note that in 'all causes of death' the SMR rises from 66 in Social Class I progressively until it reaches a figure of 165 in Social Class V. In

Table 3.16 Standardised Mortality Ratios (SMRs) by cause and social class, England and Wales, 1979–80, 1982–3 (national expected SMR would be 100).

Cause of death	Social Class					
	I	II	III N	III M	IV	V
All causes (men)	66	76	94	89	116	165
All causes (women)	75	83	93	111	125	160
Cancer of lung (men)	43	63	80	120	126	178
Cancer of lung (women)	50	73	81	122	138	170
Cancer of breast (women)	109	104	106	101	99	94
Cancer of cervix uteri (women)	29	60	73	112	124	186
Diabetes (men)	67	76	113	100	123	155
Diabetes (women)	47	59	92	114	145	247
Ischaemic heart disease (men)	70	82	104	109	117	144
Ischaemic heart disease (women)	46	75	80	122	144	194
Bronchitis (men)	34	48	85	110	115	211

(From Occupational Mortality OPCS 1987.)

women the difference is slightly less but the trend is similar. All the diseases in the table show the same type of trend, with the exception of cancer of the breast in women where there is a complete reverse. The greatest social class gradient is found in cancer of the cervix uteri where the deaths from women in Social Class V are six times greater than in Social Class I. This emphasises the importance of making certain *that women in Social Class V have smear screening tests for this condition.* At the time of this analysis (after the 1981 census), bronchitis was a condition where there was a very marked social class gradient – from 34 in Social Class I to 211 in Social Class V. As deaths from this condition fell rapidly in the 1980s, it will be interesting to see if this difference remains as great when the figures for the analysis of the 1991 census are published (probably by 1996 or 1997). There is little doubt that the reason for these differences between social classes is mainly due to living conditions and lifestyles (for instance it is known that men in Social Class V smoke much more heavily than those in Social Classes I and II, which probably explains the greater death rate fron cancer of the lung).

The unusual and atypical result in cancer of the breast in women has never been explained, but the higher rates have been consistent over all recent studies carried out following recent censuses.

Table 3.17 shows the different SMRs for various occupations and, again, wide variations are seen.

Even in the health services, it will be seen that there are wide differences in mortality – physiotherapists (80), ambulancemen (84), hospital ward orderlies (87), dentists (89), medical practitioners (97), pharmacists (121) and nurses (151). Although professional groups generally have low rates there are exceptions – judges, barristers and solicitors have an SMR of 113, almost double that of local government administrators. These differing mortality rates not only indicate particular hazards of certain occupations but are also influenced by the type of individual who is attracted to a particular job.

Value of vital statistics

Nurses are constantly concerned with the taking of various measurements used in assessing the health of the individual patient – taking temperatures, collecting specimens and assisting with biochemical or radiological investigations. Vital statistics, in their various forms, can be looked upon in the same way, for they represent the most reliable means available to estimate and measure the health of the community. It is not necessary for the nurse to become an expert in vital statistics, but a simple knowledge and understanding of their uses is likely to make their work more interesting. Community health problems change continuously and if the rudiments of the subject are understood, then the effects of these changes are likely to mean so much more.

Table 3.17 Standardised Mortality Ratios (SMRs) for all causes of death for men aged 20–64, England and Wales, 1979–80, 1982–3.

Local government		Clergymen	102
administrators	64	Librarians	108
Roadmen	67	Bus and coach drivers	111
Dustmen	69	Judges, barristers, solicitors	113
Postmen	72	Crane drivers	116
University academic staff	72	Waiters and bar staff	117
Teachers (higher education)	73	Pharmacists	121
Board and paper workers	75	Police officers	126
Physiotherapists	80	Environmental health	
Bookbinders	80	officers	127
Forestry workers	80	Miners (not coal),	
Teachers (main group)	81	quarrymen	133
Ambulancemen	84	Butchers	134
Company secretaries	86	Actors	138
Hospital ward orderlies	87	Shoe repairers	146
Railway engine drivers	88	Prison officers	147
Dentists	89	Nurses	151
Rubber and plastic workers	90	Scaffolders	159
Textile workers	91	Musicians	181
Farmers	93	Steel erectors and benders	184
Carpenters and joiners	94	Fishermen	194
Coal miners (underground)	96	Printers	202
Medical practitioners	97	Brewery, vinery process	
Masons	100	workers	266

(From Occupational Mortality OPCS 1987.)

4 Maternity services

In the UK about 760 000–790 000 births occur each year, and the task of caring for the health of each mother is an important part of the NHS.

Unlike any other specialty, the care of women in pregnancy is a normal and physiological one. This fact has helped create a very strong preventive health element, and the emphasis in all maternity services is to avoid and prevent abnormalities from occurring, and to recognise and diagnose them as early as possible so that, if they do occur, their effects will be minimised.

The maternity services are more closely coordinated than almost any other type of health care. This is essential as the maternity services are shared between the hospitals and the primary health services, assisted by midwives from the community health services.

The general principles of the NHS maternity services are:

- to promote a safe and satisfying experience of pregnancy and childbirth;
- to prevent maternal deaths;
- to reduce perinatal and neonatal deaths and, as far as possible, to prevent stillbirths;
- to eliminate disparities in all the above death rates between different sections of the population of the UK (i.e. between different socio-economic groups and between various ethnic groups) – this entails reducing inequalities of health risk associated with pregnancy in the total population as far as possible;
- to minimise impairment, disability and handicap;
- to assist parents wherever possible to participate actively during the pregnancy and birth of their children;
- to reduce unnecessary medical intervention during pregnancy and labour.

The other major aim since 1970 has been to ensure that the NHS has sufficient maternity facilities to enable every mother, if she wishes, to have her baby in hospital. This has been so successful that 99% of mothers in the UK are now delivered in hospital. It is still possible, however, for any mother who wishes to have her baby delivered at home to do so, and she has an absolute right to insist that the DHA provides her with a midwife.

Hospital confinements

The proportion of mothers having their babies in hospital varies a little with the area but overall in 1993 the average was about 99%. The following are the groups of mothers who *should always be delivered in hospital*:

- women in whom there is any abnormality. This might be a hypertensive disease of pregnancy or a malpresentation or the mother might have an illness such as diabetes;
- those who have had a previous caesarian section;
- mothers with four or more children;
- mothers over the age of 35 years;
- those who have had a low birthweight baby in a previous pregnancy;
- mothers who have primary infertility;

It is also sound practice to ensure that all mothers in their first pregnancy are delivered in hospital or in a general practitioner maternity unit.

There is an increasing tendency for mothers to be discharged home early during the first week following delivery. By 1994 over 80% of mothers delivered in hospital had been discharged home on or before the seventh day after delivery.

In 1994 the average stay in a maternity unit in hospital was about 4.7 days and in a GP unit 3.6 days. All indications are that the trend towards early discharge will increase, and some mothers are now discharged home as early as 6 hours after delivery – the Domino scheme (Domiciliary midwife in and out). In every case of early discharge, the midwife is required to call and continue to look after the mother in the puerperium (up to at least 14 days after delivery). There can be many social and community care problems created by early discharge, for no mother is fit to look after her home single-handed at such an early stage after confinement and arrangements should always be made for her to have special help.

Administration of the maternity services

In the UK, there is a strict control maintained over all midwifery services by the *United Kingdom Central Council for Nursing, Midwifery and Health Visiting (UKCC)*. This body lays down the rules for the conduct of all midwives. Under the Midwives Acts, all unqualified persons who are not either midwives or doctors (or students in training to become midwives or doctors) are prohibited from attending any woman in childbirth except to assist under the personal direction of a midwife or doctor, or in sudden or urgent emergency. This law prevents unskilled and untrained persons from attending women in childbirth *and so ensures indirectly that every woman is looked after by a fully trained and qualified person.* The rules of the UKCC are supervised locally by the DHA and include the following:

- supervision over all certified midwives in the district. This covers midwives in maternity hospitals and nursing homes as well as in the community. In practice, the detailed supervision in maternity hospitals is left to the senior staff of the hospital. No midwife may practise in the district until she has been given notice to do so by the DHA;
- power to suspend a midwife from practice if it appears necessary to do so to prevent the spread of infection. For example, it would be dangerous for a midwife who is a nasal carrier of pathogenic streptococci to continue to practise midwifery.

Codes of practice specify the records which must be kept and the standards which must be followed in midwifery practice, the drugs and anaesthetics which may be used, and at which medical emergencies the midwife has a duty to call in medical aid. The UKCC also insists that every practising midwife *must attend a refresher course every 5 years.*

Locally the DHA is responsible for arranging an adequate midwifery coverage for its area. The midwife can best be described as an expert in normal child bearing in all its aspects, working very closely with the health visitor who should wherever possible be introduced to the mother during her antenatal care (see p. 70). It is usual for every midwife to have a car. This is particularly important in order to reach patients quickly at any hour of the day or night, and to carry heavy equipment such as gas and oxygen mobile analgesia apparatus. All midwives are trained in giving gas/oxygen analgesia. A medical certificate of fitness for analgesia must first be obtained from the patient's own doctor during pregnancy. Analgesia is available today to all mothers who wish to use it. Modern apparatus is reliable and designed to allow a mother after tuition to give herself her own light gas/oxygen anaesthesia during the first stage of labour. She lies on her side, presses the mask with a pressure valve on it over her nose and breathes a mixture of gas and oxygen. As she loses consciousness her grip relaxes, the mask falls away shutting off the valve and the supply of gas is shut off. She regains consciousness and may repeat the cycle when necessary. Maternity outfits, which include all the necessary sterile dressings for the confinement and puerperium, are supplied free to each mother.

Pre-pregnancy care

Ideally the primary health care team and GP should provide information and guidance to any woman who is considering starting a family. This may naturally arise when a woman seeks family planning advice from her GP (see p. 83). Factors which then should be discussed are her lifestyle and especially smoking and alcohol intake. It is important that the woman realises that *smoking in pregnancy can result in a baby being born who is lighter in weight* and, on average, likely to have a *higher perinatal death rate*. Provided the mother gives up smoking before becoming pregnant these hazards will not occur.

During any consultation before pregnancy, the other points which should be discussed include:

- the previous obstetric history;
- any previous health problems and especially any history of *diabetes or hypertension*;
- weight guidance;
- any kind of medicinal treatment being taken by the woman.

If any personal or family problems are found, their possible effect on pregnancy should be fully discussed. If there is a history of inherited disorders in the family, then *genetic counselling* should be arranged which should be available from a local genetic counselling specialist.

Antenatal care

The prevention of most complications of pregnancy rests more with careful antenatal care than with any other factor. It is one of the main responsibilities of the midwife to ensure that adequate antenatal care is always undertaken. It is particularly important to follow up mothers who fail to attend an appointment and this must be done promptly. This is because the development of some significant symptoms may be the reason for the woman's non-attendance.

Mothers due to be delivered in hospital usually receive *shared antenatal care*. The hospital obstetrician will see the woman when booking and later organise an ultrascan and, if all is well, will only see the mother two or three times before delivery. The remainder of the antenatal care will be undertaken by the GP (if the GP has chosen to do maternity work) and the midwife. If any complication occurs the patient will then be referred immediately to the hospital obstetrician.

The pressure on most hospital antenatal clinics is so great that it is impossible for them to carry out health education or parental clinics. Mothers are encouraged to attend special health education sessions usually arranged by health visitors and midwives at health centres, group practices or at local clinics. Fathers are also encouraged to attend at least some of these sessions. In addition the National Childbirth Trust (NCT) holds parental classes in some areas.

When a mother decides to be delivered at home, there are three possibilities open to her.

- In a minority of cases, the GP carries out all the antenatal care, delivers the baby, and the midwife acts as the maternity nurse. Postnatal care is carried out by the GP.
- In most cases, the GP does the antenatal care but the midwife delivers the baby, only calling the GP in case of need. The midwife then reports the delivery to the GP who later completes the postnatal care.
- The mother may choose to have her baby delivered solely by the midwife who, in such cases, accepts full responsibility for looking after the mother in the antenatal period and in her confinement. This arrangement is now becoming very rare.

Mothers usually choose one of the first two alternatives as their own doctor is in an excellent position to help and advise in the event of complications. GPs who have had special experience in obstetrics and who undertake regular midwifery are placed on the 'obstetric list' and then are remunerated at a higher rate.

Programme of antenatal care

Good antenatal care depends on carrying out regular antenatal examinations throughout pregnancy starting with the important first examination at 8 weeks (see below). In the early stages of pregnancy, the interval between routine antenatal examinations is usually 4 weeks, from 30–32 weeks to 38 weeks the interval is 2 weeks and from 38 weeks there should be an examination weekly until delivery. If at any stage abnormal symptoms develop, the mother should be seen immediately either by the midwife or GP who examines the patient and then decides whether to seek further assistance from the hospital obstetrician.

At each regular routine antenatal examination, the following should always be carried out:

- blood pressure measurement;
- weight measurement;
- testing of the urine for protein and glucose;
- an abdominal physical examination which at the later stages of pregnancy includes checking the lie and presentation of the baby and listening to the baby's heart beat.

In the event of any problems developing, the intervals between the examinations should be reduced initially to weekly ones. This is especially important if a hypertensive disorder of pregnancy develops as this condition can rapidly deteriorate. In addition an *ultrascan should always be carried out* after about 18 weeks of pregnancy when it is usually undertaken in conjunction with the Triple Test to screen for open neural tube defects (see p. 74). The ultrascan is carried out in hospital and is used to:

- determine accurately the length of the pregnancy;
- to check whether there is a multiple pregnancy;
- to search for gross fetal abnormalities.

Some hospitals carry out an additional ultrascan at about 30–32 weeks to monitor the growth of the baby and to check for intrauterine growth retardation.

The first antenatal examination

The first antenatal examination is always especially important and should include the following:

- a complete record of the *past medical history* paying particular attention to any history of cardiovascular or chest problems, respiratory difficulties, diabetes and any past viral infections. Chest X-rays now need only to be undertaken if the history or symptoms suggest that this should be done;
- a complete obstetric history of any previous pregnancy and delivery with special reference to any difficulties or abnormalities which may have occurred either in the mother or baby;
- a physical medical examination should then be carried out and recorded together with a general assessment of fitness and weight.

In addition the following blood tests should be carried out:

- a *Wassermann or Kahn test* to make certain that the mother does not have a hidden syphilis infection. If at this stage of pregnancy it is found that the mother has a latent syphilitic infection and immediate treatment is started, then a possible congenital infection in the baby will be prevented;
- *haemoglobin* estimation to check the level in the mother. If this is lower than normal, immediate treatment should be started. This is important as haemorrhage can start later, and the results of such an event are bound to be more serious in cases where the haemoglobin level is lower than normal;

- *blood group* of the mother should always be ascertained and recorded. In an emergency, such information will be invaluable to enable a blood transfusion to be given quickly;
- *rubella serology* to detect antibodies and thus an immunity to rubella (see p. 76);
- *rhesus factor* estimation should be carried out. If the mother is Rhesus positive, then no problems will arise. If, however, the mother is Rhesus negative, difficulties may occur later affecting the health of her second and any subsequent children. If the father is Rhesus positive, which is more likely, then a further blood examination must be undertaken at the 34th week of pregnancy to check whether antibodies have developed in the mother's blood. If they have, then it is likely that the baby will develop serious haemolytic jaundice and may need an exchange transfusion. For this reason, the mother must be delivered in hospital and the neighbouring paediatric unit alerted before the birth. Even when antibodies are absent from a Rhesus negative mother's blood at 34 weeks of pregnancy, blood from the baby's umbilical cord should be collected at birth and sent to the laboratory for testing for antibodies;
- for mothers of Afro-Caribbean descent a sickle cell disease blood test should be carried out to ensure the mother is not infected;
- HIV test should always be done for any woman who has a history of intravenous drug abuse or sexual activity involving many partners.

In addition to the blood tests, *a midstream specimen of urine* should be tested to exclude a urinary infection.

Finally the first antenatal examination should end by briefly giving *health education to the mother* which should include advice on diet, and the general management of the pregnancy and lifestyle. It is particularly important to stress the extra risks to the baby if the mother smokes. The perinatal mortality rate in the babies whose mothers continue to smoke during pregnancy is consistently higher. Advice should also be given for any mother to reduce her alcohol intake.

As a result of the general health assessment carried out during the first antenatal examination, it is possible to place the mother in one of the following groups:

- mothers at low risk. These are women who have had no previous adverse history (either general medical or obstetric) and who are very healthy. This is the group where it is suitable for all the antenatal care to be carried out by the midwife and GP. Provided this pregnancy is not either the first or the fourth or subsequent ones, such women are suitable for a home delivery if they wish this;

- women at low risk as far as the pregnancy is concerned but who are likely to be at high risk during the delivery. These are mothers who previously have had no problems during the pregnancy but had a complicated delivery resulting in a caesarean section. This group can have their antenatal care managed by the midwife and GP but should always be delivered in hospital;
- mothers at high risk. This group includes mothers who have a medical condition or a past obstetric history indicating that there is a special risk of complications during pregnancy and delivery. All mothers in this group should be carefully monitored during pregnancy with special checks in addition to the usual programme of antenatal care. Such mothers should always be delivered in hospital.

It is also important to monitor carefully any pregnancies that occur in:

- very young women;
- unmarried women especially those without a settled home;
- smokers;
- women who are taking drugs or have a high alcohol intake;
- women who book their delivery late;
- any woman who has given a history of bleeding in the early stages of pregnancy.

Folic acid and neural tube defects in the baby

Chapter 14 (p. 267) describes the recent research which demonstrated a relationship between inadequate folate/folic acid intake by expectant mothers and the later development of neural tube defects in their babies. Two practical preventive initiatives are now advised:

- mothers who have already been delivered in a previous pregnancy of a baby who had a neural tube defect should take 5 mg of folic acid (in a preparation available on prescription) whilst they are planning to conceive and during the first 12 weeks of their pregnancy;
- all mothers planning a pregnancy are now advised to consume additional folate/folic acid prior to conception and during the first 12 weeks of pregnancy by eating more folate-rich foods including those fortified with folic acid and by taking a daily supplement of 0.4 mg of folic acid (which is now available in retail chemists).

Useful sources of folate/folic acid are the following foods: most vegetables but especially Brussels sprouts, spinach, green beans, potatoes, cauliflower, all of which should be boiled lightly: fruit including oranges, orange juice, grapefruit and bananas; cereals including soft grain bread fortified with folic acid, cornflakes (also fortified) and wholemeal breads. Other useful foods to supply folate/folic acid include Bovril and milk, whole or semi-skimmed.

Triple Test

The Triple Test is a blood test carried out on the mother usually at 16–18 weeks of pregnancy to check the levels of oestriol, human chorionic gonadotrophin and alpha-fetoprotein. If these are raised at 16–18 weeks of pregnancy (in the absence of a multiple pregnancy) it suggests a greater likelihood that the baby has an open neural tube defect (such as a serious spina bifida type of deformity). It is then advisable, after counselling, to carry out an amniocentesis (see p. 75) which enables the levels of these three hormones or chemicals to be calculated accurately in the amniotic fluid which surrounds the baby *in utero*. If these are raised above certain levels, the chances that the baby has an open neural tube defect are very high (in the region of 90%) and an immediate termination of pregnancy should be carried out to prevent the birth of a very severely disabled baby.

Counselling

Before the Triple Test is carried out, *skilled counselling should always be given to both parents*. The object of the test (and subsequent amniocentesis if the test proves to be positive) is to identify a baby with a severe open neural tube defect at a stage of pregnancy when termination can safely be undertaken (before 20 weeks of pregnancy). Clearly unless both parents agree to this procedure the test is of no practical value and should not be carried out. The object of counselling before the test is to make certain that the test is only undertaken when the couple are prepared to have a termination carried out if the test should prove to be positive.

Counselling should also always be undertaken of both parents after any termination because if a congenital defect is found in the fetus, such as a neural tube defect or Down's syndrome, counselling enables the parents to have explained to them the exact nature of the defect discovered in the baby and the risks of a likely recurrence in another pregnancy.

After one abnormal pregnancy resulting in a baby with a neural tube defect, the chances of a further abnormal baby in a subsequent pregnancy is 1 in 20, but after two abnormal pregnancies it rises to 1 in 8. However it would still be possible to carry out these screening tests in further pregnancies, and if this is done the chances of an abnormal child being born are minimal. It is also important to realise that even if the odds are 1 in 8 of having an abnormal child it means that in 7 of 8 pregnancies the child will be normal.

It is also important to offer counselling to the parents after any other termination of pregnancy, including abortion and natural miscarriage; to make certain that the parents have the correct advice about future pregnancies and/or birth control (see p. 83).

Screening by amniocentesis

Amniocentesis is the removal, usually during the 18th week of pregnancy, of a small amount of amniotic fluid by means of a needle inserted through the uterine wall usually via the abdominal wall. This fluid can then be examined in two ways:

- *microscopically* – the baby is surrounded by amniotic fluid in the uterus and a few cells will be cast off from the baby's skin and mucous membranes. These can be examined to give the chromosome pattern of the child (see Down's syndrome, p. 363);
- *chemically* – to estimate the level of alpha-fetoprotein (AFP) which will, at 18 weeks of pregnancy, be raised in 99% of cases of open neural tube defects.

Amniocentesis produces slight risks to the fetus. It is not easy to estimate these accurately but the most recent studies have indicated that there is approximately 1% extra risk of fetal death. This is a maximum figure and is likely to be lower. There is also an increased possibility of respiratory difficulties in the fetus at birth and of orthopaedic postural deformities which may require immediate treatment. Hence, after amniocentesis, the birth should always take place in a maternity hospital with full paediatric support.

Amniocentesis is useful in families with a history of either Duchenne muscular dystrophy or haemophilia for the sex of the unborn child can be determined. Both diseases are sex-linked conditions where the sufferer is invariably a boy although both diseases can be passed on by mothers. Clearly, if the baby is known to be a girl, there is no risk of either disease in the expected child (although a girl may pass the disease on to any male children which she may later bear).

Screening to diagnose Down's syndrome

It is possible to diagnose, by amniocentesis, whether the fetus is suffering from Down's syndrome. It is advisable only to carry out amniocentesis where the risks of Down's syndrome exceed those to the fetus during the procedure of amniocentesis (approximately 1%). In practice, this means that amniocentesis to discover Down's syndrome should only be carried out on pregnant women aged 35 years and over, or if there has been a previous Down's syndrome baby born, or if there is a family history of such births. If all such mothers were screened in this way it has been estimated that the birth of about 18–20% of babies with Down's syndrome could be prevented. The chances of any mother having a child with Down's syndrome increase as the age of the mother rises.

Rubella (German measles) and pregnancy

An attack of rubella during the first 3 months of pregnancy can result in harmful effects to the fetus. These include a higher proportion of abortion and stillbirths and an increased incidence of congenital abnormalities, especially congenital cataract in the child, congenital heart disease or deafness. Research has also shown a much higher infant mortality in children of mothers who develop rubella during the first three months of pregnancy. Active immunisation is advocated for all girls aged 11–13 years (see p. 133), if they have not previously been immunised against measles, mumps and rubella (MMR). Since 1988, a combined measles, mumps and rubella immunisation has been offered to all children at the age of 15 months. Vaccination of women of childbearing age is not recommended routinely. If an adult woman wishes to have a vaccination, a serological test, which can be carried out by the Public Health Laboratory Service, should always be undertaken. Vaccination should only be offered to those who are seronegative (approximately 10% of adult women without a history of rubella). *It is most important that a woman is not pregnant at the time of the vaccination, and does not become pregnant for at least two months after vaccination.*

Any mother who has never had rubella or has not been immunised and who comes into contact with the disease during the first three months of pregnancy should be promptly immunised with immunoglobulin. This normally prevents an attack developing and protection lasts for six weeks and so avoids subsequent congenital deformities in the child.

It is, however, essential to realise that any danger from rubella only occurs within the first three/four months of pregnancy and that a later attack does no harm. Therefore, reassurance is often needed when this occurs.

Prevention of Rhesus incompatibility by immunisation

It is now possible to prevent many of the problems of Rhesus incompatibility by immunisation with anti-D immunoglobulin of Rhesus negative women immediately after their first confinement or miscarriage. The problem in Rhesus incompatibility is due to red blood cells from a Rhesus positive child crossing the placental barrier and entering the mother's blood stream. Shortly after the birth of the first child, the Rhesus negative mother manufactures antibodies against these Rhesus positive red blood cells of her child which, in this way, are then destroyed. In second and subsequent pregnancies, these antibodies increase and, when they recross the placental barrier and enter the baby's blood stream, they lead to massive destruction of the baby's blood cells usually after birth, but in serious cases, before birth which may lead to a stillbirth.

Immunisation with anti-D immunoglobulin should be given *immediately following the first delivery* of a child or after *a first miscarriage or abortion.* An anti-D immunoglobulin then destroys the Rhesus positive red blood cells of the baby within the mother's blood stream and there is not time enough for the mother to develop antibodies. Therefore a consequent pregnancy will be like a first pregnancy and no problems will arise. It is, however, necessary in such cases to *reimmunise the mother after all subsequent pregnancies or miscarriages to prevent antibody formation.*

Recommendations in regard to treatment are as follows:

- in all cases the anti-D immunoglobulin should be given within 60 hours of delivery or termination of pregnancy (miscarriage or abortion);
- the usual dose of anti-D immunoglobulin for all Rhesus negative women having had Rhesus positive babies regardless of parity or ABO group, should initially be 100 micrograms. Further doses may be necessary for cases in which large transplacental haemorrhages have occurred;
- a standard dose of 50 micrograms should be provided for all women known to be Rhesus negative, having therapeutic abortions up to and including the 20th week of pregnancy, except for those who are sterilised at the same operation. Rhesus negative women whose pregnancy with a Rhesus positive fetus is terminated after the 20th week should receive a dose of 100 micrograms.

Diet for pregnancy

A well-balanced diet with a good proportion of high-class protein is required. Many mothers have odd ideas about diet in pregnancy and the midwife must be patient and make certain that the diet required is fully understood. At least a pint of milk should be drunk per day and foodstuffs rich in iron, calcium, phosphorus and vitamins should be eaten. One egg (completely cooked) and a good helping of meat, fish or poultry should be eaten per day. Cheese is also a most valuable food in pregnancy particularly for vegetarians.

Vitamin preparations either in the form of tablets or orange juice and codliver oil may be obtained from the local clinic, or alternatively these may be taken in the diet by fresh fruit and various fats. Good well-balanced meals will reduce the likelihood of unexplained prematurity.

It is becoming increasingly important for all expectant mothers to understand that certain foodstuffs should not be eaten by expectant mothers. This is because of the *special dangers of listeriosis to both the expectant mother and her baby*. Any food which has been associated with listeriosis should be avoided throughout pregnancy. These include many pre-cooked foods which are stored and sold as 'chilled foods'. All such foods (such as pre-cooked chicken) should always be stored below 3°C (37°F); recent studies have shown that many commercial refrigerators in shops do not achieve such low temperatures, adding to the danger of multiplication of any listeria if the food is infected. Expectant mothers should avoid eating such foods, as well as soft cheeses and pâtés. The special dangers to expectant mothers and their new-born babies are described in Chapter 8 (see pp. 159–162).

Dental care in pregnancy

Dental care in pregnancy is very important as the mother's teeth can deteriorate rapidly at this time. Every mother should, therefore, have a dental examination carried out immediately after the first antenatal visit and arrangements made for any dental treatment needed to be done at once. Because care of the teeth is so important in pregnancy, special arrangements are made to treat, at no cost, all pregnant and nursing mothers (up to one year after confinement) – this free treatment includes the provision of dentures if needed. District Health Authorities arrange for this dental treatment to be carried out by their own dental staff at clinics.

Risk to the mother as illustrated by the Report on Confidential Enquiries into Maternal Deaths

The maternal mortality rate (see p. 58) gives a measure of the risks to a mother from a pregnancy. The latest figures for the UK, for the 3 years 1988–90, show the mortality rate was 7.0 per 100 000 pregnancies which means that one mother died per 14 286 pregnancies. All maternal deaths are reported to Directors of Public Health and are then fully examined by national assessors (consultant obstetricians and preventive health experts). The latest report to be published was the second for the whole of the UK (earlier reports separately considered England and Wales, Scotland and Northern Ireland).

Although maternal deaths are now very low – the rate in 1936 was 62 times greater – then one mother in 230 pregnancies died from direct causes associated with pregnancy – the latest report still emphasised that *approximately half the maternal deaths would not have occurred if some mistake or omission had not taken place.* These examples of substandard care varied from mistakes and omissions by professionals in the NHS to a lack of cooperation on the part of the mother herself.

All nurses working in the maternity field should study carefully this report which is updated every 3 years, as these studies dramatically illustrate that these deaths are preventable in half the instances.

The details of the 1988–90 deaths indicated that errors included *lack of adequate antenatal care* and *lack of experience.* In hospitals a major factor was that junior staff rather than consultants were too often left to make a crucial treatment decision in an emergency. This was especially shown to be the case in preventing some serious cases of hypertensive disease of pregnancy from developing into eclampsia and also in cases of haemorrhage after an elective caesarian section for placenta praevia (see below).

Table 4.1 gives the details of the direct causes of maternal deaths in the UK from 1988 to 1990 (the last published report) and shows that hypertensive disease of pregnancy, pulmonary embolism, haemorrhage and ectopic pregnancy are still the commonest causes of maternal deaths.

Hypertensive disorders of pregnancy are still an important prevent-

Table 4.1 Direct maternal death – numbers and percentages, United Kingdom, 1988–90.

Cause	Numbers	Percentages
Hypertensive disorders of pregnancy	25	18.6
Pulmonary embolism	23	16.9
Haemorrhage	21	15.4
Ectopic pregnancy	15	11.0
Amniotic fluid embolism	10	7.4
Abortion	7	5.1
Sepsis (excluding abortion)	6	4.4
Anaesthesia	3	2.2
Ruptured uterus	2	1.5
Other direct causes	24	17.6
Total	136	100.0

(From the *Report on Confidential Enquiries into Maternal Deaths in the United Kingdom, 1988–90*, published in 1994.)

able cause of maternal deaths. In 1988–90, 27 such deaths occurred and substandard care was evident in 88% of them (compared with 81% in the previous report). Underlying factors were delays in taking clinical action, inadequate control of blood pressure and failure to appreciate the seriousness of signs and symptoms (often caused by too junior medical staff being left in charge). Established pre-eclampsia and eclampsia were the sole causes of death in all 27 cases. In every case but one the *blood pressure had been normal in early pregnancy*, stressing how important is *continuous antenatal care throughout pregnancy* including the checking of blood pressures and following up quickly any non-attenders in case a sudden unreported illness has been responsible for the mother not turning up at the antenatal session.

The numbers of deaths from *pulmonary embolism* (23) fell overall in the period 1988–90 compared with the numbers in 1985–87 (29). There was, as usual, a marked difference in the risks of pulmonary embolism after caesarian section compared with normal delivery. The number of deaths after vaginal delivery was the lowest ever recorded but the numbers after caesarian section has not fallen in the last 20 years, although there are now more babies being delivered in this way, i.e. this is really a hidden slow decrease.

Predisposing causes, such as *obesity* and the *increasing age of the mother*, for the dangers of pulmonary embolism increase steadily with maternal age, especially after the age of 40 years. The report recommends that all involved in the care of pregnant women or recently pregnant women should consider pain in the leg or chest or dyspnoea in an otherwise healthy patient to be due to thrombosis or pulmonary embolism until proved otherwise. Two-thirds of the deaths after caesarian section occurred after the seventh postpartum day.

Of the 22 deaths directly due to antepartum and postpartum *haemorrhage*, five were due to placenta praevia, one to coagulative failure associated with intra-uterine death and 11 to postpartum haemorrhage. The five placenta praevia deaths were in marked contrast to the nil figure reported in the last triennial analysis (1985–87). It was not that the condition was not diagnosed, but four out of the five deaths had received an elective caesarian section. The report emphasised the dangers of massive haemorrhage in such cases (in previous reports, it had been recommended that at such operations a consultant should always be present). This report also agreed with this practice and recommended that *there should be written protocols for the management of massive haemorrhage*.

Ectopic pregnancy (i.e in which the fetus is growing outside the uterus – usually in a Fallopian tube) continues to be a dangerous condition. In the UK, 15 deaths occurred from 1988 to 1990 and in seven of them it was considered there had been substandard care. The report stresses it is most important that doctors, midwives and nurses realise that there is always the possibility of an ectopic pregnancy whenever a woman of reproductive age presents with an emergency in which acute lower abdominal pain is one of the main symptoms (even in cases where pregnancy has not yet been diagnosed). Once ectopic pregnancy is diagnosed, immediate admission to hospital must be arranged and the patient operated upon immediately – it is most essential *not* to delay for resuscitation.

The role of the midwife in pregnancy, labour and the puerperium

The midwife works with mothers booked to have their babies in hospital and carries out some of their antenatal care as well as looking after those few mothers who choose to have their babies at home (see p. 70). Midwives work very closely with the maternity units in hospitals and with the mother's own GP (provided he/she is undertaking maternity services). When labour starts and the mother is admitted to hospital for delivery, the midwife is notified and is then ready to take over the care of the mother and baby when they are discharged from hospital. If this is early, then the midwife takes over the full maternity nursing care from the start (see p. 67).

In the 1% of mothers delivered at home, the midwife acts either as a maternity nurse assisting the GP delivering the patient or carries out the delivery herself (see p. 70). Once the mother reports that labour has started, the midwife visits her, carries out the examination and, upon confirming that labour has started, arranges for the care of the mother. The midwife will bring to each patient the anaesthetic apparatus plus all the equipment for the labour.

As explained earlier, the mother administers to herself gas and oxygen. The midwife reports to the GP when labour has started. As most GPs have to carry on their busy practices, the midwife continues to look after the mother, only calling the doctor if some difficulty occurs.

A high degree of surgical cleanliness is maintained by using sterile gowns, masks, cap and sheets. Increasing use is being made of disposable sterile materials and these now include towels, masks, caps and syringes. Any sterile gowns which are used remain at the patient's house to reduce any risk of carrying infection from patient to patient.

Midwives may leave the patient for a short time in the first stage of labour. They can give pethidine but because labour often progresses rapidly after giving such a drug, no midwife should leave the patient after administering pethidine.

After delivery, the midwife may have to resuscitate the child. The midwife should have a special mucus sucker to clear the air passages of the child and also a sparklet oxygen resuscitator, a most valuable and neat apparatus which supplies oxygen at a measured rate for the baby to breathe and has made the problem of resuscitation much safer and surer.

If, during the labour, the midwife meets with any abnormality, medical aid must be summoned immediately while the midwife stays to continue the delivery. Some district health authorities provide their midwives with portable radio transmitters so that they can summon medical aid without having to leave their patient. In most cases, medical aid will be provided by the doctor who is booked, but, if no doctor has been booked, the midwife sends for the nearest doctor who is on the obstetric list.

In more urgent and serious problems, the midwife may send for a special mobile hospital team, the 'flying squad'.

Use of hospital emergency team (flying squad)

Each maternity hospital has a mobile team (flying squad) consisting of an experienced obstetrician (consultant or registrar) plus an anaesthetist and an experienced hospital midwife, who will go to the home of a patient to deal with any emergency in labour. Usually such a team is taken to the patient's home by an ambulance. The most usual reasons for the flying squad to be sent for are:

- *sudden haemorrhage* (particularly postpartum haemorrhage). In this instance the flying squad helps to resuscitate the patient and for this purpose they carry blood and plasma for transfusion. They may also have to control bleeding and deal with its cause (say retained placenta). It is much safer to resuscitate the patient first and then move her to hospital;
- *a complication of labour*. An example would be difficulty in the second stage of labour such as unexpected breech presentation.

Flying squads have proved themselves to be most valuable especially in large cities and one of their great assets is that they are readily available at all times. The general practitioner may be out on his or her rounds when help is urgently needed and it is reassuring to the midwife to know that skilled help can always be obtained by calling out the flying squad.

The flying squad is called out to one in approximately 70 community births – the causes being for haemorrhage in a third of the cases, for retained placenta in half the cases and for varying difficulties in the remainder.

The cooperation card

Cooperation between all the maternity services is very important and this is helped if every mother, whether booked to have her delivery in hospital or at home, always carries with her a *cooperation card*. This is a simple record of her antenatal care, containing all the necessary information including her blood group. Then, if an emergency occurs while she is away from home, this card can be most helpful and can save valuable time.

Postnatal care

Every mother who is delivered in hospital should have a careful examination before her discharge home. The baby should also be fully examined by a paediatrician. As already explained, the midwife is responsible for the immediate aftercare of the mother and baby when they initially return home. Towards the end of the puerperium, it is a great advantage if the midwife can meet the health visitor at the home to hand over the care. Any problems which the midwife cannot deal with should be referred either to the hospital who delivered the mother or to her GP.

A full *postnatal examination should be carried out 6 weeks after delivery*. If everything has been normal, the hospital or doctor delivering the mother at home will arrange this. If the delivery was in any way abnormal (including a caesarian section), the postnatal care will always be carried out at the hospital.

The postnatal care examination is a good place to discuss with the mother the timing of her next pregnancy if she plans to have one. It is also an excellent time to discuss the whole question of *family planning* (see below). At the postnatal examination, it is usual for the GP to examine also the baby and then to mention the various screening tests for the baby (see p. 95) and the schedule for the various immunisations (see p. 130).

Family planning

Family planning should always be available to all women as part of their postnatal care. Family planning and the avoidance of unwanted pregnancies should also be available to all women of childbearing age. Recently there is increasing evidence that the proportion of unintended pregnancies has been rising steadily and reached 45% by 1989. The conception rate of those under the age of 15 years is also high (9.5 per 1000 females aged 13–15 years). The Chief Medical Officer of the Department of Health in his annual report of 1991 (published in 1992) pointed out that the Dutch teenage conception rate is now five times lower than in England and attributed this to a large extent to the recent strengthening of sex education for schoolchildren in that country. The Royal College of Obstetricians and Gynaecologists published an important report on unplanned pregnancies in September 1991 which stressed the need for all schools to have one or more teachers with special training in sex education. It is of course equally true that schoolchildren should also be taught the exact means by which HIV infection (and subsequently AIDS) is spread (see Chapter 9).

Family planning can be carried out at special clinics but increasingly GPs are undertaking family planning in their practices. Most health centres and large practices now have women GPs working there as principals so any woman wishing to consult a woman doctor about family planning can now easily do so.

The following is a brief résumé of the methods of contraception now available. Because the use of contraceptives is usually needed for most women up to the age of the menopause and immediately after (in most women up to the age of 50 years at least), it is very important that any individual contraceptive programme is carefully planned. The main reason for this is that some methods such as the contraceptive pill should not be used continuously without breaks. All GPs can prescribe oral contraceptive pills and most other forms of contraception (such as the diaphragm) on the usual prescription form, but not the condom. The following are the forms of contraception available to women:

- *combined oral contraceptive pill* (oestrogens and progesterone) which stops ovulation. It is taken for three weeks out of four. It may suppress breast milk and therefore should not be taken by any mother who is breast feeding;
- *progesterone only pill*. This is taken every day. It does not suppress breast milk and is therefore used on mothers who are breast feeding. It does not stop ovulation and is a less effective contraceptive pill than the combined one. Irregular menstruation or amenorrhoea (no periods) may follow;
- *injectable progesterones*. These are only used after rubella vaccination in the adult woman to ensure absolutely certain contraception. It is only used for 3 months. The menstrual cycle may be affected;
- *intrauterine devices* (the coil). This is usually copper-coated and can be left in for 5 years. It works by setting up a low grade inflammation. It is best fitted 6 weeks after delivery. The coil can lead to infections, heavier bleeding and, very rarely, perforation of the uterus;
- *diaphragm*. This needs special fitting and must be used with a spermicide. It is intended to cause a physical barrier which prevents sperms entering the cervix;
- *female sterilisation*. This is only advocated where the couple have already had their family or where, in an earlier pregnancy, the mother was very ill and it now is essential for her not to risk another pregnancy. The Fallopian tubes are either cut or tied or

clamped. In many instances this can be carried out through a laparoscope;

● the man can practise contraception by using a condom (not available on prescription) or be sterilised by vasectomy. Coitus interruptus (withdrawal) and the rhythm method are still used but both methods are very uncertain.

Skilled counselling is essential before female sterilisation or vasectomy to ensure that both parents realise the finality of both procedures.

Although breast feeding often delays the resumption of menstruation, it is important that mothers realise that further pregnancies can occur – in no way does breast feeding act as a contraceptive.

Social aspects

Maternity benefits

Considerable changes have occurred in these benefits during the last few years. There are now three types of maternity benefit available.

Statutory maternity pay (SMP)

This is operated by the employer and there does not need to be an intention to return to work to claim. SMP is payable if the woman has been in employment without a break for at least 6 months by her 26th week of pregnancy, and her average weekly earnings are above the amount where National Insurance contributions are paid. There are two rates of SMP. The greater amount is paid to a woman if she has been working for at least 16 hours a week full time for at least 2 years, or at least 8 hours a week part time for at least 5 years. The first 6 weeks of SMP are paid at 90% of her average earnings. After that, the lower rate is paid for the remaining 12 weeks.

For a woman who has been in the same employment for between 26 weeks and 2 years, the lower rate is paid for the whole period. To receive SMP 3 weeks' notice must be given and the employer given the maternity certificate (form MAT B1).

Maternity allowance

This is payable by the local Social Security Office for up to 18 weeks to someone who has changed jobs, or has become self employed provided that the standard rate National Insurance contributions have been paid for at least 26 weeks in the 52 weeks leading up till the 26th week of pregnancy. This maternity allowance is slightly less than the lower rate of SMP.

Maternity payment

This is paid from the social fund and is payable if the mother or partner are getting Income Support or Family Credit. The full amount is only paid if there are savings of less than £500. Applications should be made 11 weeks before the baby is due until the baby is three months old. For an adopted baby, the claim may be made up to the time he or she is 1 year old.

Free milk, prescription charges and free dental care

Free prescription charges (using an exemption certificate issued by the FHSA) and free dental care are available to all expectant and nursing mothers until 1 year after the birth of her child. The form FW 8 must first be completed – these are available from the GP, midwife or health visitor – to obtain the exemption certificate.

Free milk is also available to expectant and nursing mothers and to all children under school age where the family is below a certain income level, i.e. receiving Income Support or Family Income Supplement.

Care of the unmarried mother

Being an unmarried mother can produce special hazards for the baby and for the mother who faces more risks in pregnancy. These are mainly connected with the fact that no antenatal care may be carried out early in the pregnancy because of concealment, or because the mother may be forced to leave her home because of the unsympathetic reaction of her parents. Wherever possible special arrangements should be made to help any unmarried mother but especially very young ones, i.e. teenagers, to help heal any rift between the girl and her parents. If this can be done many problems tend to be reduced. After hospital delivery, if the mother does not wish to stay at home then it is probably best to arrange through the local social service department or reliable voluntary body for the mother to go to a suitable hostel or similar unit. Most such mothers who have no stable relationship need time to decide whether they wish to care for their child or arrange adoption. More mothers now choose to look after the child themselves and later such mothers can possibly return to their job, especially if the child can be looked after in a day nursery and if they can be provided with special sheltered housing.

In some areas special independent housing is provided for such mothers where they can live with their babies for 1½–2 years after confinement, and this has proved to be very successful. Later more permanent housing is often arranged and with the help of a local day nursery (see p. 290) the mother can return to a full-time job.

In a recent OPCS survey carried out from 1988 to 1990 in England and Wales, the effect of the marital status of the mother on infant mortality was carefully analysed. The results showed a greater mortality in the first year of life in those babies born outside marriage (see Table 4.2). Note how the infant mortality rate rises for infants born outside marriage. At present it is possible to register an infant born outside marriage in three different ways:

- jointly registered by both parents living at the same address;
- jointly registered by both parents living at different addresses;
- solely by the mother.

Clearly the distinction indicates that most parents living at the same address can be assumed to have a reasonably stable relationship while mothers living at a different address must be living apart from the father of the child. In Table 4.2 the mothers living apart are further subdivided into those mothers who solely registered the birth from those where the father still was concerned about the baby and registered the birth as well as the mother. The last group where the mother registered the child solely would indicate little or no interest by the father and probably that the father had abandoned the mother.

The impact on the IMR is quite dramatic: the IMR rose progressively to 50.6% more and 80% more, respectively, as the interest of the father (and almost certainly financial support) diminished. These figures indicate the need for extra care by the health and social services in these cases and particularly where the father of the child shows no interest at all or may not be known.

Those nurses working with mothers and young infants and especially midwives and health visitors should realise the numbers of births which occur outside marriage have been rising for many years and, in 1994 reached over 30% of all births. It is therefore obvious that this group of unmarried mothers needs more concentrated preventive health care if the preventable extra deaths in their babies are to be reduced.

Table 4.2 Effects of marital status of the mother on the infant mortality (IMR) of her child, England and Wales, 1988–90.

IMR for infants born inside marriage	IMR for infants born outside marriage		
	Jointly registered		Solely registered
	Same address	Different address	
7.3	9.8 (+35.0%)	11.0 (+50.6%)	13.1 (+80%)

(Source OPCS.)

5   Preventive child health services

The health care of infants and children is of great importance. There is much evidence that the basis of sound health later is laid down in the early years of life. Therefore the influence of the parents on any child, especially the mother, is paramount. In the first years of life, a child's learning patterns are mostly developed by copying so any bad habits in the parents (such as smoking or excessive drinking) are more likely to be repeated later in adult life. In particular divorce and marital breakdown can have a very detrimental effect on any children especially on an introverted, quiet or insecure child. It is important for all professional staff working with children to realise that such children are likely to be at greater risk. Therefore they should ensure that such children receive extra health and social care.

Care in the neonatal period (from birth to 28 days)

Feeding the baby

Much effort immediately after the birth is concerned with helping to establish a satisfactory feeding routine for the mother and baby. In the first 2–3 weeks, the main advisor is often the midwife (especially after the return from hospital of the mother and baby – see Chapter 4, p. 83). Wherever possible, breast feeding should be started. To do this much patience and encouragement are needed. The temptation to give up the effort because the difficulties may seem too great and this must be resisted even though often much anxiety is felt by the mother, who fears the baby is not getting enough milk from the breast. Usually the health visitor takes over from the midwife at the end of the puerperium and her influence in ensuring that breast feeding continues can be crucial.

As recently as 1988, a special report by the Department of Health unanimously agreed that the best food for babies is human breast milk and that, when successfully managed, breast feeding for 4–6 months offers many advantages to both the mother and infant. Since the risks of ill health are greatest when any infant is very young, breast feeding for even a short time (2–4 weeks) is still an advantage. The increased tendency for many mothers to return to work after 2–3 months, and the ease and convenience of artificial feeding have tended to reduce the incidence of breast feeding. It is, however, important to realise that the infant who is breast fed for 5–6 months has the best possible start in life. There is a lot of evidence that the incidence of all types of infection and communicable diseases is lowest in breast fed infants. In outbreaks of infantile gastroenteritis, which can be a very dangerous disease in young infants, the breast fed child almost invariably escapes. There is also evidence that the personal bond between mother and child is never closer than between the mother and her child whom she has breast fed.

Health visitors therefore do all they can to encourage breast feeding. If, however, this is not possible, then the health visitor constantly helps the mother by giving her advice regarding artificial feeding. Today the majority of artificial feeding is by the use of dried milks which are reconstituted just before the baby's feed. There are many different kinds. Suitable dried milks are available at health authority clinics at low cost. It is also usual for proprietary baby foods to be sold at such clinics.

General health advice given by the health visitor

If possible the health visitor meets and gets to know the mother during her pregnancy, at mothercraft and/or at antenatal classes. The health visitor usually takes over from the midwife the responsibility for the mother and child at the 14th day after delivery. It is best to do this at the mother's home. Increasingly in health centres and group practices, it has become usual for the link between the GP and health visitor to be very close, as the health visitor today is usually an integral member of the practice team.

At the end of the first month, usually the baby and mother have got into a sound regime and the baby is progressing satisfactorily. The mother and father are then invited to bring the baby to the nearest child health surveillance centre, which is usually at the health centre or group practice but occasionally at a health authority clinic.

Main problems of the neonatal period

There are four main problems in the first month of the baby's life:

- haemolytic disease of the newborn;
- neonatal cold injury;
- the low birth weight baby;
- congenital malformations.

Haemolytic disease of the newborn

Reference has already been made to the immunisation of the Rhesus negative mother in pregnancy to prevent haemolytic disease from developing later in her newborn baby (see p. 77). In all cases of Rhesus negative mothers whether immunised or not delivery should always take place in hospital and some blood should be taken from the umbilical cord to test for antibodies. If present these will gradually destroy the baby's red blood corpuscles by haemolysis. Immediate treatment must be started in the paediatric unit in the hospital which may include an exchange transfusion. If there is any jaundice in the baby, blood from a heel prick should immediately be tested and an estimation made of the level of bilirubin in the blood of the baby. Such a test should always be undertaken before the discharge of the baby from hospital.

If the baby is at home when the first jaundice occurs, a simple perspex device (an icterometer) which is carried by the midwife can be used to assess the depth of the jaundice. In the case of any doubt, a bilirubin test at the local paediatric unit should be arranged and treatment carried out if necessary.

Neonatal cold injury

Although the very small, low birth weight baby is liable to suffer from chilling, it is now recognised that this is also a hazard in babies of normal birth weight. If any baby in its first month of life becomes seriously chilled, its body temperature may fall dangerously low, to 32.2°C or lower. The baby then becomes quiet and difficult to rouse and feed, and is cold to touch, and later becomes oedematous. The infant may have a deceptively red complexion.

The prevention of this condition involves making certain that the temperature of the room in which the baby is sleeping does not fall below 18°C. Each midwife has a wall thermometer which should be left near the baby's cot to record the room temperature (both minimum and maximum). This check and control is most important in winter but is still needed in summer when unexpectedly low air temperatures may occur at night.

The low birth weight baby

Any baby whose birth weight is less then 2500 g is classified as 'low birth weight baby' and requires special care. Approximately 6.8% of babies come into this category. An infant's chance of survival is closely associated with the birth weight (see Fig. 5.1).

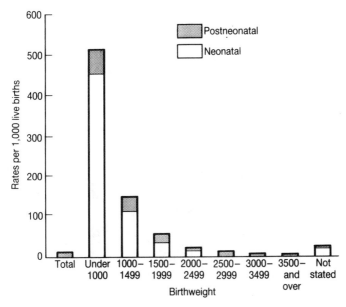

Fig. 5.1 Infant mortality rates 1988–90, combined totals by birth weight, England and Wales, per 1000 live births. (From OPCS Report *Child Mortality*, 1992.)

Note that once the birth weight falls below 1500 g (3.3 lbs) the infant mortality rate rises very sharply and especially below 1000 g (2.2 lbs), when 45% of babies die within the first 28 days of life – the baby becomes a neonatal death. It is interesting to note that the *postneonatal death rate* (from 28 days to 1 year) is also raised in these tiny babies, as shown in Fig. 5.1.

Figure 5.2 shows that the mean birth weight progressively falls as the social class rises from I to V. The figure also illustrates that there is always a lower birth weight when the birth occurs outside marriage. These figures indicate that the largest proportion of low birth weight babies are found in Social Class V when the birth occurred outside marriage.

Prevention of low birth weight babies

In many cases, the exact cause of low birth weight is unknown. However in some instances it is associated with severe hypertensive disease of pregnancy, and good antenatal care which recognises this condition very early will lessen the risk of the condition occurring. Another important cause is *the mother smoking in pregnancy* – recently there is

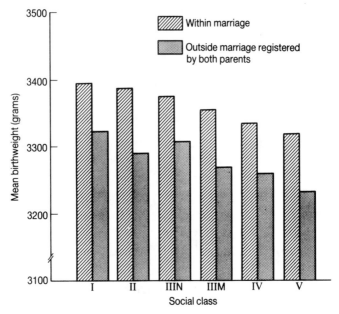

* As defined by father's occupation

Fig. 5.2   Mean birth weight in grams by social class, 1988–90, combined totals, within marriage and outside marriage, birth having been registered by both parents, England and Wales. (From OPCS Report *Child Mortality*, 1992.)

increasing evidence coming to light that smoking increases considerably the chance of a low birth weight baby. *Chronic malnutrition* in the mother is another cause and this is why the diet of mothers in pregnancy should always be carefully watched. Generally *poor living conditions* including overwork and increased frequency of various infections are also connected with a greater incidence of low birth weight babies.

Care of low birth weight babies

It is convenient to divide all low birth weight babies into two groups:

* *those under 2000 g (4.4 lbs)* who will probably need to be admitted to a special care baby unit for at least a period. *Those under 1500 g* will certainly require a prolonged stay in such a unit;
* *those between 2000 g and 2500 g* who can be looked after at home provided the home is satisfactory and there is a special domiciliary nursing service in many areas.

In the care of low birth weight babies there are five important factors:

- incubator care in special care units for the very tiny babies
- feeding
- prevention of infection
- prevention of hypoxia
- prevention of the special complications found in preterm babies.

Incubator care in special care units Special care units for low birth weight babies should be provided in all maternity and paediatric units. These units are usually designed to look after a small number of such babies. The care of the very small baby calls for skilled nursing using many modern techniques. Incubator care will be needed for the smallest babies. The value of the incubator is that it makes it easier to control the atmosphere in which the baby lives. There are three main factors:

- the *temperature* of the incubator should be maintained so that the baby's temperature is kept constant at just below 36.6°C;
- there should be a constancy in the *relative humidity* within the incubator. It is best to keep the relative humidity (the level of water vapour in the air) constant at 60%;
- the *supply of oxygen* should be controlled. As many such babies have difficulties in pulmonary ventilation (they often can develop hyaline membrane disease after birth) oxygen can be helpful. However *great care must be taken not to increase the oxygen level too high*, for if this is done, there is a danger of damaging the retina of the newborn child and producing blindness (retrolental fibroplasia). This danger can be reduced by continuously monitoring the levels of oxygen in the blood of the baby.

Feeding There are many different methods of feeding. Because of the effort of sucking, breast feeding is often not possible in very small babies, but some mothers can express their breast milk which can then be used to feed their own baby through a nasogastric tube. Various forms of artificial feeding are also used, consisting often of carefully graduated weak feeds of dried milk. These are often given more frequently than usual, every two or three hours, and are often given by nasal catheter, allowing the measured feed to flow by gravity.

Prevention of infection For all very small babies, infections represent their greatest hazard. The development of a respiratory infection in a small baby may occur so suddenly and dramatically that death can result in a few hours. The prevention of infection is therefore one of the most important tasks for nurses in charge of a special care unit. *Strict rules must always be observed.* No one other than the parents and staff working in the unit should enter a special care unit. If any staff have a cold or upper respiratory infection they should not then work on the unit until they are better. *Everyone entering the unit must wear a sterile cap, mask and gown. Handwashing by all staff must be scrupulously carried out on entering the unit and between visiting individual cots.*

The highest standards of nursing are needed. New admissions, especially if they have been admitted from home, should be separated from those already being looked after in the unit. In some units, air sterilisation is practised using ultra-violet light filters.

Prevention of hypoxia and cerebral palsy In the very small, low birth weight baby (those weighing less than 1500 g), there is a danger of periodic breathing and apnoeic spells when the baby suddenly stops breathing. Special ventilation methods are used to reduce this risk with a monitoring process examining continuously the levels of oxygen in the blood of the baby. Cerebral palsy can develop if the level of oxygen in a baby's blood falls to too low a level (hypoxia). Recent sophisticated equipment installed in some special care units has been shown to reduce the incidence of cerebral palsy by up to 40%.

Prevention of the special complications that can develop in preterm babies The special complications that can occur in very small babies include:

- respiratory distress syndrome;
- jaundice;
- intracranial haemorrhage;
- gastrointestinal problems including necrotising enterocolitis.

It is in order to prevent, control and to treat such conditions when they occur that many tiny babies (under 1500 g in weight) need to spend a long time in a special care unit. Vitamin K is used to reduce the risks of haemorrhage.

A special problem concerns the parents of very tiny babies who have to spend a long time in a special care unit. Wherever possible the mother is encouraged to become involved actively with the care of her baby although this is only practical in the later stages when the baby is progressing satisfactorily. Every effort must be made to overcome the separation problems of the mother and baby and to improve the bonding between the mother and her baby.

With the smallest low birth weight babies who have to spend many weeks in a special care unit, the strain on the parents (and especially on the mother) can be very great and much support and counselling will be needed.

Congenital malformations

Congenital malformations have been notified to the Office of Population Censuses and Surveys (OPCS) since 1964. In 1990, an important change was made and minor anomalies were no longer made notifiable and, as a result, the total notifications fell by 43% and those after stillbirths by 3%. Most of the exclusions no longer notifiable are ear and eye abnormalities, cardiovascular malformations and talipes. In 1992 in England 5618 malformations were notified and are shown in Table 5.1 below. Compared with 1991 this represented a fall of 864 (13.3%) in the total numbers per live births.

The trends in congenital malformations have generally decreased overall since 1980. The most dramatic decrease has been seen in central nervous system congenital anomalies which have fallen from 17.6 per 10 000 live births in 1980 to 4.2 in 1992. The cause of this fall is almost certainly due to the success of detecting prenatally by diagnostic ultrasound and alpha-fetoprotein screening (see pp. 74–75) and then carrying out a termination of pregnancy of those found to be affected.

Screening tests to discover unsuspected abnormalities

During the first 3 months of a baby's life, it is important to carry out various checks on the health of the child to make certain that early

Table 5.1 Congenital malformations following live births and stillbirths, numbers and rates, England, 1992.

Malformations	Live births		Stillbirths	
	Numbers	Rates*	Numbers	Rates**
Total malformations	4154	63.8	111	1.7
Polydactyly/syndactyly	741	11.4	11	0.2
Talipes	738	·11.3	4	0.1
Cleft lip/cleft palate	678	10.4	12	0.2
Hypospadias/epispadias	521	8.0	1	0.0
Cardiovascular	504	7.7	7	0.1
Chromosomal	468	7.2	16	0.2
Central nervous system	272	4.2	52	0.8
Ear and eye	232	3.6	8	0.1

* Rates per 10 000 live births.
** Rates per 10 000 total births.
(Source OPCS.)

signs of abnormalities are found so that they may be treated before they produce permanent damage. Note that these tests form part of the child health surveillance programme described in detail on p. 97. These screening tests include tests to exclude:

- *phenylketonuria* (at 6–14 days) – the Guthrie test;
- *neonatal hypothyroidism* (at 6–14 days) – using the same sample of blood as for the Guthrie test;
- *congenital dislocation of the hip* at birth, at 1 month, at 2 months and at 4 months;
- *congenital deafness* – by observation usually by the health visitor during the first 8 months, and particularly by observing the vocalisation patterns of the infant (see below).

Phenylketonuria

This is a rare metabolic disease (incidence approximately 1 in 10 000) in which the metabolism of the infant is faulty and poisonous phenylalanine metabolites are produced which eventually lead to a marked retarded mental development and the child develops severe learning disabilities. If treatment is started when the first signs of mental retardation show themselves, it is too late. However, if the disease can be diagnosed within a few weeks of birth, and the child given a special diet, this mental deterioration can be prevented.

Every child should have a simple blood test – the Guthrie test – carried out between the sixth and fourteenth day of life. Several spots of blood from a heel prick are taken from the baby and placed onto specially absorbent filter paper. In the laboratory a small disc is punched out of each blood impregnated paper and up to 100 individual discs are placed on a special agar plate containing a spore suspension of *Bacillus subtilis* and an inhibitory substance. Phenylalanase acts as an antagonist to the inhibitor; after incubation in positive tests growth of the organism will be observed around the blood disc.

At present about 95% of babies in the UK are tested for phenylketonuria.

Neonatal hypothyroidism

It is now possible to screen newborn babies for hypothyroidism which can lead to permanent brain damage within a few months and to mild or severe mental retardation. The incidence of neonatal hypothyroidism in the UK is about 1 in 5000. Provided the condition is recognised and treated *before the third month of life* 74% achieve an IQ of 90 or greater, whereas if the diagnosis is delayed until the fourth to sixth month, only 33% come into this category. The test involves measuring by radioimmunoassay thyroid hormone (T4) or thyroid stimulating hormone (TSH) of the pituitary in the baby's blood. The TSH test is more specific and is always used to make the final diagnosis, but the advantage of the T4 test is that the blood collected for the phenylketonuria test can be used for this test. It is therefore cheap and relatively easy to introduce. Such screening is now widely carried out in the UK. With widespread screening for hypothyroidism in the UK, it is estimated that about 150 infants a year will be prevented from developing brain damage and mental deterioration.

Screening for deafness

The recognition of congenital deafness is difficult and depends on careful observation of the infant during the first 8 months of life, and comparing the different vocalisation patterns in the normal and deaf child from 3 to 8 months of age: both develop in the same way up to 3 months old, making reflex sounds and responding to a loud noise, but from 3 months onwards, the deaf child's vocalisation diminishes steadily so that by 8 months little effort is being made by the child to produce sounds, although the child/infant will still remain alert, attentive and interested in surrounding features. By comparison, the normal child increases his or her sounds which become more tuneful – the child is clearly copying what is heard. This changing pattern in the deaf child is often more easily recognised by the health visitor who is visiting at intervals than by parents living with the child.

Child health surveillance

Much preventive health care is now based on *child health surveillance (CHS)*. Until the mid-1980s, this service was patchy and mainly based on child health clinics run by DHAs. However since 1990, GPs who have experience can be recognised as being fully qualified to do CHS (see Chapter 1, p. 18).

CHS is a continuous process of carefully examining and observing an infant's progress during the first 5 years. CHS should always be undertaken by a team headed by the health visitor (who should act as leader of the team), a doctor who ideally is the GP, midwives and members of the practice team especially the practice nurse. The main objective of CHS is to ensure the best possible start in life for any infant, by:

- supporting, helping and educating parents in the care of their child;
- introducing at the appropriate times preventive health methods including breast feeding, immunisations and accident avoidance;
- assessing physical, intellectual and emotional development in the infant;

- identifying behavioural problems in the infant;
- detecting illnesses and other abnormalities at the earliest possible stage;
- recognising abnormal behavioural actions on the part of the parent which may later prevent child abuse;
- building up the confidence of the parents in the team of professionals carrying out the CHS. *It is essential that parents should feel able to raise any anxiety at any time and not only at planned visits.* Listening to difficulties and problems raised by the parents is always an important part of CHS and often will reveal basic causes.

Records

All work carried out in CHS should always be recorded in two ways:

- by records kept by all the professionals involved. Routine visits at certain times should be recorded by the health visitor;
- by asking parents to keep their own records, which increases their involvement with CHS.

'At risk' groups

Although CHS should be carried out on all infants, it is important to concentrate carefully on the following 'at risk' groups as they contain a high proportion of infants who are at special risk.

- *Social factors,* including:
  — a household with a family history of child abuse;
  — unwanted and unplanned pregnancies;
  — very young parents aged 19 years and below;
  — parents with a low intelligence or who, in the past, may have attended a special school for those with learning disabilities.
- *Family history* including:
  — deafness, blindness or cerebral palsy;
  — any known congenital abnormality;
  — mental disability;
  — metabolic disorders;
  — epilepsy.
- *Prenatal or obstetric factors,* including:
  — any illness or abnormality of the mother in pregnancy such as rubella, excessive vomiting, severe hypertensive disease of pregnancy (pre-eclampsia);
  — multiple birth;
  — maternal diabetes.
- *Perinatal problems,* including:

— low birth weight (less than 2500 g);
— prematurity;
— prolonged jaundice;
— birth injury;
— convulsions;
— congenital malformation.
● Postnatal problems, including:
— babies who have a prolonged stay in a special care unit;
— difficulties in feeding and in sucking;
— any infant's failure to thrive – although there are other causes, this is *a classic sign of possible child abuse* (see Chapter 17);
— unusual and/or abnormal behaviour in the mother.

Care of children from birth to 5 years of age

All child care should ideally be linked with a CHS programme. In this, there are five specific dates when the child should attend with their mother and/or father at the CHS centre or clinic and be seen by the whole CHS team. These are:

● birth
● 6 weeks
● 8 months
● 21 months
● 39 months.

The health visitor (as leader of the CHS team) should also carry out periodic visits to the child's home for much can be learned from talking to the mother in her own home. At these visits the health visitor should check that normal progress of the infant is being maintained and any illnesses or abnormality discovered. These should then be completely investigated with other members of the practice team backed up by the local paediatric hospital staff if need be.

General points about CHS

During all stages of CHS, it is always important to involve the parents fully. Therefore it is best when seeing the child either at home or in the health centre or clinic to ask for the record which the parent holds and to discuss fully any comments made by the parents. Experience has emphasised repeatedly that the perceptive mother is usually the first to spot an abnormality in a child.

Whenever screening tests are carried out, the objectives and limitations of the test should always be fully explained to both parents. Child development is an irregular and individual process and the general trend of development is more important than a child reaching any stage or 'milestone' at a fixed time. Some normal and healthy children may be slow in some areas but will catch up later. It is never sensible to suggest that some child has failed or passed a specific CHS examination.

At the same time, there are some signs that should always alert a nurse that all may not be right. These include the following:

- at 6 weeks
    - a floppy tone and head lag;
    - no response to light stimulus;
    - nystagmus
- at 8 weeks
    - no smile
- at 6 months
    - not using both hands and the tone is floppy;
    - squint;
    - parents cannot get a response from the infant.
- at 12 months
    - child is not standing;
    - the infant is not responding to sounds;
    - the child has no grasp nor is there any hand/eye coordination;
- at 18 months
    - the child is not walking or may be drooling.
- at 24 months
    - the child does not understand language and is uncoordinated.
- at 36 months
    - the gait of the child is disturbed.

Another feature which should never be forgotten is that *often the children who need assessment are the most likely ones never to attend for a health test.* Therefore it is very important for the health visitor to visit the homes of non-attenders to check that all is fine.

General development in young children

The following general points about any child's development are worth commenting on.

Mobility

The majority of babies sit with support by the 3rd or 4th month and by the 7th sit alone. Most will stand with support by the 8th or 9th month and without support between 10 and 14 months. Walking usually follows shortly after the infant stands without support. Some crawl or creep by about 9–10 months but some do not show this.

Weight

In the past far too much emphasis was paid to weight as indicating progress. It is still useful in indicating a change in progress – a sudden loss of weight or the halting in the steady gain in weight always calls for further examination. However, due to the wide variations commonly seen in normal children, no reliance should be placed on tables giving 'normal' weights for children of different ages.

Often a baby will double its birth weight by 5–6 months and treble it about 12 months. It is certainly a mistake to stress to parents too much the baby's weight for some parents may overfeed their infant. It is interesting to note that some of the fittest babies are those who have been breast fed and are often lighter than average but are very active and alert.

Behaviour

The general behaviour of the child is an important guide to normal development. Any normal child should be happy and active and should be constantly exploring their home in an inquisitive way. It is most important that children always feel secure.

Bladder control

Sphincter control of the bladder is slow to develop. It usually does so at the end of the first year but may not be completely reliable until the child is 2½–3 years old. It is important that parents realise this for futile attempts to train the baby too young may only cause undue irritation and tensions and may later produce the opposite effect – enuresis. These and other problems should be freely discussed between the health visitor and parent.

Weaning

Weaning from either breast milk or from bottled feeds commences between 3 and 6 months of age. With the wide range of specially prepared foods now available (including tinned foods) this is simple.

Speech development

The development of speech in a child is a very important stage. The first primitive efforts to produce speech usually start at 7 or 8 months. The child begins to imitate what is heard and to associate people and objects with the sounds of speech. By 1½ years many children are using simple words and sentences, but considerable variation occurs and some very intelligent normal children (especially some boys) may speak clearly much later.

A very slow development of speech should always lead to a careful retesting of the hearing of the child. The completely deaf child hears nothing to imitate and, unless taught by special methods, will never speak. The other important cause for serious delay in speaking can be *mental retardation* – the child may suffer from a serious disability of learning. Careful testing is essential to find the cause because, if the child is very deaf, the earlier special methods of teaching are started the more likely that the child will learn speech (see p. 120).

Sudden infant death syndrome

Sudden infant death syndrome (SIDS) is a very distressing condition where death occurs without any warning and in a baby who seemed completely fit and well. The term sudden infant death syndrome or 'cot death' was introduced in 1969 and was then used to cover a wide range of infant deaths in which the term 'sudden infant death' was mentioned on the death certificate, even when another more probable cause of death was also given. Since 1986, the term has been redefined by the International Classification of Diseases as 'being confined to those cases where the only cause of death has been given as sudden infant death syndrome'.

The vast majority of sudden infant deaths in the UK occur under the age of 1 year. In 1992 in England and Wales 531 babies died under the age of 1 year, 26 aged 1–2 years, one child aged 2 years and one child aged 4 years. Of the 531 deaths under 1 year of age in 1992, 85 (16%) occurred in babies aged 6 months to 1 year, with the remaining 446 (84%) aged under 6 months. The peak age for deaths from SIDS was between 2 and 3 months when, in 1992, 113 babies (21.3%) died.

SIDS is more common in boys than in girls. In 1992 in England and Wales 339 (63.8%) boys died compared with 192 (36.2%) girls.

Between 1971 and 1982 the numbers of babies dying from SIDS rose steadily to reach 2.13 deaths per 1000 live births by 1982. Deaths remained high during the 1980s and reached a peak of 2.30 deaths per 1000 live births in 1988. Since then there has been a marked fall in deaths from SIDS (see Table 5.2).

There used to be a clear seasonal pattern in the SIDS occurring in the UK with peaks during the winter months, i.e. January–March and to a lesser extent October–December. Since 1988 there has been a steady reduction in the deaths in winter and by 1992 this seasonal incidence was no longer definite (see Table 5.3).

The cause of SIDS is still unexplained although there is general agreement that a number of different factors are probably involved. In 1991 further research focused upon the sleeping position of babies, as

Table 5.2 Sudden infant deaths under 1 year of age, England and Wales, 1988–92.

| Year | Death rates per 1000 live births | | |
	Total	Boys	Girls
1988	4.58	2.80	1.78
1989	3.87	2.32	1.55
1990	3.39	2.00	1.39
1991	2.86	1.76	1.10
1992	1.53	0.96	0.57

(From OPCS Monitor DH3 93/2.)

Table 5.3 Sudden infant deaths under 1 year of age, England and Wales, by quarters of the year.

Quarter ending	1988	1989	1990	1991	1992
31 March	581	450	390	355	139
30 June	334	268	269	259	135
30 September	277	218	221	168	109
31 December	461	404	319	212	148
Total	1653	1340	1199	994	531

(From OPCS Monitor DH3 93/2.)

there seemed to be a connection between SIDS and an infant sleeping in the prone position (with their face down). In November 1991 the Department of Health launched the 'Back to Sleep' campaign to reduce cot deaths. This campaign had four main recommendations:

- babies should not be put to sleep on their front;
- babies should not be exposed to cigarette smoke;
- they should not be overwrapped or overheated;
- breast feeding should be encouraged wherever possible.

The greatly improved 1992 returns of SIDS certainly indicates the success of this campaign and provisional returns for 1993 confirm this downwards trend.

Certain infants seem to be more liable to SIDS. A higher risk has been noted in very low birth weight babies or where a previous sibling has died from the condition. Babies born to mothers who are addicted to opiates have up to 80 times a greater risk of dying from SIDS. A further group of babies who are at high risk are those who have already nearly died from SIDS, having been found moribund and then successfully resuscitated. In such high risk cases respiratory monitoring at home with an apnoea alarm (to indicate cessation of breathing in the baby) has proved to be very useful and these are now used extensively for such infants.

Any sudden infant death is a family tragedy and help is needed for the parents to come to terms with their grief and to overcome their feelings of guilt and anger. Careful explanations are needed together with long-term counselling and support from the doctor and health visitor.

Safety of children

As the infant grows up he/she becomes more inquisitive and this can make the child especially liable to have accidents. Table 5.4 shows the fatal accidents which occurred in children under the age of 15 years in England and Wales in 1992. These are divided into two groups: fatal accidents in the home and fatal accidents outside the home.

Note that of the 411 children under the age of 15 years who died as the result of any accident inside or outside the home in 1992, 269 were boys (65.5%) and 142 (35.5%) girls. *Motor traffic accidents were responsible for the majority of deaths* – 177 in boys (66.8%) and 88 in girls (33.2%). Seat belts should always be used for children of all ages including those occupying rear seats. Baby car seats should be used for infants and should always be tethered by safety straps. Kerb drill

Table 5.4 Accidental deaths in children aged 28 days to 14 years by type and sex, England and Wales, 1992.

Type of accident	Age 28 days–4 years		Age 5–14 years		Totals	
	Males	Females	Males	Females	Males	Females
Accidents in the home						
Poisoning–liquids and solids	4	1	1	3	5	4
Poisoning–gases and vapours	1	0	0	0	1	0
Falls	7	2	4	5	11	7
Burns, scalds, explosions	36	22	14	9	50	31
Drowning	12	8	1	0	13	8
Food suffocation	4	2	0	0	4	2
Suffocation in bed/ cradle	7	2	1	0	8	2
Electric current	0	0	0	0	0	0
Total	71	37	21	17	92	54
Accidents outside the home						
Motor traffic accidents	34	21	143	67	177	88
Other traffic accidents	0	0	4	3	4	3

(From OPCS Monitors DH 4 92/3, 92/5, 93/1, 93/2.)

should be taught at an early age and parents, as well as schools, should train their children in road safety. Unlike deaths in the home, most traffic deaths occurred in the older age groups. In England and Wales in 1992, there were 146 *accidental deaths in children in the home* – 92 (63%) in boys and 54 (37%) in girls. It is important to note that it is the younger group who are at greatest risk within the home – 108 deaths occurred in this group compared with 38 in the older age group. The burns and scalds group was responsible for the largest numbers of deaths and here the 'toddler' group is particularly at risk. Health visitors and other nurses visiting a home which contains toddlers should be constantly on the watch for features which could cause such an accident. All accidents of this type are essentially preventable. As this age group always has a natural tendency to investigate the exciting world around them, it is important never to leave a toddler under the age of 5 years on their own in a kitchen if a hot cooker or hob is being used. Other special dangers are plastic bags, as many children have been suffocated by playing with these. Other hazards within the home include unprotected stairs, open upstairs windows and highly coloured medical tablets which many young children in the past have mistaken for sweets with fatal consequences. Flameproof clothing is another sensible preventive measure.

6 Health services for schoolchildren

The prevention of disease in schoolchildren is the concern of all branches of the health services. This is so important that special arrangements are made under the various Education Acts to safeguard the health of children at school. Each District Health Authority (DHA) must organise a comprehensive range of integrated health services for children including a *school health service* run in conjunction with the relevant education authority.

Each DHA has to appoint a community physician with special experience in child health who is then responsible to the local education authority for organising the local school health services. One of the most important duties of this doctor is to ensure that there is a *satisfactory system for the exchange of essential information about the health of the children* at school (including confidential records) between the local GPs and the doctors working in the school health services. Arrangements should also be made for other professionals in the education and social services to develop a good working liaison with those in the health services so that all are kept up to date on home conditions or on any special social problem which may affect the family.

There should also be a degree of integration between those working with the preschool child and those in the education and school health services. A number of staff – doctors, health visitors and nurses – are often employed in both services, many on a part-time basis and this can help coordination.

Each DHA must appoint a *senior nursing officer* who is responsible to the district nursing officer of the DHA for all the child nursing services including that in the school health services. This officer is responsible for all nursing staff working in the school health services and must work closely with the designated doctor responsible for child health.

Aims of the school health services

The move of any child to school when aged 5 years is one of the more important changes in life. The child has to leave the comparative peace and security of the home and mix with dozens of other children in the competitive atmosphere of the classroom and playground. Even for the child with brothers and sisters the move to school is important, but for the first or only child the impact of school represents a very great change.

School life in all children covers the next 11 years and many remain at school until 18 years of age when they move on to university or to other higher education.

Preventive medicine for any child of school age is largely connected with school life. In order to help children to get the most benefit from their education, the school health service, which is a highly developed preventive health service, has been built up to ensure that every child's health is safeguarded throughout his or her school career. There are two main functions of the school health service:

- to make certain that every child is *as fit as possible*. This includes many preventive health services designed to diagnose disabilities as early as possible, to allow for them to be corrected before they have a lasting effect upon the health of the child. This function also includes the promotion of *positive health* – it is not just sufficient to see that no disease occurs, but there must be a positive programme designed to make every school child as fit as possible;
- to assist with the care of various groups of disabled or handicapped children.

Nursery school

The normal child can gain much from attending a nursery school when aged three to five years. The value of such schools, which the children usually attend for half a day, is in the social contact made. The child gets used to working with others and this is especially useful and makes the entry into primary school easier. The medical care of children in nursery schools is important and is undertaken by the school health service. Special care must be taken with outbreaks of communicable disease as conditions such as dysentery can spread rapidly in nursery schools if not recognised early (see p. 162).

Steps taken to ensure every school child is as fit as possible

The present method of medical examination in schools is a combination of *full routine medical examinations* on all children either just before or immediately after entry into school (5 years) combined with *selective medical examinations during school life*. Just before leaving school (15 years) there is another full examination including a fitness test for employment. Occasionally the initial examination is replaced by a *preschool initial medical inspection* at 4 years of age. This has the advantage that a dental examination is possible earlier (when conservative dentistry is more effective) and enables any medical defect discovered to be investigated fully and treated before entry to school.

Routine medical inspections

Each school is visited at least once a year by the team carrying out the routine medical inspection – the school doctor, the health visitor and/or school nurse, and a clerk to assist with clerical work. The medical examination takes place at school, if possible in a medical inspection room. Parents are invited to be present and their presence is most important especially at the first medical inspection. It is best to summon parents on a single appointment system so that they are kept waiting as little as possible. About 12 children are examined each morning and afternoon.

A careful *medical history* is taken from the parent and this is supplemented by records from the child health service and from the general practitioner. These should provide a complete story of the child's progress from infancy with full details of any illness, medical problems, immunisations, as well as a brief record of the health of the parents and family. It is best if the health visitor who dealt with the child when a baby also looks after the school which the child attends. This is not always possible but is usually the case, for the infant's school is normally in the same district as the child's home. To have the same health visitor working with preschool children and with the infant and junior schools, means that she knows a great deal about the background of each child. Any unusual point in the medical history is noted and problems should be carefully watched.

A full *medical examination* then takes place by the school doctor. All systems are carefully examined, including the special senses. Apart from testing for abnormalities particular attention is paid to posture, nutrition and minor orthopaedic problems such as foot deformities, for example pes cavus and flat foot. The intelligence of each child is not tested routinely but if the teacher raises any doubt about a child's mental ability a special intelligence test is arranged at once.

Sight testing is carried out routinely on 5 year olds and the Keystone machine which tests visual acuity, colour vision and muscle balance is often used. If any defect is found, a full ophthalmic examination is arranged. *Any child with a squint must be treated immediately.* Treatment can be carried out at the nearest eye hospital or special orthoptic treatment can be arranged by the school health service.

The *hearing* of every child should be examined *individually* in the first medical examination when aged five. This can conveniently be carried out by a doctor or health visitor using a sweep test with a portable pure tone audiometer. This is a light, portable machine which produces sound of varying volume at frequency ranges from 128 to 8000 cycles per second. Each ear is tested independently – the child being given a small wooden mallet and asked to strike the table each time a sound is heard. Each frequency is tested starting with a loud volume of sound and gradually the volume is reduced until the child can no longer hear anything. This indicates the threshold of hearing – the lowest volume of sound at that particular frequency which the child can hear. This test is repeated for each frequency so that a pattern of hearing is established for both ears and at a number of different frequencies. It is important to test at different frequencies as occasionally there is a loss of hearing at one particular part of the sound scale (high-frequency deafness).

Testing the hearing of a 5 year old with this machine in expert hands takes between two and three minutes. About 5% of those tested initially fail the tests. All who fail should be retested immediately and this usually results in about a third of those who originally failed the test, passing it on the second occasion (they failed the first time not because of hearing loss but because they did not understand the test). Usually about 3% of the original group finally fail. These children must all be investigated further by an Ear, Nose and Throat Department to establish the cause of their hearing loss. In many cases, the hearing loss is quite small and, without a special test, might never be discovered. It is, however, most important that any hearing loss, even if small, is discovered early, otherwise it is likely to interfere with the educational progress of the child – the child will probably not be working to his or her full potential although, if intelligent, may still be progressing quite well compared with other children.

All children with a hearing loss are carefully followed up and, where necessary, a hearing aid is prescribed by the hospital department. Those with minimal hearing loss are always put at the front of the class to make certain they have the best opportunity to hear each lesson.

If any illness or disability is discovered in the routine medical examination, the parent is told about it and a note sent to the child's own general practitioner who then arranges for treatment. The school health service is really a diagnostic service and not a treatment service, although it is careful to check that the treatment ordered by the doctor is properly carried out by the child. In some cases, the treatment may affect the child's ability to play a full part in the activities of the school, for example games. Wherever possible, interference in this way is always kept to a minimum for it is important that no child should ever think some activity cannot be undertaken unless this is essential. Close liaison must be maintained between the family doctor and school doctor in this respect.

After the school medical examination, the school doctor indicates those children who need to be seen again. Whenever any disability is discovered, arrangements are always made to see the child and parent again in a few weeks after treatment. This succeeding examination will take place at one of the follow-up school clinics held weekly. All children who have been found to have disabilities should also be seen on the next routine medical examination which the doctor carries out at that school. This will normally be the following year. A perfectly normal child would not be seen by the doctor following the initial medical inspection at four or five years until the child is about to leave school (15 years).

The exceptions to this would be if a sudden illness developed in the meantime or if the parents or teachers were worried about the health of the child. In this case, the child would be seen either at the next visit of the doctor to school or be referred to the follow-up clinic.

A few examples of how routine medical inspection works are given by the following.

Normal child

The child is medically examined at school when aged 5 years and 15 years. In addition the health visitor/school nurse visits the school each term to check on minor illnesses and absentees. A questionnaire is completed by parent and teacher when the child is aged 8 years and 12 years. Selective medical examination is carried out where the answers cause concern.

Child with constant disability

A child with defective vision, or some chronic disability such as a scoliosis, would be seen when five years old at school, and then on each annual routine medical examination carried out by the doctor on the next visit to the school. Also the child may be seen at any time at follow-up clinics.

Normal child on entry to school who later develops severe illness

An example would be a child found to be quite normal on entering school at five years but who developed asthma when aged seven. This child would have been medically examined at five, found normal, and marked to be seen again at 15. However, when asthma developed at 7, the child would be referred immediately on return to the school doctor and would then be seen as regularly as needed and on each subsequent routine medical examination at the school (often called surveillance).

This careful 'watching over' process of the health of all school-children should always be carried out in such a way as to help and assist parents, general practitioners and teachers. All children are seen after any recent serious illness, or if the teacher, parent or health visitor/ school nurse is concerned because of unsatisfactory progress or difficulty of any kind.

Other functions of the school medical officer

The good school doctor will visit schools in between the more lengthy visits to carry out routine medical inspections and check up other points which are important to the health of the child. These include the following:

- *helpful advice about the hygiene in the school.* This will include examination of buildings, heating, washing facilities and kitchen premises;
- *investigation of all communicable diseases.* There are always likely to be outbreaks of communicable disease in schools, especially in infant and junior schools. Much further illness can be prevented by prompt and proper investigation. Bacteriological investigations should be carried out on the close family contacts of certain communicable diseases (such as diphtheria, dysentery, salmonella or enteric infections) and may prevent much unnecessary disease by defining carriers who may spread the disease.

Whenever a case of tuberculosis occurs within a school, complete and careful examination of all contacts (staff and children) must be carried out to make certain that an unsuspected case has not been the cause.
It is best always for all such investigations to be undertaken by the regular school doctor and health visitor for they know so much about the school and its staff and children, and will thus be able to ensure that fullest investigations are undertaken with the minimum interference to school work.

The difficult question of any possible danger of any HIV positive children in schools (see Chapter 9 for a full discussion of risks) should always be dealt with by the school medical officer. In such instances, the only risk could be in the event of an accident or nose bleed when there could be a danger from infection from blood. Sensible precautions (the provision and use of clean rubber gloves to be used in all such instances for all children) should be introduced in every school and carefully discussed with all teachers, some of whom may not understand the danger. *Health education* should always be one of the most important functions of the school health team. The aim is to *promote positive health* – to assist the teaching staff to improve the health of children as far as possible. This means encouraging certain non-athletic and underdeveloped children to improve their physique in various ways. Every school doctor should take an interest in the games schedules of the school. But it is also important not to neglect that group of children who, for one reason or another (e.g. bad eyesight) never seem able to excel at traditional ball games. Other forms of active recreation should always be encouraged and special activities such as walking, camping, cycling, rock climbing, skiing, fishing, sailing, skating and riding should, wherever possible, be part of the sporting activities of the school. To benefit from such sports is within the compass of any school today, for the Central Council of Physical Recreation runs a multitude of excellent courses in all areas of the country especially designed to introduce the older school child to such activities. Such an introduction may readily play an important part in maintaining the health of the adult later in life.

Special subjects in health education must be tackled such as sex education, care of teeth and education to prevent children starting to smoke or became involved in solvent or drug abuse (see p. 407). None of these topics are easy to put over successfully and often more can be gained by example. In this respect, the behaviour of all the teaching staff is most important – a campaign to stop children from smoking is unlikely to succeed unless staff are also prepared to help. Attempts must always be made to see that health education becomes a part of ordinary education wherever possible so that it is a continuously active process rather than a sudden strenuous campaign:

- *immunisations* should be encouraged in schoolchildren. Booster doses of diphtheria and poliomyelitis immunisation should be given to those who have had prior courses. For children who have never been immunised, primary courses of immunisation should be arranged at school. The aim should be to make it as easy as possible for the child to be immunised.

  BCG vaccination against tuberculosis should be offered to all schoolchildren aged 12 to 13 years who are then Heaf negative (see p. 133);

  Arrangements should be made to immunise all girls between the ages of 11 and 13, and who have not previously had measles, mumps and rubella (MMR) immunisation, against rubella;

- the discovery or ascertainment of all groups of *handicapped children* is another important function of the school doctor.

Routine inspections by health visitors

In addition to the health inspection visit, the health visitor visits each school frequently in order to

- note which children are absent from school so that the health visitor can pay a home visit to help and advise;
- carry out certain screening tests – repeat any hearing tests and test the vision of 7 year old children;
- carry out regular cleanliness inspections on schoolchildren.

A small percentage of all schoolchildren are found to have evidence of infestation with head lice. These infestations are mainly in the form of nits – the eggs of the head louse. Arrangements are then made for the cleansing of the child at a convenient clinic and for subsequent examination to make certain that there has not been a recurrence. It is essential for the health visitor also to visit the home, for often other members of the family are involved and, in such cases, to treat the schoolchildren only will achieve little. On such visits particular attention must be paid to examining the hair of the older members of the family.

Another disease in which it is important to treat all the family and which occasionally is found in schoolchildren is *scabies*. Modern treatment with benzyl benzoate solution is most efficient and soon controls such infestations, provided all infected members of the family are treated simultaneously.

School clinics

School clinics are provided so that schoolchildren can attend follow-up clinics and have minor ailments treated without having to spend too much time away from school. Treatment is not really the function of the school health service but there are so many problems connected with getting children's eyes tested for glasses that it has often been found most convenient for an eye specialist periodically to hold an *ophthalmic clinic* in a school clinic. The District Health Authority cooperates with the Education Committee in arranging this service. Special *orthopaedic clinics* are held in school clinics by orthopaedic consultants to treat and follow up the large number of minor orthopaedic problems always found in a school population. Such clinics are of special importance in country areas where attendance at a hospital outpatient department may be difficult.

Preventive dental treatment in schoolchildren

A comprehensive preventive dental service is an important part of the school health service. Unlike the rest of the school health service, the school dental service is both a diagnostic and a treatment service.

A visit is paid by the dental surgeon to each school every six months and every child is examined dentally and notes made of all defects.

Each child is then called for individual treatment by the dentist in the following weeks. Treatment is free and usually carried out at the dental clinic which is normally attached to the school clinic. In remote country areas dental clinics may be mounted in a mobile caravan so that the treatment centre can be taken and parked at the school. This arrangement allows treatment of every child to be carried out without taking the children away from school for long periods.

Most school dental services have facilities to carry out orthodontic treatment on children with crowded and misplaced teeth. Effective orthodontic treatment in the schoolchild can prevent many dental problems later. It is, however, important that orthodontic treatment is started early enough to enable the permanent teeth to develop correctly.

In the school dental service *dental hygienists* work under the personal direction of dentists, tackling certain tasks such as the scaling of teeth and doing some fillings.

The degree of dental decay varies considerably in different parts of the UK and is dependent mainly on whether there is natural fluoride in the water supplies. In those areas with no or little natural fluoride, dental decay is very common but can be greatly reduced by artificial fluoridation of the water supply.

Care of the handicapped school child

An important subsidiary function of the school health service is to assist in the diagnosis, discovery and special care for all handicapped schoolchildren whether the handicap or disability is physical or mental.

The education of children and young people who are handicapped or, to use a more modern phrase, have disabilities or significant difficulties was studied in detail by an expert Committee set up by the Department of Education and Science under the chairmanship of Mary Warnock. This Committee reported in 1978 and, since then, governments have generally accepted many of its recommendations and the Education Act, 1981, has changed the law where necessary.

Definition of special educational needs under the Education Act, 1981

The Education Act, 1981 accepts the recommendation of the Warnock Committee that the narrow definition of handicapped children (which only includes blind, partially sighted, deaf, partially deaf, delicate, educationally backward, emotionally and behaviourally disturbed, physically handicapped, epileptic, speech defect children) should be extended to include any child who requires some form of special educational provision (including 'remedial' education). This will mean that approximately 16–17% of the school population (one in six) will be involved at any one time (or 20% or one in five at some time during their school life). Special educational provision may take the form of special teaching techniques or equipment, a specially modified curriculum or help with social or emotional problems.

Duties of local education authorities (LEAs)

Under the Education Act, 1981, all LEAs must assess any child whom the LEA considers has a special educational need. Medical, psychological and educational advice *must* be sought in each assessment and assistance may also be obtained from social services where this is appropriate.

Once any child has been assessed to have a special educational need, the LEA will be under a legal duty to arrange special educational provision in accordance with the statement outlining that need. Parents also *must* receive a copy of the statement – indeed much emphasis in the Act is placed on parental involvement and cooperation. Parents *must* also be given the name and address of a person to whom they may apply for information and advice about their child's special educational needs.

The Education Act, 1981 requires all LEAs to provide for the needs of children requiring special education and to keep them under review. This should include making arrangements to educate children with special needs with ordinary children (i.e. integration) and parental wishes should be met wherever possible. Where it would be inappropriate for special educational provision to be made at school, LEAs can arrange for it to be made elsewhere.

An LEA can legally insist on a medical and other examination of any child whom they have reason to believe requires special education once that child has reached the age of two years.

Under the Education Act, 1981 the LEA is required to determine the special educational provision which needs to be made and to assess the child's needs. However, *parents must be involved in the making of the assessments and may appeal against the decisions.* LEAs are also empowered, with the consent of parents, to assess these special educational needs of children under two years of age and to maintain records and statements about them.

In addition, parents are able to request that the LEA assesses the special needs of their child whether or not statements or records are being maintained for them.

Recording of handicapped children

A detailed statement must be maintained for each child. This record should contain the results of multi-professional assessment and should carefully define the individual handicaps or disabilities and the child's special needs and difficulties. It should also indicate the special form of education required for the child. The LEA then has to meet such needs. Parents must be consulted in the drawing up of the record and it is a legal requirement for the LEA to review, modify and maintain the record. In the event of a disagreement between the parents and the LEA, there is an appeal to a special appeal committee and a final right of appeal to the Secretary of State.

Principles applying to meeting special educational needs

Certain basic principles apply to the education of children with special needs:

- every effort should be made to discover the extent of the disability and special needs of the child as early as possible. In some instances, such as congenital deafness, this will be within the first year of life;
- special education and care should be started early and continued well after the normal school leaving age;
- the aim should be to make each child as independent as possible;
- each child should be dealt with individually and improvisation is always helpful;
- the best solution is usually that which is as near normal as possible. All forms of integration into the ordinary school system are therefore very useful;
- the after-care of children with disabilities or significant difficulties when they leave school is most important. Wherever possible, special vocational training and/or work preparation should be arranged.

To encourage early discovery and identification of special educational needs, all DHAs, under the Education Act 1981, have a legal duty to inform parents and the LEA where they form the opinion that a child under the age of five has, or is likely to have, special educational needs. The DHA must also afford the parents an opportunity to discuss their opinion before bringing the child to the attention of the LEA.

There are many ways in which a handicapped child can be educated: in an ordinary school; in a special class in an ordinary school; in a day special school; in a residential special school; at home with a peripatetic teacher; or in a combination of these.

Discovery of disabilities and disclosure to parents

The importance of early discovery of any disability in a child has already been stressed. Depending on the nature of the handicap or problem, it may be discovered shortly after birth by the parents, doctors, health visitor, or during the first few years or not even until the child attends a day nursery, nursery school or primary school. In all instances, it is essential that a full explanation of the disability is given in a sensitive way to the parents. Many may find it difficult to grasp the full meaning and significance, especially in the case of a serious disability or mental handicap and such parents *will need constant support* and will require *information, advice and practical help.* It is best if parents have nominated to them one individual professional to act as a 'named person' who can introduce the parents to the right services, explain any problems and generally act as a guide and counsellor. For any child of preschool age, the health visitor will normally act in this capacity, although in exceptional cases (e.g. a deaf child) another professional (e.g. peripatetic teacher) may act as named person. For children with special needs at school, the head teacher should undertake this role. Parents should be encouraged to discuss their doubts and fears openly for concealment only adds to their problems.

Assessment of special educational needs

The assessment of a child with a disability or significant difficulty should always include the following:

- *parents should always be involved.* No estimation of a child's needs can be complete without the fullest help from parents. The aim should be to treat parents as partners and parents must be kept fully informed of all expert investigation;
- *multi-professional assessment should always be undertaken.* This will include expert medical examination by hospital paediatricians as well as assessment by health visitors, educational psychologists, teachers, social work staff and day nursery matrons, where appropriate. Assessment should aim at discovering how the child learns and responds over a period of time;
- there must be full *investigations of any aspect of the child's performance which is causing concern;*
- the *family and home circumstances* should always be taken into account.

Range of special education provided

The special educational needs of children are extremely complex and varied. It may be possible for even the seriously disabled to be educated in ordinary schools provided special ramps are available to accommodate wheelchairs, special teaching equipment is on hand and transport is provided to enable the child to get to school.

For most children with severe disabilities and for those who have already attended a primary school but made little progress, attendance at a special school may be needed at least for an initial period. Special schools are provided by LEAs and voluntary bodies and, under the Education Act 1981, the Secretary of State can make regulations in respect of the approval of special schools and independent schools.

In general, special schools are needed for three groups of children:

- children with *very severe or complex disabilities*. This group includes a wide range of conditions including complete blindness or deafness, severe congenital disabilities such as spina bifida and the worst cerebral palsies, and progressive diseases such as Duchenne muscular dystrophy;
- children with *severe emotional or behavioural disorders* whose behaviour is extreme and unpredictable. Such children were formerly called 'maladjusted' but this is a term no longer in general use;
- children who for various reasons have *done badly in ordinary school* and who need the more intimate atmosphere of smaller teaching groups.

Integration

Wherever possible, children with special educational needs should be educated in ordinary schools (integration). There are three forms of integration:

- *locational*. This is where a special school unit is sited within the same grounds as an ordinary school, but is run as a separate school. This is a first step in integration and is helpful in reducing isolation and stigma felt by parents and children who attend a 'special school'. It also enables seriously disabled children to attend the 'same school' as their brothers and sisters, and helps the children in ordinary schools to understand better the needs and problems of handicapped children;
- *social integration* is a further step and here the children play, eat and mix with the children from the adjacent ordinary school and may even share some of their out-of-classroom activities. Classroom teaching, however, remains separate;
- *functional integration* achieves all the above mixing but, in addition, the disabled children share most of their classes with ordinary children. Such an arrangement still allows some specialised teaching but enables the handicapped children to gain access to a wider range of teaching than is usually possible in a special school. It also enables the potential of most disabled children to be better reached.

For severely disabled children who have to spend most of their school life in a special school, it is important for them to experience some degree of social and functional integration during the last two to three years at school. This is the best way to avoid overprotection of such children which, to some degree, is inevitable for any child attending a small special school.

Special problems of the disabled child in the transitional period from school into adult life

All children with disabilities or significant difficulties meet special problems on leaving school. They are likely to find more difficulty in getting a job or in being accepted for higher education. Careful preparation is therefore important and reassessment should always take place during the last two or three years at school. As well as the usual professionals, careers guidance officers, Disablement Resettlement Officers and special social workers from the social services department should be involved.

Special linked courses whereby children may spend part of their time in a nearby college of further education and 'work preparation' schemes can be of considerable value. For disabled young persons over school leaving age, there are also Employment Rehabilitation Centres run by the Department of Employment. There are also a number of specialised residential assessment courses at special units such as the Queen Elizabeth's Foundation at Banstead Place, Surrey. *Special careers officers* are employed by most LEAs to give special help to disabled school leavers.

Young persons who have learning disabilities and have been attending special schools will usually transfer to local Adult Training Centres run by social services departments (see p. 366) and hopefully later to sheltered workshops.

Importance of further education

Many disabled young persons experience difficulties in finding work unless they can become qualified in some way. Therefore, they should, wherever possible, be encouraged to attend a college of further education or some form of higher education (polytechnic or university).

At Coventry, the LEA runs a very modern residential further education college (Hereward College). There are also a number of voluntary bodies which run excellent residential training colleges.

Special groups of children with disabilities or significant difficulties

Although handicapped children are no longer categorised, those with certain types of disabilities still require specialised help. Brief notes describing the needs of children with particular disabilities are given below.

Children who are blind or partially sighted

Blind children have no useful sight and must be educated by non-visual methods. Education in nearly all cases takes place in a residential school except in the largest cities. Blind children often start their training at the age of 2 years in the Sunshine Homes run by the Royal National Institute for the Blind.

Partially sighted children have very poor eyesight but, with special assistance, they can be taught using visual methods. Classes must be very small, not more than ten in a class, and special equipment is needed. In most instances, partially sighted children can be taught in special day schools or special classes within day schools.

Children who are deaf or partially deaf

Deaf children have no useful hearing and cannot be taught by auditory methods. *It is essential that their training and education should start very young (as soon as diagnosed)* for it is very specialised. By remarkable methods which have translated the teaching of sounds into visual tuition, it is possible to teach speech to totally deaf children who have never heard human speech. In the absence of such teaching, the totally deaf child will also be dumb, as speaking is normally learnt by the child copying what is heard. Most deaf children are educated in special residential schools.

Partially deaf children can be educated in small classes using auditory methods provided special hearing aids are used. Such tuition usually takes place in special day schools but may be carried out in residential schools.

Delicate children

This group is a large mixed group containing many medical and surgical conditions which interfere with a child's education. Chest diseases (such as asthma), heart conditions (congenital heart disease), blood diseases, diabetes and alimentary diseases make up this group, which includes any rare disease of childhood which makes a child's education difficult.

Many of these children need at first to be admitted to a residential school to allow their medical condition to be fully determined and their educational potential assessed. In many instances, education will have been very badly interrupted by repeated illnesses and the children may become very backward in their education. Many parents of such children worry so much about the child's health that they overprotect the child and this adds to the problems.

Having assessed the child in a residential school and having introduced some degree of stability into his or her education, it is often possible later to return the child to a special day school. In the case of children undergoing a series of operations, the regime at a residential school will often build up the children and help their treatment as well as maintaining, as far as possible, continuity with their education.

Children with intellectual impairment

The degree of intellectual impairment in children can vary from those who have difficulties in learning and keeping up with their peers at school to those who need long-term specialist education in order to accomplish even the most basic of everyday personal skills. Children in this last group are usually said to suffer from learning disabilities.

Many children who are handicapped in this way exhibit more behaviour difficulties than normal children. Their rate of juvenile delinquency is always higher and a continuing problem for the school health and social services. Girls may reach sexual maturity quite early and may be in moral danger, being more easily led astray. It is important therefore that this is anticipated and fully discussed with the parents or guardian to reduce such a risk. Surveys of adolescent unmarried mothers have tended to show that a greater proportion of these young people have some form of intellectual impairment.

Until recently children with intellectual handicap were classified rather rigidly as 'educationally subnormal (moderate) – ESN(M)', and 'educationally subnormal (severe) – ESN(S)' These terms are no longer used. It is now recognised that many children can achieve far more if, from the outset, all their qualities, such as their social adjustment, emotional and behavioural patterns are taken into consideration when deciding what type of educational opportunities or help may be available to them. More severe intellectual handicap or which results in learning disabilities is also covered in Chapter 19. It should be noted that whilst 'intellectual handicap' or 'impairment' are frequently used, they should not be confused with 'mental impairment' as defined in the Mental Health Act 1983 (see p. 360).

Intelligence tests

Although it should not be isolated from other aspects of a person's character and behavioural pattern, the intelligence test is a means of estimating the mental age of a child or adult. It consists of a series of tests, questions and exercises designed to demonstrate knowledge gained and reasoning power.

$$\text{The } Intelligence\ Quotient\ (IQ) = \frac{\text{mental age}}{\text{real age}} \times 100$$

Examples   A child aged 10 years who has a mental age of 12 years would have an intelligence quotient (IQ) of 120.

$$IQ = \frac{\text{mental age}}{\text{real age}} \times 100 = \frac{12}{10} \times 100 = 120$$

A child aged 10 years who has a mental age of 10 years would have an intelligence quotient of 100.

$$IQ = \frac{\text{mental age}}{\text{real age}} \times 100 = \frac{10}{10} \times 100 = 100$$

A child aged 10 years who has a mental age of 8 years would have an intelligence quotient of 80.

$$IQ = \frac{\text{mental age}}{\text{real age}} \times 100 = 80$$

It will thus be seen that a perfectly normal average child would have an intelligence quotient of 100. Above average intelligence gives an intelligence quotient over 100 and below average intelligence an intelligence quotient below 100.

Value of the intelligence quotient   Intelligence quotients vary roughly as follows:

120–125+	University entrant
115+	Bright school child
90–115+	Average school child
80–90 ⎫	Retarded school child
55–79 ⎬	Intellectual impairment
Under 50–55 ⎭	Child with learning disabilities

It·is important to realise that *these levels are guides only* and that exceptions occur in this grouping.

   In grading a backward child, it is necessary to carry out at least two or more intelligence tests and also to try the child out with a highly experienced teacher before the final decision is made. A very careful search must always be made for any signs of an accompanying physical deformity, such as deafness, which could be responsible for the low result.

   Intellectually handicapped children may need to be educated in either a residential or special day school where the curriculum contains a greater proportion of practical teaching, and where the pace of the teaching is slower than at a normal school. A child who does well in special school may later be able to move back to an ordinary school.

Children with severe emotional or behavioural disorders

A child in this group is a 'problem child' showing many behaviour difficulties. Because of this, the child may become retarded educationally, although his or her intelligence may be normal.

There are many causes of this condition. Some of these children show emotional instability and even a psychological disorder, but many just reflect unstable home conditions including marital difficulties, divorce or separation of parents.

Complete careful diagnosis of the problem is essential. This is rarely a simple procedure. Often repeated visits of the child and the parents to the *Child Guidance Clinic*, where a psychiatrist and psychiatric social worker are in attendance, will be necessary before the complete causative factors are unravelled. It is usual for the social worker attached to the child guidance clinic to be a member of the Social Services Department so that there is maximum coordination between the social work undertaken in the child guidance clinics and the community social services.

These children are best educated in ordinary schools for they gain from contact with normal children although if their home is very unsatisfactory they may have to be in residential (boarding) school. Any psychological disorders in the children must be treated appropriately. It will, however, be necessary to attempt to improve the home conditions. Because it can be hard or impossible to improve conditions in a divided home, treatment is often difficult and calls for much patience. Relapses in behaviour occur and delinquency may complicate the picture. Continued encouragement and understanding by teaching and medical staff will sometimes eventually succeed.

Failure in such children may have serious consequences later for they may drift into criminal behaviour and may even become chronic criminals. There is no doubt that much crime could be prevented by more concentrated medico-social work upon schoolchildren who exhibit extreme forms of behaviour.

Children who are physically handicapped

This group contains the very severely handicapped children. Many have serious handicaps, often with paralysis, and include children handicapped by such diseases as muscular dystrophies and other serious orthopaedic conditions. Some children may never have attended normal schools since their illness commenced. It is usual to educate such children in special residential or day schools in which the classes are very small so that each child can receive much personal attention. In those diseases which are not progressive it is important, towards the end of the child's education, to do everything possible to make him or her as independent as possible. In this respect, it is always wise to try and arrange for the child to spend the last year of school life at an ordinary school even if this can only be achieved by much improvisation – such as organising special transport. If the child can learn such independence there is more likelihood that, on leaving school, a job will be found.

Children with epilepsy

The majority of children with epilepsy can be educated in an ordinary school provided that:

● the fits do not occur very often;
● there is no marked behaviour difficulty, i.e. the emotional stability of the child is reasonably normal; and
● there is a good liaison between the school doctor and teacher who realises that no other child in the class will come to any harm from witnessing the occasional epileptic fit.

In the case of very frequent major fits or of marked emotional instability, it is wise to arrange for the child to be admitted at once to a special residential school for epileptic children for assessment and treatment. Such a school may be run in conjunction with an epileptic colony and its medical and teaching staff will have great experience of such problems. After assessment and correct treatment, in a proportion of cases, it may be possible for the child to return to an ordinary school.

It is, however, stressed that only a small proportion of children with epilepsy ever need to go to such a school, for most can be educated at an ordinary school quite satisfactorily.

Children with speech defects

Any defect of speech in a school child can be serious unless corrected. Such children may quickly develop emotional difficulties from the frustration of being unable to make themselves readily understood. This in turn will tend to aggravate their speech defect.

A most careful physical examination is needed to exclude a physical cause (defective hearing or deformities of palate) and then regular speech therapy must be started. Speech therapists are employed by each school health service to carry out this treatment by relaxation and speech training. It is most important that the child with a speech defect stays in a normal school with normal children. Special schools are, therefore, not needed.

Children with dyslexia

Dyslexia is an interesting condition in which there is a specific language difficulty which shows itself in a series of ways affecting spelling, reading and other language skills. There is always a marked discrepancy between the mental potential of the child (which is often normal) and the educational level attained. The incidence of dyslexia is as high as 3% although many minor cases are missed. In many instances the condition is not recognised until very late with consequent serious loss of learning potential. Many such children may later become language-disabled adults.

The cause of dyslexia is not fully understood but most agree that it is caused by a lesion in the central nervous system which has been present either from birth or shortly afterwards. Many children suffering from dyslexia do well if the condition is recognised early, they attend nursery schools and later receive individual teaching or teaching in very small groups in which it is possible to mould a teaching programme to an individual child.

7 Prevention of disease by immunisation

In many communicable diseases, an attack of the disease is followed by a varying period of immunity from further attacks. This does not occur in every communicable disease (for example, the common cold is followed only by a very transient immunity), but in many, the length of the immunity is substantial, lasting years or even a lifetime. Whenever a person develops an immunity in this way, the body manufactures special disease-resistant *antibodies*.

It is possible to copy this mechanism artificially by introducing into the human body modified bacteria, viruses or their products so that the individual does not suffer from the disease but does develop antibodies and, therefore, is immune to a natural attack. Artificial immunisation and vaccination relies on this principle. Immunity can be either active or passive.

In *active immunity* a modified bacteria or virus or a special product of the bacteria or virus is introduced into the body, either by injection or by mouth, which stimulates the human body to manufacture its own protective antibodies. Immunity produced in this way is always more satisfactory as it lasts a long time. Its only drawback is that it often takes 2–3 months for the human body to build up a substantial immunity.

Passive immunity is when immunoglobulin, the active constituent of human blood which contains the antibodies against the disease, is collected from a person who already has an immunity to that disease, and is then injected into the patient at risk. The great value of this method is that *it gives immediate immunity* but this is very transient and rarely lasts more than 4–6 weeks. It can also be used to increase very quickly the resistance of a patient to dangerous toxins in diseases such as diphtheria or tetanus, in a patient already in the early stages of these diseases and who has no immunity. In these cases an animal such as an ox is actively immunised, and manufactures antibodies which are then used to protect early cases. There is however the disadvantage that not only does the immunity last a very short time but that the patient may easily become sensitised to the protein of the animal and suffer serum sickness.

In preventive medicine, greater use is made of active immunisation than passive immunisation.

Active immunisation

The dangers of communicable diseases arise in two main ways:

- by a *direct invasion process* of a certain part of the body. Examples include inflammation of the lung in pertussis (whooping cough), of the small intestine in typhoid fever or of part of the central nervous system in encephalitis or meningitis;
- by the bacteria producing a very powerful poison (*toxin*), either as it grows in the body (as in diphtheria or tetanus) or after the bacteria has grown in food (as in toxin food poisoning).

Diseases caused by direct invasion are usually prevented by using an *antigen which either consists of dead bacteria or viruses or live modified ones*. Where modified live bacteria or viruses are used (as in BCG vaccination against tuberculosis or in poliomyelitis immunisation with Sabin vaccine) the live bacteria or virus has undergone a change (*mutation*) which results in it now being unable to cause the disease in the human, but it can still produce antibodies which then protect the person against the disease.

Some quite remarkable successes have been achieved by immunisation. Diphtheria and poliomyelitis are the best examples. In the 10 years before immunisation against diphtheria began in the UK in 1943, approximately 60 000 cases occurred each year. This meant that about 9–10% of persons were likely to suffer from diphtheria at some time during their life. After immunisation was introduced the incidence fell rapidly and the disease soon became very rare – immunisation has virtually eradicated diphtheria. During the 1950s on average 2800 cases of poliomyelitis occurred each year in the UK with approximately 300 deaths and many persons being left severely physically disabled. By 1970 over 20 million people had been immunised and the number of new cases had fallen to less than 10 per year – again immunisation has virtually eradicated poliomyelitis.

It is important to realise that people inherit different amounts of natural immunity. Immunisation greatly increases any person's immunity but there will still be considerable variation in any group of the population that has just been immunised. Over the following years the level of that immunity gradually falls. Obviously the person who originally had very little natural immunity will have their acquired immunity lowered more quickly. This is the reason why, after any immunisation, it is never possible to guarantee complete protection in everyone. However, those unlucky persons who do develop an attack after immunisation almost inevitably have a very mild form of the disease.

Levels of immunisation achieved in children

The levels of immunisation in children against serious communicable disease are given in Table 7.1 for England for the period 1980–91/2. Note that since late 1988, when combined vaccination against measles, mumps and rubella (MMR) was introduced, the figures for immunisation against these three diseases are combined although from 1991–2 this figure is almost entirely MMR. In the government White Paper *The Health of the Nation* (1992) a new national immunisation target of 95% was announced for 1995.

By 1993, a 95% level had been reached for diphtheria, tetanus and poliomyelitis with whooping cough, measles, mumps and rubella at 92%.

Figure 7.1 gives a clear indication of the remarkable progress that has been made in the control and eventual eradication of measles by immunisation during the period 1969–92. This graph is taken from the *Guidelines for Health Promotion No. 36* published by the Faculty of Public Health Medicine of the Royal Colleges of Physicians of the UK.

Table 7.1 Percentage of children immunised by their 2nd birthday and of children given BCG vaccine by their 14th birthday, England, 1980–91/92

Year	Diphtheria	Tetanus	Polio	Whooping cough	Measles	Mumps/ rubella	BCG*
1980**	81	81	81	41	53	—	82
1981**	83	83	82	46	55	—	78
1982**	84	84	84	53	58	—	75
1983**	84	84	84	59	60	—	76
1984**	84	84	84	65	63	—	71
1985**	85	85	85	65	68	—	77
1986**	85	85	85	67	71	—	76
1987/88**	87	87	87	73	76	—	76
1988/89	87	87	87	75	80	7	71
1989/90	89	89	89	78	84	68	36†
1990/91	92	92	92	84	87	86	90
1991/92	93	93	93	88	90	90	86
1992/3	95	95	95	92	92	92	74

* Estimated percentage.
** Estimated percentage immunised by the end of the second year after birth.
† The school BCG programme was suspended in 1989 because there were insufficient supplies of BCG vaccine.
(From the Chief Medical Officer's report *On the State of the Public Health 1993*, published in 1994, Department of Health.)

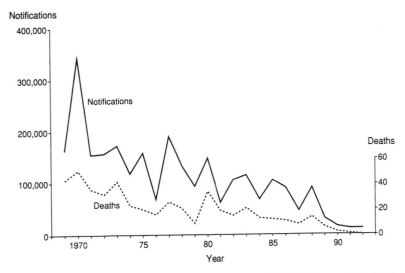

Fig. 7.1 Measles notifications and deaths, UK, 1969–92. (Source: England and Wales – OPCS, Scotland – CD(S)U and Registrar General's Office, Northern Ireland – Department of Health.)

Routine immunisation schedule for a child

The accelerated immunisation schedule for children in the UK is given in Table 7.2.

Triple immunisation against diphtheria, whooping cough and tetanus

These immunisations are combined for convenience and are given at 2 months because of the importance of protecting the infant against an attack of whooping cough at an early age when it can be dangerous. The diphtheria and tetanus portions of this immunisation are *toxoids* which protect against the dangerous and powerful toxins in both diseases. It is impracticable to inject toxin for it has many dangers. If, however, formalin is added to the toxin, its chemical composition changes and the resultant toxoid is quite harmless, but fortunately it will still acts as an efficient antigen and produces effective immunity.

Booster doses of *diphtheria and tetanus* are given to preschool children and to school leavers, but special low-dose vaccine *must be used* for school leavers and adults – this is needed to prevent adverse reactions in this age group and adults. Adults at special risk such as health staff in communicable disease units and travellers to Russia where, in 1993, 15 211 cases of diphtheria occurred, should also be protected.

Table 7.2 Active immunisation schedule for a child.

Age	Immunisation	Notes
Birth	BCG vaccine 0.1 ml intradermally	For Asian babies and for babies whose mothers have tuberculosis
2 months	Diphtheria, tetanus and pertussis 0.5 ml i.m./s.c. Poliomyelitis 3 drops by mouth Hib 0.5 ml i.m./s.c.	
3 months	Diphtheria, tetanus and pertussis 0.5 ml i.m./s.c. Poliomyelitis 3 drops by mouth Hib 0.5 ml i.m./s.c.	
4 months	Diphtheria, tetanus and pertussis 0.5 ml i.m./s.c.	
15 months	Measles, mumps and rubella 0.5 ml i.m./s.c.	For children not already protected. This can be given before entry to infant school.
15 months	Measles 0.5 ml i.m./s.c.	To be given if MMR was refused. Can be used from 6 months in a measles epidemic and then repeated at 2 years

Booster immunisations

4–5 years	Poliomyelitis 3 drops by mouth	
10–14 years	BCG 0.1 ml intradermally	If tuberculin negative
10–14 years	Rubella 0.5 ml i.m./s.c.	Girls who have not had MMR
School leavers	Poliomyelitis 3 drops by mouth Tetanus 0.5 ml i.m./s.c. New combined vaccine against tetanus and diphtheria (Td) *using low level dose for adults.* Do *not* use the diphtheria and tetanus used for preschool booster as it could be dangerous.	

i.m. = intramuscular; s.c. = subcutaneous.

Apart from the joint vaccinations against diphtheria and tetanus (see opposite) reinforcing doses should be given to adults after an injury. Protection lasts for at least 10 years and more frequent booster doses are not recommended as very frequent booster doses increase greatly the risk of severe local reactions.

Whooping cough (pertussis) vaccination is the one childhood immunisation which, in the past, had a low take up – only 41% in 1980. This was mainly caused by adverse publicity linking the immunisation with the risk of neurological symptoms and complications. Further studies have shown this risk to be very low and, by 1993, the level of this immunisation had risen to 92% (see Table 7.1). There is only one absolute contraindication to whooping cough immunisation – a severe local reaction when most of the circumference of the arm or thigh is swollen with erythema or a severe general reaction including anaphylaxis, a temperature of at least 40.5°C and/or convulsions within 72 hours of the injection. The only other group of children in whom special consideration is needed are those who showed cerebral irritation in the newborn period and those with neurological disease or where the parents or siblings have a history of epilepsy. In practice, probably less than 5% of children fall into this group who should not be immunised with whooping cough vaccine. Whooping cough vaccine *should not be given after the age of 5 years.*

It is most important to realise that all three doses of the primary immunisation, at 2, 3 and 4 months, must be given to ensure complete protection. The first of these three injections is followed immediately by hardly any protection – the first dose seems to prepare the body's mechanism for producing antibodies. The second dose is followed by a fair degree of protection but *it is the third dose which produces the most lasting immunity.* For this reason, mothers must make certain that their children have all three doses. A system of computerisation of all immunisation records helps most general practices to remind parents of the need for further immunisation in their children.

Hib disease

Hib disease is caused by the bacterium *Haemophilus inflenzae* type b (Hib) which is frequently found in the upper respiratory tract of young children. The most common symptom of this disease is meningitis but the illness may present as an epiglottis, septicaemia, osteomyelitis or pneumonia. It can now be prevented by Hib vaccination which was introduced in October 1992. Ideally this immunisation should be given simultaneously with triple vaccination but at a different site at 2, 3 and 4 months. It can also be given to children up to 4 years of age who missed their earlier protection – one dose only is needed for children over 1 year of age. This vaccination is ineffective against other causes of meningitis.

Poliomyelitis

This disease was a serious threat until widespread immunisation was introduced in the early 1960s. Since then only very occasional cases have been reported in the UK. The continued absence of this disease in any epidemic form is due to the success of poliomyelitis vaccination. Originally dead inactivated (Salk) vaccine was used but in 1962 this was superseded by Sabin oral vaccine which has the following advantages:

- it is easier to administer – by mouth rather than by injection;
- it produces an immunity not only to a clinical attack of poliomyelitis, but also to a carrier state in the small intestine;
- it is free from the dangers of allergic reactions.

There are three types of poliomyelitis virus – types I, II and III – *and all three must be included in any vaccine*. The mechanism of protection in the oral vaccine is that after each dose the small intestine is seeded with one of the particular types of virus which then grows rapidly and colonises the intestine. This is then followed by a marked immunity to that type of virus. Once the intestine has been seeded by a particular type, it cannot be colonised again with the same type, so the second dose leads to colonisation with one of the other types and the third dose with colonisation and protection against all three types. *It is essential that three doses are given to ensure complete protection*. The vaccine is conveniently given on a lump of sugar (three drops) or in a sugar solution. Care should be taken to store the vaccine in a refrigerator to maintain its potency.

Very rarely (about one in 5 million instances) a vaccine-associated paralysis may develop as a complication of poliomyelitis immunisation. This risk increases in adults over the age of 50 and the inactivated (Salk) vaccine should be given to anyone of this age if continued protection is required. Salk vaccine should also be used *to protect pregnant women and for persons who are immunosuppressed.*

Combined measles, mumps and rubella (German measles)

In the UK since 1988 a combined measles, mumps and rubella (MMR) vaccination has been the usual method of immunising children against these diseases. The immunisation is given between the ages of 1 and 2 years (see Table 7.1). The decision to include mumps immunisation for the first time was aimed at preventing two unpleasant complications – meningitis in both sexes and, in boys, orchitis.

MMR is a freeze-dried preparation which must be stored between 2°C and 8°C and protected from the light. The dose is 0.5 ml to be given by the intramuscular or deep subcutaneous route. MMR immunisation should be given even if there is a previous history of measles, mumps or rubella. Mild reactions may occur after a week and a mild parotid swelling can occur after 2 weeks but children are not infectious. If parents refuse MMR vaccination, then protection against measles can be obtained by the child having the older single antigen measles vaccine. MMR immunisation should be given to all children aged 4–5 years starting infant school if they have not already been protected.

Rubella (German measles)

Vaccination against rubella should be given to girls aged 11–13 years who did not receive an MMR immunisation at 15 months or when starting infant school at 4–5 years, to avoid any chance of contracting rubella later during early pregnancy. A single dose of freeze-dried, live attenuated virus of the Cendehill strain is used.

Routine vaccination of adult women *is not recommended* as it is uncertain whether the strain of virus can reach or harm the fetus. It is therefore most important that a woman *is not pregnant at the time of rubella vaccination and does not become pregnant for at least 2 months after immunisation*. If vaccination is requested, a screening serological test should first be undertaken by the Public Health Laboratory Service and vaccination only offered to those women who are sero-negative (before MMR started this was approximately 10%).

Tuberculosis

Immunisation against tuberculosis is carried out using a live vaccine of the Bacillus Calmette-Guérin type (BCG). This stain of bacteria is named after two Frenchmen who first discovered it at the beginning of the century. It is a modified or attenuated strain of tubercle bacillus which has lost its power to cause the disease in humans but can still produce a small trivial skin lesion after injection. This skin infection later results in an immunity against tuberculosis.

BCG immunisation is only used on people who have no skin sensitivity to tuberculin as shown by the tuberculin test (Heaf test). Four main groups of persons are immunised against tuberculosis:

● close contacts, such as other members of the family, of a case of tuberculosis. This group includes any newborn baby of parents, either of whom has had tuberculosis in the past. It also includes babies of recently arrived Asian families;
● schoolchildren aged 10–13 years who are tuberculin negative. This represents approximately 5% of schoolchildren. With the parents'

consent, all children aged 12 years are given a skin test at school. Those who are tuberculin negative are then vaccinated with BCG;
- persons who, in their occupation, are liable to run a greater risk of infection from tuberculosis. This group includes *nurses and doctors*. It is usual to give a tuberculin test to all new nursing and medical students and then to give a BCG vaccination to any who are tuberculin negative. Since BCG vaccination was started in schools for children aged 12 years, fewer nursing and medical students need BCG vaccination later;
- children of certain immigrants whose home communities have a high incidence of tuberculosis. This includes those from Pakistan, Bangladesh, India and Africa.

After vaccination with BCG, a small skin lesion develops which may suppurate for some weeks and may not clear up until a few months after vaccination. This is quite normal and all that is required is a dry dressing to cover the lesion. Sometimes BCG vaccination is followed by an axillary adenitis. This is rare and usually clears up without further complications.

BCG vaccination should not be given to children who have active eczema, local sepsis or who are HIV positive.

Hepatitis B

Hepatitis B is spread by blood, saliva, semen and vaginal secretions and can be prevented by prior immunisation. The following persons (including many health service staff) should be considered to be at high risk and should ensure that they receive protective vaccination. Three doses are required, the second after 1 month and the third after 6 months. *Persons at highest risk* include:

- staff working in renal dialysis units;
- people working in units that deal with known carriers of hepatitis B;
- personnel working in haemophiliac or blood transfusion units;
- staff in laboratories;
- nurses, doctors and dentists and students in training for these professions;
- renal dialysis patients who, when travelling abroad, receive haemodialysis outside the UK.

Other persons who may *from time to time be at risk* include:

- those working in homes and hostels for persons with a learning disability;
- health staff working in areas of the world where it is known that there is a high prevalence of hepatitis B;

- non-immune sexual contacts of carriers of hepatitis B;
- active male homosexuals;
- parental drug abusers;
- persons who suffer from a learning disability (mental handicap) and are about to enter a hostel or home for such individuals.

All the above persons should make certain they have had an immunisation against hepatitis B. Two important advisory publications have been issued by the joint UK Health Departments recently – *Guidance for Clinical Care Workers: Protection Against Infection with HIV and Hepatitis Viruses* (1990) and *Protecting Health Care Workers and Patients from Hepatitis B* (1993). *All NHS clinical and professional staff have an absolute duty to inform their prospective employer, contracting organisation and/or employment agency of all information from which it might be concluded that they are infectious carriers of hepatitis B.* In November 1993 a doctor had his name erased from the medical register for failing to report that he was a carrier. This was carried out because the General Medical Council decided that the doctor had been guilty of serious professional misconduct and the Council felt it necessary to take such serious action to protect members of the public. This action demonstrates how essential it is for staff (*including nurses at risk*) to protect themselves by insisting on having a protective immunisation. Otherwise their whole careers could be at risk if they contracted an infection and became a carrier of hepatitis B.

A small proportion of persons over the age of 40 (10–15%) do not respond to vaccination against hepatitis B, therefore post-vaccination screening at 2–4 months after vaccination should be carried out to estimate the antibody level produced by the immunisation. Those who are then found to have no immunity should be advised that, if exposure to infection then occurs, passive immunisation using hepatitis B immunoglobulin should be carried out. Any individual who is accidentally inoculated with blood products from an infected person or the sexual contacts of a recently diagnosed hepatitis B case (within 1 week of the onset of jaundice) should be given hepatitis B immunoglobulin. Note that *hepatitis B can be sexually transmitted as well as by accidental blood infection* (see chapter 9).

Anthrax

Immunisation against anthrax is now available to protect all workers at risk. These include abattoir workers and those involved with the handling of imported hides. Three doses of killed vaccine are used with second and third injections after 6 and 20 weeks. A single booster injection should be given annually.

Influenza

Influenza inactivated vaccines prepared from both influenza A and B strains of influenza virus are used to immunise certain groups of people. Changes in antigens occur periodically in this disease and vaccines are prepared using new strains which usually first appear in the southern hemisphere. The specific groups of the population at special risk who should be immunised by a single dose of influenza vaccine include:

- elderly persons;
- those with chronic cardiac, respiratory or renal disease;
- diabetics;
- individuals who are immunosuppressed (such as those on parental cortisone treatment);
- persons who live permanently in long-stay hospitals or institutions;
- health staff working in high risk areas.

Rabies

Rabies is always present on the continent of Europe and in many other parts of the world (see Chapter 8). There has always been considerable concern that rabies might spread and become endemic in the UK, however this danger has been reduced by strict legislation limiting the import of animals (the Rabies Act 1974 is designed to do this – see p. 167). Rabies can be prevented by *early active vaccination immediately after contact with an infected animal*, however the course of injections is a long and painful one. Human diploid cell vaccine should be used in a course consisting of 14 daily injections into the abdominal wall followed by a booster dose 10 days later and a final booster 20 days after that.

For persons at special risk, who may handle animals suspected of being rabid, permanent prophylactic vaccination should be carried out using two doses of duck embryo vaccine given at an interval of 4–6 weeks. Booster doses are given 6 months later and then every 3 years.

Immunisations for persons travelling outside the UK

Immunisations are advised for persons visiting certain countries outside the UK. Full details of current requirements can be obtained from the Department of Health and from travel agents and should be checked before any extensive journey abroad is started. The only disease for which immunisation at present is obligatory is *yellow fever*. This disease is limited to a narrow band of land in mid-Africa and South America and *all persons visiting such districts must first be immunised* – unvaccinated people will not be admitted.

The following are the diseases that it is wise to have protective vaccinations or immunisations against before travelling:

● typhoid and paratyphoid fevers. Prior immunisation with TAB vaccine is always a wise precaution for anyone visiting a country or district with a primitive water supply. It is also sensible to have a TAB vaccination when visiting any area of Europe if one is camping or caravanning. Two injections are given with a 4 week interval between each dose;
● diphtheria and poliomyelitis. It is wise to have a booster dose of diphtheria and poliomyelitis immunisation before visiting Third World countries and Russia.

At present *cholera* vaccine gives incomplete and short-lived protection. No country now requires cholera vaccination as a condition of entry. The Department of Health now recommends doctors in the UK not to give cholera vaccination to travellers.

Passive immunisation

Reference has already been made to the use of tetanus antitoxin which can be used to prevent the development of tetanus in persons who have never been actively immunised against this disease but who have had an injury and may have been contaminated with tetanus spores. In diphtheria only, antitoxin is a valuable therapeutic agent in the earliest stages.

The usual modern method of giving passive immunisation is to use *human blood immunoglobulin which usually contains many antibodies* against common communicable diseases.

Immunoglobulin can be used in two forms:

● normal human immunoglobulin;
● specific human immunoglobulin.

Normal human immunoglobulin

This can be used to provide immediate temporary protection in the following instances:

● to prevent an attack of *rubella* (German measles) during the first 3 months of pregnancy in a woman known to have been a contact and who has not previously had an immunisation against rubella and who has no antibodies against this disease. A dose of 2.0 g should be given which should protect her temporarily (for about

8–9 weeks) which is long enough to avoid any danger of a possible congenital malformation in her child or to cause a miscarriage;
- to prevent an attack of *measles* in an infant or young child who has previously not been immunised. This is mainly used in hospital paediatric wards for children who are already very ill with another disease (such as leukaemia). The usual dose is 0.4 g for a child under 2 years of age and 0.75 g for older children;
- to prevent an attack of *hepatitis A* in persons at special risk such as travellers to certain tropical countries, individuals who are living in a hostel in which there is an outbreak of hepatitis A or to household contacts who are already immunosuppressed, such as a person suffering from a disease being treated with cortisone.

Specific human immunoglobulin

In addition, for immediate protection from certain diseases *specific human immunoglobulin* is available. These preparations have a high antibody content, having been prepared from the blood of persons who have had recent infections or immunisations. The following are available:

- *hepatitis B virus immunoglobulin*. This can be used to protect persons at special risk after injuries from surgical needles (needlestick injuries) or bites from an infected person or babies born to hepatitis B positive mothers;
- *anti-tetanus immunoglobulin*. This is made available through regional blood transfusion centres and is used to prevent tetanus in patients who have had seriously contaminated wounds;
- *anti-rabies immunoglobulin*. This can be used for the post-exposure treatment of persons who are mainly sensitive to equine antiserum which is generally used in such circumstances;
- *anti-varicella immunoglobulin*. This is mainly used for children very ill with acute leukaemia who are on immunosuppressive therapy and who have been in contact with chickenpox.

Other information regarding immunisations

Consent to immunisations

As legally, an injection is an assault on the person, it is necessary to obtain written consent from a parent or guardian before immunising any child or young person under the age of 16 years. Consent is not required in adults.

With oral immunisation (e.g. poliomyelitis) consent is not so important although it is usual to obtain the consent of the parents in the case of children. This can conveniently be obtained by circulating letters from school.

Adverse reactions to immunisation

Severe reactions to immunisations are rare but when they do occur they are a contraindication to further immunisations. About a third of children may have mild reactions about 7–10 days after immunisation.

Severe anaphylactic reactions, although very rare, can be very dramatic and the correct treatment should always be at hand in a specially prepared pack. Emergency treatment includes the following:

- the patient should be placed on his or her left side;
- insert an airway if the patient is unconscious;
- give adrenaline 1/1000 intramuscularly (see Table 7.3 for the dosage);
- give oxygen and send for a doctor;
- if necessary, start cardiopulmonary resuscitation. A dose of 100 mg hydrocortisone may be given by intravenous injection. Repeat the adrenaline if necessary up to three doses.

Table 7.3 Dose of adrenaline 1/1000 for use in anaphylaxis.

Age	Dosage
Less than 1 year	0.05 ml
1 year	0.1 ml
2 years	0.2 ml
3–4 years	0.3 ml
5 years	0.4 ml
6–10 years	0.5 ml

Arrangements for giving immunisations

Immunisations for children can be given either by the GP (this is the most usual method, at the surgery or at a special clinic arranged in the general practice), or at the health authority child health clinic. Many GPs now arrange a special weekly time at the health centre or group practice for immunisation of children so that mothers may bring their children without having to mix with ill persons attending ordinary surgery sessions. The doctors give immunisations free as part of their service but are paid a fee for the record (see p. 26).

8 Prevention of communicable diseases

Methods of prevention have been highly developed in those diseases which are communicable or infectious (which can be passed from person to person or from animal to person).

Until about 1920–30, isolation was considered the most valuable preventive procedure and strict isolation of the patient and his or her contacts (quarantine) was widely practised. As more information was discovered as to the exact ways by which these diseases spread, it was realised that isolation is of little value in controlling the spread of many communicable diseases.

The role of the infectious or communicable disease hospital has completely changed since 1930. When isolation was thought to be essential, large infectious disease hospitals were built in out-of-the-way places, so that the isolation of the patients being treated in the hospital could be more complete. Today, the main reason for arranging admission to such hospitals or wards is not isolation, but because adequate treatment cannot be provided at home. The one exception, now that smallpox has been eradicated, is *viral haemorrhagic diseases* where complete isolation in a specially designed hospital unit is still essential. These diseases are now extremely rare in the UK and usually only occur in persons returning from West Africa.

Dangers of treating communicable diseases in ordinary hospital wards

It is very *undesirable to treat any case of communicable disease in an ordinary hospital ward or side ward* in a general hospital. Treatment of the patient can easily be carried out in an ordinary ward but the danger is that infection may spread to other patients (cross infection).

Because of this hazard, communicable diseases are now best treated in single bed units specially designed to prevent or reduce the chance of cross infection – say one or two wards each containing 10–12 single rooms but attached to a large central adult and/or paediatric hospital. Any sudden infection in a child or adult already in hospital can then be treated in the special communicable disease unit without interrupting the treatment of the main illness, as the same consultant can continue to be in charge and there will be no risk of cross infection to other patients.

Methods of spread of communicable diseases

Before the methods by which individual communicable diseases can be prevented are discussed, it is necessary to study generally the methods of spread of communicable diseases in the UK. There are three main groups:

- *airborne and droplet infections*
  - *streptococcal infections*, e.g. scarlet fever, erysipelas, puerperal infection and tonsillitis
  - *staphylococcal infections*, e.g. pemphigus neonatorum
  - *pneumococcal infections*, e.g. pneumonia
  - *diphtheria*
  - *meningitis*
  - *tuberculosis*
  - *common childhood infectious diseases*, e.g. measles, pertussis (whooping cough), mumps and rubella (German measles)
  - *legionellosis* (from hot water, air conditioning and heating systems)
- *faecal-borne infections*
  - *gastointestinal infections*
  - *typhoid and paratyphoid fevers*
  - *dysentery*
  - *infantile gastroenteritis*
  - *poliomyelitis*
  - *infective hepatitis*
- *infections spread by direct contact*
  - *from animals* – anthrax, leptospirosis, rabies, Q-fever and toxoplasmosis
  - *from milk* – undulent fever, brucellosis and tuberculosis
  - *from human to human* – sexually transmitted diseases, e.g. syphilis, gonorrhoea, hepatitis B, HIV and AIDS (heterosexual and homosexual intercourse), including anal intercourse, and minor infections
  - *by injury* – by wounds contaminated with spores deposited in the ground, e.g. tetanus
  - *via blood* – hepatitis B, HIV (AIDS)
  - *from insects* – malaria, yellow fever, plague and typhus.

As is described in Chapter 7 *immunisation* plays a very important role in preventing many of the above diseases.

Epidemiological investigation is the second method by which communicable diseases are prevented and their spread controlled.

Epidemiology is the study of all factors which affect diseases – the cause of the illness and all the conditions associated with its incidence. A full investigation is undertaken in all serious cases of certain communicable diseases so that, as far as possible, the exact method of infection and spread can be traced. If this can be done, in many instances it will prevent further cases occurring, e.g. if a *human carrier* who was the original source of infection can be found that person should be able to be prevented from causing further spread. Equally in the case of food poisoning, if the food responsible is traced immediately the risk of further infections is avoided or at least reduced.

Before any investigations can be started it is, of course, essential to know where all the cases have occurred. For this reason, the majority of serious communicable diseases are compulsorily *notifiable* – they must be reported immediately on diagnosis to the local Director of Public Health. A small fee is paid to the doctor (usually the GP) for each notification.

One important group of diseases that have never been made notifiable in the UK are the sexually transmitted diseases because it is feared that if they were made notifiable this would probably result in concealment of infections and inadequate treatment. Certainly those countries which have introduced notification of sexually transmitted diseases have a higher level of such diseases.

The following is a complete list of the notifiable diseases in the UK:

Anthrax	Plague
Cholera	Poliomyelitis (acute)
Diphtheria	Rabies
Dysentery (amoebic or bacillary)	Relapsing fever
Encephalitis (acute)	Rubella
Food poisoning	Scarlet fever
Leptospirosis	Tetanus
Leprosy	Tuberculosis
Malaria	Typhoid and paratyphoid fevers
Measles	Typhus
Meningitis	Viral haemorrhagic fever
Meningococcal septicaemia	Viral hepatitis
Mumps	Whooping cough (pertussis)
	Yellow fever

The following communicable diseases are not *notifiable*:

AIDS and HIV infections	Influenza
Chickenpox	Pneumonia
Common cold	Sexually transmitted diseases

Method of investigation

A careful history should always be taken from the patient and close contacts. Any link between the patient and other cases of the disease should be carefully investigated. If the disease is one not normally present in the UK, such as malaria or viral haemorrhagic disease, any link with someone who has recently travelled abroad should be followed up. In a gastrointestinal infection such as food poisoning or typhoid fever, a complete history of the food recently eaten should be recorded.

In any communicable disease there is always a latent period between infection and the first symptoms and signs of the disease. This is called the *incubation period*. Thus a person infected with typhoid will show no abnormal signs until about 14 days later when the first symptoms of the disease appear.

A knowledge of the likely incubation period is important for it allows the questioning to be concentrated where it is most likely to be helpful – at the start of the incubation period when the patient first became infected. When the first symptoms of typhoid appear in a patient it is necessary to go carefully over the patient's movements 14 days previously to find out how infection may have been contracted. This includes finding out what food and drink may have been consumed at that time.

Incubation periods are never easy to remember and can vary in the same disease. They can conveniently be divided into four groups.

Very short incubation periods 2–18 hours
Staphylococcal toxin food poisoning
Salmonella food poisoning
Clostridium perfringens toxin food poisoning
Short incubation periods 2–7 days
Streptococcal infections, e.g. scarlet fever, puerperal infection, erysipelas, tonsillitis
Staphylococcal infections, e.g. pemphigus neonatorum
Pneumonia
Diphtheria
Influenza
Meningitis
Dysentery
Infantile gastroenteritis
Paratyphoid fever
Anthrax
Gonorrhoea
Legionellosis

Long incubation periods 10–21 days
Typhus	(usually 8–14 days)
Viral haemorrhagic disease	(usually 10 days)
Measles	(usually 12 days)
Whooping cough (pertussis)	(usually 14 days)
Typhoid fever	(usually 14 days)

Poliomyelitis	(usually 11–14 days)
Chickenpox	(usually 17–21 days)
Mumps	(usually 17–20 days)
Rubella	(usually 17–21 days)
Syphilis	(usually 18–21 days)
Rabies	(usually 10–42 days but occasionally up to 4 months)
Hepatitis A and some non-A/non-B	(usually 18–45 days)
Hepatitis B and some non-A/non-B	(usually 60–105 days)

Exceptionally long incubation period

| AIDS | Very variable but more than 2 years and may be as long as 7–10 years |

Bacteriological and/or virological investigations are very important in communicable diseases. They aim at confirming the diagnosis and discovering which close contacts are also infected carriers.

In *airborne bacterial diseases*, nose and throat swabs can be taken. In tuberculosis, sputum tests, both by direct examination and culture, should be carried out on patients.

In the *faecal-borne diseases*, specimens of faeces or rectal swabs of patients and contacts should be examined. In most outbreaks it is usual to find some contacts who are infected but have no symptoms (carriers). In many the carrier state may only last a short time, but *if the carrier works with foodstuffs, further infections may easily result. Blood examinations* are also carried out. In the early stages of typhoid fever, a positive blood culture is usually found, allowing a complete accurate diagnosis as well as making it possible to *phage type* the particular strain of bacteria involved (see p. 154).

In virus diseases, *viral isolations* may be possible, e.g. influenza and poliomyelitis. Another method is to examine the blood very early in the illness and then about 6 weeks later when a significant rise in antibodies will be found. This test can be used for a *retrospective diagnosis* in such cases. Because of the longer time taken with viral isolation, they are less helpful than with bacterial diseases.

Carriers

A carrier is someone who is infected with a disease and who is excreting bacteria or viruses causing the disease *without suffering from any symptoms* at that time. Carriers may be *nasal, throat, faecal, blood seminal or vaginal fluids* or *urinary* and are of two kinds:

- *convalescent carriers* – people who have had the disease but who, in their convalescence, still excrete the bacteria. An example is given by a patient who has had typhoid fever, is now better but who still has typhoid bacteria in their faeces. Such persons are usually *temporary carriers*, harbouring the bacteria for some weeks only. However a few may become *permanent carriers* who intermittently carry bacteria in their faeces (or urine – see below) for all their life (chronic typhoid carrier);

- *symptomless carriers* – these are people who have never had any illness or any symptoms but who are carriers. In such cases almost certainly such individuals must have had a subclinical attack without any symptoms and a carrier state has followed. Typhoid carriers are occasionally of this type. Symptomless carriers can either be *temporary or permanent*. Symptomless carriers are particularly dangerous as there is no way of indicating they may represent a serious hazard, particularly if they work as a food handler.

Following the first infection with HIV (see Chapter 9) a carrier state develops leading eventually in the majority of cases to AIDS. In most carriers of HIV, the virus is present in the blood and in seminal and vaginal fluids and can therefore very easily infect others either by contamination with blood or during sexual intercourse.

Types of carriers

Anatomically, carriers can be divided into the following types:

- *nasal carriers*, e.g. streptococci, diphtheria, staphylococci;
- *throat carriers*, e.g. diphtheria, meningococci, streptococci;
- *faecal carriers*, e.g. typhoid, salmonella, poliomyelitis, dysentery;
- *urinary carriers*, e.g. typhoid;
- *blood carriers*, e.g. hepatitis B, HIV;
- *sexual carriers*, e.g. hepatitis B, HIV.

It is important to realise that most typhoid carriers excrete typhoid bacilli in the faeces and in rare cases in the urine intermittently. Usually the faeces are positive for about 2 weeks then negative for 3–5 weeks and then positive again. Because of this pattern, repeated faecal examinations in typhoid fever are necessary, otherwise a chronic carrier could easily be missed because the examination was carried out during the period when no bacteria were being excreted. For this reason, carriers in typhoid fever are especially dangerous and have been responsible for many large-scale outbreaks.

Special screening tests

X-rays form an important part of any investigation into an outbreak of tuberculosis.

Detailed methods of preventing communicable diseases

Airborne infections

Streptococcal infections

These include such varied diseases as scarlet fever, erysipelas (an acute skin condition), puerperal pelvic infection, tonsillitis, cellulitis and septicaemia. The usual method of infection is from either a patient or suspected case or from a nasal or throat carrier. It is also important to realise that the same type of bacteria may cause scarlet fever in one patient, tonsillitis in another and even puerperal pelvic infection if a woman recently confined is infected. A careful search should always be made to discover any *unknown carriers* by examining bacteriologically nasal and throat swabs.

In especially dangerous infections such as puerperal pelvic infection great care should be taken to ensure that aseptic conditions are always maintained during and after confinement. *No midwife with a nasal or throat infection should ever be allowed to attend a mother in her labour.* In such circumstances the midwife must remain off duty until better and until bacteriological examinations of her nose and throat are clear. If an unexpected streptococcal puerperal infection occurs nasal and throat swabs of all who attended her birth must be examined to make certain that none of them are carriers.

Some of the most dangerous infections that can follow surgical operations are streptococcal infections. The stringent preventive measures taken in all surgical theatres to ensure aseptic conditions including preparation of the patient's skin and theatre aseptic techniques are all examples of preventive measures taken to reduce the chances of streptococcal infections.

In certain serious accidents, it may be impossible to prevent infection gaining access into a patient's tissues. In such cases, prophylactic treatment with chemotherapy and antibiotics is started as a further preventive measure.

Staphylococcal infections

Some of the most dangerous neonatal cross infections in the nursery units of maternity units are caused by penicillin-resistant staphylococci (pemphigus neonatorum). Preventive measures include the following:

- *early recognition* to enable the case to be promptly removed from the unit;
- *strict barrier nursing techniques* after the first case has been diagnosed;

- *early discharge* of mothers and babies so that the time for possible cross infection is kept as short as possible;
- in those outbreaks that are not immediately controlled, *the stopping of all new admissions* and eventually closing the unit temporarily so that the chain of infection is broken.

Diphtheria

Immediately a case of diphtheria is diagnosed and removed to hospital, an investigation should be started to discover the source of the infection. Nasal and throat swabs of all close contacts (members of the family and all classmates at school in the case of a child) should be taken. Other members of the family should be excluded from school until the bacteriological tests are complete and also other members of the family are excluded from work if there is a risk of spread, for example a food handler.

Daily visits should be paid by the health visitor or practice nurse to check that no one else has developed any symptoms as it is not only important to prevent the spread of the disease but also to diagnose it early, when treatment is so much more effective. Other children in the family and close contacts should be given a booster immunisation and those who have never been immunised should be given their first immunising dose.

If any of the contacts are found to be a carrier a virulence test must be carried out on the diphtheria bacteria isolated. A minority of diphtheria bacteria are avirulent – they are incapable of causing disease. No carrier should be implicated as a possible cause of the infection until he/she has been confirmed to be carrying *virulent diphtheria bacteria*.

Any contacts who develop early suspicious signs should immediately be given a protecting dose of diphtheria antitoxin. An early small dose of such antitoxin is of great importance in reducing the severity of the attack. The main method of preventing diphtheria is to ensure as many children as possible are protected by immunisation. The level of immunisation in the UK has already reached over 95% and the next aim is to reach 95% by 1995. Travellers to certain countries, particularly Russia, face extra hazards from infection from diphtheria and therefore should always be immunised and have a recent booster dose (see p. 129).

Tuberculosis

The total number of cases of tuberculosis which are notified in England and Wales (and in the UK) has been rising steadily since 1987 (see Table 8.1). The former steady fall of tuberculosis which had been

Table 8.1 Numbers of total and respiratory cases of tuberculosis notified in England and Wales, 1987–92.

	1987	1988	1990	1991	1992
Total tuberculosis	5086	5164	5204	5436	5799
Respiratory tuberculosis	4010	4022	3942	3950	4205

(From various OPCS Monitors in the MB 2 series.)

recorded since the early 1950s has clearly been reversed. The almost certain cause of the latest increase is the increasing numbers of AIDS patients – because AIDS destroys the immunity of the body all communicable diseases but especially tuberculosis are more likely to develop.

The proportion of total tuberculosis is greater in males (57%) than in females (43%) but in respiratory tuberculosis the proportion is greater still where in males 60% of the cases occur.

The incidence of tuberculosis is greater in some ethnic groups. A survey carried out in England in 1988 showed that 40% of the notifications are of either Indian, Pakistani or Bangladeshi origin. (Since 1988 the numbers of notifications in these groups have fallen by about 6% annually but the rate is still 25 times greater than in the white population (see Chief Medical Officers Report for 1991). Another difference noted in these patients from the Indian subcontinent who have tuberculosis is that there is a greater amount of non-respiratory tuberculosis, especially abdominal tuberculosis and tuberculous adenitis. Because of this greater incidence, the Department of Health recommends that all persons (adults and children) coming from India, Pakistan or Bangladesh should have a Heaf test (a skin sensitivity test) on arrival and, if negative, should have a BCG vaccination. Also any newborn babies should be vaccinated within a few days of birth.

Doctors and nurses caring for AIDS patients should constantly consider whether tuberculosis has developed as a result of their reduced resistance. Periodic chest X-rays should therefore be carried out and all staff looking after these patients should always have a BCG vaccination unless their skin sensitivity test shows a positive result.

The majority of cases of tuberculosis today are caused by direct infection from one human being to another by droplet (airborne) infection. The control and prevention of tubculosis depends on:

* tracing the source of the infection;
* taking steps to reduce the chance of infection;
* immunising those at risk.

Tracing the source of the infection

Tuberculosis does not spread like measles, by chance, short-lived contact, but usually follows repetitive contact such as that which occurs among the members of the same household, classroom or office. When any new case occurs, it is essential to search for the cause of the infection among close contacts. In all instances an examination *must* include a chest X-ray of all adults over the age of 15 years and, for children under this age, a skin sensitivity test. It is most important that every close contact is examined. This is because the cause of the infection could be someone who may have slight symptoms and is afraid to have an X-ray. Equally the source of infection could easily be in someone with no symptoms at all.

Because there is a preponderance of tuberculosis infection at present in men in the UK over the age of 45 years, every effort must be made to X-ray this group. It is important to realise that a person may have a heavily infected sputum (and therefore be a most likely source of infection) and yet be able to lead a normal type of life. Therefore, the absence of symptoms must never be used as an excuse to dispense with an X-ray.

Steps to reduce the chance of infection

Housing Overcrowded housing and sleeping accommodation produces conditions which favour the spread of the disease. No patient should ever sleep in the same room as another member of the same family. The one exception is where the patient is a married person; in this case, the couple can share the same room but should have twin beds. It is most important that no parent with tuberculosis should sleep in the same room as a child. Equally, no child with tuberculosis should share a room with other children.

If the house is not large enough to allow the patient to have a separate bedroom, immediate rehousing is essential to avoid infection spreading through the family. Most local housing authorities have special priority housing schemes which enable patients to be rapidly rehoused in such circumstances.

Occupation No person who has tuberculosis should be employed in an occupation in which there is a chance of spreading tuberculosis if a relapse occurs. This means that work should not be undertaken as a food handler or in close association with young children under the age of 12 years such as teaching or nursery nursing. Consequently no person is allowed to enter teacher training unless he/she has a clear chest X–ray. Periodic check-ups for teachers are also encouraged. Likewise all staff employed in children's homes should be X-rayed before commencing their employment. It is illegal for a person with open tuberculosis to be employed in the food trade.

Follow-up   Careful follow-up of all patients is important not only during treatment which normally takes place at home but also for some considerable time after the end of treatment. This follow-up usually takes place at a chest clinic and includes X-rays and should also be accompanied by home visits carried out by special nurses to ensure that the social factors at home have not deteriorated. If this occurs there is a greater chance of a relapse.

Pregnancy in a patient whose tuberculosis is controlled is likely to do no harm but it is essential that everything is done to help the mother meet this extra challenge. Delivery should always take place in hospital and arrangements should be made for her to have a prolonged convalescence after delivery. The baby must be vaccinated with BCG immediately. If the problem is known in good time, before 6 months, it is usually possible to make satisfactory arrangements for the care of the baby and family, but if the problem is only discovered in the puerperium, the mother may ignore the convalescent period to look after her family and baby, and risk permanent damage to her health and may spread infection to her family.

Measles, mumps and rubella (German measles)

The prevention of these diseases rests mainly with active immunisation of young children (see p. 132). The success already achieved in England and Wales (and also in the whole of the UK) is excellent and is clearly shown in Fig. 8.1 below.

By 1993 the level of active immunisation in the UK had reached 95%. Passive immunisation is used very occasionally where an attack of these diseases would be likely to be more dangerous than normal (see p. 138).

Acute meningitis and encephalitis

From 1988 there was a marked increase in the number of cases of acute meningitis and/or encephalitis which reached a peak in 1988 when 2987 cases were notified. Since then the numbers have fallen slightly – in 1992 there were 2605 cases notified including 34 cases of acute encephalitis.

Figure 8.2 shows the incidence of the commonest form of bacterial meningitis – meningococcal meningitis. This form represents 36.1% of all the bacterial types of meningitis. The remainder includes *Haemophilus influenzae* (27.1%) and *Streptococcus pneumoniae* and a mixed group of 18.5% containing other streptococci and eight cases of *Listeria monocytogenes*.

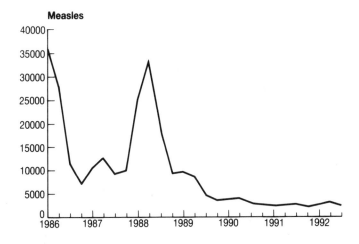

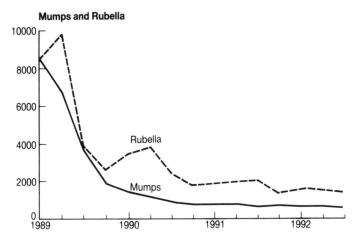

Fig. 8.1 Cases of measles 1986–94 and of mumps and rubella 1989–94, England and Wales. (From OPCS Monitor MB2 93/4.)

Among the viruses which cause meningitis/acute encephalitis, echo-viruses are responsible for the majority (63.5% in 1991), followed by Coxsackie A and B (18.2%), while mumps only accounted for 2.4% of the viral causes in 1991. This is a remarkable improvement from 1988 when mumps was responsible for 20.7% of all viral meningitis/ encephalitis and clearly confirms the success of MMR immunisation in preventing mumps and its complications.

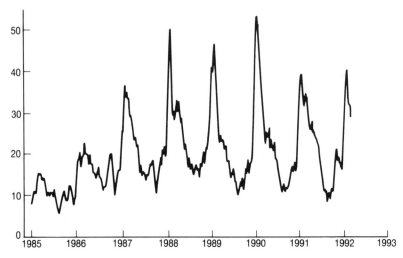

Fig. 8.2 Notifications of meningococcal meningitis: 5 week moving average, England and Wales, 1985–92. (From the Chief Medical Officer's Report, Department of Health, 1991, published 1992.)

Legionellosis

Legionellosis is a serious respiratory disease which first appeared in Spain and the USA in the 1970s. Table 8.2 shows the reported cases in England and Wales from 1980 to 1991.

Note that a substantial proportion of cases occur in persons who

Table 8.2 Cases of legionellosis, numbers England and Wales, 1980–91

Year	Total confirmed cases	Associated with travel abroad
1980	182	79
1981	142	63
1982	138	57
1983	159	48
1984	150	56
1985	210	56
1986	189	89
1987	209	109
1988	278	82
1989	240	91
1990	188	91
1991	110	52

(From The National Surveillance Scheme for Legionellosis, supplied by the Communicable Disease Surveillance Centre.)

contracted the infections abroad. The worst outbreak recorded in the UK was in 1985 when 101 cases (with 25 deaths) occurred in Stafford District Hospital and was traced to water contamination in water-cooled air conditioning and heating systems.

Method of spread The disease is caused by the bacteria *Legionella pneumophilia* and, so far, 14 serogroups have been identified. The bacteria is found in natural and artificial water supplies. It is an airborne infection and domestic hot water systems, jacuzzis, showers, industrial water-based coolants and water-cooled air conditioning systems have all caused outbreaks.

The prevention of legionellosis depends on the design and operation of hot water systems, and especially those which may lead to the entry of contaminated airborne particles into a ventilation system from a cooling tower (this was the mechanism found to have been reponsible for the Stafford outbreak).

Cooling towers require regular cleaning and treatment with biocides and also hot water systems should use calorifiers to ensure storage temperatures remain above 50°C.

In 1991 a joint Department of Health and Health and Safety Executive Working Group considered the prevention and control of legionellosis. Their main recommendations were concerned with the design and maintenance of cooling towers and hot water systems and the ways of maintaining high standards. The Health and Safety Executive also published an approved Code of Practice for the prevention and control of legionellosis which came into effect in January 1992.

Faecal-borne infections

Typhoid and paratyphoid fevers

At present about 140–180 cases of typhoid fever and 80–100 cases of paratyphoid fever are notified annually in England and Wales. Typhoid is spread by water and food; paratyphoid is spread by food.

The prevention of both typhoid and paratyphoid depends on:

- full immediate investigation of all cases to discover the source of the infection;
- food control including sampling at docks (on import of the food), pasteurisation of milk supplies and ice cream, prohibition of infected shellfish;
- environmental hygiene especially among all food handlers;
- immunisation of holiday visitors to certain countries where the risk of infection is high – Africa, Far East and the country areas of many European countries including Italy and Spain.

In both diseases, infection is introduced into water and food by another human being who is either suffering from the disease or is a carrier. Most infections result from carriers and anyone who handles food in any capacity can be a very real danger. Personnel employed in water companies, if they come into contact with the actual supply of water, can also be a danger.

The investigation of any case or outbreak of both diseases should always start with a careful history concentrating upon the start of the incubation period – 14 days in typhoid and 7 days in paratyphoid. Details of food and drink consumed are critical. Because of the length of the incubation period in typhoid the patient may find it difficult to remember and further visits for questioning may be important after the patient has discussed their movements with the family.

Immediate stool examinations must be carried out on all close contacts and especially on kitchen personnel. If a carrier is discovered, the typhoid bacteria must be typed by phage typing. It is possible to divide typhoid and paratyphoid bacilli into different phage types, and the type isolated is then compared with the type causing the outbreak. If the types are dissimilar, then the carrier could not have been responsible. If the type is the same, the carrier could have been the source of the infection, however, the discovery of a carrier of the same type does not prove that the person is the cause and further investigations must be undertaken.

The large typhoid epidemics of the past were mainly *water-borne* and were caused by water supplies which had not been properly purified. Careless methods of sewage disposal and lack of purification led to the last serious water-borne outbreak in Zermatt, Switzerland, in 1963 when 434 cases of typhoid occurred.

In the UK, where water supplies are all purified and sterilised, the main vehicle of infection is now food supplies which usually have been infected by a carrier. For this reason all known cases of typhoid and paratyphoid are very carefully followed up with stool examinations every 2 weeks for at least 6 months. This is because most carriers are intermittent so check-ups are needed over a long period. About 5% of typhoid cases become chronic carriers – usually faecal carriers but occasionally urine carriers who are more dangerous. Animals are not a source of typhoid but paratyphoid infections have been traced to cows.

Once a carrier is diagnosed, a careful check is kept on the occupation undertaken by the individual and other members of the family. No chronic typhoid or paratyphoid carrier is legally allowed to be employed in the food trade or to work in a kitchen or place where infection could be passed on. Members of the family of any carrier must be protected periodically by immunisation with TAB vaccine.

In 1945 a serious outbreak of typhoid in Aberystwyth in Wales was caused by home-made ice cream being infected by a carrier. Now by law all ice cream must be pasteurised, which is a heat treatment process that destroys any pathogenic bacteria present.

In 1964, an extensive outbreak of typhoid occurred in Aberdeen. Over 400 cases occurred with five deaths. The most probable cause was a large commercial tin of corned beef which contained typhoid bacteria. It is thought that the bacteria gained entry to the can after it had been sterilised. This probably occurred by the tin being cooled by unchlorinated river water. To prevent any possible recurrence, it is essential that all water used for cooling in any canning process should be pure chlorinated water.

Safety of nursing staff TAB immunisation should be given to all nursing staff looking after typhoid or paratyphoid patients in communicable disease hospitals to protect them from the danger of cross infection. For this reason, all cases of typhoid or paratyphoid should be treated in special communicable disease units and never in general wards.

Food poisoning

The main causes of food poisoning are:

- *chemical causes* such as tin or antimony;
- *bacterial toxin* food poisoning
  - *staphylococcal* toxin
  - *Clostridium perfringens* toxin;
- *salmonellosis*.

Incidence

Food poisoning notifications increased rapidly from 1985 to 1989 but there were few changes in the next 3 years (see Fig. 8.3).

The majority of food poisoning outbreaks are salmonellosis. All cases of food poisoning must be immediately investigated to discover, if possible, the cause. Such an investigation, if successful, will normally suggest ways and means of avoiding a recurrence.

Chemical food poisonings are very rare today and are only likely to occur if totally unsuitable containers (such as those made from galvanised iron) are used to cook food.

Toxin food poisonings

Staphylococcal toxin food poisoning results when foods are infected with certain strains of *Staphyloccus aureus* and are then stored in warm conditions enabling the bacteria to multiply within the food. This then

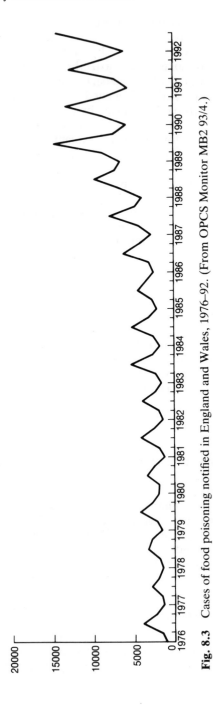

Fig. 8.3   Cases of food poisoning notified in England and Wales, 1976–92. (From OPCS Monitor MB2 93/4.)

produces an *enterotoxin*, a poison which acts upon the stomach and occasionally the central nervous system. An interval of at least 12 hours must occur between infection of the food and its being eaten to allow sufficient toxin to be produced to lead to food poisoning. Staphylococci usually contaminate foods from either a skin or nasal lesion in a food handler. They do, however, also attack the skin of animals and, in the cow, may lead to a staphylococcal infection of the udder with subsequent contamination of the milk.

Once staphylococcal food poisoning toxin has been produced in any foodstuff, it is very difficult to destroy by heat as it is heat stable. This means that even boiling a foodstuff already contaminated would only destroy a very small and insignificant amount of the toxin and would not render the food safe.

As staphylococci are usually present in the noses of 10% of persons chance infection of any food with staphylococci may inevitably occasionally occur. However this type of food poisoning can be avoided by ensuring that all foods are eaten within an hour or two of preparation or are always stored in refrigerated conditions and that a *high degree of personal hygiene* is maintained. Hands must be frequently washed and habits avoided that would encourage transfer of staphylococci from the nose and mouth of the food handler to foodstuffs.

Great care must always be taken to prevent any food handler who has an acute or chronic skin infection, infected cut, boil, or paronychia from handling food. Legal regulations specify that all cuts must be covered with a waterpoof dressing to avoid contaminating foods. It is of course better to exclude such staff from handling any foods at all.

Clostridium perfringens toxin food poisoning is less severe than staphylococcal toxin food poisoning but is much more common. The toxin, which is also heat stable, is produced by the multiplication of *Clostridium perfringens*, a spore-bearing anaerobic bacterium. The spores of the organism are widespread – in soil and often in faeces. However, being an anaerobic bacterium it will only multiply in the absence of oxygen. For this reason, it mainly produces food poisoning in meats and stews and soups made by low temperature simmering.

Spores of *Clostridium perfringens* are found in many meats and therefore invariably gain entry to kitchens. Infections with this type of food poisoning will only be avoided if the following rules are strictly observed:

- avoid precooking of meats;
- avoid storing any food between 10°C and 49°C for more than 3 hours;
- if meats are to be precooked, it is essential that they are rapidly cooled below 10°C in a domestic refrigerator;
- care must be taken when gutting animals such as rabbits to avoid

contamination of the flesh with faeces from the intestine of the animal (which will probably contain spores of this bacterium).

Salmonellosis food poisoning

Salmonellosis is the commonest type of food poisoning. It is an infective gastroenteritis in which the small intestine is attacked by one of the *Salmonella* bacteria producing an inflammation. There are over 1000 different serotypes but in 1992 the commonest found in the UK were *Salmonella enteritidis* (63.5%), *Salmonella typhimurium* (17.3%) and *Salmonella virchow* (4.4%).

Method of spread

There are six main sources of infection with salmonellosis:

- human cases and contacts
- eggs of chickens and ducks
- pigs
- chickens
- domestic animals and rodents
- untreated raw milk.

Any one of these sources may lead to contamination of food but fortunately a very heavy infection is necessary to lead to salmonella food poisoning. This means that to produce infection in humans it is necessary to have two factors: there has to be infection of the foodstuff *and* incorrect storage of the food – the food has to be stored for at least 12 hours at normal room temperature which allows rapid multiplication of the invading salmonella bacteria in the food. If the food is stored in a refrigerator there will be virtually no such multiplication. In addition it is wise to avoid using duck eggs in cooking as they may be very heavily infected with *Salmonella typhimurium*.

Whenever an outbreak of salmonellosis occurs, a complete investigation must take place to find, if possible, the source of the infection. The incubation period of salmonellosis is very short, about 8–18 hours, so questioning should concentrate on food eaten at that time. A particular search should be made for faecal carriers. If a carrier is found of the same serotype, it must not be assumed that he or she is necessarily the cause, for such a carrier may also have been affected either with or without symptoms. All carriers must stop handling food immediately and not do so again until they have been cleared. The carrier state in salmonellosis usually only lasts a few weeks and it is unusual for a carrier to be permanent.

Any foodstuff which is precooked and then stored for a lengthy period before consumption, such as cooked and prepared meats, may be dangerous if storage has been faulty and the food was infected. That is why many more cases of salmonella food poisoning occur in warm weather when storage of food out of the refrigerator means that the warm conditions will hasten the growth of bacteria in the food, so that within 10–12 hours the food is heavily infected.

Naturally infected foods can also cause infections. For example, in the past serious outbreaks have been caused by heavily contaminated eggs and coconut products from abroad. With the latter, an effective method of heat treatment has been devised rendering even infected imports safe.

Prevention

Salmonella food poisoning can best be avoided by the following measures:

- extreme care being taken in the preparation of food and with personal hygiene among food handlers. This reduces the chances of a carrier accidentally contaminating any food;
- all food being prepared immediately and any left over food being thrown away. In this respect, it is most undesirable to prepare a sweet today for lunch tomorrow, unless it is immediately stored in a refrigerator;
- where food such as meat pies is stored for any length of time it must be stored at a low temperature (below 4°C) preferably in a refrigerator;
- gamma radiation from a cobalt-60 source should be used to destroy salmonella organisms in frozen egg, coconut, imported meats and in animal feeding stuffs;
- pasteurisation of liquid milk;
- avoidance of eating raw or lightly boiled eggs;
- ensuring that frozen chickens are completely defrosted before cooking;
- never storing cooked meats next to fresh meats.

Listeriosis

From 1986 to 1988 listeriosis rose rapidly in the UK and reached a peak figure of 281 cases in England and Wales in 1988. Cases of listeriosis then fell to 115 in 1990 and to 125 in 1991 (see Fig. 8.4).

Listeriosis is a bacterial infection caused by *Listeria monocytogenes* which is very common in soil, animals and poultry and which, in certain circumstances, can cause disease in humans. Transference of *Listeria* infections is mainly by foodstuffs and particularly by those where the

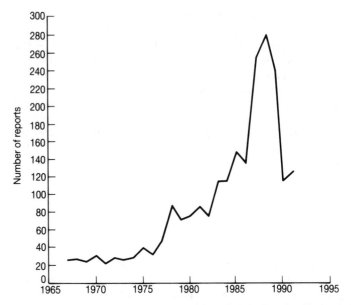

Notes: i. For the years 1967–79 the number of reports includes those from Northern Ireland.
For the years 1980–91 it includes reports from England and Wales only.
ii. For the years 1967–82 the number of reports includes only those to CDSC. For the years
1983–91 it includes those to CDSC and the Division of Microbiological Reagents and Quality
Control (DMRQC)

Fig. 8.4 Cases of listeriosis, England and Wales, 1965–91. (From Communicable Diseases Surveillance Centre (CDSC).)

preparation does not involve any cooking or heating process. Unlike most bacteria which cause food poisoning *Listeria* bacteria can increase slowly at refrigerated temperatures. Three groups are at special risk:

• pregnant women;
• their newborn infants;
• adults who are receiving immunosuppressive treatment.

Listeria monocytogenes is widely present in nature – surveys have shown that 29% of healthy persons carry the bacteria in their stools. There is a seasonal incidence with the disease being common in early summer.

Types of listeriosis

During pregnancy When the disease attacks pregnant women, it usually shows two or more febrile episodes – the woman has some or all of the following symptoms: headache, general malaise, pharyngitis, conjunctivitis, abdominal or low back pain. Occasionally the febrile attack may be misdiagnosed as pyelonephritis. Blood culture at this stage is usually positive. If ampicillin is given promptly, the fever quickly subsides but the woman may relapse. The second episode usually follows later in pregnancy when a 'flu-like illness with a low pyrexia develops. This is often followed by the birth of a premature baby who may also be infected (see below). It is thought that this secondary episode is probably caused by a reinfection from the placenta.

The mother usually recovers completely, but the outlook for the infant is often very serious or fatal.

Neonatal infections   Two methods of infection occur:

- haematogenous transplacental transmission;
- intrapartum infection as the baby traverses the birth canal.

In pregnant women with listeriosis, bacteria are often present in the vagina. About 50–75% of perinatal infections occur each year in the UK. In newborn infants, two forms of the disease are seen:

- a septicaemia within 2 days of birth; the premature baby is particularly likely to show respiratory distress and rashes may occasionally also be seen;
- a meningo-encephalitis may develop after the fifth day following the birth. Occasionally a slowly developing hydrocephalus may also follow.

Up to a third of infected babies are stillborn. If prompt treatment is given with ampicillin, about 50% mortality occurs. If however treatment is started late or not at all, the mortality rises to over 90%. Provided the baby was at least of 36 weeks gestation when born, sequelae are most unlikely in those babies who recover.

Disease in adults other than pregnant women   Central nervous system infections are the most likely forms of listeriosis seen in adults other than pregnant women. Fever of a low grade is usually present and focal neurological signs may develop such as cranial nerve palsies or hemiparesis. Occasionally there is a progressive loss of consciousness eventually leading to coma.

In immunosuppressed adults who develop any form of meningitis, infections with listeriosis are among the commonest causes. Treatment is with ampicillin and should be continued for at least 1 month after the fever has subsided. The prognosis for adult forms of listeriosis is good provided that treatment is started at once.

Prevention

The main preventive measures are that vulnerable persons (pregnant women and immunosuppressed adults) should avoid eating the following foods:

- soft ripened cheeses such as Brie, Camembert and the blue vein types;
- cooked ready-to-eat foods should be reheated until piping hot rather than eaten cold;
- paté.

Dysentery

In 1991 there was a sudden increase in the level of dysentery cases in England and Wales and this peaked in 1992 (see Fig. 8.5). No reason has been found for this increase although it may reflect a natural periodicity in this disease as previously very high levels were recorded in 1977 and 1984–5.

The bacillary dysentery caused by *Shigella sonnei* (often called Sonne dysentery) is the commonest form of dysentery found in the UK. It is a mild, short-lived gastroenteritis which is only serious in young babies or in debilitated elderly persons.

Sonne dysentery is spread by direct contamination from person to person in a closed community, such as a ward or nursery. It usually spreads slowly at first, but as soon as a substantial proportion of persons are infected it spreads more quickly. The best way to avoid outbreaks is to diagnose cases of dysentery early and to isolate all cases and carriers. These preventive measures are especially important in day nurseries and hospital wards. All cases of diarrhoea must be bacteriologically examined, (stool specimens) to make certain that any early cases are identified – there is always a proportion of symptomless carriers among the close contacts but usually they are carriers for only 2–3 weeks.

By careful investigation and isolation of early cases and carriers, serious outbreaks will usually be avoided. If, however, a widespread outbreak has been allowed to develop, isolation will then achieve little. The aim therefore should always be to diagnose the first cases. This can only be done if it becomes a routine measure to examine bacteriologically the stools of all patients or those attending at a day nursery who develop diarrhoea, however mild or trivial.

Infantile gastroenteritis

This is a general term used for any gastroenteritis in young infants. The exact cause of some outbreaks is uncertain but in others, infection has

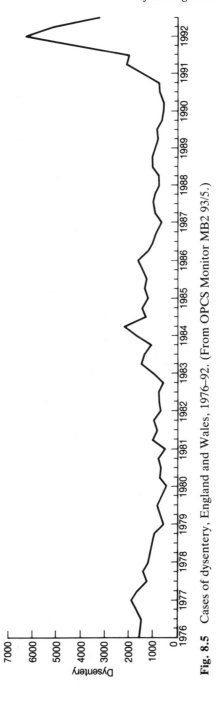

Fig. 8.5 Cases of dysentery, England and Wales, 1976–92. (From OPCS Monitor MB2 93/5.)

been traced to certain pathogenic strains of *Escherichia coli* including 0 26, 0 55, 0 111, 0 125, 0 126, 0 127, 0 128 and 0 129. Many enteroviruses (echoviruses and Coxsackie B virus) have also been identified as causes. The virus responsible for many attacks of infantile gastroenteritis can be identified using an electron microscope. Serologically the virus, which has been given many names including reovirus-like agents, orbivirus, rotavirus and duovirus, is related to the virus of calf diarrhoea. As soon as the problems of culturing this virus *in vitro* are overcome, it is hoped that it will be possible to develop a prophylactic vaccine.

Prevention

These attacks can best be prevented by complete investigation when they occur and by arranging for all young babies and infants to spend as little time as possible in hospital or in a residential nursery unit. There is no doubt that many attacks result from cross infection – the bacteria or virus spreading rapidly from infant to infant in a ward or nursery. It is therefore most important that the initial cases are isolated immediately and that no child with any history of diarrhoea is ever admitted to a clean infants' ward but goes straight into the isolation unit.

Once infection has occurred, especially the serious type of infantile gastroenteritis, new admissions should be immediately stopped and the ward emptied as soon as possible by discharging the mothers and babies home early. In this way it is possible to prevent what can turn out to be a disastrous outbreak with many infant deaths.

Any attempt to stop the spread and to control serious infantile gastroenteritis by barrier nursing nearly always fails. This is probably because of the intensity of infection and the role infected dusts play in spreading this disease.

Another very effective measure is to encourage breast feeding in as many babies as possible. In outbreaks it is interesting that many breast fed babies escape, and every effort should be made to keep breast feeding going if a baby develops the disease. If the breast fed baby has to enter hospital then the mother should also be admitted so that breast feeding can continue.

Poliomyelitis

The success of the immunisation programme against poliomyelitis which started over 35 years ago means that the UK is free from indigenous poliomyelitis caused by the wild virus. However in most years there are one to three cases associated with receipt of the vaccine (vaccine-associated recipient cases) or with contact with the vaccine

(vaccine-associated contact cases). In 1989 and 1990 there was one such case and in 1991 and 1992 there were three.

There is still a risk to travellers to certain Third World countries. In such instances, it is a wise to have a booster dose before leaving the UK. For those over the age of 50 years it is safer to use the inactivated Salk vaccine for this booster dose, given by injection.

Poliomyelitis has a well-defined seasonal incidence. Cases usually occur in late summer and early autumn – in the UK in August, September and early October. Poliomyelitis is a *faecal-borne disease* and is spread by direct contact from person to person and particularly those living in the same household. Although infected, the majority of close contacts show no symptoms and only rarely does clinical poliomyelitis result. When a case of poliomyelitis occurs, it is wise, as far as possible, to segregate the members of the household from the general population. Child contacts should certainly be kept away from school for at least 3 weeks. By isolating the family in this way, the chance of spreading infection is undoubtedly reduced.

In addition, as soon as any case is confirmed immediate immunisation using oral vaccination should be given to all contacts at home, school and work, and all people living within approximately a quarter of a mile radius of the patient.

This procedure not only serves to boost their immunity but also blocks the entrance of 'wild' virus into their intestines and thus helps to reduce further the chances of infection. Household contacts should be placed under surveillance for 3 weeks. They should be visited by the practice nurse or health visitor to check whether they have any symptoms. If any abnormality develops, the patient should be put to bed and kept as quiet as possible. This is important because violent exercise in anyone in the earliest stages of poliomyelitis can result in a severe attack. As a further precaution any close contact should avoid strenuous exercise for 3 weeks. Close family contacts should not go on walking tours or any similar activities at this time. Restrictions among the general population regarding swimming are probably useless in preventing the spread of poliomyelitis. However swimming can be a form of strenuous exercise and therefore should be avoided for 3 weeks by close contacts.

As already explained, by far the most effective preventive measure is to ensure 90% or more of all persons under the age of 40 are protected by oral vaccination (see p. 132).

Cholera

Although classic cholera last appeared in epidemic form in the UK in 1866, recently there have been a number of outbreaks in Westernised countries from the El Tor strains. Since 1986 there have been about

10–25 cases notified in the UK each year; almost invariably the infection occurred abroad. In 1990 19 cases were reported, 22 in 1991 and 25 in 1992. The speed of air travel facilitates the spread of this disease which usually has a short incubation period – 3–5 days.

El Tor cholera bacteria remain in the stools of patients for at least 14 days and occasionally up to 3 months.

Prevention

This mainly depends on purification of water supplies and safe disposal of sewage and this is the main reason why infection in the UK is extremely unlikely to occur. In epidemics abroad (on the Indian subcontinent) water and milk must be boiled (unless it is pasteurised) and careful segregation of all patients arranged. As already explained, immunisation is no longer recommended because it has been shown to be ineffective.

Direct spread from animals

Anthrax

Anthrax is now a rare disease in the UK – there was one case in 1989, two in 1990, none in 1991 and one in 1992. It is caused by a spore-bearing anaerobic bacterium with a marked tendency to produce spores as soon as it comes into contact with oxygen – hence the spores are widespread and are present in hides, untreated imported wool and the bones of some animals. It is usually caught by direct spread from the hide, wool or bones of imported animals. It is only seen in persons whose occupation brings them into contact with animals and animal products. The main groups of people at risk are dockers handling hides and wool sorters.

Prevention

This depends on the following measures:

- special treatment of wool imports to kill any anthrax spores;
- protective clothing worn by personnel handling hides and bones;
- immunisation against anthrax for all workers at risk (see p. 135).

As a further safeguard, the dangers of anthrax are explained to all those working in occupations in which there is a danger of contracting the disease. Diagrams of early symptoms are prominently displayed so that if anyone develops a skin lesion it will be recognised and diagnosed early. All workers also carry a special card to show to their general practitioner so that the doctor will know of the special risks which their occupation carries. The early diagnosis of anthrax is most important as modern treatment can quickly cut short an attack.

Leptospirosis

Leptospirosis, caused by *Leptospira icterohaemorrhagiae*, is primarily a disease of rats. About 20–30 cases are notified each year in the UK. Infection in humans results from the skin being contaminated with rat urine. It is mostly seen in abattoir and sewage workers who are most likely to come into close contact with rats. All workers should be warned of the dangers and of the importance of a high standard of hygiene. It is especially important that they avoid contaminating their skin with water which may have been infected by rat's urine. It is especially dangerous to walk barefoot in such places.

Rabies

Rabies (hydrophobia) is a rare disease in the UK. Two cases occurred in 1987 and 1988 but none since then. There is still a considerable amount of rabies on the continent where it is known many wild animals are infected, including foxes (the vast majority) but also rodents and some otters. There has been an epizootic (an animal epidemic) in foxes in the last 20 years which spread from Germany, Switzerland, Austria and Denmark to Belgium and France. An interesting campaign of oral vaccination against rabies was introduced in 1986, attempting to immunise wild animals (see p. 253). About 75% of all animal outbreaks have occurred among wild animals with the remainder found in domestic animals. Dogs are most commonly affected in this group but cats and bovines have also been infected.

Prevention

The virus of rabies is found in the saliva of rabid animals. After a bite from a rabid animal, the virus spreads in humans to the central nervous system producing the characteristic symptoms. The disease is very dangerous with a high mortality and anyone who has been bitten by a rabid animal must be immunised (see p. 136). The incubation period is 2–6 weeks but may be much longer.

Rabies Act 1974

Under this Act there is a compulsory 6 months quarantine period for all animals entering this country. Effective precautions must also be taken against transmission of the disease within quarantine kennels. All dogs and cats entering quarantine must be vaccinated on entry with a proved potency tested inactivated vaccine; they must also be revaccinated after 1 month of quarantine to extend immunity.

Dogs and cats are allowed to enter the UK but only at a limited number of ports. Animals landed illegally may be destroyed on landing and the Act provides for severe penalties including up to 1 year imprisonment.

Further orders provide for a wide range of measures to control any outbreak of rabies in the UK. These include the destruction of foxes, controls over the movement of domestic pets and their vaccination, the seizure of strays and the banning of hunting and cat and dog shows.

Prophylactic vaccination against rabies (see p. 136) should be offered to all persons who are at risk in their work, including:

- those employed in quarantine kennels;
- those working in quarantine premises in zoos;
- agents who are authorised to carry such animals;
- those working in research and acclimatisation centres where primates and other imported mammals are housed;
- those working in ports where animals are imported regularly.

Booster immunisation should be given every 2–3 years.

9 AIDS, sexually transmitted diseases and viral hepatitis

Acquired Immune Deficiency Syndrome (AIDS)

AIDS is caused by infection with a long-acting virus, human immunodeficiency virus (HIV), which prevents the human immune system from functioning properly. The disease first appeared in Africa but soon spread to the USA and can now be found in most countries in the world. The first clinical cases were described in Los Angeles in 1981.

AIDS represents the most serious threat this century in the field of communicable diseases because of its unique features. The virus renders the body susceptible to attacks from other infecting agents – bacteria, viruses, worm and protozoal infections – by virtually destroying the body's normal immune systems. This also means that the usual range of protective immunisations are not effective in combatting and preventing common communicable diseases. In addition certain unusual cancers are also found in some patients with AIDS.

Stages in the development of AIDS

AIDS develops in a number of stages with usually a long interval between infection with HIV and the subsequent development of clinical AIDS. The first stage is *infection with HIV*. The stage of infection is usually symptomless but, if symptoms do appear, they are non-specific and similar to glandular fever – malaise, lethargy and sore throat. The proportion of patients who progress further is still not known accurately but the present estimates (which are being constantly changed) indicate that only a proportion (about 35–75%) will do so. In these it is usual for there to be a long latent period of at least 7–10 years before the next stage towards AIDS develops.

The next stage is *lymphadenopathy* in which discrete lymph glands are enlarged (to more than 1 cm in diameter) at two or more sites (excluding the inguinal lymph glands) Most persons at this stage remain well but a proportion later develop the more serious next two stages. As the disease develops more accurate information will be known about the proportion of patients who progress to full clinical AIDS and the time factors involved.

AIDS-related complex is the next and more serious stage and indicates that the patient's immune system is becoming seriously impaired. Symptoms that develop include *continuous or intermittent fever, weight loss of at least 10%, great fatigue* and *night sweats*. Most of these patients progress to full AIDS.

The final stage is the development of *full clinical AIDS* which is fatal. The person may develop very serious opportunistic infections. These include:

- generalised herpes simplex
- severe herpes zoster (shingles)
- continuous and severe diarrhoea
- more loss of weight
- unusual forms of cancer.

Opportunistic infections

Opportunistic infections are those that usually are harmless to humans but, because the body's immune system has been seriously damaged by earlier invasion with HIV, now become recognisable and serious diseases. Because of the inability of the body to respond in the normal way by producing an increasing immunity, these become very serious and can lead to the death of the patient. These opportunistic infections include the following:

- various helminth and protozoal infections, for example *toxoplasmosis* or *Pneumocystis carinii* which both cause pneumonia, *strongyloidosis* which also causes pneumonia or may affect the central nervous system, and *cryptosporidiosis* which presents with diarrhoea;
- various virus infections, for example *aspergillosis* and *candidiasis* which both affect the oesophagus and lungs, *Cryptococcus* which affects mainly the meninges but also the bones, lungs, and genitourinary tract, and *histoplasmosis* which affects the lungs, spleen, liver and gastrointestinal tract;
- many unusual and atypical bacterial infections, for example atypical *mycoplasmosis*;
- certain fairly common viral infections which usually cause trivial attacks in normal persons such as herpes simplex can become very serious in the AIDS patient. Life-threatening disseminated herpes simplex may develop in this way.

Unusual forms of cancer

These include the following:

- *Kaposi's sarcoma* which presents as a flat or raised reddish–purple lesion on any part of the skin or hard palate;
- *cerebral lymphoma*;
- *non-Hodgkin's lymphoma*;
- *lymphoreticular malignancy* which starts more than 3 months after an opportunistic infection.

Methods of spread of HIV

There are three main ways HIV (and therefore AIDS) can be spread:

- *by sexual intercourse.* HIV virus is commonly found in seminal fluid and in vaginal secretions of those who are infected. This means that both homosexual and heterosexual persons are at risk if one partner is infected;
- by *blood to blood contamination*, thus by blood transfusion when the donor blood or blood products are infected with HIV. A number of haemophiliac patients in the UK have been infected in this way. *All blood and blood products used for transfusion, whether collected in this country or abroad, are now heat treated and therefore safe.* However there are still many countries in the world (particularly in Africa) where blood transfusion is very hazardous. Any 'at risk' patients who may require a blood transfusion periodically should certainly avoid such travel. Nurses, particularly those working in accident and emergency departments, should realise the potential danger of any unprotected contact with the blood of a patient and surgical gloves should always be worn when treating people who have been involved in traffic accidents and other patients who are bleeding. Staff in renal dialysis units should also take similar precautions.

  Many intravenous drug abusers are infected with HIV having picked up the infection by sharing syringes. Minute amounts of blood are often left in the needle or syringe and can lead to person to person spread if the earlier user has the HIV virus in their bloodstream. As will be explained later in this chapter (see p. 181), such careless use of syringes is also a common method of spreading hepatitis B virus. New sterile syringes are essential for all injections (including therapeutic ones). Home 'sterilisation', carried out by boiling glass syringes and needles, has been shown repeatedly to be unsafe, particularly against viral infections;
- by *the maternal–fetal route*, either by infection during pregnancy

via the placenta, by infection of the baby during birth by contact with an infected mother's vaginal secretions or later via breast milk.

The development of HIV infection and AIDS in the world

In 1992, the 8th International Conference on AIDS was held in Amsterdam and one of its main themes was the changing development of AIDS worldwide. When AIDS was first discovered in 1981, it was primarily a disease affecting homosexual men. In the UK by 1993, the cumulative total of AIDS cases that had been identified showed that 92.6% were men. This reflected the fact that initially, early in the 1980s, the vast majority of HIV infections had occurred in homosexual men. The first differences noticed were when contaminated blood products were given mainly to haemophiliac patients leading to some becoming infected by HIV and later getting full AIDS. Since the introduction of compulsory heat treatment for all imported blood products (including Factor VIII and Factor IX used to treat haemophiliacs) no further infections by this route have occurred in the UK. At present all 'at risk' groups such as intravenous drug users and homosexual men have been excluded from acting as blood donors.

The next group to be infected were intravenous drug abusers and some of these have already developed AIDS. This is one of the reasons for the high concentrations of HIV infected persons in some large cities such as London and Edinburgh in the UK and New York and Los Angeles in USA.

Since then the situation has developed further and the present (1994) position can be summed up as follows:

- AIDS is now a full *pandemic* (a worldwide epidemic);
- the density of infection varies in different parts of the world. It is worst in Africa where it is widespread. For instance, in some African cities at least a third of all adults are infected with HIV. In one study in Kigali in Rwanda, 25% of women with only one life partner were found to be infected with HIV, presumably by their steady partner. In this study, the youngest age groups were even worse – in the 19–23 years age group 38% were found to be HIV positive. Another part of the world where HIV is spreading rapidly is in South-East Asia and unless effective preventive action is taken at once, it is likely that by 2003 it will be as bad as Africa. In the USA 47 500 new infections of HIV occurred in the first 6 months of 1994. In the USA AIDS is growing fastest in the south among Black and Hispanic people;
- women are now being infected as much as men;
- infection is spreading from high risk groups now to the general population in all parts of the world including the UK;

- by 1992, 2 million cases of AIDS had already occurred worldwide and it is expected that the pandemic will grow rapidly and that by the year 2000 at least 12 million cases of AIDS will have occurred, and the numbers may reach 15 million;
- the proportion of persons acquiring HIV infection through heterosexual sex is rising rapidly. In fact, by 1994 at least 50% of new HIV infections in the UK occurred in this way. By the year 2000, it is estimated by experts that the proportion becoming infected with HIV by heterosexual intercourse will reach 85–90%;
- the perception of the risks of HIV infection by the majority of ordinary people in highly developed countries is still probably similar to the findings of a recent American survey which states 'American adults believe that the risk of AIDS is irrelevant since they are currently monogamous or celibate. They do not consider it a lifetime risk;'
- a further complication now emerging is that the AIDS epidemic is likely to be followed by an epidemic of *tuberculosis*: the World Health Organization (WHO) reported in 1993 that '30–50% of persons who have AIDS in the developing countries now also have tuberculosis.'

Levels of AIDS in the UK

In England, to the end of December 1993, 7890 persons (7306 men and 584 women) had developed AIDS with 5203 deaths. Table 9.1 gives details of the cumulative totals for England classified in a way which shows how they had become infected.

Table 9.1 represents the earliest infections probably up to the mid-1980s when undoubtedly the majority of HIV infections were in homosexual men and certainly does not indicate the likely future trends in HIV infection in the UK. Figure 9.1 is more helpful in this respect for it shows that the spread by heterosexual sex is increasing quite rapidly.

The levels of AIDS in 12 European countries is shown in Fig. 9.2 which shows the numbers of cases of AIDS per million of the population. Note that the level in the UK is the same as Germany and that only Greece, Portugal and Ireland have lower figures. The highest rates are in France and Spain where the incidence is three times higher than in the UK.

Prevention of AIDS – the importance of health education

The only certain way to avoid AIDS is to understand fully the mechanisms of infection and then to avoid running the known risks. This entails improving the health education of the whole population. An important starting point in any campaign is to ensure that all

Table 9.1   Cumulative totals of AIDS cases by exposure category, England, to 31 December 1993.

How persons probably acquired the virus	Number of cases				Numbers of deaths
	Males	Females	Total	%†	
Sexual intercourse					
Between men	6010	–	6010	76	4058
Between men and women					
'High risk' partner*	25	62	87	1	47
Other partner abroad**	417	278	695	9	354
Other partner UK	42	32	74	1	37
Not known	4	2	6	<1	3
Injecting drug user (IDU)	187	85	272	3	164
IDU and sexual intercourse					
between men	127	–	127	2	85
Blood					
Blood factor (e.g. haemophiliacs)	342	5	347	4	293
Blood or tissue transfer (e.g. transfusion)					
Abroad	10	38	48	1	24
UK	17	18	35	<1	17
Mother to child	45	46	91	1	46
Other (undetermined)	80	18	98	1	63
Total	7306	584	7890	100	5203

* Includes men and women who had sex with injecting drug users, or with those infected through blood factor treatment or blood transfusion, and women who had sex with bisexual men.
** Includes persons without other identified risks who are from, or have lived in, countries where the major route of HIV-1 transmission is through sexual intercourse between men and women.
† Does not add up to 100 because of rounding. (Source: Communicable Disease Surveillance Centre (CDSC).)

professionals in the NHS completely understand that the risk is *not* confined to small groups such as homosexual men or drug abusers but is far wider – anyone is likely to be at risk if they ignore the known dangers. Still far too many members of the general public do not realise the potential dangers facing everyone. Nurses and other health staff should act as health educators to their partners and patients whenever the opportunity arises.

In 1986, the UK Government mounted a widespread health education campaign aimed at informing the general public about the dangers of AIDS and its methods of spread. Over £20 million was spent on all forms of publicity, and an explanatory leaflet was delivered

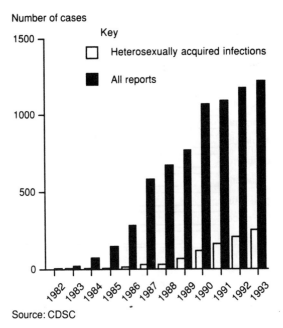

Source: CDSC

Fig. 9.1 AIDS cases: total numbers and numbers where infection was probably acquired through sexual intercourse between men and women, England, to 31 December 1993. (From the Chief Medical Officer's Report *On the State of the Public Health 1993*, Department of Health.)

to every household. As with all other large-scale health education campaigns, the effectiveness of the message depended on supplementation at a later date by health staff in their day-to-day contact with patients and their families. It is of particular importance to teach young persons at school and in further education colleges and universities about the true dangers of AIDS and how these can be avoided.

The following are the practical steps which should be taken to avoid developing AIDS:

- *the need to limit sexual contacts*. The greater the number of sexual partners, the greater the chance of infection with HIV. This cannot be overemphasised – even if all the other preventive steps are taken (use of condoms, etc.) no other preventive method is better than a monogamous relationship (one sexual partner of the other sex for life is ideal) or celibacy. It is important to realise that any heterosexual relationship could be dangerous if either partner is HIV positive and this fact is not known by the other partner or is concealed from them. The same is true of homosexual relationships where anal or oral sex represents the main danger;

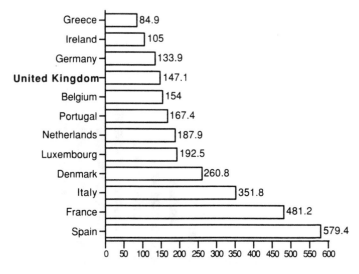

Rates per million population

Source: European Centre for the Epidemiological Monitoring of AIDS

Fig. 9.2   Reported AIDS cases in Europe: cumulative rates to December 1993. (From the Chief Medical Officer's Report *On the State of the Public Health 1993*, Department of Health.)

- the use of the condom in any casual sexual contact is essential for the safety of both partners. The objective of using a condom is to prevent the partner coming into contact with seminal or vaginal fluids. Oral sex should also be avoided. The Government campaign not only stressed the value of condoms but helped to make condoms more widely available. Travellers should always take stocks with them as condoms purchased in some countries may be unreliable;
- realising that the only reason why there is, at present, a greater risk in any male homosexual relationship is because there is now a much higher proportion of homosexual men who are HIV positive;
- recognising there is a special danger of contamination from any used syringe. The only certain way to avoid this danger is always to use a new sterile disposable syringe for every injection. After use, the disposable syringe should always be carefully destroyed (so that it cannot be used again). 'Home sterilisation,' of glass syringes has been shown to be inadequate as far as viruses are concerned. There has been much debate regarding the suggestion that known

drug abusers should be provided with free sterile syringes (as has been the practice in The Netherlands and Edinburgh) and certainly this would reduce the danger of spreading HIV infection in such persons;

● a clean pair of rubber gloves should always be kept in the glove box of the car so that if one comes across a road accident and goes to help one will be protected from contamination from blood. This is particularly important for nurses and those trained in first aid who are far more likely to offer help in such circumstances.

Sexually transmitted Diseases (STDs)

Sexually transmitted diseases are those which are spread mainly by sexual intercourse – one partner infecting the other. There are three serious STDs:

● urethritis and related diseases
● gonorrhoea
● syphilis.

In addition, *candidiasis (thrush), genital herpes* and *trichomoniasis vaginalis* are also sexually transmitted. As explained below (see p. 181.) certain viral hepatitis infections can also be spread by sexual intercourse. Table 9.2 gives the six most common types of STDs recorded in England in 1991 and 1992.

There was a further fall in non-viral STDs in 1992. It had been feared that gonorrhoea in men was increasing but the figures indicated a further fall. Herpes simplex virus infections continued to increase.

Table 9.2   Sexually transmitted diseases reported in England, 1991 and 1992.

Condition	Males		Females		Total	
	1991	1992	1991	1992	1991	1992
Non-specific urethritis and related diseases	53 348	48 044	18 227	16 883	71 575	70 234
Syphilis	885	848	464	464	1349	1312
Gonorrhoea	11 399	7 289	8744	5539	18 683	14 288
Candidiasis (thrush)	9541	9104	50 094	516 118	59 963	60 722
Herpes simplex (1st attack)	6152	6140	7122	7877	13 274	14 017
Trichomoniasis	334	371	5929	5472	6263	5843

(From the Chief Medical Officers Reports, 1992 and 1993.)

Non-specific urethritis and related diseases

In men, this usually presents as a urethritis (urethral discharge), but in women over 90% are symptom free – a few later develop a urethritis or pelvic genital infection. The incubation period is 10–28 days. In approximately 70% of cases *Chlamydia trachomatis* can be isolated; in the remainder the cause is not usually found. In women, this is the commonest cause of pelvic inflammatory disease and subsequent infertility. Occasionally arthritis can develop as a late complication. Tetracycline is mainly used to treat non-specific genital infection.

Gonorrhoea

Gonorrhoea has an incubation period of 3–10 days (usually 5 days). In men the first symptoms are a urethral discharge with some pain on micturition. In women, about 60% have no symptoms and the remainder have a vaginal discharge.

Treatment is with penicillin but, increasingly, patients are also given tetracycline to clear up any non-specific genital infection.

In both non-specific infections and in gonorrhoea, *follow-up* should always be undertaken after 3 weeks to assess treatment and after 3 months to make certain that a double infection with syphilis has not occurred. What can happen in this case is that the initial treatment with antibiotics may suppress the development of the characteristic chancre of primary syphilis but not cure the disease.

The dramatic way that cases of gonorrhoea have fallen from 1980 to 1992 is shown in Fig. 9.3.

Syphilis

This is potentially the most dangerous STD, but fortunately, treatment with penicillin in the primary stage (usually developing about 3 weeks after infection) or in the secondary stage (after about 8 weeks) will prevent the very serious complications from developing. Treatment early in pregnancy of a woman already infected with syphilis will also prevent any danger of congenital syphilis in her child.

The first signs of syphilis usually occur after an incubation period of 9–90 days (usually 21 days) with the development of a painless chancre at the site of the infection. Confirmation of the diagnosis is by bacteriological examination identifying the presence of the spirochete *Treponema pallidum*.

The number of cases of syphilis have been falling steadily in the UK for many years.

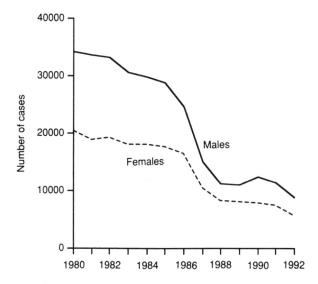

Fig. 9.3 All gonorrhoea: number of new cases seen at NHS genitourinary medicine clinics, England, 1980–92. (From the Chief Medical Officer's Report *On the State of the Public Health*, Department of Health, 1993.)

Other STDs

The other STDs mentioned in Table 9.2 are usually mild, but genital herpes may be confused with cystitis. Candidiasis (thrush) is a fungal infection leading to an intense irritating white creamy discharge. Treatment is with pessaries of nystatin, clotrimazole or econazole and is usually very effective. Trichomoniasis also causes a vaginal discharge which is treated with metronidazole; the male partner should be treated at the same time.

Prevention of sexually transmitted diseases depends on:

- complete and efficient diagnosis and treatment of all cases;
- the searching out of suspected cases; and
- avoidance of casual or promiscuous sexual intercourse.

Diagnosis, especially of gonorrhoea, is not simple in women. This means that an infected woman can remain so for a lengthy period without realising it. In doubtful cases hospital out-patient attendance is desirable so that bacteriological smears may be taken and blood tests examined.

On diagnosis of a STD, a careful history should always be taken and arrangements made for the cohabiting partner to be medically examined as soon as possible. To carry out this important contact tracing, specially trained nurses and social workers are attached to all STD departments. Their task is to trace the cohabiting partner and persuade him or her to attend for examination as soon as possible.

Better education is needed so that everyone realises that only by self control and avoidance of casual sexual experience will all STDs (including HIV infections and AIDS) be prevented. It is especially important that people realise that without bacteriological tests it is impossible even for a doctor to exclude the possibility of a STD in any person. This should be explained to all people who may otherwise be misled into believing they can tell when a contact is or is not infected.

Viral hepatitis

Viral hepatitis is notifiable and the number of cases notified in England and Wales have trebled in the 6 years from 1987 to 1992 (see Table 9.3).

Hepatitis A

This type of hepatitis has an incubation period of between 3 and 5 weeks. It is spread by the faecal/oral route and usually follows person to person contact. Many food-borne outbreaks have been reported, and during the incubation period there is a heavy excretion of virus in the stools and careless personal hygiene amongst food handlers is often responsible for the spread of infection. *Hepatitis A is rarely sexually transmitted but this mode of spread can occur after oral/anal contact, usually in homosexual men.*

Hepatitis A does not result in liver failure and complete recovery is normal although it may be many weeks before the patient feels really

Table 9.3 Notifications of viral hepatitis, England and Wales, 1987–92.

	1987	1988	1989	1990	1991	1992
Hepatitis A	1836	3190	5278	7316	7430	8993
Hepatitis B	444	390	432	435	488	498
Hepatitis non-A/non-B	249	363	256	169	157	164
Hepatitis other/not known	850	1120	1105	1087	785	484
Total	3379	5063	7071	9007	8860	10 139

(From various Monitors in the MB2 series.)

well again. A vaccine against hepatitis A was introduced in the UK in 1992. It is useful for travellers to tropical and other countries where living conditions may be primitive.

Passive immunisation using immunoglobulin can be given to close contacts and has been used to control hepatitis A outbreaks in nursery schools and homes for those with learning disabilities.

Hepatitis B

Hepatitis B is a sexually transmitted form of the disease which is spread by infected body fluids such as semen, vaginal secretions, saliva and breast milk and can also be spread through contaminated blood. It has a variable incubation period between about 7 and 15 weeks.

Infection with blood or blood products can occur in the following ways:

- accidental contamination of health staff during surgical operations (needle stick injury) or when assisting with renal dialysis;
- first aid help during traffic and other accidents when there is haemorrhage. Clean rubber gloves should always be worn on such occasions and, as has already been stressed, it is sensible for all nurses to have a pair of clean rubber gloves in their car;
- needles and syringes shared by intravenous drug abusers;
- tattooing and ear piercing, cases have very occasionally been traced to these sources.

It is important for all nurses to realise that blood carriers of hepatitis B are not uncommon. About 5–10% of all cases become chronic blood carriers and may remain as life-time carriers. If any nurse become such a carrier *she/he has an absolute duty to report this fact to their employers.* If the nurse fails to do this she/he is likely to be accused of *serious professional misconduct.* Already in the case of one doctor which came before the GMC late in 1993, failure to report the fact that the doctor was a hepatitis B carrier resulted in the doctor's name being erased from the Medical Register. Although this body has no jurisdiction over nurses, this decision cannot be ignored for it seems to have established an important principle for all professional health workers in the NHS who have close daily contacts with patients.

In the UK, the carrier rate among persons who have had an attack of hepatitis B is only 0.1% but in Africa and the Far East up to 20% of those recovering from hepatitis B have become chronic carriers. Nurses who are going to work in these countries should always be immunised against hepatitis B before they leave the UK (see Chapter 7, p. 134 for details of the effective vaccine now available).

Hepatitis B has similar clinical features to other forms of hepatitis –

fever and fatigue with jaundice. Complete recovery occurs in most patients but a small proportion (5–10%) develop liver damage or even liver failure and a late complication is that a primary cancer of the liver becomes more likely. Treatment includes a low-fat/high energy diet and no alcohol should be drunk until all the liver function tests are normal.

Non-A/non-B hepatitis (sometimes called hepatitis C)

This is becoming the commonest form of hepatitis in many countries of the world following blood transfusion using blood that has not been heat treated. The long-term consequences of this form of hepatitis can be very serious as chronic liver damage has been reported in 30–50% of cases. Both long and short incubation periods have been reported in this form of hepatitis.

10 Prevention of non-communicable diseases

With non-communicable diseases, the greatest barrier to prevention is that so little is known about the causes of these diseases. Research into causation is continuously being carried out and the various preventative factors are slowly being unravelled. It is, however, a very complicated study as usually there is a multiplicity of factors involved. Even in diseases whose cause is as yet hardly understood, wide differences exist between the incidence and mortality in the various social classes of the population (as shown on p. 63) suggesting that conditions and other environmental factors concerned with the differing lifestyles of the various social classes may increase or diminish the dangers of developing such diseases.

Sometimes important factors only come to light by a steady increase in a disease leading to greater research which finally discovers an important causative factor. An example of this is *cancer of the lung*, the increase of which has been shown to be connected with cigarette smoking. Another example is *cancer of the bladder*. Here epidemiological studies have demonstrated there is a higher incidence of this cancer amongst workers in the dyestuffs industry and indicated that three aromatic amines, α-naphthylamine, β-naphthylamine and benzidine, are potent carcinogens. It was also found that antioxidants made from α- and β-naphthylamines were widely used in the rubber and cable industries. Since the use of these naphthylamines was banned, the incidence of bladder cancers in men who started in this industry after the ban was introduced has fallen dramatically, although the incidence in those men who were already employed before the ban still shows a marked increase.

Prevention of non-communicable diseases can always be considered from three aspects:

- complete prevention of the disease ever occurring in any individual (*primary prevention*);
- early detection by screening of the disease in a person who, as yet, has no symptoms (*secondary prevention*);
- prevention of complications from a disease which already existed

before the effects had produced disability or handicap (*tertiary prevention*).

Unless the correct treatment is carried out for many non-communicable chronic diseases such as diabetes mellitus, asthma and hypertensive disease, many serious long-term complications and disabilities may occur.

Ischaemic heart disease

The incidence of ischaemic heart disease increased markedly from 1950 to the mid-1980s in the UK but has fallen slightly since then. Much research has been carried out throughout the world to discover the cause of this condition. Although much has yet to be cleared up, it is now known that considerable differences occur throughout the world (see Table 10.1).

Table 10.1 Deaths from ischaemic heart disease in men in 1989 (unless otherwise stated) in various countries of the world per 100 000 population.

Japan	43.0	USA (1988)	220.9
Spain	90.1	Germany	227.4
Portugal	99.8	Australia (1988)	260.9
France (1988)	103.4	New Zealand (1987)	276.2
Netherlands (1987)	140.4	Ireland (1988)	287.0
Israel (1987)	168.3	England and Wales	335.8
Canada (1988)	208.1	Scotland	391.5
Austria	218.2		

(From The World Health Organization Annual Statistics.)

Factors associated with ischaemic heart disease

There are many factors associated with the incidence of ischaemic heart disease including the following (see also p. 52):

- *genetic history* – members of some families undoubtedly have a greater risk of developing ischaemic heart disease. In some instances this is connected with an abnormally high blood cholesterol level. For anyone with such a family history, it is very important that all the factors below are in their favour;
- *physical activity* – the more physically active a person is, the less likely they are to develop ischaemic heart disease, and vice versa;
- *a high fat intake* – the more fat that is eaten the greater the risk; therefore all persons should reduce their fat intake (see p. 201 for the simplest ways to do this). It also reduces the risks if *unsaturated*

vegetable fats are used (such as margarine and cooking fats made from sunflower and soya extracts instead of butter and lard). A high level of saturated fats is associated with higher levels of blood cholesterol;

- *a high intake of vegetable fibre is beneficial* (see p. 195 for a list of foods containing a high level of fibre);
- *overweight* – gross overweight increases the risks of developing ischaemic heart disease (see p. 200);
- *cigarette smoking* – smoking considerably increases the risks not only of ischaemic heart disease but also of other vascular diseases such as intermittent claudication. Unlike many diseases associated with smoking (such as cancer of the lung and chronic bronchitis and emphysema) the connection between smoking and heart disease is not very cumulative which means that stopping smoking even in someone who has smoked for many years is likely to reduce the risks substantially after some months. This fact is a valuable point to make when attempting to persuade an older individual who has been smoking for many years to give it up;
- *stress* – it is not easy to be certain of the role of stress in the development of ischaemic heart disease but anyone who is finding it increasingly difficult to cope with their job or with life's responsibilities may be at greater risk. This is probably connected with the fact that frustration, anxiety, aggression and tension (all often associated with stressful situations) are accompanied by a rise in blood pressure, and by the liver releasing temporarily cholesterol and fatty acids into the blood. Also some individuals respond to stress by over-eating and become obese, adding to their risks. If a person can cope well and enjoys their job, it is very unlikely that the individual is at special risk from ischaemic heart disease.

Sex differences

There are some marked differences between the sexes as regards the chance of developing ischaemic heart disease *early in life*. Attacks below the age of 45 are normally *only seen in men*. Women seem to be protected by their natural circulating female sex hormones until after the menopause. Then the risks of heart disease in women gradually rise until at approximately the age of 70 the incidence is similar in both sexes. Any woman receiving hormone replacement therapy after the menopause will prolong this period of protection. Any woman who has had her ovaries removed early in life is usually given hormone replacement therapy.

Aspirin

There is much evidence that small daily doses of aspirin reduce the risks of ischaemic heart disease and stroke especially in persons at high risk. Those who develop gastric symptoms after taking soluble aspirin can prevent these problems by taking enteric coated aspirin (sold commercially under the name 'Nu-seals'). This product must be taken on its own and never with alkalis (which are present in many medicines taken for indigestion). This type of tablet protects the sensitive person with its acid-proof coat which means that the aspirin never comes into contact with the sensitive stomach mucosa. The protective covering melts as soon as the tablet reaches the duodenum and small intestine and the aspirin is absorbed without creating any problems.

There are two important diseases which ischaemic heart disease is more likely to follow:

- *hypertension* – it is most important that anyone with persistent high blood pressure has effective treatment. Otherwise an attack of ischaemic heart disease may follow;
- *diabetes* – persons with either type of diabetes (the insulin dependent one as well as the milder form) are at greater risk than normal of developing an attack of ischaemic heart disease.

Prevention of ischaemic heart disease

The following are the simplest and most effective ways of reducing the chance of suffering an attack of ischaemic heart disease:

- *avoid being overweight* – persons who are grossly overweight have a considerably increased chance of having an ischaemic heart attack;
- *regular physical activity* seems to be associated with a decreased risk. Persons in a sedentary job should make every effort to be active – walking briskly wherever possible is sensible. An active lifestyle is desirable; sudden bursts of very violent exercise should be avoided;
- *do not smoke* – there is very clear evidence that ischaemic heart attacks occur more commonly in smokers;
- *reduce the intake of fat in the diet* as well as ensuring that adequate supplies of *vegetable fibre* are eaten.

These simple rules are more important than relying on regular estimations of blood cholesterol levels or undertaking routine medical check-ups unless it is known that the individual is at special risk. It is always useful to have a blood cholesterol test to discover the very small percentage of persons with exceptionally high levels in whom the risk of an eventual heart attack is very high. These individuals should always then be referred to a cardiologist and given special counselling along the lines indicated above.

Methods of reducing fat in the diet

The best ways to reduce the fat intake in any diet are to:

- choose the leanest cuts of meat and trim any visible fat;
- use at least semi-skimmed milk (only for adults);
- eat plenty of fish and poultry (with the skin removed);
- avoid eating made up meats such as corned beef, salami and meat pies;
- grill, microwave, steam, poach or boil foods rather than fry them; drain off any excess fat;
- eat margarines labelled 'high in unsaturates';
- reduce the amounts eaten of the following foods – crisps, chocolates, cakes, pastries and biscuits;
- choose low fat cheeses or cottage cheese.

Effective emergency treatment

It is important that *effective emergency treatment and aid be given by paramedics and ambulance crews* sent to patients who have had a sudden attack of ischaemic heart disease. In 1990 the NHS introduced nationwide defibrillators into the equipment of emergency ambulances. By the end of 1991, all qualified ambulance staff had been fully trained in the use of the defibrillator. A system of further training was then started to ensure that by 1996, 60% of all qualified ambulance staff will be trained to paramedic standard. By April 1991, 2251 ambulance staff in England and Wales had already been trained in this way and it is now expected that the target will be reached well before 1996. There is no doubt that such an advance will reduce the immediate death rate after an attack of ischaemic heart disease.

The cancers

The true causative nature of cancers is, as yet still unknown. Yet many new features are now coming to light. There are many different factors which are likely to predispose a person to the development of a cancer in addition to their genetic make-up. Many of the known factors are connected with some *repetitive form of irritation*. It is known, for instance, that various *skin cancers* can be caused by excessive exposure to ultraviolet light from the sun or by chronic irritation from oils.

Excessive radiation resulted in many cancers in the pioneers of radiology before that hazard was understood. Smoking cigarettes is well known to be connected with the development of many different cancers – the commonest being cancer of the lung but it also has been shown to increase the chances of developing cancer of the bladder and cancer of the cervix uteri in women. Another very clear connection is that between *inhalation of asbestos dusts* and cancer of the lung. As a result, the use of asbestos has been prohibited in the UK. A clear link that has also been established as a cause of cancer of the bladder is the exposure of workers to benzene and naphthylamine derivatives, as in the cable industry.

Another very interesting connection is that between the development of a primary cancer of the liver and the *chronic carrier state of hepatitis B* (see p. 182). Another further fascinating example is given by oesophageal cancers found in an area from Northern Iran through the southern republics of Russia to western China (see Chapter 12).

Most cancers show their highest incidence in Social Class V and their lowest in Social Class I (Fig. 10.1). The exception is cancer of the breast in women (see p. 192).

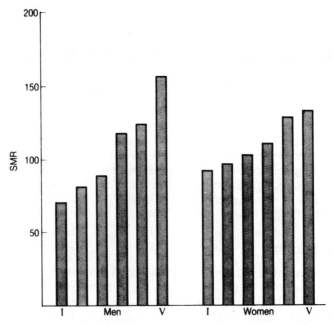

Fig. 10.1 Mortality from malignant neoplasms by social class in men and women aged 20–64 years, England and Wales, 1979–80. (From *Occupational Mortality*, OPCS, 1987.)

Prevention of cancers depends on many factors including:

- *the removal of the precipitating cause* such as stopping smoking or avoiding excessive sun bathing and protecting the skin with a sun cream of at least factor 15 or 20;
- *protection from radiation* especially for personnel likely to be exposed in their jobs such as radiographers, some nurses and some scientists;
- *early and radical treatment of a precancerous condition* (this is the basis of cervical screening to prevent cancer of the cervix uteri in women (see p. 190).

International cancer mortality

There are marked variations in the cancer mortality in different countries in the world (see Table 10.2). Many of these are too great to be explained by varying degrees of diagnosis and treatment. Note that exceptionally low rates of cancer mortality (and incidence) occur in Japan except that the rate of cancer of the stomach is very high there. When cancer rates for Japanese individuals who have migrated to the USA are studied, the rates are similar to those of local Americans suggesting that the main factors are environmental (including diet) rather than genetic.

Cancer of the cervix uteri

Cancer of the cervix uteri in women was responsible for 1668 deaths in 1992 in England and Wales. From 1988 to 1992 these deaths fell steadily

Table 10.2 Cancer death rates in different countries per 100 000 population, 1991.

Site	USA	Austria	France	Netherlands	UK	Australia	Japan
Stomach							
Males	6.8	26.0	15.8	16.3	21.9	10.6	50.3
Females	4.4	22.6	10.5	10.0	13.9	6.3	28.2
Lung							
Males	73.5	66.5	67.6	16.2	97.6	56.1	43.0
Females	35.9	18.0	9.6	11.7	42.3	18.6	15.4
Breast							
Females	33.5	41.8	34.8	25.4	53.4	28.4	9.2
Cervix uteri							
Females	3.5	5.1	2.9	1.6	7.0	4.2	2.9
Leukaemia							
Males	8.1	8.1	8.9	8.8	7.8	7.4	5.6
Females	6.2	7.3	7.3	5.7	6.7	5.6	3.8

(From World Health Organization Annual Statistics.)

by about 20% per year. Table 3.16 (see p. 63) shows a marked variation between the six social classes – deaths steadily rise from Social Class I to V. In Social Class V women not only smoke more cigarettes (a powerful predisposing cause) but also have the lowest rates of cervical smear tests carried out. Both factors show their effect in an increased mortality.

Prevention

The widely used *cervical smear* screening test (exfoliative cytology) can detect a precancerous condition of the cervix. The test is simple: a vaginal speculum is passed and a direct smear is obtained from the cervix and examined histologically. If there are abnormal mitotic changes in the nuclei of the epithelial cells, a complete gynaecological examination is carried out to ascertain whether a precancerous condition exists. If these investigations confirm a precancerous condition, the appropriate treatment is carried out *before an invasive cancer develops*. This is often a simple laser treatment which totally destroys these dangerous cells. Usually such smears are collected by GPs. Since the introduction of target payments there have been remarkable improvements in the percentage of women now having the smear test. In 1990–1 74% of women aged 20–64 were tested in England and Wales compared with 43% in 1988–9. It is expected that, as a result of the larger numbers of women now being examined there will be a further fall in mortality from this cancer.

Cancer of the lung

Deaths from cancer of the lung increased rapidly and steadily from 1947 in the UK until the mid-1980s. In England and Wales, for instance, deaths from cancer of the lung were 9204 in 1947 and reached a peak of 35 739 in 1986. Initially deaths in men greatly outnumbered those in women – in 1947 84.2% occurred in men but by 1992 the distribution between the sexes was 67.3% in men and in women (see Table 10.3).

Note that *deaths in women are increasing whereas in men they are falling*. In young persons under the age of 21 years more women smoke

Table 10.3 Deaths from cancer of the lung, numbers and percentages in England and Wales, 1965–92.

	1965	1974	1986	1992
Males	22 231 (84.2%)	26 400 (80.0%)	26 423 (71.8%)	22 668 (67.3%)
Females	4168 (15.8%)	6600 (20.0%)	10 374 (28.2%)	10 994 (32.7%)

(From various OPCS Monitors in the MB2 series.)

than men. If this trend continues, then it can be expected that the numbers of deaths in women due to cancer of the lung will increase. Cancer of the lung is not easy to treat effectively – it leads to death of the person within 2–3 years in all but 5–7% of cases. Marked differences occur in the incidence of cancer of the lung in different countries. Table 10.4 shows the levels in seven leading countries; it will be noted that the UK has the highest rate.

Much research has been carried out in various parts of the world to discover the factors that lead to cancer of the lung. All these investigations have shown that cigarette smoking is the commonest cause. It has also been shown that death rates from cancer of the lung increase steeply the more any individual smokes. Indeed *heavy cigarette smokers have a death rate from cancer of the lung 30 times greater than non-smokers.*

The Royal College of Physicians has studied the problem in depth and clearly states that 'cigarette smoking is an important cause of lung cancer. If the habit ceased, the number of deaths caused by this disease should fall steeply in the course of time'. Research in USA has also shown that there are highly abnormal cells in the sputum of heavy smokers which show many abnormal changes and which may be pre-cancerous. The interesting and encouraging feature is that, if smoking stops then within a short time there is a fall in the numbers of such cells in the sputum and eventually they disappear. This strongly suggests that giving up smoking is likely to reduce the chance of developing cancer of the lung.

If the level of cancer of the lung in the UK is to be significantly reduced, it is *most important that young women realise the increased risks smoking produces.* Otherwise although mortality in men is likely to continue to fall gradually, that in women will rise and may well counterbalance the improvement in the male mortality and the total numbers of deaths may stop falling. Professional women and *especially those in the health services* have a particular responsibility to give a lead

Table 10.4 Mortality from cancer of the lung per 100 000 population in various countries 1991.

Country	Males	Females
Japan	43.0	15.4
Australia	56.1	18.6
Austria	66.5	18.0
France	67.6	9.6
USA	73.5	11.7
Netherlands	76.6	35.9
United Kingdom	97.6	42.3

(From World Health Organization Annual Statistics, 1992.)

in this respect. If they do not smoke or give the habit up, the example provided to their patients and to the public in general is bound to be of value in the campaign to reduce the lethal habit of smoking.

The Royal College of Physicians has suggested the following seven courses of action:

- more education of the public and especially schoolchildren concerning the hazards of smoking;
- restriction of tobacco advertising;
- more effective restriction of the sale of cigarettes to children;
- wider restriction of smoking in public places;
- an increase in tax on cigarettes;
- informing purchasers of the tar and nicotine content of the smoke from cigarettes;
- investigating the value of anti-smoking clinics to assist those who find difficulty in giving up smoking.

The reduction of cancer of the lung is a key target in the White Paper *The Health of the Nation* together with the reduction of smoking (see Chapter 11).

Passive smoking

Recent research has shown that the inhaling of the smoke produced by cigarette smokers (passive smoking) produces a definite extra risk of developing lung cancer. It is estimated that in the UK approximately 600 persons die each year as a result of passive smoking.

Cancer of the breast

Cancer of the breast is an important cause of death in women – in 1992 in England and Wales it was responsible for 13 786 deaths, and it is the commonest cancer in women. Table 3.16 (p. 63) shows an unusual inverse Standardised Mortality Ratio curve demonstrating mortality is highest in Social Class I and lowest in Social Class V. However, there is a much wider range of mortality in different countries (see Table 10.5). The full reasons for these differences are unknown but in countries where breast feeding is common there has been much speculation that this may be a factor in the lower incidence, although this has never been proved. The high rate in the UK emphasises the need to prevent deaths from this cause. This is why so much is now being done to encourage mammography (see below) especially in women aged 50–64 years of age. Although the modern contraceptive pill has been shown to be quite safe, no woman should take it continuously for longer than 10 years without a break, as this may be a contributing factor.

Table 10.5   Cancer of the breast, females, deaths per 100 000 in different countries, 1989.

Australia	Japan	Netherlands	USA	France	Austria	United Kingdom
8.4	9.2	25.4	33.5	34.8	41.8	53.4

(From The World Health Organization Annual Statistics.)

The best chance of reducing the mortality from cancer of the breast in women is to diagnose the condition as early as possible. Recent research strongly suggests that women whose breast cancers are detected when they are smaller than 15 mm have a much higher survival rate than those where the size of the cancer on diagnosis is 15 mm or larger. This is why *mammography* is so valuable as it enables very small breast cancers to be detected. The *type of breast cancer* present is also an important factor – the most rapidly developing and serious breast cancers are those types which occur in pregnancy and lactation.

Mammography

The Forrest Committee in 1986 published a report which pointed out the value of mammography screening for breast cancer in women. Following this report, an NHS Breast Screening Programme (NHSBSP) was set up for women aged 50–64 years of age. In 1991 the Advisory Committee of the NHSBSP reviewed all the recent trials and reported that the views expressed in the original Forrest Report that mammography screening for women aged 50–64 reduced mortality substantially had been confirmed by long-term follow-up.

As yet there is no evidence that women under the age of 50 should be screened routinely, but at present there is consideration being given to a possible extension to age 69 years. Women over the age of 64 may be screened by the NHS on request. As there is a higher rate of breast cancer in women who have a family history of this condition, mammography may be offered to these women under the age of 50. The decision whether to screen should be made on clinical grounds and should not be part of the routine NHS screening process.

The 1991 detection rate of breast cancer by mammography was 6.2 per 1000 women who had the mammography test. The success of any mammography screening programme depends on the quality of the service. The NHSBSP recommends that the minimum acceptable standard should be that 70% of women who have been invited actually attend and that a rate of 75% should be achievable.

Mammography should be carried out every 3 years. Any women found to have suspicious shadows are then further examined by ultrasound imaging and fine needle aspiration which enables the final diagnosis to be made histologically.

It is particularly important to follow up with mammography any woman who has already had one breast cancer as research studies have shown that there is a 4–6 times greater risk that a primary cancer will develop in the opposite breast.

Cancer of the stomach

In England and Wales in 1992, 8285 persons (4994 men and 3291 women) died from cancer of the stomach. Deaths from this type of cancer have been steadily falling – between 1982 and 1992 they fell by 18.9% in England and Wales. It is interesting to note the following in regard to cancers of the stomach:

* there is a marked variation between the mortality in the social classes – the SMR rises from 50 in Social Class I to 158 in Social Class V (see Fig. 10.2);
* there is a well-marked geographical distribution in the UK with the highest rates in the rural areas of North Wales;
* there is an association between chronic gastric irritation (in the form of a chronic gastritis or previous gastric ulcer) and the subsequent development of a cancer of the stomach. Also it is known that persons with pernicious anaemia have three times the incidence of cancer of the stomach compared with the general population;
* genetic factors may be significant and persons with blood group A have a 20% greater incidence;
* diet probably plays an important part and the high levels in Japan may be connected with this factor.

Cancer of the large bowel (colon and rectum)

Cancers of the large bowel (colon and rectum) are the second commonest cause of cancer deaths in the UK and these figures are continuing to increase slowly. In 1992 in England and Wales there were 11 781 deaths from cancer of the colon (5531 in men and 6250 in women) and 5622 deaths from cancer of the rectum (3218 in men and 2404 in women). These figures represent a 8.9% increase compared with the figures in 1982.

There are definite regional variations in the incidence and mortality of large bowel cancers in England and Wales. The SMR for the RHAs in London averages 89 compared with an average of 111 for the RHAs of Mersey, North Western, West Midlands and Northern. In Scotland there is a similar varied distribution.

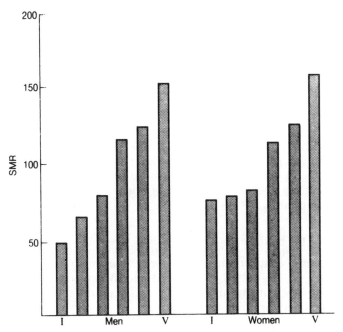

Fig. 10.2 Mortality from cancer of the stomach by social class in men and women aged 20–64 years, England and Wales, 1979–80, 1982–3. (From *Occupational Mortality*, OPCS, 1987.)

Large bowel cancers are much commoner in the Westernised countries of Europe and North America than in Africa and south Asia. Differences in diet are thought to be responsible and particularly the large amounts of vegetable fibre eaten in Africa and south Asia (see below).

Prevention

The most effective way to reduce the incidence of these cancers is to ensure one's diet contains:

- a low fat content;
- a low meat consumption;
- a high vegetable fibre content. This can best be achieved by ensuring that the diet contains plenty of *fruit, vegetables, salads of all types* and making certain that *wholemeal breads* are eaten rather than white bread. Vegetable fibre seems to protect the large bowel through being indigestible. After digestion has been completed at

the distal end of the small intestine, the fibre collects and then has to be moved down the colon into the rectum prior to being ejected as the solid matter in the faeces. This process involves the colon and rectum with a constant normal workload which seems to be beneficial. In African tribes eating large amounts of fibre (about seven times the usual fibre intake of the average British individual) the incidence of large bowel cancers is very low.
• a low consumption of refined carbohydrate such as sugars.

There is little doubt that if everyone increased their normal fibre intake and reduced amounts of fat and meats in the diet the level of large bowel cancers would be reduced in the UK. It is helpful also to take fibre additives (usually in the form of bran) but with a good natural fibre intake this is not essential.

Cancer of the bladder

More cases of cancer of the bladder occur in men than in women, in a ratio of 2 to 1. In 1992 in England and Wales 5094 deaths were reported, 3482 in men and 1612 in women. Many different causes have been identified including the following:

• *smoking* has been shown to be an important contributory factor;
• *occupation* – particularly in the rubber and cable industries due to exposure of workers to *benzidene* and *naphthylamine* derivatives;
• infestation of the bladder by *Schistosoma haematobium*; this is a common cause of bladder cancer in Egypt and Tanzania.

There is a marked social class gradient seen in this cancer (see Fig. 10.3).

Bronchitis

In the last 20 years and particularly since 1980 there has been a remarkable drop in the number of deaths from bronchitis in the UK. This is very clearly seen in Table 10.6.

Table 10.6 Deaths from bronchitis, emphysema and asthma in England and Wales, 1981–92

	Males	Females
1981	13 482	5651
1988	6666	3971
1992	4657	3204

(From various OPCS Monitors in the DH2 series.)

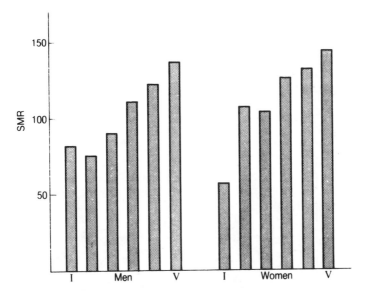

Fig. 10.3 Mortality from cancer of the bladder by social class in men and women, England and Wales, 1979–80, 1982–3. (From *Occupational Mortality*, OPCS, 1987.)

This fall represents a drop of 66.9% in men and of 43.3% in women. This difference is probably due to the greater reduction in the numbers of men now smoking. The numbers of women have fallen to a lesser extent. The social class gradient is very marked in both sexes (see Fig. 10.4).

Hypertensive disease

The mortality from hypertensive disease has fallen rapidly and steadily from 1961 to 1992, as shown in Table 10.7.

Table 10.7 Deaths from hypertensive disease in England and Wales, rates per 1 000 000 population, 1961–92.

Year	Males	Females
1961	31.7	40.5
1966	21.6	27.7
1971	17.6	20.4
1976	14.2	16.8
1980	10.6	12.0
1985	7.9	10.1
1992	5.4	6.7

(From various OPCS Monitors.)

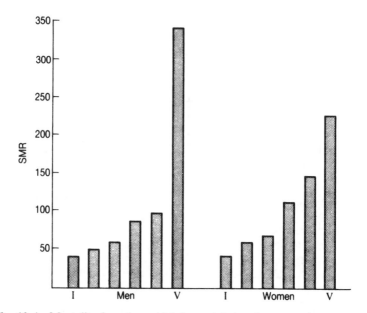

Fig. 10.4 Mortality from bronchitis by social class in men and women aged 20–64 years, England and Wales, 1979–80, 1982–3. (From *Occupational Mortality*, OPCS, 1987.)

Note that there has always been greater mortality in women than in men. There are also marked regional differences in mortality – the RHAs of Mersey, Yorkshire and North Western show a death rate 60% of that in S.E. Thames and S.W. Thames. There are also very definite social class differences – the mortality in Social Classes I and II being 2–3 times lower than in Social Classes IV and V.

The are three main reasons for the fall in mortality from hypertensive disease:

● greatly improved treatment methods;
● better early diagnosis leading to earlier treatment and less serious medical problems;
● changes in the lifestyles of people and especially the reduction in smoking in men that has occurred over this period.

Diabetes

Diabetes is a disease which has a trend quite different from most diseases in that mortality has been steadily increasing from 1980 to 1992 in the UK. Table 10.8 shows this trend very clearly.

Table 10.8 Deaths from diabetes, England and Wales, 1980–92.

	1980	1982	1984	1985	1987	1988	1992
Males	1993	1979	2687	3156	3327	3380	3565
Females	2788	2555	3682	4296	4310	4492	4502
Total	4781	4534	6369	7442	7637	7872	8067

(From various OPCS Monitors.)

Note that consistently the *mortality in women is greater than in men*. Over the 12-year period 1980–92 the total number of deaths rose by 69.4% but in men the rise was 78.8% and in women 61.4%. Diabetes occurs in two forms:

• the more serious insulin-dependent type which is almost invariably seen in persons under the age of 35. In this form of diabetes there is a *strong hereditary factor*. Research has found that if one twin develops insulin-dependent diabetes the chance of the other twin getting the same disease is five times greater in identical twins than in non-identical twins;
• the 'adult' form which can start at any age but is commonest in middle-aged and elderly persons and which is controllable by diet and medication. There is a greater incidence of this type of diabetes in persons who are *overweight or obese*. During the 1939–45 war there was a marked fall in this form of diabetes which was almost certainly connected with rationing, as people were less likely to overeat then than today. It is interesting to note that the prevalance of this 'adult' form of diabetes is twice as high in persons of Asian or Caribbean origin as in the general population.

Prevention

There is considerable scope to reduce the incidence of the 'adult' form of diabetes by:

• controlling overweight and especially obesity;
• increasing physical activity;
• ensuring that a balanced diet is taken.

There is considerable evidence that nearly half those with the milder 'adult' form of diabetes are undetected. A number of such cases are found by investigating a sudden loss of weight or by having a routine urine test.

It is always very important that all persons with diabetes (especially the insulin-dependent form) are effectively treated and followed up and monitored as many may be at risk of developing serious complications such as blindness, renal failure, cardiovascular diseases and peripheral vascular diseases. All these risks can be reduced by sound glycaemic control.

Another important aspect of tertiary prevention in diabetics is to check that the prescribed treatment is being properly carried out. It is here that regular visits by the practice nurse and other nursing personnel can be useful. Many patients have improperly understood the treatment and diets prescribed and a series of home visits by the practice nurse can be invaluable and can prevent serious complications from developing later.

Obesity

Gross overweight is associated with an increased tendency to develop the following diseases:

- diabetes;
- ischaemic heart disease and heart failure;
- degenerative arthritis in weight-bearing joints;
- hypertensive disease;
- gall bladder disease;
- colonic diseases.

Figure 10.5 shows a graphic illustration of the relationship between the height and weight of an individual. Note that five different groups are identified:

- underweight;
- normal weight;
- overweight;
- fat;
- obese.

It is always best for anyone to be in the normal band but if a person is plumpish in build, this may be very difficult or impossible. In such a case it is acceptable for the person to be in the 'overweight' band. The bands which should be avoided are the 'fat' and especially the 'obese' one. Anybody who is consistently in the obese band is *at high risk of developing one of the diseases listed above.*

Treatment for overweight

Perhaps one of the most important features is, if possible, to ensure that the individual is properly motivated, i.e. is determined to lose weight. Once that has been established, the aims should be as follows:

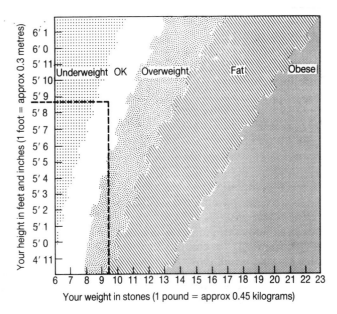

Fig. 10.5 Diagram illustrating weight and height.

- to lose weight gradually – if an average loss of weight over a period of time of about half a kilogram (about 1 lb) per week can be achieved and maintained then up to 25 kilogram (nearly 4 stone) can be lost in a year!
- to understand as much as possible about the calories in different foods and drinks. Simple calorie guides (booklets) are useful as they educate the individual and especially demonstrate foods that should be avoided;
- to aim at taking approximately 1100–1300 calories a day, for a period of about 8 weeks at a time and then have a break for 2 weeks before returning to the restricted calorie regime;
- to remember to count the calories of everything which passes the lips – food and drink and especially alcohol (most alcoholic drinks contain at least 100 calories);
- to have three simple meals a day and to avoid snacks between meals;
- to take plenty of vegetable fibre – fruit, green vegetables and salads. Many of these contain very low calorie amounts and are extremely useful in making up bulk in foods without adding too many calories;
- to take most calories early in the day rather than late in the

evening; avoid very small breakfasts and snack lunches and wherever possible have light evening meals;

- if unsuccessful try many different approaches – some individuals are helped by a group approach (such as Weightwatchers) but this is only likely to be of lasting value when it becomes a constant feature;
- avoid crash diets or any special efforts (such as 'health farms'). What is required is constant control and understanding of the calorie intake in ordinary foods under normal living conditions.

Epilepsy

The problems created by epilepsy include the following:

- to find an effective treatment which will control the fits;
- to help the patient to overcome the social disadvantages which too often accompany epilepsy;
- treatment must be continuous and always calls for much care and patience to ensure that the best combination of drugs is found;
- unfortunately many stigmas are still attached to the patient with epilepsy, mainly due to ignorance on the part of the public who mistakenly believe that it is connected with mental illness and may cause dangerous behaviour. The truth is that such behaviour is extremely rare. For this reason many patients conceal their disease which often adds to their problems.

Particular care should be taken with the rehabilitation of people with epilepsy. The question of stigma must never be overlooked or underestimated. By better understanding, which follows social after-care and preventive work, it is often possible to prevent someone who suffers from epilepsy from losing their job, and this adds to the stability in their life.

Much still needs to be done both individually with patients and collectively to educate the general public as to the true nature of this disease. Reference has already been made in Chapter 6 to the educational problems in epilepsy (see p. 124).

Diseases connected with occupation and the environment

A number of diseases have, in the past particularly, been caused by contact with various poisons, irritants and dusts especially in people working in very close contact with chemicals. Safety measures in industry are generally the responsibility of the Health and Safety

Executive (HSE) and other government departments such as the Department of Health (DH) and the Department of the Environment (DOE). In 1987 a Small Area Health Statistical Unit was set up by the DH, DOE and HSE. Its principal objects were:

- to investigate possible links between pollution from industrial installations and ill health in the community;
- to develop methods of analysing and interpreting industrial statistics relating to small areas (down to post-code levels).

In 1990 an independent group, the Health Advisory Group on Chemical Contamination Incidents, was set up. Its main tasks are to provide advice on:

- the extent to which illness occurring in an area following an incident is attributable to the toxic properties of the contaminating chemicals;
- the likelihood of prolonged or delayed health effects;
- any diagnostic or therapeutic measures which should be offered to those affected, or to the whole population of the area;
- any epidemiological or clinical investigations required to determine the nature and extent of exposure of members of the public and effects;
- any long-term surveillance required.

Strict standards are laid down regarding the uses of all dangerous chemicals, solvents and gases in industry which could lead to illness. These include the following:

- dangerous metals such as lead, phosphorus, mercury, arsenic, manganese, antimony, cadmium, nickel, copper and aluminium;
- oils, pitch and tar;
- dangerous gases such as ammonia, benzol, carbon dioxide, carbon monoxide, carbon tetrachloride, chlorine, nitrous fumes, petrol, phosgene, sulphur dioxide, sulphurated hydrogen and trichlorethylene;
- dangerous solvents;
- radiation hazards in industry.

Illnesses from industrial poisons vary greatly, from blood disorders to cancers of the skin and to occupational dermatitis. In some instances, such as those who are continuously working with lead, regular routine blood tests must be carried out to make certain that no hidden changes are occurring in the blood which could be a sign of cumulative poisoning.

Some industrial dermatitis can be avoided by all workers having a medical examination before they start work on hazardous jobs. In this way it is possible to prevent certain susceptible persons ever running these risks. This practice has been very useful in ensuring that persons with a previous or family history of dermatitis are never employed in a process in which dermatitis is a hazard.

Prevention of dust diseases

The chronic inhalation of certain dusts eventually leads to the development of pathological lesions in the lungs. The most dangerous dusts are those containing minute particles of *silica* or *asbestos*.

The term *pneumoconiosis* is used to describe diseases caused by these dusts. Industries in which dusts are hazards include a section of the coal-mining industry where extraction of coal includes mining in areas where silica dust occurs. Many of these mines are now no longer operating but the level of pneumoconiosis was very high in workers from some mines in the past and especially before preventive measures were taken. *Silicosis* is a fibrotic lung disease in which the lung tissue is slowly destroyed and replaced by fibrosis. Emphysema eventually follows with loss of vital capacity and leads to invalidism. Respiratory tuberculosis is a common complication.

In the few mines and quarries where there is still a risk to workers, strict preventive measures are in force, including the following:

- regular medical examinations, including a chest X-ray, of all personnel employed in any occupation in which pneumoconiosis is a risk;
- immediate suspension from work of anyone found to be suffering from pneumoconiosis, including those with the earliest of radiological signs, or from tuberculosis, together with the payment of a special financial benefit.

As well as these medical examinations, dust diseases can be prevented by undertaking the following precautions:

- the replacement of a dangerous dust with a harmless one. An example is the replacement of sandstone grinding wheels by carborundum (sandstone grinding gives rise to silica dusts);
- dust suppression by good general ventilation, by exhaust ventilation sited over the process, or by introducing a wet process in which dusts are kept to a minimum;
- personal protection for all workers by the wearing of masks. This is only practical for short periods. Generally reliance should never be placed on workers wearing protective masks.

The inhalation of asbestos dust is very dangerous for, after a period, asbestosis develops. This disease is rather similar to silicosis but also increases markedly the risk of developing cancer of the lung. The various preventive measures mentioned above have greatly reduced the risks of pneumoconiosis. Also the shutting of a number of mines where the risks were very high has reduced the chances of workers developing pneumoconiosis.

Prevention of accidents

Increasing attention has been paid in recent years to all forms of accidents both in the home and at work.

Traffic accidents

In England and Wales in 1992, 4566 persons (3303 males and 1263 females) were killed in accidents on the roads. This represents an improvement of 9.7% on the numbers killed in 1982 – the year of the introduction of compulsory seat belt legislation. This in real terms is a greater improvement than it first appears bearing in mind the increased numbers of motor vehicles on the road in 1992 compared with 10 years earlier.

Home accidents

Reference has already been made in Chapter 5 to the importance of preventing accidents in the home in children (see Table 5.3 p. 103). The other age group which is particularly liable to home accidents are persons over the age of 75 years. Table 10.9 demonstrates the steep rise of these accidents in elderly persons. If the over-75 year age group is further analysed the highest proportion of accidents occur in those over 85 years of age. Another very serious consequence of home

Table 10.9 Deaths from home accidents by age and sex, England and Wales, 1992.

Age group	Males	Females
0–14	115	90
15–44	566	174
45–64	360	190
65–74	266	229
75+	630	1436
Total	1937	2119

(From OPCS Monitors DH4 92/3, 92/5, 93/1, 93/2.)

accidents in elderly persons is that, in many instances, the accident is the beginning of a sudden decline leading eventually in many cases to invalidism or death.

It is interesting to note the high number of deaths in women over the age of 75 years compared with men. This is connected not only with the fact that at such ages there are many more women than men alive but also because the *degree of handicap and disability is greater in elderly women than men of the same age* (see Chapter 18, p. 327). Many of these accidents could have been prevented by the following measures:

- improved lighting, especially on stairs, landings and passages. In many elderly persons over 80, their balance depends increasingly on sight and in dim light many are very vulnerable (see p. 377);
- renewal of faulty equipment and furnishings: worn carpets, broken stair rods, carpets not properly secured, trailing wires from electrical appliances and loose floor boards;
- ensuring that visual defects in elderly persons are corrected by suitable spectacles *and that very old persons wear them*;
- better understanding by older persons of the increased dangers of home accidents as sight deteriorates. More effective health education particularly by practice nurses and health visitors who visit the homes of elderly persons to check on their health would be of great benefit.

The prevention of accidents is one of the key targets in the White Paper (see Chapter 11).

Prevention of mental illness

The exact cause of most mental illness is not yet fully understood. However a great deal is already known about some of the most important factors related to its development. These include the following:

- *intrinsic factors* connected with the individual, and particularly:
  - *— hereditary factors;*
  - *— developmental factors;*
- *extrinsic factors* to do with the person's occupation, home and lifestyle and surroundings.

Intrinsic factors are complicated. Hereditary factors are more of an inherited predisposition to develop mental illnesses than being born with such an illness. The predisposition may never result in a mental illness and the likelihood of such illness developing even in someone with a predisposition depends more on stages in the individual's life and/or on environmental (extrinsic) factors.

The most likely times for mental illness to develop in any individual are *puberty, pregnancy, the menopause, late middle age and in retirement.* *Mental illness* is the commonest cause of days lost from work in women but only the fourth commonest in men.

Extrinsic or environmental factors are even more complicated, as each person continuously selects different features from the environment. The more unsatisfactory and insecure the surroundings of anyone, the more likely it is that mental illness will develop, but each person will react differently when placed in the same surroundings.

Once a mental illness has started, the longer it continues the more likely it is to become permanent, regardless of the detailed circumstances associated with its commencement. It is, therefore, important to diagnose the earliest signs of mental illness – say in a child – for early diagnosis will help in the treatment.

Many 'functional' disorders are due to the effect of adverse social problems in childhood, or to very rigid or ill-judged moral or cultural standards, or to rejection by one or both parents. Many such problems are dealt with by social workers, health visitors and school nurses in their ordinary work. More arrangements are now being made to introduce preventive psychiatry into child care services, and many authorities now arrange for psychiatrists to carry out sessions in the routine work in community homes dealing with deprived and delinquent children and young persons (see Chapter 16). GPs in their child health surveillance work are now referring certain disturbed young children to the local paediatric psychiatrist as soon as the problem comes to light because early correction of any adverse factors at home can have a very beneficial effect on the child and hopefully may prevent possible later mental health problems.

It is impossible to protect anyone from all mental or physical trauma in life – in fact, attempts to do so may well encourage a mental breakdown. It is, however, always possible to alter or attempt to change any environment which may be adversely affecting a person in one way or another, and this can assist in preventing an impending mental illness.

The occupation and work which a person does can have an important effect on mental stability. Much mental illness can be averted by suitable employment for that individual. Therefore careful selection together with medical and/or psychological testing before people are placed in various occupations can help to avoid subsequent difficulties and possible mental illness.

Finally, it is important that sensible advice is always given to mentally disordered persons. Health education programmes should always be aware of the dangers of wrong advice which may have been handed down to the young person or child from parents and grandparents. Many needless fears can be generated in this way and these, in some-

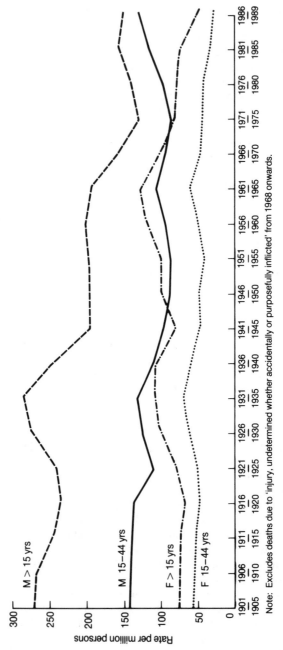

Fig. 10.6 Suicide rates, England and Wales, 1901–89. Note: Excludes deaths due to 'injury, undetermined whether accidentally or purposefully inflicted' from 1968 onwards. (Source: OPCS.)

Note: Excludes deaths due to 'injury, undetermined whether accidentally or purposefully inflicted' from 1968 onwards.

one already predisposed to mental illness, may be the spark which starts off the illness.

Suicide

In 1992 in England and Wales 3952 persons committed suicide (3049 males and 903 females). This distribution is the usual – 77% men and 23% women. Since 1975 there has been a general downwards trend in suicides. However one age group (young men aged 15–44) is the exception; since 1975 the suicide level of this age group has been increasing (see Fig. 10.6).

Many factors connected with suicide have been reported, including mental illness, alcohol and drug abuse, employment and unemployment, marital breakdown and AIDS. However the most consistent factor is *mental illness*. A recent study reported that the life-time risk of suicide in mentally ill persons is 15% despite the majority of these being in contact with the psychiatric services. One recent audit showed that 81% of those committing suicide had received in-patient psychiatric care in the past. The commonest types of mental illness connected with suicide are psychotic depression and schizophrenia. The second commonest group in which suicide occurred was in alcohol and drug abuse – 10%. While it might be expected that suicide in young men might follow AIDS or HIV infection, the rise in the suicide rate in young men long predated the AIDS epidemic. Many people have suggested a connection between suicide and unemployment in young men but there is little evidence to support this – while there was a fall in unemployment in the UK from 3 million to 1.6 million in the late 1980s, there was no corresponding dip in the suicide rate among young men.

In 1991 a Confidential Enquiry into suicide and homicide by mentally ill people was set up by the Under-Secretary of State for Health. It is led by the Royal College of Psychiatrists and involves other professional groups.

Homicide and violence by mentally ill persons

People with severe mental illness only very rarely commit homicide or are violent. Yet when such a case is widely reported in the media the wrong impression can easily be given that mental illness is often associated with violence or homicide. The government has set up the new Confidential Enquiry (see above) to ensure that everything is being done to prevent such tragedies from occurring.

The reduction of suicide has become a key target in the White Paper *The Health of the Nation* (see Chapter 11).

11 A strategy for health – the Government's initiative: The Health of the Nation

For many years, experts in public health and preventive medicine have pointed out that any nation's health can only be effectively and permanently improved if there is a sensible and practical plan or strategy to achieve consistent improvements in health over a number of years.

In the past, history has often shown that a nationwide threat to existence (such as a major war) can stimulate great advances in health. The 1939–45 war was no exception and saw many such examples (often introduced under the guise of helping the war effort), including:

- the development of an effective universal free blood transfusion service;
- the development of antibiotics especially penicillin,
- the introduction of diphtheria immunisation which virtually wiped out the threat of that disease;
- the introduction and rapid advance of chest surgery:

Many of these were accelerated because the nation could not afford high mortality which was primarily preventable. Yet the benefit of these advances has of course continued, benefiting millions since that emergency.

At the end of the war, the NHS was begun (in 1948) and has undoubtedly helped by providing an excellent comprehensive health service to all the nation irrespective of the financial means of the patient at time of need. Nearly two generations later, there is plenty of evidence of continued great advances in health – life expectation has steadily increased, infant and perinatal mortality are at lowest ever levels, diphtheria and poliomyelitis are now very rare and it is likely that measles, mumps and rubella are on the way to becoming equally rare. Many cancers can now be prevented in some way either by early recognition when in a precancerous state or by modifying one's lifestyle to avoid causative factors. Yet the NHS has never been under greater strain and new life-threatening diseases like HIV/AIDS have suddenly emerged. All recognise that prevention is ideal and that it is always better than cure, yet until 1992 no general strategy for health had ever been introduced in the UK. Then, in July 1992, an important White Paper was introduced by the Secretary of State for Health called *The Health of the Nation*. It laid out for the first time, five key areas and many targets to aim at up to the year 2000 and beyond.

The five key areas are

- coronary heart disease and stroke;
- cancers;
- mental illness;
- HIV/AIDS and sexual health;
- accidents, especially to children, young persons and those aged 65 and over.

Coronary heart disease and stroke

The main *objective* is to reduce the level of ill health and death caused from coronary heart disease (CHD) and stroke and the risk factors associated with them. Please note that for all risk factors in this chapter the baseline is the average of 3 years centred round year 1990 unless otherwise stated.

The main *targets* aimed at are:

- to reduce the death rate for both CHD and stroke in people under 65 by at least 40% by the year 2000;
- to reduce the death rate for CHD in people aged 65–74 by at least 30% by the year 2000;
- to reduce the death rate from stroke in people aged 65–74 by at least 40% by the year 2000.

The various risk factors for these diseases have already been discussed in Chapter 10 (p. 184). The White Paper also adopts a number of *risk factor targets* for CHD and strokes, these are:

- to reduce the mean systolic blood pressure in the adult population by at least 5 mmHg by year 2000 (the baseline to be derived from the new survey now being carried out);
- to reduce the average percentage of energy derived from saturated fatty acids by 35% and the total fat consumed by 12% by the year 2000;
- to reduce the proportion of men and women aged 16–64 who are obese by at least 25% and 35%, respectively, by the year 2005 (baseline 1986–7);
- to reduce the proportion of men drinking more than 21 units of

alcohol and women drinking 14 units per week by 30% by the year 2005;
- to reduce smoking in both men and women (see targets below).

Cancers

There are three main *objectives* – to reduce ill health which is:

- caused by breast and cervical cancers;
- caused by skin cancers by increasing awareness of the need to avoid excessive exposure to ultraviolet light (mainly by the direct rays of the sun);
- caused by lung cancer by reducing smoking prevalence and tobacco consumption throughout the population.

The main *targets* for cancer are:

- to reduce the death rate for breast cancers in the population invited for screening (today women aged 50–65) by at least 20% by the year 2000;
- to reduce the incidence of invasive cancer of the cervix uteri by at least 20% by the year 2000;
- to halt the year-on-year increase in the incidence of skin cancer by the year 2005.

In relation to the *risk factors* connected with smoking the *targets* are:

- to reduce the prevalence of cigarette smoking to no more than 20% by the year 2000 in both sexes (this represents a reduction of one-third on the 1990 figures);
- to reduce the consumption of cigarettes by at least 40% by the year 2000;
- to reduce the smoking prevalence of 11–15 year olds by at least 33% by 1994.

In addition the target aim is to persuade at least 33% of women smokers to stop smoking at the start of their pregnancy by the year 2000.

Mental illness

The main *objective* is to reduce ill health and death caused by mental illness. To make a start to achieve this objective, three *specific targets* have been drawn up. These are:

- to improve significantly the health and social functioning of mentally ill people;
- to reduce the overall suicide rate by at least 15% by the year 2000;
- to reduce the suicide rate of severely mentally ill persons by at least 33% by the year 2000.

In addition to the last two specific targets, the White Paper identified three broad areas for action to assist in the achievement of the first target above.

- To tackle the lack of information on the prevalence and outcomes of mental illness so that, in the future, more precise targets for mental health improvement can be set. A national survey has been commissioned by the Department of Health which will be undertaken by OPCS. Already the pilot study for this has been completed – it was based on five centres throughout the UK. At the same time the Royal College of Psychiatrists together with other professional groups are working on standardised assessment procedures to measure symptom states, social disability and the quality of life of mentally ill persons.
- A comprehensive system of psychiatric service is being developed under the Mental Health Task Force which was set up in 1992 to oversee the completion of the transfer of mental health services from the older isolated mental hospitals and asylums to a more balanced range of locally based mental health services. At the same time, new and more effective information systems are being developed to monitor the mental health services on how to ensure continuity of services.
- The final thrust is to improve the development of good mental health practice in *primary health care teams* (*general practice*) so that with further training, they will improve their ability to recognise early psychiatric depression, severe anxiety and suicide risk. At the same time, health authorities are being encouraged to develop better *audit systems of suicides* with a view not only to prevent suicides but to improve the support systems for persons with mental illness living in the community.

HIV/AIDS and sexual health

In the field of HIV, AIDS and sexual health *six objectives* were identified in the White Paper:

- to reduce the incidence of HIV infection;
- to reduce the incidence of other sexually transmitted diseases (STDs);

- to develop further and to strengthen the monitoring and surveillance of the developing situation in the UK;
- to provide effective services for diagnosis and treatment of HIV and other STDs;
- to reduce the number of unwanted pregnancies;
- to ensure the provision of effective family planning services for those people who want them.

The main targets for HIV/AIDS and sexual health include reducing:

- the incidence of gonorrhoea by at least 20% by 1995 as an indicator of HIV/AIDS trends (the 1993 figure showed this has been achieved);
- by at least 50% the rate of conception among the under 16s by the year 2000 (baseline 1989).

The following *risk factor* for HIV/AIDS was also included:

- to reduce the percentage of injecting drug abusers who share injecting equipment in the previous 4 weeks from 20% in 1990 to no more than 10% by the year 2000.

Accidents

The prevention of accidents was the last key area highlighted in the White Paper. The overall *objective* is to reduce the ill health, disability and death caused by accidents.

To achieve this objective, three main targets were chosen. They are:

- to reduce the death rate from accidents among children under 5 by at least 33% by the year 2005;
- to reduce the death rate from accidents among young people aged 15–24 by at least 25% by the year 2005;
- to reduce the death rate from accidents among people aged 65 and over by at least 33% by the year 2005.

It will be noticed that the Government's strategy to promote preventive health runs parallel to the principles laid down in health audit (see Chapter 2). Having first defined the main objective in the five key areas, all the targets represent the stage in audit called 'setting the standards to be aimed at' (see Fig. 2.1, p. 37). Note also that all these standards are *specific numerate ones* which subsequently can quite easily be checked. It could be criticised that some are empirical but at least the standards have now been defined in a way that everyone in the NHS can understand and work towards achieving in the time scales set down.

Clearly this is only the first stage in setting up a national strategy for health in the UK, and in time these standards will be refined and updated.

In the White Paper setting out this plan, it was pointed out that a major theme of the strategy is the formation of a 'healthy alliance' in which different organisations and individuals are to be brought together to exchange ideas so that health issues may be tackled more effectively. The concept of 'healthy settings' was also introduced, when the White Paper identified seven settings where action should be taken to achieve the targets mentioned above. These are healthy:

- cities
- schools
- hospitals
- workplaces
- homes
- prisons
- environments.

Since the publication of the White Paper, many working groups have met involving all the above settings and in many instances have included voluntary bodies, individuals and NHS professionals and managers. In these meetings many 'second order' priorities have been discussed, some of which will undoubtedly later be chosen to become key areas. However at first the five key areas already outlined are to be the top priorities. Included in the areas which later may become first priorities are:

- maternal and child health
- food safety
- oral health
- child immunisation.

However as all these areas are already well-established preventive health topics in which considerable progress has already been made, it was felt that less well-developed areas might better be chosen next to be given key area status. These include:

- rehabilitation
- the health of elderly persons
- asthma
- back pain
- drug misuse.

It is likely that it will first be necessary to carry out research before sound national numerate targets could be set in these areas.

Already much work has been undertaken by the Department of Health to implement these health strategies. Generally the publication of the White Paper has been widely welcomed by the World Health Organization, many health care professionals, voluntary bodies and local authorities as an important innovation to improve the health of the UK. But however praiseworthy is the objective of this publication, it will only succeed if all health professionals and especially nurses recognise the importance of what is being attempted and give it their support not only by understanding its aims but by their example showing the general public that this effort is worthy of support.

12 The role of the nurse in prevention of ill health with special reference to primary health care and health education

The role of the nurse in the prevention of ill health is always very important. So often it is the nurse, whether working in hospital or in the community as a practice nurse, health visitor, midwife or community or district nurse who sees the patient frequently and for long periods in the informal surroundings of their home. It is therefore the nurse who often gets closest to patients and who therefore can do much in her/his approach. The nurse also usually deals with the minor complications of the illness and is in a perfect position to prevent further problems from developing.

It is also the nurse who can often reduce the impact of stigma which can so often become one of the most damaging aspects of any chronic illness or disability, whether it is primarily physical or mental. It is therefore important that all nurses fully understand the details of and the potentials for preventing ill health and the complications of many illnesses and accidents.

Types of prevention

There are three types of prevention – *primary, secondary* and *tertiary*.

Primary prevention is the complete avoidance of disease. This includes persuading families and individuals to take advantage of preventive measures such as immunisations against certain diseases. Many of these are given to infants and young children but a number are given to adults who may be in a hazardous position because of their occupation (see Chapter 7, pp. 134–5) or who may need protection as they are about to visit a country in which an unusual disease is commonplace and which can be prevented by prior immunisation (see p. 137). All types of health education are important and essential parts of primary prevention. The various lifestyles of people such as their diet or whether they smoke or drink too much or whether they are overweight or never take any exercise can make certain illnesses much more likely. The fluoridation of water supplies or the use of tooth-pastes containing fluorides are further examples of primary prevention.

Secondary prevention (often called 'screening') is aimed at detecting the very earliest signs of diseases before any symptoms become apparent. Many of these screening tests are carried out on infants and toddlers (e.g. tests to discover congenital dislocation of the hip, phenylketonuria and hypothyroidism – see p. 96). Nurses play a crucial role in all these – not only in carrying them out but in persuading parents that all are most important. They also follow up parents and families to make quite sure that any necessary treatments are properly and regularly carried out. The efficiency and conscientious-ness of the nurse is often the main factor that can prevent the condition or illness from developing its potentially damaging effects.

Screening is also very important in adults. For example the detection of early hypertension (raised blood pressure) enables effective treatment to be started before any permanent damage has been done. Provided the correct treatment is continued for as long as the blood pressure remains high (which may be for life) the most serious stage of the disease may never be reached. Glaucoma is a further example and everyone over the age of 45 years should have an eye test at regular intervals which includes the measurement of intraocular pressure every 2–3 years. Cervical cytology is another example (see p. 190).

Mammography (see p. 193) is a most valuable screening test especi-ally in women aged 50–65 or in a woman who has already had a cancer in one breast. Mammography enables breast cancer to be detected and treated at a very early stage when the results are most likely to be successful.

Tertiary prevention is concerned with persons already suffering from some chronic (long-standing) disease. Tertiary prevention aims at avoiding and preventing serious complications from occurring. This is done by treating the disease in such a way that permanent handicaps do not develop, hence preventing permanent disability. In many of these diseases, complications develop insidiously over many years and their prevention calls for much painstaking work. An essential feature of most tertiary prevention is to ensure that patients understand about their condition or illness and how any illness can very slowly develop and eventually damage their health and lead to serious disabilities. Much of this process involves patient health education and is best carried out by nurses in the practice team and especially when they can visit the patient in their own home. The success or failure of tertiary prevention usually can mean the difference between the patient even-tually being able to lead a reasonably normal life or becoming an invalid. Hence tertiary prevention is crucial to the quality of life of such patients. Tertiary prevention is at its most effective in the management of chronic disease. More and more practice nurses are now working with GPs in the running of clinics for patients with chronic diseases such as asthma, diabetes, and hypertension and this work plays an important part in preventing the development of many disabilities in these patients. This was confirmed by the report of the Medical Research Council (published in 1985) of the trial of the treatment of mild hypertension which emphasised the valuable role played by nurses in coordinating the treatment of this condition. It is likely that as the proportion of very elderly persons living in the community increases (see p. 372) the need for tertiary prevention will become even greater.

Health education

All three forms of prevention depend on being able to convince parents, children and adults that it is important to prevent diseases or to mitigate their effects. The practice of health education involves persuading individuals to make the most sensible choices and is a continuing process throughout all the stages of life. In the end, the success of health education depends on the person concerned making balanced decisions based on logic – rejecting what is obviously unwise and choosing what is sensible. In many cases the decision is not clear cut. Most people will have to modify and change what they choose to do a number of times during their life as evidence accumulates suggesting that a particular habit or practice is more hazardous to health than was previously thought. Everyone, both children and adults, should be encouraged to adopt a flexible approach and it is therefore important that any nurse involved in health education likewise never adopts an authoritarian and rigid attitude. Advice that has to be modified as new facts emerge is likely to alienate many persons and will undermine their future confidence. At the same time, the nurse should guide and lead and, in doing so, must necessarily take some responsibility for that individual's health.

Health education falls into three main groups:

● individual health education;
● group health education;
● mass media health education.

In most cases the final decision made by the individual depends on features from all three categories of health education but especially individual and mass media health education. In many instances advertising (or persuasion) in the mass media can be said to prepare the individual to make some decision or to take some action – for example to choose one type of food rather than another, accept advice to change a potentially dangerous habit such as smoking, or to use a condom because of the danger of HIV and AIDS. Individuals may seek expert advice before deciding that a suggested change in lifestyle is justified. In a health matter that 'expert advice' is very likely in the first instance to be a nurse working in the community (practice nurse, health visitor, midwife, district or community nurse) or even a nurse who happens to be a close neighbour or friend. Although the advice may be sought in an unofficial or casual way, the effectiveness of the reply and the advice given may well be crucial to the person's final decision. Hence, the role of nurses is very important in the practical prevention of ill health whether it be primary, secondary or tertiary prevention.

This chapter provides details of the various preventive procedures commonly used in the community and particularly in general practice where the practice nurse, health visitor and district or community nurse play so active a part in ensuring that members of the public understand exactly the best ways to avoid disease and to prevent its various complications. In practice, much primary and secondary prevention is carried out simultaneously and these two forms of health education are discussed together. Subdivisions have been made into prevention in:

- infants and children under 16 years;
- young adults (aged 16–25 years);
- adults (aged 25–64 years);
- elderly persons.

Primary and secondary prevention

Infants and children under 16 years

Infants and children provide one of the best opportunities to prevent many diseases. In this respect the roles of the health visitor and practice nurse are crucial. Individual preventive health measures are initiated in many ways through constant individual health education. Regular home visits by the health visitor or practice nurse allows an accurate assessment to be made and enables practical advice to be given on many important topics including infant feeding, general management of the infant or child and on the avoidance of accidents. All this is in addition to the normal advice that is given to parents in their visits to the health centre or group practice. These visits to the home by the nurse should soon build up a good relationship with the parent and child and create an atmosphere of trust which is so helpful and necessary in health education. All the various immunisations described in Chapter 7 which are given to infants are also good examples of primary prevention. Most serious communicable diseases like diphtheria and poliomyelitis are now very rare and measles and mumps are already diminishing fast and are likely to become equally rare in the future – all due to the success of immunisation.

Next the health visitor or practice nurse carries out a number of screening tests within the home including tests to exclude congenital dislocation of the hip, phenylketonuria and hypothyroidism (see p. 96). Follow-up examinations are either carried out at subsequent home visits or at special sessions at the health centre including those arranged for child health surveillance examinations. These visits to the health centre/group practice may also provide an opportunity for group health education when small groups of mothers (say five to eight) are encouraged to take part in a discussion on a particular subject. Visual aids, including videos and overhead projection of slides can be helpful on such occasions. Group health education is especially valuable as it enables mothers and others to realise that others are experiencing similar problems to their own and this can not only be reassuring but helpful in suggesting alternative approaches.

Mass media health education

Leaflets, booklets, posters, radio and television all can play an important part in teaching health education. Once an interest has been aroused, the impact of such information is greater when there is an opportunity to discuss it further with a health visitor or practice nurse. The combination of mass media and individual health education can be very effective – mass media information raises interest in the subject but it is individual health education that is the more decisive.

Social pressures within any group can also become a powerful influence towards change. For example, if it is generally accepted in a group that smoking by an expectant mother is likely to be detrimental to her baby, the mother who continues to smoke is likely to feel under considerably more pressure to give up the habit.

Occasionally a natural opportunity presents itself to a group to discuss some subject in depth. For instance, a sudden local cot death is likely to become the centre of interest and discussion or a serious case of child abuse (physical or sexual) which has been widely reported in the press locally may provide the health visitor or practice nurse with the perfect opportunity to raise the subject and to get the group to discuss it together in a very natural way. Advice given at such a time is likely to make a bigger impact. This demonstrates how good effective health education should be a *continuous process* involving many people in their ordinary lives.

Another technique that health visitors and practice nurses may find useful is to identify 'at risk' groups of infants in whom the level of problems such as congenital abnormalities is likely to be higher than normal (see p. 98).

Most general practices now have computerised records of their patients and these can be most valuable in providing practice nurses and health visitors with information which could help in the prevention of health problems. For instance, it known that cancer of the cervix uteri in women is much commoner in Social Classes IV and V than in I and II. This means that a special effort should always be made to persuade women in these vulnerable groups to attend for smear tests even if the special efforts made reduce the final figures of cervical tests carried out. In such an example more prevention of cervical cancer would be likely to be the result rather than just counting the numbers who are examined, as most may well be in the low risk groups in Social Classes I and II.

Young adults (16–25 years)

Independence is very precious in early adult life and most young adults are eager to demonstrate that they are now making their own decisions. It is also a time of much questioning of rules and customs. Mass media health education can have a marked effect at this stage of life provided it is subtle and not authoritarian, because that kind of approach can be counterproductive in this age group. Many social habits which can have an important effect on later health are determined at this age. Smoking and alcohol may be experimented with and the outcome – whether the young adult persists to become a permanent smoker or heavy drinker – may well be determined. There is usually little contact with the health services for those aged 16–25 years unless some physiological event like pregnancy occurs. At the same time most young persons are eager to learn more about health and its problems and many will be reading widely.

This is the time when sexual behaviour is becoming very important and there will be opportunities for individual health education especially in further education, university or in work situations. Great concern is being expressed at the present time about the spread of HIV and AIDS and the potential threat which these sexually transmitted infections and diseases pose to future generations. It is most important that all young adults fully understand the facts and perhaps the most important of these is that although initially HIV (and subsequent AIDS) was primarily found in homosexual males, now *transmission of HIV is commonest in heterosexual relationships in the UK*. It is vital that young adults understand this change. A certain amount of 'trial and error' is bound to take place, hence it is essential to stress the value of condoms (providing a physical barrier to infection) and that casual sexual contacts should be avoided thereby reducing the risks of HIV infection. If the message is presented in a clear lucid way, it is more likely that young people will adopt sensible sexual behaviour, e.g. one monogamous sexual relationship.

An especially important time for nurses to practise health education is when pregnancy occurs for the first time. This is discussed further in the next section although it is recognised that such education is important for and applicable to young adults who are about to embark on parenthood. However in at least 30% of young persons, a first pregnancy will occur when the partners are unmarried, although a small proportion may marry later. Abortion is an option that may well be considered and the nurse often has a difficult task in giving balanced advice on the subject. The nurse must always be very careful to respect the confidentiality of any information received. Whether or not the parents are involved must be left to the young person. Unless confidentiality is always absolute, a person's confidence in nurses and other health professionals may be destroyed and the potential to help in the future may be lost.

Adults (aged 26–64 years)

As mentioned above, health education should be a continuous process. Many of the points discussed below may well be equally applicable to young adults.

To many people, marriage and setting up a new home together is a crucial step in their lives. Usually both partners bring to their new life principles and habits learned in their parental homes. In the first months and years, many of the essentials of their future life together are determined – their sexual life, the pattern of their day-to-day routine, including diet and nutrition, habits such as smoking or alcohol consumption, their recreation, sport and exercise, their holidays and general attitude to life. Their first experience of illness together and their reaction to it will also be important. Pregnancy is another challenge for it forms an essential part of the maturation process of any marriage. It will inevitably lead to many reappraisals by the couple and many changes in the pattern of their life together.

Increasingly all health care professionals are realising that the first pregnancy, and particularly the antenatal period, is an ideal time for health education. Once any couple realise that the future health and well-being of their expected child is largely in their own hands, health education is likely to be very effective. It is important to involve and not isolate the father-to-be both in the preparation for and in the birth itself.

Prevention of congenital abnormalities

Screening early in pregnancy is increasingly used to identify possible congenital abnormalities in the baby. This is especially important for couples known to be at high risk of having such a baby. The techniques used include:

- examining the blood of the mother early in pregnancy for some 'marker' which suggests that the baby is probably abnormal (e.g. neural tube defects – see p. 74);
- combining the above test with an amniocentesis which will show with certainty whether or not the baby is abnormal (e.g. Down's syndrome and for most cases of cystic fibrosis.)

In *Down's syndrome* a blood test on the mother is first carried out to estimate the level of alpha-fetoprotein and human chorionic gonado-trophin. If this test is normal, then the incidence of Down's syndrome in the expected baby is likely to be low even in women over the age of 35. This initial test has reduced the need to carry out an amniocentesis on all expectant mothers over the age of 35 years and has thus also reduced the chance of precipitating a miscarriage of a normal child by carrying out an unnecessary amniocentesis. In one health authority where this test was introduced, the incidence of Down's syndrome has fallen from 1.1 per 1000 to 0.4 per 1000.

The screening test for *cystic fibrosis* first concentrates on detecting couples both of whom are carriers of the gene for cystic fibrosis. In such cases the chances of having a child with cystic fibrosis are 1 in 4 (25%). The test consists of examining DNA from the mouth wash of both parents. Because only 75% of the gene mutations responsible for cystic fibrosis can be detected by this test, in positive cases it would be wise to follow up with an amniocentesis to examine the baby's blood to see if the child is affected, when a termination of pregnancy could be carried out. As explained later, this type of screening must be accompanied by counselling of both parents to ensure they realise that it is only worthwhile in couples who agree to a termination in the event of a positive result.

Because cystic fibrosis occurs more commonly in some families, the testing of close relatives planning to have a family can be very useful (*cascade screening*) to discover persons who may be at high risk of having a child with cystic fibrosis (if their partner also carries the gene for the condition).

In all families that already have had a case of *Duchenne muscular dystrophy* 50% of all boys born later will on average be affected – hence the knowledge of the sex of the expected baby is important. The same type of incidence occurs also in *haemophilia* – the inheritance is of a male dominated sex linkage – the illnesses only occur in the males but the females act as carriers. Duchenne muscular dystrophy is a particularly distressing condition as in all boys who are affected the baby is perfectly normal at birth but symptoms start before the age of 5 years and then the child progressively deteriorates so that the boy is chairbound by the early teenage years and dies before the age of 25. In such circumstances many families would prefer to terminate a pregnancy if it is known the baby is a boy.

Most expectant mothers are very keen to do anything which will give their expected baby the best possible chance in life. Many will be prepared to give up smoking once they realise the extra risks which are then attached to the baby. Because of the other danger later of passive smoking (for example it is now known that many chest conditions such as asthma are commoner in children in families where smoking occurs) the father also may be persuaded more easily at such a time to stop smoking. Many sacrifices have to be made by anyone wishing to become a caring parent and the attitudes of both parents during the pregnancy may be the starting point of a sounder and happier relationship, or the opposite. There may be ignorance regarding the subject of sex during the pregnancy and this should be discussed openly with both parents to avoid unnecessary decisions which may later lead to resentment and/or guilt.

Much importance is placed on the nutrition of the mother during the antenatal period (see p. 77) and on the feeding of the baby. This provides an excellent opportunity for health education in what is not only important for the baby and mother but for all the family in the future. The value of protein intake, vitamins (taken both in natural foods and in supplements), fibre intake, calcium (it is the early years of life that this is so essential to reduce the possibility of osteoporosis later in life), fluid consumption and that not too much salt is added to foods all should be considered. A real attempt should always be made to explain why certain foods are so important, for example why vegetable fibre is so essential for the healthy functioning of the colon and therefore for reducing the chances of diverticulitis or cancers. Most parents will make the correct choice if only they fully understand the reasons – in other words most mistakes are made because of ignorance. All nurses have an important responsibility to explain this for nurses often are trusted and will be carefully listened to and their advice usually followed.

Many women begin to put on excess weight during their first pregnancy or in the following years. The avoidance of obesity is one of the more essential preventive lessons which should be learned at this stage of life. Explanations should stress that all individuals are different in the way they burn up their calories – some will rarely put on excessive weight whilst others will rapidly do so even if taking the same diets. A reappraisal of the type of food eaten is of value after any pregnancy.

Every effort should be made to encourage anyone who has a tendency to be overweight to learn how foods vary greatly in their calorie content. A simple booklet under such titles as *Your greatest guide to calories* can be invaluable. Anyone who uses such a guide will quickly realise which type of foods should be avoided.

Obesity (see also p. 200) is a constant threat to some people and the problem of overweight can easily get out of hand, especially for persons in the 35–50 year age group. Any information learnt earlier can therefore be very useful. It is never too early to emphasise that gross overweight is associated with a considerable reduction in life expectancy – such individuals will always be heavily penalised in regard to life assurance premiums.

Blood pressure checks are valuable later in life and it is a wise precaution for everyone to have their blood pressure checked every 2–3 years after the age of 30. Early hypertensive disease (see p. 198) usually produces no symptoms and it is always an advantage to identify such disease early so that effective treatment to lower the blood pressure to normal limits can be started.

Osteoporosis is a disease which mostly affects elderly women. The young developing child should always have plenty of calcium in their diet. However no one can benefit from calcium diets after the age of 25. Increasing evidence now suggests that *hormone replacement therapy* following the menopause (for no longer than 10 years) will markedly reduce the incidence of osteoporosis later in life. Such treatment is particularly important and helpful for women who are at 'high risk' of developing osteoporosis. These are women who:

- had started their periods late and who had an early menopause;
- are very inactive in their life-style;
- have a thin and lightly built physique;
- take alcohol regularly and who smoke;
- have taken steroids in the past;
- are of Asian race; recent research has shown that Asian women who live in the UK are at higher risk of developing osteoporosis.

Occasionally there is a special need for *immunisation* to be carried out in adults (see p. 135, 136) and for certain persons at special risk in their work. These include many health workers such as nurses in dialysis units or in accident and emergency units, surgeons and theatre staff and those working in blood transfusion units. All should be immunised against *hepatitis B* (see p. 135).

Secondary prevention by screening in adults

This is especially important in:

- cancer of the cervix uteri (see p. 190);
- cancer of the breast in women (mammography; see p. 193);
- cancer of the colon (see p. 194);
- glaucoma. This condition can gradually develop after the age of 40 and will present no symptoms for 7–9 years. The only certain way to diagnose a rising intraocular pressure is to test this in a routine eye test. This is carried out in the eye test by any optician and it is important that such an examination be carried out every 2–3 years on everyone after the age of 40–45 years.

General criteria for screening

The following criteria are always important if any screening test is to be effective and acceptable:

- the disease being searched for should always be one which has potentially serious consequences (it should either be *life threatening* or lead to some serious *disability or handicap*;
- the screening test should always be
  — simple to carry out and unequivocal in interpretation;
  — objective and never subjective;
  — completely safe and should never produce any fear or apprehension;
- all screening tests must be accompanied by counselling so that the person undergoing the tests fully understands the nature of the test. In the event of the test being positive treatment must be started immediately.

Elderly persons

All three forms of prevention, primary, secondary and tertiary, are important in elderly persons. However tertiary prevention becomes essential to prevent further serious deterioration in anyone with a disability or chronic medical condition over the age of 75 years.

The special health problems found in elderly persons include the following.

Eyesight

Serious impairment of sight and blindness are mainly found in persons over the age of 60 years. Early recognition and treatment are important for all conditions but the practice nurse should especially be on the lookout for *cataract*. This is commonly found in persons over the age of 75. Simple questioning by the practice nurse will often identify those suffering from cataract. Two signs are particularly indicative that cataract is probably developing:

* the person may notice it is easier to see in a dim light. The explanation is that in a dim light the iris of the eye opens more and this allows the peripheral part of the lens of the eye (which is usually clearer and more normal) to transmit more light;
* the individual may have found that they have had to have their spectacles changed more frequently.

The modern cataract operation to replace the lens in the eye with a plastic one is very simple to carry out and often it is done today by day surgery with the consequent minimum of disturbance for the elderly person.

It is important to remember that a large contributory factor in many falls seen in elderly persons is failing vision. Any fall in an elderly person is serious as fractures occur more readily in old people (especially in elderly women because there may be a degree of osteoporosis) and so often any fall is the starting point of a progressive and serious decline from which the elderly person may never recover.

Deafness

Deafness is considerably commoner in persons over the age of 60 years. If failing hearing is suspected, a full audiometric test should be carried out. If the hearing loss is confirmed, then usually a hearing aid is fitted. It is then important for the practice nurse to explain that all hearing aids can be very disappointing at first. The reason is because nearly always hearing is lost differentially – appreciation of the high notes (which are the consonants in speech) are lost to a greater degree than the low notes (the vowels in speech). Any hearing aid, being an amplifier, magnifies all sounds equally so that the high notes can now be heard but they are drowned by the low notes. This is very confusing and often leads to the hearing aid being discarded as useless. What needs to be done is that the elderly person should persist with the hearing aid even if at first it does not seem to help. After a few weeks the brain will adjust to the new mix of sounds and understanding of speech will improve significantly. Deafness is often considered to be a minor problem but progressive deafness, unless treated properly, always has serious consequences as it leads to social isolation.

Foot problems

Minor foot problems are common in elderly persons and can result in considerable limitation of mobility. If they are discovered early and then treated effectively, independence can usually be maintained. Lack of mobility can often produce other difficulties – isolation may well develop and, in a number of cases, nutritional problems may follow as the elderly person finds it impossible to travel far to shop. Certainly osteoporosis is more likely to develop in immobile women and then even minor accidents can result in fractures. Arrangements should be made early in the development of foot problems for the elderly person to attend a *chiropodist* (see p. 382).

Nutritional problems

After the age of 75 years, nutritional problems become commoner especially in those whose partner has recently died. Many of these difficulties are caused by the survivor (usually the widow) settling for snack meals (e.g. tea and toast) once the discipline of preparing proper meals has eased now that the individual is living alone. A simple explanation by the practice nurse can usually correct this tendency and once the elderly person realises that a proper balanced diet with adequate protein, vegetables and fruit is still important, then usually normal eating habits return. It is however important for the practice nurse to check this at a later date otherwise serious vitamin and other deficiencies can quite easily develop. In this respect a number of studies have shown that on admission to hospital, some very old persons (in the mid or late eighties or older) were found to have various nutritional deficiencies including advanced anaemias.

Accidents in the home

Accidents in the home (mostly falls) are a particular hazard to persons over the age of 80 years. Many are caused by a combination of poor eyesight and inadequate lighting. All nurses when talking to a patient at home or in hospital who is over 80 should always discuss accident prevention. Another cause of accidents in very old persons is to do with the slow deterioration in the balancing mechanism in the dark (when the levels of fluid in the semi-circular canals in the inner ear come into play). It is essential that, when such an elderly person has to get up at night, a hand torch is always used enabling them to balance through the mechanism of sight.

Confusional states

There are two different types of confusional states found in old persons – the acute confusional states and Alzheimer's disease.

The *acute confusional states* all have a specific cause and when diagnosed correctly and the cause effectively treated, the patient recovers completely. The causes include the following:

- *chest and other infections*: in persons over 80 years of age the usual symptoms of these infections do not always occur – for instance, pyrexia is usually absent but instead the person suddenly becomes very confused;
- *dehydration*: many very old people reduce their fluid intake and thus become dehydrated. Again the usual symptoms often do not occur but the person becomes confused. Once this has been corrected, the individual returns to normal;
- *hypoxia*: there are many causes of a lack of oxygen to the main organs of the body, including heart and vascular diseases and certain chest conditions. Elderly patients who develop hypoxia also become very confused. Again if the hypoxia is relieved by oxygen etc. these elderly persons become lucid and their confusion disappears;
- *certain medications* (such as cimetidine, β-blockers, anticholinergics and levodopa) when given to persons over 80 years of age are destroyed more slowly by the body so, by a process of accumulation an overdose eventually occurs. This is usually shown by the patient starting to become confused. As soon as the dose has been reduced and the patient is again in equilibrium, the confusion disappears. It is most important that nurses point out these possible problems to relatives and others caring for such patients at home and to the patient where appropriate.

The situation is always different in *Alzheimer's disease* where there is a gradual and insiduous onset of confusion. The great difference between the two forms of confusion is that in the acute confusional states the patient is always worried as they realise all is not right – they can appreciate that they are confused. In Alzheimer's disease the patient does not realise that they are behaving in an odd or eccentric way – the patient has no insight and there is usually an absence of anxiety. There is no understanding on the part of the patient as to what is happening as their ability to comprehend common features of life is disappearing. The outlook and prognosis in Alzheimer's disease is always poor – inevitably there is a steady deterioration until the patient does not recognise their husband or wife or close relatives.

The ability to diagnose correctly the acute confusional states is very important as the cause in every instance is specific and once diagnosed and rectified, the patient quickly returns to normal. Many relatives confronted with confusion in an elderly relative tend to assume that the condition is the start of Alzheimer's disease, but if the correct diagnosis has been made that it is an acute confusional state, this can be very reassuring. Equally if the correct diagnosis is that the person is suffering from Alzheimer's disease then this should make clear the future problems and dangers. As Alzheimer's disease is steadily progressive, the close relatives have a very difficult task. Eventually full-time care in a psychogeriatric unit will be necessary.

Hypothermia

The danger of hypothermia in elderly persons can be reduced by effective health education, especially by practice nurses and district/ community nurses involved in the treatment and care of such persons in their own homes. Those who are at greatest risk are those who are:

- living alone;
- relatively immobile;
- ill or have recently been ill.

Most elderly people at greatest risk have a diminished sense of cold and do not feel uncomfortable sitting in a room that is too cold. Another important factor is that a number of old people believe that to remain in good health it is essential to sleep in a bedroom with the window open, even in the coldest of weather in winter. This is totally untrue – in fact the opposite is more likely but such habits are often difficult to change. Perhaps the best time to do this is much earlier in life (perhaps when looking after their young children). Sound health education advice at such a time can do much to dispel this mistaken myth and can prevent the danger of hypothermia much later in life.

Tertiary prevention

Tertiary prevention (which is the same as the prevention of serious complications following a chronic illness) is mainly possible with adults and especially with those over the age of 65 years. Many types of patients respond to tertiary prevention including those with the following diseases:-

- ischaemic heart disease and peripheral vascular diseases;
- hypertensive disease;
- asthma and bronchitis;
- diabetes mellitus;
- many forms of arthritis and especially rheumatoid arthritis;
- persons recovering from strokes;
- all very painful chronic conditions;
- accident cases.

The main aim of tertiary prevention is to avoid permanent handicaps and disability as these can quickly reduce the quality of life. To be completely successful tertiary prevention should form part of a continuous process which starts after the beginning of the illness. Tertiary prevention certainly includes *effective rehabilitation* which is mainly concerned with ensuring that the patient, if possible, regains his or her full function. But tertiary prevention goes beyond rehabilitation, as some patients can never regain their full function and are left with some permanent disability. It is then that the attitude and approach of the person is crucial. In many cases considerable improvisation is required before the individual can again lead a normal life. A positive attitude is absolutely essential and all nurses should do everything to promote such an approach especially in the advice they give. Any tendency to self pity is likely to be disastrous and may soon lead to a bitter individual and this will probably add social isolation to their problems.

In teaching those patients struggling to overcome a chronic painful illness (such as rheumatoid arthritis or the results of a stroke) to lead useful and reasonably normal lives, the most influential health workers are those in constant contact with the patient's home. This is often the practice nurse and/or the district/community nurse. Close relatives and friends of the patient may also need help to understand that over-protection should be avoided at all costs if independence is not to be lost. Respite care may also be required for those relatives constantly looking after the patient. Tertiary prevention can be further assisted and supplemented by various community agencies which encourage such persons to remain actively independent. For example, attendence at a day centre run by the health, social services or voluntary body can help in making certain that the person is not overprotected. It often helps because contact at such a centre with others who may be far more seriously handicapped can provide encouragement to someone who, for the first time, can see how much has been achieved by enterprising people who have found ways of coping with far worse handicaps.

One of the most serious difficulties for anyone to overcome, especially if the disability is the result of a sudden accident is inertia. Too often the patient and relatives feel that all is lost and that it is a waste of time attempting to carry on a normal life. Tertiary prevention will only succeed if such a negative attitude is overcome. Many different approaches will usually be needed. Day centres aim at not only getting patients out of their home and mixing with others but also at motivating individuals and discovering what is most likely to interest them.

Importance of anticipating future problems

The secret of successful tertiary prevention lies in being able to anticipate future problems, not only in the medical and nursing fields but in the environmental ones. Housing can be very important; living in the right type of accomodation can make all the difference to anyone trying to cope with some serious problem. For anyone with a handicapping illness, especially if it is progressive and one in which mobility tends to become more restricted, it may be essential eventually for the patient to avoid stairs and steps. An adaptation to the ground floor may be possible so that the patient can remain in their home even if they can no longer climb stairs. Patients should always approach the local social services department for advice. Many such departments have occupational therapists who specialise in this field and are skilled in assisting disabled persons to remain at home. In illnesses such as multiple sclerosis, patients may gradually lose their mobility, and anticipation of such difficulties can provide time for the problem to be solved before it becomes too serious and this may enable the patient to continue to lead a reasonably normal life. Remember in a progressive disease such as multiple sclerosis total mobility may eventually be lost, making it very important that the patient at that stage is already living on the ground floor with all necessities at hand.

Social security financial benefits for ill and disabled persons

An understanding of the various supportive financial benefits which are available to ill and disabled persons is most important for practice nurses and district/community nurses. The two main financial benefits are:

- Disability Living Allowance, available for persons disabled before the age of 65 years (see p. 330); it has two elements:
  — care element;
  — mobility element;
- Attendance Allowance – available after the age of 65 for persons who need a great deal of help with their personal care (see p. 331).

Such information should be an essential part of health education and can be crucial in preventing further rapid deterioration of the patient and family. All nurses should at least know the scope of such financial help although the minutiae of claiming benefits can be left to social workers and others working in the welfare benefits field. Nurses should realise that the potential value of such financial help is often lost because many professionals are ignorant of the scope of this help. Yet these benefits are specifically designed to help everyone who is seriously ill or disabled irrespective of their financial means. The numbers of persons who apply for such financial help are considerably lower than the proportion of such people in the country. It is up to everyone working in the health and social services to make certain that the 'take up' of this valuable financial help is improved. Although financial benefits and allowances can never compensate anyone for a serious illness or disability, they can make life much more comfortable for the patient and family.

Palliative care

Palliative care is active total care offered to a patient with a progressive disease and his/her family when it is recognised that the illness is no longer curable. It concentrates upon:

- the quality of life of the patient;
- providing relief from pain and other distressing symptoms;
- integrating the psychological and spiritual aspects of care;
- offering to support the patient's family to enable them to cope during the illness;
- continuing that support during the period of bereavement following the death of the patient.

A detailed study of palliative care by the Standing Medical Advisory Committee and the Standing Nursing and Midwifery Committee was commissioned by the Department of Health during 1991 and the report was published in 1992. This report covered all aspects and concluded that 'the best palliative care is provided when a multidisciplinary approach is taken'. The role of the primary health care team, GP, practice nurse and district nurse, was considered to be paramount and was considered to be the mainstay of support to the patient and family. In addition, the report emphasised the special roles of hospices, hospital palliative support teams, day centres and particularly the specialist Macmillan nurses.

The approach should always be a positive one, in contrast to the negative attitude summed up in the phrase 'nothing more can be done'.

The report also stressed that the care of patients with advanced disease will largely fall on nurses, and many training courses will be needed to equip nurses with the skills palliative care requires. These include:

- pain control;
- analgesia;
- personal aspects of terminal care;
- symptom management by the patient and carer;
- wider legal and ethical issues.

Palliative care should always be a continuous part of health care and not a distinct and separate service. Dying is a normal part of life and therefore the health service that is closest to the public, primary health care, should always be a dominant feature of palliative care. Many models of palliative care are developing. There is much unevenness of provision throughout the NHS. Although palliative care is concerned with serious cancer cases primarily, such a service should be available to all patients suffering from incurable diseases likely to lead soon to their death. One very important feature of the best models of palliative care is that they not only provide relief from pain and other symptoms but, as far as possible, encourage the patient to choose what he or she wants to do and to lead as normal a life as possible in comfortable and congenial surroundings.

Palliative care should always aim at helping the relatives, especially in the period of bereavement following the death of the patient. This can be a difficult time often made worse by the inability of most people to talk about the deceased. Nurses and especially those working in the community practice or district nurses need to understand the problems of bereavement. This report correctly states that 'relatives need to feel they have permission to talk and the primary health care team (e.g. the GP, practice and district nurse) are in the ideal position to be listeners'.

Organisation of health education

The Secretary of State for Health has overall responsibility for the policy and development of health education. Centrally, many functions are delegated to the Health Education Authority. Locally the District Health Authority, through its District Medical Officer, is responsible for health education and for the distribution of health education material.

In addition to the role of health care professionals already described in this chapter, the following staff also have an important role in health education:

- health education officers. Over half of all health authorities employ such staff. Many of these officers have had training in nursing, health visiting or the teaching profession. Their main function is the organisation and promotion of health education by:
  — training staff to carry out group or individual health education;
  — collecting and distributing suitable material and information;
  — assessing and evaluating the impact of the health education undertaken;
- general practitioners have many opportunities for health education as the majority of patients have great faith in their doctor's advice. It is important that each doctor realises the oppor-

tunities there are of carrying out health education during their daily work in their practice;

- teachers also have a widespread influence on the lives of their pupils. School life always plays an important part in health education, as any success with children moulds the attitudes of future generations. If children learn how best to avoid disease and maintain good health at school, they are most likely to ensure their own children benefit in the same way;
- social workers are also involved in health education indirectly when dealing with children, physically handicapped persons and those with learning difficulties and with elderly persons.

It will be understood from this list that *health education is a multidisciplinary task* and that the role of the professional health education officer is mainly to help others to play a useful role.

The Health Education Authority

The Health Education Authority is the national body set up to organise health education with an annual budget which comes from a direct grant from the Department of Health, the Scottish Office, the Welsh Office or from the Department of Health, Northern Ireland. The main functions of the Health Education Authority include the following:

- advising on priorities for health education;
- advising and carrying out national or local campaigns in cooperation with health authorities or local authorities;
- producing information and publicity material and publishing articles of interest to those engaged in health education;
- sponsoring and undertaking research including epidemiological and statistical research, cost–benefit analysis and evaluation;
- acting as the national centre of expertise in health education;
- encouraging and promoting training in health education work;
- cooperating with local education authorities in schools, colleges and universities;
- maintaining contact with and advising various national voluntary bodies engaged in specialised aspects of health education work.

Voluntary bodies and commercial organisations

Many different bodies are involved nationally in health education, especially in the field of accident prevention e.g. the Royal Society for the Prevention of Accidents (ROSPA), and in cancer education.

Commercial organisations mainly prepare visual aids and other material for use in health education – videos, films, overhead projection slides etc. Although this material may be self-advertising as well as having a health education content, much of this commercial advertising is discreetly carried out and the material can be very useful.

13 The world's health problems – the work of the World Health Organization (WHO)

The control of international health has become increasingly important in a world in which the rate of travel from one country to another is becoming progressively faster. The international controlling body for health in the world is the *World Health Organization (WHO)* which was set up in 1946. By 1993, there were 170 member states plus one associate member in WHO including all the major powers in the world. The headquarters of WHO is at Geneva and there are six regions (see Fig. 13.1):

- Africa with headquarters at Brazzaville;
- Americas with headquarters at Washington, DC;
- East Mediterranean with headquarters at Alexandria, Egypt;
- Europe with headquarters at Copenhagen;
- SE Asia with headquarters at New Delhi;
- West Pacific with headquarters at Manila, Philippines.

Each region has its own Regional Advisory Committee on medical research and there is also a single Global Advisory Committee.

Although WHO is concerned with all aspects of health, it has always paid particular attention to preventive medicine. It also has always played an important role in stimulating and assisting in the development of the preventive health services in under-developed and Third World countries. The main principle that has been constantly followed by WHO since its creation is that 'health is now a world responsibility – for health, like peace, is one and indivisible'.

The Executive Board of WHO meets twice a year in Geneva and a World Health Assembly meets annually. Examples of successful cooperation among all member states include the eradication of smallpox from the world and the acceptance in 1978 of a new universal aim for year 2000 'Health for all by Year 2000'.

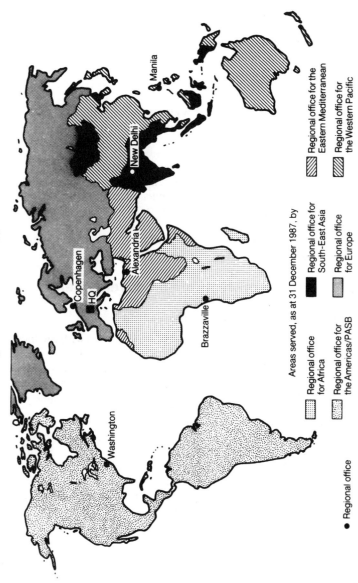

Fig. 13.1   World Health Organization regions.

The work undertaken by WHO

The work of WHO falls under the following four headings:

- Health promotion and health care.
- Disease prevention and control.
- Information and teaching.
- Research.

Special priorities

In 1991 the Director General of WHO drew attention to the following five special areas needing priority in addition to the well-established essentials of primary health care:

- the health of humankind in a changing environment;
- proper food and nutrition for a healthy life;
- integrated disease control as a part of overall health care and human development;
- dissemination of information;
- intensified health development action in, and in support of, countries most in need.

General health protection and development

Women's health protection and development

During the last few years WHO has been concerned with the increased participation of women in health matters. Efforts have been made by WHO to promote more leadership of women in the provision of health services throughout the world. Two special problems have been studied by WHO in 1990–1:

- the widespread incidence of nutritional anaemias in women in many countries throughout the world. Recent studies have shown that about half of pregnant women and a third of non-pregnant women in the world are suffering from nutritional anaemias. A further problem is that there has not been much improvement since 1980;
- the prevention of the transmission of HIV infection to women. WHO have been testing the efficiency of the female condom in trials in Europe during recent years.

Food and nutrition

WHO has continued to make the integration of food and nutrition policies in primary health care one of its top priorities with special emphasis on the training of all community health workers.

During 1990–1 a task force from WHO reviewed the value of health education in food safety. It found that 20–50% of travellers suffer from diarrhoea or other food-borne diseases. A guide on safe food for travellers has been prepared by WHO in a leaflet which has been widely disseminated.

During 1991, WHO established a databank on food-borne diseases which collects information on their incidence, and developed an expert system for the identification of causative agents in food-borne diseases.

Oral health

Reports from the WHO global databank for oral health have shown that the numbers of decayed, missing or filled teeth (DMFT) in developing and industrialised countries, which had been rising until 1984, had fallen from 1984 to 1990 with a small rise in developing countries in 1991 (see Fig. 13.2).

Accident prevention

Work has continued on accident prevention in many countries; much of this has been integrated into two centres:

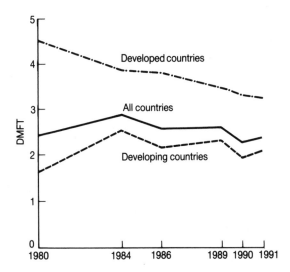

Fig. 13.2   Mean numbers of decayed, missing or filled teeth (DMFT) at 12 years, 1980–91 (weighted averages by size of population). (From *The Work of WHO 1990–91. Report of the Director General.*)

- in Amsterdam, The Netherlands for domestic safety;
- in Atlanta, Georgia, USA for injury prevention.

Protection and the promotion of health for specific groups

Maternal and child health including family planning

WHO has continued to be very active in this field and especially in maternal and newborn infant care, child health, growth and development, adolescent health, and in health aspects of family planning (including infertility).

It is in the developing countries that the main concern still occurs. A few developing countries have succeeded in bringing down maternal mortality but many others still fall short of the targets set by WHO. The main problems include:

- severe anaemia
- haemorrhage
- eclampsia
- unsafe abortion
- under-utilisation of family planning services.

Many research and epidemiological studies have been carried out into maternal mortality. Common protocols have been introduced for eclampsia, the evaluation of maternal nutrition, the management of labour and for the treatment of retained placenta. In 1991, a handbook was published on the latest available information on maternal mortality, called *Maternal Mortality – a Global Handbook*.

Protection and promotion of mental health

WHO has continued to be very active in many countries in the field of mental health. Many countries have now formulated national mental health programmes, including Brazil, Chile, China, Cyprus, Dominican Republic, Omar, Philippines, Tunisia and Uruguay.

WHO has reviewed areas of special interest, such as mental health and deviance in inner cities. Many steps have been taken to improve communication between mental health workers and others. Guidelines have been devised for clinicians, research workers, general practitioners and child health workers. Some 150 centres in 50 countries have collaborated in this work.

Efforts have been started to measure the quality of life of people in certain groups at risk, including:

- persons suffering from certain diseases (diabetes, chronic arthritis and AIDS);
- populations exposed to special stress such as refugees in camps, children in orphanages;
- those caring for chronically ill persons;
- people who have difficulty in communication such as those with dementia.

A Task Force has been set up by WHO in Europe on mental health promotion and education mainly aimed at strengthening the collaboration between health and education authorities. Training in behavioural sciences has been advocated and a document produced on the integration of a mental health component into general nursing education.

Suicide and parasuicide continues to be of special concern to WHO. Both are increasing in many countries and preventive measures are urgently needed. WHO has convened an expert meeting in Europe and initiated a global study of parasuicide.

Prevention and control of drug abuse

Because excessive and uncontrollable use of alcohol and drugs has become increasingly common in many countries. WHO has been studying assessment procedures and is reviewing the type of treatment being provided in different settings. Much training material for workers in primary health care and in the community and in social services has been prepared for use in national programmes. A regional drug abuse surveillance system has been developed in the Americas as well as a 10 country study on the detection and management of alcohol-related problems.

Disease prevention and control

Immunisation

In 1991, progress in national immunisation programmes in the world accelerated and for the first time more than 80% of children in their first year of life received three doses of combined diphtheria, pertussis and poliomyelitis immunisation. Figure 13.3 shows the immunisation coverage of children in their first year of life in all the WHO regions.

WHO has estimated that at least 1.7 million deaths from measles, neonatal tetanus and pertussis could be prevented through immunisation. WHO has managed to arrange an impressive degree of support for immunisation at global and regional levels of many organ-

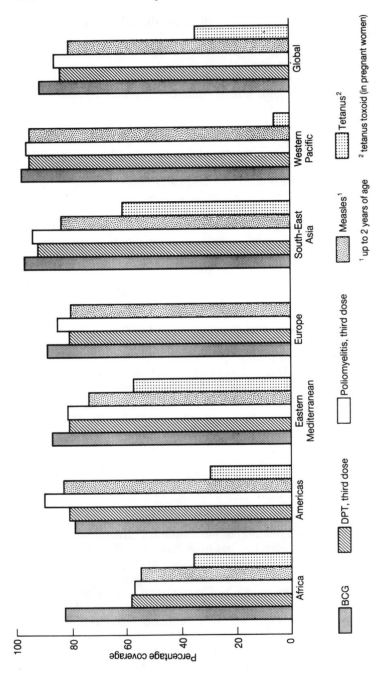

Fig. 13.3 Immunisation coverage of children in the first year of age, by WHO region, August 1991. (From *The Work of WHO, Biennial Report of the Director General.*)

isations including UNICEF, the World Bank, UNDP Rotary International and many others.

However the success of immunisation programmes cannot be assumed. Social and economic problems severely constrain the growth of health services in many countries. Outbreaks of poliomyelitis still occur in South-east Asia and Western Pacfic regions and neonatal tetanus and measles were once again major killers of children in 1990–1.

WHO has made an estimate of the numbers of deaths due to measles, tetanus and pertussis and of the numbers of cases of poliomyelitis prevented by immunisation in the developing countries. This is shown graphically in Fig. 13.4.

Malaria

Malaria still remains one of the world's major health problems. *Over 40% of the world's population are still exposed to varying degrees of malaria risk.* Excluding Africa, 5.2 million cases of malaria were reported in 1991. Africa is the worst affected and accounts for 80% of clinical cases reported and for 90% of all parasite carriers in the world. Unfortunately in African rural areas, there has been a rapid develop-

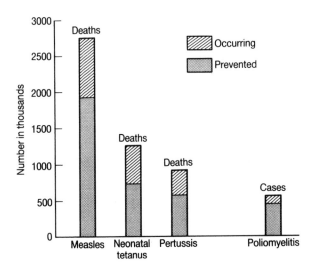

Fig. 13.4 Number of deaths due to measles, neonatal tetanus and pertussis and number of poliomyelitis cases occurring and prevented by immunisation in developing countries, 1990. (From *The Work of WHO. Biennial Report of the Director General, 1990–91.*)

ment of resistance to chloroquine and there is also evidence of such resistance in Indonesia and Papua New Guinea.

The WHO Collaborating Centre on the Epidemiology and Control of Malaria is based in Rome and has carried out many epidemiological studies with a view to developing better vector control.

WHO has established a database on malaria. Each year 1400–1550 cases of malaria occur in the UK with about 10–12 deaths – all are individuals who have just returned from visits abroad, particularly to Kenya, Malaysia, Tanzania and Zambia which are all areas where there is an increasing prevalence of the strain of *Plasmodium falciparum* resistant to chloroquine. For anyone visiting such areas *mefloquine* should be used instead as the preferred prophylactic drug. Mefloquine has the advantage that it is taken once a week but should *not* be used for any woman who is pregnant or for children.

For tourists and travellers visiting heavily infected malaria areas, WHO has stressed that the possibility of malaria should always be considered if a febrile disease occurs on return, not only within the first few weeks but *within the following year*.

Diarrhoeal diseases

WHO continues to give high priority to the control of diarrhoeal diseases in developing countries. The most practical and effective control of diarrhoeal diseases in such countries is now based on oral rehydration salts (ORS) which is a simple, cheap and effective way to reduce mortality from diarrhoeal diseases. In 1991 a new target was set to halve diarrhoeal mortality in developing countries by the year 2000 (see Fig. 13.5).

It was agreed with UNICEF that the availability to all developing countries of an adequate supply of oral rehydration salts should be the main objective rather than support for a more limited local supply. The production of such salts in 1990–1 in developing countries increased slightly and now 64 such countries are producing the salts.

In addition WHO is promoting breast feeding as a further effective way to prevent diarrhoeal diseases in developing countries.

Cholera spread in 1991 to Latin America for the first time this century and extensive epidemics also occurred in Africa. More deaths from cholera occurred in 1991 than in the previous five years. WHO has set up a Global Task Force on cholera to coordinate WHO's reponses to the epidemic.

Tuberculosis

Tuberculosis is again becoming a major communicable disease in the world and, in 1990, no less than 8 million new cases occurred with 3 million deaths (see Table 13.1).

The decline in incidence of tuberculosis in industrialised countries which has been occurring for many decades has been halted. In America, tuberculosis is again increasing mainly because of the interaction

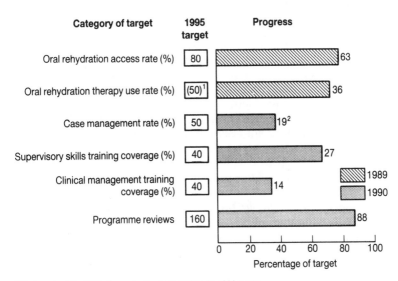

Category of target   **1995 target**   **Progress**

Oral rehydration access rate (%) — 80 — 63

Oral rehydration therapy use rate (%) — (50)[1] — 36

Case management rate (%) — 50 — 19[2]

Supervisory skills training coverage (%) — 40 — 27

Clinical management training coverage (%) — 40 — 14 — 1989 / 1990

Programme reviews — 160 — 88

0   20   40   60   80   100
Percentage of target

[1] No target set for 1995. Progress shown in relation to 1989 target.
[2] Based on survey results from 17 countries and global rate of use of oral rehydration therapy (ORT).

Fig. 13.5 Progress in reaching targets of the Diarrhoeal Diseases Control Programme. (From *The Work of WHO. Biennial Report of the Director General, 1990–91.*)

Table 13.1 Global tuberculosis: estimated cases and deaths, 1990

Region	Prevalence of infection	New cases (thousands)	Deaths
Africa	171 000	1398	656
Americas[1]	117 000	564	220
South-East Asia	426 000	2480	932
Eastern Mediterranean	52 000	594	163
Western Pacific[2]	574 000	2557	894
Industrialized countries[3]	382 000	409	42
Total	1 722 000	8002	2907

[1] Excluding Canada and the United States of America.
[2] Excluding Australia, Japan and New Zealand.
[3] Australia, Canada, Japan, New Zealand, United States of America and all European countries.

of tuberculosis and HIV infections but the reasons for the increase in some European countries and Japan are not yet clear. In Africa the problem is very serious – over 3 million people there are infected with both the tubercle bacillus and HIV infection (2.4 million persons in Sub-Saharan Africa alone). In many countries in Africa the cases of tuberculosis reported have doubled in the last few years. Because of this, less than half the cases of tuberculosis are being detected and less than half those diagnosed are being cured.

The main objectives of the WHO tuberculosis prevention programme were to draw up new global tuberculosis control strategies, develop tools for implementing them, provide support for programmes of tuberculosis control, to single out high priority research areas and to implement field studies on AIDS-related tuberculosis.

The latest strategy of WHO is based on achieving by the year 2000:

- an 80% cure rate among sputum-positive cases under treatment;
- a 70% detection rate;
- a concentration of well-managed local programmes of short-course chemotherapy;
- wherever possible to encourage national programmes to operate through the primary health care system. This should strengthen the local health infrastructures and assist in the development of an effective curative component in primary health care.

Aids, HIV infection and sexually transmitted diseases

The AIDS epidemic which first appeared to be mainly confined to homosexual men has now evolved into a pandemic affecting millions of men, women and children in all continents of the world. Heterosexual spread of HIV infections is growing in importance throughout the world and already by 1994, it is the predominant mode of spread in Sub-Saharan Africa, Asia and parts of Latin America. Women therefore are becoming increasingly infected, and WHO estimates that by the year 2000 there will be an equal number of HIV infections in both sexes (see Fig. 13.6).

HIV infection from blood transfusion has been virtually eliminated from all industrialised countries and is declining elsewhere following WHO's Global Blood Safety Initiative. But *HIV transmission through needle sharing by injecting drug users is increasing in many countries*.

The confirmed numbers of AIDS cases worldwide had reached 400 000 by the end of 1991 but it is known that there is considerable under-diagnosis and under-reporting. WHO estimates that by the end of 1991 more than one million cases of AIDS had occurred and 8–10 million HIV infections in adults plus 500 000 paediatric cases of AIDS due to perinatal infections, more than 90% of them in Sub-Saharan

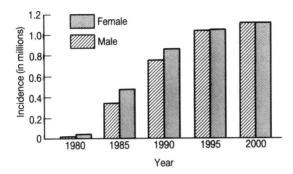

Fig. 13.6 Estimated or projected annual global adult incidence of HIV infection, by sex, 1980–2000. (From *The Work of WHO. Biennial Report of the Director General, 1990–91.*)

Africa. By the year 2000, WHO expects there will be 12–18 million AIDS cases and 30–40 million HIV infections worldwide.

During the period 1993–2010, AIDS may in some countries (e.g. in Africa) increase the child death rate by as much as 50%, eliminating all the gains in child survival from 1973–1993. In addition to the great increased health care costs, the pandemic will have an overwhelming socio-economic impact.

WHO has identified six priorities for AIDS prevention:

* to strengthen national AIDS programmes;
* to plan for the social and economic consequences of AIDS which not only threaten individuals, families and communities but the economic stability of many developing nations;
* to develop more effective interventions for halting the spread of AIDS and for caring for infected persons;
* to accelerate biomedical research aimed at producing safe, practical, effective, affordable and universally available vaccines and drugs;
* to support human rights and to oppose discrimination and stigmatisation as irrational to HIV-infected persons and a danger to public health;
* to fight complacency so that all countries confront the AIDS pandemic.

An excellent example of a poster to help reduce discrimination is given in Fig. 13.7.

There has been an unprecedented response to the AIDS threat from all governments in the world. By 1991, all member states had a national

I HAVE AIDS
PLease hug me

I can't make you sick

J.keeler

AIDS HOT LINE FOR KIDS
CENTER FOR ATTITUDINAL HEALING
19 MAIN ST., TIBURON, CA 94920, (415) 435-5022

Fig. 13.7 An American poster urges people not to discriminate against people with AIDS.

AIDS programme. WHO also reports that there has been large-scale pledges of financial support for funds which are channelled through the WHO Trust Fund for Global Programme on AIDS.

Campaigns to promote the use of condoms under national AIDS programmes have been mounted, specially in Africa. Financial support has come from the World Bank, UNICEF, UNFPA and the United States Agency for International Development. Special condom quality assurance laboratories have been established in the African Region of WHO enabling local programmes to monitor the rate of condom deterioration.

WHO has continued to cooperate in the development of a safe blood supply in developing countries, since up to 10% of all HIV infections in such countries are caused by transfusion of blood and blood products. In spite of all the efforts of WHO, discrimination and stigmatisation still exists in some countries. WHO has continuously advised that such practices are dangerous, as infected persons then conceal their infection. Attempts to keep HIV travellers out of a country, and to detect and confine infected nationals, are dangerous because they can never be 100% effective but may delude the public into believing that precautions are no longer necessary.

WHO has continued to coordinate World AIDS Day held on 1 December (the first such publicity programme was in 1988). Each year the effort highlights a new message. In 1990 it was 'Women and AIDS' in an effort to emphasise the spreading problem in women. In 1991 it was 'AIDS: Sharing the Challenge', which underlined the need for individuals, groups, communities, non-governmental organisations agencies of UN and all nations to join together in fighting the AIDS pandemic.

Other sexually transmitted diseases

WHO remains extremely active in the field of other sexually transmitted diseases. WHO's strategy to reduce these diseases aims:

- to join with programmes for mother and child care to reduce natal and perinatal infections;
- to control sexually transmitted diseases generally in primary health care;
- to improve family planning;
- to strengthen the health laboratory infrastructure;
- to provide essential drugs;
- to emphasise that *changes in sexual behaviour are still the essential strategy* for primary prevention of most infections.

Particular problems in sexually transmitted diseases including the following:

- drug resistance to commonly used antibiotics (such as penicillin and tetracyclines) used to treat gonorrhoea and chancroid is becoming increasingly common. This means that these conditions now must be treated with more expensive antibiotics such as cephalosporins and quinolones;
- as infection with sexually transmitted diseases is often asymptomatic, active case finding must be undertaken in high risk groups such as pregnant women;

- hepatitis B infection in industrialised countries is mainly sexually transmitted but in the developing world only 25–30% of such infections are acquired sexually. In these countries the disease is mainly transmitted in the perinatal period and in childhood. As hepatitis B is the only sexually transmitted disease for which an effective vaccine is available, WHO has drawn up at a recent meeting in Geneva a consensus statement on how hepatitis B should be controlled.

Zoonoses

WHO has given high priority to the prevention of zoonoses (diseases which are spread through and from animals). Of particular interest to the UK are rabies, leptospirosis (see p. 167) and the major food-borne diseases related to animals and animal products such as salmonellosis (see p. 158) and brucellosis (see p. 269).

Rabies

The successful introduction in 1986 of oral vaccination of foxes in Europe has continued and been extended. Figure 13.8 shows the range of this preventive initiative by 1991. This cross-border oral vaccination now covers all Germany, most parts of France, parts of the Czech and Slovak Republics and over the Austrian border into former Yugoslavia.

WHO is also involved in similar delivery of vaccine to immunise various wild animal species in the Americas. In Ecuador, Sri Lanka and Tunisia, dog vaccination programmes have led to a marked reduction in cases of human rabies. The effect of such vaccinations in Sri Lanka since 1976 is shown in Fig. 13.9.

Control and surveillance of viral and bacterial diseases

Viral hepatitis B

Viral hepatitis B can now be prevented by a safe and effective vaccine (see p. 134) – this could be described as the first vaccine against a potential cause of cancer. This is because *chronically infected carriers of hepatitis B are at high risk of serious liver disease from cirrhosis and primary liver cancers.* More than one million carriers from hepatitis B die in the world in this way every year.

More than 30 countries have now introduced new hepatitis B vaccinations into their infant immunisation programmes and another 20 are planning to follow suit.

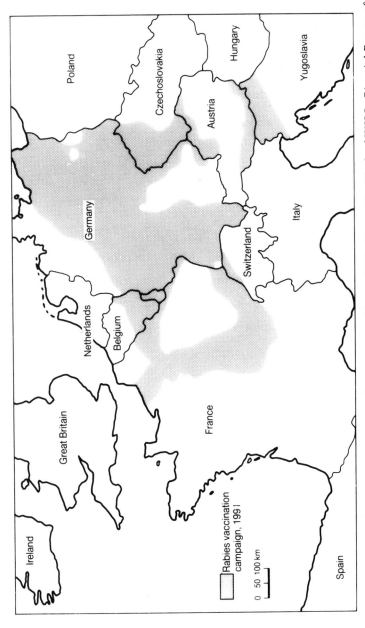

Fig. 13.8 Area in Europe for coverage by oral vaccination of foxes, 1991. (From *The Work of WHO. Biennial Report of the Director General, 1990–91.*) Please note this map was drawn prior to recent developments involving border changes in Eastern Europe.

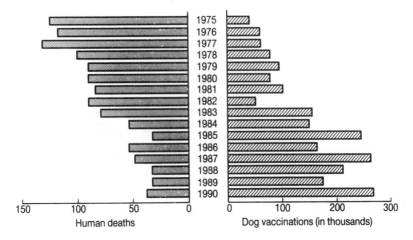

Fig. 13.9   Effect of dog vaccination in reducing the number of deaths from human rabies in the AGFUND project area in Sri Lanka. (From *The Work of WHO. Biennial Report of the Director General, 1990–91, published 1992.*)

Viral haemorrhagic fevers

Viruses causing haemorrhagic fever with renal syndrome have now been shown to be present in many parts of the world. WHO is continuing efforts to develop simple methods of rapid diagnosis.

Yellow fever

Yellow fever is re-emerging as a *major health threat in Africa*. Routine immunisation was abandoned in 1960 in favour of emergency measures taken after the start of an outbreak. Since then, a series of epidemics of varying severity have occurred, as shown in Fig. 13.10.

A new and disturbing epidemiology trend in some recent epidemics is that the majority of cases have occurred in children under the age of 14 years.

Recently, the Global Programme on Immunisation reviewed the position and have recommended that countries in endemic areas should incorporate yellow fever vaccination into their routine immunisation programmes.

Legionellosis

In cooperation with the WHO Collaborating Centre in Stockholm, a project has been launched to establish a surveillance system for

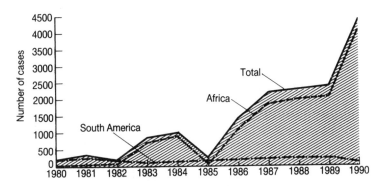

Fig. 13.10 Yellow fever: number of cases notified to WHO, 1980–90. (From *The Work of WHO. Biennial Report of the Director General, 1990–91, published 1992.*)

Legionella infections in travellers, using data available through an international network in Europe.

Prevention of blindness

Some 80 member states, most of them in developing countries, now benefit from WHO support in implementing national blindness preventive programmes based on a primary health care approach. As cataract is the cause of more than 50% of blindness in most countries, it is becoming a major challenge in the fight against blindness. There is a backlog of 13.5 million cases needing cataract surgery by 1992 with an estimated 1000 cases per million population occurring each year. Because of the magnitude of the problem and of the resources needed the introduction of intraocular lens implant surgery in developing countries will have to increase gradually.

Cancer

The global programme for the reduction of cancer throughout the world has two main components:

- *cancer control* – this has three elements: *primary prevention*, *early detection* and *palliative care*. The basic concepts adopted by WHO are that one-third of all cancers are preventable, one-third are curable if detected and treated at an early stage and that cancer is becoming an increasing problem in developing countries;
- research into the *epidemiology* of cancers, *aetiology* (cause of cancers), *prevention* and the *mechanisms of carcinogenesis*. This

component in practice is the responsibility of the International Agency for Research on Cancer.

Primary prevention

WHO gives support to cancer prevention in all its regions. WHO has pointed out that national programmes provide an ideal entry point for anti-tobacco activities, which many countries would not undertake on their own. *About 30% of cancer worldwide is associated with tobacco use – either smoking or chewing.* WHO has advised that anti-tobacco measures should be carried out by all countries including health education especially of schoolchildren, legislation and taxation, and the setting up of national anti-smoking committees made up of a wide range of interests.

At least one-third of cancers are related to diet. WHO has helped to lay down guidelines for diets which are likely to result in a reduction of cancers especially in industrialised countries. WHO is supporting a research project in China aimed at primary prevention of hepatocellular cancer by vaccinating newborn infants against hepatitis B.

Early detection

The work of WHO is always aimed at early detection of cancers particularly cancers of the breast, cervix, mouth and skin. This is generally carried out in primary health services.

Cancer of the cervix uteri is the commonest cancer found in women in developing countries. As it can be cured if it is discovered in time, special efforts are being made by WHO to design methods for early detection especially in developing countries where national screening programmes which are effective are rare and where most cases which are discovered are at a late and incurable stage.

Palliative care

WHO has produced pain relief guide-lines (published in the WHO Technical Report series No. 804, 1990) which are being used to great benefit for patients with incurable cancers in many countries.

Information and teaching

Both these subjects have always been of great importance to WHO. Every possible means of dissemination of information on health has been used by WHO. Another feature has been the WHO special days when one particular health subject has been highlighted throughout the world. Figure 13.11 shows the various health topics used on one

Fig. 13.11 WHO's Special Days. (From *The Work of WHO. Biennial Report of the Director General, 1990–91*, published 1992.)

particular day in the year to emphasise some important feature on health during 1990 and 1991.

WHO has used modern audiovisual technology to make its objectives and important health issues better known. For instance, a major teleconference on AIDS was organised by WHO in the region of the Americas in 1991. A film and video library has been built up by WHO to provide broadcasters with the footage they require.

An excellent working contact has been established between representatives of the media and WHO experts with press meetings bringing together journalists and health care workers and those responsible for national health care programmes in developing countries. In addition regular briefing sessions for journalists are held at WHO Headquarters.

The teaching and training of health workers has always been an essential part of the work of WHO and many training visits are arranged for health service staff in all countries each year.

Research

Many of the research efforts of WHO which cover a wide field are carried out in close collaboration with the Global Advisory Committee on Health Research. This is aimed at developing a clear research strategy and promoting harmonious science aid research policies. Three Task Forces were set up by WHO in 1990 to study 'the role of health research in the strategy for health for all by year 2000'. These will consider the following:

- health service research;
- monitoring of emerging areas in science and technology;
- investigation of evolving problems of health research.

WHO has also agreed that priority should be given to:

- optimum use of limited resources;
- improvement of health policy and management;
- promotion of innovation and experimentation;
- the acquisition of new knowledge for local and general benefit.

Those who then considered the evolving problems which are likely to be of special relevance to health services throughout the world have identified four priority issues:

- development perspectives of home habitat;
- quality of life and health indicators;
- access to health services;
- ethics and equity.

Health for All by the Year 2000

This historic concept and principle was laid down at a WHO meeting at Alma-Ata in 1978. The position 10 years later was assessed at a meeting of 22 senior health experts at Riga in 1988. The WHO's total commitment to the principles of Health for All by Year 2000 (HFA) was renewed and it was recommended that, in order to accelerate progress towards that goal, countries should take the action as outlined in Table 13.2.

Table 13.2   Action recommended by the World Health Organization in order to attain the goal of Health for All by Year 2000 (HFA).

---

1. Maintain HFA as a permanent goal of all nations up to and beyond the year 2000
   Reaffirm Health for All as a permanent objective of all nations, as stressed in the Alma-Ata Declaration, and establish a process for examining the

longer term challenges to Health for All that will extend into the 21st century.

2. **Renew and strengthen HFA strategies**
   Each country should continue to monitor its own health problems and develop its own health strategies in the spirit of Health for All. This will reveal its most pressing health problems and identify the most seriously underserved and vulnerable populations. Programmes should be directed towards those populations in the spirit of equity, inviting their active participation in the development and implementation of the strategies.

3. **Intensify social and political action for HFA**
   Intensify social and political actions necessary to support shifts in policy and allocation of resources required to progress toward Health for All, including the involvement of other sectors, non-governmental organisations, communities and other interested groups. Seek mechanisms for promoting new partnerships for health among them and with governments.

4. **Develop and mobilise leadership**
   Give strong emphasis in every country to developing and stimulating the interest in HFA.

5. **Enable the people to share in decision-making and action for health**
   Empower people by providing information, technical support, and decision-making possibilities, so as to enable them to share in the opportunities and responsibilities for action in the interest of their own health. Give special attention to the role of women in health and development.

6. **Make intersectoral collaboration a force for HFA**
   Support the creation of sustained intersectoral collaboration for health by incorporating health objectives into sectoral policies and activating potential mechanisms at all levels.

7. **Strengthen district health systems based on PHC**
   Strengthen district health systems based on primary health care, as a key action point for focusing national policies, resources and local concerns on the most pressing health needs and underserved people.

8. **Plan, prepare and support health manpower for HFA**
   Change educational and training programmes for health personnel emphasising relevance to health services' requirements by locating learning experiences in functioning health systems based on primary health care. Provide strong moral and resource support for personnel, particularly those working in remote or difficult circumstances.

9. **Ensure development and rational use of science and appropriate technology**
   Emphasise the applications of science and appropriate technology to the critical health problems that threaten populations in all parts of the world, and strengthen research capacities of Third World countries, with emphasis on research aimed at improving the health of the most deprived people.

10. Overcome problems that continue to resist solution

Establish priority programmes aimed at overcoming serious problems where underdevelopment or disturbances of development are major contributing factors and progress has been very limited, such as: high infant, child and maternal mortality rates; substance abuse, such as tobacco and alcohol; and the imbalance between population growth and environmental and socio-economic resources. Develop improved approaches through primary health care emphasising intersectoral action.

14 Nutrition and environmental health

Nutrition

Nutrition and public health are inseparable, as a well-balanced and adequate food supply is essential for complete health. A balanced diet must contain adequate protein, essential vitamins, certain mineral salts and plenty of fibre as this has a protective action against colonic diseases and ischaemic heart disease. As the Western world has developed foods rich in animal proteins, more fat has been eaten and carbohydrates rich in sugar have become popular. However there is mounting evidence that such a diet is not ideal and the marked increase in ischaemic heart disease, certain colonic diseases and obesity over the last three decades has been connected with this trend. At present, there is a move towards diets in which dairy fats are reduced and foods rich in fibre are increased. Nutritional problems are (i) worldwide; (ii) national; and (iii) individual.

Worldwide problems

The task of providing an adequate food supply for the rapidly increasing world population is one of its major social problems. *Protein malnutrition* is one of the main public health hazards in developing countries. As food supplies are increased, a further complication is that this improvement in nutrition leads to an increase in population which, in turn, makes heavier demands upon the food supply. Indications show that food supplies are not keeping pace with the increase in world population. The solution lies both in controlling the growth of the world's population and in increasing its food supply by various improvements in agriculture, pest control and research to discover more suitable crops and animal stocks.

The national problem

The national nutritional problems of the United Kingdom are complex, but for many years a national nutritional policy has been accepted which ensures that the following conditions are met:

- all essential foodstuffs should be available to the whole population at reasonable cost, and present in variety;
- certain priority foods should be provided for certain sections of the community. Examples include vitamins and subsidised dried milks for mothers and young infants, free school meals for children whose families are in need, and subsidised meals on wheels and lunch clubs for elderly people;
- standards of milk production are controlled nationally – areas are designated where all herds must be free from tuberculosis; a Brucellosis Incentive Scheme is in operation and regulations introduced for the pasteurisation of milk supplies and other products (e.g. ice cream);
- minimum standards are maintained for many foodstuffs and constant sampling ensures that these are reached;
- many foods are fortified to guarantee adequate supplies of vitamins;
- adulteration of foodstuffs is prevented by extensive legislation on such aspects as food preservatives or additives;
- foodstuffs must be free from disease and this is achieved by meat and food inspection both at ports and at abattoirs and markets;
- food handlers must be clean and must not contaminate the food – food hygiene;
- continuous health education should be carried out to teach the public about nutrition.

The individual problem

The individual nutritional problems are directly related to the type, amount and variety of foodstuffs consumed. Foods must supply the energy needs of the body in the form of calories and the proteins necessary for growth and tissue replacement; hence the correct proportion of proteins, carbohydrates and fats must be present in the diet which should also contain adequate amounts of vitamins, minerals and fibre.

Components for an adequate diet

Proteins

Proteins may be of animal or vegetable origin. The best are obtained from milk, egg, meats, fish, kidney or liver, for such foods contain large amounts of essential amino acids. The amount of protein required varies – a child uses about one-third of his or her protein requirements for growth, but an adult requires relatively little for replacement of tissue. Generally, it is accepted that an adult requires a minimum of 70 g of protein daily, although this amount may often be exceeded. Unlike fats and carbohydrates, proteins cannot be stored in the human body. In adults it is possible to obtain large quantities of proteins from vegetable sources, but for children, a high proportion of proteins should be of animal origin.

Fats

Fats are a concentrated form of energy and some are vehicles for the fat-soluble vitamins A and D. Fats are easily stored and form the main reserve of energy. The main sources of fat are butter, eggs, cream, cheese and fatty meats. Apart from herring, salmon and trout, there is very little fat in fish.

Carbohydrates

These are the starches and sugars – bread, potatoes, cane sugar, glucose. They are the cheapest form of food and the body can metabolise them rapidly to produce energy. As family income diminishes, so the amount of carbohydrate in the diet increases. Roughly half the energy requirements of the body are obtained from carbohydrates. Fats and carbohydrates are to some extent interchangeable, the latter being necessary for the proper metabolism of fats. Carbohydrates are stored in concentrated form, glycogen, in the liver and muscles and this can be rapidly broken down into glucose to provide energy in an emergency.

Mineral salts

Many different mineral salts are needed by the body including those given below.

Calcium is required for ossification, clotting of the blood and for regulating muscular contraction, especially of the heart muscle. The best sources of calcium are milk and cheese. Most vegetables and fruits contain satisfactory amounts. Note that meat, fish, sugars, fats and highly milled cereals are deficient in calcium. It is most important that the growing child has good supplies of calcium. If any child's intake of calcium is too low, osteoporosis, especially in females, is more likely to develop later in life (after the age of 60 years).

Phosphorus is also required for ossification and for the proper metabolism of fat. With the exception of butter and sugar, most foods are excellent sources of phosphorus.

Iron is required to form the haemoglobin of the blood. Only a few foods – egg yolk, liver, whole grains, beans, kale and some fruits – are satisfactory sources of iron. It is absent in butter and present in only very small quantities in milk.

Iodine is necessary for the proper functioning of the thyroid gland and for preventing goitre. Fish, milk, and leaf vegetables are good sources.

In addition, potassium, copper, magnesium, manganese, zinc, boron, fluorine, selenium, molybdenum are also required in minute traces. The function of many of these is obscure and they are often referred to as 'trace elements'.

Fibre

Fibre is the cellulose element in food and, in general, is not absorbed, being excreted in the stools (it forms the main bulk of bowel motions). Fibre is valuable for two reasons. Firstly it contains certain chemicals which are absorbed and which are very useful in fat metabolism. Provided that plenty of fibre is eaten, fats from dairy products are unlikely to increase the chance of ischaemic heart disease. Secondly, fibre is necessary for the satisfactory health of the large bowel (colon). In Third World countries where people have to take large quantities of fibre to obtain their proteins, diseases such as diverticulitis are unknown.

Fibre occurs naturally in salads, most vegetables (especially in their skins), fruit and wholemeal flour and brown bread. Many breakfast cereals are fortified with fibre in the form of bran.

Vitamins

These are organic compounds whose presence in small quantities is necessary for correct growth and health. Many different vitamins have been isolated but the most important are fat-soluble vitamins and water-soluble vitamins.

Fat-soluble vitamins

These include vitamins A, D and K. *Vitamin A* is present in many animal fats in liver, eggs, fish-liver oils, and is introduced into most butters and margarines. The yellow plant pigment carotene, which is found in green vegetables and carrots, is transformed into vitamin A by the body. Vitamin A deficiency causes a degeneration of surface epithelium which can lead to *night blindness* due to a deficiency of visual purple, *xerophthalmia* which is a drying and thickening of the cornea and later to *keratomalacia* which is a softening and inflammation of the cornea leading to opacity and blindness, and to *hyperkeratosis* of the skin. These conditions are rarely seen in the United Kingdom but are common in the Middle East.

Vitamin D is the vitamin which controls the deposition of calcium and phosphorus in bones. The best natural sources of vitamin D are cod and halibut liver oils, but the vitamin can be produced by the action of ultraviolet rays upon ergosterol. Vitamin D deficiency in infants leads to *rickets* and in adults to *osteomalacia*, a disease where, due to inadequate utilisation of calcium, there is a softening of the bones. This condition is endemic in underdeveloped countries and may affect pregnant and lactating women. It is extremely rare in European countries. Rickets has been largely eliminated from this country by the introduction of vitamin D fortification of margarine and butter and by ensuring that all babies are given vitamin drops.

Vitamin K is necessary for maintaining the prothrombin level of the blood and therefore for promoting clotting. It is synthesised by bacteria in the intestinal tract and also is present in many vegetables (spinach, cauliflower, cabbage, kale). Vitamin K deficiency is seen as a hypoprothrombinaemia in haemorrhagic disease of the newborn produced by a deficiency of intestinal synthesis of the vitamin.

Water-soluble vitamins

These include the *vitamin B complex* which contains at least four important factors – vitamin B_1 (thiamine), vitamin B_2 (riboflavin), nicotinic acid, and vitamin B_{12} (cyanocobalamin) – and *vitamin C*.

Vitamin B_1 (thiamine) is present in whole grain cereals and acute deficiency (*beri-beri*) is found in tropical countries. There are two forms, dry beri-beri characterised by a polyneuritis and wet beri-beri with cardiac failure. In the United Kingdom, *thiamine deficiency is usually seen in chronic alcoholics* who are taking a high carbohydrate diet with a very low intake of the vitamin. The symptoms usually are those of a peripheral neuritis.

Vitamin B_2 (riboflavin) is found in milk, eggs, liver and kidney. Deficiency of this vitamin shows itself as a dermatitis of the seborrhoeic type affecting the skin around the nose, mouth and ears. There may also be a sore tongue, an angular stomatis and vascularisation of the cornea which may eventually lead to a corneal opacity.

Nicotinic acid is found naturally in whole grain cereals excluding maize. Deficiency produces the clinical syndrome of *pellagra* seen in the maize-eating communities of eastern Europe and Asia. In the United Kingdom nicotinic acid deficiency is occasionally seen in conjunction with chronic alcoholism.

Vitamin B_{12} is found in whole grain cereals. A deficiency causes pernicious anaemia as, in the absence of Castle's intrinsic factor from the gastric secretion, vitamin B_{12} in the diet is not absorbed.

Vitamin C (ascorbic acid) is present in green vegetables, fresh fruit, oranges, tomatoes and blackcurrants. Note that milk, including human milk, is a very poor source. Deficiency leads to scurvy in which bleeding occurs in mucous membranes. Today, in the United Kingdom, vitamin C deficiency is occasionally seen in old people living on their own because often they neglect their diet, especially during the winter. Spontaneous haemorrhages appear, teeth may become loose and skin purpura may be present. Preventive measures include arranging a varied diet containing plenty of fresh vegetables and fruit. Because of the deficiency of this vitamin in milk *it is essential to give all babies, whether breast or bottle fed, vitamin C additives.* Convenient forms include orange juice or rose hip syrup.

Folic acid is a heat-sensitive vitamin that is easily destroyed by cooking. It is present in salad crops (lettuce), raw or lightly cooked vegetables, fortified breakfast cereals, bread, potatoes, fruit and nuts. Deficiencies can occur after an upper bowel obstruction, any haemolytic condition or after taking antifolate drugs such as the antibiotic trimethoprim. (See also pp. 73, 267 for the importance of adequate folate/folic acid in pregnancy.)

Calorie requirements of the diet

Every diet must contain a minimum quantity of protein (preferably first-class proteins) and a balance of carbohydrates and fats to give sufficient calories as well as adequate mineral salts and vitamins.

The calorie requirement of the body varies in men and women depending upon the energy needed for the performance of heavy work and to maintain body temperature, especially in cold climates. As a rough guide, a minimum daily calorie requirement for a person at rest is approximately 1400 to 1550 calories. For light work about 2000 to 2750 calories are needed and for heavy work approximately 3000 calories. In pregnancy, women usually require about 2500 calories daily and this must be increased to approximately 3000 calories during lactation.

About 300 calories come from the 70 g of protein in the diet. The balance is made up from both fats and carbohydrates and it is always best to ensure a balance of these in varied foods. In old age, calorie requirements are less.

Recent developments in the nutritional field

In 1991 an important report by the Committee on Medical Aspects of Food Policy (COMA) introduced a new approach to Dietary Reference Values. This extended the recommended values not only for micronutrients and protein and but also for those other components of the diet which contribute to dietary energy – the macronutrients fat and carbohydrate and also included for the first time the non-starch which makes up 'dietary fibre'.

At the same time COMA gave not just one figure but three figures in an attempt to represent more accurately for any population group the variation requirement of different individuals. These three groups are:

- the *Lower Reference Value* which would meet some people's needs;
- the *Estimated Average Requirement* for the group;
- the highest intake which some individuals might need (called the *Reference Nutritional Intake*).

It is hoped that this new classification will give a better indication of what might be required for an assessment and provision of diets and food supplies and also provide an improved basis for food labelling.

These new Dietary Reference Values will provide a better set of goals which should enable the Government and various commercial interests to work towards an improved common nutritional objective.

In the Department of Health's report *The Health of the Nation* published in 1992, it was proposed that a Nutritional Task Force should be created which would help to meet the nutritional elements of the target to reduce ischaemic heart disease and strokes These include:

- specific targets to reduce the contributions of total fat and of saturated fatty acids to food energy (by 12% and 35%, respectively);
- a substantial reduction in the amount of obesity in the UK;
- reduce the systolic blood pressure in the adult population by lowering the intake of sodium (mainly by reducing common salt intake).

Folic acid and the prevention of neural tube defects

In 1991 the Medical Research Council published the results of a study which showed that folic acid given to women who previously had had a baby with a neural tube defect such as spina bifida or anencephaly, gave a 72% protection against the recurrence of this congenital malformation in a subsequent pregnancy. The Chief Medical and Nursing Officers of the Department of Health immediately advised that any woman who had already had a child with such a neural tube defect should take 5 mg (or 4 mg if such a preparation became available) of supplementary folic acid daily *while she was planning to conceive and during the first 12 weeks of a pregnancy* (see Chapter 4).

Nutrition of elderly people

In 1992 the Department of Health published a report from the Committee on Medical Aspects of Food Policy on the *Nutrition of Elderly*

People. This report emphasised the need for a balanced diet and healthy eating and regular physical activity for elderly persons. It also stressed that, in elderly people, it is essential that food should always include an adequate intake of all nutrients, especially if the amount of food consumed begins to fall. It also pointed out that there is an increased risk of vitamin D deficiency in any old person who cannot go out of doors and that very old persons are very vulnerable to nutritional deficiencies, especially if they suffer from repeated episodes of ill health.

Food control

Many diseases that affect animals can also attack humans. The prevention of such illnesses depends on the care and control of food production and on the various inspections taking place to avoid contaminated food ever being eaten by humans.

Food inspection at ports

As much of the food in the United Kingdom is imported from abroad, careful inspection is made of all food arriving at the port of importation. Each consignment is inspected and sampled and can be imported only if the port health staff are satisfied as to its high standard.

All meat imported has to have a special certificate of purity from the country of origin and, in addition, is carefully examined by meat inspectors. If any disease is found, the complete carcass is given a very careful further examination. If the disease is only local, and the diseased portion can be completely removed, this is done. But, if the disease is widespread, the whole carcass is condemned and either has to be re-exported or destroyed, or stained and sent for animal foodstuff after complete sterilisation. Certain meats are prohibited meats and cannot be imported. These include the following:

- scrap meat which cannot be identified;
- meat comprising parts of the wall of the thorax or abdomen from which any part of pleura or peritoneum has been detached;
- meat, except mutton and lamb, from which a lymphatic gland has been removed;
- the head of an animal without a submaxillary gland.

Tinned goods are sampled and examined and a small sample is sent to a bacteriologist for a full and complete bacteriological examination to check on the sterility of the product. If the results are unsatisfactory, the whole consignment is condemned.

All types of foodstuffs are examined in the same careful way.

Meat inspection

Continuous meat inspection is undertaken on all meat produced and eaten in the United Kingdom. After slaughter in the abattoir a systematic and careful inspection of all carcasses is undertaken by specially trained inspectors. If any disease is found, it is dealt with in the same way as already described in port meat inspection.

Forty years ago *tuberculosis* was common in cattle in the United Kingdom. Although it is now rarely seen, it is still important to take steps to avoid meat infected with tuberculosis from ever coming into a kitchen. If this occurs infection is very likely as working surfaces, such as tables, will soon become contaminated. The pathogenic bacteria in the meat might be destroyed by heat in the cooking, but other foodstuffs would rapidly be infected via the contaminated working surfaces. The Aberdeen typhoid epidemic of 1964 was probably spread in this way – from a contaminated counter in a cooked meat department of a supermarket. For this reason, contaminated meat is only allowed to be used for animal foodstuffs provided it is sterilised and thoroughly stained with a dye to make such meat easily recognisable.

There are also a number of infectious conditions in animals which lead to the condemnation of the meat including various forms of *salmonellosis, septicaemia, anthrax, pyaemia* and *actinomycosis*.

Prevention of disease by control of milk supplies

Milk is a very important and essential part of our food supplies and forms the basis of all infant feeding. Milk supplies have always been particularly liable to lead to the spread of infectious disease for the following reasons:

- the cow may suffer from two diseases which can be passed on to humans via her milk – *tuberculosis* and *brucellosis*;
- milk supplies may be contaminated in the process of collecting and distributing milk. In the past, before modern clean methods of milk distribution were perfected, epidemics traced to such causes included *typhoid, paratyphoid, diphtheria, scarlet fever* and other *streptococcal infections, food poisoning, dysentery, gastroenteritis* and *brucellosis*.

It is now extremely rare for infection of any kind to be traced to milk. This improvement has resulted from two factors:

- a successful nationwide campaign to eradicate tuberculosis and other diseases from all dairy herds;

- the large scale pasteurisation of milk supplies and the use of other heat treatment methods (see below).

Pasteurisation of milk means the subjection of the milk to heat treatment for a specified time so that any live pathogenic or disease-producing bacteria are killed. The usual process of pasteurisation is the *High Temperature Short Time process* in which milk is retained at a temperature of not less than 71.5°C (161°F) for 15 seconds and then immediately cooled to a temperature of not more than 10°C (50°F). Immediately after pasteurisation the milk is bottled by machine and sealed so that no further chance of contamination can occur. Thus the milk is delivered to the householder completely safe and free from infection.

Sterilised milk is milk which has been filtered and homogenised, and then maintained at a temperature of not less than 100°C (212°F) for such a period as to comply with the turbidity test. In practice, after filtering and homogenising, the milk is poured into bottles and heated to 108°C (227°F) for 10–12 minutes.

Ultra-heat-treated (UHT) milk has been retained at a temperature of not less than 132°C (270°F) for a period of not less than one second, and then immediately placed in sterile containers in which it is supplied to the consumer.

As a further precaution, any person working in a dairy shop who develops a communicable disease must notify the local 'proper officer' who is generally the local Director of Public Health who can prohibit the sale of milk if it is likely to cause disease, until it has been heat-treated. There is also power to prohibit any person who is an open infectious case of tuberculosis from working in a dairy or milking cows on a farm.

Sampling to prevent adulteration of milk and food supplies

The possible adulteration of food supplies is very carefully guarded against by the continuous sampling of all foodstuffs. At the beginning of the century, there was widespread adulteration of food in the United Kingdom and this led to disease due both to dangerous additives to food and the lowering of nutritional value of some foods.

The adding of water to milk is fortunately easily detected by a test on the freezing point of milk – the adulterated milk has a higher freezing point. Sampling of milk supplies goes on all the time and very heavy penalties are given to the rare offenders.

Only very limited preservatives are allowed to be added to certain foods. As preservatives could mask staleness of food and encourage incorrect food storage, making food poisoning attacks more likely, it is illegal to add preservatives to the majority of foods, including all milk products. Examples of foods to which limited preservatives may be added are sausages, jams, and pickles.

Environmental health inspectors carry out sampling without warning, on shops and stores selling food, drugs and drink. Samples are tested for purity and for any evidence of adulteration. This constant vigilance has resulted in a very high standard being maintained in all food products, and cases of adulteration are very rare. Recently a few instances have been traced where items of food, particularly baby foods, have been intentionally adulterated with items like glass in a vindictive attempt to damage the reputation of major international firms. All parents should carefully examine baby foods and their packaging and immediately report anything suspicious.

Special precautions for special foodstuffs

Certain foodstuffs, for example shell-fish and ice cream, are particularly liable to contamination which may result in disease in humans, and special precautions are necessary to avoid this.

Shell-fish   Many shell-fish are eaten raw. For this reason, special precautions must be taken to ensure that shell-fish do not become contaminated with pathogenic bacteria. Unfortunately shell-fish can contain *typhoid* and *paratyphoid bacilli* if they have been collected from a sea-shore or sea which is grossly contaminated with sewage. A number of outbreaks of typhoid fever have been caused in this way.

Special regulations are enforced, preventing the collection of shell-fish from dangerously polluted beaches. Shell-fish can be purified by immersion in specially prepared tanks for two to three weeks.

Ice cream   Ice cream is particularly liable to spread infection because, although bacteria will not multiply at the low temperatures necessary for ice cream, the bacteria present in ice cream will be preserved at such temperatures. This means that a disease like *typhoid fever*, which can easily be spread by a tiny infecting dose, could be spread widely by ice cream which has become contaminated with typhoid bacilli. This is what happened in the Aberystwyth ice cream typhoid outbreak in 1945 when over 100 cases of typhoid occurred.

To prevent any possible recurrence, all *ice cream must, by law, now be pasteurised* and then cooled and left at a temperature not above 9.3°C (45°F) until frozen.

Special preventive measures relating to food handlers

Under various Food Hygiene Regulations special precautions must be taken by all food handlers in shops and stalls to avoid spreading disease. These include the following precautions:

- steps must be taken to avoid food becoming contaminated – food must be covered, protected from flies and contact with the public;
- no open food – that is food not in a tin or jar – must be placed lower than 18 inches (45 cm) from the ground;
- anybody handling food must keep their person and clothes clean;
- any open cut or abrasion must be covered by a waterproof dressing to avoid staphylococcal lesions in whitlows, boils, etc. from contaminating food and causing food poisoning;
- all food handlers must refrain from spitting and smoking;
- all wrapping paper must be clean – newspapers are not allowed except for uncooked vegetables;
- any food handler who becomes aware that he or she is suffering from *typhoid* or *paratyphoid fever, salmonella* infection, *dysentery* or *staphylococcal* infection, must notify the 'local Director of Public Health.

In addition there are widespread regulations about food premises, all designed to reduce the chance of infection. These include regulations about the provisions of washing facilities with hot and cold water, and working surfaces to prevent accumulation of bacteria in cracks on unsuitable types of surfaces. Standards are also laid down for the construction of premises and the temperature at which foods may be stored.

Further regulations concern many aspects of the transport and handling of foodstuffs.

Environmental health

Housing and town planning

The house a person lives in has an important influence upon that individual's life and well-being. It also has a significant effect upon health.

A satisfactory house must reach certain physical standards, such as being free from dampness, being well lighted and ventilated, having reliable heating preferably which is automatic, having a proper water system including hot water system and bath, an adequate internal toilet, sinks and proper drainage system, adequate means for preparing, storing and cooking food. These physical standards are invariably found in modern houses, but some older houses, especially in industrial areas, lack some of them.

The house must also be suitable for the family living there – not only must it be large enough, but it should be sited in an attractive way not being too close to other houses, and form an integral part of a group of houses or area. No family living in an inadequate house will be able to enjoy life completely. Nor will all the families of a large area be able to live properly unless all the necessary community services – shops, churches, schools, doctors' houses, health centres and hospitals, community centres, cinemas, etc. – are present. In communities such as a country town which has developed over many years, often centuries, all such facilities will usually be present, having been added to the community gradually.

It is in the area which has developed quickly in which many of these facilities are missing. Examples include 'slum' areas and some new housing estates.

It is now known that it is best to plan a whole neighbourhood unit in all urban development. Developments should not be too large, and a neighbourhood unit for about 10 000 persons is considered ideal. Within such a development not only should the necessary houses be built but essential services such as shops, schools, churches, community centres, library, police station, clinics, health centres etc. should be provided.

Effects of bad housing on health

What effect does poor housing have upon the health of those living in it? It is not difficult to demonstrate that the health of people living in poor housing areas is inferior to those living in good areas. There is a greater amount of communicable disease present and, when the children develop the usual childhood diseases, there is a higher incidence of complications. Overcrowding, which is usually present in poor housing and living conditions leads to a greater spread of communicable diseases. Unsuitable housing makes the individual more liable to disease, as the incidence of infection is more likely, rather than actually producing disease.

Many poor houses are damp – either from defective roofs or gutters allowing rain water to enter the house, or by rising dampness percolating upwards from the ground, due to the absence of a dampproof course. Damp living conditions lead to an exacerbation of various *rheumatic problems* so commonly found later in life, a *higher child mortality*, and a greater incidence of serious chest conditions such as *acute bronchitis*. Such conditions also aggravate *chronic bronchitis* in the elderly. Dampness always has a most *depressing effect* on the occupants of the home, who see their efforts at redecoration ruined, and leads to much unhappiness and aggravation of minor mental and emotional disorders.

The overcrowding effect of poor housing has a stultifying effect upon the proper development of the family. No family can hope to reach its full potential in such conditions and families give up because the effort to overcome the difficulties becomes too great. The extra strain of looking after a child with learning difficulties (mental handicap) in such conditions is tremendous and is always difficult. Poor housing cannot be said to be a cause of mental illness but it certainly is a contributory factor and has a very bad and often disastrous effect on the mentally ill person living there. Even after the acute state of the mental illness has passed, unsatisfactory home conditions can retard recovery.

The *level of accidents* both in children and old persons is much higher in those living in poor houses. This is due to bad lighting and steep unsuitable stairs which predispose to accidents resulting from falls. Overcrowding is also associated with an increased number of scalds and burns.

Poor housing conditions not only predispose the individual to attacks of some diseases but may also be an important factor in the correct management of illness. A patient with angina of effort or a chronic cardiac condition must be able to avoid stairs. In a modern house, it is usually possible to arrange this by turning a downstairs room into a temporary bedroom and this works quite well, especially if there is a downstairs lavatory. But in a poor house, this would be impossible and the management of such a case is made difficult. Either the patient would have to climb steep stairs or stay permanently upstairs; there is also the complication that there is not usually an inside lavatory. In such a house, the management of various forms of malignant disease is made very difficult. A case of a person with a colostomy, for instance, will produce many extra problems in the absence of a bathroom, internal lavatory and proper washing facilities.

Local authorities realise the importance of doing all they can to provide good houses. It is usual for the housing authority to give special priority for urgent housing for really important medical reasons, so that the effect of poor housing on health can be minimised. Tuberculosis infection can be prevented by the rapid rehousing of a patient's family if they are living in an overcrowded house.

Methods of dealing with unsatisfactory houses

Unsatisfactory houses can be dealt with in a number of ways:

- slight defects can be put right by serving an abatement notice on the owner;
- individual unfit houses can be demolished or repaired;
- houses or parts of houses may be closed;
- large Clearance Areas can be defined. This is the usual method used for large scale slum clearance. The Department of the Environment holds a local inquiry where the council has to provide

public evidence of unfitness of houses and where owners can bring their own evidence;
● houses in multiple occupation can be controlled;
● special measures can be used to improve houses.

All these methods are used by the environmental health inspectors who are responsible for this work.

Atmospheric pollution and health

Although the control of atmospheric pollution has improved markedly in recent years many large cities and towns, especially those in industrial areas, had, in the past, their atmosphere constantly polluted by smoke and other fumes in the air. It is known that the health of the people living in such areas was affected by this atmospheric contamination.

Atmospheric pollution is probably a small factor in the production of lung cancer, for it is known that the level of lung cancer is higher in industrial areas than in country areas. It is a minor problem compared with cigarette smoking, but it is a factor.

However, the most serious danger to health occurs in those unfortunate people who have some degree of *chronic bronchitis* and *emphysema*. Many of these are elderly and their respiratory and cardiac function is impaired. The British climate, with its damp misty winter days, always tends to make such patients worse but really serious medical problems arise when atmospheric pollution in the form of a smoky fog (smog) occurs.

To such patients even minor pollution increases their symptoms while a major fog, lasting a few days, often brings them very near complete collapse. For instance, in the historic smog of London in December 1952, it is estimated that just under 4000 patients with chronic bronchitis died. The inhalation of smoky particles and/or sulphur gases commonly present in industrial areas both play a part in aggravating the chronic bronchitic's condition.

Since the Clean Air Act came into force in 1956, local authorities have progressed towards the ideal of clearing the atmosphere of much of its pollution. It was hoped to achieve this by two means:

● preventing the building of any new factory plant unless its means of producing heat or power are completely smokeless. Prior approval of all such plans must be given by local authorities before any building construction can start;
● introducing smoke control areas in which it is an offence to produce any smoke at all or to burn ordinary coal. Before any part of a town can be made such an area, all the houses must have cooking

and heating methods which are smokeless. This may mean replacing old grates with modern ones capable of burning smokeless fuel. A more satisfactory method is to change to other forms of power such as oil, gas or electricity.

Control of water supplies

In the United Kingdom the control of water supplies, their purification and cleanliness has been so reliable that one hardly considers that this is an important health safeguard. The disastrous epidemic of typhoid in Zermatt, in Switzerland, in 1963 provides a reminder of the dangers which face any population which ignores stringent high safety standards.

There are two bacterial diseases easily spread by water – *typhoid fever* and *cholera*. Cholera is a disease, seen mainly in the East, which can spread because of grossly inadequate water and sewage systems. Its epidemic spread today in this country is virtually impossible.

However typhoid fever could quite easily be spread by water unless constant care is taken to ensure that the purification of water is complete. This entails the following measures:

- storage of water in reservoirs;
- filtration of water;
- sterilisation of water using chlorine to make certain that any bacteria not removed by filtration are killed.

In addition, great care is always needed to make certain that no employee in a water works contaminates the supply. In particular, *it is essential to make certain that no typhoid carriers are ever employed in a water works*. Careful medical tests including agglutination blood tests are carried out on all such employees to reduce the chance of a carrier not being detected among the staff of the water works. The last serious water-borne outbreak of typhoid fever in this country was in Croydon in 1937 when 290 cases of typhoid fever occurred. It was caused by a urinary carrier contaminating the water supply while he assisted in work on a deep well forming part of Croydon's water supply.

Very high standards are maintained in the water supplies in this country and further large-scale outbreaks of water-borne typhoid are most unlikely to occur. The most vulnerable supplies are probably some country ones especially during the crowded holiday months of July and August. Constant sampling of all water supplies is an extra safeguard.

Skin contact with water contaminated with rats' urine can lead to the development of leptospirosis (see p. 167).

The freedom of infection from water supplies in this country is no guide to the hazards of many foreign countries. Many cases of typhoid occur each year in travellers who have visited the Indian subcontinent, Italy, Spain and North Africa especially when these visitors have stayed in remote country areas or have taken camping holidays. If such a holiday is planned, it is essential either to (i) sterilise all water with a simple camp sterilisation outfit; or (ii) be protected with a course of TAB inoculation before starting. This protects against typhoid fever and paratyphoid fever (see pp. 136–7).

Fluoridation of water supplies

It is known that the variation in dental caries found in different areas is connected with the content of natural fluoride in the water consumed by the people of that area (see p. 114).

In localities where the natural fluoride content of the water supply is low, fluoride can be added to the water supply to bring the level to about one part of fluoride per million parts of water. This has been done in many parts of the world and has always been followed by a substantial reduction in the amount of dental caries in the children in that area. After pilot trials, the Department of Health has advised that all water supplies should have fluoride added to them where the natural supply of fluoride is deficient. It is known that if this is done, there should be a reduction of at least 60% in the dental caries. A number of areas have already introduced artificial fluoridation.

In 1991 the results of the Third Decennial Adult Dental Health Survey of the United Kingdom were published. They showed there had been steady and substantial improvements in the 10 years 1978–88. The proportion of adults with some natural teeth rose from 70% to 79% and by the year 2008 it is likely to reach 90%. From 1978 to 1988 the number of decayed teeth fell by 36% despite a population growth of 11%. The most dramatic improvements were in young adults.

A considerable proportion of this improvement is probably due to increased fluoridation of water supplies.

15 The structure of the social services

The 'social services' in the UK cover many different types of services which mainly fall into three well-defined groups:

- *personal social services* which are provided by *large local authority social service departments* – in the metropolitan districts in the large conurbations or in the London boroughs and in the county councils in the rest of England and Wales (see Fig. 15.2, p. 287). These services include a wide range of statutory, community and residential services for children, physically disabled, mentally disordered (the mentally ill and those with learning disabilities), homeless and elderly persons. All the hospital social services are also provided by these social service departments in local authorities although such work is entirely undertaken within the hospitals. These types of services are described in Chapters 15–22. Centrally these services are the responsibility of the Secretary of State for Health and the Department of Health;
- the *probation and aftercare service* which is attached to the courts and works mainly with adult offenders who, as part of their sentence, are placed on probation. In addition, much of the aftercare work for discharged prisoners is undertaken by this service. Note that most of the aftercare work with juvenile offenders (delinquent children) is carried out by the local authority *social service departments* (see Chapter 15). The probation service is quite separate from the local authority services and, like the prison service, is centrally the responsibility of the Home Secretary and the Home Office;
- *voluntary bodies*. There are many well-established voluntary bodies providing social services of all kinds on a national and local basis. They include many specialist organisations working with children such as the National Society for the Prevention of Cruelty to Children (NSPCC), Barnardo's, National Children's Homes and the Family Welfare Association. There are many groups dealing with all aspects of elderly persons' services such as Age Concern. In the field of services for disabled persons there are many specialist bodies including the Central Council for the Disabled

and the British Council for the Rehabilitation of the Disabled. In addition, there are large numbers of voluntary bodies working in the field of blind and deaf persons, with spastics, with people with epilepsy, etc. Then there are the voluntary organisations dealing with those who are mentally disordered (mentally ill people) and those with learning disabilities (formerly called mentally handicapped). Locally, Councils of Social Service and Rural Community Councils undertake a coordinating role in respect of many small voluntary bodies or local branches of the large national organisations;

- nationally the government department which is mainly responsible for voluntary bodies is the Department of Health, and in some instances this department encourages voluntary work in the field of social care by providing small grants to voluntary bodies especially in respect of research and experimental schemes. Examples of such grants include financial help provided in this way to reduce and to prevent alcohol abuse;

- a further example of voluntary work is the service provided by the Citizens' Advice Bureaux. These services first came into existence in the 1939–45 war to help with various queries about rationing and missing relatives, etc. Their role has now been widened to include *consumer protection, explanation of various pension rights and the provision of legal advice.* They are particularly valuable in helping families who are unwilling to seek help from the statutory services (such as the local authority Social Service Departments) because perhaps they may feel aggrieved for some reason – they may have been evicted for rent arrears or are generally resentful of the way they have been treated in the past by the local authority or other statutory services. For this reason, some local authority Social Service Committees give small financial grants to the local Citizens' Advice Bureaux to enable them to continue to help clients who would otherwise be unlikely to seek help. Centrally there is a National Association of Citizens' Advice Bureaux linked to the local bureaux by a regional committee.

Central Government control of local authority social services

In England the main Government department concerned is the Department of Health and the Secretary of State for Health is responsible for all the social services. As this minister is also responsible for all the health services and is a full member of the Cabinet, such an arrangement helps to achieve a coordinated central policy for both the social services and for all the health services. In Wales the Secretary of State for Wales is responsible and the main Government department (the Welsh Office) is based in Cardiff. In Scotland the local authority departments are called Departments of Social Work and the Government minister is the Secretary of State for Scotland with the main Department again in charge of both the health and social services (the Scottish Office) situated in Edinburgh.

The role of the Department of Health in controlling social services is similar to that already described for the health services (see p. 2). The Department of Health is primarily concerned in assisting the development of social services in three main ways:

- *advisory*. From time to time important advisory memoranda on various social services are issued by the Department of Health. These deal with every aspect of the personal social services including the balance between community-based and residential services;
- *policy and planning*. Policy and planning of the social services is an essential function of the Department of Health as it helps to achieve a coordinated approach of both the health and social services. An excellent example is in the case of mentally ill persons now being cared for in mental hospitals. The aim in the future is that many of these people will be able to be discharged from hospital into the community, but this will only be possible if there is a parallel development of community social services to carry on supervising them and, in some instances providing the homes to look after them. In practice this means more day care provision will be required as well as an increase in hostels and homes. Special financial arrangements have been made by the Department of Health to enable social service departments to provide these extra services by transferring money from the health services to the social services (see p. 282). The central structure of the Department of Health is organised to ensure there is integration of planning between the social and health services;
- *financial*. This is another important indirect method of control of the social services. Special financial allocation is made by the Government (acting on the advice of the Secretary of State) in the *block grant* which is paid to local authorities so that social and other services can be maintained. The costs of the day-to-day social services (*revenue costs*) is financed by:
  — the block grant;
  — the council tax.

Community care

The biggest change in the organisation of local authority social services since 1991 has been the introduction of much extended and wider community care services. In 1986, Sir Roy Griffiths began a comprehensive review of all forms of community care on behalf of the Secretary of State for Health and his report, in 1988, was called *Community Care: An Agenda for Action*. The main objective of these changes has been to ensure that the personal social services run by local authorities kept up with the reforms and objectives of the NHS. Since 1991 both services have increasingly concentrated on providing help and assistance to families and individuals in their own homes and within the local community as far as possible.

This process was started in 1989 when the government published an important White Paper on community services entitled 'Caring for People: Community Care in the Next Decade and Beyond'. This publication identified six key policy objectives:

- to promote the development of domiciliary, day and respite services to enable people to live in their own homes wherever feasible and sensible;
- to ensure that those providing services make practical support for carers a high priority;
- to make proper assessment of need and good care management the cornerstone of high quality community care;
- to promote the development of a flourishing independent sector alongside good quality public services;
- to clarify the responsibilities of agencies and so make it easier to hold them to account for their performance;
- to secure better value for taxpayers by introducing a new funding structure for social care in the community.

The National Health Service and Community Care Act 1990 passed legislation which brought into effect the various reforms of the NHS as outlined in Chapter 1 and also outlined a programme of changes in the procedures and financial grants which were to be introduced into the local authority social services to strengthen and extend them so that the above objectives could be achieved.

Gradually, from 1991 to 1993, the following changes have been introduced into local authority personal social services:

- the establishment of new methods of inspection and checking of standards by introducing *quality assurance units* into social service departments which should ensure as far as possible a constantly high standard of community services whether these are run by local authorities, voluntary bodies or by the private sector;
- the introduction of new *specific financial grants* by the Government to make certain that some special financial provisions are transferred from the NHS to local authorities when mentally

disordered patients who previously had been cared for permanently in mental hospitals move out of them to live in special hostels or homes in the community. The original Griffiths report recommended that such specific grants should be be made available to meet a significant proportion of the cost of most community care programmes for a wide range of clients but this was not agreed by the Government, who limited the use of specific grants to:

— the care of mentally ill patient (at the 70% rate);
— local funding of voluntary bodies providing a service for drug and/or alcohol abusers;
— increasing the grants for the training of social service staff by 25–30%.

From 1992 to 1993 the detailed planning of these changes took place between the local health authorities and the local authorities supplying personal social services locally.

The final stage which was introduced in April 1993 was to transfer from the Department of Social Security to local authorities in charge of the personal social services the responsibility for paying financial grants to assist persons living in voluntary and private elderly persons' homes and others such as those who are physically or mentally disordered who live in homes or hostels. A large block grant to meet these costs is now made directly to the local authority who then must administer this financial assistance.

It is hoped that these changes will ensure that the private residential provision for elderly persons as well as the local authorities' own forms of residential care will in future develop logically and complement each other to provide the best possible care in the community.

These detailed changes have carefully been planned by the local health authorities working very closely with the local authorities in the Joint Care Planning Committees (see p. 13). In 1992–3 the Government reminded local authorities that there were eight key tasks to be accomplished:

- agreeing the basis for the required assessment systems for individuals in need;
- clarifying and agreeing for continuing care for new residents in residential and nursing homes, including making arrangements for respite care when needed (note that in future as already mentioned local authorities will monitor private nursing homes as well as elderly persons' homes and hostels);
- ensuring the robustness and mutual acceptability of discharge arrangements;
- clarifying the roles of general practitioners and primary health care teams in community care programmes;

- ensuring that adequate purchasing and charging arrangements are in place in respect of individuals receiving residential or nursing care;
- ensuring that staff are suitably trained – wherever possible on a joint basis;
- ensuring that financial and management systems can meet the new demands after April 1993;
- informing the public of the arrangements made by the local authority for assessment and provision of community care.

Structure of local authority social services

Because of the National Health Service and Community Care Act 1990 local authorities have altered many of their management structures to meet their new responsibilities. There has been generally a need to divide the staff of social service departments into two divisions:

- *those who provide services* (*the providers*) – this group will include staff running various residential homes for persons in need such as children's homes, those for physically disabled people, homes for mentally disabled persons, day centres of all types, day nurseries, workshops, home helps, meals and transport services;
- *those who purchase these services* – these are mainly the social workers and other professional staff who assess the needs of individuals, sort out priorities and then arrange for the required services to be provided. This division is referred to as '*the purchasers*' as it arranges which service is needed and transfers the cost to those providing the care whether this is carried out within the social service department itself or by voluntary bodies or in the private sector.

The new management structure of local authority social services now has many similarities when compared with the management in the reformed NHS (see pp. 5, 6) – in both there is a distinction between those who are providing services and those who require them.

In the social service field the providers are now especially to be found in the private and voluntary sectors (this is most obvious in the residential field). To some extent local authority social service departments will act in the future in both capacities as purchasers and providers (as for the time being do District Health Authorities with hospital provision to the NHS) but their more important function will eventually be as purchasers. The crucial role of quality assurance will clearly become a top priority for them as will also the setting and controlling of standards of community care.

The detailed organisation of a social service department varies according to the type (conurbation, town or country area) but generally they are now arranged into various divisions as illustrated in Fig. 15.1). Note that there are two main methods locally of supplying social community care – by purchasing the services and by providing that care directly. The 'purchasers' are all centred in the social services department (with the assistance of financial specialists from the local authority's treasurers department) but the 'providers' are shared between the private sector, various voluntary organisations and directly by parts of the social services department.

Within the purchasing division, there are three important sections:

- *social workers and other professional staff* who are the main point of contact with members of the public requiring social care. In most social service departments there are various teams of social workers covering areas or districts usually working from small centres within the area or district. These teams assess the services required and then arrange for their provision either directly by other sections of the department or by voluntary bodies or private organisations;
- *a quality assurance unit* which concentrates upon ensuring high standards of care. This section of the department is responsible for assessing standards of care both in the private and voluntary sectors and also checks those social services which the department directly provides (such as the care in their own elderly persons' homes). There is particular emphasis on those who are carrying out quality assurance work to do it in an *entirely independent manner* – 'at arms' length' to quote government guidance – so that a quite separate administration is set up within each social services department to carry this out. The introduction of quality assurance to check constantly the standards and levels of social care in the community both in services provided directly by the department and within the voluntary and private sectors should assist in more cooperation between all who are responsible for community care and at the same time improve overall standards;
- a *financial section* which has the responsibility of negotiating contracts for community care which is to be provided either in the private or voluntary sectors (specialist officers from the local authority's treasurer's department are attached to this section to assist with this task). A further responsibility of this section is to manage and distribute the large sum of money now entrusted to the local authority from the Department of Social Security to subsidise the large numbers of elderly persons living in privately managed homes. By introducing this system, the government is hoping that there will evolve a better system of meeting the ever-increasing need for residential accommodation as the numbers of

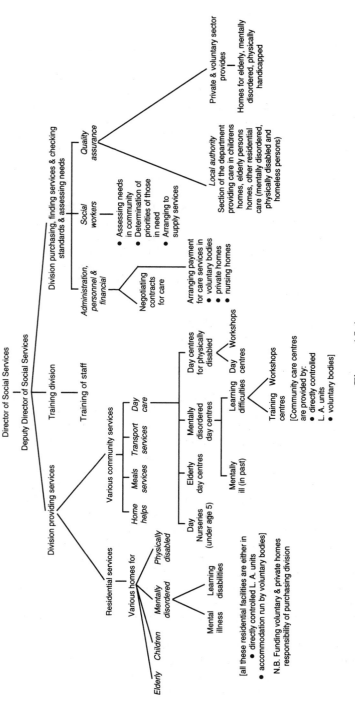

Figure 15.1

very old persons in the community rise rapidly in the next two decades (see p. 372).

Types of social services provided by local authorities

Each major local authority must have a Social Services Committee to control its social services (the full list is given below), and must appoint a Director of Social Services who is the chief officer in charge of the Department of Social Services which administers all the services.

Local authority social services are run by the County Councils in England and Wales, by the Metropolitan District Councils within the large conurbations of West Midlands, Greater Manchester, West Yorkshire, South Yorkshire and Tyneside, and by the London Boroughs in London (see Fig. 15.2). In Scotland the departments are called Social Work Departments and are controlled by the Regional Local Authorities. In Northern Ireland there is a unified structure, which is outside local political control, which deals with the social services and all the health services. There are four Boards set up to administer the local social and health services (see Chapter 1, p. 29).

The following is a summary of the types of social services provided either directly by the social services department or by voluntary or private organisations:

- *all child care services*. These include child care protection and all connected services, and acceptance of parental responsibility for children committed to the care of the local authority because their parents for any reason either cannot or are not capable of looking after their children themselves. The service also undertakes preventive work with children and their families. A wide network of family placements is arranged in which a child is cared for in a family environment (see Chapter 15);
- *prevention and treatment of child abuse* (see Chapter 16);
- *day care for children under 5 years of age*. This includes day nurseries, playgroups and child minders many of whom are provided by private or voluntary organisations;
- *care for the mentally disabled* including those who have had mental illness and those with learning difficulties. All types of community services are provided – community day centres, training centres, workshops and specialised housing. Some of these, especially in the housing field, are provided in the voluntary and private sectors (see Chapter 19);
- *care of elderly persons* within the community – this includes all the field work services which are available in the community and the provision of all forms of residential care. Although all social

Fig. 15.2 Social Services Authorities, England.

services still provide directly a considerable amount of elderly persons' homes, the majority are now provided privately – there has been a marked increase in private homes for elderly persons since 1990 (see Chapter 20, Table 20.2);

- *provision of home helps and good neighbours* (see Chapter 21);
- *provision of meals services* either to the home of a person (meals on wheels) or in various luncheon clubs. These are services in which voluntary groups play an important part;

- *care of unsupported mothers.* This is another area where voluntary bodies play a significant part in some authorities (see Chapter 21);
- *work in the field of alcohol and drug abuse.* Once again voluntary organisations are very active in this work (see Chapter 22);
- *the provision of hospital social workers* stationed and working in the hospitals.

Training of social workers

The standards of training of social workers is the responsibility of the Central Council for Education and Training in Social Work (CCETSW). This Council is responsible for the promotion of training in all fields of social work. Training to be a social worker usually involves 2 years' academic work and is carried out in universities and commercial colleges. Each social services department should have a training unit and special training officers.

There is also a National Institute of Social Work based in London.

Liaison between the health and social services

Many of the social services in the local authority represent the main supporting services within the community for persons recovering from illness or suffering from some chronic disabling condition. Many of the necessary aids, gadgets or adaptations for disabled persons which are so essential for the successful rehabilitation of many disabling conditions (e.g. arthritis, paraplegia, multiple sclerosis and spasticity) are supplied by local social service departments.

The closest liaison must therefore be developed and maintained. The extended community care initiative described earlier in this chapter also requires good cooperation between the health and social services. This is particularly the case in the following:

- *mentally ill persons* who have spent long periods in mental hospitals. Under the special financial grant arrangements now made for this class of patient, at least 70% of the cost of maintaining them in the community by the local authority either in their own accommodation or in residential care provided by a voluntary organisation or privately will be transferred from the NHS to help to establish community care;
- *drug abuse patients and/or alcohol-dependent patients* being treated in hospitals may also be eligible for special financial grants;
- *elderly persons* who represent an ever-increasing number of patients using hospital services. Special grants do not apply for this group, however, their successful rehabilitation back into their

own homes after accidents and severe illnesses which have resulted in a lengthy hospital stay depends a great deal on the coordination between the local hospital and social services, as most of these persons will require much supportive help, meals provision and many forms of day care (see Chapter 20).

The closest liaison between the two services must therefore be developed and maintained. On the health side, a community physician is usually appointed with responsibility for liaison – sometimes called a Specialist in Community Medicine (Social Services) – and on the social services side a senior officer is appointed to take charge of the hospital social work services and to be responsible for integration.

Local arrangements should be made to assist day-to-day cooperation. Social workers should visit health centres and group practices from time to time so that they can meet not only the general practitioners but also the health visitors, practice nurses, district/community nurses and other staff there.

There should also be working links created between social workers and the hospital services through the permanent medical social workers at all hospitals and especially at geriatric and mental hospitals.

The locally designated community physician responsible for coordination acts as medical advisor to the social services department and consequently becomes acquainted with all the medical problems of that department. It is particularly important that practice nurses and health visitors work closely with social workers for many of the problems they both deal with are also important to the social services department and vice versa. Both find themselves working with difficult 'problem families' but each deals with different aspects – the health visitor and practice nurse from the preventive health viewpoint while the social worker deals with various social difficulties. This coordination is especially important in preventing and in treating child abuse.

In child abuse (see Chapter 17) the closer the two groups work together, the better will be the results. Case conferences to consider individual cases should always be arranged in all instances for such meetings enable sound links to be forged between social services and the health, education, probation, police and voluntary bodies. As explained in Chapter 17, it is only by improving cooperation between all these services that mistakes will be avoided.

16   Care of children in need

All local authorities, through their Social Services Committees and departments, have special responsibilities for providing child care services for supervising and looking after children and young persons under the age of 18 years. In much of this work the social services department is attempting to find the best possible alternative arrangement for care of the child in the absence of the parents – either because the parents have abandoned the child, the child is an orphan, or because the parents have been found incapable of looking after the child properly. Every attempt is made in trying *to settle the child in a suitable family placement in order to provide the child with as normal a home as possible*. For this reason, large institutional homes are no longer used.

Special help is given to parents who, because of social reasons, cannot look after their children during the daytime. Most of this help is given in day nurseries or day care centres, playgroups or with a child minder.

Day nurseries and day care centres

Day nurseries are provided by Social Service Departments to help care for young children when this care cannot be provided at home due to social circumstances. Such reasons would include sudden illness of the mother leading to her admission to hospital, a single mother who has to go out to work to support her family, or a widower or widow with a small child.

Under the Children Act 1989, the duties of local authorities have been extended and they must now provide day care and supervised activities for preschool children and for school aged children outside school hours and in the holidays for children in need: Such children are defined in the Act as 'children who need services to secure a reasonable standard of health and development' and includes children who are disabled. In future all social service departments, together with the local authority education department, must publish a review of these services every three years.

Day nurseries look after children from a few weeks old up to the age of five years when they can go to school. In some cases, the need for care is temporary while an acute social crisis occurs in the family. It is usual for about 50 children to be looked after in each nursery. 'Family groups' are set up in each nursery so that about ten children are looked after together covering an age range from six months to five years. Babies under six months of age are looked after separately.

Each nursery has a trained matron and deputy matron plus a number of trained nursery nurses. The staff are responsible for all aspects of care of the children including their health which must be carefully supervised. Special attention is paid to ensure that:

● every child is fit when admitted;
● every child is fully immunised; and that
● any case of communicable disease is immediately investigated.

Dysentery or gastro-enteritis can be particularly serious if they spread in a day nursery (see p. 162) and any child with diarrhoea must be sent home until all bacteriological tests are normal.

Day nurseries are being increasingly used for young handicapped children (with various disabling conditions e.g. spina bifida) to help with their development. It is best if such children are looked after in ordinary day nurseries rather than being segregated in a special nursery. Where a day nursery has a number of handicapped children it will be necessary to employ larger numbers of staff. Nursery nurses qualify after a two year course and by gaining the certificate of the Nursery Nurses Examination Board.

Private day nurseries, playgroups and child minders

Many private day nurseries, playgroups and child minders look after children and each Local Authority, through its Social Services Committee, is responsible for ensuring that proper standards of staff, fire precautions and accommodation are provided. Each such unit must be registered with the Local Authority and inspected from time to time to check that the correct standards are being maintained. All people caring for more than one child in their own home, whether for profit or not, must be registered with the local authority.

Since 1989, the number of children looked after in registered private day nurseries has increased substantially, by nearly 71%. There has been a smaller increase in the numbers attending registered private playgroups and child minders and in children under the age of 5 years attending school either full or part time. Over the same period, there has been a decrease of 7% in the numbers of children attending local authority day nurseries (see Table 16.1).

The large increase in the use of private day nurseries is a reflection of the 'market influence' introduced in community care. It has meant that

Table 16.1   Numbers on registers of day nurseries, playgroups, child minders and nursery education for children under the age of 5 years in England 1989–92

	1991	1992	1993
LA day nurseries	30 302 (3.8%)	28 400 (3.5%)	27 100 (3.1%)
LA playgroups	2589 (0.3%)	1600 (0.1%)	1600 (0.1%)
Reg. day nurseries	77 092 (9.6%)	91 600 (11.1%)	111 000 (12.6%)
Reg. playgroups	420 526 (52.2%)	409 800 (50.6%)	394 400 (44.9%)
Reg. child minders	233 272 (28.8%)	254 300 (30.7%)	300 800 (34.4%)
Pupils in nursery schools	42 101 (5.2%)	42 158 (5.1%)	43 635 (4.9%)

(From Health and Social Services Statistics, Dep. of Health, 1994.)

social service departments had to increase their methods of ensuring that the correct standards of care are maintained (quality assurance). Most social service departments now have efficient sections dealing with this essential work (see p. 284).

Child care services

These services primarily look after children who need care and protection because of the neglect, abandonment or inability of the parents to cope due to some sudden emergency (illness, separation, etc.) or exposure to moral danger. The Children Act 1989, identifies the type of children (called children in need) for whom the local authorities' child care services are designed. A child is considered to be in need if any of the following situations arise:

- if the child is unlikely to achieve or maintain, or have the opportunity of achieving or maintaining, a reasonable standard of health or development without the provision of the services of the local authority;
- if the health or development of the child is likely to be significantly impaired, or further impaired, without the provision of such services for the child;
- if the child is disabled.

The Children Act 1989 defines a child as disabled 'if he or she is blind, deaf or dumb, or suffers from a mental disorder of any kind or is substantially or permanently handicapped by illness, injury or congenital deformity or such other disability as may be prescribed'.

In all cases the first consideration is *the need to safeguard and promote the welfare of the child.* Every social services department must investigate fully each case which comes to their knowledge. Social workers undertake this inquiry.

The Children Act 1989 simplified existing child care legislation in the United Kingdom and has introduced some very important changes. The basis of the Act is the principle that children generally are best looked after within the family with both parents playing a full part and, if possible, without resort to legal proceedings. This principle is expressed in the Act by the following:

- a new concept of *'parental responsibility'* (replacing 'parental rights');
- the ability of unmarried fathers to share that responsibility by agreement with the mother;
- local authorities now have a duty to give support for children and their families;
- local authorities now have a duty to return a child who is being looked after by them to his or her family unless this is against the child's interests;
- for a child who is looked after, away from home, by the local authorities they now have a duty to ensure contact between the child and his or her parents whenever possible.

Parental responsibility

In the past, child care law spoke of 'parental rights' where a child taken into care had the parental rights transferred to the local authority. The Children Act 1989 abolishes this arrangement. In the future, whenever a child is taken into care permanently, the local authority will accept parental responsibility. All decisions about parental authority must be made by the courts (Magistrate, County or High Courts, depending on the complexity of the case). It is not possible, as formerly, for a local authority to assume parental responsibility as this question must be determined by the Court. This allows maximum opportunity for decisions to be challenged, questioned and properly discussed.

Parental responsibility will be conferred on both parents if they are married and on the mother if not. A father who is not married to the child's mother may acquire parental responsibility if the mother agrees. If both parents are in agreement, this can be done by a simple agreement and without going to Court.

Children away from home

When the local authority has to arrange for a child to live away from home (for any period) because the natural parents are unable to look after him or her properly or need respite, it is preferable that *voluntary arrangements* be made. In such instances, the parents retain their parental responsibility and act as partners with the local authority or with those caring for their child. The parents should participate in the child's care and in decisions made, and they should also retain contact so that the child can return to them as soon as possible.

All administrative measures to exercise compulsion on a child being looked after, whether to limit contact with a parent or to prevent the parent recovering the child, are abolished by the Children Act 1989. The Act also now recognises that *a child's racial origin, culture and language are important factors* to be taken into consideration by the local authority looking after the child.

Every local authority must prepare the child for the time he or she leaves school until the age of 21 years. A *complaints procedure* must be introduced by every local authority and must contain an independent element.

The child's interests are paramount

This overriding principle which has been an important benchmark in all child care since 1976 has been further strengthened by the Children Act 1989, which contains a checklist of matters to be considered in all Court proceedings. Heading this list is the fact that the Court must have regard to the child's wishes and feelings. With the Court's permission, a child may seek a Court Order about his or her future.

In local authority proceedings, such as the application for a care order, the child is always to be a party to the proceedings. Generally the Court will appoint a '*guardian ad litem*' and it will always be the guardian's duty to represent the child in these proceedings and to safeguard the child's interests. The child will also be entitled to separate legal representation.

Court orders

The Children Act 1989 gives power to a Court to make the following orders.

Care Orders and Supervision Orders – to determine parental responsibility. The sole ground for a Care Order is one of 'harm' or 'likely harm' to the child.
Residence Orders – to decide with whom the child will live.
Contact Orders – to decide what form of contact the child is to have with other people.
Specific Issue Orders – to deal with any other particular matter in relation to the child.
Prohibited Steps Orders – to prohibit anything being done in relation to the child, for example to ensure that a parental responsibility order by the Court is carried out.

Further Court Orders can be made regarding the protection of the child (see below), Education (see p. 296) and Family Assistance (see p. 298).

Protection of children

The Children Act 1989 gives wide powers to Courts to intervene to protect children at risk of harm within the family, provided the child is suffering or is likely to suffer significant harm because of a lack of reasonable parental care or because he or she is beyond parental control. In such cases the Court can do the following:

- Order the assessment of a child where there is real suspicion of harm (*Child Assessment Order*).
- Order the removal or retention of a child in an emergency (*Emergency Protection Order*).
- Order that a child be put under local authority care or supervision pending a full investigation and hearing of the proceedings (*Interim Care and Supervision Orders*).
- Make *Private Law Orders* altering the arrangements about with whom the child lives, regulating his or her contact with other people, determining any particular matter relating to his or her upbringing and prohibiting any particular step being taken.

Note that the Act defines the test of reasonable parental care as 'that care which a reasonable parent would provide for the child concerned'. It is important to realise that a standard of care which would be reasonable for a normal healthy child may not be reasonable if the child has particular social needs because, say, he or she has brittle bones, is asthmatic, or mentally disabled.

Child Assessment Order

If an assessment of a child is needed to decide whether significant harm is likely and it is clear there is not an emergency an application can be made by the local authority for a Child Assessment Order which lasts up to seven days. The main difference between this order and many others is that it does not convey parental responsibility to the holder. It is hoped that this order will be helpful where there is concern about the child, but the parents and carers are uncooperative and an application for a care or supervision order would not be appropriate.

Emergency Protection Order

This order has replaced the Place of Safety Order and is used where there is reasonable cause to believe the child is likely to suffer significant harm unless

- removed from where he or she is to another place; or
- kept where he or she is.

An Emergency Protection Order is also used where it is impossible to carry out full enquiries because the parents unreasonably withhold access to the child and there is reasonable cause to believe that access is required as a matter of urgency.

Emergency Protection Orders are mainly used in serious suspected or proved cases of child abuse. The practical application of this order is discussed fully in Chapter 17 (see p. 316).

Private Law Orders

In disputes between parents a Private Law Order to protect the child may be sought by a parent or others who have some legal responsibility for the child.

Age limit

In all cases where parental responsibility has been transferred to a local authority, this *ceases when the young person reaches the age of 18 years*.

Further powers of Courts

The Children Act 1989 gives power to a Court to make an Education Supervision Order when a child of school age is not being properly educated. This means that, in future, a care order cannot be made in such cases.

Child care provisions

Local authority accommodation

A local authority must provide accommodation for a child in need in their area who requires it as a result of any of the following:

- there being no person who has parental responsibility for the child;
- the child is lost or has been abandoned;
- the person who has been caring for the child being prevented (whether permanently or not, and for whatever reason) from providing the child with suitable accommodation or care.

The range of options which a local authority can use includes the following:

- *a family placement* with a family, relative or another suitable persons. Under previous child care law this was usually referred to as 'boarding out';
- *placement in a community, voluntary or registered children's home*;
- *other appropriate arrangements*, for example for older young persons hostels or semi-independent living or arrangements for rented accommodation.

In many instances the local authority looks after the child for quite a short time during a family crisis (perhaps a few weeks). The most appropriate method of care is used – family placement or the child stays in a small home or even an admission unit if the period is very short. Children rarely suffer from any deprivation in such cases and it is usual for other members of the family either to remain with the child or to visit regularly. If the crisis lasts some months then the aim of the local authority is to attempt to keep the family together, preferably in a family placement.

Care Order

When a Court passes a Care Order the parental responsibility is transferred to the local authority. Such cases are the more serious ones involving grave neglect, abandonment or moral danger to the child. Once parental authority has been transferred the only way that the natural parents can reclaim their child is by petitioning the same Court which made the original Order to revoke it. The Court must then decide whether the parents are now responsible enough to justify returning the child to their care. If the Court decides they are not, the child remains in the care of the authority; if the Court decides they are responsible enough, the parents will have the child returned to them.

Preventive social and rehabilitation work with children

Increasing emphasis is being laid on the importance of preventive work in child care. This depends upon the social services taking action early enough to enable them to prevent a child coming into care or appearing before a Court.

There is a great deal of evidence that everything must be done to avoid family breakdown. As this will be made more likely if the family gets into debt and is made homeless, there is power for the Social Services Committee to make financial payments to prevent a child coming into care. These may even include the payment of rent arrears. Much of this financial help is concentrated on ways which are likely to prevent child delinquency – holiday adventure schemes or clubs, etc.

The social services department and its social workers should also do all in their power to try to rehabilitate each child in its care so that the child may eventually return to the family.

Family Assistance Orders

Under the Children Act 1989, a Court may make a *Family Assistance Order* in family proceedings. This enables a social worker or probation officer to be made available to give advice and assistance and, where appropriate, befriend the person named in the order – this may be the child, a parent or guardian of the child or any person with whom the child lives. Before such an order may be made, each person named in it must give his or her consent. Such an order may last up to six months and is designed to give expert advice to families, especially in separation and divorce cases.

Types and methods of child care

The needs of every child should be carefully assessed on admission into care and each child should be placed according to that assessment.

The aim in child care is to look after every child in the way which is best suited to his or her needs. Supervision is always carried out by trained social workers and *each case must be reviewed every six months*. The ideal is to care for each child in conditions and environment as near normal as possible.

It is usual for a child to go to an *Admission Unit* where any special needs are carefully assessed. There are five main ways in which a child can be looked after:

- *a family placement*. The child lives with a family just as if the child was in his or her own home. This is an ideal arrangement and is used wherever possible, particularly in long stay cases. The person with whom the child lives is called a local authority *foster parent* and such people are very carefully chosen to ensure the right type of person is used. All children in a family placement must be visited regularly and *at least once every six weeks by social workers* from the social services department. The frequency of such visiting is very carefully controlled by the Department of Health;
- *a family group home*. Placement of a child in such a home, containing four to six children of different ages, is the next best type of care wherever family placement is not possible. It aims to look after the child in small units where life can be very similar to that in any large family. These homes are scattered throughout a community and made inconspicuous so that the child's living conditions can be kept as near normal as possible;

- *a small children's home.* Children who do not seem suitable for either family placement or life in a family group home may be cared for in small children's homes, containing from 12–18 children. Many of the children living in these homes later progress to other forms of care. A certain amount of assessment can be undertaken in such homes and an unstable child often settles well;
- *in a child's own home under supervision.* This arrangement is often used during the rehabilitation of children to see if they can now settle back into their own home;
- *a children's home run by a voluntary body.* Examples include Barnado's and the National Children's Home.

Need for continuous review

In all instances it is most important to review each child's progress regularly and to attempt to rehabilitate that child so that eventually it may be possible to return that child home.

With the disturbed child who has had a difficult home background, this may mean many different stages have to be passed through. Such a child may go to a reception centre, small children's home, family placement, a short trial back at home (which may or may not succeed) and much patience is always needed. The eventual success or failure will only be seen when that child becomes an adult; the constant aim is to help children to develop and mature so that they grow into responsible, mature and happy adults.

Community homes

All types of children's homes and the former remand homes and approved schools are now called community homes. Some of these have education provided on the premises (see below).

Special residential units

The larger local authorities social services departments usually provide five special residential units – an admission unit; a residential nursery; a reception centre; a community home with education on the premises for children on remand or for assessment (former remand homes); and a community home with education on the premises for treatment (former approved schools).

Admission unit

The admission unit is the place into which all urgent cases are admitted. The number of children looked after varies, but many look after 45–50 children. Children needing short-term care, especially if the emergency is likely to be short lived, are often cared for in admission units but others are carefully assessed in the admission unit to decide which type of care is best suited to the child. Once this has been decided the child goes on to the appropriate care which may be either residential nursery, reception centre, family placement or admission to a family group or small children's home.

Residential nursery

Small children under the age of 5 years and babies may be looked after in a residential nursery immediately following admission. Many of the short-term care cases will stay there while in care, but some of the older children may later leave for family placement or other forms of child care.

During the past few years, more social service departments have been closing their residential nurseries and relying on using a carefully selected panel of foster parents to look after babies in care. It has been found that such an arrangement is best for it enables a one-to-one relationship to be established between the foster parent and infant.

Reception centre

Some children need a longer period of assessment or may have difficulty in settling down and these are looked after at a reception centre. Some of these children are maladjusted and the regime of the centre allows a longer and more expert assessment of the child to be undertaken.

Community homes with education on the premises (CHEs)

Separate community homes are run by the larger social services departments for children on remand or for assessment or for treatment. Originally their main function was to accommodate children on remand for some serious offence while full investigations (especially psychiatric) took place. Today the most important function undertaken is *the assessment of each child* who is committed to the care of the local authority by a Court (because of conviction on some serious offence).

Many children who pass through such community homes are maladjusted or disturbed having come from an unsatisfactory home. It is, therefore, important to have staff in charge who are trained in dealing with such children and each community home should make arrangements for a psychiatrist to be available to help and advise.

Entry into such a community home used to follow the decision of a juvenile court sentencing the child. Now the decision in such a case is usually made by a case conference of social workers after assessment at a suitable assessment centre which indicates that a stay in such a community home would be beneficial for the child.

Education for children in care

In all community homes with education on the premises, including admission units and reception centres, the local education authority may run one or two classes at each centre which the children can attend or the teachers may be employed by the social services department.

Once the child is transferred to other types of care – family placement, family group or small children's home – the children attend normal schools in the community and, if this is still practicable, the same school that they attended before coming into care.

Juvenile proceedings

Following the Children Act, care orders may no longer be imposed as a sentence in criminal proceedings. The fact that a child has committed an offence may be evidence that he or she is suffering, or is likely to suffer, significant harm so a local authority may apply for a care or supervision order in respect of the child. 'Harm' includes behavioural or social development. Supervision orders may still be made in criminal proceedings and these often include a residential requirement for a child or young person to live in the local authority accommodation provided for up to six months.

Intermediate treatment

A juvenile court can place a child on a supervision order and attach to it an order for the child to attend a local scheme of intermediate treatment. The principle underlying intermediate treatment is that wherever possible it is better to keep the young offender within the family and community than to attempt to resolve problems away from the situation in which they arose. At the same time intermediate treatment aims at the following:

- providing a more realistic method of working with the young offender than removing him or her from home;
- avoiding the side effects of institutionalisation which so often may follow placing the young person in a residential home;
- avoiding some of the difficulties of reintegration into the community when the child has been admitted to a residential home.

Increasingly intermediate treatment is chosen as an alternative to admitting a child to a community home with education on the premises (CHE). It is usual to arrange that the young person on intermediate treatment undertakes useful tasks such as car maintenance in the hope that energies will be channelled into the development of skills. A short period of residential care (not longer than a few weeks) may be arranged and wherever possible this is linked to the other programme of help to the young person.

Probation orders

Probation orders for young persons under 17 years have been replaced by *supervision orders* which may be made in both criminal and care proceedings. These supervision orders are now administered by social services departments.

Adoption services

Every Social Services Authority (County Councils, Metropolitan Districts and London Boroughs) must establish and maintain within its area an adoption service designed to meet the needs, in relation to adoption, of children who may have been adopted, their parents and guardians and adopters. The local authority may either do this directly or via an approved adoption society or agency. Any adoption service should always include facilities for:

- assessing children and prospective adopters;
- placing children for adoption;
- counselling people with problems relating to adoption.

Most of the adoption work undertaken by the local authority should be carried out in conjunction with the other social services for children in their area.

The responsibility for approval and registration of adoption societies and agencies in England and Wales is that of the Secretary of State for Health. The legal status of an adopted child is exactly similar to that of a child born to the adopters – the adopted child becomes a permanent and full member of a new family.

Unless the child is related to the adopter or has been placed with them by a High Court order, an adoption order cannot be made unless the child has had his/her home with the applicants for at least 12 months.

The following are some of the most important points about adoption that all nurses should know about:

- a legal adoption is by an adoption order granted by a Court of Law;
- generally an adoption order can only be made in relation to a child (that is a person who has not yet attained the age of 18 years);
- an adoption order cannot be made in relation to a child who is or who has been married;
- the child must either live in England and Wales or outside Great Britain when the application is made. The courts in England and Wales have no jurisdiction to make an adoption or freeing order in relation to a child in Scotland;
- persons who may adopt a child include single persons if they have attained the age of 21 years, live in the UK, Channel Islands or in the Isle of Man;
- a child cannot be adopted by more than one person unless the couple are married;
- a married person may adopt singly if they are separated and the separation is likely to be permanent or, if the spouse is by reason of ill health incapable of making an application to adopt;
- a parent (mother or father) may make a joint application with the spouse to adopt provided they have attained the age of 18 years and their spouse at least 21 years. Stepparents may now make a similar application;
- normally a male person cannot singly adopt a female child;
- an adoption order may contain such terms and conditions as the Court thinks fit;
- all Court hearings must be in private;
- the child must be at least 19 weeks old and have been in the care of the applicant for at least three consecutive months;
- the applicant must notify the local authority if the adoption has not been arranged through an adoption agency;
- the person whose consent is necessary must fully understand the nature of the consent;
- parental consent to adoption may be dispensed with where a parent cannot be found or is incapable of giving agreement or where the child has been seriously ill-treated;
- once a local authority has decided to seek adoption for a child in its care, it may then place the child with prospective adopters registered with the authority or another agency. These prospective adopters then can make an application for an adoption order;
- alternatively the local authority can make an application to the Court for an order freeing the child for adoption prior to any adoption application;
- every adoption must be in the best interests of the child;
- adoption must *not* be arranged for reward;
- social workers must visit prospective applicants during at least three months before the order is made;

- cohabiting couples cannot jointly adopt a child;
- parental consent is now given before the adoption order is made. This procedure frees the child for adoption and, in this way, is less traumatic for both parents and the adopters;
- any foster parent who has looked after a child continuously is entitled as of right to apply for a residence order which means that the child cannot be removed suddenly if the child has lived with the foster parent for at least three years during the previous 5 years and last lived with him/her within 3 months of the application;
- if the parents agree to adoption, the Court appoints a Reporting Officer who then visits the parties and reports back to the Court. Where there is no agreement, the Court appoints a *Guardian ad litem* who is an officer who safeguards the interests of the child on behalf of the Court.

Health considerations

It is important for nurses to realise that there are important health considerations relating both to the child who is being adopted and for the adopting parents. The adopting parents should know all about the general health of the child and of any defects of sight, hearing, speech or intelligence of the child. Serological tests for syphilis and HIV infection should also be carried out. In the same way, the adopting person should be in good health and be suitable temperamentally and psychologically to care for a child and have a sound family history. Also there should not be too great a difference between the age range that a natural parent would be in and the person or couple making the application to adopt. Medical circumstances which suggest caution in agreeing to an individual adopting would include a history of mental illness or instability, tuberculosis and any other serious chronic disease.

Access to birth records

Adopted persons over the age of 18 years have a legal right to information about their birth records. The local social services department and adoption agencies have a duty to provide counselling. People adopted after 12 November 1975 must be given an opportunity to see a counsellor but need not do so. Those adopted before that date must see a counsellor before being given the information they seek.

The Registrar General is required to set up an Adoption Contact Register which enables persons who have been adopted to obtain information about their birth parents so that, if they wish to do so, they can contact their natural parents and relatives.

The staff of the Registrar General have to be satisfied about the identity of the adopted person making the enquiry. The Register is only open to people over the age of 18. A fee is charged for this service. It is now possible for counselling interviews to take place either in the UK or outside the UK by a body that has notified the Registrar General that it is willing to provide counselling and which the Registrar General is satisfied is suitable to conduct counselling.

17   Child abuse

Since the late 1960s, increasing interest has centred upon child abuse and much research and investigation has taken place into this subject. Child abuse can occur as neglect, physical abuse, sexual abuse or emotional abuse (see p. 308 for further details). A fifth form, 'grave concern' was added in 1989 to indicate where there is a significant risk of any of the above-mentioned forms of child abuse. Of these, the two main forms of abuse are:

- *physical abuse*, the deliberate physical injury to a child;
- *sexual abuse* where a child is sexually interfered with in the home surroundings. Although the majority of child sexual abusers are men or youths, and often a male relative (father, step-father, cohabitor, elder brother), occasionally a woman is involved, either as the abuser or in consenting to or arranging for the abuse to take place.

Both child physical and sexual abuse are now known to have existed for a long time but it is only since 1970 that the degree of abuse has been appreciated. In the case of child sexual abuse, the controversy in Cleveland in 1987 when no fewer than 464 cases of alleged child sexual abuse were reported in a population of approximately 550 000 over a few months highlighted the problem. Widespread investigations followed, including an Inquiry set up by the Secretary of State and presided over by Lord Justice Butler-Sloss. The recommendations of this Inquiry and the subsequent advice from the Department of Health have now emphasised many important facts and principles about both child sexual abuse and child physical abuse, its recognition and diagnosis and its treatment. At the same time, the Department of Health issued an important booklet entitled *Working Together* which is essentially a guide to arrangements for inter-agency cooperation to protect children from both forms of abuse. In this chapter the important essentials of the recommendations of the Butler-Sloss Inquiry and the Department of Health's advice are fully described.

There are some striking similarities as well as differences between the two forms of child abuse. The *similarities* between child physical abuse and child sexual abuse include the following:

- both physical and sexual abuse are found in *all types of families and social classes*. Although cases are commoner in certain social groups in society, many instances of child abuse will be missed if it is assumed the cases never, or very rarely, occur in those families usually described as the 'pillars of society'. Such judgements should never be used for professionals must realise that instances of both child physical abuse and child sexual abuse do occur throughout the whole strata of society;
- both conditions *usually start gradually and are progressive*. This means that unless the child abuse is recognised early and properly treated, not only will the abuse get worse but other children in the family may also be abused. (Indeed, children born into the family in the future may eventually be affected);
- *child abuse can become self-generating*. The child who has been abused may later become an abuser when he or she becomes a parent. This characteristic is often seen in child physical abuse but, as yet, not enough research has been undertaken to see to what extent this pattern may also occur in child sexual abuse. However because all human beings are so much influenced by their earliest experiences in life, it should never be assumed that a person who is known to have been sexually abused as a child will never become a sexual abuser as an adult.

The *differences* between child physical abuse and child sexual abuse are most obvious when the effects on the child are studied:

- in any case of child physical abuse, progressive injury to the child is likely to occur and therefore a proportion are in acute danger. Hence delay over diagnosis and effective treatment can lead to severe injury and even death in some children. Therefore, in the investigation and treatment of child physical abuse, the safeguarding of the child is paramount at all times but particularly early in the development of the syndrome. For this reason short-term separation of the child from the family to allow the fullest investigation to take place is still justified in serious cases;
- in most cases of child sexual abuse the damage to the child is primarily *emotional*. All suspected cases must be fully investigated but there is never the degree of urgency to protect the child by immediate separation from the family as there is in serious cases of child physical abuse. Indeed routine removal of the sexually abused child from the family may increase the child's emotional difficulties. In Cleveland in 1987 it was the routine removal of so many children from their families following suspected sexual abuse that produced so many disturbing factors. The suspicion of child sexual abuse is a very emotive accusation which can easily destroy

marriages and family life, particularly if accompanied by the removal of the child, even if the suspicion is later shown to have been unfounded.

Recognition of child abuse (physical and sexual)

The Department of Health's publication *Working Together* defines and classifies child abuse into the following five categories.

- *Neglect.* The persistent or severe neglect of a child (for example by exposure to any kind of danger, including cold and starvation) which results in severe impairment of the child's health or development, including non-organic failure to thrive.
- *Physical abuse.* Physical injury to a child, including deliberate poisoning, where there is a definite knowledge or reasonable suspicion, that the injury was inflicted or knowingly not prevented.
- *Sexual abuse.* The involvement of dependent, developmentally immature children and adolescents in sexual activities they do not fully comprehend, to which they are unable to give informed consent, or that violate the social taboos of family roles.
- *Emotional abuse.* The severe adverse effect on the behaviour and emotional development of a child caused by persistent ill-treatment or rejection. All abuse involves some emotional ill-treatment. This category should be used where it is the main or sole form of abuse.
- *Grave concern.* Children whose situations do not currently fit the above categories, but where social and medical assessments indicate that they are at significant risk of abuse. These could include cases where another child in the household has been harmed or the household contains a known abuser.

Stages of work in child abuse cases

There are three main stages in the management of the individual case of child abuse (physical or sexual) (i) recognition and investigation; (ii) assessment and planning; and (iii) treatment and review.

Recognition and investigation

The diagnostic signs of physical child abuse are described on pp. 315–316, and of child sexual abuses on pp. 319–320.

In both forms of child abuse, once any professional suspects that child abuse is occurring, it is essential *to refer this concern to either the social services department, police or National Society for the Prevention of Cruelty to Children (NSPCC)*. Whenever any person alleges child abuse a full investigation must be undertaken and every allegation must be considered serious unless proved otherwise. Once the facts have been identified, the question 'Is the child still in danger?' must be asked. If this appears to be so, an *Emergency Protection Order* must be obtained immediately from a Court (see p. 314). It is essential to act urgently in the worst cases of physical child abuse for any procrastination can be disastrous.

Once the child is not in immediate danger (either because the child has been removed from the household under an Emergency Protection Order or because of the nature of the case), the next step in all cases is to call a case conference. This should be set up immediately (within 24 hours), either by the social services department or by the NSPCC in those areas where this body acts as the main specialist for child abuse. Any professional can request such a conference. Every case conference should include those already concerned with the case – the paediatrician, the family doctor, the social worker, the health visitor, the police, a teacher from the school (if the child or a brother or sister is still at school), the NSPCC inspector and, if relevant, the probation officer. *Parents should also be invited, where practicable*, to attend part, or if appropriate, the whole of case conferences unless, in the view of the Chairman of the conference, their presence will preclude a full and proper consideration of the child's interests. *Parents should be informed of the outcome of a case conference as soon as is practicable* and this information should be confirmed in writing.

The case conference decides whether the case is child abuse and determines the next action. In any case conference it is *most important that all such decisions are made jointly and not by any individual professional*. It has often been shown that the only way to ensure the wisest decision is made is to do so after the sharing of all the information and facts. In the past, many mistakes have been made by failing to follow this principle.

Once the case conference has decided that there is a case of child abuse (either physical or sexual) the name and address of the child and family must be entered on the local Child Protection Register (see p. 313) and the parent informed in writing that this action has been taken.

By 1991, 47 800 children had been placed on Child Protection Registers (see Table 17.1).

Note that in 1991, there were slightly more girls (50.8%) than boys (49.2%). The largest groups were 1–4 years (32.4%) and 5–9 (32.0%) and in both groups there were slightly more boys. From the age of 10 years onwards girls are abused more often than boys – by age 16 and over twice as often.

From 1988 to 1991 the distribution of the types of child abuse

Table 17.1 Children and young persons on Child Protection Registers, England and Wales, 1990, 1991 and 1992 (numbers and rates).

Age (years)	Boys			Girls		
	1990	1991	1992	1990	1991	1992
Numbers (thousands)						
Under 1	1.5	1.5	1.4	1.4	1.5	1.2
1–4	7.7	8.1	6.5	6.9	7.3	6.1
5–9	7.5	7.8	6.7	7.3	7.5	6.3
10–15	4.9	5.5	4.9	6.6	6.8	6.1
16 and over	0.5	0.6	0.5	1.1	1.2	1.0
All children	22.1	23.5	20.0	23.3	24.3	20.7
Rates (per 1000 children in each age group)						
Under 1	4.2	4.5	3.8	4.2	4.5	3.6
1–4	5.7	5.9	4.7	5.6	5.6	4.6
5–9	4.6	4.7	4.0	4.7	4.8	4.0
10–15	2.7	3.0	2.6	3.8	3.9	3.4
16 and over	0.7	0.8	0.7	1.7	1.9	1.7
All children	3.8	4.0	3.4	4.2	4.3	3.7

(From Social Trends Central Statistical Office, 1993.)

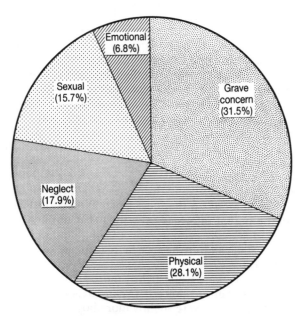

Fig. 17.1 Children on child protection registers by reason, England, 1992, percentages. Total number 38 100. (From Health and Personal Social Service Statistics, Department of Health, 1993.)

recorded changed slightly. Grave concern has increased in incidence to reach 47% while sexual abuse has fallen from 15% to 11%.

Assessment and planning

Once any child has been identified as having been abused and his or her name entered on the Child Protection Register, then either the social service department or the NSPCC should be responsible for all future child care.

The next stage is to appoint a *key worker*, who has three main functions:

- to carry out all aspects of care for the child and family;
- to prepare a multidisciplinary plan for the child and family, including a comprehensive social and medical assessment, and short-term and long-term objectives;
- to act as the leading professional for all inter-agency work. The Key Worker should indicate exactly what the role of other agencies should be (each agency should confirm their acceptance of their appointed tasks). Once this plan has been drawn up and accepted, it should be recorded in the notes of the case conference.

Treatment and review

The treatment of physical child abuse is different from sexual child abuse and these are therefore described separately (see p. 317 and pp. 320–321).

Child protection duties of social services departments of local authorities

The Children Act 1989 makes it clear that, to ensure that children will be protected, the local authority (through its social service department) is *under a duty to investigate fully in the following circumstances*:

- where they have reasonable cause to suspect that a child who lives or is found in their area is suffering or is likely to suffer significant harm;
- where they have obtained an emergency protection order in respect of a child;
- where they are informed that a child who lives or is found in their area is subject to an Emergency Protection Order or is in police protection;
- where a Court in family proceedings directs them to investigate a child's circumstances;

- where a local education authority notifies them that a child is persistently failing to comply with directions given under an Education Supervision Order.

The aim of the investigation should be to establish whether the local authority needs to exercise any of its powers under the Children Act 1989 with respect to the child.

Inter-agency coordination in child abuse

If child abuse is to be effectively reduced, it is essential that coordination between the social services, health services, education services, police services and voluntary services (especially the NSPCC) is made efficient in all districts. Two features have evolved to assist in this coordination – Area Child Protection Committees and Child Protection Registers.

Area Child Protection Committees

In each district, an *Area Child Protection Committee* has been set up on the advice and direction of the Department of Health. The main function of the Area Child Protection Committee (formerly called the Area Review Committee) is to act as a policy forming body to ensure that the arrangements for dealing with both forms of child abuse (physical and sexual) are satisfactory.

Each Area Child Protection Committee should include representatives of the appropriate Local Authority (especially the Director of Social Services, who usually acts as the Convenor and Secretary, and the Director of Education), the Health Services (especially paediatric and other consultants, the District Medical Officer, the District Nursing Officer, plus the specialists in community medicine dealing with social services and child health) and a senior police officer, senior inspector of the NSPCC and a representative of the Chief Probation Officer. Area Child Protection Committees should meet regularly (four times per year) and should undertake the following duties:

- review local practice and procedure for dealing with such cases with special reference to inter-agency guidelines to be followed;
- ensure that immediate hospital admission for children at risk is accepted;
- approve written instructions defining the exact duties and responsibilities of professional staff in connection with non-accidental injury;
- provide education and training programmes for staff in the health and social services;

- review the work of case conferences;
- inquire into the circumstances of cases which appear to have gone wrong and from which lessons could be learned;
- ensure that procedures are in operation to safeguard continuity of care between neighbouring areas and in those instances when families move to another area;
- agree arrangements for the operation of the Child Protection Register.

Child Protection Registers

A central register of information is essential in each district to ensure there is an effective means of recording and sharing information about child abuse. The register is usually maintained by the social service department but, in those few districts where the NSPCC acts as specialists for child abuse, the latter would organise the register. The following information is always recorded:

- identification of the child and family and details of any other children in the household (names and addresses, etc.);
- the nature of the child abuse;
- the key worker and core group. In addition, a record of the general practitioner, the health visitor, name of the child's school, details of the original referral, investigations and treatment plans and review and date of deregistration (if applicable) would also be maintained.

The register is absolutely confidential – queries are always dealt with by the 'ring back principle'. There should be arrangements to share information between neighbouring authorities. A most important feature of registers is that they should be *readily accessible at all times*. It should be possible to consult the register on a 14 hour basis so that doctors, nurses, social workers in the community can obtain information which is reliable and up to date. The ability of a doctor in a accident and emergency department or a health visitor or social worker in the community to seek out information from such a register could be vital to an early and effective diagnosis of child abuse. Notes of all referrals to the register are made and, where two separate enquiries are made within 18 months, the two professionals concerned should be informed so that they can contact each other in order to discuss the circumstances.

Note that the discovery that a child or family is already on the Register does not prove that the present incident is child abuse, but does call for extra special care and vigilance.

Urgent protection of children at risk

In a proportion of cases of child abuse it is essential to ensure that the child in question is protected from further abuse. This is more often necessary in child physical abuse whilst the early investigations take place but is also important in cases of child sexual abuse where the child is being intimidated or assaulted.

The Children Act 1989 introduced the *Emergency Protection Order* which must be obtained from a Court, and lasts for not more than 8 days, although in certain circumstances it can be extended for a further seven days. The Order directs that the child must either be moved (to a safe place such as a hospital or children's home) or detained (this would cover the child who is already in hospital and who is likely to suffer if he or she is returned home). There is a right of appeal to the Court for the order to be discharged after 72 hours and there are also powers for obtaining a medical or psychiatric examination. Subject to Court direction, the person responsible under the order for the child *must allow reasonable contact with the child by specified persons*.

There is a legal duty on the local authority to investigate the child's circumstances where the child has been made subject to an Emergency Protection Order. Under the Children Act 1989, the Court is given power to assist in the discovery of children who may be in need of emergency protection by ordering disclosure of information and by issuing warrants (to authorise entry to search the premises). It also provides for cases where there may be another child on the premises to be covered by an Emergency Protection Order.

A further safeguard for children in urgent need of protection is given in the Children Act 1989. This allows *a child to be taken into police protection for up to 72 hours* where a constable believes that the child might otherwise suffer significant harm. The constable must ensure that the case is inquired into by an officer who has been designated for this purpose by the chief officer of the police area.

Child physical abuse

Child physical abuse is the deliberate injury of a child, usually by parents, step-parents or cohabitors. Formerly this abuse was called non-accidental injury and originally baby battering until it was recognised that it can occur to children of all ages, although the majority of serious cases occur to children under the age of 8 years.

Many different factors are known to accompany child physical abuse. In some of the worst cases criminal neglect by parents and others may be connected with other forms of antisocial behaviour – assaults, drunkenness, frustration, bad living conditions. There is a higher proportion of cases in single parent families, many of whom inevitably have to accept unsatisfactory and overcrowded living conditions where unsympathetic neighbours or landlords are constantly complaining about babies and infants who seem to be crying a great deal.

There is certainly a greater proportion of child physical abuse by parents who:

- themselves were physically abused as a child;
- are very young and under the age of 20 years (such parents often have to face very unsatisfactory living conditions and poverty, and may also be immature and much less tolerant of the problems which all young children inevitably produce); and
- are suffering from some psychiatric illness, which may be characterised by their inability to cope with everyday problems, and especially those of infants and young children.

Diagnosis and early recognition

Child physical abuse can present itself in many ways but usually starts by one or both parents, a step-parent or cohabitor slapping, hitting, punching or severely shaking the child, causing bruises and occasionally more serious injuries. The following conditions may be seen.

- minor bruises which show that the child has been gripped tightly or shaken.
- minor injuries (especially facial bruises) probably caused by slapping or hitting the child. The type of injury is usually similar, 70% being soft tissue injuries to the head and face. There may be 'finger bruising' in which the outlines of the fingers which slapped the child are clearly seen within the bruised area. Such bruising tends to pick out the bony prominences. In many cases, the lips are thick and bruised and there is a torn upper lip frenum. Ribs are frequently bruised or broken and X-rays often indicate that these injuries have been caused in the past. Occasionally small burns may be present.
- an unexplained failure of the child to thrive.
- unusual behaviour by the parents. This may take many different form – over-anxiety and frequent attendance with the child at clinics or surgeries, plausible explanations of an injury which does not fit the case, or unnatural lack of concern for the child's condition.

Repetitive and progressive abuse

Child physical abuse is repetitive and progressive. Many cases show similar characteristics; stress of various kinds is common including poverty (in one survey 80% of abusers were in receipt of income support), unemployment (many fathers batter their children when engaged in maternal tasks), overcrowding and unsatisfactory housing conditions and many have unstable marriages. Another interesting finding is that the parents are often very young (about four years below the national average). Studies have shown that teenage parents are less tolerant and have a low tolerance towards the baby's crying. A high proportion of the women involved are pregnant at the time.

A number of parents shown to be responsible for child abuse are mentally disturbed or inadequate emotionally. It is interesting that the 'innocent' parent (usually the mother) does not do more to protect her child; the most likely explanation is that she has never learnt how to stick up for herself and for her children. Certainly many of the parents involved never received any affection when they were children and consequently find it very difficult to relate as a normal parent does towards their child.

Any additional stress will tend to precipitate problems – moving house often results in much loneliness and resentment and battering is then more likely.

Early diagnosis of child abuse depends upon the alertness of many professional staff including general practitioners, paediatricians, health visitors, practice nurses, district nurses, midwives, social workers and the staff of many voluntary organisations including the NSPCC. Because injury to the child is always a dominant feature, all those working in casualty or accident departments of hospitals should be especially vigilant. Once there is a reasonable degree of suspicion of physical child abuse, the child should at once be admitted to a hospital (or very occasionally a children's home) for diagnosis and for the child's own safety. In many instances, an Emergency Protection Order should be obtained from a court (this can most easily be arranged by the Social Services Department) but the child may be just 'provided with accommodation'. In all cases an immediate case conference should be arranged (see p. 309).

In those instances in which the professional worker does not feel that the suspicions are firm enough to arrange immediate admission to a hospital, it is still advisable to hold a case conference to decide on the next action. If suspicion is very slight, in every instance the nurse should, at least, undertake the following:

- consult the family doctor;
- discuss the details of the case with a senior colleague;
- make a record of such consultations and discussions;
- make enquiries to find out if the child and family are on the Child Protection Register.

Treatment and rehabilitation

Most cases of child physical abuse will initially be in the care of the paediatrician who will be responsible for the assessment and treatment of the case in hospital. Assessment should include both physical and psychiatric investigations. Skeletal surveys should be undertaken in doubtful cases. Case conferences will continue to be held and should indicate the most likely methods of treatment. These should vary considerably in different cases and may include the following:

- receiving the child into *statutory* care by the local authority (by Court Order). In the very worst cases there will also be prosecution of the parents;
- providing the child with accommodation. This may be risky in some cases because parents may suddenly remove the child from hospital or the children's home. Therefore, in all cases where this is done the Social Services Department must always be prepared to seek an urgent Emergency Protection Order if that need arises;
- arranging for the child to remain under supervision in the home by a Supervision Order obtained from a court;
- returning the child home with planned help to the parents.

In all instances the aim is to ensure that the short- and long-term interests of the child are met as far as possible. It is important to realise that, although there are a number of serious cases of intentional injury and neglect that can only be properly treated by permanent removal of the child from the parents, the majority of cases are quite different. In these the physical child abuse has been caused by many other factors – bad living conditions, unemployment, poverty, threat of eviction (especially if babies cry repeatedly) and by minor psychiatric illnesses. *These parents urgently require help and if this can be satisfactorily given they may be assisted to develop into perfectly satisfactory parents and families.* However, the causative factors *must* be discovered. In many instances, the temporary provision of residential care (in a residential nursery or children's home) may be required to enable the parent to be treated.

Day care

Many people who have been found to ill-treat their children are young and often very isolated and lonely. In a number of instances the mother herself had an unhappy childhood or was brought up in a broken home.

A very useful method of helping is to admit the child to a day nursery or play group and then to arrange for the mother to help in the group.

In this way, the mother is assisted to make new friends and to obtain the support she needs. Indirectly she will be taught to improve her relationship with her own child from the example of care she will see in the nursery or play group. More and more social services departments are now developing day care which can be extended to older children in the same family who come along to the unit after school.

Many girls' schools now arrange for senior girls to help periodically in play groups and day nurseries, and thus to learn more about the methods of care of young children. This is particularly important because the incidence of child abuse is highest in teenage mothers.

Some local authorities have arranged to deal with many cases in nurseries close to a paediatric department which makes the development of special working arrangements between the health and social services departments easier.

Periodic review of long-term cases

Some of the most difficult problems are found in long-term cases. It is absolutely essential that periodic reviews of such cases are undertaken. These must involve the many professional workers who would normally be concerned with the care of that child and especially general practitioners, teachers, school nurses, health visitors, practice nurses, education welfare officers, social workers (including those working in child guidance) as well as those working with voluntary agencies in that area. In all older children (and some of the worst cases of child abuse occur in older children) it is most important that the levels of communication between teaching staff, and others concerned with the child in school and health visitors, practice nurses and social workers are always good.

The statutory duty to protect and care for all children who are in need is that of the Director of Social Services and his or her staff, or the NSPCC in those few areas where this organisation acts as specialists in child abuse for the whole area. Unless there is an effective network of information between all staff working in education, health and social services, action by the social services department may be delayed until it is too late to prevent further injury. For this reason, long-term cases should never be written off until a case conference agrees that no further risk remains. Unless this multidisciplinary team approach is always used, mistakes of the past will be repeated.

In any serious case of doubt, a doctor or nurse should always arrange immediate hospital admission for the child to enable more detailed investigations to be undertaken. In cases of difficulty, the problem should always be reported by telephone to the Director of Social Services or District or Area Social Services Officer.

Child sexual abuse

Although child sexual abuse has always existed, detailed studies have only recently been undertaken. The incidence in the Cleveland controversy was an alleged 464 cases in a population of 550 000 (a rate of 84 per 100 000). Not all of these were proven cases. In Liverpool, a city with a population of 479 000, studies have been going on since 1980 and these indicate that about 13% of the 600–700 case conferences held each year were child sexual abuse cases. Such an incidence would be of the order 16.0 per 100 000 and this is probably more realistic than the Cleveland figures.

Child sexual abuse is an extremely emotive subject and it is never easy to involve the parents in any investigation without risking complete destruction of their own personal relationships. In physical child abuse any parent may inadvertently raise suspicion by natural discipline of a child, but to introduce a sexual element in the affection given by a parent or other adult to a child of either sex is to suggest something which most parents would find offensive. Certainly there is no doubt that most people feel greater abhorrence towards anyone who has been found to abuse sexually a child compared with physical abuse instances, especially if the physical abuse has been of a minor nature or if there are extenuating circumstances.

Diagnosis and recognition

Diagnosis of child sexual abuse is always difficult. It mainly depends on the professional being aware that there is a possibility of sexual abuse, especially in certain circumstances. Apart from the few cases where a child unequivocally alleges sexual abuse in the clearest terms, the diagnosis is rarely clear cut and is usually only reached after a lengthy period of assessment. Even where a child has made an unambiguous accusation, this is often later retracted when the seriousness of the disclosure is realised.

There is no simple test to confirm child sexual abuse except when semen is found or blood from a different group from that of the child. Very careful assessment, observation and investigation by many different professionals is needed. A multidisciplinary approach is most important to ensure a balance between over-enthusiasm and zeal and failure to act in time. Doctors, social workers, nurses, health visitors, teachers and the police all have a part to play.

The starting point in the diagnosis of child sexual abuse should be the raising of suspicion that it may be occurring. It is helpful to consider three types of suspicion – serious, moderate and mild.

Serious suspicion should be raised in the following instance:

- when the child makes clear verbal allegations of sexual abuse. If the allegation is spontaneous, it would be most unusual for it to be a fabrication.

Moderate suspicion is justified in the following instances if:

- the child makes an allegation of sexual abuse in ambiguous terms (so that it is not clear precisely what occurred);
- a child is sexually provocative to adults or discloses detailed knowledge of sexual matters in conversation, fantasy or drawings or appears preoccupied with sexual fantasies and behaviour;
- a child responds to questioning by describing sexual abuse but has not made a spontaneous allegation;
- a child shows a specific fear of a father, step-father or sexually mature older brother;
- a child is living in cramped circumstances and the mother is known to be a prostitute – but it should be noted that a particular family setting should never, on its own, be grounds for serious suspicion.

Mild suspicion should be aroused in the following instances if:

- a child shows behavioural or emotional disturbance for which no other cause can be found;
- a child shows unexplained changes in behaviour;
- a child makes a suicide attempt;
- a child runs away from home when there is no obvious cause;
- there is an unusually close relationship between the father or step-father and the child and, at the same time, there is marital discord in the home.

The test of reflex anal dilatation has been considered to indicate sexual abuse. However, the Butler-Sloss report clearly states that *there is no proof of a direct link between reflex anal dilatation and the diagnosis of sexual abuse*, although its presence does raise the level of suspicion.

Management and treatment

Unlike child physical abuse, child sexual abuse does not necessarily call for an immediate emergency response or for the removal of the child from the household. The one exception is where the child is liable to assault or intimidation – then care away from the home must be provided promptly.

Much support and counselling is needed for the parents and family and a specialist social worker skilled in this role can be invaluable. It may well be that, initially, it would be best for the abuser to leave the family home, at least for a period while further investigations take place. Obviously all treatment must ensure that the interests of the child be given priority. But one crucial question must be asked: *Should treatment also strive to keep the family together?* The answer will depend on individual circumstances and the flexibility of the family's attitudes. It is also always important to endeavour to find out the views of the child.

Many different patterns of treatment are at present being tried and no doubt the best alternative will eventually evolve. In many instances, the solution may turn out to be very individual with a variety of solutions being tried. The abuser may be required to live away from home but still be able to support and have access to the family. On the other hand, the split between the parents may be complete. Whether it is worthwhile attempting to reconcile the parents must depend on their attitude. Expert advice and counselling will always be most important. The Butler-Sloss Inquiry suggested that *specialist assessment teams* could be set up with advantage. These would include a social worker, a doctor and a specialist police officer working together. This team would carry out the initial assessment and then indicate which course of action would be most likely to be in the best interests of the child.

It is clear that, at present, there is little expertise in dealing with child sexual abuse in either the social, health or police services. The model of treatment for physical child abuse is clearly not appropriate to many cases of child sexual abuse. The development of successful forms of treatment will be most likely to occur if prejudice and revulsion are not allowed to cloud the issue. What is needed is the evolution of a series of models of treatment (mainly by trial and error) until some are shown to have the best chance of success. *The test of success must be in the long-term results – when a child who is known to have been sexually abused grows up into a normal loving caring adult and parent with good personal relationships, happy with his or her own family and children.*

18 Care and rehabilitation of disabled people

The Department of Health is centrally responsible for the community social services for disabled or physically handicapped people.

Locally each major local authority (County Council, Metropolitan District Council or London Borough) is responsible through its Social Services Committee. The chief officer in charge of these services is the Director of Social Services (see p. 284).

In addition, there are large numbers of national and local voluntary bodies working for the handicapped; examples include the Royal National Institute for the Blind, the Royal Association for Disability and Rehabilitation (RADAR), SCOPE (previously the National Spastics Society), the national Multiple Sclerosis Society, and various Deaf and Dumb Associations. Most local authorities give monetary grants to help such voluntary bodies.

Relationships between health services and social services

Medical, nursing and social services all attempt to help the disabled in different ways. Doctors and nurses carry out their treatment in hospitals or in the community while the social services are more concerned with rehabilitation and with helping them to lead an active life and to overcome their social problems or difficulties. It will follow from this that doctors, nurses and social workers must work closely together if the best results are to be obtained.

Generally social services concentrate upon aids to normal life within the community – housing, adaptations to houses, employment, special workshops, transport, various aids and gadgets, handicraft centres, social centres and clubs and holidays. For these reasons, most social services provided by local authorities are in the community while many medical and nursing services are in the hospital. District and community nurses, health visitors and general practitioners also are actively engaged in helping many handicapped people in their own homes. It is *most important that the social worker links up with these medical and nursing services*; this is best done by social workers visiting hospitals and general practitioners to ensure that a continuous working arrangement is maintained at all times. The eventual success with any individual handicapped person is closely connected with the degree of such cooperation between doctors, nurses and social workers. Eventually it is hoped that social workers will work closely with primary health care teams.

Legislation

Disabled Persons (Employment) Acts, 1944 and 1958

These Acts are designed to help all disabled people. A 'disabled person' is defined as one 'who on account of injury, disease or congenital deformity, is substantially handicapped from obtaining or keeping employment'. Every employer who employs 20 or more people must, under the above-mentioned Acts employ a minimum of 3% of disabled persons among his staff. The names of all disabled persons are held on a register.

Although the wide definition of disabled people has reduced the effectiveness of this Act, it has helped to increase the opportunities for employment of handicapped people.

Chronically Sick and Disabled Persons Act, 1970

The Chronically Sick and Disabled Persons Act, 1970 gives many special responsibilities to local authorities in respect of those who are substantially and permanently disabled (including those who are mentally handicapped). The main duties of local authorities include the following.

- *Information*. Local authorities must ensure (i) that they are adequately informed of the numbers and needs of disabled persons so that they can properly plan and develop their services, and (ii) that the handicapped and their families know what help is available to them by general publicity and personal explanations.
- *Provision of services*. Local authorities, when satisfied that certain services are necessary to the disabled person, can provide the following services:
  — practical assistance in the home;
  — radio, television, library or similar recreational facilities in the home;
  — recreational facilities outside the home and assistance in taking advantage of educational facilities;
  — specialised travelling facilities for disabled persons;
  — assistance in carrying out adaptations to the home;

- — facilitating the taking of holidays;
- — meals at home or elsewhere;
- — a telephone and any special equipment necessary for its use.
- **Housing.** Every local authority must have regard to the special needs of the disabled and any new houses planned must show that special provision is made for them. This clearly gives housing authorities a duty to plan and provide special housing accommodation for handicapped people.
- **Premises open to the public.** There are a series of requirements for public buildings. These deal specially with the following facilities for the disabled.
  - — Providing means of access to and within the buildings and in the parking facilities and sanitary conveniences. Such provision must be considered before planning permission is given.
  - — Need for a local authority to provide public sanitary conveniences.
  - — Need for anyone providing sanitary conveniences in premises open to the public for accommodation, refreshment or entertainment, to make provision, as far as is practicable, for the disabled.
  - — Adequate sign-posting for the above provisions from outside.
  - — Need to provide facilities for access, parking, and sanitary conveniences suitable for disabled people as far as is practicable at school, university and other educational buildings.

In addition, there are special clauses about Advisory Committees for the handicapped either nationally or locally and these insist that members of *such committees must include persons with experience of work for the disabled and people who are themselves disabled.*

Many local authorities have provided excellent services (especially telephones) for the handicapped, but some have been slow to assist.

National Assistance Act, 1948, Section 29

This gives the local authorities the responsibility of providing a further wide range of social services for disabled people including home training, occupational therapy and many other domiciliary services.

Disabled Persons (Services, Consultation and Representation) Act 1986

This Act aims at improving the effectiveness of services for mentally and physically disabled persons by introducing an 'advocacy' service. When disabled people cannot represent themselves because of their disability, an 'advocate' or representative is appointed to act on their behalf.

Much of the Act is concerned with improving the effectiveness of Section 2 of the Chronically Sick and Disabled Persons Act 1970 (see above) by way of the following:

- ensuring that any help for the disabled person is coordinated properly;
- requiring the *local authority to assess the needs of every disabled person when requested to do so*;
- insisting that the *results of such an assessment are given in a written statement*, including explanations of the various decisions of the local authority;
- ensuring that the *local social service department gives the disabled person all proper help* (including 'interpretation assistance' for a deaf and dumb person) and *considers every case on its merits*.

In addition, the Act includes important provisions to help disabled young people in the difficult transfer period immediately after leaving school.

The Act also ensures that every social service department must periodically publish general information about the services it provides for disabled persons under the 1970 Act.

Incidence of disability

Six important surveys looking into the levels of disability in Great Britain were carried out from 1985–1988. These found that there were about 6.2 million people who were disabled in the country – 7% (422 000) were in residential establishments with the remainder living in the community. It was estimated that almost 14% of people living in private households had at least one disability. Among those living in private households, musculoskeletal complaints, especially arthritis, were the commonest reported. Ear and eye problems and diseases of the circulatory system, were also found in many cases. For those in residential establishments, mental problems, especially forms of senile dementia, were most commonly found, followed by arthritis and strokes.

These surveys focused on the types of disability and 13 distinct types were found: locomotion; reaching and stretching; dexterity; personal care; continence; seeing; hearing; communication; behaviour; intellectual function; consciousness; eating, drinking and digesting; and disfigurement.

The results are shown graphically in Fig. 18.1. Ten degees of severity were chosen, category 1 being the least severe up to category 10, the

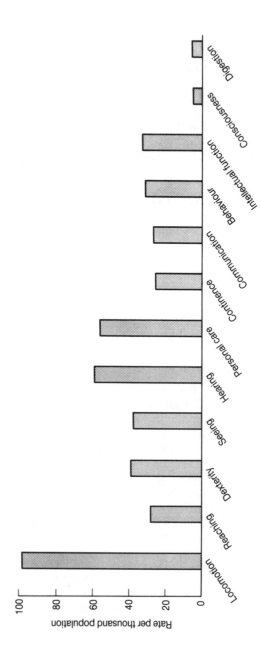

Fig. 18.1 Estimates of prevalence of disability among adults by type of disability, Great Britain. (From the OPCS Surveys, 1985–8.)

most severe. Two hundred and ten thousand persons were identified in category 10 and the numbers then progressively increased through the categories until 1 199 000 persons were found in category 1. Most disabled persons had more than one disability. Just under one-half of the most severely disabled people lived in private households.

One of the most striking findings was that the rate of disability rose steeply with age (see Fig. 18.2). The incidence of disability accelerates after the age of 50 and later rises rapidly after the age of 70. Almost 70% of disabled persons were over 60 years of age and almost 50% were aged 70 and over. Also there is a connection between the severest disability and age. In fact 40% of the disabled persons in categories 9 and 10 were over 80 years of age. *The numbers of disabled persons is likely to rise significantly in the next three decades as the projections of those who then will be aged 85 and over in Great Britain show that they will rise steeply (see p. 372).*

The surveys also showed that there were consistently *more disabled women than men in Great Britain.* This is partly due to the fact that women, on average live 5–6 years longer than men. But there must be other reasons for the rate of disability in women being greater than in men.

These surveys were followed in 1991 by the Department of Health:

- establishing an Advisory Group on Rehabilitation;
- arranging for the integration of the Disablement Services

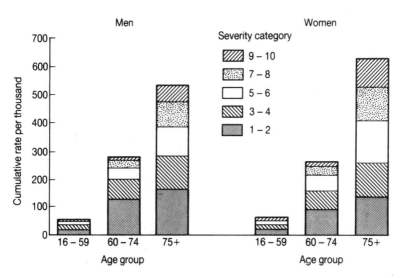

Fig. 18.2 Estimates of prevalence of disability among adults by age and severity category for men and women. (From OPCS Surveys, 1985–8.)

Authority (formerly the Artificial Limb and Appliance Service) into the general structure of the NHS;
- introducing an initiative to improve rehabilitation services for persons with a brain injury which was fully established in 1993;
- commissioning a research project on the Epidemiologically Based Needs Assessment of Young Adults with Physical Disabilities;
- undertaking a review of the continence services in Great Britain.

General principles for helping disabled people

In the rehabilitation of all disabled people there are certain basic principles which are important. No social service can succeed if they are ignored, and it is essential to understand them, for they carry the secret of success and can quite simply be modified for every disabled person. There are four main principles:

- the problems of every handicapped person are *highly individual and personal*;
- the best solution for any handicapped person is that which is *as near normal as possible*;
- a large amount of *improvisation* will probably be necessary;
- *great determination and singleness of purpose* is usually essential for success.

An individual approach

The difficulties of any disabled person vary with each individual. This is because the problems depend on:

— the age of the person – there is a very high incidence of disability in persons over the age of 75 years (see p. 327),
— the nature and extent of the disability,
— the reaction of the disabled person to the handicap.

Thus, many blind people are able to hold down an important job whilst others who are blind may be unable to carry out successfully quite a simple occupation. The disability is the same, complete blindness, but the end result and size of the individual problem varies greatly.

The reaction of disabled people to these difficulties depends very much on the attitude of those who have tried to help in the early and crucial stages. A correct approach and attitude of mind here are essential. What is wanted is an understanding, which very often means something quite different from ineffective and maybe sentimental sympathy. Often the best approach is a fairly tough one which promises the person little but many hard struggles and disappointments.

For these reasons, individual visiting and assessment are always a most important first step in rehabilitation. As the social background of the disabled person – their home and their family – plays a significant part in overcoming the handicap, it is important that assessment includes these.

Maintaining normality

There is a very simple rule to follow in determining what any handicapped person should attempt to do. The best solution is always the one which is as near normal as possible.

This basic principle applies to all aspects of life including education and occupation. A person with no handicap usually works in an industry or in an office and is not in any way protected. This is also the best solution for any handicapped person.

If difficulties are found in suggesting the next stage in rehabilitation, a useful indicator is given by considering what occupation the person would be following if he or she was not disabled. The aim should always be for the rehabilitation process to progress towards this goal.

The constant hope given by successfully reaching various stages in rehabilitation will do much to counteract any attitude of self pity in the handicapped person which must be avoided at all cost.

Improvisation

Just as the problems of each handicapped person differ, so will the solutions. Hence, an ability to improvise in overcoming the inevitable and unexpected difficulties is most important. Those working with disabled people cannot afford to be narrow minded, too set in their ways or hidebound by convention. All the most successful are resilient and often unconventional people to whom improvisation comes naturally.

Determination

It is always easy to find an excuse for failure when dealing with disabled people. Therefore, to succeed, it is important to *concentrate solely upon success*, however remote this might seem to be. If possible, the disabled person and those immediately around him or her, should be fired with an enthusiasm to succeed irrespective of the difficulties and inevitable disappointments ahead. A complete singleness of purpose should be encouraged for this often helps to overcome difficulties.

Special financial help available to seriously disabled people

Disability Living Allowance

Persons who are suffering from a serious illness or disability and need help with personal care or mobility may be able to obtain the Disability Living Allowance. This is a non-contributory tax-free benefit payable from the Benefit Agency. The Disability Living Allowance has two elements:

- a care element;
- a mobility element.

To qualify for the Disability Living Allowance, a person must be under the age of 66 and provide evidence that the help he/she needs started before their 65th birthday.

In addition to qualify for the *care element* the individual must fall into one of the following groups – that he/she needs:

- help with washing, dressing and using the toilet;
- help to prepare a cooked main meal (this does *not* apply to someone under the age of 16 years);
- someone to be at home with them to keep an eye on them;
- someone with them when they are on dialysis;
- that the person is not expected to live longer than 6 months because of an illness.

To qualify for the *mobility element*, the person must require help with mobility because he/she:

- cannot walk at all;
- has had both legs amputated above the ankle or at the ankle or that he/she was born without legs or feet;
- has difficulty with walking;
- is both deaf and blind and needs someone with them when out of doors;
- is seriously mentally impaired with severe behaviour problems;
- can walk but needs someone with them when out of doors.

Normally a medical examination is not required (unless the claim is being made because of a terminal illness when the doctor should complete Form DS 1500) provided that satisfactory evidence is available explaining the degree of the problem.

To obtain the Disability Living Allowance a person normally must have needed help for *at least 3 months and must be likely to require that help for a further 6 months or more.* However *persons who are not expected to live longer than 6 months do not have to wait 3 months and also will be given special priority.* Such individuals also qualify for help with personal care automatically even if no help is required.

Once a person qualifies for the Disabled Living Allowance, it will be paid for the rest of that person's life, irrespective of age, provided the need for the help remains.

Attendance Allowance

After the age of 65, the Attendance Allowance can be paid if the person meets the qualifications outlined above for the care element of the Disabled Living Allowance.

No financial help is given with mobility if the person's need commenced after the age of 65 although anyone already qualified for the mobility element before 65 will continue to receive it irrespective of age provided the need remains.

To obtain the Attendance Allowance *a person must normally have needed that help for 6 months.* However anyone who is not expected to live longer than 6 months because of an illness does not have to wait 6 months and also receives special priority. Such a person would qualify for help with personal care automatically even if no help was required.

Motability

This is the name of a voluntary organisation formed on the initiative of the government to assist disabled persons to get maximum value for money in using the mobility element of the Disability Living Allowance to acquire a car. Two schemes are available: a leasing scheme; and a hire purchase scheme.

In the first, a new car is leased for 3–4 years in return for surrendering the mobility element for this period and, in most cases, also paying a 'once and for all' advance rental. Full details of both schemes can be obtained from RADAR, Mortimer Street, London W1.

Invalid Care Allowance

This is a weekly cash benefit for people under pension age (16–64 years for a man, 16–59 years for a woman) who spend at least 35 hours a week looking after someone who is receiving either an Attendance Allowance or a Constant Attendance Allowance (following an industrial accident or as a result of an industrial disease). If the individual has children or supports another adult, extra benefit is payable.

Main groups of disabled

The main groups of disablement for which local authorities provide
social services include the following:

- blindness and partial sightedness;
- total deafness from birth, including the deaf and dumb;
- hardness of hearing, acquired deafness, usually late in life;
- congenital disabilities, spina bifida or spastic diplegia;
- paraplegia and hemiplegia;
- various paralytic diseases (e.g. multiple sclerosis, muscular dystrophy, poliomyelitis);
- strokes;
- serious arthritic conditions – rheumatoid arthritis, spondylitis,
  severe osteoarthritis;
- epilepsy;
- accident cases.

Social services available for disabled people

The following are the social services provided by local authority social
services departments and voluntary bodies working with them.

Social worker support and assessment

Social workers are available to assess and advise disabled persons at
home. Initially each person is registered and his or her needs carefully
assessed and catalogued. Social workers are usually attached to area
social work teams and include specialists trained to work with the blind
and who can teach Braille, and to work with the deaf and dumb using
sign and finger language.

Social workers work closely with other community workers such as
health visitors, practice nurses, district nurses and general practitioners. Special services such as meals-on-wheels and home helps can
be arranged by the social worker.

Employment for disabled people

There are two main ways in which disabled people can be employed
full time: (i) in ordinary or 'open' industry; (ii) in special sheltered
employment.

'Open' industry refers to ordinary occupations where each disabled
person works with and under exactly the same conditions as a person
with no handicap. Full wages are paid without any subsidy.

This is always the best solution, but is, unfortunately, only possible for a proportion of the employable handicapped. The success of placing a disabled person in open industry will depend on the employment opportunities of the area and the efforts of the social services department and Disablement Resettlement Officers (DROs) of the Department of Employment to find openings in local industries. It should be possible to place many intelligent well trained disabled persons in most industries. With the blind, special Blind Persons Resettlement Officers are employed to assist finding places in industry for the handicapped (see p. 340).

Sheltered employment is subsidised employment (full-time) arranged either in a special workshop or in a home workers scheme (details for the blind on p. 341). The Department of Employment runs special Remploy workshops for handicapped people and some local authorities run their own workshops. There are also many voluntary bodies who run sheltered workshops usually with financial help from local authorities.

Industrial therapy services

Many local authorities run industrial therapy services and, in this way, assist disabled persons with their rehabilitation. Reference is made later to such services provided for those with learning difficulties (see p. 367) and similar services are made available to physically disabled people. The aim of these services is mainly to train and prepare physically disabled individuals for full-time work.

Handicraft centres

Handicraft centres are also provided by local authorities for disabled people and are usually staffed by handicraft instructors. The main aim of such centres is to assist those who are disabled to enjoy recreational facilities although complete rehabilitation towards eventual full-time employment may not be possible.

Occupational therapy services

Most local authority social services departments employ occupational therapists. These may be on a *domiciliary basis* where the occupational therapist calls on each disabled person at home from time to time, or the services may be provided at *special rehabilitation centres*. In such cases the disabled persons are often brought to the centre by special transport.

The concept of the work of occupational therapists has changed and much more emphasis is now placed on *teaching disabled people to live with their handicaps* rather than instruction in craft work. In this way they are helped to overcome their muscular difficulties by the use of various aids or machines including knitting and fretsaw machines, various looms and treadle lathes. A number of crafts are also taught at such centres.

Occupational therapists also train people with a disability in special training kitchens and these are especially useful to the handicapped housewife to help her become more independent. Various aids and gadgets are tested out in these kitchens so that later the correct aid can be fitted in the person's own kitchen. Attendance at such centres may be on a full-time or part-time basis. As well as the training undertaken at each centre, the *social value of disabled people meeting each other and becoming less isolated is also important.*

Much chronic invalidism can be caused by the disabled person becoming more and more withdrawn as he or she stays permanently at home meeting only close friends or family. If the handicapped person is brought to a rehabilitation or handicraft centre, his or her confidence is helped by meeting other people and seeing what can be achieved, and further deterioration can be prevented. Domiciliary occupational therapy services are also provided by many health authorities.

Aids centres

Permanent aids centres containing a wide range of equipment suitable for the disabled have been established in London by the Disabled Living Foundation and by some local authorities. These aids centres set out to enable disabled people and their families to see for themselves the range of equipment available. It is usual to staff such units with experienced occupational therapists and to run the centre on an appointment system as it usually takes 1½ to 2 hours to demonstrate all the equipment available.

Disabled people and their families wishing to visit such centres should contact either the Disabled Living Foundation, 346 Kensington High Street, London W8, or the local Director of Social Services.

Transport

Mobility for handicapped people is very important. Individual problems depend very much on the type of handicap. Various adaptations can be made to cars so that they can be safely driven by hand controls only.

Individual transport

Individual transport for severely disabled people is the responsibility of the government. *Direct provision, through the NHS, is now avail-*

able only to war pensioners and very special cases. All other severely handicapped persons use the mobility element of the Disability Living Allowance when appropriate (see p. 330). The production of Invacars has ended but those who have such a vehicle can continue to use them. Anyone using an Invacar may transfer to the mobility element of the Disability Living Allowance without medical examination or age limit. Local authorities provide the run-in, drive and base for the garage which is erected by the Department of Health.

Local authorities often provide *temporary wheelchairs* on loan to help those who have a transient need – less than six months. In permanent cases, after this period, the District Health Authority should provide the wheelchair.

Group transport

Local authority social services departments provide various vehicles, personnel carriers, mini-buses, etc., to carry the disabled from their homes to various centres. Many of these vehicles are fitted with hydraulic lifts so that wheelchairs with their occupants can easily be loaded and unloaded.

The success of many of the activities and services provided by local authorities (various centres and clubs, etc.) depends to a large extent on the efficiency of transport services for disabled people which must be adequate to meet the needs of the area.

Holidays and outings

Many voluntary bodies and local authorities arrange special holiday schemes for disabled persons. These have become more and more ambitious in recent years and include holidays abroad, with arrangements made as regards transport and all holiday activities. Special staff go with the handicapped group which usually contains many severely handicapped people in wheelchairs.

Some local authorities also help handicapped people by subsidising ordinary holidays arranged by the disabled person him or herself with a small monetary grant. This enables the disabled person to arrange a more expensive type of holiday (for example, to stay at a hotel with a lift).

Emphasis today is on the *provision of normal holidays* in which the non-handicapped members of the family can share with the disabled individual. There are, however, a number of special holidays arranged and some local authorities have special seaside holiday homes for the disabled.

Social centres and clubs

Many voluntary bodies run special social centres and clubs for disabled people. Local authorities usually give financial support to such centres or provide a central club which voluntary bodies may use at no cost. Transport can be provided by the local authority.

Housing for disabled people

The design of the home occupied by the individual disabled person is very important. Many adaptations are needed to enable a severely handicapped person to live normally – larger doors, no steps, large bathrooms and toilets and special fitments.

It may be possible to *adapt the home* or to introduce special aids (see below). But with the most severely disabled, for example the paraplegic, it is usually easier and cheaper for the local housing authority to *build specially designed bungalows* which incorporate such adaptations.

In the case of an individual who suffers a paraplegia following an accident and who is consequently admitted to a regional hospital spinal centre, it is most important that the housing requirements are considered shortly after admission and not left until just before the patient is discharged home. Most patients will remain in such hospitals for at least 6 months and it is essential to ensure that the local authority has all this time to solve the housing difficulties which often are considerable. Certain adaptations may be needed at the patient's home or even rehousing, either of which may take months to achieve.

Minor adaptations, aids and gadgets

Under the Chronically Sick and Disabled Persons Act, 1970, local authorities help by providing (usually at a subsidised cost) minor adaptations including the following:

- *ramps or handrails*;
- *hoists* in bedrooms and bathrooms for those paralysed in the legs so that they can become more independent and mobile;
- *modifications to table implements*; knives, forks, spoons, to make them more easily used by people whose grip is weak or whose hands are deformed;
- various *kitchen fitments* for disabled people. These include many gadgets for one-handed people or those who only have power in one hand, and other aids for those whose balance is poor (e.g. slings to be fitted to sinks to allow such people to stand supported by the sling);

- *kitchen management and planning* are most important. The height of various working surfaces and the design of kitchen furniture are examples. Many rehabilitation centres are fitted with model kitchens for disabled people so that the occupational therapist can see which equipment best suits the person before steps are taken to fit out the individual's own kitchen. Various kinds of cooking stoves can be tried in such demonstration kitchens;
- various *personal aids in dressing* are all important so that the independence of the disabled person is improved. In all this work, the aim is always to make the disabled person as normal as possible and, in this respect, anything that engenders independence is valuable.

Other social services which are available include meals-on-wheels (see p. 386) and home helps (see p. 391) for which charges are usually made.

Telephones

Under the Chronically Sick and Disabled Persons Act, 1970, most local authorities help by providing a telephone (and paying rent) for those who are severely disabled and who live alone. Standards vary but *most local authorities give top priority to disabled people living alone who cannot go outside even in fine weather.* Telephones are also provided for special medical cases. Any nurse coming across such a disabled person who urgently requires a telephone should report the case to the local Director of Social Services.

Rehabilitation of disabled people

This is a joint enterprise involving the medical services, the Department of Employment and local authority social services departments and, in children and young persons, the education authority.

Rehabilitation usually starts in the hospital, in the rehabilitation or orthopaedic departments and then transfers to *rehabilitation centres* run by local authorities or special hospitals. Special transport usually brings the patient to the centre and makes it possible to extend more quickly the range of rehabilitation. At the centre, there are many and various machines and aids such as knitting machines, fretsaw machines, looms, as well as a training kitchen. There are also opportunities to follow many crafts.

The rehabilitation centre is usually open all day and people can attend for half a day or a full day. It is usual for the kitchen to be used by a disabled person learning to cook, and in this way meals are prepared for themselves and others attending the centre.

One of the most valuable parts of the centre's regime is the *social life* provided, whereby disabled people meet others. In many long and chronic illnesses or disabilities, there is a tendency for any person to become more and more withdrawn and to stay permanently at home, meeting only family and close friends. Even when the physical disability improves, the individual very often continues to stay at home and this factor can make it difficult or impossible to rehabilitate the person back to normal life. Attendance at the occupational therapy centre and travelling to it can greatly increase self-confidence and prevent permanent invalidism. Once a week at the centre, a social evening is arranged so that those attending the centre can relax together playing games, table tennis and dancing.

Rehabilitation from centre to workshops and industry

The aim of the occupational therapist is to transfer eventually the disabled person either directly into open industry or to a special sheltered workshop. The latter are run by social service departments, various voluntary bodies supported by local authorities by financial grants and by the Department of Employment through the special Remploy factories (see p. 333). These workshops are sited throughout the country and are designed to provide permanent work for severely disabled people.

Another very important link in the rehabilitation chain is the Employment Rehabilitation Centres run by the Department of Employment. These are designed to teach disabled person a new trade skill and are of great importance to those people who have had to learn a new job because the one for which they are trained is now unsuitable for them.

Note that the highest unemployment rates are always in unskilled workers. If such persons also suffer from a physical disability, their chances of finding permanent employment are usually very slight. For this reason, *all disabled people should, if possible, be taught an industrial skill suitable to their handicap and ability* and the Centre is equipped to do this.

There must also, at all times, be complete coordination between the occupational therapist and the Disablement Resettlement Officer.

Social services for blind and visually handicapped persons (including partially sighted people)

Registration

Proper registration of blind and partially sighted people is essential. In 1990, there was a major revision of Form BD 8 which is used for the certification of blind and partially sighted persons. This followed the recommendations in the Working Group report to the Minister for the Disabled published in 1989. The epidemiological section of Form BD 8 has been revised to enable the collection of better information on the causes of blindness and partial sight. The new form is designed to improve service delivery at local level, inter-agency collaboration and statistical information, and should be a significant step forward in providing services to visually handicapped persons.

In 1991 there were 136 200 persons registered as blind in England. Of these 79.3% were aged 65 and over and 8.7% aged 50–4 emphasising that *blindness mainly occurs in late middle-aged and elderly persons*. There is an even greater tendency for the newly blinded to be elderly – only 8% of them are under 50 years of age while 82% are aged 65 years and over.

Individual assessment

The problems facing any blind person vary greatly from individual to individual. The age at which blindness develops is a major factor. The child born blind has to learn to live their whole life as a blind person – being educated as a blind person, employed as a blind person and face the difficulties of retirement and old age with the same handicap. Many elderly persons going blind over the age of 70 years have only the last years of their life to lead as blind people – education and employment never present any difficulties. Obviously in the intermediate age group, there are different problems.

The personality, past training, intelligence and the home conditions will all have a marked effect on either reducing or increasing the difficulties facing the blind person.

Each blind person must be carefully and individually assessed by expert social workers (usually called *home teachers for the blind*) whose task it is to unravel each problem and arrange for help. The attitude of the social worker can do a great deal to minimise the difficulties of each blind person.

With newly blinded young adults (rather than with aged newly blinded), assessment is never easy, for often the blindness has suddenly occurred leaving the person uncertain, with some self pity and often they are bitter. Such newly blinded people should always be sent to a *special assessment centre* such as the one at Queen Elizabeth Homes of Recovery, Torquay, which is run by the Royal National Institute for the Blind. Here, under expert guidance, the person spends from four to six weeks while being assessed. Any self pity is quickly lost and the individual soon realises that life as a blind person can still be full and interesting. After a visit to this home, most newly blinded people return to their own home with a new and essential spirit of hope. Any industrial training then becomes easier.

Even when the blind person has settled down well, the social worker should make periodic home visits and continue assessment in an unobtrusive manner. Only in this way is it possible to ensure that the wide social services available to blind people are properly used.

Employment

About 10% of the blind people in the United Kingdom are between the ages of 16 and 50 years, and it is in this group that the problem of employment occurs. Full-time employment of blind people includes employment in 'open-industry', or an occupation in sheltered employment, either in workshops or in home workers schemes.

Employment in 'open industry'

The term 'open industry' is used to denote employment in an ordinary job (in industry or commerce) where the blind person works with, and is treated the same as, sighted people. No special arrangements are made as regards remuneration. There are many different types of occupations in which the intelligent, highly trained blind person can make a success, including a number of industrial processes such as capstan lathe operatives, telephone operators, piano tuners, etc.

The placing of blind people successfully in open industry depends on two important factors:

- having a helpful and sympathetic employer who is prepared to try out one or two blind people; and
- being able to train the blind person not only before the job starts but actually while carrying it out.

In both respects, the work of the *Blind Persons Resettlement Officers* of the Department of Employment is invaluable. These officers include highly trained blind persons who arrange for the placement of blind people in industry. They liaise with the employers and find out what vacancies exist locally, in open industry, which would be suitable for a blind person. The Resettlement Officer then assesses the potential of the blind persons wishing to enter open industry and trains those selected. The officer then introduces each blind person to the new post and stays to help with the training. In this way, this officer is able to guide the blind person through the most difficult part of the job, the beginning, and help in the settling down period. Afterwards visits are paid to the factory from time to time to check how the blind person is doing. If any difficulties occur in the meantime, the employer can call upon the Blind Persons Resettlement Officer to help sort them out. There is no doubt that this service helps many blind people to find and retain employment in industry.

Following the general principle already mentioned, *the aim should always be to try and place as many blind people as possible in 'open industry'* – an employment solution which is normal. It is encouraging to note, in many areas, a steady increase in the proportion of blind people in open industry.

Occupation in sheltered employment

For those blind people who cannot, for some reason, manage to hold down a job in 'open industry', the next alternative is to try and place them in what is known as 'sheltered employment'. This is specially subsidised full-time occupation applicable to blind persons only.

If possible, the blind person needing sheltered employment should be sent to a *special workshop for the blind*. Here, after a period of training in a suitable occupation, he or she is employed in the workshop. There are many traditional trades for blind persons in workshops including basket making, rug making, brush making, chair caning, machine knitting. The blind person is employed at the workshop full time, just as in an ordinary factory. Specially trained sighted foremen assist in the finishing-off of articles, and arrange the marketing of the products.

Each blind worker receives the usual wage for the occupation although, because of the handicap, the worker might not have been able to earn this wage 'on piece rates'. The difference between what is actually earned and is paid is called 'augmentation' and is paid by the local authority. Provided certain conditions are met, the Department of Employment will make a grant equal to 75% of the financial deficiency each year to the authority for each approved worker in sheltered employment. Certain capital grants are also available to voluntary bodies who provide satisfactory sheltered employment.

Home workers schemes are mainly found in rural areas and smaller towns where it is not possible to collect enough blind people together to form a sheltered workshop. Under the scheme the blind worker is provided with materials at home and makes a certain quota of goods which are later collected and marketed. Provided the individual averages a certain minimum output per week, *augmentation of wages* is paid as in the workshops. An example would be a blind person employed at home as a machine knitter; the knitting machine is provided by the local authority together with materials and orders.

Blind persons are employed in similar occupations in home workers schemes as in the workshops. Although many blind home workers schemes are excellent, they do not provide such a satisfactory solution as workshop schemes. In particular, it is often difficult to supervise the blind people satisfactorily and the blind persons themselves miss the company that they meet in a workshop. It is also more difficult for the blind person to concentrate on a high level of production – most homes contain too many distractions.

General social services for blind persons

- *Part-time occupations.* Some elderly blind people are keen to fill in a portion of their day by having a part-time occupation. This is usually arranged by the home teacher who helps organise any marketing assistance for articles produced. There are various arrangements to cope with this problem and many towns have a *disabled persons shop* which sells the products made in this way.

  Augmentation is never given to blind people working part time as it is only intended to help and encourage those engaged in full-time work.

- *Learning to read.* An important part of any social service for the blind is concerned with home tuition in reading. There are two forms of embossed type.
  - *Moon.* Raised letters, easy to learn but a very slow and inefficient method of reading which, for this reason, is not often taught.
  - *Braille.* This is the usual method of reading used by the blind. It is a complicated system of embossed dots arranged in a rectangular pattern. Braille is taught to all blind children and younger blinded adults, and to elderly persons who have both the ability and desire to learn. It takes an intelligent blind person at least six months fairly hard study to learn Braille and, for this reason, is beyond the ability of many elderly persons who go blind in later life. A useful indicator of the likelihood of an elderly person, who has recently developed blindness, learning Braille is given by finding out how much and what type of reading was undertaken before sight was lost. If the individual was an avid reader, it is always important to persevere with Braille. If, however, the blind person was a most casual reader of the simplest and widely illustrated newspapers, it is not likely that Braille will ever be learned. All persons recently blinded under the age of about 50 years, and all young persons should always be taught Braille.

- *Substitutes for reading.* The Royal National Institute for the Blind have a large *library of recorded tapes of books* and will lend a standard tape recorder to each blind and partially sighted person wishing to take advantage of this service. The person borrows the tape recording of the required book, plays the tape and, in this way, can have a continuous and changing supply of books read aloud to him or her. Each local authority makes a contribution to the Royal National Institute for the Blind for each person in its area who is using this service.

- **Radios for the blind.** The radio is a most useful service and greatly enjoyed by all blind people. There is a special voluntary society financed by the traditional appeal over the radio each Christmas Day, whose object is to ensure that every blind person is provided with a radio. Maintenance is arranged by local authorities.
- **Special aids.** Special aids in the home are available for the blind. A good example is the special braille form of 'regulo' which can be fitted to gas stoves to help the blind person when cooking.
- **Provision of guide dogs for the blind.** A society exists which provides and trains special guide dogs which can be used by the blind. The selection and training of the dog and blind person is lengthy and costly and necessarily limits the number of blind people who can be helped in this way. Only a few breeds are suitable for training, for example, retrievers. The service is particularly valuable for active blind people living alone. Local authorities meet the cost of training and provision of guide dogs.
- **Holidays and hostels.** The provision of special holiday homes for the blind is another general social function. Many of these are run by voluntary bodies, and local authorities assist by contributing and paying for the blind people from their area who use them. The holiday homes are specially adapted and make it possible for blind people to have a holiday of their own. The difficulties and dangers of going alone to ordinary hotels and boarding houses may prohibit blind people from taking holidays.

There are a few specially designed permanent hostels for elderly blind people. But many more old people who are blind are looked after very satisfactorily in ordinary elderly persons hostels – perhaps two blind people in a hostel containing 40 sighted elderly persons – and in many ways the blind people seem to enjoy such hostels more.

- **Financial help.** Although local authorities cannot help blind people by direct money grants, there are *special pension facilities* available to blind people. It is the responsibility of the social workers employed by local authorities to make certain that the blind people understand what these are:
  — for all blind persons aged 16 years and over, the income support rates are increased;
  — there are special income tax allowances for blind persons less any tax free disability payments.
- **Voting.** A blind person has a right to vote by post in parliamentary and local elections or to have the ballot paper marked with the help of a sighted person.
- **Free postage.** Free postage is allowed for a number of 'articles for

the blind' including embossed literature, paper for embossing, and for recordings acting as an alternative to an embossed book.
- **Television licence.** There is a reduction in the cost of any television licence.

Social services for other groups of disabled people

The social services described in detail above, provide a useful basis for a discussion of the services available to other disabled persons. In all groups, it is always important to arrange for the following:

- as complete a system of *registration* as possible;
- *individual assessment* by means of home visiting so that the difficulties and problems of the person can be separately assessed in the surroundings of his or her own home.

Compared with the other social services described for blind people, there are many differences for other disabled groups and these will now be discussed separately.

Social services for the deaf and dumb

The general term deaf and dumb describes people who are *born completely deaf* and who, in the past, *never developed any speech*, not because of a defect of voice production, but because normal speech is only learnt by copying what is heard – a process impossible in the congenitally deaf. With very modern methods of teaching, it is now possible to teach speech to most congenitally deaf children.

The problems of the group as a whole are *mainly connected with the isolation from which they suffer*. The need of most deaf and dumb people is, therefore, connected with arranging the following:

- suitable *interpreter services* in obtaining a job or in sorting out any difficulty. Finding and keeping a suitable occupation is not usually a difficult problem for deaf and dumb people, provided they receive help, especially in interpretation from a trained social worker;
- *clubs and recreational facilities*. Many deaf and dumb people use a mixture of sign and finger language by which they converse with each other. Because of this, they enjoy mixing with other deaf and dumb people rather than non-handicapped people with whom they often find it difficult to communicate.

Lip reading is also used to understand speech and many deaf and dumb people find television very enjoyable.

Most of the social services for deaf and dumb people are carried out by voluntary societies, many of which are connected with church bodies. There is an historical reason for their welfare which was originally started in the nineteenth century by the church, with the object of providing special church services which deaf and dumb people could follow. Today welfare services have developed widely to include all types of social services, but there are still special religious services held weekly for deaf and dumb people in many places.

Social services for the hard of hearing

People who develop deafness, having in the past enjoyed good hearing, are usually referred to as 'hard of hearing'. This term indicates that although deaf, such disabled people have normal speech and listen either by lip reading or with the help of a hearing aid.

The greatest proportion of people who are hard of hearing are elderly, as deafness, like blindness, usually develops seriously in old age. It is important to ensure the following:

- that correct assessment of hearing is undertaken from time to time;
- that hearing aids are provided and are well maintained so that they are constantly helpful.

The assessment of hearing is usually carried out in an Ear, Nose and Throat department of a hospital, or in a special centre, such as those found in the school health service of large authorities. Hearing should always be tested by a pure tone audiometer. Coarse tests often used, such as listening to speech or the ticking of a watch, are of very limited value and of no use at all in assessing the degree of deafness to different frequencies of sound.

Probably there is no more neglected health aid than a *hearing aid*. The fitting of a hearing aid needs patience to ensure that it is fully understood by the deaf person. One of the problems is that, for most people, the loss of hearing is differential – the notes at high frequencies are lost to a greater degree than those at low frequencies. As the consonants in speech are in the high frequency range of sound and the vowels much lower, it is the consonants which are usually missed, rendering speech difficult to understand. When the hearing aid is fitted, it amplifies both high and low frequencies equally; hence the consonants can be heard but seem to be drowned by the vowels. This leads to many elderly people thinking the hearing aid is useless. The solution is to persist for weeks with the aid until the brain slowly adjusts and speech once again becomes intelligible.

Social services for paralytic conditions

These include both progressive conditions (multiple sclerosis, muscular dystrophies) and non-progressive states, often the sequelae of accidents. Many of these individuals need a variety of community services outlined on pp. 332–338. Occupation should be possible for those whose mobility is maintained and especially for mild cases. Much of the social help this group requires is assistance with housing, transport and the fitting of various aids to enable them to live more normal lives within the community.

Paraplegia

Many of these cases result from accidents in which the spinal cord is permanently injured. The extent of the paralysis will depend upon the site of the injury – the lower the site the better the outlook and vice versa. All will be paralysed from the waist down, but if this is the main lesion (i.e. if the arms are unaffected) then up to 80% of patients should be able to lead reasonably normal lives and be able to follow an occupation. Such disabled people can, with the aid of suitable mechanised transport, become quite mobile and will usually develop tremendous power in their arms to compensate and soon learn how to improvise.

Sporting facilities have always been an important part of the social facilities provided for paraplegics. This is because the strengthening of compensatory muscles is an essential part of training those with paraplegia to overcome their disability. Following the lead given by Stoke Mandeville Hospital both national and international sporting events are held each year culminating in the Paraplegic Olympics which are held in the same year as the Olympic Games. Many different sporting activities are suitable including archery, basket ball, etc. Some local authorities assist paraplegics by providing suitable premises and sports centres where these activities can take place.

Cerebral palsy (spasticity)

Many spastic disabled people need similar services to those with other paralytic or crippling diseases. Most of these conditions date from birth and, therefore, suitable education and training facilities for the young adolescent are important. Speech defects also pose special difficulties and may lead to the erroneous impression that the person is unintelligent.

Recent work has emphasised that it is better to look after spastics in conjunction with other disabled people. About 25% of spastics also suffer from epilepsy and, therefore, for this group the services outlined below may also be important.

Epilepsy

People with epilepsy present many problems not met with in other groups of disabled people. This is not due to the unusual difficulties of treating epilepsy, but to the ill-informed and unfair attitude of the public generally.

Most people with epilepsy suffer from minor degrees of the illness and are well controlled and can quite satisfactorily be employed in most professions and occupations. In fact, there are many examples of people who have mild epilepsy succeeding in most occupations. But the public have an unreasonable fear of people with this disease because, quite wrongly, they assume that the person with epilepsy may be dangerous. Some people even think the disease is some form of mental illness. All this adverse public reaction leads to many patients with epilepsy concealing the fact that they have had occasional epileptic seizures, because they fear that if it is known they have epilepsy, they may lose their jobs or find it difficult to find employment. The strain of concealing these facts is considerable, especially as a sudden unexpected attack of epilepsy at work, could, at any time, lead to discovery. For this reason, many patients in good posts live in constant fear of discovery and this often leads to the development of other difficulties including a minor anxiety state.

To help anyone with epilepsy, it is important to realise this difficult background and to try and arrange for the employer or prospective employer to know the full facts and that the epilepsy, if properly controlled, may be no hazard. It is usual for those with epilepsy to have some form of warning of an impending attack and, apart from avoiding one of the few dangerous occupations which are rarely sought after, there are few jobs which are not suitable.

It is, however, essential that a constant and careful watch is kept on each person with epilepsy to make sure that the treatment received is controlling the disease.

The final success of any treatment depends on complete rehabilitation. Because of this, it is helpful to attach a specially trained social worker to any hospital which treats serious epilepsy, so that all the social aspects of the illness – home, occupation, etc. – can be carefully investigated. In this way, much preventive work can be done and many problems can be avoided or corrected before they can have a serious effect.

Occasionally, it is necessary to admit to an epileptic colony the rare person whose epilepsy is uncontrollable or whose home is quite unsuitable. Most epileptic colonies are run by voluntary bodies and local authorities meet the cost. Although most people in colonies have to stay there permanently, every effort is made to rehabilitate them sufficiently to return to community life if at all possible.

Driving

If the person has had an epileptic fit in the last three years he/she will be barred from holding a driving licence. If the epilepsy is fully controlled, then after three years' absence of any seizures, the individual will be able to regain their driving licence.

Special medical assessment and treatment centres for epilepsy

Important special centres for medical assessment of difficult cases of epilepsy have been set up for children at Oxford (based on the Park Hospital for Children) and for adults at York and Chalfont (Bucks). Skilled assessment in difficult cases is essential and such units are just beginning to probe some of the complicated facets of epilepsy.

19 Care of mentally disordered persons

Mentally disordered persons are a large group of people suffering from two separate problems:

- those who have, or in the past have had, *some form of mental illness the main feature of which is that their emotional reactions are unstable, at times illogical, unbalanced and may be unpredictable.* This group has no direct connection with the individual's level of intelligence and will include a full range of people from the most brilliant through the normal range to the duller;
- those who have a *learning disability* because their intelligence is limited and is well below the normal range. The terminology of this group is confusing. The Mental Health Act 1983 is applicable to only a small proportion who are carefully defined as either 'severely mentally impaired' or 'mentally impaired' (see p. 360). The majority were originally referred to as 'mentally handicapped' but this by convention was changed first to 'those with learning disabilities (mental handicap)' and now has been shortened to 'those with learning disabilities'. In this group the most usual cause is that the person was born with a low intelligence quotient (see p. 121). In many instances the condition is linked with inheritance and in some, such as Down's syndrome, is known to be due to a genetic abnormality (trisomy on chromosome 21).

Although the aetiology (the causative factor) is different in those who are mentally ill from those who have learning disabilities, the services for both were moved closer together by the Mental Health Act 1959. The reason for this was that both the emotional stability and the level of intelligence of the individual can often play an important part in assessing the likelihood or not of extra problems developing in both the mentally ill and in those with learning disabilities. For example, in the case of someone who has learning difficulties (in which the level of intelligence is seriously retarded) the chances of their ability to live normally and maybe independently will to a large extent also depend on the persons's emotional stability. If, as in the case of most people with Down's syndrome, that is normal, there is a much better chance of them leading a reasonably normal life and hopefully carrying out a simple occupation. If, however, there is even a moderate degree of emotional instability, this may well prove to be impossible.

In the same way, an extremely clever person may be able to manage to live 'normally' even though he or she is extremely emotionally unstable – their extreme intelligence enabling them to behave just within the bounds of the law, and others will usually excuse their odd behaviour as being 'very eccentric'. If however the person who is very mentally unstable happens to be dull and relatively unintelligent (even if this falls short of being classified as having a learning disability) social rejection and consequently serious problems are more likely to follow.

Another important reason for not completely separating those with mental illness from those with learning difficulties is that since the mid 1960s, it has been shown that the best results are obtained when the care of both is carried out in the community (either in their own home if possible or in a specialised home or hostel) rather than as an inpatient in a hospital. This is the main reason for the current emphasis on *community care* for both those who have mental illness and those with learning disabilities. Extensive research has shown that if good community care can be carried out the individual is much happier and the end result is far more normal and satisfactory. It is important never to make the mistake of believing that the motive in developing community care is economy – that is not so, as *in most instances good community care is more expensive than hospital care.*

Main aims of all treatment and long-term care for those who are mentally disordered

The main aims and principles governing the treatment and care of those who are mentally disordered (whether they are mentally ill or have learning disabilities) can be summed up as follows:

● *preventing wherever possible any stigma attached to these conditions.* It is illogical to attach any stigma to mental disability as both types are extremely common. At least 439 persons per 100 000 are actually admitted to a mental hospital every year (that is one in 227 people). In addition it has been calculated that one in 10 persons at some time during their life will seek advice from a GP for an illness that is primarily mental rather than physical. Surveys in Wessex and Camberwell (London) have indicated that 235 people per 100 000 (or one in 425) have an IQ less than 50 (almost all of these would be classified in the group as 'those with learning disabilities'). This means that there are few families who do not have some relative who has been or is either mentally ill or who has learning disabilities;

- *attempting to reduce stigma in every possible way*, by arranging for district general hospitals to have a mental health department so that anyone being investigated and treated for mental illness is not necessarily segregated and therefore possibly stigmatised. Also it is hoped that the basis of treatment in all physical illness will eventually be copied when treating mentally ill persons. In physical illness as far as possible many of the initial investigations are carried out on an outpatient basis and hospital admission is only arranged when the treatment cannot be undertaken at home, (i.e. a serious operation is required). Once the acute treatment is over the person returns home even if the outlook is poor – even in a steadily progressive disease such as a serious cancer the patient returns home if at all possible.

There are of course important differences between mental disorders and physical illnesses. In mental illness there may be a question of protecting the patient and the community from some of the effects of the illness – for example there may be a danger of suicide which is a special problem in endogenous depression, or if there is any insomnia in puerperal depression. Occasionally violent behaviour is noted (even sometimes criminal behaviour) which means that special arrangements have to be made to admit a few persons compulsorily to a mental hospital or mental department and to retain them there (custodial care). Many mental disorders are longstanding which adds to the problems. However more and more persons suffering from serious mental diseases such as schizophrenia are now spending most of their time at home or being supported in some way in the community, although occasionally they have to return to hospital if they relapse.

Before the 1950s, mental hospitals were almost entirely asylums – places where the inmates could be cared for. Treatments were limited and many patients remained in these hospitals for years and became totally institutionalised. The introduction of tranquillisers and better rehabiliation and support in the community has changed all this. The main aim today is to use hospital admission in all mental disorders only for assessment and early treatment. Once the patient has been stabilised they return home as soon as possible. Here treatment is continued by visiting GPs or outpatient departments and the use of *community psychiatric nurses and aftercare services in day centres*. These and other forms of community care are essential to avoid isolation and eventually a relapse. Occasionally it is still necessary to arrange an emergency hospital admission but wherever this is possible, it is done on an informal basis. It is only when this proves impossible that such persons today will be admitted to a hospital compulsorily.

The *core objective of all services for the mentally disordered in both the health and social services is to develop all forms of community care*

*to help persons who are either mentally ill and those with learning
disabilities to remain in normal circulation outside the hospital.*
It is still occasionally necessary to arrange a special hospital admission usually for a short period but this has already become the exception rather than the rule. However it is now realised that already steps
are needed to ensure that patients who are suffering from mental
illness are not discharged before adequate community care facilities
are available (see below – the Secretary of State's statement in August
1993 about the intention to introduce legislation to create 'supervised
discharge').

Community care services for mentally disordered persons

The development of community mental health and social care services
started in the 1960s and evolved slowly until the National Health and
Community Care Act 1990 was passed. This accelerated the rate of
development of community care, making it a top priority. In fact the
specific financial grants which the Griffiths report of 1988 recommended were the only patient/client care grants implemented (see
pp. 281–2). These have made certain that the majority of the funding
necessary for the development of community care for a mentally ill
person who formerly was looked after in a hospital will be transferred
from the NHS budget to local authorities to assist them to meet these
new increased responsibilities. At the same time, as already explained
in Chapter 15 (p. 282), the Government emphasised the need to use
private community services especially in the home/hostel field to
ensure the fullest use is made of existing services whether provided
publicly or privately.

The increased development of widespread community care services
since 1990 has made it possible for treatment to be continued while the
person remains at home. Where home conditions are not suitable, the
individual may live in a *special hostel/home* provided either by the
social services department locally or by a voluntary organisation.
Occasionally *boarding out* may be arranged with sympathetic persons
who understand mental disability. Another excellent arrangement is
to provide *sheltered flats* where two mentally disordered persons can
live together quite independently. For those with learning disabilities
initially considerable supervision and training will be required but
once such persons have settled in, it is quite usual for them to cope very
well with a minimum of supervision especially if they continue to
attend a day centre.

Successful community care will only be possible if a wide range of
supporting services (especially social service help) are available –
social workers skilled in aftercare work, hostels, special homes, adult

training centres, day centres, clubs, special workshops, occupational therapy, and job placement services leading, if possible, to full- or part-time employment being obtained in ordinary industry or if this is impossible in special workshops. On the health side, community care can be provided by primary health care teams (GPs, practice nurses, health visitors and district nurses), and community psychiatric nurses supported by consultants from the local mental health departments and hospitals. All must work closely together so that all complement each other.

Supervised discharge and other initiatives announced by the Secretary of State for Health in August 1993

The Secretary of State for Health announced in August 1993 a new 10 point plan for developing successful and safe community care:

- strengthened powers to supervise the care of patients detained under the Mental Health Act 1983 who need special support after they leave hospital. These comprise:
  - a new power of supervised discharge; and
  - extending from six months to one year the period during which patients who have been given extended leave under existing arrangements can be recalled to hospital;
- publication of the Department of Health team's report of its review of the 1983 Mental Health Act;
- publication of an improved version of the *Code of Practice*, which spells out clearly the criteria for compulsory admission under the 1983 Act;
- fresh guidance to ensure both that *psychiatric patients are not discharged from hospital inappropriately* and that *those who leave get the right support* from the different agencies;
- *better training for key workers* in their duties under the care programme approach. This will cover the new Code of Practice and guidance, and will take account of the lessons from the cases which have gone wrong, and from the Royal College of Psychiatrists' confidential inquiry into homicides and suicides by mentally ill people;
- encouraging the development of *better information systems*, including special supervision registers of patients who may be at risk and need most support;
- a review by the Clinical Standards Advisory Group of standards of care for people with schizophrenia, both in hospital and in the community;

- an agreed work programme for the Government's Mental Health Task Force, which supports health authorities in moving to locally based care;
- ensuring the health authority and GP fundholder purchasing plans cover the essential needs for mental health services;
- the London Implementation Group will take forward an action programme to help improve mental health services in the capital, identifying and spreading the best practice.

Supervised discharge and other changes

Supervised discharge is undoubtedly the main reform in the new programme. Under supervised discharge patients will be subject to conditions, including a *treatment plan negotiated with the patient and their carers, and a requirement to attend for treatment periodically*. A named key worker would be appointed who is immediately responsible for that patient's case. He/she must ensure that the procedures agreed in advance of the discharge from hospital are followed and that decisive action is taken if the patient does not cooperate.

The patient will have the right to appeal against the conditions attached to his or her discharge to a Mental Health Review Tribunal. Patients and their carers must and will be closely involved with determining their treatment plan. It is most important that patients and their carers are clear about what their treatment in the community involves.

Failure to comply with the conditions would lead to an immediate review of the case. If necessary, the patient could be recalled to hospital under the existing provisions of the Mental Health Act 1983.

Both the introduction of supervised discharge and the lengthening of the period of extended leave will require primary legislation to implement.

Compulsory hospital admissions

About 10% of mentally ill patients enter hospital compulsorily. In most of these persons, the reason for the admission is acute and serious. Under the Mental Health Act 1983, only persons who cannot be persuaded to enter hospital informally can be compulsorily admitted. Three types of compulsory admission are used.

- *Admission for observation in an emergency* (Section 4 of the Mental Health Act 1983). This section is used for acute emergencies, *only lasts 72 hours* and requires either (i) an application by the nearest relative or by a specially trained social worker, or (ii) one medical recommendation. The applicant must examine the patient within 24 hours of making the application and the admission must be carried out within 24 hours of the medical examination.

- *Admission for assessment* (Section 2 of the Mental Health Act 1983). Again the application can only be made by the nearest relative or by a specially trained social worker. Recommendations from two doctors are needed, one of whom must be approved as having specialist knowledge of the type of mental disorder from which the patient is suffering. Both doctors must examine the patient at the same time or within a period of seven days.

  Such a patient may be admitted and detained in hospital for a *period not exceeding 28 days*. There is an opportunity to appeal against detention under Section 2 of the Mental Health Act 1983 within the first 14 days of detention and then the case must be reviewed by a Mental Health Review Tribunal (see p. 356).

- *Admission for treatment* (Section 3 of the Mental Health Act 1983). This is the least common method of compulsory detention and is usually used for patients who have already been admitted to hospital under Section 2 but who need further detention in the interests of their own health or safety or with a view to the protection of other persons and who need to be kept in hospital for treatment. This method of admission and detention can be used for persons suffering from mental illness or from severe mental impairment or psychopathic disorder. However in the latter two instances, such patients may only be detained if they can benefit from treatment.

  Admission under Section 3 *lasts for six months and then for one year at a time. Any patient who has been compulsorily detained for three years without a Mental Health Review Tribunal must then be referred to the Mental Health Review Tribunal.*

Mental Health Act Commission

This Commission was set up in 1983. Its main responsibilities include the following:

- the exercise of general protective functions for detained patients;
- the visiting and interviewing of detained patients;
- ensuring that patients are informed of their rights;
- examining the lawfulness of detention;
- investigating complaints.

Mental health review tribunals

There are many safeguards to make certain that no patient is retained in hospital compulsorily unless it is essential. Special Mental Health

Review Tribunals, consisting of a senior lawyer as president, a psychiatrist and a lay member, are set up in each area to deal with requests for discharge from patients. After hearing the application the tribunal may direct the patient's discharge. *It must do so* if it is satisfied that any of the following conditions are met:

- that the patient is no longer suffering from mental illness, psychopathic disorder, mental impairment or severe mental impairment;
- that it is not in the interests of the patient's health or safety, nor for the protection of other persons, that the patient should continue to be detained;
- in the case of a psychopathic disorder that, if released, the patient would not be likely to act in a manner dangerous either to others or to him or herself.

Ordinary informal hospital admissions for those who are mentally ill

The majority (90%) of all hospital admissions for mentally ill persons are made by the GP arranging for the patient to go into hospital informally in exactly the same way as for physical illness. The decision is usually made after a discussion between the GP and the consultant psychiatrist at the local mental department. In long-standing cases well known to the psychiatrist all arrangements are usually made by a phone call but in new cases, the psychiatrist will usually first see the patient either on a domiciliary visit or at the local outpatient department.

Social services for the mentally disordered

Role of local authorities

The social services departments of local authorities are responsible for developing widespread community social services for the mentally disordered (mentally ill and those with learning disabilities). These fall mainly into three categories:

- social work support provided by specially trained social workers;
- day care facilities to help with the reintegration of anyone who has had mental illness or has learning disabilities. These include social rehabilitation, occupational therapy, industrial therapy and workshop provision;
- residential facilities for those who have no satisfactory home.

It is convenient to discuss social services for the mentally ill under the following headings.

- Prevention
- Housing
- Hostels
- Occupation
- General aftercare
- Day care
- Hospital admissions.

Prevention of mental illness

Much preventive work in the mental health field is concerned with the *avoidance of further breakdown.*

In many instances, however, the *extrinsic factors* (see p. 207) connected with the patient's environment especially at certain times of life, for example puberty, pregnancy, menopause, old age, *are the precipitating cause* of the start of the mental illness or a further breakdown.

Because of the extreme importance of the early years of life on the subsequent development of any person, it is most important to recognise early, if possible, *unusual signs of insecurity in a child*, as this is likely to indicate unsatisfactory home conditions. Most maternity and child health services today have a close link with a child psychiatrist and child psychiatric social worker so that health visitors may discuss such cases and get help with their preventive work.

Social work support should be available to such a home at any time and the decision about who is best fitted to provide this should be made after joint discussion between doctors, health visitors, community psychiatric nurses and social workers. In the same way, close liaison should always be maintained between child guidance staff who are helping schoolchildren with emotional or behavioural disorders and social workers who may have to provide aftercare later.

Housing and conditions at home

Housing conditions which are unsatisfactory for the mental development of a child may be quite different from those precipitating physical illness. The home may be very well provided with the physical essentials of life, but the *important mental factor of stability, love and affection* may be missing. Some of the worst environments are those homes in which parental strife is continuous and unending, perhaps eventually leading to separation or divorce. For this reason the health visitor or social worker must pay particular attention to any home with such a background.

Even when early recognition of mental health problems has been made, it is never easy to change that home so that it becomes satisfactory. But it is always a great help to know the problem exists and it is usually possible to prevent the effects of the poor home conditions being very detrimental to the child.

The value of the right type of home is just as important for anyone who has had a mental illness and has been successfully treated in hospital. *It may be better for such a person to go to a special hostel on discharge from hospital rather than return to an unsuitable home.*

Small homes (hostels)

Homes can be of various types and are provided by either the social services department privately – or by a voluntary body. The aim should always be to achieve *maximum integration between those living in them and the ordinary community*. This is easier if the hostels are small, accommodating 6–8 persons and if they are scattered throughout the area rather than built together. As far as possible, hostels should be like ordinary houses; they can be established successfully in the older larger house or by modifying two or three adjacent terraced houses together on a modern council estate. *Boarding out* can also be useful as an alternative to an unsuitable home provided sympathetic and understanding hosts can be found – because of this difficulty few successful boarding out schemes have yet been introduced by local authorities.

Occupation

A carefully chosen occupation can do much to prevent a person developing a mental illness or having a relapse, and is always an important factor in rehabilitation.

Many large industrial firms and HM Forces carefully examine all new entrants to assess as far as possible the type of personality, intelligence, aptitude and emotional stability, so that the individual can be fitted into the most suitable occupation. This is an important part of any occupational health service, for correct selection of occupation can avoid many breakdowns.

Having fitted the new entrant into a job, it is equally important that the worker is carefully watched in the early period of employment so that any signs of undue strain are recognised. This is also a valuable part of all student health services at universities for it is known that serious mental illness in students can be avoided by ensuring early recognition of signs of stress.

A *Disablement Resettlement Officer* (DRO) (see p. 333), a specially trained officer of the Department of Employment, will assist in finding employment for all disabled people, including those who are mentally disabled. It is often difficult to find employment for persons who have had a mental illness. They may have lost their original job and there is usually a resistance among employers to re-employ them for fear they will again break down and perhaps dislocate their staff. It is important that any unavoidable delay should not depress the person who has just left a mental hospital. *Occupational therapy* at a special rehabilitation centre or *attendance at a day centre should always be provided* as this will not only help in training the individual in physical skills (see below) but, perhaps more importantly, it will do much to *restore self-confidence* and get the person used to meeting others and prepared for normal working conditions.

Social workers assist the Disablement Resettlement Officer in trying to find suitable jobs for those recovering from mental illnesses. Some social services departments have found it useful to employ a full-time officer to do this task. Much of this work is slow, and in one year such an officer may only find employment for a few patients. Work is needed not only in finding jobs, but in meeting employers, and constantly helping to educate the public in the problems of mental illness. The successful placement of one such person may well lead to another post being found in the same firm.

General aftercare

Most people who have had a mental illness will need long-term help and follow-up aftercare, usually provided by the person's own GP, who should work closely with the social worker. All social aspects – home, family, occupation, etc. – play an important part in aftercare and the social worker must ensure that close cooperation exists so that the person who has recovered from a mental breakdown is given every opportunity to return to normal life as quickly as possible.

Day care facilities for the mentally ill

Day care facilities play an increasingly important role in the rehabilitation of many former mental hospital patients. The centres should provide a wide opportunity for the individual to meet many different people and thus improve their social rehabilitation. Many such people lack confidence and their self-respect has been shaken by their illness. They need to gain confidence by demonstrating that they can manage quite well on their own (when they are away from their families). Daily attendance at such centres which are reached by a bus or train journey helps in regaining self-confidence.

The recent rapid growth of day centres for mentally ill persons is shown in Table 19.1. It will be noted that the numbers of places at day centres for those who are mentally ill have increased in the decade

Table 19.1   Numbers of day centres for mentally ill: places in England, 1981–91.

1981	1985	1986	1987	1988	1989	1990	1991
4907	5414	5545	5839	6113	6396	6979	7841

(From Health and Personal Social Service Statistics, 1993.)

1981–91 by 59.8% – a reflection on the emphasis which has been placed on community care.

The functions of such centres often overlap with those of day hospitals and sheltered employment. *Occupational therapy* should be available at day centres. As well as helping with the problems of readjusting to the demands of work, *cultural and educational activities* such as a study of art, music, drama or literature should also be provided at day centres. Those attending day centres should be encouraged to help in their daily running and organisation.

Homelessness and mentally disordered persons

Homelessness is a special problem in mentally disordered people (especially those with long-term mental illness) who have have had no home or family support. Many of these persons gravitate towards large cities and especially to London. In an attempt to prevent such people from becoming homeless and destitute, four multidisciplinary teams have been set up in London by the Department of Health to reintroduce homeless people to mainstream mental health services. Specialist hostel provision has been developed to supplement that already provided by voluntary organisations and statutory services. Longer term accommodation will be provided through the Housing Corporation.

Social services for persons with learning disabilities

'Learning disabilities' is a colloquial term in general use. It is not a legal term. The Mental Health Act 1983 introduced two terms: 'severe mental impairment' and 'mental impairment'. Both are similar but vary in degree. 'Mental impairment' is defined as a state of arrested or incomplete development of the mind which includes significant impairment of intelligence and social functioning and *is associated with abnormally aggressive or seriously irresponsible conduct.*

Note that all persons who are mentally impaired will also have learning disabilities but only a small proportion of those with learning disabilities are also mentally impaired. It all depends on whether or not there is also 'abnormally aggressive or seriously irresponsible conduct'. Mental impairment is a legal term and only *those who are mentally impaired can be dealt with under the Mental Health Act 1983.*

There is a tendency to classify people who have learning disabilities according to their intelligence level, by means of an intelligence test (see pp. 121–122). However, it is well known that intelligence tests often give unreliable results. These tests take no account of the individual as a whole – the personality, behaviour and skills – and the results can vary according to the motivation of the person being tested and the particular test used.

The basis for determining whether or not someone has a learning disability depends on the following:

• an estimate of the person's intelligence;
• a social test to judge the ability of the individual to make full use of their intelligence (i.e. a test of performance). Generally children who are 3 years or more behind their average age group in school probably have a learning disability unless there is another reason for their learning difficulties such as deafness or they have had a prolonged absence from school because of illness;
• the emotional stability of the person. The more unstable the individual the more likely that person will function at a lower level and that could be crucial in borderline cases.

The range of intelligence in those with learning disabilities is wide. Generally those with an IQ less than 50 will all have learning disabilities provided there are no reasons for a false result such as deafness. With an IQ of above 50 the individual's level of functioning eventually will determine whether that person suffers from learning disabilities or not. This decision will depend on the following:

• their home and living conditions. Those with an excellent home with a patient and helpful family may eventually be able to function above the level of learning disabilities even with an IQ as low as 50–55. If their home is totally unsuitable then a level of 60–65 IQ will not always be sufficient to lift them out of the learning disabilities group;
• their emotional stability. This is very important for with very stable persons whose IQ is just over 50 it may still be possible for them to function above the learning disability group. However a very emotionally unstable individual with an IQ as high as 75 may not be able to function above the learning disability level.

Persons with an IQ below 45 are quite unable to lead an independent life and to guard themselves against exploitation and common dangers. They are occasionally referred to as having 'special needs' or needing 'special care'. Many are multiply handicapped, need nursing services and require constant supervision. They often have a reduced life-span.

Incidence of those with learning disabilities

In the UK it is estimated that approximately 235 persons per 100 000 suffer from learning disabilities. About 51–55% live at home and the remainder in special hospitals or in residential accommodation.

Causes of learning disabilities

Most cases of learning disabilities are present at birth and generally result from a mutation in which the individual is left with an incomplete development of the mind. Such persons may belong to a recognised group such as *Down's syndrome* which is caused by a chromosome abnormality, but there may be no discernible origin. A number of cases are associated with *cerebral palsy* which is mainly caused by anoxia (lack of oxygen to the baby often earlier in pregnancy). Although in such cases there may be a connection between the degree of spasticity and the intelligent quotient, this is not invariable for *a few very severely spastic persons have normal intelligent quotients*.

Reference has already been made to the rare metabolic disease *phenylketonuria* (see p. 96) in which the baby is born normal but the defective metabolism soon produces a poisoning of the brain leading to developmental delay within a few months. If phenylketonuria is diagnosed early – within 6 weeks of birth – and the child is then fed on a special diet, there is every hope that subsequent development will be normal. It is for this reason that the blood of all babies is tested by the midwife on the tenth day and between 4 and 6 weeks of delivery to make certain that every case is discovered early. It is equally important to recognise *hypothyroidism* shortly after birth by screening every baby early in life and then treating any abnormality that might be found – otherwise, if hypothyroidism is present and not treated, it will lead gradually to the infant being affected with a learning disability.

Learning disabilities occasionally develop following a severe infection of the brain or meninges especially if the diagnosis has been delayed. For this reason, it is essential that any symptoms of brain irritation are immediately fully investigated so that effective treatment can quickly be started if it turns out to be a case of meningitis.

Prevention of learning disabilities

The opportunities to prevent handicap are increasing. The following is a list of likely ways to avoid it.

- **Genetic counselling.** The aim in genetic counselling is to identify where there is a high risk of the transmission of hereditary disease leading to learning disabilities. At present this is usually only possible after the birth of one affected child (unless there is a family history as in Huntington's chorea). In some cases it may be possible to estimate the risks of another disabled child being born. If these are high because one parent is a carrier of an abnormality which is likely to show itself in other children, then the parents can seek family planning help to prevent conception of another child.

It is possible to predict the chances of any parents having a Down's syndrome child. In a few instances there seems to be a family tendency to such births, shown by either a family history of such children or by the mother already having given birth to a Down's syndrome child. In such families genetic counselling is of considerable help. *The incidence of Down's syndrome also progressively increases with the age of the mother (see Table 19.2).*

- *Amniocentesis* (removal of a small quantity of amniotic fluid). Chromosome abnormalities can be detected at 16 weeks, in time to enable a termination of pregnancy to be carried out if investigations show that the fetus is abnormal. This is advised routinely for pregnant women aged 35 years and over and for anyone who has already had a Down's syndrome baby (see p. 75).
- *Immunisation of girls against rubella.* Immunisation between the ages of 11–13 years of a girl, who did not have an MMR vaccination as an infant, will prevent a possible rubella infection later in the first three months of a pregnancy which could lead to brain damage in the baby. Since 1988, all young children have been offered an MMR immunisation before the age of 15 months (see p. 132).
- *Use of anti-D immunoglobulin* to prevent haemolytic disease of the newborn (see p. 77).
- *Expert care in labour and the puerperium* to reduce the risk of hypoxia and brain damage to the infant.
- *Intensive care during the neonatal period* for babies of low birth weight including the continuous monitoring of blood oxygen levels.
- *Screening* to prevent phenylketonuria (see p. 96) and other metabolic diseases.
- *Earlier completion of families* to reduce the chance of a child with a congenital mental disability such as Down's syndrome from being born. Table 19.2 illustrates how the chance of a baby being born with Down's syndrome rises as the age of the mother increases.

Importance of coordination and a multidisciplinary approach

Although this section mainly describes social services, it is essential to realise that the *medical, educational, psychological and social needs* should always be considered together. No single profession can tackle

Table 19.2 Incidence of Down's syndrome by age of mother (from Hook E.B. and Chambers G.M. (1977) *Birth Defects* **3A**, 123–141).

Mother's age	Risk	Mother's age	Risk	Mother's age	Risk
20	1/1923	30	1/885	40	1/109
21	1/1695	31	1/826	41	1/85
22	1/1538	32	1/725	42	1/67
23	1/1408	33	1/592	43	1/53
24	1/1299	34	1/465	44	1/41
25	1/1205	35	1/365	45	1/32
26	1/1124	36	1/287	46	1/25
27	1/1053	37	1/225	47	1/20
28	1/990	38	1/177	48	1/16
29	1/935	39	1/139	49	1/12

successfully all the problems and the use of an *assessment team* is important.

In young children the paediatrician, psychiatrist, child psychologist, health visitor, practice nurse, social worker and educationalist may all be involved as well as the family doctor. Older children need educational, social and vocational assessment. Adults may require repeated assessments from psychiatrists, clinical psychologists, general practitioners and social workers. Much of this assessment will take place in hospitals, schools, training centres, workshops or in the individual's own home.

Community social services

Many of the main social services of local authorities aim to provide a supportive community care service in which persons with learning disabilities and their families are encouraged to live a more normal life. If possible such individuals should be trained to follow a full-time occupation.

Since the introduction of the Education (Handicapped Children) Act 1971, the care of a child with learning disabilities up to the age of 19 years is undertaken by the education services (see p. 121).

Many varied types of assistance are provided by social services departments of local authorities including the following:

- social work support and counselling;
- practical help – home help, day nurseries, laundry services, sitters-in, etc.;
- training and day centres for adults;
- occupational therapy centres;
- workshops for adults;

- employment in ordinary industry;
- small homes (hostels);
- short-term or respite care;
- holidays and recreational activities – clubs, etc.

Social work support and counselling

Parents and families need much help to adjust to the problems of caring for a child with learning disabilities. Many professionals are involved – doctors, health visitors, teachers and social workers. Much of the domiciliary visiting in the community is undertaken by social workers especially after initial diagnosis and assessment.

Although education authorities are now responsible for the education of these children in special schools, much of the social work for this group, for example visiting at home, is carried out by social workers from the social services department. This has the great advantage of improving coordination between the education and social services departments and enabling continuity of care to be maintained when the child reaches the age of 19, ends formal education and then comes under the direct supervision of the social services department.

Key workers

The latest initiative issued by the Secretary of State for Health (see p. 353) contained much emphasis on the importance of allocating a *named key worker* to any person who is mentally disordered (mentally ill or suffering from a learning disability) and is being looked after in the community. When such a person is first discharged from hospital into the community, it is essential that the key worker should be appointed so that it is clear to all – the person with the learning disability, their family or close friends – so that they can in difficulty turn to a professional who will be able to help them. It is expected that most key workers will be social workers with special training who will then be responsible for giving advice, support and assistance when needed.

Practical help in the community for those with learning disabilities

Most families facing the problem of caring for a person with learning disabilities may need the assistance of a *home help* (see p. 391), *a day nursery* (see pp. 290–291) and *laundry services. Sitters-in* can also be of great practical help to enable the parents to get a short break. *Respite care* in which the person who has learning difficulties is admitted for a week or fortnight to some residential care to allow the parents to take a holiday break is also invaluable and is an essential element of an effective community care scheme. The key worker should be able to arrange all these services when they are required.

Training centres for adults

Adult training centres or social education centres are provided by social service departments and designed to carry on the training of people with learning disabilities who have left special school. Most are mixed but there are some single sex centres. The main task of the centre is to concentrate on training in some skill to enable most to move to a special workshop and a few to ordinary employment. A few adults with learning disabilities may find it difficult to adjust themselves to such training, but with the modern workshop whose tasks are more diverse, most should be able to benefit (see p. 367).

Social training should continue in the adult training centres and all should concentrate on mastering the skills of helping to run a home and to enjoy various hobbies and pastimes. It is very often in these training sessions that a simple concept of numbers is understood.

The development of adult training centres and special care units by local authorities has continued at a steady rate (see Table 19.3). This has been at a slower rate of 30% from 1981 to 1991 than that seen with the mentally ill (see Table 19.1) but the reason for this is that the main development of adult training centres and special care units for those with learning disabilities took place from 1965 to 1981.

Table 19.3 Numbers of adult training centres and special care units for people with learning disabilities: places in England, 1981–91.

1981	1985	1986	1987	1988	1989	1990	1991
43 627	48 824	50 374	51 782	53 032	54 221	55 897	56 723

(From Health and Personal Social Service Statistics, 1993.)

The importance of *inducement and constant encouragement* must be recognised. Individuals must be given targets to achieve and not just left to work at their own pace. The *potential of many people with learning disabilities is far higher than usually expected*, but full potential will only be reached by training which constantly encourages each individual to improve.

Family therapy

Any training given in a centre should always be linked with home life for people with learning disabilities enjoy participating domestically.

The disabled person's family, too, may need continuing support. They should be encouraged to include their disabled member in all their activities since stimulation and a loving and secure environment, as with all children, will help development. In addition to home visits by professionals, informal family group meetings allow ideas to be exchanged, problems to be aired and are also social occasions. Problems occasionally arise as puberty develops in people with learning disabilities. It should always be carefully explained to parents that close supervision must be maintained on the activities of their child at home. In particular, it is most important that every parent of a girl who has learning disabilities realises that her handicap will make her more vulnerable to the advances of unscrupulous men.

Occupational therapy centres

Some occupational therapy centres are also used to help those with a learning disability, giving them an opportunity to become involved in many different activities. These include various handicrafts and also training in group activities. If possible evening clubs should be arranged and run in such a way that the people with learning disabilities themselves do much of the organisation (see p. 370).

Workshops

During the 1980s there was widespread development in the setting up of *sheltered workshops* within or close to adult training centres by local authorities, where adults with learning disabilities are employed. The type of work varies, but examples include:

● carrying out tasks which can only be undertaken by hand and which those with learning disabilities can cope with; occasionally these are contracted out to the workshops by industry;
● fixing a pourer into the top of a salt container;
● stamping tight the top of another container;
● assembling packs of picnic cups;
● assembling ball-point pens.
● manufacturing 'own products' such as the making of wooden and soft toys or furniture which are then sold locally.

Because of the necessity to fit the regime into that of industry, the workshop remains open for the whole of the year. Although the workshop is, in effect, a place of employment for many people with learning disabilities, the training processes still continue. This is often seen in the method of payment adopted. One successful scheme is to base weekly payment upon a 'points' system, in which points, which represent part of the maximum wage, are added for good steady work and rate and standard of production, and deducted for bad behaviour, lateness or non-attendance. In this way people employed at the workshop quickly learn the importance of hard work and good behaviour.

Inducement is an essential part of workshop training and the method of financial remuneration used should encourage better productivity, hard work and better social behaviour. It is usual to arrange that the maximum 'wage' be equal to the maximum amount each may earn without having any deduction made from income support. At present, this means each person with learning disabilities employed at the workshops may earn a small sum of money per week without any deduction being made in income support.

One of the most encouraging and remarkable changes which has always been reported following the successful introduction of workshops for such persons has been the great improvement in the behaviour and outlook of those attending. Almost without exception, they become better behaved, easier to control and seem to be very delighted to realise at last they are 'earning' – they obviously feel they have made a great step forward by having shown they have a useful occupation. There is little doubt that the introduction of such workshops has done much to improve the opportunities and facilities for the adult with learning disabilities.

Employment in open industry

Until recently few opportunities occurred for mentally handicapped people to move on from workshops to working in ordinary industry. Successful workshops report that it should be possible to find work in ordinary industry for at least 10% of those with learning disabilities who have been trained in the workshops. The success of this must depend to some extent on the employment opportunities in the district and the present high level of unemployment is making it very difficult. It is, however, important to recognise the employment potential of these people which, in a minority, includes successful employment in ordinary industry, especially when unemployment falls to lower levels.

Small homes (hostels)

Most social services departments provide special homes where those with learning disabilities can live when, for any reason, they have to leave home. In some cases there is a need to provide a home (hostel) where the individual can live during rehabilitation after discharge from hospital. It is most *important that no-one is ever kept in hospital any longer than is absolutely necessary, otherwise they become institutionalised* and further rehabilitation becomes more difficult.

The term 'home' is often used instead of 'hostel' because it is hoped that it will not give the impression of impermanence or of a certain austerity. All should provide a homely atmosphere and be friendly. The purpose of the home should be to provide a permanent substitute family home.

The size of each home varies, but it should not exceed 20 and many excellent ones are much smaller containing four to five individuals.

It is important that all persons with learning disabilities living in the home partake of ordinary duties just as if they were living with their own family. These include the cooking of breakfast and the preparation of a light evening meal.

Every effort should be made to *integrate these homes completely within the community* – children should attend normal special schools (i.e. not a school solely for the residents), adults should go out to work either in ordinary industry or in special workshops and special care units. The activities of the residents should be as nearly the same as those people in a normal home environment.

Short-term or 'respite' care

Very many children with learning disabilities are looked after in their own homes by devoted parents. There is, however, a great deal of strain involved and many parents find the continuous caring process produces considerable problems for the family. It is important that the devotion of such parents is not continued in such a way that matrimonial difficulties occur, and that other normal members of the family are not neglected.

One of the most useful aids in preventing this danger is for social services departments to provide 'short-term' respite care in which special temporary arrangements are made to look after the child with learning disabilities for a short period (two to three weeks to enable the parents and family to get a complete break). It has been found that such short-term care helps such parents considerably and enables them to return refreshed to the arduous task of looking after their handicapped child.

It is also important to provide some shorter breaks for parents by arranging for experienced 'sitters in' who can look after the child while the parents have an evening out. In some instances it helps to arrange residential care for one night or even for a weekend.

Special care units

These units are designed to look after the more profoundly disabled persons with learning disabilities, some of whom are multiply handicapped and may even be incontinent. They are usually sited adjacent to the normal adult training centre and require some special nursing staff. They do enable even these grossly handicapped persons to live at home and these units also give the parents essential respite during the day time from the very arduous task of caring for their very handicapped child.

Services provided by hospitals

A certain proportion of profoundly handicapped persons with learning disabilities are unable to settle at home even with the assistance of the special care units and other forms of community care. A few therefore will always have to remain in special small hospital units because they cannot even learn simple social habits or because of their extreme emotional instability, behavioural problems and incontinence.

However the main aim should always be to keep such individuals within the community wherever possible, but even with the most sophisticated community services, a few very handicapped persons cannot manage to live at home. For this small group, permanent hospital care is and will always be needed.

Holidays and recreational activities

Most social service departments provide social centres or clubs for people with learning disabilities where they can pursue pastimes and form a club. Such activities are valuable in helping them to gain confidence, to enjoy themselves and to get used to meeting people. Social workers often attend such centres and, in this way, keep in touch with their clients.

Holidays of various kinds are also arranged. Some of these are traditional type holidays but others are of a more ambitious type (i.e. adventure type of holidays, camping, etc.).

Special legal powers covering mentally disordered people

Criminal proceedings

In criminal proceedings, courts have power to authorise the admission and detention of a mentally disordered person found guilty of offences by the Courts. A *Hospital Order* may be made if the court is satisfied that, on the written or oral evidence of two doctors (one of whom must be specially approved), the offender is suffering from mental illness, severe mental impairment, mental impairment (see p. 360) or psychopathic disorder warranting hospital treatment. This order authorises the removal of a patient to hospital within 28 days. The

Court may, if necessary, make an order for the detention of the patient in residential accommodation provided by a Local Authority, a hospital or mental nursing home, a residential home for mentally disordered persons, a police station or any other suitable place where the occupier is willing to receive the patient.

Alternatively, the Court may make a *Guardianship Order* instead of a Hospital Order if it is thought that the client should be cared for within the community. It is usual in such cases for local authorities to assume the office of Guardianship.

Protection and management of property and affairs

Any person who becomes mentally incapable of managing his or her own affairs cannot legally authorise anyone else to do this. If power of attorney has been given to another person before the mental illness then such authority will probably become inoperable because of the illness. In such cases, the *Court of Protection* exists to protect and manage the affairs and property of any person who is mentally incapable of doing so. The Court of Protection usually appoints a *receiver* – often a close relative (parent, brother or sister) – to administer the patient's affairs under the direction of the Court. This will continue until the Court of Protection is satisfied, on medical evidence, that the patient is now fit again. Application to the Court of Protection (at 25 Store Street, London WC1) can be made by a close relative or by instructing a solicitor to make such an approach.

20 Care of elderly persons

The proportion of elderly persons in the UK has been steadily rising since 1900 and by 1992, those aged 65 years and over has reached 9 138 000 or 15.76% of the population – 59.9% in this age group are women (5 472 000) and 40.1% are men (3 666 000).

The Office of Population Censuses and Surveys (OPCS) calculates population projection figures for England and Wales. The latest estimates for the period 1991–2031 show that the largest increases will occur in the age group 85 years and over. The latest figures are given in Table 20.1.

These figures represent a massive increase in the numbers of persons aged 85+ in the years to 2031 and will cause many extra problems for the health and social services for the incidence of disability is very high in this age group (see p. 327), and persons of this age need more hospital and other medical care and also considerable supportive services.

Figure 20.1 shows where and with whom the elderly lived in England in 1976, and these results are likely to be similar today. Note that 94% of all old persons lived at home, the remaining 6% in hostels/homes, hospitals, etc.; 28% of old people lived alone and only 12% lived with children (today this figure would probably be lower). In fact, over two-thirds of all elderly households contained no-one under the age of 65 years and at least one-third of all elderly people had never had any children or their children had not survived – they have no near immediate next generation family.

Table 20.1 Projections of numbers of persons aged 85 and over from 1991 to 2031, England and Wales, thousands.

	1991	2001	2011	2021	2031
Males	211	294	380	485	699
Females	601	793	924	974	1235
Total	812 (1.59%)	1087 (2.05%)	1304 (2.40%)	1459 (2.65%)	1934 (3.5%)
	1 in 62	1 in 49	1 in 42	1 in 38	1 in 29
Total Population	50 955	52 885	54 299	55 129	55 240

(From OPCS Monitor PP2 94/1.)

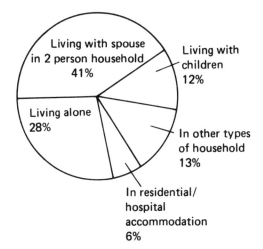

Fig. 20.1 Where and with whom the elderly lived in England, 1976.

Special problems of elderly people

An excellent research project was carried out in Aberdeen in 1980 by Taylor and Ford who studied the elderly persons in that city to find out which old people were at most risk. They divided their results into three groups, as follows:

- *At high risk:*
  — very old persons (over the age of 80) – these represented 15% of the sample;
  — those who had recently been discharged from hospital – 13% of the sample;
  — those who had recently moved – 13.7% of the sample.
- *At moderate risk:*
  — those on low incomes;
  — those recently widowed;
  — those living alone;
  — those in social class V.
- *At low risk:*
  — those living in isolated situations;
  — those who have never married;
  — those who had never had any children.

It is interesting and important to note that those at greatest risk were not in the groups usually classified as those who are likely to be at the

greatest risk – those living alone or those in poor financial circumstances. It is also important for any nurse working in the community to
realise that anyone in the 'greatest risk' group shown above should be
carefully watched and extra visits carried out where possible for most
problems in elderly people are much easier to solve when discovered
early.

Another finding in this survey was that it is a mistake to assume that
'the elderly' make up a homogeneous group. In fact, the only characteristic that is similar to all old persons is their age and apart from
that, they always represent a completely mixed group with very individual problems often requiring specific solutions. For these reasons,
careful individual assessment is always needed.

Prevention of social and medical problems in old age

The avoidance of many social and medical problems in elderly persons
depends on the earliest recognition of warning signs and social difficulties. All social service departments employ social workers and other
care staff solely to help old persons with advice, to visit them when
necessary, to support them and, if the need arises, to arrange various
community help including home helps, meals services, chiropody
services, occupational therapy services as well as day centres and day
care centres. It is important that all this work is carried out in close
association with the many other persons working in the community
and especially with those in the primary health care team – doctors,
practice nurses, health visitors, community nurses. Links should also
be maintained with those working in the churches, voluntary workers,
friendly visitors and all other community workers so that those elderly
persons in special need can be found quickly. Neighbours can always
play an important part in alerting professionals that some elderly
person is at special risk. Any person living nearby should, in some way,
ensure daily that the old person is all right. In villages and small towns,
such surveillance is natural and tragedies rarely occur. However in
large cities old persons living alone are likely to be at much greater risk.

Planning for retirement

Many of the difficulties in retirement can be eased by good planning.
Generally it is wise to stay in the same district close to well-known
friends. Human relationships are worth more in old age than being in
some attractive place particularly if the individual has to live alone as a
widow or widower.

Large companies are increasingly arranging pre-retirement semi-
nars for their employees. These are normally held within 2–5 years of

retirement and usually include the partner of the employee. Topics covered include social security benefits, company pensions, health, leisure, part-time work, the home in retirement and at least two long sessions on all aspects of financial planning. *It is also essential to check that everyone has made a will as many complications and problems can follow whenever anyone dies intestate.*

Health advice

Health advice which can either be given at the pre-retirement seminar or by the individual's own GP should cover the following points:

- the importance of maintaining a clear-cut sense of purpose in retirement;
- the value of an active lifestyle. Sensible physical activity can reduce the chances of developing an ischaemic heart attack and also can help to keep arthritic joints mobile;
- continued intellectual activity is always important and can be crucial in maintaining an active mind;
- weight control. Gross overweight causes many problems as it increases the risks of developing ischaemic heart disease and diabetes. It also aggravates any degenerative arthritis present in the hips, knees and back;
- nutritional problems can occur especially in late retirement as the person may then have to live on their own after the death of their spouse or partner. A well-balanced varied diet with plenty of vegetable fibre, a low fat content and a good fluid intake is important;
- various *screening tests* should continue to be carried out including *cervical smear tests* until the age of 70, and *mammography tests* from 50 to 65 and then afterwards if there is a family history of breast cancer. Regular *eye tests* every 2–3 years including the checking of intra-ocular pressure are essential (as this is the only way to make certain of avoiding the later development of glaucoma as any warning symptoms occur very late or not at all);
- protection of the skin against excessive ultraviolet sunlight especially on the tip of the nose and face by using sun creams with *at least a factor as high as 15*;
- having medical checks immediately on noticing any unexplained loss of weight;
- having a blood pressure test every 2–3 years;
- caring for the feet – many serious mobility problems can arise later by neglecting the care of even relatively trivial foot defects;
- the importance of recognising early *warning signs* which need immediate medical investigation. These include *persistent cough,*

sudden hoarseness of the voice, loss of weight, breathlessness, frequency of micturition and sudden change in the rhythm of the bowel motions;

- a sudden alteration in any *skin mole* – it may change colour, bleed, become larger or itch excessively – all these are indications for a full medical investigation;
- a hearing loss should never be ignored. If a hearing aid is fitted, it is important to emphasise the need for persistence in its use. As the high notes are nearly always lost to a greater degree than the low notes the amplifying effect of a hearing aid can result in speech suddenly becoming difficult to understand and many elderly persons immediately come to the wrong conclusion that the hearing aid is useless. If they persist with the aid for a few weeks their brain adjusts to the new sounds and they will get benefit from the aid;
- for persons over the age of 65 years it is sensible each October *to have an immunisation against influenza*. Mortality from this disease is always higher in older persons and protection in this way is valuable;
- the home of all elderly persons should always be well heated. Bad habits such as insisting on keeping the bedroom windows open in very cold weather can quickly aggravate chest infections and lead to ill health. The homes of all elderly persons should whenever possible by heated by an automatic heating system. This enables the individual even in an emergency to heat the home properly.

It is also very useful to discuss at some length the importance of recognising and treating *psychotic depression* early. Many elderly persons are reticent even to consider the possibility of mental illness although all the statistics show that *mental illness is considerably commoner in elderly persons*.

It is vital to treat depression at once otherwise there is a real risk of suicide – this is always very tragic as with treatment the results are excellent and the patient should recover completely within a few weeks. Another important point to emphasise is that any development of confusion should always be immediately reported to the GP. This is especially important in very old persons – over 80 – as acute confusional states become much commoner then and, as most have quite specific causes (see p. 379), effective treatment will nearly always quickly cure them. It is also helpful to explain that the symptoms of Alzheimer's disease usually start gradually – the development of the disease is quite different from the sudden onset of a confusional state. This can be very reassuring to the relatives who nearly always first jump to the wrong conclusion that the problem is Alzheimer's disease.

Another helpful topic that can be discussed with women who are attending a pre-retirement seminar and are still in their early fifties is the option of *hormone replacement therapy*, especially if they are in one of the high risk groups for osteoporosis (see p. 226).

The prevention of accidents in the home

Elderly people living at home either with a family or on their own are more likely to have accidents and especially falls. Any such fall will probably be more serious in an elderly person because:

* it is more likely to result in serious injury and in the development of various fractures;
* any fall can become the start of a general deterioration in that elderly person.

Three main types of falls are seen in elderly persons:

* those associated with vertigo (dizziness);
* those caused because old people are usually more liable to trip up;
* most elderly persons have considerable difficulty in regaining their balance after a trip.

A contributory factor is that in most people over the age of 80 years their labyrinthine function is faulty which means that they cannot balance in the dark. As this defect is slowly progressive, anyone over the age of 75 should always either put on the light or use a hand torch if they have to get up at night so that they can continue to use their sight to balance.

Extra care should always be taken by an elderly person who changes his or her spectacles to bifocals, for these make it more difficult to focus in the area around the feet. Consequently objects seen previously may now become potential obstacles and lead to falls. Anyone with a special liability to fall should learn to walk with some support from a solid object (handrail, chair or a piece of furniture or use a Zimmer walking frame). Intelligent anticipation of the causes of falls can do much to prevent them.

Cold-associated ill health (hypothermia)

Elderly persons tend to react to the effects of cold badly. A prolonged cold spell in winter always coincides with an increased number of deaths in elderly persons. Severe hypothermia is relatively rare but deaths from respiratory diseases, heart attacks and strokes in old people increase in very cold weather and are often now spoken of as 'cold-associated deaths'. Those at greatest risk are:

* over 70 years of age – the older the individual the greater is the risk;
* elderly people over 75 years taking certain medicinal drugs including tricyclic antidepressants and phenothiazines;

- those already suffering from some other disease including diabetes, hypothyroidism, strokes, Parkinsonism, confusional states and alcohol dependence;
- any sudden illness such as pneumonia will increase the risk temporarily.

Whatever the cause, it is *most important that the condition is recognised early* and that all staff dealing with elderly persons at risk know the early signs of hypothermia. The person does not look cold and certainly does not shiver. The hands and face often look warm and are red or reddish purple in colour. The individual is often drowsy, very inactive and the speech may become slow and slurred. The hands, feet and face feel cold and the body temperature (as measured on a specially low recording thermometer) is usually well below 35°C (95°F).

Once the condition is recognised, emergency treatment must be started. Treatment is often difficult and unsatisfactory. *Rapid warming is very dangerous in elderly people with hypothermia* and must be avoided at all costs. The aim should be to limit the warming up of the elderly person to 0.6°C per hour. The room temperature should be kept warm and a few extra blankets applied but no direct heat.

Prevention of hypothermia

The prevention of hypothermia involves realising that the condition can develop insiduously. Three important factors should be stressed:

- elderly persons should always be accommodated in warm conditions;
- encouragement should be given to elderly people to move around during the daytime. It is wrong for them to sit all day even if they are in a warm room;
- it should be realised that hypothermia is always more likely to occur in a person already ill. Therefore any nurse looking after an ill old person at home should always be on the look-out for its occurrence.

Mental illness in elderly persons

Mental illness is commoner in elderly persons. Any type of mental illness may be seen in old people but there are two special problems – Alzheimer's dementia and the acute confusional states.

Alzheimer's dementia

It has been estimated that in the UK about 500 000 persons suffer from Alzheimer's dementia. This disease always starts slowly and insidiously and shows the following signs and symptoms:

- there is a slow progressive decline in the ability of the individual to understand the common features of life;
- there is a general deterioration of higher cortical function. Although they remain alert, they find it more and more difficult to think and behave logically;
- the individual becomes increasingly confused although anxiety is completely absent. The person clearly does not understand what is happening and does not realise how odd their behaviour is becoming – normal insight is eventually completely lost.

Because of the slow nature of the early symptoms and the absence of any specific pathological test, Alzheimer's dementia may be difficult to diagnose with certainty early in the disease. It can start any time after about age 50 and progressively deteriorates until eventually the patient cannot even recognise close members of their family.

One form of Alzheimer's dementia is associated with a gene deficiency which is located on chromosome 21. This is the same chromosome associated with Down's syndrome which explains why Alzheimer's dementia is much commoner in those with Down's syndrome in late middle age.

No known curative treatment exists for Alzheimer's dementia. In the early stage of the disease it is always best to keep the patient at home but the strain on the relatives becomes greater and greater. *Forms of respite care are essential for the carers* who are always under great strain. Eventually as the person deteriorates it becomes impossible for the relatives to cope and the person must be admitted to a psychogeriatric unit. This stage however may not be reached for some years.

Acute confusional states

These usually develop suddenly and are mainly seen in people over the age of 70. Sudden confusion is the main feature and as the patient realises that all is not right, anxiety and agitation also commonly occur (this is in striking contrast to those developing Alzheimer's dementia).

In all the confusional states there is always an underlying precipitating factor. These differ widely and include the following:

- *dehydration* – some very old persons do not drink enough fluids and this can lead to an attack;

- *medicines/drugs* – a number of commonly prescribed medications can precipitate a confusional state in very old people unless the dosage is reduced as the patient reaches 75 years. The commonest medicines that can do this include cimetidine, beta blockers, anticholinergics, many tranquillisers and barbiturates;
- *infections* – in very old persons infections such as pneumonia, influenza, urinary infection, etc. are often not accompanied by a fever as in younger people but instead they produce a confusional state. Once the condition is effectively treated, this confusion disappears and once again the person becomes lucid;
- *hypoxia* (oxygen deficiency) can produce a confusional state in a very old person mainly by starving the brain of oxygen. Cardiac failure and respiratory deficiency can affect elderly people in this way;
- *psychotic depression* in very old persons can be accompanied by a confusional state;
- *alcohol excess or alcohol withdrawal* have both been found to produce a confusional state in this age group;
- *intrinsic brain damage* caused by cerebral tumours, secondary cancers in the brain, strokes and cerebral trauma have all been identified as causing confusional states;
- *the development of uraemia* can lead to confusion.

The early diagnosis of a confusional state in very old persons is very important as most can be promptly and effectively treated and the patient will then quickly return to normal. The reason why certain medicines can produce these attacks is that the rate of their destruction in the body slows down after the age of 75. This means that *these drugs slowly accumulate and eventually reach a state where the person is receiving what is equivalent to an overdose.* Occasionally this condition is referred to as an *iatrogenic* disease (doctor induced) and all nurses looking after very old patients should always be on the look-out for such a complication. In all confusional states it is best to treat the patient at home amongst familiar surroudings.

In all cases a close watch should be kept on the amount of fluids being taken by the patient during treatment as if dehydration develops it can soon become a further cause of confusion and, in this way can prolong the attack even after the initial factor producing the original confusional state has been corrected.

Health services for elderly persons

All the normal primary health care services and district nursing services are available to elderly persons at no extra cost as there are no prescription charges for women aged 60 years and over and for men aged 65 years and over. In recognition of the extra medical work involved in providing medical services for elderly persons, there is an increased per capita fee paid to GPs for all patients on their lists aged 65 and over.

Special problems seen in elderly persons living at home

Often an illness or accident is the starting point of a rapid deterioration in any old person living at home, hence *any illness or accident in an elderly person must be treated seriously* even if at first it seems trivial.

Rehabilitation is *more important in elderly persons* because there is a tendency for many elderly people never to get back to normal after a serious illness. Rehabilitation can be hastened by arranging for the elderly person to attend a rehabilitation unit. Physiotherapy and occupational therapy at such units will assist them to regain their mobility during convalescence and can be especially useful to elderly persons whose rheumatism and arthritis have inevitably been aggravated by them staying in bed during an illness.

Convalesence on return home can be aided by arranging a full-time home help for a short period and then gradually reducing that help, as the elderly person takes over the routine tasks. In this way, it is often possible to nurse an elderly person through a serious illness without eventual loss of function and independence.

Incontinence can be a difficult problem in some elderly persons. The following are important:

- making certain that medical or surgical treatment will not help;
- encouraging an elderly person to empty their bladder regularly. There is evidence that a number of those who suffer from incontinence just forget to go to the toilet. In homes where attendants remind people from time to time the level of incontinence falls;
- the use of suitable clothing. A number of old people suffer from urgency and cannot undo their clothing in time. There is a wide range of special clothing designed and available from the Disabled Living Foundation or aids centres which can help with this problem. Buttons are replaced with 'velcro' and many garments have front openings although designed in such a way as to look normal.

Geriatric hospitals

Geriatric hospitals and geriatric wards in general hospitals help and are widely available for the investigation, treatment and rehabilitation of elderly people. The main differences between geriatric and acute hospitals are the special facilities which geriatric hospitals have for the following:

- linking up with the local social services. *Social factors in the life of an elderly person often determine the seriousness of an illness and its prognosis*;
- emphasising the importance of *active rehabilitation* for all elderly persons. There is a real danger that bed rest required in the treatment of an acute disease will tend to prevent full recovery in an elderly person unless very active steps are taken to assist them to become fully active in convalescence. For this reason good rehabilitation facilities are always part of any geriatric ward.

Day hospitals

Day hospitals have been developed to help with the rehabilitation of elderly patients. They act as a half-way stage between hospitals and home. Patients are brought there by transport and return home in the evening. Elderly persons may attend daily or on a specified number of days per week. Physiotherapy and occupational therapy are usually provided.

The main value of the day hospital is that they:

- allow an elderly person to be safely discharged home earlier, thus encouraging independence;
- assist with the active rehabilitation of the patient;
- help to establish a better link between the geriatric unit and the community services for elderly people.

Community hospitals

In country districts community hospitals have helped to develop a day hospital approach for some patients. These hospitals also provide *short-term 'respite care'* for bedridden elderly persons being looked after at home enabling the family to take a break. They also are useful for terminal cases and are usually staffed by the local GPs.

Chiropody

At present chiropody is provided privately and to a limited extent by District Health Authorities. In some instances the service is given at luncheon clubs, day care centres and clubs where elderly persons congregate.

Foot defects can have a serious effect on the mobility of an elderly person. To obtain maximum benefit, it is important that chiropody treatment is regularly arranged *once every six to eight weeks*, otherwise the condition of the elderly person's feet may quickly deteriorate.

Day surgery

Day surgery in which the patient comes to a hospital unit early in the day, has some surgical procedure carried out, then rests and returns home in the evening has developed considerably since 1980. In 1979–80, 570 000 cases were dealt with by day surgery but a decade later, in 1989–90, over 1 million patients a year were being treated by day surgery. There are three main reasons why day surgery is being encouraged:

- medical advances now make it possible to carry out certain surgical procedures more quickly and easily, sometimes with minimal invasive techniques (with the smallest of incisions) and using local or regional anaesthesia rather than a general anaesthetic. This can be very useful in elderly patients;
- it is preferable for any patient to return to his/her home and family rather than stay in hospital;
- recent research has shown that it is more cost effective than in-patient treatment.

Social services available to elderly persons living in their own homes

There are many special social and supportive services available to an elderly person living in his/her own home. The main aim should always be to encourage an old person to maintain their sense of purpose in life and to keep as active and independent as possible. Most elderly people find the early years of retirement very enjoyable provided they have a sufficient income and a satisfactory home to live in. It is after the age of 75–80 that problems are more likely to arise. Sensible anticipation can reduce many of these.

Interests, hobbies and part-time work

Every retired person should be encouraged to cultivate some hobby, past-time or interest. It is best if this process has been started before retirement. The advantages are many – contact with people, widening of interests, mental stimulation, physical activity and a sense of satisfaction. It is also useful for an elderly person to become involved in some part-time work (either voluntary or paid). Even during periods of high unemployment, many opportunities can be found. It does not matter if the elderly person has little experience in the particular field provided they have an affinity and are reliable. Many retired people can be extremely understanding, patient, helpful and sympathetic, making them very suitable for dealing with the general public. To the elderly person themself, part-time work can be invaluable for it gives the person a clearer cut sense of purpose as well as the satisfaction of knowing they are still needed.

For any elderly person who, in some way, is becoming more and more physically handicapped (perhaps with a degenerative arthritis) the motivation of work can be most important as it seems to make the individual more determined to keep going for as long as possible.

Financial help

Pensions and allowances

State retirement pensions and extra financial help are provided by the Department of Social Security. Many elderly people need help and advice as most old persons and families only have an imperfect understanding of the range of pensions and allowances available. There are two very useful free telephone enquiry lines open to the public throughout the UK. Anyone can ring these lines to discuss any general pension or allowance (both contributory or non-contributory) or benefit. The numbers are:

0800 666 555 – for general enquiries

0800 882 200 – for enquiries about financial assistance for those with physical and/or mental disabilities.

A telephone queueing system is in operation for these lines. It is therefore best to ring the number and wait. A useful method is to make notes about the enquiry, dial the number and wait either reading or writing a letter. Never replace the receiver, wait and ring again in a few minutes as this means one will constantly go to the back of the queue.

Retirement pension

The retirement pension is a state benefit that is paid to everyone who has:

- reached state pension age (60 for women and 65 for men) *and has*
- paid or has been credited with enough National Insurance contributions (39 years for women and 44 years for men for the full pension). If contributions have been paid or credited for a shorter period (minimum 10 years) a proportionately smaller pension will be paid.

A married woman can qualify for a retirement pension either:

- if she meets the above conditions or
- on her husband's qualifications. In this instance she must be 60 years old *and* her husband must be 65 years old.

If the elderly person goes into an NHS hospital the retirement pension is reduced after six weeks. If however the person is living in a local authority elderly persons' home, the pension is reduced immediately.

Income support

Income support is a benefit anyone (elderly or not) may be able to get if their total income is insufficient. Income support is a non-contributory benefit and can, in certain circumstances, be paid to persons receiving a retirement pension.

Disability Living Allowance and Attendance Allowance

Any disabled person whose needs for special financial help starts under the age of 65 can apply for the Disabled Living Allowance (see pp. 330–331). For any disability which starts *after the age of 65*, there is no special financial help available for mobility but the Attendance Allowance (which is comparable to the 'care' element of the Disability Living Allowance) can be claimed if the person requires special help at home during the day and/or at night. Any elderly person who is in doubt whether they qualify should ring the freeline 0800 882 200.

Housing accommodation

Reference has already been made of the importance of any elderly person living in satisfactory housing in which they will be able to cope even if they become very limited by physical disabilities (see p. 272).

Sheltered housing

This can be very useful for frail elderly persons who can no longer cope at home. Most local authorities and some voluntary bodies provide excellent sheltered housing particularly for frail people living on their own. Most of the sheltered housing units provided are specially adapted flats with alarms fitted.

Supportive housing

Some local authorities are now introducing special units – supportive housing – where even more support can be given to the frail elderly person than in sheltered housing. In addition to a midday meal, two or three hours of domestic help are provided daily, yet the old person retains his or her own 'front door' and thus remains more independent than in an elderly persons' home.

Community services available to assist elderly persons living in their own homes

Numerous special services are supplied by social services departments to assist elderly persons living in their own homes. In all instances, the constant aim is to ensure that the elderly person remains as independent as possible. In most cases it is important to provide these services early enough so that they can prevent more serious difficulties from developing. These community services include the following.

Home helps

One of the main functions of home helps is to assist elderly persons in their own homes and, in this way, enable them to remain there much longer even though they are getting more and more frail. (A detailed account of the role of home helps is given in Chapter 21, p. 391.)

Good neighbour schemes

A number of local authorities have introduced 'good neighbour' schemes to help frail elderly people at home (see Chapter 21, p. 392 for full details).

Home care programmes

Elderly persons living on their own are particularly vulnerable when they have just been discharged home from hospital after an illness. Home care programmes have been devised to support elderly people at such times (see Chapter 21, p. 392 for full details).

Meals services

Social service departments provide two types of meals services for elderly people:

- *meals-on-wheels* provide a hot two-course meal delivered to the home of the elderly person, usually three to six times a week according to need. A small charge is usually made for this service;
- *luncheon clubs* are for less frail elderly people who can attend at some local hall or club from three to six times a week and there obtain a hot meal. Luncheon clubs are especially useful as the elderly person is encouraged to meet others, gets exercise on their journey to the hall and not only gets the benefit of a hot meal, but also has the opportunity to make friends. A similar charge is usually made for the meal at the luncheon club.

Day care centres

These have been described as 'homes without beds' as they are intended to look after frail elderly persons who are in need of care and attention which would usually be provided in an elderly persons' home. Transport collects and brings the elderly person to the day care centre and takes them home in the evening. The elderly person spends the day at the centre where meals and other services are provided (such as bathing, hairdressing and laundry etc.).

This type of care is particularly useful where a frail elderly person is living with young relatives who go out to work during the day. It is also useful for any elderly person living alone and can prevent much loneliness as well as making it possible for the elderly person to stay in their own home. It is usual for an elderly person to come to the day care centre two to three times a week. A small charge is usually made.

Clubs and day centres

There are many types of clubs and day centres run by social services and by voluntary bodies (especially Age Concern). These provide a place which the elderly person can visit at any time for company, have a light meal and, in many cases can enjoy some leisure activity. Attendance is usually free but charges are made for meals etc.

Holidays and outings

Most local authorities, through their social service departments, arrange special holidays and outings for elderly people and this is also widely supported by voluntary bodies. Holidays are especially important to help elderly persons living alone and also for those living with relatives, for holidays enable each to have a break. In this way, a holiday can be of great value to both the elderly person and the family.

Concessionary fares

Facilities for unrestricted travel on buses in off-peak times can do much to maintain the independence of elderly people and also can help them to keep in touch with members of their family who may have been rehoused some distance away (to a pensioner living on the retirement pension alone bus fares out of large cities can be very expensive and out of their reach). Schemes vary throughout the country – some local authorities provide a free bus pass while others provide a certain number of tokens that can be exchanged for bus tickets. The usual age group qualifying for such help are women aged 60 and over and men 65 and over.

British Rail Senior Citizen's Railcard

British Rail has a scheme whereby anyone who is aged 60 years or over can buy a special railcard for £16 (1994). This enables the person to obtain usually about one-third off the price of a rail fare.

Residental homes for elderly persons

From 1978 to 1992, there was a complete change in the pattern of provision of residential homes for elderly persons in the UK. Table 20.2 illustrates this clearly. The figures are for England and Wales but similar changes have occurred in Scotland and Northern Ireland.

Table 20.2 Residential homes for persons over the age of 65 years, England and Wales, places and percentages, 1978–93.

Type of home	1978	1983	1986	1990	1992	1993
Local authority	102 804	103 598	101 704	89 340	71 369	63 400
	(67.7%)	(60.2%)	(49.8%)	(37.9%)	(30.3%)	(27.4%)
Private	24 657	42 142	77 557	119 883	132 063	134 500
	(16.2%)	(24.5%)	(37.9%)	(50.8%)	(56.4%)	(58.1%)
Voluntary	24 526	26 468	25 121	25 633	31 483	33 700
	(16.1%)	(15.3%)	(12.3%)	(11.3%)	(13.3%)	(14.5%)
Total	151 987	172 208	204 382	234 856	234 915	231 600

(From Health and Personal Social Service Statistics, 1994.)

Note that over the period 1978 to 1993 there has been a large increase in the numbers of places provided overall, of 79 613 (52.4%). The greatest increase has been in the numbers of places provided in the private sector as well as in the proportion between the three types of elderly persons' home. In 1978 local authorities provided the majority of places (67.7%) with private homes at 16.6% and voluntary homes at 16.1%. By 1993, it was the private sector who provided the majority at 52.4% while the local authorities had fallen to 27.4% and the voluntary bodies to 13.3%.

This change has been encouraged by the Government's emphasis upon community care (see Chapter 15, p. 281). This indicated that local authorities in future should act not only as providers of residential care but should assist in the development of private residential homes. At the same time, there has been a greater concentration on local authorities developing satisfactory and up-to-date methods of ensuring the quality of care remains high in all residential homes whether private, local authority or voluntary homes (quality assurance).

To this end, the Registered Homes Act 1984 came into effect together with the Residential Care Homes Regulations made under the Act. At the same time, with sponsorship from the Department of Health, the Centre for Policy in Ageing drew up a Code of Practice for the running of all residential homes. This emphasised five basic principles:

- the maintenance of the personal dignity of all residents;
- the importance of access of space which the resident can call his or her own;
- that choice is essential;
- autonomy – as far as possible, the Code of Practice recommended that residents should have a say in the way the home was run. Rules should be kept to a minimum and mainly be, as in a good hotel, limited to instructions in case of a fire or other emergency;
- responsible risk taking should be accepted and in particular over-protection should be avoided.

This Code of Practice illustrates perfectly the principles to be followed to ensure, as far as possible, residents can enjoy a good quality of life in a residential home.

Residential homes in the UK include many purpose-built ones (these are mainly run by local authorities) and many large converted houses. If possible there should be a high proportion of single rooms with a few double ones. Larger rooms are not desirable. A particular problem with elderly persons' homes is that a large proportion of the residents are extremely frail. Most are over 80 years old and women outnumber men by at least 3 to 1. A few are confused and some incontinence occurs. Some are mentally disturbed and can cause difficulties as they are often verbally aggressive.

In all homes, local authority and private, every resident subscribes to their cost. Each person is asked if they can afford the cost and, if they can, they pay the full cost. If not each resident is assessed. If their only income is the retirement pension then they are left with a small sum as pocket money and the balance has to be paid. Any capital below £3000 is ignored but if the capital exceeds that sum, the full cost must be paid until that capital has been reduced to £3000. The local authority then meets the balance in local authority homes. In private homes the Government under the community care programme pays to each large local authority (the ones who run the local social services) a large sum to enable them to subsidise to a predetermined amount those whose income and capital are insufficient.

The capital rule means that most elderly prefer, if at all possible, to remain in their own homes. The Government would prefer such a strategy and under the community care initiative supporting services (including respite care) are being increased in both the health and social services. With the large expected increase in the numbers of very old people over 85 years of age it is clear that it would be more sensible to aim at keeping most persons of this age in their own homes with support rather than admit them to an elderly persons' home. Anyway most persons of this age would prefer to stay in their own home if at all possible.

Occasionally the question arises whether a particular elderly person is so disabled that they should be cared for in a hospital or in a nursing home rather than in an elderly persons' home. Generally the answer is that the frailest elderly person who can reasonably be looked after in an elderly persons' home should be able to at least get up daily, dress even if only with assistance, make their way across a room with help and eat a meal without assistance. Anyone unable to do this would generally be deemed to need specialised hospital or nursing home care.

Emergency compulsory removal of an elderly person from their own home

Very occasionally it is necessary to consider removing compulsorily an elderly person from their own home because it is dangerous for the individual to stay at home and they refuse to enter a hospital or elderly persons' home. Fortunately very few elderly persons are removed in this way as most readily agree or can be persuaded. The cases that have to be removed are those who have badly neglected themselves and include those suffering from late cancers and others who are afraid to go to a hospital.

Action is taken under Section 47 of the National Assistance Act 1948 and the Amendment Act of 1951 which gave power for compulsory removal of aged and certain other people to hospitals or other institutions. It is only possible to remove those who are:

- suffering from grave chronic disease or being aged, infirm or physically incapacitated, are living in insanitary conditions, *and*
- are unable to devote to themselves, and are not receiving from other persons, proper care and attention.

The social services department arranges the removal but first the local Director of Public Health must arrange for a doctor to certify that it is in the interests of the person to do this. If the magistrate (or Court) is satisfied, the removal to hospital or elderly persons' home is then carried out.

21 Other community social services

Home helps

Every social service department must provide a home help service which is adequate for the needs of the area. The aim of the service is to provide assistance in an individual's home when, because of age, infirmity, acute or chronic illness (physical or mental), the person cannot look after themselves or their home. The service can also be used in some maternity cases.

The majority of home helps (about 88%) care for elderly persons in their own homes (see p. 386). Other groups include disabled younger persons and those with acute or chronic illness. Ocasionally home help services can also be used to help care for physically or mentally disabled children, to allow the parent to spend more time with a handicapped toddler. This can be especially important *for a child who is born deaf.* Provision of a home help to assist with housework and shopping can allow the parent to spend more time teaching the child lip reading – this is particularly important while the child is aged 1½–5 years.

It is usual to make a charge for home helps but there is a sliding scale of assessment according to income; those on income support or those whose only income is the retirement pension are usually given the service free.

The duties of a home help will vary with each case but include many of the tasks normally associated with housework – cleaning rooms, preparing meals and, in a family, looking after the children. Home helps can be provided full or part time depending on the circumstances. Apart fron emergency work, most home helps are provided part time, perhaps amounting to two or three sessions per week. This is important when assisting elderly persons over a long periods of time as *it is essential to encourage these people to continue to do as much as they can for themselves,* thus helping to keep them active for as long as possible. In emergency illnesses or in maternity cases, a full-time home help for a short period of time may enable a young family to be kept together and thus avoid taking the older children into short-term care. This type of support is especially valuable where there are no relatives to help (apart from the father who has to continue to go out to work).

Links between home helps and community teams

Any home help soon gets to know very well the client and family that she is visiting and can learn a great deal about their personal problems. It is, therefore, important that *all home helps form part of the balanced community team* and, in particular, *work in close contact with social workers*. To help achieve this, most social service departments arrange for home helps to be deployed by the social work districts. Then any useful information the home help has learnt about his or her clients can easily be passed on to the social workers so enabling the fullest social support to be arranged.

The local home help organiser must coordinate closely with GPs, community and practice nurses, health visitors and many others who require the assistance of home helps from time to time in their work. Occasionally a home help is needed to tackle a particularly difficult, dirty or heavy task to clean up a home which has become extremely dirty due to neglect or illness of the occupant. Many social service departments arrange for special teams to do this work and many provide special equipment. In many instances, male home helps are used for these tasks. It is usual for those tackling such exceptionally difficult and dirty tasks to be given extra remuneration for such work.

Good neighbour schemes

Usually the demand for home helps outstrips its provision and some authorities have experimented with alternative methods of help such as 'good neighbour schemes'. Local volunteers are sought, often from among fit elderly persons, who agree to carry out a number of light duties, for example shopping, cooking and light cleaning and generally keeping an eye on the old person to prevent them gradually deteriorating without anyone knowing about it. Most volunteers live close by so no travelling is involved. Some schemes arrange for the volunteer to be paid a small sum, say £6–8 per week as an honorarium, provided the service is given constantly.

Home care programmes

One of the most critical times for many elderly persons occurs when when they are discharged home from hospital after an illness or accident. In such a situation an elderly person living on their own will often deteriorate rapidly. What is needed is good support to be provided on discharge home for a short time – say for about 4 weeks. This gives the elderly person a chance to get back to normal gradually. One such service aims at providing a home help and a meals-on-wheels service plus any home nursing services on discharge from hospital for 4 weeks. At the end of this period, those needing continued assistance have to apply through the normal services. Such a programme has to be organised in close coordination with the geriatric hospital unit but has already proved to be very helpful in encouraging continued independence and, in this way, has prevented many elderly persons from being admitted permanently to an elderly persons' home.

Care of homeless persons

Homelessness is a very complex subject. It is found mainly in three groups of people:

- *families with young children*. These have usually become homeless because the family has been evicted from their accommodation usually for non-payment of their rent or because of a family row in the case of a family living with close relatives. Very occasionally it is due to an emergency which could not have been avoided such as a fire or flood;
- *mentally ill persons* who have left hospital recently and who have no family to support them and have not been able to settle;
- *rootless persons* – these include a few persons who have chosen to lead a nomadic life and some young persons (often teenagers) who have left their families and have moved to large cities and conurbations, failed to find any employment, may have become drug abusers and because of this have gravitated towards crime or prostitution.

The homeless problem is always worse in the large cities although recently it seems to be increasing in rural areas. Homelessness leads to many extra problems particularly as persons may drift into being homeless and a vicious circle develops.

In an attempt to help those families and ill and vulnerable people who are at greatest risk, the law was changed in the late 1970s by the introduction of the Housing (Homeless Persons) Act 1977. This introduced two new concepts and divided those who are homeless into two groups:

- *priority cases* and *other cases*. Priority cases include anyone who has one or more children living with them, anyone made homeless because of an emergency (fire, flood, etc.) and a household which *includes anyone who is elderly, mentally handicapped or suffers from a physical disability*. In addition *battered wives* and *pregnant women* are priority cases;
- homeless persons are also divided into those made *homeless by chance* and those made *homeless intentionally*.

Duties of housing authorities to those who are homeless

To those with a priority need

Provided the homelessness was not intentional, the local housing authority must provide permanent accommodation which enables the family to live together as soon as possible.

If the homelessness was intentional, the local housing authority must:

• provide accommodation to the household on a temporary basis;
• give advice and assistance.

To those who do not have a priority need (whether intentional or not)

For those cases where the local housing authority must give advice and assistance, the Code of Guidance published by the Government at the time of bringing in the 1977 Act indicated that such help should include registering the family on the housing list, giving assistance through a housing centre or referring the case to housing associations or voluntary bodies. Advice should also be given regarding lists of accommodation agencies, hostels and possible accommodation in the private sector.

Most homeless families need a great deal of continuous assistance and support although some are difficult to help – perhaps due to the low intelligence of the parents. After rehousing, careful aftercare work will be needed, otherwise the family are often likely to fall into debt again and repeat their mistakes.

Initially some homeless families are rehoused in sub-standard housing and then progress towards normal council housing when the family has shown themselves capable of managing their own affairs and keeping up with their rent. Even at this stage, such families need support from social workers, Family Service Units, and other voluntary workers.

Prevention of homelessness

The prevention of homelessness is very important because once homelessness has become firmly established, a vicious circle of social problems can start including longstanding debt, a nomadic lifestyle and a family that will eventually find it very difficult to settle anywhere.

The following are the more important factors in the prevention of homelessness:

• the avoidance of large rent arrears and other forms of debt. For those on income support, arrangements may have to be made for the rent to be paid directly by the Benefits Agency;

- continuous support should be given after rehousing wherever possible by voluntary bodies such as Family Service Units;
- regular visiting by a specialist social worker can help to ensure that the family does not get into debt again;
- better surveillance for those mentally ill persons who have recently been discharged from hospital and who have no home or family. Community psychiatric nurses are extremely useful in such cases particularly to check that the individual is taking their medication regularly. Many of the breakdowns and consequent erratic behaviour are due to the patient stopping their medication when discharged. This is particularly important with those who do not have the support of a caring family. The recent decision of the Secretary of State for Health to introduce legislation to create a system of 'supervised discharge' from mental hospital units for certain patients is aimed at preventing this group drifting into a chronic state of homelessness (see p. 353). Such a group has many problems for some recently discharged mental patients are notoriously difficult to help;
- the early assistance of young persons who leave home and move to large conurbations. Many of these sleep rough and drift into crime because of their shortage of money. Drug abuse and prostitution can then quickly follow and, in a relatively short time, a chain of circumstances has developed which are difficult to change.

Treatment of homelessness

This is never easy. It involves both housing and social service authorities, the mental health care services, the probation services and many specialised voluntary bodies such as Shelter and the Family Service Units.

For those who are priority cases under the 1977 Act, the aim should always be to rehouse and resettle them quickly. This is often best done through a series of stages, as follows:

- temporary accommodation should be provided immediately to care for their family by providing them with shelter and accommodation. The housing authority should next promptly rehouse the family. The temporary accommodation in the past in many large cities like London has consisted of the 'bed and breakfast' type which is in cheap, run down hotels and this has never been satisfactory. The aim now is wherever possible to rehouse the family at once even if only into a poorer type of housing temporarily;
- moving the family next to permanent housing accommodation. This should always be accompanied by skilled help and supervision from social service departments and voluntary bodies such as

Family Service Units who can help the family to settle into a better routine;

- once the family has settled down and is paying rent regularly (in rent arrears cases), then a move should be made into the final rehousing in a satisfactory area. It is a mistake to leave homeless families for long periods in very poor run-down housing. Then usually there is a danger of a drift back into unsatisfactory habits and the circle of deprivation starts again and the family ends up facing the same problems.

Avoidance of rent arrears

Because rent arrears are often the starting point of difficulties which eventually end in the homelessness of the family, it is helpful to list the actions which can prevent rent arrears and eventually eviction. These include:

- an early warning system after a few missed payments should be started to enable special arrangements for rent collection to be made and for social services advice to be given;
- if rent arrears are still accumulating, housing authorities should check whether tenants are eligible for housing benefit;
- there should be a vigorous pursuit of rent arrears and this should include selective visiting to prevent rent arrears getting greater;
- for families on income support this will include an element for rent and arrangements should be made for this to be paid direct;
- if there are also serious family and social problems, it may be possible to assist by payment of rent arrears using powers of Section 1 of the Children and Young Persons Act 1963 (to avoid the children in the family being taken into care);
- transfer to cheaper accommodation to help reduce the rent problems.

For those persons with a mental disability and with no home or family, early prevention of homelessness is very important. A survey carried out in London in 1986–7 showed there was a high proportion of single homeless persons who were psychologically disturbed. The findings showed that:

- 25% had a history of schizophrenia;
- 14% had alcohol dependence;
- 11% had personality disorders;
- 6% had mood disorders.

Another study showed the level of schizophrenia at a higher level of 37%. None of this group are usually easy to deal with and few respond well to help. Certainly a great deal of patient and continued support will always be required. It is important to realise that for some 'custodial care' will be required. The development within the mental health field of community care was certainly responsible for great successes and there are now many persons living satisfactorily in the community who, but for the reforms, would have stayed permanently in mental hospitals. However there are still a few chronically mentally disturbed persons including those with serious personality disorders who will always require the support of hostels (such as those run by the Salvation Army) in which three features are always evident:

- a wide range of odd and bizarre behaviour is tolerated;
- there is a general attitude of non-intrusiveness on the part of the staff and other residents;
- there is a wide degree of personal freedom for the residents to lead their own eccentric lives.

It is clear to all professionals whether working in the health or social services field that there will always be a need for dedicated voluntary bodies to continue to work in this field.

For those whose homelessness is intentional and who do not have priority, every help and advice should be given by the housing authority. This group does however contain some persons who have little intention of conforming and because of this are extremely difficult to help. Many voluntary bodies including Shelter and the Salvation Army do excellent work with this group but almost invariably certain individuals never settle down.

Specialist advice and assistance for homeless families and unsupported mothers

Family planning

Family planning (see p. 83) for all homeless families should always be carefully considered as too many children at too short intervals in any family are likely to aggravate problems. In the most intractable problem families, it is best to arrange a domiciliary family planning service to ensure the mother receives correct and effective family planning advice.

Care of unsupported mothers

The care of unsupported mothers who are homeless (including the unmarried mother) is also the responsibility of social service departments who can make arrangements often in conjunction with voluntary bodies for residential care of some mothers. As with other types of homelessness it is always desirable to do everything to educate the homeless mother to prevent a recurrence. It follows from this that *the unsupported mother needs a considerable amount of supportive social work and advice.*

Hospital social workers

Since 1974 the employment and control of hospital social workers rests with the local social service departments although all hospital social workers are stationed in the hospitals. Hospital social workers are attached to all large hospitals with considerable specialisation and concentration in mental, geriatric and paediatric fields. Those specialising in mental health work are often specially qualified *psychiatric social workers*.

There are four main areas of work for hospital social workers:

- *medical casework*. This is concerned with the adjustment of the patient and family to the disease in question. This is the largest and most important part of hospital social work. It mainly involves working with the patient in hospital (including in-patient and out-patient work). It may also necessitate the hospital social worker visiting the patient's home. All types of work are covered – work with children including child abuse; with elderly persons, many of whom may be living alone; terminal cases especially the cancers. An illness in the parent in a one parent family often produces many extra problems to solve and coordination must be carried out with the child care section of the local social services department. Another very important group are accident patients especially those suffering from serious burns or those who have very special problems such as paraplegics. In these careful planning can avoid extra difficulties in the future especially where considerable alterations are now necessary in the patient's accommodation in their own home. Many social problems following a mental illness can be reduced by the anticipation of a good hospital social worker and their role can be crucial in many of these cases;
- *environmental help*. This involves arranging how the patient's home can be improved to help him or her to cope with the illness. This is more important, of course, in certain chronic disabling conditions and may involve complete rehousing of the family or the adaptation of the home either structurally or the introduction of certain aids such as a stair lift or special kitchen equipment to ensure the maximum independence of the patient;
- special arrangements may be needed to provide *immediate assist-*

ance to the patient or the relatives. This includes advising about any claims for special financial benefits such as claiming the Disability Living Allowance for a patient under the age of 65 or the Attendance Allowance for someone aged 65 and over. Convalescent arrangements or accommodation for relatives visiting dangerously ill relatives are also duties of the hospital social workers' staff;

- *Liaison* with various other social work agencies is another area of work tackled by hospital social workers.

22   Alcohol and drug abuse

Alcohol abuse can be defined as 'dependence upon alcohol to such a degree that the person shows noticeable disturbance or an interference with bodily or mental health'. It is both a medical and social problem in its origin and manifestations for it interferes with interpersonal relationships and with the normal economic and social functioning of the individual affected and the family.

Alcohol abuse

Incidence and trends

There has been a large increase in the consumption of alcohol in the UK since the late 1950s. Pure alcohol consumption in England and Wales rose from 6.88 litres per head of population in 1970 to 8.95 litres in 1991 (this represents a 30% rise over this period). This increase has also been accompanied by a change in the type of alcohol drunk. This is shown in Table 22.1.

These figures show a marked move away from beer drinking to wine and spirit drinking over this period. Estimates for the UK suggest that at least 1 million people have a serious alcohol problem and that more than 10 000 premature deaths occur each year which are associated with alcohol abuse.

The publication *Health of the Nation* in 1992 included a *target to reduce the proportion of heavy drinkers*, that is men who are exceeding a weekly average of 21 units of alcohol and women who are drinking more than 14 units, by 30% by the year 2005.

Table 22.1   Type of alcohol consumed in England and Wales, 1970 and 1992.

	1970	1992
Beer/lager	72%	53%
Spirits	17%	22%
Wine	9%	21%
Cider	2%	4%

(From the Chief Medical Officer's Report, Department of Health, 1992.)

Social class and alcohol consumption

The 1987 OPCS survey on 'Drinking in England and Wales' showed no clear-cut pattern of alcohol consumption in different social classes. However the General Household Survey of 1988 demonstrated that there was a consistent association between household income and alcohol consumption. In particular, *as household income increases, its members are less likely to be abstainers and more likely to be heavy drinkers.*

Causes of alcohol abuse

Alcohol abuse is *not a specific disease* – in certain circumstances anyone can be affected. *Social factors are always very important.* There is a higher incidence in persons who are single, widowed or divorced. The usual average age for men to show the first signs of alcohol abuse is the mid-40s but in women it is higher. For serious cases of alcohol abuse, men outnumber women in a ratio of 5 to 1. Certain occupations are at special risk – commercial travellers, business executives, lawyers, publicans and seamen, while the level in doctors is higher than average. No particular personality is susceptible although there is a higher incidence in both excessively shy people and in gregarious extroverts.

Development of alcohol abuse

Alcohol abuse usually develops gradually over a lengthy period of time. Most cases start as social drinkers who gradually increase the amount they consume. In an attempt to control the amount of alcohol that is drunk regularly (which is the essential factor in the development of alcohol abuse) the 'unit of alcohol' is now used as an indicator.

1 unit of alcohol = ½ pint of ordinary beer or lager
                 = 1 single measure of spirits (whisky, gin, vodka, etc.)
                 = 1 glass of wine
                 = 1 small glass of sherry
                 = 1 measure of vermouth or an aperitif.

All the above drinks contain approximately the same amount of alcohol.

A safe amount of alcohol per week is up to 21 units for men and 14 units for women. If the drinking is evenly spread throughout the week a slight increase is unlikely to lead to long-term harm, but then the person is on the borderline limit and a gradual increase to heavier drinking can easily occur.

It is important to realise that *the safe limit for women is lower than for men.* This is because the water content in the body measures 55–65% in men but only 45–55% in women and, as alcohol is spread throughout the body fluids, the higher water content in men means that the alcohol is more diluted than in women. Hence higher concentrations of alcohol accumulate in women than in men and there is a greater danger of damage to the liver.

Serious alcohol abuse

There are two types of serious alcohol abuse:

• problem drinkers;
• dependent drinkers.

Problem drinker

This is a person who drinks heavily and *experiences serious physical and/or mental symptoms.* Loss of appetite and poor food intake are commonly present. This stage may last a long time and is often accompanied by many social, family, occupational and social problems. If treatment is started early, it may be possible to reverse the increasing list of problems; however relapses are common and these tend to lead to more family and social problems which often means that support diminishes and a vicious circle starts.

Dependent drinker

A dependent drinker *is one who has a compulsion to drink.* In the early stages, there is an increased tolerance to alcohol but later this changes to a reduced tolerance. If alcohol is then stopped, withdrawal symptoms occur. These symptoms are relieved by more drinking and this then seems to take precedence over other activities. *At this stage, even if drinking stops for a period such persons tend to start drinking again.*

In both types of alcohol abuse, the late stages are often accompanied by much illness including cirrhosis of the liver and peripheral neuropathy. Severe memory loss with dementia finally occurs with severe withdrawal symptoms (dementia tremens).

Prevention of alcohol abuse

The prevention of alcohol abuse depends on the following steps being taken:

- *early careful control of the amount of alcohol being consumed.* If the amounts referred to on the previous page are adhered to, permanent health problems will not occur;
- *avoidance of drinking alone*;
- *simple disciplines* when taking alcohol regularly – a couple who like a late night drink realising it is best to have a drink or two about half an hour before going to bed. The earlier drinks are taken, the more likely too much will be consumed;
- *the substitution of non-alcoholic drinks* at times in a social atmosphere;
- strict adherence to the *'no drink and drive' principle.* Public opinion is increasing on never drinking when driving and the increasing penalties are having an effect. The consequences for anyone who loses their driving licence can be very serious (including the loss of a job in many occupations);
- the *example of parents* is crucial in moulding the drinking habits of their children;
- the *care and vigilance of doctors, nurses and social workers* in recognising the early stages of alcohol abuse when it may be possible to reverse the process.

Diagnosis of alcohol abuse

Early diagnosis of alcohol abuse depends on the recognition of a combination of social and medical signs. Increasing absenteeism, a decline in job efficiency, worsening marital disharmony, and self-neglect are always suggestive of alcohol abuse. A clear indication of an inability to keep to a sensible drinking limit, missed meals, blackouts and nocturnal sweating followed by early morning drinking are usually confirmatory signs of serious alcohol dependence.

Treatment of alcohol abuse

Treatment is never easy and success depends on:

- obtaining the complete cooperation of the drinker;
- an acceptance of the individual concerned that a serious drinking problem exists;
- early diagnosis;
- support from the family.

The first aim of treatment is to reverse any physical, mental and social damage. Any alcohol dependence must be tackled next. In the UK there are a number of special *detoxification units* and their use should be combined with *home detoxification* where the GP helps to coordinate the care. Here voluntary bodies such as Alcoholics Anonymous and special Community Alcohol Teams can be a great help especially during rehabilitation and aftercare. This is most important as relapses may easily occur then.

Drug abuse

Drug abuse is serious as it can lead to drug dependence. The World Health Organization defines drug dependence (the term that has replaced drug addiction) as 'a state, psychic or physical, which results from the interaction between a living organism and a drug which is characterised by behavioural and other responses that always includes a compulsion to take the drug on a continuous or periodic basis in order to experience its psychic effects and sometimes to avoid the discomfort of its absence.'

Three types of drug dependence occur:

- *intermittent consumption* without the development of tolerance;
- *daily use of drugs* by mouth, injection or inhalation (solvent abuse) to obtain their psychic effect;
- in patients *receiving drugs prescribed medically*. In this instance, the drug is taken to avoid psychological and/or physical withdrawal symptoms. Drugs producing such reactions include the barbiturates, tranquillisers and hypnotics.

Contributory factors leading to drug abuse

The following contributory factors are usually connected with the misuse of drugs:

- *personality*. Immature, inadequate and unstable individuals who often come from a broken family or have had an unhappy childhood and who may have shown truancy and/or criminal tendencies are more likely to become drug abusers;
- *'peer pressure'*. Few want to be the 'odd one out' in any group and a number of young persons start to take drugs for this reason;
- *availability of drugs*. Anyone who has easy access to drugs may begin to use them. Consequently there is a higher incidence of drug abuse in *doctors and nurses* than in the general population. Although this danger is now well known, it still occasionally occurs in spite of the various precautions and safeguards which have been introduced;
- *experimentation*. An increasing number of young persons start to use drugs from curiosity – to experience themselves the effect of these drugs. In those who are wealthy enough to afford to buy

them easily, or who belong to an unconventional group in society, the temptation to experiment may be great and this can become the starting point of serious drug abuse.

It is important to realise that *drug dependency occurs in all social classes and the range of behavioural problems which are caused is very wide.*

Types of drugs which can cause drug abuse

A large number of drugs can cause drug abuse including the following:

- narcotics such as heroin, morphine and methadone
- cocaine
- amphetamines
- lysergic acid diethylamide (LSD)
- barbiturates
- cannabis
- solvents (the solvent most frequently used now is butane but originally glue was the commonest solvent abused)
- tranquillisers.

The use of the most dangerous habit forming drugs, such as the narcotics and cocaine, in health care are very carefully controlled by law. They must always be kept under lock and key and their use must always be recorded. Tranquillisers are not so strictly controlled and their widespread use has become a problem although adverse symptoms are only produced when attempts are made to change or to withdraw the drug.

A further problem which developed in the 1980s is *the danger from HIV infection (and later AIDS) and hepatitis B* from the sharing of syringes used to give drugs by injection.

The present estimates suggest that the total number of drug abusers in the UK exceeds 100 000 but a much smaller number take their drugs by injection. Most drug abusers are to be found in London and other larger cities and their surrounding conurbations – Edinburgh, Glasgow, Manchester and Liverpool and their satellite communities.

Aspects of drug dependence

There are three important aspects in drug dependence:

- *physical dependence.* Physiological changes occur eventually which hinder any attempts to stop taking the drug as *serious withdrawal symptoms* develop and these can only be relieved by

further consumption of the drug. These physiological changes in the body are the basis of drug dependence or addiction;
- *psychological dependence*. This is found in all types of drug abusers. It may be present in combination with physical dependence as in the case of narcotics or may be the main reason for the dependence as with the tranquillisers or barbiturates. Psychological dependence develops because *the person mistakenly believes it would no longer be possible to exist without taking the drug*. The symptoms which then follow any attempt to withdraw the drug are mainly psychosomatic;
- *tolerance*. When a drug is consumed on a regular basis, the same dose produces less effect. This is commonly seen with most narcotics like morphia, hence there is a need to increase the dosage to obtain the same effect. This in turn heightens dependency.

Diagnosis and recognition of drug abuse

The diagnosis of drug abuse depends on the following:

- recognition of the suggestive *signs and symptoms of drug dependency*;
- a doctor or nurse realising that any patient already receiving treatment with a drug known to be able to produce dependency is at some risk;
- recognising the *social problems* which commonly follow any drug dependency.

Signs and symptoms

These include malnutrition with vitamin deficiencies, extreme anxiety, insomnia, fits, blackouts, recurrent infections, repetitive incidences of trauma (falls, etc.), peripheral neuritis and/or the symptoms of liver disease.

Social problems

These include all forms of family and/or marital disharmony. Most cases are first recognised by the family who should always be consulted and carefully listened to as, in this way, many suggestive signs and symptoms come to light which otherwise would probably have been missed. The possibility of a drug abuse problem should be raised when any young person suddenly shows criminal tendencies. Association with criminal behaviour, especially in young persons, is a common drug-related social problem, as this is often the only way they can obtain enough money to buy more drugs.

It is always wise to realise that the possibility of drug abuse is more likely in any 'at risk' family such as a family known to have a history of drug abuse. The incidence of drug abuse in the children of drug abusers is always higher than normal.

Drug dependency in patients

Any patient who is a frequent attender at the GP's surgery, either for minor complaints or for certificates for absence from work should be considered as a possible drug abuser. Any elderly patient who has been on a drug which is known to produce drug dependency, should be considered to be at risk. In very old persons (over the age of 80) most drugs are broken down by the body less effectively and therefore accumulation of the drug can occur with consequent overdosage.

Any doctor who suspects that a person being treated has drug dependency *must by law notify the Chief Medical Officer of the Home Office Drugs Branch* within 7 days (The Misuse of Drugs Act 1971).

Prevention of drug abuse

A better understanding of the potential dangers of all forms of drug abuse is crucial for the prevention of this condition. Health education is also important and it is most effective when it is reinforced by sound family support. It is essential never to give the impression that it is only the 'hard drugs' (the narcotics) that are dangerous. Most persons who become dependent on 'hard drugs' started by using 'soft drugs' such as cannabis. Having enjoyed the feeling of well-being which cannabis commonly produces, they can soon be persuaded to try other more dangerous drugs and, in this way, eventually become dependent on narcotics. Health education *must stress that any drug abuse is potentially dangerous*. It should also emphasise that many solvents can be dangerous when sniffed and inhaled especially in a confined space. At present approximately 100–135 deaths occur each year due to the inhalation of volatile substances. Figure 22.1 shows clearly how these deaths increased during the 1980s.

At first it was sniffing of glue that predominated but recently the inhalation of fuel gases, especially of butane in the form of lighter refills, has emerged as the major cause of deaths. Certain aerosols are the second most commonly abused volatile product. In 1992 the Department of Health launched a national publicity campaign on solvent abuse. At the same time the Department published a booklet entitled *Solvents – a Parent's Guide* which was widely distributed in an attempt to raise the public awareness of the dangers of solvent misuse. Television can also be most helpful in getting this message across, particularly when repeated in different forms such as drama episodes.

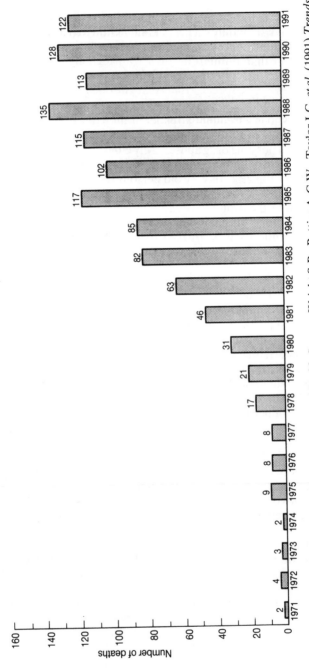

Fig. 22.1 Volatile substance abuse deaths, UK, 1971–90. Source: Wright S.P., Pottier A.C.W., Taylor J.C. *et al.* (1991) *Trends in Deaths Associated with Abuse of Volatile Substances 1971–1989.* London: Department of Public Health Sciences: St. George's Medical School (Report No. 4). (From the Chief Medical Officer's Report *On the State of the Public Health*, Department of Health, 1990.)

Probably one of the most effective forms of prevention is a stable and happy family. Certainly there is a much higher incidence of all forms of drug abuse in broken families or where both parents work full time and leave their children on their own for long periods. Young persons who run away from home and often end up in large conurbations are always at special risk. As mentioned in Chapter 21 (see p. 397) single homeless young persons tend to become drawn into drug abuse and need special support and counselling to prevent this.

Treatment and management of drug abuse

The treatment of drug abuse may involve special drug dependency clinics, day centres and specialist social services and the GP and primary health care team.

An essential prerequisite for the successful treatment of anyone who has drug dependency is for the *individual to be determined to stop taking drugs*. Therefore, a sensible first step should be to emphasise this and then to *obtain a written statement to this effect (the contract) which is then signed by the patient*. The objective of the treatment is then absolutely clear. At the same time, the professional involved in the management and treatment must realise the following:

- *moralistic and judgemental attitudes must be avoided* for these have often been shown to be totally counterproductive;
- although the patient being treated may genuinely want to give up the drug habit, this will always be difficult and relapses may occur. Therefore as well as any positive treatment prescribed, the *social lifestyle of the patient and his/her family must be carefully considered*.

Many of the dangers of a relapse may be closely connected with past contacts and friends of the person. In many instances, once the initial stages of treatment have been successfully overcome, *it is better for the patient to move away from the area where the dependence started*. A move to a new district enables a fresh start to be made.

The basis in the early stages of treatment is to keep the individual in a specialist unit and to substitute a less dangerous drug for the original one, slowly breaking the dependence. An example of this technique is the use of methadone in persons already dependent upon heroin.

Once the person has come off all drugs *close follow-up and support are essential*. A number of useful self-help agencies can help at this stage, including Narcotics Anonymous and Families Anonymous.

Index